10e

AWARD-WINNING

Business English

Mary Ellen Guffey

Emerita Professor of Business
Los Angeles Pierce College

Carolyn M. Seefer

Professor of Business
Diablo Valley College

SOUTH-WESTERN
CENGAGE Learning

Australia • Brazil • Japan • Korea • Mexico • Singapore • Spain • United Kingdom • United States

SOUTH-WESTERN
CENGAGE Learning™

Business English, Tenth Edition
Mary Ellen Guffey, Carolyn M. Seefer

Vice President of Editorial, Business: Jack W. Calhoun

Editor-in-Chief: Melissa Acūna

Senior Acquisitions Editor: Erin Joyner

Senior Developmental Editor: Mary Draper

Editorial Assistant: Kayti Purkiss

Vice President of Marketing: Bill Hendee

Senior Marketing Communications Manager:
 Sarah Greber

Senior Content Project Manager: Kim Kusnerak

Media Editor: John Rich

Frontlist Buyer, Manufacturing: Miranda Klapper

Production Service: S4Carlisle Publishing Services

Copyeditor: Patsy Fortney

Compositor: S4Carlisle Publishing Services

Senior Art Director: Stacy Jenkins Shirley

Internal Designer: Grannan Graphic Design

Cover Designer: Grannan Graphic Design

Cover Image: ©Masterfile

Senior Rights Account Manager--Text:
 Mardell Glinski Schultz

Senior Photography Editor: Jennifer Meyer Dare

For product information and technology assistance, contact us at
Cengage Learning Customer & Sales Support, 1-800-354-9706

For permission to use material from this text or product,
submit all requests online at **www.cengage.com/permissions**
Further permissions questions can be emailed to
permissionrequest@cengage.com

Library of Congress Control Number: 2009938873
ISBN-13: 978-0-324-78974-4
ISBN-10: 0-324-78974-2

Student Edition ISBN 13: 978-0-324-78975-1
Student Edition ISBN 10: 0-324-78975-0

South-Western Cengage Learning
5191 Natorp Boulevard
Mason, OH 45040
USA

Cengage Learning products are represented in Canada by Nelson Education, Ltd.

For your course and learning solutions, visit **www.cengage.com**
Purchase any of our products at your local college store or at our preferred online store **www.CengageBrain.com**

Printed in the United States of America
2 3 4 5 6 7 13 12 11 10

Dear Student:

Many of you will be entering or returning to the world of work soon, and you want to brush up your language skills. **Business English** can help you refresh your knowledge of grammar and usage so that you will be confident in today's workplace where communication skills are increasingly important.

Business English has helped thousands of students over the years improve their oral and written communication skills. It has been the leading book in the field for nearly three decades because it works. Its three-level approach makes grammar less intimidating and easier to grasp. This approach provides small learning blocks that proceed from simple to complex, thus helping you understand and remember.

Within the textbook, you will find tried-and-true learning tools as well as new features to ensure that you improve your grammar, punctuation, and usage skills.

Mary Ellen Guffey

- **New Homework Help!** In this Tenth Edition, we bring you an outstanding new interactive feature—**Online Reinforcement Exercises**. This means that you can complete your homework faster and more confidently. At **www.meguffey.com** are half of the textbook exercises so that you can try out your skills, see the answers immediately, and receive helpful explanations.
- **Three-level approach** presents grammar guidelines in segments proceeding from easier, more frequently used concepts to less frequently used concepts.
- **Ample end-of-chapter reinforcement exercises** enable you to apply your learning so that you can internalize and retain your new skills.
- **Pretests and posttests** keep you informed about your needs and your progress.
- **Self-help exercises** give you even more opportunities to improve through practice.
- **Frequently asked questions** present everyday language queries such as those you might face in your career—with answers from the authors.
- **Writer's Workshops** offer you guidelines, model documents, and writing tips necessary to compose e-mails, memos, letters, and short reports.
- **Learning Web Ways** takes you to Web sites with step-by-step instructions that help you develop your Internet skills.
- **Chat About It** promotes classroom and distance-learning discussions related to chapter concepts.
- **Exceptional Web Resources** include chapter quizzes, PowerPoint reviews, flash cards, Editor's Challenge, WebCheck reviews, and more at **www.meguffey.com**.

Carolyn Seefer

Business English reviews the grammar, punctuation, and usage guidelines necessary for you to succeed in your business or professional career. The textbook is not only a friendly teaching and learning tool but also a great reference for you to keep handy on the job.

One student remarked, "**Business English** is a gift to any student who really wants to learn how to use the English language proficiently."

Cordially,

Mary Ellen Guffey   *Carolyn M. Seefer*

Guffey...
It's Just That Easy!

Market-leading and student-oriented, *Business English, 10e,* continues to give you the most current and authoritative coverage of grammar and mechanics. Award-winning author Mary Ellen Guffey provides unparalleled student resources to help you throughout your course. With the book's three-level approach, reinforcement exercises, and additional online resources and support at **www.meguffey.com**, you will find that learning business English can be *just that easy.*

Technology With Guffey...
It's Just That Easy

More than ever, Mary Ellen Guffey and coauthor Carolyn Seefer have focused on making digital resources easy to use with *Business English, 10e*. New for this edition, the authors offer **www.meguffey.com**, an exciting new student Web site with numerous resources to help you understand and remember what you are learning.

- **Brand NEW Student Support Web site –** **www.meguffey.com** gives you one convenient place to find the support you need. You can study with resources such as self-teaching grammar/mechanics review, PowerPoint slides, chapter review quizzes, online reinforcement exercises, and other learning tools.

"Guffey's *Business English* and student Web site provide the tools for making teaching and learning easier. We never consider any other English texts. We love Guffey!"

Carol Middendorff
Clackamas Community College,
Oregon City, Oregon

www.meguffey.com

For students who purchase a new book, this **premier student Web site** offers the following resources:

- **Chapter Review Quizzes** highlight chapter concepts and give you immediate feedback with explanations for right and wrong responses.

- **Online Reinforcement Exercises** provide half of the textbook exercises in an interactive format so that you can complete your homework online and receive immediate feedback for all of your responses.

- **Ms. Grammar** strengthens language skills with chapter synopses and interactive exercises.

- **PowerPoint** chapter slides provide a quick review of chapter concepts.

- **SpeakRight!** helps you learn to pronounce 50 frequently mispronounced words.

- **SpellRight!** provides interactive exercises that review all 400 words in Appendix A of the textbook.

- **WebCheck exercises** provide additional reinforcement for the most challenging chapter concepts

- **Editor's Challenge** presents error-filled letters, memos, e-mail messages, and reports for you to correct.

- **Self-Check Diagnostic Grammar Quiz** assesses strengths and weaknesses. Different from the diagnostic test in the textbook, this quiz is meant to pique interest.

- **Flash Cards and Glossary** review key terms from each chapter and help you internalize concepts.

- **Bonus Bloopers** supply even more language mishaps from actual written and oral expression that challenge you to detect the problems and remedy them.

- **Writing Help** in the form of links to OWLs (online writing labs) guides you to the best Internet grammar services where you will find exercises, handouts, and writing advice.

HOW DO YOU SIGN UP FOR WWW.MEGUFFEY.COM?

When you purchase a new textbook, you have access to the resources at the premium Web site. All of these resources are provided to students who purchase new books. Others may purchase access at the Guffey premium Web site at www.meguffey.com.

Learning With Guffey...

It's Just That Easy!

You will find multiple resources to help make learning business English easier. From the three-level approach to new online reinforcement exercises, Guffey has updated and created new ways to keep you interested and engaged. With all of these options, learning can be *just that easy.*

Popular Three-Level Approach

Dr. Guffey's approach to learning grammar starts with a solid foundation of basic information and then progresses to more complex concepts step-by-step. When using this approach, you build your confidence by learning small, easily mastered learning segments. Reinforcement exercises, self-checks, and writing exercises will help you along the way.

Lively Reinforcement Exercises

Dr. Guffey knows that you learn by doing. That's why each chapter of **Business English** includes a variety of tools, including self-help exercises aligned with the three-level approach.

Self-Check Exercises and Unit Reviews. The first exercise in each level of each chapter is self-checked to help you determine immediately whether you comprehend the concepts just presented.

Self-Help Exercises. Special worksheets enable you to check your own learning as you review and internalize chapter concepts.

Writing Exercises. Each chapter includes a short writing exercise that encourages you to apply chapter concepts in composing sentences.

Writer's Workshops. Six workshops feature composition tips and techniques necessary to develop work-related writing skills.

Learning Web Ways. Step-by-step exercises help you to gain familiarity and build skills in using helpful Web sites.

New Features With Guffey...

It's Just That Easy!

NEW! Online Reinforcement Exercises

Half of the exercises are now ready for students at our premium Web site, **www.meguffey.com**. Available to anyone with a new book, these exercises help you complete your homework by checking your answers immediately. Best of all, you receive an explanation for every answer.

NEW! Frequently Asked Questions

One of the most popular features of ***Business English*** has been its questions and answers patterned on those received at grammar hotline services across the country. In this edition, Hotline Queries has been transformed into Frequently Asked Questions, similar to the FAQs at many Web sites.

These questions—and suggested answers from Dr. Guffey and Professor Seefer—illustrate everyday communication problems encountered in the contemporary work world. In easy-to-read question-and-answer form, the authors explain important distinctions in English grammar, usage, style, and vocabulary. Updated items related to current events appear in this Tenth Edition.

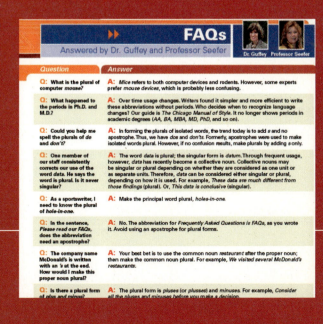

FAQs — Answered by Dr. Guffey and Professor Seefer — Dr. Guffey, Professor Seefer

Question	Answer
Q: What is the plural of computer *mouse*?	**A:** *Mice* refers to both computer devices and rodents. However, some experts prefer *mouse devices*, which is probably less confusing.
Q: What happened to the periods in Ph.D. and M.D.?	**A:** Over time usage changes. Writers found it simpler and more efficient to write these abbreviations without periods. Who decides when to recognize language changes? Our guide is *The Chicago Manual of Style*. It no longer shows periods in academic degrees (AA, BA, MBA, MD, PhD, and so on).
Q: Could you help me spell the plurals of *do* and *don't*?	**A:** In forming the plurals of isolated words, the trend today is to add *s* and no apostrophe. Thus, we have *dos* and *don'ts*. Formerly, apostrophes were used to make isolated words plural. However, if no confusion results, make plurals by adding *s* only.
Q: One member of our staff consistently corrects our use of the word *data*. He says the word is plural. Is it never singular?	**A:** The word *data* is plural; the singular form is *datum*. Through frequent usage, however, *data* has recently become a collective noun. Collective nouns may be singular or plural depending on whether they are considered as one unit or as separate units. Therefore, *data* can be considered either singular or plural, depending on how it is used. For example, *These data are much different from those findings* (plural). Or, *This data is conclusive* (singular).
Q: As a sportswriter, I need to know the plural of *hole-in-one*.	**A:** Make the principal word plural, *holes-in-one*.
Q: In the sentence, *Please read our FAQs*, does the abbreviation need an apostrophe?	**A:** No. The abbreviation for *Frequently Asked Questions* is *FAQs*, as you wrote it. Avoid using an apostrophe for plural forms.
Q: The company name McDonald's is written with an *'s* at the end. How would I make this proper noun plural?	**A:** Your best bet is to use the common noun *restaurant* after the proper noun; then make the common noun plural. For example, *We visited several McDonald's restaurants*.
Q: Is there a plural form of *plus* and *minus*?	**A:** The plural form is *pluses* (or *plusses*) and *minuses*. For example, *Consider all the pluses and minuses before you make a decision.*

New Features With Guffey... It's Just That Easy!

NEW! More Bloopers!

Because students and instructors loved our Spot the Blooper feature in previous editions, we have expanded the number of bloopers from newspapers, magazines, and other sources. You'll see real examples of mangled sentences, misused words, and creative punctuation. You are challenged to explain the mishaps and correct them.

Spot the BLOOPER

Using the skills you are learning in this class, try to identify why the following items are bloopers. Consult your textbook, dictionary, or reference manual as needed.

Blooper 1: Pitcher Roger Clemens, testifying before Congress about steroid use in baseball, said, "In Andy and I's conversation, he obviously disremembers."

Blooper 2: AT&T sent this notice to its customers: "AT&T supports the human spirit through it's sponsorship of the US Paralympic Team."

Blooper 3: Headline on a flyer from the American Automobile Association offering a free U.S. road map to new members: "Your's free."

Blooper 4: United States Secretary of Education Arne Duncan said of a friend and mentor, "He gave my sister and I the opportunity to start a great school on the South Side of Chicago."

Blooper 5: In an *Entertainment Weekly* interview, Barack Obama was asked if he and Michelle argue about anything. He replied, "She likes *American Idol*, her and the girls, in a way that I don't entirely get."

Blooper 6: Tennis star Venus Williams, commenting at Wimbledon about her upcoming match against her sister Serena: "Now it's every Williams for themself."

Blooper 7: WSB-TV presented the results of Georgia's educational proficiency test that all students are required to take. The reporter, after talking with a student, said, "Her and most of her classmates flunked the test."

Blooper 8: Senator Charles Schumer in a letter to *The Wall Street Journal*: "Democrats like myself do not oppose all new domestic oil supplies."

Blooper 9: From an ad in the Winnetka [Illinois] *Talk*: "The Northbrook Community Nursery School held it's gala on May 7 .... The school would like to thank all of it's donors."

Blooper 10: Paris Hilton wore a T-shirt that said "Thats Hot" on the front and "Your Not" on the back.

Chat About It

Your instructor may assign any of the following topics for you to discuss in class, in an online chat room, or on an online discussion board. Some of the discussion topics may require outside research. You may also be asked to read and respond to postings made by your classmates.

Discussion Topic 1: People frequently misuse pronouns. For example, they have trouble knowing whether to choose *I or me, he or him, she or her,* and so on. Why do you think pronouns are so troublesome? After reading Chapter 6, what did you discover about your pronoun use? What types of mistakes have you been making? How will your pronoun use change?

Discussion Topic 2: The pronoun is one of the most frequently misused parts of speech in the English language. Some people don't know the rules, but others misuse pronouns intentionally. For example, you might not be comfortable saying *This is she,* or you might think that *everyone except him and me* doesn't sound right. Have you ever misused pronouns intentionally? If so, why did you do it? Do you think your

NEW! *Chat About It.*

To encourage classroom discussion and build online rapport among distance learners, the Tenth Edition provides Chat About It. Each chapter offers five questions that encourage you to discuss chapter concepts and express your ideas orally or in written comments at the student course site.

NEW! Trivia Tidbits.

This edition provides marginal notes with captivating factoids about the history and use of the language.

Object of a Verb

As you learned in Chapter 3, objects of action verbs can be direct or indirect. A **direct object** is a noun or pronoun that answers the question *What?* or *Whom?* An **indirect object** is a noun or pronoun that answers the question *To whom?, To what?, For whom?,* or *For what?* When pronouns act as direct or indirect objects of verbs, they must be in the objective case.

> Please ask *her* where she would like to go for dinner.
> Can you meet *them* at the airport at 10 a.m.?
> The attorney sent *them* an important e-mail message.
> The network supervisor issued *her* a new password.

Trivia Tidbit

Nine words account for about 25 percent of all written and spoken English. Two of these words are the pronouns *you* and *it*. The other seven words are *and, be, have, of, the, to,* and *will.* Can you identify the parts of speech for the letter group?

Object of a Preposition

As you learned in Chapter 2, a preposition is a word in a position *before* its object. The **object of a preposition** is a noun or pronoun. The objective case is used for pronouns that are objects of prepositions.

Updates With Guffey...

It's Just That Easy!

Wondering what has changed since the last edition? The authors have made it easy to see what has been updated in every chapter.

Overall Improvements

- Added a new margin note feature, Trivia Tidbit. This feature contains a variety of interesting facts about the English language that can be used to spark invigorating classroom discussion.
- Reviewed every entry to be certain that it coordinated with the most recent editions of Clark and Clark's *Handbook for Office Professionals*.
- Moved Spot the Blooper margin notes to a stand-alone section at the end of each chapter. This change will allow the bloopers to be used more easily for classroom discussion, group activities, and other assignments. Added many relevant and timely grammar/usage bloopers to pique interest. Increased the number of bloopers for each chapter to ten.
- Changed the name of the Hotline Query feature to "FAQs About Business English" to make it more contemporary. Increased the number of FAQs to ten per chapter.
- Added a new feature to the end of each chapter, Chat About It. This feature contains five discussion topics per chapter that can be used in traditional and online classrooms to generate discussion in campus classes, provide a forum for expressing ideas, and create sense of community in distance learning classes. Many discussion topics require outside research.
- Based on feedback from instructors, removed the Editor's Challenge exercises from each chapter. Developed new Editor's Challenge feature at the student Web site.
- Added model documents to each Writer's Workshop for student use when preparing writing assignments. These model documents demonstrate proper grammar, spelling, mechanics, and format.

- Scrutinized every sentence to be sure it was concise, clear, and readable at a level appropriate for users of this book.
- Updated all reinforcement exercises and examples with references to current business topics, business history, workplace professionalism, and other relevant information. This content expands student business-related knowledge while improving their business English skills.
- Increased the number of Pretest and Posttest items for each chapter to ten, and increased the number of Reinforcement Exercises to ten per section for most exercises to allow for additional practice and easier grading.
- Added an opening quotation related to business English and writing to the beginning of each chapter. This quotation can be used to generate classroom discussion.
- Reduced the number of margin notes in each chapter to give the textbook a cleaner, less cluttered look in order to improve readability.

Chapter 1

- Emphasized the importance of having an up-to-date print dictionary by listing words that were added to the most recent edition of the *Merriam-Webster's Collegiate Dictionary*.
- Updated lists of archaic, obsolete, colloquial, slang, nonstandard, and dialect words to show more current examples.
- Incorporated information about the electronic dictionary programs included in Web forms, blogs, wikis, and social networking sites.
- Presented information about adding spell-check programs to a browser or Google toolbar and about downloading dictionaries to MP3 players and cell phones.
- Modified instructions for using spell-check programs so that students can use the instructions in either Word 2003 or Word 2007.
- Included information about the most reliable handheld electronic dictionaries on the market.
- Revised and expanded the list of online dictionaries to describe the top eight dictionary Web sites, including Google Dictionary and Wiktionary.
- Revised illustrations and exercises to include current and lively examples.
- Enhanced margin notes with information about the history of English-language dictionaries, recommendations for learning more about the history of dictionaries, and information about how words are added to dictionaries.

Chapter 2

- Placed greater emphasis on the reasons for learning how to identify parts of speech.
- Added new bloopers to illustrate misuse of some parts of speech.
- Introduced new FAQs About Business English (formerly Hotline Queries) section by explaining what FAQs (Frequently Asked Questions) are.
- Added discussions to FAQs about the words *peaked* versus *piqued* and *forward* versus *foreword*.
- Changed many exercises to update and freshen references.
- Expanded exercise that requires students to write sentences using the same word as different parts of speech, a concept that many students find difficult.
- Revised the Learning Web Ways exercise to reflect the current Purdue Online Writing Lab (OWL) Web site.

- Added Chat About It discussion topics related to chapter content, including acronyms and abbreviations, the value of being able to identify parts of speech, capitalization of technology-related words, e-mail salutations, and palindromes.
- Restructured entire chapter for a clearer and more logical presentation of the concepts. Sentence patterns and types are now discussed before sentence faults.
- Reorganized "Sentence Elements" section to make this topic easier to understand.
- Reformatted example sentences to more clearly identify the simple subjects and simple predicates.
- Added new section on recognizing phrases and clauses to help students build complete sentences, use a variety of patterns, and avoid common sentence faults. This new section includes many examples of phrases, independent clauses, and dependent clauses to help students differentiate among these sentence building blocks.
- Added new section on sentence variety that introduces students to simple, compound, complex, and compound-complex sentences. This new section contains varied examples of each kind of sentence
- Added discussions to FAQs about the words *alot* versus *a lot* and *thru* versus *through*.
- Reformatted reinforcement exercises as needed to make it easier for students to complete them.
- Added a reinforcement exercise to cover new chapter concepts, including phrases, independent clauses, and dependent clauses as well as simple, compound, complex, and compound-complex sentences.
- Added a brief proofreading exercise to Writer's Workshop 1 to allow students to practice using proofreading marks.
- Revised Writing Application 1.1 in Writer's Workshop 1 to make instructions clearer. Converted sample introductory letter to a model, error-free document that students can use as a guide for preparing Writing Application 1.1.
- Placed more emphasis on the fact that apostrophes are used to make nouns possessive, not plural.
- Added plural forms of metric measurements.
- Double-checked every plural form to ensure that the most current forms are presented.
- Expanded the list of nouns borrowed from foreign languages to include three new words.
- Added coverage of the use of *lb.* as the abbreviation for pound to the FAQs.
- Added a reinforcement exercise for students to distinguish between concrete and abstract nouns.

- Added a reinforcement exercise about special nouns that are usually singular, are usually plural, or may be singular or plural.
- Reorganized chapter content to better group noun possessive concepts according to difficulty and usage.
- Added section on various ways to show noun possession, including verbs, prepositional phrases, and the possessive case.
- Simplified process for making nouns possessive, reducing it from five steps to three steps.
- Added a new section about making people's names possessive. Simplified this concept by removing information about the traditional versus popular forms.
- Added a new section about generic academic degrees, such as bachelor's degree and master's degree.
- Added discussion to the FAQs about the traditional versus popular forms for making proper nouns possessive.

Chapter 6
- Added more references to previous chapters to allow students to see connections between the concepts presented.
- Expanded discussion of possessive pronouns versus contractions.
- Added discussions to the FAQs about *apart* versus *a part* and *backup* versus *back up*.
- Revised Learning Web Ways exercise to introduce students to Bartleby.com Great Books Online.

Chapter 7
- Updated the list of suggested multipurpose unisex pronouns.
- Replaced the term *common gender* with *gender-biased* to reflect current terminology.
- Added discussion of sports teams and musical groups as antecedents.
- Removed discussion about *many a* as an antecedent to reflect contemporary usage.
- Added discussions to the FAQs about *your* versus *you're*, writing indefinite pronouns as one word or two, and *fiancé* versus *fiancée*.
- Completely revised Learning Web Ways exercise to give students even better practice in learning how to critically evaluate Web content.

Chapter 8
- Relocated the text material on helping verbs from Chapter 9 to Chapter 8 where it more logically fits.
- Added a section outlining action, linking, and helping verbs so that students can better understand these three categories of verbs.
- Improved discussion of helping verbs by adding reference to those verbs that express necessity or possibility.

- Added discussion to the FAQs about *premier* versus *premiere*.
- Scrutinized Reinforcement Exercises to make sure that all new concepts in the chapter are adequately covered in the proper level.
- Updated Learning Web Ways exercise to change discussion from grammar hotlines to Web-based FAQs.

Chapter 9
- Moved the helping verbs section to Chapter 8 where it improves comprehension.
- Explained more clearly that the present participle is formed the same way for both regular and irregular verbs.
- Strengthened list of Frequently Used Irregular Verbs by adding a column to show the present participle of irregular verbs.
- Expanded list of irregular verbs to include even more verbs that are challenging to students.
- Omitted passive form of progressive and perfect tenses to reflect common usage.
- Added discussions to the FAQs about *suppose* versus *supposed* and *cannot* versus *can not*.
- Revised Learning Web Ways to present discussion of online netiquette.

Chapter 10
- Changed the chapter title to "Subject-Verb Agreement" to reflect common terminology.
- Moved discussion of subjects preceded by *each* and *every* to Level 1 to place all references to subjects joined by *and* together.
- Removed discussion of *many a* to reflect current usage.
- Added discussion of subjects joined by and that represent one person or thing.
- Separated "Company Names and Titles" section into two separate sections for clarity.
- Added discussion of sports teams and musical groups as subjects.
- Included reference to titles of artistic works such as songs as subjects.
- Reorganized the section on "Indefinite Pronouns as Subjects" to increase comprehension. Separate discussion and examples are now included for indefinite pronouns that are always singular, always plural, or singular or plural.
- Added "percentages" to the discussion of fractions and portions as subjects.
- Reorganized the section on "Who Clauses" to create separate sections for plural *who* clauses and singular *who* clauses. Also added reference to that clauses.
- Added discussion to the FAQs about *anxious* versus *eager*.
- Presented new Learning Web Ways exercise that focuses on using social networking sites for business-related purposes.

- Provided an e-mail message that students can use as a model when completing the writing applications in the Unit 3 Writer's Workshop.

Chapter 11
- Reorganized the chapter to make the introduction of topics more pedagogically sound.
- Added a list of the most commonly used adverbs that do not end in *ly*.
- Moved discussion of whether to use adjectives or adverbs from Level 2 to Level 1 so that students are presented with this concept before studying comparatives and superlatives.
- Reformatted the section on comparative and superlative forms so that adjectives and adverbs are discussed separately. This new organization will improve student comprehension.
- Added *less/least* to the discussion of comparatives and superlatives.
- Moved sections on articles, demonstrative adjectives, possessive adjectives, and double negatives from Level 1 to Level 2 so that all modifiers deserving special attention are discussed in one level.
- Increased the number of examples of compound adjectives and ensured that all examples of compound adjectives reflect current usage.
- Added discussion and examples of hyphenated compound adjectives in which part of the compound adjective is implied.
- Moved the coverage of commonly confused adjectives and adverbs from Level 2 to Level 3.
- Deleted the section on absolute modifiers to reflect current usage.
- Added discussions to the FAQs about *desert* versus *dessert* and *awhile* versus *a while*.

Chapter 12
- Added a section discussing prepositional phrases, including several examples.
- Added additional idioms to the list including *appreciation for, convenient to, convenient for,* and *respect for*.
- Scrutinized each idiomatic expression to ensure that is complies with current usage guidelines.
- Added discussion to the FAQs about *onto* versus *on to*.

Chapter 13
- Converted all exercises to multiple-choice format to make it easier for students to respond.
- Expanded list of conjunctive adverbs.
- Added discussion to the FAQs about *perspective* versus *prospective*.

Chapter 14
- Included discussion of the importance of the serial comma.
- Added a definition for direct address.
- Revised list of parenthetical expressions to include expressions that students are most likely to use.
- Added discussion of Roman numerals added to names in "Degrees and Abbreviations" section.
- Added discussion to the FAQs about *emigrate* versus *immigrate*.
- Substantially increased number of reinforcement exercises to give students additional practice with commas

Chapter 15
- Added discussion of conjunctive adverbs used as parentheticals.
- Removed discussion of using commas to separate two short, closely related independent clauses to avoid confusion about what constitutes a comma splice.
- Included instructions for presenting long quotations of two sentences or more that will take up more than three lines.
- Added examples to show students how to punctuate in locations near abbreviations such as *i.e.* and *e.g.*
- Removed section on "Independent Clauses With Coordinating Conjunctions" to avoid the confusion that this optional rule causes.
- Explained the difference between mixed and open punctuation.
- Omitted section covering use of the colon in works cited and bibliographies to reflect current usage.
- Added discussions to the FAQs about spacing after colons and about *lessee* versus *lessor*.

Chapter 16
- Revised section on polite requests and included additional examples to make this concept clearer for students.
- Reorganized section on abbreviations to add headings that increase clarity.
- Included information about spacing after periods and other end punctuation.
- Added a new section about using the hyphen to form compound words, to form words with prefixes, to form compound numbers, and to divide a word over two lines.
- Added a new section on using the apostrophe to show possession, to form contractions, to take the place of omitted letters or figures, and to serve as the symbol for feet.
- Added discussions to the FAQs about spacing after colons and periods.
- Modified the Writer's Workshop to incorporate the 6 Cs of Business Communication, adding completeness and confidence.

Chapter 17
- Included many marginal notes about how capitalization differs in various languages.
- Reorganized Level 1 to begin chapter with the most basic capitalization rule of all: the first word in sentence.
- Added a new section about capitalizing the pronoun *I*.
- Added information about capitalizing days of the week.
- Changed rule regarding academic degrees when they are used after and in conjunction with a person's name to comply with the most up-to-date guidelines.
- Removed the rule about capitalizing seasons when they are personified.
- Created a separate section that discusses capitalization of business correspondence components, including salutations, complimentary closes, and subject lines.
- Added discussion and example of capitalization of titles appearing in a displayed list.
- Expanded the section on numbered and lettered items by adding capitalization of the word *vitamin*.
- Added discussion about capitalizing government offices/agencies and schools/colleges within universities.
- Expanded section on ethnic references to include coverage of cultural, language, and religious references.
- Added discussions to the FAQs about unconventional capitalization in company and product names.

Chapter 18
- Reorganized the section on general rules for expressing numbers to improve clarity.
- Added section about using commas in numbers.
- Added a new section about international time and the 24-hour clock format.
- Included marginal notes about number expression with temperatures and metric figures.
- Added discussion to the FAQs about differences between American and British English.

ACKNOWLEDGMENTS

We are indebted to many individuals for the continuing success of **Business English.** Instructors across the country have acted as reviewers or have sent us excellent ideas, constructive insights, and supportive comments. We are particularly grateful for the consultation of the following people:

Paige P. Baker,
Trinity Valley Community College

Joan W. Bass,
Clayton State University

Julie G. Becker,
Three Rivers Community College

Amy Beitel,
Cambria-Rowe Business College

Margaret Britt,
Copiah-Lincoln Community College

Leila Chambers,
Cuesta College

Connie Jo Clark,
Lane Community College

Robin Cook,
Sawyer School

Maria S. Damen,
University of Cincinnati/Raymond Walters College

Betty Dooley,
Clark State Community College

Cathy Dropkin,
Eldorado Colleges

Judy Ehresman,
Mercer County Community College

Valerie Evans,
Cuesta College

Diane J. Fisher,
The University of Southern Mississippi

Marye B. Gilford,
St. Philips College

Barbara Goza,
South Florida Community College

Margaret E. Gorman,
Cayuga Community College

Helen Grattan,
Des Moines Area Community College

Ginger Guzman,
J. Sargeant Reynolds Community College

Joy G. Haynes,
Chaffey College

Marilyn Helser,
Lima Technical College

Nancy A. Henderson,
North Harris College

Janet L. Hough,
Spokane Community College

Marilynne Hudgens,
Southwestern College

Iva A. Upchurch Jeffreys,
Ventura Community College

Edna V. Jellesed,
Lane Community College

Tina Johnson,
Lake Superior College

Evelyn A. Katusak,
Broome Community College

Lydia J. Keuser,
San Jose City College

Marilyn Kilbane,
Cuyahoga Community College

Donna Kimmerling,
Indiana Business College

Jared H. Kline,
Southeastern Community College

Ann Marie Klinko,
Northern Virginia Community College

Shelley Konishi,
Kauai Community College

Linell Loncorich,
Hutchinson Technical College

Jane Mangrum,
Miami-Dade Community College

Shirley Mays,
Hinds Community College

Darlene McClure,
College of the Redwoods

Timothy A. Miank,
Lansing Community College

Carol Vermeere Middendorff,
Clackamas Community College

Anita Musto,
Utah Valley State College

Paul W. Murphey,
Southwest Wisconsin Technical College

Jaunett S. Neighbors,
Central Virginia Community College

Mary Nerburn,
Moraine Valley Community College

Jackie Ohlson,
University of Alaska

Mary Quimby,
Southwestern College

Jana Rada,
Western Wisconsin Technical College

Susan Randles,
Vatterott College

Carol Jo Reitz,
Allentown Business School

Judith R. Rice,
Chippewa Valley Technical College

Kathie Richer,
Edmonds Community College

Benelle Robinson,
Ventura Community College

Maria Robinson,
Columbia College

Sally Rollman,
Shoreline Community College

Jan Sales,
Merced College

Linda Serra,
Glendale Community College

Mageya R. Sharp,
Cerritos College

Susan Simons,
Edmonds Community College

Marilyn Simonson,
Lakewood Community College

Lynn E. Steffen,
College of Lake County

Letha Strain,
Riverside College

Susan Sutkowski,
Minneapolis Technical College

Evelyn Taylor,
Cincinnati Bible College

Michelle Taylor,
Ogeechee Technical College

Robert Thaden,
Tacoma Community College

Dorothy Thornhill,
Los Angeles Trade Technical College

James A. Trick,
Newport Business Institute

Susan Uchida,
Kauai Community College

June Uharriet,
East Los Angeles Community College

Lois A. Wagner,
Southwest Wisconsin Technical College

Fred Wolven,
Miami-Dade Community College

Many professionals at South-Western, a part of Cengage Learning, have helped propel **Business English** to its prominent position in the field. For their contributions in producing the **Tenth Edition,** we sincerely thank Jack Calhoun, Melissa Acuna, Erin Joyner, Kim Kusnerak, John Rich, Stacy Shirley, and especially Mary Draper, my incomparable developmental editor. Special thanks go to Jane Flesher and Catherine Peck, Chippewa Valley Technical College, for their enormous help in preparing student online materials.

Author Accessibility

No business communication or English book on the market offers more instructor support and author interaction than **Business English.** Through teaching seminars, e-mail, author Web sites, personal messages, and online newsletters, we try to stay in touch with those of you in the trenches. Our goal is to be accessible and responsive authors who provide relevant, practical, and quality materials for immediate classroom use. As always, we are delighted to receive comments about your course and suggestions for improving this book from messages left at our Web site (Talk to the Authors).

Dr. Mary Ellen Guffey
Emerita Professor of Business
Los Angeles Pierce College

Professor Carolyn M. Seefer
Professor of Business
Diablo Valley College

Contents

In the following sentences, you will find faulty grammar, punctuation, capitalization, and number expression. For each sentence underline any error. Then write a corrected form in the space provided. If you must add punctuation, also show the word that appears immediately before the necessary punctuation mark. Each sentence contains one error.

Example: Manufacturers know that the size and design of a product like the iPod <u>is</u> critical to its success. _____are_____

LEVEL 1

1. Businesspeople are sending more e-mail messages than ever before, that's why writing skills are increasingly important. _____

2. A network security workshop next month in Seattle, Washington will help our firm learn techniques for keeping our network safe. _____

3. In it's latest online announcement, our Information Technology Department said that even the best-protected information sometimes is lost, erased, or corrupted. _____

4. Louis and I certainly appreciate your taking our calls for us when he and me are away from the office. _____

5. A summary of all of our customers' comments for the past month were given to the manager and her last week. _____

6. Every field employee, as well as every manager and department head, are eligible for tuition reimbursement. _____

7. For you Mr. Johnson, we have a one-year subscription to *The Wall Street Journal*. _____

8. I plan to go to law school after i complete my undergraduate degree. _____

9. We couldn't barely believe that our colleagues agreed to the plan. _____

10. In the spring Kathy took courses in history, english, and management. _____

LEVEL 2

11. Please collect all of the graduates names and e-mail addresses so that we can keep them informed of job opportunities. _____

12. Either Jimbo or she will be working overtime on the next two Friday's. _____

13. Of the forty-six orders placed by customers last week, only 9 were filled on time. _____

14. If you expect a three-week vacation, you must speak to the Manager immediately.

_____

15. You should have saw the warehouse before its contents were moved to 39th Street.

_____

16. Your job interview with the manager and her will last for a hour.

_____

17. Before her trip to the East last summer, my mother bought an Olympus Camera.

_____

18. We need only 20 44-cent postage stamps to finish the mailing.

_____

19. Your account is now 90 days overdue, therefore, we are submitting it to an agency for collection.

_____

20. We feel badly about your missing the deadline, but the application has been lying on your desk for 15 days.

_____

LEVEL 3

21. Under the circumstances, we can give you only 90 days time in which to sell the house and its contents.

_____

22. The cost of the coast-to-coast flight should be billed to whomever made the airline reservation.

_____

23. Los Angeles is larger than any city on the West Coast.

_____

24. The number of suggestions made by employees are increasing each month as employees become more involved.

_____

25. Our school's alumni are certainly different than its currently enrolled students.

_____

26. Courtney is one of those efficient, competent managers who is able to give sincere praise for work done well.

_____

27. Because she looks like her sister, Kendra is often taken to be her.

_____

28. If I were him, I would call the Cortezes' attorney at once.

_____

29. Three employees will be honored, namely, Lucy Lee, Tony Waters, and Jamie Craig.

_____

30. If you drive a little further, you will come to the library on the right side of the street.

_____

Unit 1

Laying a Foundation

1 Reference Skills

© Steve Hix/Somos Images/Corbis

2 Parts of Speech

© Pixland/Jupiterimages

3 Sentences: Elements, Varieties, Patterns, Types, Faults

© Getty Images/liquidlibrary/Jupiterimages

"Businesses are crying out—they need to have people who write better."

—Gaston Caperton
Business executive and president, College Board

Chapter 1

Reference Skills

OBJECTIVES

When you have completed the materials in this chapter, you will be able to do the following:

- Understand the content of business English and its relevance to you and your career.
- Describe several types of dictionaries, including print, electronic, and online.
- Use a dictionary confidently to determine spelling, meaning, pronunciation, syllabication, accent, word usage, and word history.
- Select a dictionary to suit your needs.
- Anticipate what information is included in dictionaries and what information is not.
- Understand the value of reference manuals.

Each chapter begins with a brief pretest. Answer the questions in the pretest to assess your prior knowledge of the chapter content and also to give yourself a preview of what you will learn. Compare your answers with those at the bottom of the page. When you complete the chapter, take the posttest to measure your improvement. Write *T* (true) or *F* (false) after the following statements.

1. Online dictionaries have made printed dictionaries obsolete. _____

2. Dictionary diacritical marks help readers pronounce words correctly. _____

3. The usage label *colloquial* means that a word is no longer in use. _____

4. Some online dictionaries provide audio pronunciations of words. _____

5. Reference manuals provide information about punctuation and hyphenation. _____

6. Good communication skills can help you succeed in your job. _____

7. To be considered an expert, you must know all of the answers to questions in your field. _____

8. A college-level dictionary contains no more than 75,000 entries. _____

9. A print dictionary should be no older than five years to be considered up-to-date. _____

10. The *etymology* of a word refers to its history. _____

Business English is the study of the language fundamentals needed to communicate effectively in today's workplace. These basics include grammar, usage, punctuation, capitalization, number style, and spelling. Because businesspeople must express their ideas clearly and correctly, such language basics are critical.

Why Study Business English?

What you learn in this class will help you communicate more professionally when you write and when you speak. These skills will help you get the job you want, succeed in the job you have, or prepare for promotion to a better position. Good communication skills can also help you succeed in the classroom and in your personal life, but we will be most concerned with workplace applications.

Increasing Emphasis on Workplace Communication

In today's workplace you can expect to be doing more communicating than ever before. You will be participating in meetings, writing business documents, and using technology such as e-mail and instant messaging to communicate with others.

1. F 2. T 3. F 4. T 5. T 6. T 7. F 8. F 9. T 10. T

Communication skills are more important than ever before, and the emphasis on writing has increased dramatically. Businesspeople who never expected to be doing much writing on the job find that e-mail and the Web force everyone to exchange written messages. As a result, businesspeople are increasingly aware of their communication skills. Misspelled words, poor grammar, sloppy punctuation—all of these faults stand out glaringly when they are in print or displayed online. Not only are people writing more, but their messages travel farther. Messages are seen by larger audiences than ever before. Because of the growing emphasis on exchanging information, language skills are more relevant today than ever before.

What Does This Mean for You?

As a businessperson or professional, you want to feel confident about your writing skills. This textbook and this course can sharpen your skills and greatly increase your confidence in expressing ideas. Improving your language skills is the first step toward success in your education, your career, and your life.

When Jennifer M. enrolled in this course emphasizing language basics, she did not plan to become an expert in the subject. After finishing the course, she didn't think of herself as an expert. When she started to work, however, she discovered that many of her fellow workers considered her an English expert. Most of them had no training in grammar, or they had studied it long ago. Their skills were rusty. Jennifer found that even her boss asked her questions. "Do I need to put a comma here?" "Should this word be capitalized?" Because she was a recent graduate, her coworkers assumed she knew all the answers. Jennifer didn't know all the answers. But she knew where to find them, and this ability made her more valuable in her workplace.

One of the goals of your education is to know where to find answers. You should also know how to interpret the information you find. Experts do not know *all* the answers. Attorneys refer to casebooks. Doctors consult their medical libraries. And you, as a student of the language, must develop skill and confidence in using reference materials. You can become a language expert not only by learning from this textbook but also by learning where to find additional data when you need it.

Dictionaries

Using reference materials should become second nature to you. Dictionaries and online resources are invaluable when you must verify word spellings and meanings, punctuation style, and usage. If you have your own personal library of reference materials, you can find information quickly. At the minimum you need a current desk or college dictionary and a good reference manual. Another helpful reference book is a **thesaurus**. This is a collection of **synonyms** (words with similar meanings) and **antonyms** (words with opposite meanings). Many helpful resources are now available digitally, whether online or in a software program such as MS Word.

A **dictionary** is an alphabetical list of words with their definitions. Most dictionaries contain pronunciation guides, parts of speech, **etymology** (word history), labels, and other information, which you will learn about in this chapter. You can purchase dictionaries in almost every language. Bilingual dictionaries, such as English-Spanish and Italian-French, are increasingly popular in today's global marketplace. Dictionaries dedicated to topics such as American Sign Language (ASL), slang, and acronyms are also available. In addition, many fields, such as law and medicine, have specialized dictionaries that contain vocabulary specific to that field.

Businesspeople today make use of both print dictionaries and online dictionaries. Even with the availability of online dictionaries, many prefer to have a print dictionary handy to look words up quickly and easily. First, you will learn about print dictionaries, including how to select one and how to use it. Then, you will learn about using an electronic dictionary, such as the one that comes with your word processing software. Finally, you will learn how to use online dictionaries.

Selecting a Print Dictionary

Not all print dictionaries are the same, as you will notice when you shop for one. To make a wise selection, you should know how to distinguish among three kinds of print dictionaries: pocket, desk, and unabridged. You should also know when your dictionary was published (the copyright date), and you should examine its special features.

Pocket Dictionary

As its name suggests, a **pocket dictionary** is small. Generally, it contains no more than 75,000 entries, making it handy to carry to class and efficient to use. However, a pocket dictionary doesn't contain enough entries to be adequate for postsecondary or college reference homework. In addition, the information provided about each word in a pocket dictionary is generally limited.

Trivia Tidbit

The first American dictionary, *A Compendious Dictionary of the English Language*, was written by Noah Webster and published in 1806.

Desk or College-Level Dictionary

A **desk** or **college-level dictionary** generally contains over 170,000 entries plus extra features. For college work you should own a current desk or college-level dictionary. The following list shows some of the best-known dictionaries in this category. Notice that the titles of two dictionaries contain the name *Webster*. Because names cannot be copyrighted, any publisher may use the word *Webster* on its dictionary. Definitions and usage in this textbook are based on *Merriam-Webster's Collegiate Dictionary*. Publishers often rely on this dictionary as their standard. Many readers, however, prefer *The American Heritage College Dictionary*. It provides more plural spellings, more usage labels, more readable entries, and more opinions about appropriate usage than most other dictionaries. However, any one of the following dictionaries is a good choice for postsecondary and college students:

> *Merriam-Webster's Collegiate Dictionary* (the standard dictionary for definitions and usage in this textbook)
>
> *The American Heritage College Dictionary*
>
> *Random House Webster's College Dictionary*
>
> *Webster's New World College Dictionary*
>
> *Oxford American College Dictionary*

Unabridged Dictionary

An **unabridged dictionary** is a complete dictionary. **Abridged dictionaries**, such as pocket and desk dictionaries, are shortened or condensed. Because unabridged dictionaries contain nearly all English words, they are large, heavy volumes. Schools, libraries, newspaper offices, and organizations concerned with editing or publishing use unabridged dictionaries. One of the best-known unabridged dictionaries is *Webster's Third New International Dictionary*. It includes over 450,000 entries and claims to be America's largest dictionary. Another

Study Tip

To *abridge* means to "shorten"; a bridge shortens the distance between points. An "unabridged" book has not been shortened.

famous unabridged dictionary is the *Oxford English Dictionary* (*OED*). This 20-volume set shows the historical development of all English words; it is often used by professional writers, scholars of the language, and academics. CD-ROM versions are available for easy computer searching.

Copyright Date

If the copyright date of your current dictionary shows that it was published five or more years ago, consider investing in a more recent edition. English is a responsive, dynamic language that admits new words and recognizes changes in meaning, spelling, and usage of familiar words. These changes are reflected in an up-to-date dictionary. For example, the following words were added to the *Merriam-Webster's Collegiate Dictionary* in 2008: *infinity pool, kiteboarding, malware, mental health day, pretexting,* and *webinar.*

Features

In selecting a dictionary, check the features it offers in addition to vocabulary definitions. Many editions contain biographical and geographical data, abbreviations, standard measurements, signs, symbols, foreign words and phrases, and information about the language. Some also contain CD-ROMs and access to special online features.

Using a Print Dictionary

Study Tip

Many of the tips for using a print dictionary can also be applied when using an online dictionary.

Whether you purchased a new one or you are using a family dictionary, take a few moments to become familiar with it so that you can use it wisely.

Introduction

Before using your dictionary, take a look at the instructions located in the pages just before the beginning of the vocabulary entries. Pay particular attention to the order of definitions. Some dictionaries show the most common definitions first. Other dictionaries develop meanings historically; that is, the first known meaning of the word is shown first.

Guide Words

In boldface type at the top of each dictionary page are two words that indicate the first and last entries on the page. When searching for a word, look *only* at these guide words until you locate the desired page. Using this technique will save you a lot of time.

Syllabication

Most dictionaries show syllable breaks with a centered dot, as you see in Figure 1.1 for the word *signify.* Compound words are sometimes troublesome to dictionary users. If a compound word is shown with a centered dot, it is one word, as in *work•out* (workout). If a compound word is shown with a hyphen, it is hyphenated, as in *old-fashioned.* If two words appear without a centered dot or a hyphen, they should be written as two words, as in *work up.* If you find no entry for a word or phrase in a college-level dictionary, you may usually assume that the words are written separately, for example, *ball field.* For newer terms, such as *home page* or *spyware,* you should check an online dictionary.

Pronunciation

Diacritical marks are special symbols that help you pronounce words correctly. A detailed explanation of pronunciation symbols is found in the front pages of a dictionary. A summary of these symbols may appear at the bottom of each set of pages. If two pronunciations are possible, the preferred one is usually shown first.

FIGURE 1.1
Dictionary Entry

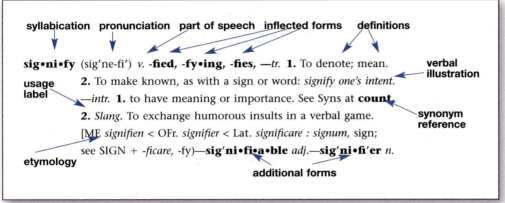

Source: © 2010 by Houghton Mifflin Harcourt Publishing Company. Reproduced by permission from *The American Heritage College Dictionary, Fourth Edition.*

Accent

Accent refers to the syllable of a word that gets the most emphasis or stress when you pronounce it. Most dictionaries show accents with a raised stress mark immediately following the accented syllable, as shown for the syllable *sig* in Figure 1.1. Other dictionaries use a raised stress mark immediately *preceding* the accented syllable (*'sig ni 'fi*). Secondary stress may be shown in lighter print (as illustrated on the syllable *fi* in Figure 1.1), or it may be shown with a *lowered* accent mark (*'sig ni ,fi*).

Etymology

Etymology shows the history of a word. College-level dictionaries often provide a brief word history in square brackets [ ]. For example, the word *signify* has its roots in Middle English, Old French, and Latin. Keys to etymological abbreviations may be found in the introductory notes in your dictionary. Do not confuse the etymological definition shown in brackets with the actual word definitions.

Trivia Tidbit

The primary language from which English evolved during the fifth and sixth centuries AD is German.

Part of Speech

Following the phonetic pronunciation of an entry word is an italicized or bold-faced label indicating what part of speech the entry word represents. The most common labels are the following:

adj	(adjective)	*prep*	(preposition)
adv	(adverb)	*pron*	(pronoun)
conj	(conjunction)	*v* or *vb*	(verb)
interj	(interjection)	*vt* or *v tr*	(verb transitive)
n	(noun)	*vi* or *v int*	(verb intransitive)

Spelling, pronunciation, and meaning may differ for a given word when that word functions as different parts of speech. Therefore, check its grammatical label carefully. If the parts of speech seem foreign to you at this time, do not worry. Chapter 2 and successive chapters will help you learn more about the parts of speech.

Study Tip

For a fascinating look at the making of the *Oxford English Dictionary*, read *The Professor and the Madman* by Simon Winchester.

Labels

Not all words listed in dictionaries are acceptable in business or professional writing. **Usage labels** warn readers about the use of certain words. In the dictionary entry shown in Figure 1.1, notice that one meaning for the word *signify* is labeled *slang*. The following list defines *slang* and other usage labels:

Label	Example
archaic: words surviving from a previous period	*twixt* (meaning "between")
obsolete: words no longer in use	*darg* (meaning "a day's work")
colloquial or *informal**: words used in casual writing or conversation but not in formal speech	*how come* (meaning *why*)
slang: very informal words that quickly go out of fashion	*off the hinges* (meaning "great," "outstanding")
nonstandard and *substandard*: words not conforming to usage among educated speakers	*ain't*
dialect, *Brit.*, *South*, *Scot*, etc.: words used in certain countries or regions	*fixing* (verb used in the American South to mean "getting ready to do something")

Some dictionaries no longer use the labels colloquial *or* informal.

If no usage label appears, a word is considered standard; that is, it is acceptable for all uses. However, it should be noted that many lexicographers have substantially reduced the number of usage labels in current editions. **Lexicographers**, by the way, are those who make dictionaries.

Inflected Forms
When nouns, verbs, adverbs, or adjectives change form grammatically, they are said to be **inflected**, as when *child* becomes *children*. Because of limited space, dictionaries usually show only irregular inflected forms. Thus, nouns with irregular or unusual plurals (*wife, wives*) will be shown. Verbs with irregular tenses or difficult spelling (*bring, brought*) will be shown. Adverbs or adjectives with irregular comparatives or superlatives (*good, better, best*) will also be shown. But regular noun plurals, verb tenses, and comparatives generally will *not* be shown in dictionaries. Succeeding chapters will elucidate regular and irregular parts of speech.

Synonyms and Antonyms
Synonyms, words having similar meanings, are often provided after word definitions. For example, a synonym for *elucidate* is *explain*. Synonyms are helpful as word substitutes. **Antonyms**, words having opposite meanings, appear less frequently in dictionaries; when included, they usually follow synonyms. One antonym for *elucidate* is *confuse*. The best place to find synonyms and antonyms is in a thesaurus.

Using Electronic Dictionary Programs
Most word processing programs today come with a dictionary/thesaurus feature that helps you locate misspelled words as well as search for synonyms and antonyms. In addition, most e-mail programs now include a spell-check feature that uses an electronic dictionary. You may even be able to program your e-mail program to automatically spell-check your messages when you press the **Send** button. Many Web forms (such as online employment applications) completed online contain built-in spell-checkers. In addition, blogs, wikis, and social networking sites include spell-checkers. You can even add a spell-check tool to your browser or Google toolbar.

Trivia Tidbit

Words are added to the dictionary according to usage. Before a word is added, dictionary editors must prove that it is widely used.

REFERENCE SKILLS

Locating Misspelled Words

An **electronic dictionary**, also called a **spell-checker**, compares your typed words with those in the computer's memory. MS Word uses a wavy red line to underline misspelled words as you type them. If you immediately recognize the error, you can quickly key in the correction. If you see the red wavy line and don't know what's wrong, you can right-click on the word. This displays a drop-down menu that generally shows a variety of options to solve your spelling problem. If one of the suggested spellings appears correct, you can click it and the misspelled word is replaced.

Many writers today rely heavily on their spell-checkers; in fact, many may rely too much on them. The real problem is that spell-checkers won't catch every error. For example, spell-checkers can't always distinguish between similar words, such as *too* and *two*. That's why you should proofread every message carefully after running it through your spell-checker. In addition, important messages should be printed out for proofreading.

Searching for Synonyms and Antonyms

Electronic dictionary programs often include an online thesaurus showing alternative word choices. Let's say you are writing a report and you find yourself repeating the same word. With MS Word you can right-click the word and select **Synonyms** from the drop-down menu. A number of synonyms will appear in a dialogue box. If you see an appropriate synonym, simply click the word to replace the original word. You can also select **Thesaurus** from the dialogue box to access the complete thesaurus feature. A good online thesaurus can be a terrific aid to writers who want to use precise language as well as increase their vocabularies.

Using Online and Other High-Tech Dictionaries

An increasing number of electronic resources are available on the Web, on CD-ROMs, and as handheld devices. The Web provides an amazing amount of information at little or no cost to users. Many excellent online resources, some of which are described in Figure 1.2, are similar to their print counterparts. The big differences, though, are that most of the online versions are free and many also provide audio pronunciations of words. Some even give you hyperlinked cross-references. Online dictionaries are especially useful because they can be updated immediately when new words or meanings enter the language.

Online dictionary sites offer many features. Figure 1.2 provides a list of some of the most notable and recommended online dictionary sites. Want a quick definition for a word? Simply go to Google and type the word *define*, a colon, and the word you would like defined (example, *define:supercilious*). A list of definitions from a variety of online sources will appear.

If you don't want to bother searching the Web to look up a word, you may purchase one of many **CD-ROM dictionaries** that can be installed on your computer. *Merriam-Webster's Collegiate Dictionary & Thesaurus, Electronic Edition* and the *Oxford English Dictionary on CD-ROM* give you access to large databases of words that can be easily searched electronically. Many print dictionaries also come bundled with a CD-ROM version of the text. You can even download dictionaries to your MP3 player or cell phone.

Handheld electronic dictionaries offer another efficient way to check spellings, find meanings, and look up synonyms. Many students and businesspeople find handhelds easy to use. They are especially appealing to people struggling with a different language, such as tourists, interpreters, emigrants, and immigrants. Some of these devices provide audio pronunciations. Franklin Electronics, Sharp, and Zelco make some of the most popular handheld devices on the market.

FIGURE 1.2
Notable Online Dictionaries

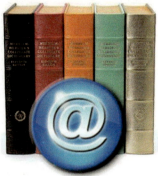

An amazing number of Web sites offer free dictionaries and usage advice. If any of the URLs for the sites listed here have changed, just put the name into a search tool (**www.google.com**) and you should find it.

- **Merriam-Webster Online (http://www.m-w.com).** Offers audio pronunciations (click on the red speaker icon next to any word to hear its pronunciation), etymologies, and authoritative definitions of a vast number of words. Provides word games and essays on the history of English and the processes involved in the making of dictionaries. The "Word of the Day" feature can help you increase your vocabulary. You can even have vocabulary words delivered via e-mail or podcasts.

- **Wiktionary (http://www.wiktionary.org).** A part of the online encyclopedia Wikipedia, this collaborative project aims to create a free, open-content dictionary in every language, including meanings, etymologies, pronunciations, sample quotations, and synonyms and antonyms. This site also contains a thesaurus, a rhyme guide, and other related tools.

- **Google Dictionary (http://www.google.com/dictionary).** An online dictionary with an extremely simple interface. Type in a word, and Google Dictionary will provide definitions from a variety of online sources.

- **OneLook Dictionaries (http://www.onelook.com).** Claims to index approximately 13 million words contained in more than 975 dictionaries (at this writing). Accesses computer/Internet, science, medical, technological, business, sports, religion, and general dictionaries. Allows wildcard searching if you are unsure of an exact spelling.

- **Encarta World English Dictionary (http://www.dictionary.msn.com).** Not only defines and pronounces words but also links to atlases, maps, and encyclopedia articles from Microsoft's *Encarta*. Also features a message board where you can ask questions, share information, and offer advice.

- **TheFreeDictionary.com (http://www.thefreedictionary.com).** Claims to be the most comprehensive dictionary in the world. In addition to a standard dictionary, the site has links to computer, medical, legal, and financial dictionaries, as well as dictionaries in a variety of languages. You will also find links to dictionaries of acronyms, abbreviations, and idioms. In addition, you will find links to Wikipedia, a literature reference library, and other valuable resources. You can even customize your FreeDictionary homepage by adding the tools you want, including a personalized word list, Word of the Day, Article of the Day, In the News, This Day in History, Quotation of the Day, Today's Birthday, weather, and games such as hangman, a spelling bee, and a matching game.

- **Dictionary.com (http://dictionary.reference.com/).** Provides links to a variety of references, including English dictionaries, foreign language dictionaries, thesauruses, online translators, and language-related articles. Users can also access a word-of-the-day feature, vocabulary games, podcasts, reverse dictionaries, and a resource center.

- **YourDictionary.com (http://www.yourdictionary.com/).** Calls itself "The last word in words." Provides definitions, thesaurus entries, spelling, pronunciation, and etymology results for each word you enter. Also provides language and translation tools, word games, links to specialized dictionaries, a language forum, and wildcard searching. You can even follow YourDictionary on Twitter.

Reference Manuals

In addition to one or more printed dictionaries, every writer should have a good reference manual or handbook readily available.

Career Tip

For use now and on the job, invest in a good reference manual, such as Clark and Clark's *HOW 12: A Handbook for Office Professionals* (Cengage Learning).

Reference Manuals Versus Dictionaries

A reference manual generally contains helpful information not available in a dictionary. Two popular reference manuals are *How 12: A Handbook for Office Professionals* and *The Gregg Reference Manual*. Most reference manuals provide information such as the following:

- **Punctuation.** Detailed explanations of punctuation rules are presented logically. A well-written manual also provides ample illustrations of punctuation usage so you can readily find solutions to punctuation dilemmas.
- **Hyphenation.** Dictionaries provide syllable breaks. Words, however, cannot be divided at all syllable breaks. A reference manual supplies rules for, and examples of, word division. Moreover, a good reference manual explains when compound adjectives such as *up-to-the-minute* should be hyphenated.
- **Capitalization.** Complete rules with precise examples illustrating capitalization style are shown.
- **Number style.** Deciding whether to write a number as a figure or as a word can be difficult. A reference manual provides both instruction and numerous examples illustrating number and word styles.
- **Commonly confused words.** Do you have trouble deciding whether to use *affect* or *effect*, *its* or *it's*, *than* or *then*, or *principal* or *principle*? Reference manuals contain complete lists of commonly confused words to help you choose the right one.
- **Abbreviations.** What is the two-letter state abbreviation for Arkansas? Can the abbreviation *a.m.* be written with uppercase letters? Should you add periods to the abbreviation *FBI*? A good reference manual can help answer your questions about using those tricky abbreviations and acronyms.

Other topics covered in reference manuals are contractions, literary and artistic titles, forms of address, letter and report formats, employment application documents, information sources, and file management. In addition, some manuals contain sections devoted to English grammar and office procedures. This textbook is correlated with the widely used *Handbook for Office Professionals* (Cengage Learning) by Clark and Clark.

Reference Manuals Versus Your Textbook

You may be wondering how a reference manual differs from a business English textbook such as the one you are now reading. Although their content is similar, the primary difference is one of purpose. A textbook is developed *pedagogically*—that is, for teaching—so that the student understands and learns concepts. It includes teaching and learning exercises. A reference manual is organized *functionally*, so that the reader finds accurate information efficiently. A well-written reference manual is complete, coherent, and concise.

Most of the language and style questions that perplex businesspeople and students could be answered quickly by a trained person using a reliable dictionary and a well-written reference manual.

Spot the BLOOPER

What is a **blooper**? Television producer Kermit Schaefer first defined the word *blooper* to describe mistakes made on television, radio, and film. Today the word *blooper* is used to describe any embarrassing blunder. In this textbook we use the word *blooper* to refer to language mistakes made in writing and speech. At the end of each chapter, you will find a list of written and spoken bloopers. Many of these bloopers appeared in prestigious publications or were spoken by highly respected individuals. Using the skills you are learning in this class, try to identify why these are bloopers. Consult your textbook, dictionary, or reference manual as needed.

Blooper 1: On résumés that crossed the desk of personnel expert Robert Half: "Instrumental in ruining entire operation for a Midwest chain of stores." "Here are my qualifications for you to overlook." "Hope to hear from you shorty."

Blooper 2: CBS News anchor Dan Rather speaking on CNN's *Larry King Live*: "Cable news is revelant, of course, but I think network news is, if anything, even more revelant."

Blooper 3: A flyer promoting a square dance weekend in Daytona Beach lists the location as the Dessert Inn Hotel.

Blooper 4: Sign in a souvenir shop in York Beach [Maine]: "You brake it, you pay for it."

Blooper 5: Public meeting notice in the *Daily Express* [Newport, Vermont]: "Interrupters will be there to help the deaf community."

Blooper 6: Magazine advertisement for a dentist in Monterey, California: "You wear your smile everyday. Make it the best!."

Blooper 7: Sign at Cambridge University in Great Britain: "Entrance to Collage Car Park Only."

Blooper 8: Photo caption in the *News-Sentinel* [Lodi, California]: "Remains of buildings, including the house George Washington lived in when he was president, are seen at the sight of an archaeological dig in Philadelphia."

Blooper 9: Headline in the sports section of *The Quad-City Times* [Davenport, Iowa]: "State titles allude Q-C area teams."

Blooper 10: Article about college football in the *San Francisco Chronicle*: "Bowl results are often sited as evidence, but the conference with the best winning percentage in bowl games the past three years is the Western Athletic Conference."

1 Reinforcement Exercises

Note: At the beginning of every set of reinforcement exercises, a self-check exercise is provided so that you will know immediately whether you understand the concepts presented in the chapter. Do not look at the answers until you have completed the exercise. Then compare your responses with the answers shown at the bottom of the page. If you have more than three incorrect responses, reread the chapter before continuing with the other reinforcement exercises.

 A. (Self-check) Write *T* (true) or *F* (false) after the following statements.

1. Because all dictionaries contain similar information, it doesn't matter which type of dictionary you purchase or use. _____

2. Students and office workers would find an unabridged dictionary handy to carry with them. _____

3. The label *archaic* means that a word is informal and may be used in casual writing and conversation. _____

4. Knowing which syllable is accented can help you pronounce words correctly. _____

5. Dictionaries usually show noun plurals only if they are irregular. _____

6. Rules for using abbreviations may be found in a reference manual. _____

7. All dictionaries show definitions in historical order. _____

8. Today's spell-check programs can be used to locate all misspelled words in a document. _____

9. Print dictionaries are not needed by college students today. _____

10. Some print dictionaries come bundled with a CD-ROM version of the text. _____

Check your answers at the bottom of the page.

Use a desk, college-level, electronic, or online dictionary to complete the following exercises. The definitions, pronunciations, and usage in this book come from *Merriam-Webster's Collegiate Dictionary*.

 B. Select the letter that provides the best definition or synonym for each word shown.

1. pandemic (adj)   a. famous   c. notorious
                b. widespread   d. panoramic _____

2. entomology (n)   a. study of words   c. study of insects
                b. study of fossils   d. love of outdoors _____

3. imminent (adj)   a. impending   c. famous
                b. old   d. stubborn _____

4. integrity (n)   a. value   c. perseverance
                b. honesty   d. loyalty _____

1. F 2. F 3. F 4. T 5. T 6. T 7. F 8. F 9. F 10. T

5. ostentatious (adj)   a. annoying   c. eager

                            b. rude   d. showy   _____

6. feasible (adj)   a. possible   c. likeable

                            b. unlikely   d. difficult   _____

7. supercilious (adj) a. large   c. haughty

                            b. silly   d. circuitous _____

8. tepid (adj)   a. lukewarm   c. fast

                            b. fearful   d. lazy   _____

9. meander (v)   a. to follow a winding course   c. to say something unflattering

                            b. to misplace   d. to arrive   _____

10. inept (n)   a. unprepared   c. unaware

                            b. unfit   d. inescapable _____

C. Write the correct form of the following words. Use a current dictionary to determine whether these compound words should be written as one or two words or should be hyphenated.

Example: print out (n)   printout_____

1. co worker   _____   **6.** work place   _____

2. in as much as   _____   **7.** first class (adj.)   _____

3. in depth   _____   **8.** first class (n)   _____

4. on line   _____   **9.** day care   _____

5. out of date   _____   **10.** Web site   _____

D. For each of the following words, write the syllable that receives the primary accent. Then give a brief definition or synonym of the word. If more than one pronunciation appears in your dictionary, use the first one given, which is generally the preferred pronunciation.

Word	Syllable	Definition or Synonym
Example: judicious	di	prudent, exhibiting sound judgment
1. comparable	_____	_____
2. desert (n)	_____	_____
3. desert (v)	_____	_____
4. indefatigable	_____	_____
5. irrevocable	_____	_____
6. posthumous	_____	_____
7. Caribbean	_____	_____
8. electoral	_____	_____
9. mischievous	_____	_____
10. chimera	_____	_____

E. Select the letter that most accurately completes the sentence.

1. The word *chauvinism* derives from Nicholas *Chauvin*, a Frenchman known as a(n)

    a. fanatical bomb thrower   c. extreme misogynist (woman hater)

    b. excessive patriot   d. radical critic of Napoleon   _____

2. If Angelica attends a training session and reports that it was *superficial,* she means that it was
    a. shallow and without substance   c. super helpful
    b. extremely entertaining   d. fun but worthless

    _____

3. The abbreviation for the Occupational Safety and Health Administration is
    a. O.S.H.A.   c. Osha
    b. OSHA   d. OS&HA

    _____

4. Which of the following is correctly written?
    a. American novel   c. american novel
    b. American Novel   d. american Novel

    _____

5. When businesspeople talk about *malware,* they are referring to
    a. computer equipment   c. a flu-like virus
    b. goods that are not durable   d. software that disrupts computer functions

    _____

6. If an expression is *redundant,* it is
    a. repetitive   c. obsolete
    b. clever   d. awkward

    _____

7. The word *spam,* which now means "unsolicited e-mail," derives from
    a. a slang term for an annoying person   c. users who hate receiving it
    b. *Monty Python's Flying Circus*   d. senders who want to remain anonymous

    _____

8. Because Sophia wanted to _____ that all of her friends received her new e-mail address, she sent everyone a special announcement.
    a. assure   c. insure
    b. ensure   d. advice

    _____

9. The word *irregardless* is given what label in the dictionary?
    a. archaic   c. nonstandard
    b. slang   d. dialect

    _____

10. What is a *lift* in British dialect?
    a. a rise   c. a forceful, aggressive athlete
    b. a type of hair style   d. an elevator

    _____

F. **Writing Exercise.** All employers seek workers with good writing skills. In this book you will find unit workshops devoted to developing your writing skills. In addition, each chapter will include a short writing exercise. Let's say that a friend asks you to explain what a reference manual is and why it might be useful. Write two or three complete sentences with your explanation.

_____
_____
_____
_____

In two or three complete sentences, tell whether you prefer a print or an online dictionary. Explain why.

_____
_____
_____
_____

To make sure you enter the work world with good online skills, this book provides a short Web exercise in each chapter. If your instructor assigns this exercise, you will need access to a computer with an Internet connection. Additionally, your computer must have a Web browser, such as Microsoft Internet Explorer or Netscape Mozilla Firefox. These programs enable you to see and use Web pages.

All Web pages have addresses called **URLs** (uniform resource locators). URLs must be typed exactly as they are shown, including periods (.), hyphens (-), underscores (_), slashes (/), tildes (~), and upper- or lowercase letters. URLs are often enclosed in angle brackets < > when they are shown in print. You do not need to include the angle brackets when typing a URL.

The following exercise introduces you to an online dictionary. A major advantage of an online dictionary is that it presents the latest information. It also provides pronunciation if your computer has sound capability.

Goal: To gain confidence in using an online dictionary.

1. With your Web browser on the screen, key the following URL in the location box or address bar: **http://www.m-w .com**. Press **Enter**.

2. Look over the Merriam-Webster OnLine home page. Move up and down the page by using the scroll bar at the right. Ignore any advertisements.

3. Scroll to the top and move your cursor to the **Merriam-Webster OnLine Search** box. Make sure that "Dictionary" is the selected reference.

4. Type the word *pretexting* in the search box. Click **Search**.

5. Scroll down to see the definition for *pretexting–noun*.

6. Click the red speaker icon to hear the word pronounced. Then close the box.

7. Print a copy of the definition page by clicking **File** (upper left corner of your browser). Click **Print** and **OK**. Save all printouts to turn in.

8. Click **Back** (arrow in upper left corner of browser) to return to the search page.

9. In the **Merriam-Webster OnLine Search** box, key the word *firewall* and click **Search**. Notice that the dictionary shows that this word is spelled as two words. Read the definition. Print a copy.

10. Click **Back**. Using either the **Dictionary** or **Thesaurus** feature, look up one word from Exercise E. Print the definition or synonym.

11. Click **Word of the Day** (left navigation panel). Read about the word. Print a copy.

12. Click **Word Games** (left navigation panel). Choose one word game to play. (**Hint:** scroll down to see them all.) Print one page showing the game you selected.

13. Explore the rest of the site as time permits.

14. End your session by clicking the **X** box (upper right corner of browser).

15. As your instructor advises, send an e-mail message summarizing what you learned or turn in all printed copies properly identified.

Chat About It

At the end of each chapter in this textbook, you will find five discussion questions related to the chapter material. Your instructor may assign these topics to you to discuss in class, in an online chat room, or on an online discussion board. Some of the discussion topics may require outside research. You may also be asked to read and respond to postings made by your classmates.

Discussion Topic 1: Prepare an introduction to deliver to your classmates so that they can get to know you. Include the following in your introduction: your name, where you live, where you work, information about your family and friends, why you are taking the class and what you hope to learn, your major, your career goals, and anything else of interest.

Discussion Topic 2: Why do you think that excellent communication skills are in such demand in today's workplace? How will these skills help you succeed on the job? How will understanding the fundamentals of business English help you to communicate more effectively?

Discussion Topic 3: Choose one of the online dictionaries listed in Figure 1.2 and explore the site in detail. What features did you find on the site? What features did you especially enjoy and why? What features would be most useful to a business English student? What features would be most useful on the job?

Discussion Topic 4: Read the introduction to your print dictionary. What information does it contain? How will this information help you use your dictionary better? When sharing your findings with the class, be sure to let them know what specific print dictionary you have.

Discussion Topic 5: Now that you have had a chance to read about reference materials that can help you with this course and on the job, find one online reference not mentioned in the chapter that would be helpful for business English students. Share the following information about the reference with the class: complete title of reference, Web site address (URL), brief description of the reference and why you chose it, and an explanation of how you would use the online reference on the job and/ or how business English students would find it beneficial.

Posttest

Write *T* (true) or *F* (false) after the following statements.
Compare your answers with those at the bottom of the page.

1. The best dictionary for a college student's assignments is a pocket dictionary. _____

2. When searching for a word in a dictionary, to save time look only at the guide words until you locate the desired page. _____

3. The etymology of a word is usually contained within square brackets. _____

4. The usage label *slang* means that the word may be used in certain regions only. _____

5. A reference manual can help you determine whether to use *capital* or *capitol* in a sentence. _____

6. Today's technology has made writing less important. _____

7. Most dictionaries show syllable breaks with a centered dot. _____

8. The abbreviation *vb* in a dictionary indicates that a word is "very beneficial." _____

9. A nonstandard word is one that does not conform to usage among educated speakers. _____

10. To determine whether to write a number as a word or figure, it is best to consult a dictionary. _____

"Whatever your program in college, be sure to include courses in writing and speaking. Managers must constantly write instructions, reports, memos, letters, and survey conclusions. If this comes hard to you, it will hold you back."

—James A. Newman and Alexander Roy
Climbing the Corporate Matterhorn

Chapter 2

Parts of Speech

OBJECTIVES

When you have completed the materials in this chapter, you will be able to do the following:

- Define the eight parts of speech.
- Recognize how parts of speech function in sentences.
- Compose sentences showing words playing more than one grammatical role.

Study the following sentence and identify selected parts of speech. For each word listed, underline the correct part of speech. Compare your answers with those at the bottom of the page.

The customer and I critically evaluated information on the company Web site.

1.	The	a. preposition	b. pronoun	c. conjunction	d. adjective
2.	customer	a. noun	b. pronoun	c. verb	d. adjective
3.	and	a. preposition	b. conjunction	c. adjective	d. adverb
4.	I	a. noun	b. pronoun	c. interjection	d. adjective
5.	critically	a. adjective	b. conjunction	c. preposition	d. adverb
6.	evaluated	a. adverb	b. noun	c. verb	d. adverb
7.	information	a. pronoun	b. adjective	c. verb	d. noun
8.	on	a. preposition	b. conjunction	c. adjective	d. adverb
9.	company	a. noun	b. adverb	c. pronoun	d. adjective
10.	site	a. pronoun	b. noun	c. adjective	d. verb

As you learned in Chapter 1, this book focuses on the study of the fundamentals of grammar, current usage, and appropriate business and professional style. Such a study logically begins with the eight parts of speech, the building blocks of our language. This chapter provides a brief overview of the parts of speech. In future chapters you will learn about each part of speech in greater detail.

The Eight Parts of Speech

Why is it important to learn to identify the eight parts of speech? Learning the eight parts of speech helps you develop the working vocabulary necessary to discuss and study the language. You especially need to recognize the parts of speech in the context of sentences. That is because many words function in more than one role. Only by analyzing the sentence at hand can you see how a given word functions. Your boss is unlikely to ask you to identify the parts of speech in a business document. Being able to do so, however, will help you punctuate correctly and choose precise words for clear, powerful writing. Using the parts of speech correctly will also help you sound more professional and intelligent on the job. In addition, understanding the roles different parts of speech play in written and oral communication will be helpful if you learn another language.

Nouns

In elementary school you probably learned that a **noun** refers to a person, place, or thing. In addition, nouns name qualities, feelings, concepts, activities, and measures. Nouns can be proper or common. **Proper nouns** are capitalized, and **common nouns** are not, as you can see in the following list. You will learn more about this concept in Chapter 4.

1. d 2. a 3. b 4. b 5. d 6. c 7. d 8. a 9. d 10. b

Persons:	Amelia, Dr. Villano, attorney, president
Places:	New York City, Heathrow Airport, university, island
Things:	novel, surfboard, bicycle, iPod
Qualities:	patience, honesty, initiative, enthusiasm
Feelings:	happiness, anger, confusion, euphoria
Concepts:	knowledge, freedom, friendship, patriotism
Activities:	kiteboarding, dancing, management, eating
Measures:	week, million, inch, kilometer

Nouns are important words in our language. Sentences revolve around nouns because these words function both as subjects and as objects of verbs. To determine whether a word is really a noun, try using it with the verb *is* or *are*. Notice that all the nouns listed here would make sense if used in this way: *Amelia is young, New York City is in New York, bicycles are popular, kiteboarding is fun,* and so on. In Chapter 4 you will learn four classes of nouns and rules for making nouns plural. In Chapter 5 you will learn how to show that a noun possesses something.

Pronouns

Pronouns are words used in place of nouns. As noun substitutes, pronouns provide variety and efficiency to your writing. Compare these two versions of the same sentence:

| **Without pronouns:** | Scott gave the book to Kelli so that Kelli could use the book to study. |
| **With pronouns:** | Scott gave the book to Kelli so that *she* could use *it* to study. |

In sentences pronouns may function as subjects of verbs (for example, *I, we, they*) or as objects of verbs (for example, *me, us, them*). They may act as connectors (for example, *that, which, who*), and they may show possession (for example, *mine, ours, hers, theirs*). Only a few examples are given here. More examples, along with functions and classifications of pronouns, will be presented in Chapters 6 and 7. You will also learn to use pronouns properly in these chapters.

Please note that words such as *his, my, her,* and *its* are classified as adjectives when they describe nouns (*his car, my desk, its engine*). This concept will be explained more thoroughly in Chapters 6 and 11.

Verbs

Verbs express an action, an occurrence, or a state of being.

Jason *built* an excellent Web site. (Action)

It *has* many links. (Occurrence)

He *is* proud of it. (State of being)

Action verbs show the physical or mental action of the subject of a sentence. Some action verbs are *run, study, work,* and *dream.* **Linking verbs** express a state of being and generally link to the subject words that describe or rename them. Some linking verbs are *am, is, are, was, were, be, being,* and *been.* Other linking verbs express the senses: *feels, appears, tastes, sounds, seems, looks.*

Study Tip

To test whether a word is truly a verb, try using it with a noun or pronoun, such as *Kim eats, she seems,* or *it is. He food* doesn't make sense because *food* is not a verb.

Verbs will be discussed more fully in Chapters 8 through 10. At this point it is important that you be able to recognize verbs so that you can determine whether sentences are complete. All complete sentences must have at least one verb; many sentences will have more than one verb. Verbs may appear singly or in phrases. When verbs are used in verb phrases, **helping verbs** are added.

Stacy *submitted* her application to become a management trainee. (Action verb)

Her résumé *is* just one page long. (Linking verb)

She *has been training* to become a manager. (Verb phrase; helping verbs *has* and *been* are added)

Stacy *feels* bad that she *will be leaving* her current colleagues. (Linking verb and verb phrase; helping verbs *will* and *be* are added)

Adjectives

Words that describe nouns or pronouns are called **adjectives**. They often answer the questions *What kind?*, *How many?*, and *Which one?* The adjectives in the following sentences are italicized. Observe that the adjectives all answer questions about the nouns they describe.

Small, *independent* businesses are becoming *numerous*. (What kinds of businesses?)

We have *six* franchises in *four* states. (How many franchises? How many states?)

That chain of health clubs started as a *small* operation. (Which chain? What kind of operation?)

He is *energetic* and *forceful,* while she is *personable* and *outgoing*. (What pronouns do these adjectives describe?)

Adjectives usually precede the nouns they describe. They may, however, follow the words they describe, especially when used with linking verbs, as shown in the first and last of the preceding examples. Here is a brief list of words used as adjectives:

effective	green	sensitive
excellent	intelligent	small
expensive	long	successful

Three words (*a*, *an*, and *the*) form a special group of adjectives called **articles**. Adjectives will be discussed more thoroughly in Chapter 11.

Adverbs

Study Tip

To remember more easily what an *adverb* does, think of its two syllables: *ad* suggests that you will be adding to or amplifying the meaning of a *verb*. Hence, adverbs often modify verbs.

Words that modify (describe or limit) verbs, adjectives, or other adverbs are **adverbs**. Adverbs often answer the questions *When? How? Where?* and *To what extent?*

Today we must complete the project. (Must complete the project *when*?)

Mitch approached the intersection *cautiously*. (Approached *how*?)

He seems *especially* competent. (*How* competent?)

Did you see the schedule *there*? (*Where*?)

The prosecutor did not question him *further*. (Questioned him *to what extent*?)

Some of the most commonly used adverbs follow:

carefully	now	really
evenly	only	too
greatly	rather	very

Many, but not all, words ending in *ly* are adverbs. Some exceptions are *friendly*, *costly*, and *ugly*, all of which are adjectives. Adverbs will be discussed in greater detail in Chapter 11.

Prepositions

Prepositions join nouns and pronouns to other words in a sentence. As the word itself suggests (*pre* meaning "before"), a preposition is a word in a position *before* its object. The **object of a preposition** is a noun or pronoun. Prepositions are used in phrases to show a relationship between the object of the preposition and another word in the sentence. In the following sentence, notice how the preposition changes the relation of the object (*Ms. Laham*) to the verb (*talked*):

Brian often talked *with* Ms. Laham.

Brian often talked *about* Ms. Laham.

Brian often talked *to* Ms. Laham.

Some of the most frequently used prepositions are *at, by, for, from, in, of, to,* and *with*. A more complete list of prepositions can be found in Chapter 12. You should learn to recognize objects of prepositions so that you won't confuse them with sentence subjects. You will learn more about the difference between verb subjects and objects in Chapter 10.

Conjunctions

Words that connect other words or groups of words are **conjunctions**. The most common conjunctions are *and*, *but*, *or*, and *nor*. These are called **coordinating conjunctions** because they join equal (coordinate) parts of sentences. Other kinds of conjunctions will be presented in Chapter 13. Study the examples of coordinating conjunctions shown here:

Yukie, Dan, *and* Kristi are all looking for jobs. (The conjunction *and* joins equal words.)

You may be interviewed by a human resources officer *or* by a supervising manager. (The conjunction *or* joins equal groups of words.)

Interjections

Words expressing strong feelings are **interjections**. Interjections standing alone are followed by exclamation marks. When woven into a sentence, they are usually followed by commas.

Wow! Did you see what she wrote in her e-mail message? (Interjection standing alone)

Well, I guess that means the meeting is over. (Interjection woven into a sentence)

Career Tip

To sound professional, credible, and objective, most business writers avoid interjections and exclamation marks in business and professional messages.

Summary

The following sentence illustrates all eight parts of speech.

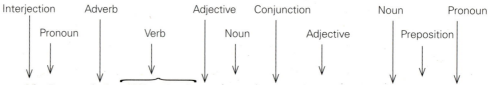

| Interjection | Pronoun | Adverb | Verb | Adjective | Noun | Conjunction | Adjective | Noun | Preposition | Pronoun |

Oh, I certainly will submit a résumé and application letter to them.

You need to know the functions of these eight parts of speech in order to understand the rest of this textbook and profit from your study of language basics. The explanation of the parts of speech has been kept simple so far. This chapter is meant to serve as an introduction to later, more fully developed chapters about the different parts of speech. At this stage you should not expect to be able to identify the functions of *all* words in *all* sentences.

A word of caution: English is a wonderfully flexible language. As noted earlier, many words in our language serve as more than one part of speech. Notice how flexible the word *mail* is in these sentences:

Our *mail* is late today. (Noun—serves as subject of sentence)

This pile of *mail* must be delivered today. (Noun—serves as object of preposition)

Please read your *mail* soon. (Noun—serves as object of verb)

Mail the letter today. (Verb—serves as action word in sentence)

The *mail* system in the United States is efficient. (Adjective—used to describe *system*, which serves as subject of sentence)

Spot the BLOOPER

Using the skills you are learning in this class, try to identify why the following items are bloopers. Consult your textbook, dictionary, or reference manual as needed. Also think about what part of speech each blooper demonstrates.

Blooper 1: A high school principal quoted in the *San Francisco Chronicle*: "He had some personal issues his mother and him were working on."

Blooper 2: From *The Wall Street Journal* comes a report that Marshall Field's, the big Chicago retailer, announced it would serve hot chocolate to "tiresome" shoppers.

Blooper 3: Headline in a small-town newspaper: "Stolen Painting Found by Tree."

Blooper 4: Letter to the editor of the *San Francisco Chronicle*: "Me and my siblings are not thugs and gangsters. We all have degrees and are doctors, technology workers, DNA researchers—the people who are defining the future."

Blooper 5: In a *Washington Post* article: "What drains out is an intensely sweet juice that is fermented into a pricey wine found on the desert lists of the finest restaurants."

Blooper 6: The aviation magazine *Air Classics* referred to baseball as "America's national past time."

Blooper 7: From the Web site of Ipsos, a company that conducts online consumer surveys: "Here are just a few highlights to peak your interest."

Blooper 8: In a column in *The Denver Post,* columnist Julia Martinez discussed a proposed history of Denver for which the city's mayor "is supposed to write the forward."

Blooper 9: When the great American opera singer Beverly Sills died, *The New York Times* said that she made her debut in 1969 "at the most scared of all Italian opera houses, La Scala."

Blooper 10: An editorial in *The New York Times* about the state of the schools in Washington, DC: "The imbalance is particularly disturbing, given that the District's children fair worse at school than children in other big cities."

Businesspeople and professionals are very concerned about appropriate and professional English usage, grammar, and style. This concern is evident in the number and kinds of questions posted to discussion boards and Web sites devoted to proper English usage. Among the users of these discussion boards and Web sites are business supervisors, managers, executives, professionals, secretaries, clerks, administrative assistants, and word processing specialists. Writers, teachers, librarians, students, and other community members also seek answers to language questions. The questions that are asked online are often referred to as **Frequently Asked Questions,** or **FAQs** (pronounced "facks").

Selected questions and Dr. Guffey and Professor Seefer's answers to them will be presented at the end of each chapter. In this way you, as a student of the language, will understand the kinds of everyday communication problems encountered in business and professional environments.

Representative questions come from a variety of reputable grammar-related discussion boards and Web sites. You can locate sites that present these FAQs by using the search phrase grammar FAQs in Google (www.google .com). Many Web sites exist where you can browse questions and answers and post your own questions.

Question	Answer
Q: We're having a big argument in our office. What's correct? *E-mail, e-mail, email,* or *Email? On-line* or *online? Website, Web site, web site,* or *website?*	**A:** In the early days of computing, people capitalized *E-mail* and hyphenated *on-line.* With increased use, however, both of these forms have been simplified to *e-mail* and *online.* The letter *e* in *e-mail* should be capitalized only if the word is first in a sentence. In regard to *Web site,* we recommend the capitalized two-word form. Capitalizing *Web* is logical since it is a shortened form for *World Wide Web.* These are also the forms noted by the *Merriam-Webster's Collegiate Dictionary* (our standard reference). You might want to check with your company's in-house style manual for its preferred style for all of these words.
Q: Should I capitalize the word *Internet?* I see it written both ways and am confused.	**A:** We recommend writing the word with a capital *I* (*Internet*). However, we are in a time of change with regard to the proper spelling and writing of Web-related words. For example, *Wired News* was the first to spell *Internet, Web,* and *Net* using lowercase letters; others may follow. For now, though, you should continue to capitalize *Internet* and *Web* because that is the format many style manuals and dictionaries recommend.
Q: What is the name of a group of initials that form a word? Is it an abbreviation?	**A:** A word formed from the initial letters of an expression is called an **acronym** (pronounced ACK-ro-nim). Examples: *scuba* from *self-contained underwater breathing apparatus,* and *PIN* from *personal identification number.* Another example of an acronym is *OSHA* (pronounced *Oh-shah*), which stands for *Occupational Safety and Health Administration.* Acronyms are pronounced as single words and are different from abbreviations. Expressions such as *FBI* and *NFL* are **abbreviations,** not acronyms. Notice that an abbreviation is pronounced letter by letter (*F, B, I*), whereas an acronym is pronounced as a word. Shortened versions of words such as *dept.* and *Ms.* are also considered abbreviations.
Q: What's the difference between *toward* and *towards?*	**A:** None. They are interchangeable in use. However, we recommend using the shorter word *toward* because it is more efficient.
Q: Is *every day* one word or two in this case? *We encounter these problems every day.*	**A:** In your sentence it is two words. When it means "ordinary," it is one word (*she wore everyday clothes*). If you can insert the word *single* between *every* and *day* without altering your meaning, you should be using two words, as in your sentence.

Question	Answer
Q: Should an e-mail message begin with a salutation or some kind of greeting?	**A:** When e-mail messages are sent to company insiders, a salutation may be omitted; however, including a salutation will personalize your message. When e-mail messages travel to outsiders, omitting a salutation seems curt and unfriendly. Because the message is more like a letter, a salutation is appropriate (such as *Dear Courtney, Hi Courtney, Greetings,* or just *Courtney*). Including a salutation is also a visual cue that identifies the beginning of the message. Some writers prefer to incorporate the name of the recipient in the first sentence (*Thanks, Courtney, for responding so quickly.*)
Q: In e-mail messages is it acceptable to use abbreviations such as *IMHO* (*in my humble opinion*), *LOL* (*laughing out loud*), and *TIA* (*thanks in advance*)?	**A:** Among close friends who understand their meaning, such abbreviations are certainly acceptable. But in business messages, these abbreviations are too casual and too obscure. Many readers would have no idea what they mean. **Emoticons** (or smileys) such as :-) are also too casual for business messages. Worst of all, abbreviations and emoticons make business messages look immature and unprofessional.
Q: Tell me it's not true! I just heard that the word *d'oh,* which is uttered frequently by the Homer Simpson character, was recently added to the *Oxford English Dictionary.* Surely this is an urban legend.	**A:** It's true. The word *d'oh* was recently added to the *Oxford English Dictionary,* long considered the foremost authority on the English language. Its editors decided that the word *d'oh* is so universally accepted that it warranted formal recognition. This certainly proves what an effect popular culture has on our language. However, keep in mind that not all words appearing in dictionaries are appropriate for business messages.
Q: I just included this sentence in a cover letter and am wondering whether it is correct: *Your ad for a Web content specialist peaked my interest.*	**A:** We hope you haven't sent this letter yet! In this sentence you should have used *piqued* instead of *peaked.* The verb *pique* comes from a French word that means "to excite or arouse," as in "to pique your curiosity." Also don't confuse these two words with *peek,* which means "to take a brief look."
Q: Is there a difference between the words *forward* and *foreword*? How do I decide which to use?	**A:** The word *forward* has many uses. As an adverb it means "toward or at a place, point, or time in advance" (*from this day forward*). As an adjective it means "presumptuous or bold" (*it was forward of her to ask whether she got the job*). As a verb it means "to transmit" (*please forward the message to me*). The word *foreword,* on the other hand, can be used only as a noun, meaning "the preface or introduction of a book" (*the famous scholar wrote the foreword*).

2 Reinforcement Exercises

Online Homework Help! For immediate feedback on odd-numbered items, go to **www.meguffey.com.**

A. (Self-check) Complete these statements.

1. Names for persons, places, things, qualities, feelings, concepts, activities, and measures are
   a. verbs   b. adjectives   c. nouns   d. pronouns   _____

2. Words that substitute for nouns are
   a. adverbs   b. adjectives   c. interjections   d. pronouns   _____

3. The part of speech that answers the questions *What kind?* and *How many?* is a(n)
   a. adverb   b. adjective   c. preposition   d. conjunction   _____

4. Words such as *slowly*, *very*, and *tomorrow* that answer the questions *How?* and *When?* are
   a. adverbs   b. adjectives   c. nouns   d. conjunctions   _____

5. *I, you, they, hers*, and *he* are examples of
   a. pronouns   b. nouns   c. adverbs   d. adjectives   _____

6. *Wow, well*, and *oh* are examples of
   a. pronouns   b. prepositions   c. interjections   d. adjectives   _____

7. *And, or, nor,* and *but* are
   a. adverbs   b. prepositions   c. interjections   d. conjunctions   _____

8. Words such as *by, in*, and *of* that join noun or pronoun objects to other words in sentences are
   a. adverbs   b. prepositions   c. conjunctions   d. adjectives   _____

9. Words that express an action, an occurrence, or a state of being are
   a. verbs   b. nouns   c. interjections   d. adverbs   _____

10. *The, a,* and *an* are a special group of adjectives called
    a. joiners   b. articles   c. limiters   d. descriptors   _____

Check your answers below.

B. In each of the following groups of sentences, the same word is used as different parts of speech. For each sentence indicate the part of speech for the italicized word.

Example: We have little *time* in which to make a decision.	noun
Officials will *time* the runners in the marathon.	verb
Factory workers must punch a *time* clock.	adjective

1. Max had to *dress* quickly to make it to work on time.   _____

2. Does your company have a *dress* code?   _____

1.c 2.d 3.b 4.a 5.a 6.c 7.d 8.b 9.a 10.b

3. She decided to wear a suit instead of a *dress* to the interview. _____

4. Doug prefers a casual *work* environment. _____

5. Susan arrives at *work* early each morning. _____

6. The entire department will *work* overtime to finish the project. _____

7. Volunteers do important *work* in the community. _____

8. Advertisements promised instruction from a *master* teacher. _____

9. Few students can *master* Web design in a short course. _____

10. Warren Buffet is a *master* in the field of investing. _____

C. A word can often function as more than one part of speech, depending on how it is used in a sentence. This writing exercise will give you an opportunity to use the same word in different ways.

Write complete sentences using the word *contract* as the part of speech indicated.

1. (noun) _____

2. (verb) _____

3. (adjective) _____

Write complete sentences using the word *set* as the part of speech indicated.

4. (noun) _____

5. (verb) _____

6. (adjective) _____

Write complete sentences using the word *desert* as the part of speech indicated.

7. (noun) _____

8. (verb) _____

9. (adjective) _____

Write a complete sentence using the word *dessert* as the part of speech indicated.

10. (noun) _____

D. Read the following sentences and, taking into account the function of each word within each sentence, identify the part of speech of each word shown. Use a dictionary if necessary.

The e-mail message contained a virus, but it was quickly deleted.

1. **The** _____   6. **but** _____

2. **e-mail** _____   7. **it** _____

3. **message** _____   8. **was** _____

4. **contained** _____   9. **quickly** _____

5. **virus** _____   10. **deleted** _____

Wow! She immediately determined the cause of the company network problem.

1. **Wow!** _____
2. **She** _____
3. **immediately** _____
4. **determined** _____
5. **the** _____

6. **cause** _____
7. **of** _____
8. **company** _____
9. **network** _____
10. **problem** _____

E. In each of the following sentences, identify the verb. Each sentence contains only one verb. As an added challenge, try to identify whether the verb is action or linking.

1. Many colleges now offer free lectures on YouTube. _____

2. Google Earth provides satellite images of geographic areas around the world. _____

3. The hotel manager selected four trainees from many applicants. _____

4. Her outgoing voice mail message sounds professional. _____

5. Please deliver the computers and printers be fore April 4. _____

6. The manager and the human resources director studied all job descriptions carefully. _____

7. Words are the most powerful drug in the world. _____

8. Antonia felt bad that too much month was left at the end of her money. _____

9. She dreams about a bright future. _____

10. I am very pleased about your new job! _____

F. FAQs About Business English Review. In the space provided, write the correct answer choice.

1. Those research statistics are available on the _____.
   a. internet   b. Internet   c. InterNet   _____

2. Experts suggest that users check their _____ at regular intervals.
   a. Email   b. E-mail   c. email   d. e-mail   _____

3. We are considering subscribing to an _____ databank to aid research.
   a. on-line   b. online   c. on line   _____

4. Our _____ has been completely updated.
   a. Web site   b. website   c. web site   d. web-site   _____

5. All computer files must be backed up _____ to prevent possible loss.
   a. everyday   b. every day   c. every-day   _____

6. Backing up files is an _____ occurrence in most organizations.

    a. everyday   b. every day   c. every-day   _____

7. Which of the following is an acronym?

    a. U.S.A.   b. IRS   c. PIN   d. RSVP   _____

8. Which of the following is an abbreviation?

    a. laser   b. scuba   c. radar   d. DVD   _____

9. Your statement during the interview has _____ my curiosity.

    a. piqued   b. peaked   c. peeked   _____

10. When you receive the announcement, please _____ it to me.

    a. foreword   b. forward   c. for-ward   _____

    G. Writing Exercise. In three or four complete sentences, explain why it is important to understand the parts of speech for this course and later on the job.

    _____

    _____

    _____

    _____

    In three or four complete sentences, explain the difference between nouns and verbs. Which do you think is more important to a writer?

    _____

    _____

    _____

    _____

▶▶ Learning Web Ways

Many colleges and universities offer online writing labs (OWLs). These Web sites offer helpful resources for students and businesspeople. You can read online or download handouts that provide help with punctuation, spelling, sentence construction, parts of speech, and writing.

Goal: To learn to use an online writing lab.

1. With your Web browser on the screen, key the following URL in the location box or address bar: **http://owl .english.purdue.edu/owl/**. Press **Enter** to access The OWL at Purdue site.

2. Scroll down to reveal the site's 15 areas as listed in the navigation menu to the right. Notice that you can click each option to reveal a drop-down menu showing the complete contents of each area; clicking the plus sign next to each option will also reveal the drop-down menu. Clicking the menu item a second time or the minus sign closes the drop-down menu.

3. Click **The Writing Process**.

4. From the drop-down menu, click **Proofreading Your Writing**.

A document about proofreading will display in the main window.

5. Read the information on the page. When you get to the bottom, you will see a menu for links to all five sections of the proofreading document. Be sure to click each link to access the complete document. Read all five sections.

6. Print a copy. (You can click the **Full Resource for Printing** icon to print any document.)

7. Select other topics from the menu to the right to look over.

8. End your session by clicking the **X** box in the upper right corner of your browser. Turn in your printout or send an e-mail message to your instructor summarizing what you learned.

▶▶ Chat About It

Your instructor may assign any of the following topics for you to discuss in class, in an online chat room, or on an online discussion board. Some of the discussion topics may require outside research. You may also be asked to read and respond to postings made by your classmates.

Discussion Topic 1: For this discussion assignment you will be sharing your favorite acronyms and abbreviations with the class. Select five acronyms and five abbreviations. Label each item clearly so that you show whether it is an acronym or an abbreviation. For each item, provide the following information: what the acronym or abbreviation stands for, the phonetic pronunciation (if necessary), and a brief description. All acronyms and abbreviations must be written in the correct format, including proper use of lowercase letters, capital letters, and periods. Consult your dictionary or reference manual if needed.

Discussion Topic 2: Explain how you think being able to identify parts of speech will help you on the job, in school, and in your personal life.

Discussion Topic 3: Although it is recommended that you capitalize the word *Internet* and *Web site*, many publications and online sites are beginning to write these words using lowercase letters. Do you think these words should be capitalized when written? Why or why not? Defend your answer.

Discussion Topic 4: Do you think including a salutation in an e-mail message is important?

Why or why not? Do you use salutations when writing your e-mail messages? How do you feel when you receive a message that addresses you by name? How do you feel when the salutation is omitted?

Discussion Topic 5: As mentioned in Chapter 2, a *palindrome* is a word, phrase, or sentence that reads the same backward and forward, such as *civic*, *mom*, *dad*, and *level*. Palindromes can be single words, phrases, complete sentences, poems, names, or long blocks of text; and palindromes exist in almost every language. Do a Web search to find an interesting palindrome, and then share it with your classmates. If you are creative, you could even try writing your own!

Posttest

Identify the parts of speech in this sentence by underlining the correct choice. Compare your answers with those at the bottom of the page.

Paul eagerly waited for the moment when **he** would become **a college graduate**.

1.	Paul	a. pronoun	b. interjection	c. noun	d. adjective
2.	eagerly	a. adverb	b. adjective	c. verb	d. conjunction
3.	waited	a. adverb	b. verb	c. preposition	d. adjective
4.	for	a. conjunction	b. pronoun	c. preposition	d. interjection
5.	the	a. adverb	b. conjunction	c. interjection	d. adjective
6.	moment	a. verb	b. noun	c. adverb	d. adjective
7.	he	a. pronoun	b. verb	c. noun	d. adjective
8.	a	a. adverb	b. adjective	c. preposition	d. interjection
9.	college	a. adjective	b. adverb	c. noun	d. verb
10.	graduate	a. adverb	b. verb	c. pronoun	d. noun

"I'm not a very good writer, but I'm an excellent rewriter."

—**James Michener, author**

Chapter 3

Sentences: Elements, Varieties, Patterns, Types, Faults

OBJECTIVES

When you have completed the materials in this chapter, you will be able to do the following:

- Recognize basic sentence elements including subjects and predicates.
- Differentiate among phrases, dependent clauses, and independent clauses.
- Distinguish simple, compound, complex, and compound-complex sentences.
- Identify four basic sentence patterns.
- Punctuate statements, questions, commands, and exclamations.
- Use techniques to avoid basic sentence faults such as fragments, comma splices, and run-on sentences.

Write the correct letter after each of the following items to identify it. End punctuation has been omitted.

> a = phrase   c = independent clause
> b = dependent clause

1. Saudi Arabia relies on its citizens to find Web sites to block _____

2. Even though countries like China use the government to censor the Web _____

3. In the course of one day _____

4. Students and religious figures tend to be most active in flagging offensive sites _____

5. Should rely on software _____

Write the correct letter after each of the following groups of words to identify it.

> a = correctly punctuated sentence   c = comma splice
> b = fragment   d = run-on sentence

6. Jennifer who was recently hired as a management trainee. _____

7. Guitar Center's stock price increased this year, JetBlue's decreased. _____

8. On the ground floor of our building are a café and a bookstore. _____

9. Some employers monitor their employees' e-mail others do not want to bother. _____

10. Although many employees start at 6 a.m., which explains the empty parking lot. _____

To be a good writer, you must be able to construct effective sentences. **Sentences** are groups of words that express complete thoughts. In this chapter you will review the basic elements of every sentence. In addition, you will learn to recognize sentence patterns and types, and you will learn how to differentiate among phrases and clauses. This knowledge will be especially helpful in punctuating sentences and avoiding common sentence faults. The Writer's Workshop following this chapter introduces proofreading marks, which are useful in revising messages.

Sentence Elements

Understanding the important role of sentence elements—including subjects, predicates, phrases, and clauses—is the first step toward writing complete and correct sentences.

Writing Complete Sentences

To be complete, sentences must have subjects and predicates, and they must make sense.

1. c 2. b 3. a 4. c 5. a 6. b 7. c 8. a 9. d 10. b

Must Have a Subject

Every sentence must have a subject. A **simple subject** is a noun or pronoun that tells who or what the sentence is about. The **complete subject** of a sentence includes the simple subject and all of its **modifiers** (words that describe or limit). You can locate the subject in a sentence by asking, *Who or what is being discussed?*

> *Rebecca* wanted out of her dead-end job. (Who is being discussed? *Rebecca*)

> *Positions* in many companies are advertised online. (What is being discussed? *Positions*)

You will learn more about locating subjects in Chapter 10.

Must Have a Predicate

Every sentence must have a predicate. A **simple predicate** is a verb or verb phrase that tells what the subject is doing or what is being done to the subject. The **complete predicate** includes the verb or verb phrase and its modifiers, objects, and complements. Objects and complements will be explained in more detail later in this chapter.

Here are some examples of complete sentences. The simple subject in each sentence is underlined once, and the simple predicate is underlined twice. Notice that a sentence can have more than one simple subject and more than one simple predicate.

Simple Subject	Simple Predicate
The new CEO of the company	introduced himself and outlined his future plans.
All employees in the company	may choose from a benefits package.
She and I	will be applying for jobs after graduation.
The person who sent the e-mail	might have been a customer.

Notice in the preceding examples that the verbs in the predicate may consist of one word (*received*) or several (*will be applying*). In a **verb phrase** such as *will be applying*, the **principal verb** is the final one (*applying*). The other verbs are **helping**, or **auxiliary**, **verbs**. The most frequently used helping verbs are *am, is, are, was, were, been, have, has, had, must, ought, can, might, could, would, should, will, do, does,* and *did.*

Study Tip

Many linking verbs also serve as helping verbs. Note that a verb phrase is *linking* only when the final verb is a linking verb, such as in the phrase *might have been.*

Must Make Sense

In addition to a subject and a predicate, a group of words must possess one additional element to qualify as a sentence. The group of words must be complete and make sense. Observe that the first two groups of words that follow express complete thoughts and make sense; the third does not. In the following examples, the simple subjects are underlined once; and the simple predicates are underlined twice.

> Athletic shoe makers convinced us to buy $150 tennis shoes. (Subject plus predicate making sense = sentence.)

> Anthony now owns different athletic shoes for every sport. (Subject plus predicate making sense = sentence.)

> Although sports shoe manufacturers promote new versions with new features. (Subject plus predicate but NOT making sense = no sentence.)

Recognizing Phrases and Clauses

Sentences are made up of phrases and clauses. Learning to distinguish phrases and clauses will help you build complete sentences, use a variety of patterns, and avoid common sentence faults in your speaking and writing.

Phrases

A group of related words without a subject and a verb is called a **phrase**. You have already been introduced to verb phrases and prepositional phrases. It is not important that you be able to identify the other kinds of phrases (infinitive, gerund, participial); however, being able to distinguish phrases from clauses is very important to a business writer.

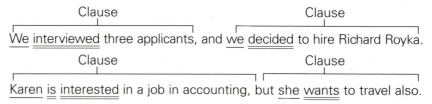

Verb phrase	Prepositional phrase	Prepositional phrase

The alarm *was coming from another part of the building.*

Clauses

A group of related words including a subject and a verb is a **clause**.

Clause	Clause

We interviewed three applicants, and we decided to hire Richard Royka.

Clause	Clause

Karen is interested in a job in accounting, but she wants to travel also.

Clauses may be divided into two groups: independent and dependent. **Independent clauses** are grammatically complete. **Dependent clauses** depend on their meaning for independent clauses. Dependent clauses are often introduced by words such as *if, when, because,* and *as.*

Dependent clause	Independent clause

When employees need help, Adam solves our technology problems.

Sentence Varieties

Sentences may be divided into four groups: simple, complex, compound, and compound-complex. One important way to improve your writing is to use a variety of these kinds of sentences.

A **simple sentence**, shown in the following example, contains one independent clause (complete thought) with a subject (underlined once) and predicate (underlined twice):

> Our team completed the project.

A **compound sentence** contains two complete but related thoughts. The two independent clauses may be joined by a (a) conjunction such as *and, but,* or *or;* (b) semicolon; or (c) conjunctive adverb such as *however, consequently,* and *therefore.* You will learn more about conjunctive adverbs in Chapter 13. You will also learn to use semicolons properly in Chapters 13 and 15. Notice the punctuation in these examples:

> The team project was challenging, and we were happy with the results.

The team <u>project was</u> challenging; <u>we were</u> happy with the results.

The team <u>project was</u> challenging; however, <u>we were</u> happy with the results.

A **complex sentence** contains an independent clause and a dependent clause (a thought that cannot stand by itself). Dependent clauses are often introduced by words such as *although*, *since*, *because*, *when*, and *if*. When dependent clauses precede independent clauses, they always are followed by a comma. You will learn more about punctuating dependent clauses in Chapters 13 and 15.

When <u>we finished</u> the team project, <u>we held</u> a team party.

A **compound-complex sentence** contains at least two independent clauses and one dependent clause. Because these sentences are usually long, use them sparingly.

Although this team <u>project is</u> completed, soon <u>we will begin</u> work on another; however, <u>it will be</u> less challenging.

Sentence Patterns

Another way business communicators can add variety to their writing is to use different sentence patterns. Four basic patterns express thoughts in English sentences. As a business or professional writer, you will most often use Patterns 1, 2, and 3 because readers usually want to know the subject first. For variety and emphasis, however, you can use introductory elements and inverted order in Pattern 4.

Pattern No. 1: Subject–Verb

In the most basic sentence pattern, the verb follows its subject. The sentence needs no additional words to make sense and be complete.

Subject	Verb
We	worked.
Everyone	is studying.
She	might have called.
Employees	are being informed.

Pattern No. 2: Subject–Action Verb–Object

When sentences have an object, the pattern is generally subject, action verb, and object. Objects of action verbs can be direct or indirect. A **direct object** is a noun or pronoun that answers the question *What?* or *Whom?*

Subject	Action Verb	Direct Object
Luke	needed	a new car. (Needed *what*?)
He and a friend	questioned	the salesperson. (Questioned *whom*?)
The sales manager	provided	good answers. (Provided *what*?)

Pattern No. 2 may also use an **indirect object** that answers the question *To whom?*, *To what?*, *For whom?*, or *For what?* Notice that a sentence can have both an indirect object and a direct object.

Subject	Action Verb	Indirect Object	Direct Object
This dealership	promises	customers	good prices.
The manager	handed	him	the keys.
The technician	gave	the vehicle	a tune-up.

Pattern No. 3: Subject–Linking Verb–Complement

In Pattern No. 3, the subject comes before a linking verb and its complement. Recall from Chapter 2 that common linking verbs are *am, is, are, was, were, be, being,* and *been.* Other linking verbs express the senses: *feels, appears, tastes, sounds, seems, looks.* A **complement** is a noun, pronoun, or adjective that renames or describes the subject. A complement *completes* the meaning of the subject and always follows the linking verb.

Subject	Linking Verb	Complement	
The instructor	was	Connie Murphy.	(Noun complement)
Our customers	are	friends.	
Your supervisor	is	she.	(Pronoun complement)
The callers	might have been	they.	
My job	is	challenging.	(Adjective complement)
These Web sites	will be	useful.	

Pattern No. 4: Inverted Order

In **inverted sentences**, the verb comes before the subject. You might use inverted order for variety or emphasis in your sentences.

Sitting in front is Michele.

Working hardest was the marketing team.

In questions, the verb may come before the subject or may be interrupted by the subject.

What is his e-mail address?

Where should the invoice be sent?

In sentences beginning with *here* or *there*, the normal word order is also inverted.

Here are the applications.

There were three steps in the plan.

Punctuating Four Sentence Types

Because sentences express complete thoughts, they must include **end punctuation**. The punctuation you choose to end a sentence depends on whether the sentence is a statement, question, command, or exclamation.

Statements

A **statement** makes an assertion and ends with a period.

> <u>Laws</u> <u>require</u> truth in advertising.

> <u>Manufacturers</u> today <u>must</u> <u>label</u> the contents of packages.

Questions

A **direct question** uses the exact words of the speaker and requires an answer. It is followed by a question mark.

> How many e-mail messages <u>do</u> <u>you</u> <u>receive</u> each day?

> What <u>are</u> your peak message <u>hours</u>?

Commands

A **command** gives an order or makes a direct request. Commands end with periods or, occasionally, with exclamation points. Note that the subject in all commands is understood to be *you*. The subject *you* is not normally stated in the command.

> <u>Shut</u> the door. ([You] <u>shut</u> the door.)

> <u>Insure</u> your home against fire loss. ([You] <u>insure</u> your home...)

Exclamations

An **exclamation** shows surprise, disbelief, or strong feeling. An exclamation may or may not be expressed as a complete thought. Both subject and predicate may be implied.

> Wow! <u>We</u> just <u>had</u> an earthquake!

> What a wonderful time <u>we</u> <u>had</u>!

> How extraordinary [<u>that</u> <u>is</u>]!

Study Tip

Don't be tempted to punctuate statements as questions. For example, *I wonder whether he called* is a statement, not a question.

Sentence Faults

Writing complete and grammatically correct sentences can be challenging. To be successful in your career, you must be able to write complete sentences that avoid three common faults: fragments, comma splices, and run-ons. You can eliminate these sentence faults by recognizing them and by applying the revision techniques described here.

Fragment

A **sentence fragment** is an incomplete sentence. It may be a phrase or a clause punctuated as if it were a complete sentence. Fragments are often broken off from preceding or succeeding sentences. Avoid fragments by making certain that each sentence contains a subject and a verb and makes sense by itself. You can remedy fragments by (a) joining them to complete sentences or (b) adding appropriate subjects and verbs. In the following examples, the fragments are italicized.

Fragment: *Because Zara controls every link of its supply chain.* That is why it has become one of the world's biggest clothing retailers.

Revision: Because Zara controls every link of its supply chain, it has become one of the world's biggest clothing retailers. (Join the fragment to the following complete sentence.)

Fragment: We are looking for a new wireless carrier. *One that offers unlimited minutes on a 3G network.*

Revision: We are looking for a new wireless carrier that offers unlimited minutes on a 3G network. (Join the fragment to the preceding sentence.)

Fragment: My college offers many majors in business administration. *Such as accounting, finance, human resources, and marketing.*

Revision: My college offers many majors in business administration such as accounting, finance, human resources, and marketing. (Join the fragment to the preceding sentence.)

Fragment: The deadline for the project was moved up three days. *Which means that our team must work overtime.*

Revision: The deadline for the project was moved up three days, which means that our team must work overtime. (Join the fragment to the preceding sentence.)

Fragment: *Although Ayla will give him some tough competition.* Stephen is confident he will get the promotion.

Revision: Although Ayla will give him some tough competition, Stephen is confident he will get the promotion. (Join the fragment to the following sentence.)

Fragment: *Etiquette guidelines for employees visiting the Web site Second Life, where the company has a business presence.*

Revision: IBM has issued etiquette guidelines for employees visiting the Web site Second Life, where the company has a business presence. (Add a subject and verb.)

Comma Splice

A **comma splice** results when two sentences or independent clauses are incorrectly joined or spliced together with a comma. Remember that commas alone cannot join two sentences or independent clauses. Comma splices can usually be repaired by (a) adding a conjunction, (b) separating into two sentences, or (c) changing the comma to a semicolon.

Comma Splice:	Virginia is the office manager, Michael is the receptionist.
Revision:	Virginia is the office manager, *and* Michael is the receptionist. (Add a conjunction.)
Comma Splice:	Let us help you find out whether you are underpaid, visit us at PayScale.com.
Revision:	Let us help you find out whether you are under-paid. Visit us at PayScale.com. (Separate into two sentences.)
Comma Splice:	No stock prices were available today, the market was closed for the holiday.
Revision:	No stock prices were available today; the market was closed for the holiday. (Change the comma to a semicolon.)
Comma Splice:	Many applicants responded to our advertisement, however, only one had the required certification.
Revision:	Many applicants responded to our advertisement; however, only one had the required certification.

Run-On Sentence

A **run-on sentence** joins two independent clauses without proper punctuation. Run-on sentences can usually be repaired by (a) separating into two sentences, (b) adding a comma and a conjunction, or (c) adding a semicolon.

Run-On:	The work ethic in America is not dead it is deeply ingrained in most people.
Revision:	The work ethic in America is not dead. It is deeply ingrained in most people. (Separate into two sentences.)
Run-On:	Sachi thought she had passed the exam she was wrong.
Revision:	Sachi thought she had passed the exam, but she was wrong. (Add a comma and a conjunction.)
Run-On:	Many freelance workers take part in "coworking" this allows them to share office space and socialize with other freelancers.
Revision:	Many freelance workers take part in "coworking"; this allows them to share office space and socialize with other freelancers. (Add a semicolon.)

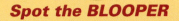

Spot the BLOOPER

Using the skills you are learning in this class, try to identify why the following items are bloopers. Consult your textbook, dictionary, or reference manual as needed.

Blooper 1: Menu at Pizzagram Plus in Guilderland, New York: "Our food is cooked to order. We appreciate your patients."

Blooper 2: From a Nabisco advertisement: "Honey Wheat Thins is the perfect choice because of it's slightly sweet honey taste."

Blooper 3: From a set of bylaws: "Each condominium unit may have a reasonable number of household pets. Which at the desecration of the Association do not create a nuisance to other owners." [Did you spot two bloopers?]

Blooper 4: In an article in the *Statesman-Journal* [Salem, Oregon]: "Three people were arrested after an early morning robbery at a Mission Street coffee shop in a London double-decker bus."

Blooper 5: A headline on the *Washington Post* online site: "CIA more fully denies deception about Iraq."

Blooper 6: A classified ad in the Gainesville [Florida] *Sun* offers a two-year-old stallion for sale for $500 and a three-year-old "mayor" for $1,000.

Blooper 7: Filene's Department store ran an ad that said "One Day Sale—This Friday, Saturday, and Sunday."

Blooper 8: In an article in *Sporting News*: "Jazz musician Wayne Tisdale will make his first musical appearance since having a portion of his right leg amputated at halftime of the Sooners basketball game against Virginia Commonwealth next month."

Blooper 9: A *San Francisco Chronicle* photo caption: "Bruce Springsteen denies rumors that he and his wife, Patti Scialfa, are splitting up on his Web site."

Blooper 10: A wedding announcement in *The Houston Chronicle*: "Amber was escorted by her father wearing a strapless silk wedding gown designed by Marianne Lanting carrying a tropical floral bouquet." [Did you spot two bloopers?]

Question	Answer
Q: This sentence doesn't sound right to me, but I can't decide how to improve it: *The reason I am applying is because I enjoy editing.*	**A:** The problem lies in this construction: *the reason…is because….* Only nouns or adjectives may act as complements following linking verbs. In your sentence an adverbial clause follows the linking verb and sounds awkward. One way to improve the sentence is to substitute a noun clause beginning with *that: The reason I am applying is that I enjoy editing.* An even better way to improve the sentence would be to make it a direct statement: *I am applying because I enjoy editing.*
Q: My colleague says that this sentence is correct: *Please complete this survey regarding your satisfaction at our dealership, return it in the enclosed addressed envelope.* I think something is wrong, but I'm not sure what.	**A:** You're right! This sentence has two independent clauses, and the writer attempted to join them with a comma. But this construction produces a comma splice. You can correct the problem by adding *and* between the clauses, starting a new sentence, or using a semicolon between the clauses.
Q: My boss wrote a report with this sentence: *Saleswise, our staff is excellent.* Should I change it?	**A:** Never change wording without checking with the author. You might point out, however, that the practice of attaching *-wise* to nouns is frowned on by many language experts. Such combinations as *budgetwise, taxwise,* and *productionwise* are considered commercial jargon. Suggest this revision: *On the basis of sales, our staff is excellent.*
Q: At the end of a letter I wrote: *Thank you for recommending me to this company.* Should I hyphenate *thank you?*	**A:** Do not hyphenate *thank you* when using it as a verb (*thank you for recommending*). Do use hyphens when using *thank you* as an adjective (*I sent a thank-you note*) or as a noun (*I sent four thank-yous*). Because *thank you* is used as a verb in your sentence, do not hyphenate it. Notice that *thank you* is never written as a single word.
Q: A fellow worker insists on saying, *I could care less.* It seems to me that it should be *I couldn't care less.* Who is right?	**A:** You are right. The phrase *I couldn't care less* has been in the language a long time. It means, of course, "I have little concern about the matter." Recently, though, people have begun to use *I could care less* with the same meaning. Most careful listeners realize that the latter phrase says just the opposite of its intent. Although both phrases are clichés, stick with *I couldn't care less* if you want to be clear.
Q: How should I address a person who signed a letter *J. R. Henderson?* I don't know whether the person is a man or a woman, and I don't want to offend anyone.	**A:** When you can't determine the gender of your reader, include the entire name in the salutation and omit the personal title (*Mr., Ms., Dr.*). In your letter you should use *Dear J. R. Henderson.*
Q: My friend insists that the combination *all right* is shown in her dictionary as one word. I say that it's two words. Who's right?	**A:** *All right* is the only acceptable spelling. The listing *alright* is shown in many dictionaries to guide readers to the acceptable spelling, *all right.* Do not use *alright.* By the way, some people remember that *all right* is two words by associating it with *all wrong.*

Question	Answer
Q: **If I have no interest in something, am I** *disinterested?*	**A:** No. If you lack interest, you are *uninterested.* The word *disinterested* means "unbiased" or "impartial" (*the judge was disinterested in the cases before him*).
Q: **I have always spelled** *alot* **as one word. Is that acceptable?**	**A:** No, this word should always be written as two words: *a lot.* In fact, the word *alot* (written as one word) does not exist. Also, don't confuse this word with the verb *allot,* which means "to assign as a share or portion" or "to distribute."
Q: **I used the word** *thru* **in a proposal, and my boss told me to change it to** *through.* **What is wrong with using** *thru?*	**A:** Some people use *thru* as a variant of *through*; however, this usage is informal and should be avoided in business writing. Your boss was correct to have you change it.

3 Reinforcement Exercises

Online Homework Help! For immediate feedback on odd-numbered items, go to **www.meguffey.com**.

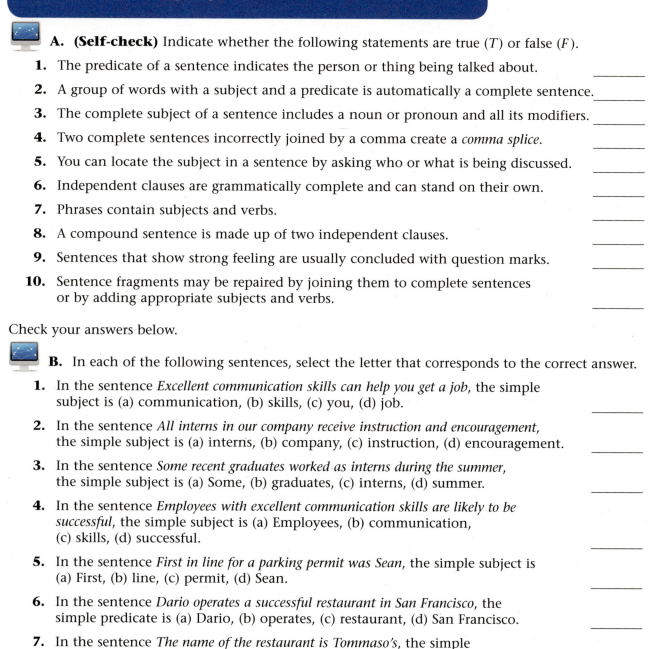

A. (Self-check) Indicate whether the following statements are true (*T*) or false (*F*).

1. The predicate of a sentence indicates the person or thing being talked about. _____

2. A group of words with a subject and a predicate is automatically a complete sentence. _____

3. The complete subject of a sentence includes a noun or pronoun and all its modifiers. _____

4. Two complete sentences incorrectly joined by a comma create a *comma splice*. _____

5. You can locate the subject in a sentence by asking who or what is being discussed. _____

6. Independent clauses are grammatically complete and can stand on their own. _____

7. Phrases contain subjects and verbs. _____

8. A compound sentence is made up of two independent clauses. _____

9. Sentences that show strong feeling are usually concluded with question marks. _____

10. Sentence fragments may be repaired by joining them to complete sentences or by adding appropriate subjects and verbs. _____

Check your answers below.

B. In each of the following sentences, select the letter that corresponds to the correct answer.

1. In the sentence *Excellent communication skills can help you get a job*, the simple subject is (a) communication, (b) skills, (c) you, (d) job. _____

2. In the sentence *All interns in our company receive instruction and encouragement*, the simple subject is (a) interns, (b) company, (c) instruction, (d) encouragement. _____

3. In the sentence *Some recent graduates worked as interns during the summer*, the simple subject is (a) Some, (b) graduates, (c) interns, (d) summer. _____

4. In the sentence *Employees with excellent communication skills are likely to be successful*, the simple subject is (a) Employees, (b) communication, (c) skills, (d) successful. _____

5. In the sentence *First in line for a parking permit was Sean*, the simple subject is (a) First, (b) line, (c) permit, (d) Sean. _____

6. In the sentence *Dario operates a successful restaurant in San Francisco*, the simple predicate is (a) Dario, (b) operates, (c) restaurant, (d) San Francisco. _____

7. In the sentence *The name of the restaurant is Tommaso's*, the simple predicate is (a) name, (b) of, (c) restaurant, (d) is. _____

8. In the sentence *Tommaso's offers authentic Italian food*, the simple predicate is (a) Tommaso's, (b) offers, (c) authentic, (d) food. _____

1. F 2. F 3. T 4. T 5. T 6. T 7. F 8. T 9. F 10. T

9. In the sentence *Customers appreciate the quality of the food*, the simple predicate is (a) Customers, (b) appreciate, (c) quality, (d) food. _____

10. In the sentence *Dario is a dynamic entrepreneur*, the simple predicate is (a) Dario, (b) is, (c) dynamic, (d) entrepreneur. _____

C. Indicate whether the following word groups are phrases (*P*), independent clauses (*I*), or dependent clauses (*D*). (Remember that phrases do not have both subjects and verbs.) Capitalization and end punctuation have been omitted.

Example: in the spring of this year   **P**

1. when you account for cultural differences _____
2. Microsoft and Google approved of the new Internet regulations _____
3. recently they acquired an option to purchase the property _____
4. before anyone had an opportunity to examine it carefully _____
5. during the middle of the four-year fiscal period from 2008 through 2012 _____
6. if you want to apply for the job _____
7. the merger was approved by stockholders _____
8. should have been in the room _____
9. because we recommend new tax regulations _____
10. is counting on a raise _____

D. A **simple sentence** has one independent clause. A **compound sentence** has two or more independent clauses. A **complex sentence** has an independent clause and a dependent clause. Indicate whether the following sentences, all of which are punctuated correctly, are simple, compound, or complex. **Hint:** A sentence is not compound unless the words preceding and following a conjunction form independent clauses. If these groups of words could not stand alone as sentences, the group of words is not compound.

1. Sharon Forrester conducted research on blogs and shared her findings with other department members. _____

2. Sharon Forrester conducted research on blogs, and she shared her findings with other department members. _____

3. Management trainees are sent to all our branch offices in this country and to some of the branch offices in South America and Europe. _____

4. Fill in all answer blanks on the application, and send the completed form to the human resources director. _____

5. When you receive a response, please let me know. _____

6. In 1994 Southwest Airlines issued the industry's first e-ticket. _____

7. Before arriving at the airport, many airline passengers now check in online for their flights. _____

8. Chesley Sullenberger maintained control of his disabled US Airways plane and successfully landed it in the Hudson River. _____

9. If you have sensitive data on your mobile phone, erase or encrypt it before throwing or giving the phone away. _____

10. The best companies embrace their mistakes and learn from them. _____

E. Writing Exercise. Study the following examples. Then fill in the words necessary to complete the four sentence patterns.

Pattern No. 1: Subject–Verb

Example: The boss   called.   **Example:** The blog was   updated.

1. The football team _____
2. Our office _____
3. Students _____

4. Health costs _____
5. The committee _____
6. E-mail messages _____

Pattern No. 2: Subject–Action Verb–Object

Example: Administrative assistants use software.

7. Licia answered the _____
8. FedEx delivers _____
9. Salespeople sold _____

10. Congress passes _____
11. Stock pays _____
12. Students threw a _____

Pattern No. 3: Subject–Linking Verb–Complement

Fill in noun or pronoun complements.

Example: The manager is.   Stephen.   **Example:** The recipient was   she.

13. The applicant was _____
14. Chandra is the new _____

15. The caller could have been _____
16. The president is _____

Fill in adjective complements.

Example: The salary is   reasonable.

17. My investment was _____
18. New York is _____

19. Our new supervisor is _____
20. The report could have been _____

F. From the following list, select the letter that accurately describes each of the following sentences and add appropriate end punctuation.

    a. statement   c. question
    b. command   d. exclamation

Example: Take appropriate steps to prevent hacker attacks.   **b**

1. School and work holidays should always be scheduled on Mondays and Fridays _____
2. Do employers and workers contribute jointly to the retirement fund _____
3. How exciting this proposal is _____
4. Use Google to receive tens of thousands of hits in a nanosecond _____
5. We wonder whether our new marketing campaign will be successful _____
6. What a terrific view we have from the observatory on the tenth floor _____
7. Do you know whether Susan Simons received the purchase order _____
8. Turn off the power, close the windows, and lock the doors before you leave _____

9. Many college students spend a semester studying abroad _____

10. To succeed in the job interview, research the company thoroughly _____

G. For each of the following groups of words, write the correct letter to indicate whether it represents a fragment, a correctly punctuated sentence, a comma splice, or a run-on sentence.

a. correctly punctuated   c. comma splice
b. fragment   d. run-on sentence

Example: Because the office will be closed on Friday.   **b**

1. Anyone doing business in another country should learn what kinds of gifts are expected and when to give them. _____

2. Russian children usually open gifts in private, however, Russian adults usually open gifts in front of their gift givers. _____

3. In Thailand a knife is not a proper gift it signifies cutting off a relationship. _____

4. Because a large percentage of all U.S. corporate profits are now generated through international trade. _____

5. Making eye contact in America is a sign of confidence and sincerity. _____

6. Although Italians, Middle Easterners, and Latin Americans stand very close to each other when talking. _____

7. Which means that we will have to learn how to negotiate when in Chile. _____

8. Being on time is important in North America in other countries time is less important. _____

9. Filipinos take pride in their personal appearance, they believe a person's clothing indicates social position. _____

10. In many countries people do not address each other by given names unless they are family members or old friends. _____

H. Writing Exercise. Revise the following sentence fragments.

Example: If I had seen the red light at the intersection. I could have stopped in time.

    If I had seen the red light at the intersection, I could have stopped in time.

1. Because I am looking for a position in hotel management. That's why I am interested in your job posting.

2. We are seeking a management trainee. Someone who has not only good communication skills but also computer expertise.

3. During job interviews candidates must provide details about their accomplishments. Which is why they should rehearse answers to expected questions.

4. Although an interviewer will typically start with general questions about your background. Be careful to respond with a brief history.

_____

_____

5. A candidate who provided a wide range of brief stories about specific accomplishments. That's who was hired.

_____

I. **FAQs About Business English Review.** In the space provided, write the letter of the correct answer choice.

1. The reason we are moving is _____ we need more space.
a. because   b. that   _____

2. I _____ care less whether Craig becomes manager.
a. could   b. couldn't   _____

3. Is it _____ if I leave work early today?
a. all right   b. alright   _____

4. It is important to have a(n) _____ judge during a trial.
a. uninterested   b. disinterested   _____

5. We would like to _____ for your careful work.
a. thank-you   b. thank you   c. thankyou   _____

6. Always send a _____ note after a job interview.
a. thank-you   b. thank you   c. thankyou   _____

7. Which of the following represents better expression?
a. On the basis of taxes, we are in a good position this year.
b. Taxwise, we are in a good position this year.   _____

8. I am completely _____ in reading romance novels.
a. uninterested   b. disinterested   _____

9. As soon as you are _____ with the copy machine, let me know.
a. through   b. thru   c. threw   _____

10. She put _____ of careful preparation into her résumé.
a. alot   b. allot   c. a lot   _____

J. **Writing Exercise.** On a separate sheet, write complete sentences illustrating each of the following ten forms: a statement, a question, a command, an exclamation, a sentence with a direct object, a sentence with a complement, a simple sentence, a compound sentence, a complex sentence, and a sentence in inverted order. Identify each sentence.

A number of search tools—such as Google and Yahoo—are available at specialized Web sites devoted to searching. These tools help you find Web pages related to the search term you enter. Anyone using the Web today must develop skill in using a search tool.

Goal: To become familiar with a search tool.

1. With your Web browser on the screen, key the following URL: **http://www .google.com**. Press **Enter.**

2. Look over the Google home page. Notice the categories it will search: **Web, Images, Maps, News, Shopping, Mail,** and **more** (includes **Video, Groups, Books, Scholar, Finance, Blogs, YouTube, Calendar, Photos, Documents, Reader, Sites,** and **even more**). Click each one and study what is available.

3. Click **Web** to return to Web searching.

4. In the search term box, type "*sentence fragments*" as your term. Enclosing an expression in quotation marks ensures that the two words will be searched as a unit. Click **Google Search** or press **Enter.**

5. Google presents a screen showing the first ten hits it has located. Click any of the hits that seem most helpful to someone studying sentence structure. To return to the list, click the **Back** button in the upper left corner of your browser.

6. Select the most helpful site. Print one or more pages (click **File, Print,** and **OK**).

7. End your session by clicking the **X** in the upper right corner of your browser.

8. On the page(s) you printed, explain why the site you found was helpful and why it was better than others you visited. Turn in the page(s) you printed or send an e-mail to your instructor summarizing your response.

▶▶ Chat About It

Your instructor may assign any of the following topics for you to discuss in class, in an online chat room, or on an online discussion board. Some of the discussion topics may require outside research. You may also be asked to read and respond to postings made by your classmates.

Discussion Topic 1: Why is it important to write in complete sentences when communicating professionally? What does writing proper sentences communicate about you to others in the workplace?

Discussion Topic 2: Do Web research to find out four interesting facts about your major, program of study, or career. Write one sentence about each fact (four total sentences) using the four different sentence patterns (Pattern No. 1, Pattern No. 2, Pattern No. 3, and Pattern No. 4). Label each sentence for clarity. Share your sentences with your classmates, and be prepared to critique your classmates' sentences.

Discussion Topic 3: What technology tools do you use to communicate in writing on the job and in your personal life? When using these tools, do you write in complete sentences? Why or why not?

Discussion Topic 4: Marilyn vos Savant, an American writer and magazine columnist, said, "When our spelling is perfect, it's invisible. But when it's flawed, it prompts strong negative associations." Do you agree? Why or why not?

Discussion Topic 5: As mentioned in this chapter, a *portmanteau* is created when two words are combined to form one word. Two common portmanteaus are *brunch* (*breakfast + lunch*) and *motel* (*motor + hotel*). Can you think of others? Do a Web search to find five interesting portmanteaus, and then share them with your classmates. Try to find words that are unique and have not yet been shared by others in your class.

Posttest

Identify the sentence type of each of the following numbered items.

a = simple   c = complex
b = compound   d = compound-complex

1. If you are late for the meeting, please enter quietly. _____

2. Many Americans have gotten rid of their landlines and are using cell phones at home in an effort to save money. _____

3. Leaving your cell phone on in a movie theater is rude, but some people do it accidentally. _____

4. When your application is processed, we will let you know; in the meantime, please contact your references. _____

5. Jennifer is on a leave of absence and plans to return to work in February _____

Write the correct letter after each of the following numbered items.

a = correctly punctuated sentence   c = comma splice
b = fragment   d = run-on sentence

6. The computer arrived Wednesday the printer is expected shortly. _____

7. On the fifth floor is the Human Resources Department. _____

8. If you agree to serve on the committee. _____

9. On Monday my e-mail box is overflowing, on Friday my box is empty. _____

10. Because Christine, who is one of our best employees, was ill last week. _____

1.c 2.a 3.b 4.d 5.a 6.d 7.a 8.b 9.c 10.b

Begin your review by rereading Chapters 1–3. Then check your comprehension of those chapters by writing *T* (true) or *F* (false) in the following blanks. Compare your responses with the key at the end of the book.

1. Because of advances in technology, you can expect to be doing more communicating than ever before in today's workplace. _____

2. All dictionaries use the same plan for showing the order of definitions. _____

3. College-level dictionaries often provide in square brackets the brief history or etymology of a word. _____

4. Usage labels such as *obsolete*, *archaic*, and *informal* warn dictionary users about appropriate usage. _____

5. Most dictionaries show noun plurals only if the plurals are irregular, such as the word *children*. _____

6. Most dictionaries show syllable breaks with a hyphen. _____

7. Accent marks may appear before or after stressed syllables. _____

8. The usage label *obsolete* means that a word is no longer in use. _____

9. The terms *unabridged* and *college-level* refer to the same kind of dictionary. _____

10. Online dictionaries often provide audio pronunciations of words. _____

Read the following sentence carefully. Identify the parts of speech for the words as they are used in this sentence.

Wow! The applicant was very impressive in the interview, and we will hire her.

11.	**Wow!**	a. noun	b. interjection	c. pronoun	d. adjective	_____
12.	**The**	a. conjunction	b. preposition	c. adjective	d. adverb	_____
13.	**applicant**	a. adjective	b. pronoun	c. interjection	d. noun	_____
14.	**was**	a. adverb	b. verb	c. conjunction	d. preposition	_____
15.	**very**	a. adverb	b. adjective	c. pronoun	d. interjection	_____
16.	**impressive**	a. verb	b. adverb	c. adjective	d. noun	_____
17.	**in**	a. preposition	b. interjection	c. adverb	d. conjunction	_____
18.	**interview**	a. pronoun	b. adjective	c. verb	d. noun	_____
19.	**and**	a. adjective	b. interjection	c. conjunction	d. preposition	_____
20.	**we**	a. pronoun	b. noun	c. adjective	d. preposition	_____

For each of the following statements, determine the word or phrase that correctly completes that statement and write its letter in the space provided.

21. In the sentence *Excellent communication skills can help you get a job*, the simple subject is (a) communication, (b) skills, (c) you, (d) job. _____

22. In the sentence *Here is your paycheck*, the simple subject is (a) Here, (b) is, (c) your, (d) paycheck. _____

23. In the sentence *The CEO addressed the enthusiastic crowd*, the simple predicate is (a) CEO, (b) addressed, (c) enthusiastic, (d) crowd. _____

24. In the sentence *I feel bad about your accident*, the complement is (a) I, (b) feel, (c) bad, (d) accident. _____

25. The sentence *She sent many e-mail messages* represents what sentence pattern? (a) subject–verb, (b) subject–action verb–object, (c) subject–linking verb–complement, (d) subject–linking verb–object. _____

From the following list, select the letter to accurately describe each of the following groups of words. End punctuation has been omitted.

a. phrase   c. dependent clause

b. independent clause

26. In the spring of next year _____

27. Although he wore sandals, white socks, and a T-shirt with a beer company's logo _____

28. Claudia volunteers regularly for her local elementary school _____

29. Should have been in today's newspaper _____

30. When the workweek is over _____

From the following list, select the letter to accurately describe each of the following groups of words.

a. simple sentence   c. complex sentence

b. compound sentence   d. compound-complex sentence

31. Many companies feature profit-sharing plans, but some employees are reluctant to participate. _____

32. PepsiCo ran three commercials during the Super Bowl; however, not one was devoted to its core brand. _____

33. Although Alan Greenspan no longer heads the Federal Reserve, he is still influential in shaping economic policy. _____

34. Because he is a student, Mark works part-time; however, he plans to work full-time over the summer. _____

35. Chandra was hired by a local retailer and will start her new job on Monday. _____

From the following list, select the letter to accurately describe each of the following groups of words.

    a. complete sentence   c. comma splice

    b. fragment   d. run-on

36. Armando hates receiving "spam," he uses filters to avoid unwanted messages.   _____

37. Since the founding of the company.   _____

38. Turn on your computer when you arrive, and leave it on all day.   _____

39. That company's products are excellent that is why we use them exclusively.   _____

40. Susie loves her job, however, she also enjoys her free time.   _____

FAQs About Business English Review

Write the letter of the word or phrase that correctly completes each statement.

41. We appreciate your work; _____ for completing the report early.   _____

    a. thankyou   b. thank-you   c. thank you

42. Is it _____ to leave my computer on overnight?   _____

    a. all right   b. alright

43. I learn something new _____.   _____

    a. everyday   b. every day   c. every-day

44. The reason I am late is _____ my car stalled.   _____

    a. because   b. that

45. Which of the following is an acronym?   _____

    a. FBI   b. Dr.   c. scuba

46. A famous economist wrote the _____ to the textbook.   _____

    a. forward   b. foreword

47. Please send your cover and résumé to me by _____.   _____

    a. email   b. e-mail   c. E-mail

48. I know that _____ of messages we receive are spam.   _____

    a. allot   b. alot   c. a lot

49. We had to go _____ security before boarding our flight.   _____

    a. through   b. thru   c. threw

50. The new CEO's remarks _____ the interest of employees.   _____

    a. peaked   b. peeked   c. piqued

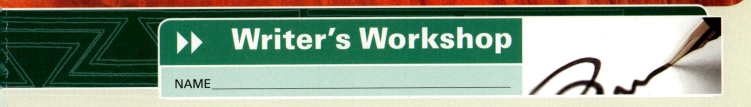
Developing Proofreading Skills

As you complete a set of chapters (a unit), you will find a workshop exercise that introduces various techniques to help you improve your writing skills. This first workshop emphasizes proofreading skills. You will learn about proofreading marks, which are often used by writers to edit printed material. Study the basic symbols shown here. See the inside back cover of your textbook for a more comprehensive list.

≡ Capitalize	∜ Insert apostrophe	⊙ Insert period
⌒ Delete	⅄ Insert comma	/ Lowercase
∧ Insert	⊼ Insert hyphen	⌒ Close up space

Example:

Proof reading marks are used by writers an editors to make corrections and revisions in printed copy they use these standard Marks for clarity and consistency. If you are revising your own work Youll probably use these mark only occasional. In many jobs today however you will be working in a team environment Where writing tasks are shared. Thats when its important to able to aply these well known marks correctly.

Practice:

Now it's your turn! Use the proofreading marks above to edit the following e-mail message. You will insert ten proofreading marks.

> Marcus,
>
> Thank-you for letting me know about our up coming meeting. Im sure that it will be productive and the company will benefit as a result. I have alot of good ideas to share you an the others. when you have a rough draft of the agenda please send it to me by email

Proofreading Tips

- Use your computer's spell-checker. But don't rely on it totally. It can't tell the difference between *it's* and *its* and many other confusing words.
- Look for grammar and punctuation errors. As you complete this book, you will be more alert to problem areas, such as subject-verb agreement and comma placement.
- Double-check names and numbers. Compare all names and numbers with their sources because inaccuracies are not always visible. Verify the spelling of the names of individuals receiving the message. Most of us dislike when someone misspells our name.
- For long or important documents, always print a copy (preferably double-spaced), set it aside for at least a day, and then proofread when you are fresh.

Writing Application 1.1. Using Figure 3.1 as a model, write a similar introductory personal business letter to your instructor. Explain why you enrolled in this class, evaluate your present communication skills, name your major, describe the career you seek, and briefly tell about your current work (if you are employed) and your favorite activities. Give a hard copy of the letter to your instructor, or send it by e-mail. Your instructor may ask you to write a first draft quickly, print it, and then use proofreading marks to show corrections before preparing your final copy. If so, double-space the rough draft; single-space the final copy. Turn in both copies.

FIGURE 3.1

Personal Business Letter, Block Style

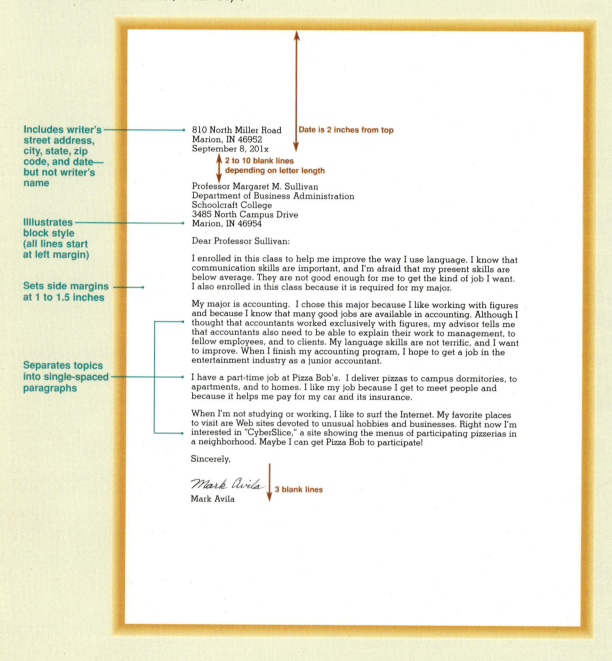

Includes writer's street address, city, state, zip code, and date—but not writer's name

Illustrates block style (all lines start at left margin)

Sets side margins at 1 to 1.5 inches

Separates topics into single-spaced paragraphs

810 North Miller Road
Marion, IN 46952
September 8, 201x

Date is 2 inches from top

2 to 10 blank lines depending on letter length

Professor Margaret M. Sullivan
Department of Business Administration
Schoolcraft College
3485 North Campus Drive
Marion, IN 46954

Dear Professor Sullivan:

I enrolled in this class to help me improve the way I use language. I know that communication skills are important, and I'm afraid that my present skills are below average. They are not good enough for me to get the kind of job I want. I also enrolled in this class because it is required for my major.

My major is accounting. I chose this major because I like working with figures and because I know that many good jobs are available in accounting. Although I thought that accountants worked exclusively with figures, my advisor tells me that accountants also need to be able to explain their work to management, to fellow employees, and to clients. My language skills are not terrific, and I want to improve. When I finish my accounting program, I hope to get a job in the entertainment industry as a junior accountant.

I have a part-time job at Pizza Bob's. I deliver pizzas to campus dormitories, to apartments, and to homes. I like my job because I get to meet people and because it helps me pay for my car and its insurance.

When I'm not studying or working, I like to surf the Internet. My favorite places to visit are Web sites devoted to unusual hobbies and businesses. Right now I'm interested in "CyberSlice," a site showing the menus of participating pizzerias in a neighborhood. Maybe I can get Pizza Bob to participate!

Sincerely,

Mark Avila

3 blank lines

Mark Avila

Unit 2

Knowing
the Namers

© ImageShop/Corbis

4 Nouns

© Caterina Bernardi/Corbis

5 Possessive Nouns

© Getty Images/Thinkstock/Jupiterimages

6 Personal Pronouns

© Getty Images/Goodshoot/Jupiterimages

7 Pronouns and Antecedents

"Of all the arts in which the wise excel, nature's chief masterpiece is writing well."

**– André Breton,
French writer (1896–1996)**

Chapter 4

Nouns

OBJECTIVES

When you have completed the materials in this chapter, you will be able to do the following:

LEVEL 1 ● Recognize four classes of nouns.
● Make regular and irregular nouns plural.

LEVEL 2 ● Spell challenging plural nouns ending in *y*, *o*, and *f*.
● Form the plurals of proper nouns, surnames, compound nouns, numerals, letters, degrees, and abbreviations.

LEVEL 3 ● Recognize and use correctly foreign plural nouns.
● Make special nouns plural.

Pretest

Underline any incorrectly spelled nouns in the following sentences. Each sentence contains one error. Write the correct spelling in the space provided.

1. Several attornies were assigned to the case. _____

2. The two bottom shelfs contain business history books. _____

3. We are considering two logoes for our new business start-up. _____

4. Both of our CPAs asked for leave of absences in June. _____

5. Based on all the criterion, several diagnoses were given. _____

6. Several boxs of office supplies were delivered today. _____

7. Our family has gone skiing the past three Februaries. _____

8. Bill Clinton was president of the United States for most of the 1990's. _____

9. Our firm hired three new CPA's this year. _____

10. How many crisises can our economy handle? _____

One way to ensure that you are writing well is to understand the importance of nouns in sentences. As you will recall from Chapter 2, nouns *name* persons, places, things, qualities, feelings, concepts, activities, and measures. In this chapter you will learn to distinguish concrete from abstract nouns and common from proper nouns. The principal emphasis, however, will be on forming and spelling plural nouns, an area of confusion for many business writers.

Beginning with this chapter, we present concepts in levels, progressing from basic, frequently used concepts at Level 1 to more complex and less frequently used concepts at Level 3. This unique separation of concepts will help you understand, retain, and apply the information taught in this book.

LEVEL 1

Classes of Nouns

As the "namers" in our language, **nouns** perform an important function. They often serve as sentence subjects. In addition, nouns can serve as objects of verbs and objects of prepositions. Although nouns can be grouped into many categories, this chapter focuses on four classes that are important to business writers: concrete, abstract, common, and proper nouns.

Concrete and Abstract Nouns

Concrete nouns name persons, places, and things that you can actually see, hear, feel, taste, or smell. **Abstract nouns** name qualities, feelings, and concepts that are difficult to visualize. Because concrete nouns are precise, they are more forceful in writing and talking than abstract nouns.

Career Tip

Successful job applicants fill their résumés with concrete expressions and quantifiable data rather than abstractions. Instead of *Worked as lab assistant,* try *Assisted over 300 students and 25 faculty members using Word, Excel, and Access in computer lab.*

1. attorneys 2. shelves 3. logos 4. leaves of absence 5. criteria or criterions 6. boxes 7. Februarys 8. 1990s 9. CPAs 10. crises

Concrete Nouns

apple	highway	river
cell phone	kitten	surgeon
dictionary	laptop	teacher

Abstract Nouns

accuracy	happiness	success
ethics	memory	technology
freedom	personality	value

Common and Proper Nouns

Common nouns name *generalized* persons, places, and things. Because they are general, common nouns are not capitalized. **Proper nouns** name *specific* persons, places, and things. They are always capitalized. Rules for capitalization are presented in Chapter 17.

Common Nouns

candy	organization	roller coaster
company	printer	software
magazine	professor	television

Proper Nouns

Milky Way candy bar	Phi Beta Lambda	Cyclone roller coaster
American Airlines	Epson Stylus	Windows NT
BusinessWeek	Dr. Virginia Green	Sony Bravia

Making Nouns Plural: The Basics

Singular nouns name *one* person, place, or thing. **Plural nouns** name *two* or more. In Level 1 you will learn basic rules for forming plurals. In Level 2 you will learn how to form the plurals of nouns that create spelling problems, and in Level 3 you will learn how to make foreign nouns and special words plural.

Plural of Regular Nouns

Most regular nouns, including both common and proper nouns, form the plural with the addition of *s*.

advantage, advantages	issue, issues	passenger, passengers
computer, computers	Janice, Janices	password, passwords
contract, contracts	Miller, the Millers	supplier, suppliers

Plural of Nouns Ending in *s, x, z, ch,* or *sh*

Nouns ending in *s, x, z, ch,* or *sh* form the plural with the addition of *es*.

blintz, blintzes	fax, faxes	Valdez, the Valdezes
business, businesses	lunch, lunches	virus, viruses
dish, dishes	tax, taxes	BUT: quiz, quizzes

Trivia Tidbit

The oldest word in the English language that is still used today is the common noun *town*.

Plural of Irregular Nouns

Irregular nouns form the plural by changing the spelling of the word. Dictionaries show the plural forms of irregular nouns, but you should be familiar with the most common irregular noun plurals, such as the following:

child, children	man, men	tooth, teeth
foot, feet	mouse, mice	woman, women

WARNING: Do not use apostrophes (') to form plural nouns. Instead, use the apostrophe to show possession. (Chapter 5 discusses possessive nouns in detail.)

Incorrect:	Many executives and CEO's earn big salary's.
Correct:	Many executives and CEOs earn big salaries.

In using plural words, do not confuse nouns with verbs (*He saves* [verb] *his money in two safes* [noun]). Be especially mindful of the following words:

Nouns	Verbs
belief, beliefs	believe, believes
leaf, leaves (foliage)	leave, leaves (to depart)
loaf, loaves (of bread)	loaf, loafs (to be idle)
proof, proofs	prove, proves

Now complete the reinforcement exercises for Level 1.

LEVEL 2

Challenging Noun Plurals

You can greatly improve your ability to spell challenging nouns by studying the following rules and examples.

Common Nouns Ending in *y*

Common nouns ending in *y* form the plural in two ways.

a. When the letter before *y* is a vowel (*a, e, i, o, u*), form the plural by adding *s* only.

attorney, attorneys	journey, journeys	toy, toys
delay, delays	monkey, monkeys	valley, valleys

b. When the letter before *y* is a consonant (all letters other than vowels), form the plural by changing the *y* to *i* and adding *es*.

country, countries	library, libraries	quality, qualities
currency, currencies	party, parties	supply, supplies

Common Nouns Ending in *f* or *fe*

Nouns ending in *f* or *fe* follow no standard rules in the formation of plurals. Study the examples shown here, and use a dictionary when in doubt. When dictionaries recognize two plural forms for a word (such as *calves, calfs*), they usually show the preferred form first.

Add *s*	Change to *ves*	Both Forms Recognized
brief, briefs	half, halves	calves, calfs
belief, beliefs	knife, knives	dwarfs, dwarves
chief, chiefs	leaf, leaves	scarves, scarfs
staff, staffs	shelf, shelves	wharves, wharfs
sheriff, sheriffs	wife, wives	

Common Nouns Ending in *o*

Nouns ending in *o* may be made plural by adding *s* or *es*.

a. When the letter before *o* is a vowel, form the plural by adding *s* only.

duo, duos	ratio, ratios	tattoo, tattoos
portfolio, portfolios	studio, studios	video, videos

b. When the letter before *o* is a consonant, form the plural by adding *s* or *es*. Study the following examples and again use your dictionary whenever in doubt. When dictionaries recognize two plural forms for a word, the preferred one usually appears first.

Add *s*	Add *es*	Both Forms Recognized
auto, autos	echo, echoes	avocados, avocadoes
casino, casinos	embargo, embargoes	cargoes, cargos
kimono, kimonos	hero, heroes	commandos, commandoes
logo, logos	potato, potatoes	mosquitoes, mosquitos
memo, memos	tomato, tomatoes	tornadoes, tornados
photo, photos	torpedo, torpedoes	volcanoes, volcanos
taco, tacos	veto, vetoes	zeros, zeroes

c. Musical terms ending in *o* always form the plural with the addition of *s* only.

alto, altos	cello, cellos	solo, solos
banjo, banjos	piano, pianos	soprano, sopranos

Proper Nouns and Surnames

Most proper nouns form the plural by adding *s* or *es* (*February, Februarys*) depending on the ending of the noun. When making proper nouns and **surnames** (last names) plural, don't change the original spelling of the word. Simply add *s* or *es* to the end. Note that when the word *the* appears before a surname, the name is always plural (*the Kennedys*).

a. Most proper nouns become plural by adding *s*.

Awbrey, the Awbreys	Germany, Germanys	Leno, the Lenos
January, Januarys	Lowenthal, the Lowenthals	Elizabeth, Elizabeths

b. Proper nouns and surnames that end in *s, x, z, ch,* or *sh* are made plural by adding *es*.

Bush, the Bushes	Rex, Rexes	Paris, Parises
Finch, the Finches	Rodriguez, the Rodriguezes	Williams, the Williamses

Compounds

Compound words and phrases are formed by combining words into single expressions. Compounds may be written as single words, may be hyphenated, or may appear as two words.

Trivia Tidbit

When we begin to use two words together, these words often progress from two words to a hyphenated word to a single word. For example, the words *to morrow* were once written as two words before becoming hyphenated (*to-morrow*) As this compound word became more common, the hyphen was dropped and it became one word (*tomorrow*). Can you think of others?

a. When written as single words, compound nouns form the plural by appropriate changes in the final element of the word.

bookshelf, bookshelves	notebook, notebooks	printout, printouts
footnote, footnotes	photocopy, photocopies	walkway, walkways

b. When written in hyphenated or **open form** (as two or more separate words), compounds form the plural by appropriate changes in the principal (most important) noun.

account receivable, accounts receivable	board of directors, boards of directors	leave of absence, leaves of absence
attorney-at-law, attorneys-at-law	editor in chief, editors in chief	president-elect, presidents-elect
bill of lading, bills of lading	father-in-law, fathers-in-law	runner-up, runners-up

c. If the compound has no principal noun, the final element is made plural.

cure-all, cure-alls	no-show, no-shows	start-up, start-ups
go-between, go-betweens	show-off, show-offs	trade-in, trade-ins
know-it-all, know-it-alls	seven-year-old, seven-year-olds	write-up, write-ups

d. Some compound noun plurals have two recognized forms. In the following list, the preferred plural form is shown first.

attorney general: attorneys general, attorney generals

court-martial: courts-martial, court-martials

cupful: cupfuls, cupsful

notary public: notaries public, notary publics

teaspoonful: teaspoonfuls, teaspoonsful

Numerals, Alphabet Letters, Isolated Words, and Degrees

Numerals, alphabet letters, isolated words, and degrees are made plural by adding *s*, *es*, or *'s*. The trend is to use *'s* only when necessary for clarity.

a. Numerals and uppercase letters standing alone (with the exception of *A*, *I*, *M*, and *U*) require only *s* in plural formation (no apostrophe).

9s and 10s	all Bs and Cs	three Rs
2000s	three Cs of credit	W-2s and 1040s

b. Isolated words used as nouns are made plural with the addition of *s* or *es*, as needed for pronunciation.

ands, ifs, or buts	pros and cons	yeses and noes
ins and outs	whys and wherefores	(*or* yeses and nos)

c. Academic degrees are made plural with the addition of *s* only (no apostrophe). Notice that degrees are written without periods or spaces. You will learn more about degrees and other abbreviations in Chapter 16.

AAs	EdDs	MDs
BSs	MBAs	PhDs

d. Isolated (standing alone) lowercase letters and the capital letters *A*, *I*, *M*, and *U* are made plural with an *'s* for clarity. Without the apostrophe, these letters might be confused with other words, such as the verb *is* or the abbreviation *Ms*.

A's	M's	p's and q's

Abbreviations

Abbreviations are usually made plural by adding *s* only (no apostrophe) to the singular form.

bldg., bldgs.	DVD, DVDs	No., Nos.
CPA, CPAs	FAQ, FAQs	wk., wks.
dept., depts.	mgr., mgrs.	yr., yrs.

The singular and plural forms of abbreviations for units of measurement are, however, often identical. Notice that some of these abbreviations end in periods, and others do not.

doz. (dozen or dozens)	km (kilometer or kilometers)
ft. (foot or feet)	kW (kilowatt or kilowatts)
in. (inch or inches)	oz. (ounce or ounces)

Some units of measurement have two plural forms.

lb. or lbs. (pounds)	qt. or qts. (quarts)	yd. or yds. (yards)

Now complete the reinforcement exercises for Level 2.

LEVEL 3

Foreign Nouns and Special Plurals

Selected nouns borrowed from foreign languages and other special nouns require your attention because their plural forms can be confusing.

Nouns From Foreign Languages

Nouns borrowed from other languages may retain a foreign plural. A few, however, have an Americanized plural form, shown in parentheses in the following list. Check your dictionary for the preferred form, which will be listed first.

Singular	Plural
alumna (*feminine*)	alumnae (pronounced a-LUM-nee)
alumnus (*masculine*)	alumni (pronounced a-LUM-ni)
analysis	analyses
axis	axes

Study Tip

Language purists contend that the word *data* can only be plural (*the data are*). However, see the FAQs About Business English for another view.

bacterium	bacteria
basis	bases
beau	beaux (or beaus)
crisis	crises
criterion	criteria (or criterions)
curriculum	curricula (or curriculums)
datum	data
diagnosis	diagnoses
emphasis	emphases
formula	formulae (or formulas)
hypothesis	hypotheses
matrix	matrices (matrixes)
medium	media (or mediums)
memorandum	memoranda (or memorandums)
nucleus	nuclei (or nucleuses)
parenthesis	parentheses
phenomenon	phenomena (or phenomenons)
stimulus	stimuli
vita	vitaes

Special Nouns

Some nouns ending in *s* or *es* may normally be *only* singular or *only* plural in meaning. Other special nouns may be considered *either* singular *or* plural in meaning, whether they end in *s* or not. Notice that many of the nouns that are usually singular refer to games, fields of study, or diseases. Many of the nouns that are usually plural refer to clothing and tools. Those nouns that may be singular or plural often refer to animals or nationalities.

Study Tip

You can practice these special nouns by using them with the singular verb *is* or the plural verb *are*. For example, *Mathematics is my favorite subject* (singular); *scissors are useful* (plural).

Usually Singular	Usually Plural	May Be Singular or Plural
billiards	clothes	Chinese
dominos	earnings	corps
economics	goods	deer
genetics	pliers	headquarters
kudos	proceeds	offspring
mathematics	scissors	politics
mumps	thanks	sheep
news	trousers	statistics

Now complete the reinforcement exercises for Level 3.

Spot the BLOOPER

Using the skills you are learning in this class, try to identify why the following items are bloopers. Consult your textbook, dictionary, or reference manual as needed.

Blooper 1: Newspaper headline in Thatcham, Berkshire, England: "Newbury Bride To Be Found Dead."

Blooper 2: Article title in *Experience Life* magazine: "One of America's most celebrated chef's gives credit where credit is due."

Blooper 3: From the *Democrat and Chronicle* [Rochester, New York]: "Foremans and supervisors will receive training."

Blooper 4: Icing on a cake for a network party celebrating the thirtieth anniversary of the hit show *Happy Days*: "Happy Day's."

Blooper 5: In an advertisement for Accelerated Schools in Colorado's *Rocky Mountain News*: "STUDENT'S DON'T HAVE TO FAIL."

Blooper 6: Advertisement for Kimberly Woods Apartment Houses, San Jose [California]: "Make the Jones Jealous."

Blooper 7: The *San Jose Mercury News* printed a photo of a plaque located on the Stanford University campus that reads "The Stanford's purchased 'the farm' from the Gordon's in 1876."

Blooper 8: From *The Journal* [Bath County, Ohio] announcing honors for two female graduates: . . . the award goes "to an alumni who has made a significant contribution or given extraordinary service."

Blooper 9: A headline in the *San Francisco Chronicle*: "Numbers put face on a phenomena."

Blooper 10: A banner ad for Mother's Day on the Web site of a worldwide florist service: "Thank's Mom."

Question	Answer
Q: What is the plural of computer *mouse?*	**A:** *Mice* refers to both computer devices and rodents. However, some experts prefer *mouse devices*, which is probably less confusing.
Q: What happened to the periods in Ph.D. and M.D.?	**A:** Over time usage changes. Writers found it simpler and more efficient to write these abbreviations without periods. Who decides when to recognize language changes? Our guide is *The Chicago Manual of Style*. It no longer shows periods in academic degrees (*AA, BA, MBA, MD, PhD*, and so on).
Q: Could you help me spell the plurals of *do* and *don't?*	**A:** In forming the plurals of isolated words, the trend today is to add *s* and no apostrophe. Thus, we have *dos* and *don'ts*. Formerly, apostrophes were used to make isolated words plural. However, if no confusion results, make plurals by adding *s* only.
Q: One member of our staff consistently corrects our use of the word *data*. He says the word is plural. Is it never singular?	**A:** The word *data* is plural; the singular form is *datum*. Through frequent usage, however, *data* has recently become a collective noun. Collective nouns may be singular or plural depending on whether they are considered as one unit or as separate units. Therefore, *data* can be considered either singular or plural, depending on how it is used. For example, *These data are much different from those findings* (plural). Or, *This data is conclusive* (singular).
Q: As a sportswriter, I need to know the plural of *hole-in-one.*	**A:** Make the principal word plural, *holes-in-one*.
Q: In the sentence, *Please read our FAQs*, does the abbreviation need an apostrophe?	**A:** No. The abbreviation for *Frequently Asked Questions is FAQs*, as you wrote it. Avoid using an apostrophe for plural forms.
Q: The company name McDonald's is written with an *'s* at the end. How would I make this proper noun plural?	**A:** Your best bet is to use the common noun *restaurant* after the proper noun; then make the common noun plural. For example, *We visited several McDonald's restaurants*.
Q: Is there a plural form of *plus and minus?*	**A:** The plural form is *pluses* (or *plusses*) and *minuses*. For example, *Consider all the pluses and minuses before you make a decision*.
Q: I know the abbreviation for *pound* is *lb.*, but that doesn't make sense to me because none of the letters match. Why do we use this abbreviation?	**A:** The abbreviation *lb*. actually stands for the Latin word *libra*, which refers to the basic unit of Roman weight, from which our present-day pound derives.
Q: I don't have a dictionary handy. Can you tell me which word I should use in this sentence? A [*stationary/ stationery*] *wall will be installed.*	**A:** In your sentence use *stationary*, which means "not moving" or "permanent" (*she exercises on a stationary bicycle*). *Stationery* means "writing paper" (*his stationery has his address printed on it*). You might be able to remember the word *stationery* by associating *envelopes* with the *e* in *stationery*.

4 Reinforcement Exercises

LEVEL 1

Online Homework Help! For immediate feedback on odd-numbered items, go to **www.meguffey.com**.

Note: At the beginning of each level, a self-check exercise is provided so that you may immediately check your understanding of the concepts in this chapter. Do not look at the answers until you have finished the exercise. Then compare your responses with the answers shown at the bottom of the page. If more than three of your answers do not agree with those shown, reread the chapter before continuing with the other reinforcement exercises.

A. (Self-check) Select the letter for the correctly spelled plural noun.

Example: Computer (a) virus, (b) viruses, (c) virus's can cause a network to crash. _____b_____

1. We received two confirmation (a) fax, (b) fax's, (c) faxes this morning. _____

2. Investors purchased numerous rare Chinese (a) tea, (b) tea's, (c) teas. _____

3. Most manufacturers employ (a) children, (b) childs, (c) childrens to test new toys. _____

4. Wachovia has three (a) branch, (b) branches, (c) branch's in that neighborhood. _____

5. The economic downturn has affected many (a) business, (b) business's, (c) businesses. _____

6. The condition will not change unless Congress passes a law with (a) tooths, (b) teeth, (c) teeths in it. _____

7. One administrative assistant may serve six (a) bosses, (b) boss's. _____

8. Our state legislators passed several new (a) tax's, (b) taxs, (c) taxes to meet the budget deficit. _____

9. French carmaker PSA Peugot Citroën builds the cleanest (a) car's, (b) cars sold in Europe. _____

10. I have never seen so many (a) klutzes, (b) klutzs, (c) klutz's on one dance floor! _____

Check your answers below.

B. Select the letter for the correctly spelled plural noun.

Example: The advertising agency submitted several (a) sketches, (b) sketch's of the design. _____a_____

1. The tennis match turned out to be a battle of the (a) sex's, (b) sexes. _____

2. After several (a) brushes, (b) brush's with success, Charlie Shi finally reached his goal. _____

3. News (a) dispatchs, (b) dispatch's, (c) dispatches from Europe reported new trade agreements. _____

4. Business students were required to take three (a) quiz's, (b) quizzes, (c) quizes this morning. _____

1.c 2.c 3.a 4.b 5.c 6.b 7.a 8.c 9.b 10.a

5. We need to hire seven additional waiters and (a) waitresses, (b) waitress's. _____

6. Each employee received three free (a) pass's, (b) passes to the exhibit. _____

7. Courtenay Redis purchased two different (a) lens, (b) lenses,
(c) len's for her new camera. _____

8. She has three different (a) accounts, (b) account's with her bank. _____

9. People who run their businesses out of coffee shops and (a) cafés,
(b) café's are called "laptop nomads." _____

10. Three (a) mices, (b) mouses, (c) mice just ran right through the kitchen! _____

C. Writing Exercise. Write plural forms for the nouns listed. Use your dictionary as needed.

1. employee _____   **11.** waltz _____

2. louse _____   **12.** hunch _____

3. watch _____   **13.** goose _____

4. witness _____   **14.** bias _____

5. franchise _____   **15.** glitch _____

6. quota _____   **16.** service _____

7. lunch _____   **17.** gas _____

8. foot _____   **18.** woman _____

9. glass _____   **19.** committee _____

10. marsh _____   **20.** ox _____

D. Concrete nouns name persons, places, and things that you can actually see, hear, feel, taste, or smell. **Abstract nouns** name qualities, feelings, and concepts that are difficult to visualize. Indicate whether the underlined nouns in the following sentences are abstract (*A*) or concrete (*C*).

Example: Our company serves pizza for lunch every Friday   C

1. Philip M. Parker has written over 300,000 books using special automated
software he created. _____

2. Patriotism increased in the United States after September 11. _____

3. A study by Expedia shows that 87 percent of Americans would prefer their
relatives to stay in hotels while visiting. _____

4. The television show *Survivor* has popularized the phrase "voted off the island." _____

5. The poet's brilliance showed during the reading of her latest poem. _____

6. Historian David McCullough said, "Real success is finding your lifework
in the work that you love." _____

7. When people lose faith in financial institutions, sales of home safes increase. _____

8. Most parents show unconditional love for their children. _____

9. Plumbers became very popular after the presidential debates in 2008. _____

10. Reporting the company's fraudulent practices took great courage. _____

A. (Self-check) Select the letter for the correctly spelled plural noun.

1. Two (a) attornies, (b) attorneys were disbarred for unethical behavior. _____

2. The supervisor approved three (a) leaves of absence, (b) leave of absences, (c) leaves of absences. _____

3. You will find the files for our past cases on the upper (a) shelfs, (b) shelf's, (c) shelves. _____

4. Small businesses can afford few administrative (a) luxurys, (b) luxuries. _____

5. The (a) Simmonses, (b) Simmons's, (c) Simmons' bought a vacation home in Maine. _____

6. Students had to show their (a) IDs, (b) ID's before they were admitted. _____

7. Two (a) bailiff's, (b) bailiffs are assigned to the courtroom. _____

8. Our organization is prepared to deal in foreign (a) currencies, (b) currencys. _____

9. Reece earned all (a) As, (b) A's last semester. _____

10. The four (a) sisters-in-laws, (b) sister-in-laws, (c) sisters-in-law get together every month for lunch. _____

Check your answers below.

 B. Select the letter for the correctly spelled plural noun.

1. Several (a) CEO's, (b) CEOs will attend a conference on improving corporate communication. _____

2. Many (a) companys, (b) company's, (c) companies believe strongly in the importance of being socially responsible. _____

3. We compared the liquidity (a) ratios, (b) ratio's, (c) ratioes of the two companies. _____

4. President Krista Johns wanted a manager with contemporary (a) believes, (b) beliefs, (c) belief's. _____

5. The reunification of the two (a) Germanies, (b) Germany's, (c) Germanys occurred in 1990. _____

6. Most (a) MBA's, (b) MBAs have taken classes in business ethics. _____

7. Do the (a) Wolf's, (b) Wolfs subscribe to *BusinessWeek*? _____

8. Sales are increasing with all Pacific Rim (a) countries, (b) countrys, (c) country's. _____

9. Two of our publications managers were former (a) editor in chiefs, (b) editors in chief, (c) editors in chiefs. _____

10. Congress established the Small Business Administration in the (a) 1950s, (b) 1950's. _____

11. Computer users must distinguish between zeros and (a) O's, (b) Os. _____

1.b 2.a 3.c 4.b 5.a 6.a 7.b 8.a 9.b 10.c

12. We will tabulate all (a) yes's and no's, (b) yeses and noes before releasing the vote. _____

13. The two (a) boards of directors, (b) boards of director, (c) board of directors voted to begin merger negotiations. _____

14. President Lincoln had four (a) brother-in-laws, (b) brothers-in-laws, (c) brothers-in-law serving in the Confederate Army. _____

15. We didn't expect so many (a) no-show's, (b) no-shows. _____

16. The legal staff filed all of its (a) brief's, (b) briefs on time. _____

17. Stevie Nicks sang three (a) solos, (b) solo's during the Fleetwood Mac concert. _____

18. How many (a) vetos, (b) veto's, (c) vetoes did the president have during his administration? _____

19. Pacific Grove, California, celebrates the return of the monarch (a) butterflys, (b) butterflies, (c) butterfly's every October. _____

20. We have three (a) Max's, (b) Maxs, (c) Maxes in our department alone! _____

C. Write plural forms for the nouns listed. Use a dictionary if you are unsure of the spelling.

1. balance of trade _____
2. half _____
3. bill of sale _____
4. IPO (initial public offering) _____
5. subsidiary _____
6. M _____
7. Wednesday _____
8. liability _____
9. Sanchez _____
10. valley _____

11. know-it-all _____
12. ATM _____
13. C _____
14. No. _____
15. governor-elect _____
16. if _____
17. logo _____
18. ft. _____
19. dept. _____
20. q _____

D. Writing Exercise. Write complete sentences using the plural form of the nouns shown in parentheses.

1. (Alvarez) _____

_____

2. (standby) _____

_____

3. (do and don't) _____

_____

4. (portfolio) _____

_____

5. (hero) _____

_____

6. (witness) _____

_____

7. (attorney) _____

_____

8. (belief) _____

_____

LEVEL 3

A. (Self-check) Select the letter for the correctly spelled plural noun.

1. She received two different (a) diagnosis, (b) diagnoses, (c) diagnosises from two different doctors. _____

2. Many (a) sheep, (b) sheeps are raised for their wool. _____

3. Moving lights and other (a) stimulus, (b) stimuli affect the human eye. _____

4. Black holes are but one of the many (a) phenomenon, (b) phenomena of astronomy. _____

5. Numerous (a) crises, (b) crisis, (c) crisises within education will only be worsened by budget cuts. _____

6. Fund-raisers contacted all (a) alumnus, (b) alumni of Colorado State University. _____

7. The most important (a) criterion, (b) criteria for making our decisions are expense and safety. _____

8. We will need a good pair of (a) plier, (b) pliers, (c) plier's to complete the job. _____

9. Almost all humans are born with 33 (a) vertebrae, (b) vertebra, but most have only 24 by adulthood. _____

10. (a) Economics, (b) Economic, (c) Economic's is a subject studied by all business majors. _____

Check your answers below.

B. Select the letter for the correctly spelled plural noun.

1. Substantial (a) datum, (b) data, (c) datas show that tobacco can lead to a number of health problems. _____

2. The private girls' school will honor its illustrious (a) alumna, (b) alumni, (c) alumnae. _____

3. Several (a) species, (b) specie's, (c) specie are on the verge of extinction. _____

1.b 2.a 3.b 4.b 5.a 6.b 7.b 8.b 9.a 10.a

4. Eunice Smith's proposal contains six (a) appendixes, (b) appendix. _____

5. Page references are shown in (a) parenthesis, (b) parentheses. _____

6. Bernard Berton requested information about two related (a) curricula, (b) curriculum. _____

7. Many of Galileo's (a) hypothesises, (b) hypothesis, (c) hypotheses were rejected by his peers. _____

8. Use (a) ellipses, (b) ellipsis, (c) ellipsises to show omitted words in a passage. _____

9. Scarlett O'Hara had many (a) beau, (b) beaux. _____

10. Dr. Binsley's master's and doctoral (a) theses, (b) thesis, (c) thesises are both available online. _____

C. Indicate whether the nouns in parentheses (a) are usually singular, (b) are usually plural, or (c) may be singular or plural. Use your dictionary as needed.

1. economics	_____	11. kudos	_____
2. deer	_____	12. proceeds	_____
3. goods	_____	13. mumps	_____
4. thanks	_____	14. scissors	_____
5. fish	_____	15. means	_____
6. billiards	_____	16. earnings	_____
7. news	_____	17. Vietnamese	_____
8. species	_____	18. sheep	_____
9. clothes	_____	19. headquarters	_____
10. offspring	_____	20. jeans	_____

D. Skill Maximizer. To offer extra help in areas that cause hesitation for business and professional writers, we provide Skill Maximizers. In the following sentences, underline any noun errors. Each sentence contains one error. For each sentence write a corrected form in the space provided.

1. Regular dental checkups will help you have healthy tooths. _____

2. We heard wolfs howling in the woods last night. _____

3. The Japanese are renowned for their advances in electronic's and other technologies. _____

4. Many banks have installed multilingual ATM's to serve their customers. _____

5. Her goal is to earn all As this semester. _____

6. The huge number of inquirys resulting from the news announcement overwhelmed their two Web sites. _____

7. Although many stimulus are being studied, scientists have not yet determined an exact cause of the bacterial mysteries. _____

8. Unless the IRS proves that the Kellys owe federal taxs, no penalty can be assessed. _____

9. Both woman asked for leaves of absence during the week of June 7. _____

10. Idaho is famous for its potatos. _____

11. Our directory lists RNs and MD's separately. _____

12. The company had record earning last quarter. _____

13. After numerous brushs with the law, Mark became a consultant to a security company. _____

14. The Ruiz's named three beneficiaries in their insurance policies. _____

15. Because of many glitches in our software, e-mail messages arrived in irregular batchs. _____

16. Despite the new flexible hours for Mondays through Thursdays, all employee's must put in a full workday on Fridays. _____

17. The Williamses discussed all the pro's and cons of the transaction before signing the contract. _____

18. Many companies' investment portfolioes lost millions last year. _____

19. Dylan and his two brother-in-laws opened a business together. _____

20. Hillary received four W-2's from her employers. _____

E. FAQs About Business English Review. In the space provided, write the correct answer choice.

1. Many people now use wireless (a) mouses, (b) mouse devices, (c) mices with their computers. _____

2. Despite the manufacturer's list of (a) dos and don'ts, (b) do's and don't's, (c) do'es and don'ts, we managed to blow a fuse. _____

3. She rides her (a) stationery, (b) stationary bike every morning before work. _____

4. Many artists' works are featured on the free e-mail (a) stationery, (b) stationary offered with Outlook Express. _____

5. For a fast answer to common questions about our Web site, please consult our (a) FAQ's, (b) FAQs. _____

6. He has visited (a) McDonald's restaurants, (b) McDonaldses all over the world. _____

7. We will discuss the (a) plus's and minus's, (b) pluses and minuses of going completely wireless. _____

8. The correct abbreviation for *pounds* is (a) pd., (b) pnd., (c) lb. _____

9. *The Chicago Manual of Style* recommends writing academic degrees (a) with periods (e.g., M.B.A.), (b) without periods (e.g., MBA). _____

10. The (a) datum, (b) datums, (c) data suggest that red wine can reduce cholesterol levels. _____

Many Web sites provide summaries of information about well-known companies. Some sites, such as Yahoo Finance, allow you to see a capsule of information at no charge. For more extensive information, you must subscribe. You can find information such as a company's addresses (Web and land), the names of its current officers, its subsidiary locations, its products, and its competition. You can even learn its annual revenue and other financial information. In this short exercise you will search for information about the Coca-Cola Company.

Goal: To learn to search for company data on the Web.

1. With your Web browser open, key the following URL in the address bar: **http://finance.yahoo.com/**. Press **Enter.**

2. Look over the Yahoo! Finance home page. Find the **Finance Search** box at the top of the page.

3. In the **Finance Search** box, key "Coca-Cola." As you begin to type, a drop-down menu will appear. Select the first item on the list, *KO The Coca-Cola Company*. Click **Get Quotes**.

4. Wait for the search results. When the **Search Results** page is fully loaded, scroll down to the **Business Summary** section at the bottom of the page and click the **Company Profile** link to see a summary of company information.

5. Read about Coca-Cola's main products. What types of products does it sell? In what year was it founded? Where is it headquartered? Who is the company's CEO?

6. Print one page from the **Profile** section.

7. Click the **View Financials** link. What is Coca-Cola's most recent gross profit? What is its most recent net income? What is the current price of its stock? Print one page from the **Financials** section.

8. End your session by clicking the **X** in the upper right corner of your browser. Turn in all printed copies or send an e-mail to your instructor summarizing what you learned.

▶▶ Chat About It

Your instructor may assign any of the following topics for you to discuss in class, in an online chat room, or on an online discussion board. Some of the discussion topics may require outside research. You may also be asked to read and respond to postings made by your classmates.

Discussion Topic 1: You learned in Chapter 4 that successful job applicants fill their résumés with concrete expressions and quantifiable data rather than abstractions. Why do you think concrete expressions and quantifiable data are more powerful and persuasive on résumés?

Discussion Topic 2: Employers look for various traits in job applicants, including *reliability*, *initiative*, and *flexibility*. These words are all nouns that name qualities. Assume you had to tell an employer about your five greatest

strengths. What strengths would you name and why? Be sure to express these strengths as nouns.

Discussion Topic 3: In 1992, when Dan Quayle was vice president of the United States, he served as a judge in a spelling bee at an elementary school in Trenton, New Jersey. During the spelling bee, he corrected student William Figueroa's accurate spelling of the noun *potato*, telling him to add an *e* to the end. Although he was relying on cards provided by the school, which included the misspelling, Quayle has been criticized and ridiculed for years for not being able to spell the word *potato* correctly. Is this criticism and ridicule justified? Why or why not?

Discussion Topic 4: William Strunk and E. B. White's classic book *The Elements of Style* states that "the steady evolution of the language seems to favor union: two words eventually become one, usually after a period of hyphenation." This statement often applies to nouns. For example, the word *wild life* became *wild-life* and then

wildlife. Find three similar examples and share them with the class. Also explain why you think this phenomenon occurs in our language.

Discussion Topic 5: Many English nouns are borrowed from other languages, including those listed in Level 3 of this chapter. Select five nouns that do not appear on this list and share the following information with your classmates: the singular form, the plural form (traditional and Americanized forms if applicable), and the language from which the noun was borrowed.

Posttest   Underline any incorrectly spelled nouns. Each sentence contains one error. Write the correct form.

1. The Valdez's vacation each year in Cabo San Lucas.   _____

2. Nine woman and three men belong to the book club.   _____

3. The children were warned to be careful of the sharp knifes.   _____

4. Three bunches of red tomatos look ripe enough to eat.   _____

5. Gray wolves are reported to live in the two vallies.   _____

6. In the 2000s many companys will be seeking MBAs.   _____

7. After several business crises, we hired two attornies.   _____

8. Several memoes about the new procedure have been sent to employees.   _____

9. How many sister-in-laws does he have?   _____

10. We purchased several DVD's for training purposes.   _____

1. Valdezes 2. women 3. knives 4. tomatoes 5. valleys 6. companies 7. attorneys 8. memos 9. sisters-in-law 10. DVDs

"Write with nouns and verbs, not with adjectives and adverbs. The adjective hasn't been built that can pull a weak or inaccurate noun out of a tight place."

—William Strunk Jr., E. B. White

Chapter **5**

Possessive Nouns

OBJECTIVES

When you have completed the materials in this chapter, you will be able to do the following:

LEVEL 1
- Distinguish between noun plurals and possessive nouns.
- Follow three steps in using the apostrophe to show ownership.

LEVEL 2
- Distinguish between descriptive nouns and possessive nouns.
- Make compound nouns, organization names, people's name, and abbreviations possessive.
- Avoid awkward possessives.

LEVEL 3
- Show possession with time and money.
- Understand incomplete possessives.
- Show separate and combined ownership.
- Write generic academic degrees correctly.

Underline any incorrect possessive forms. Write correct versions in the spaces provided.

1. Our survey covered many companys officers across the country. _____

2. Some students loans carried lower interest rates than yours. _____

3. Mr. Browns CPA firm will open in June. _____

4. The Perrys stock portfolio contains a variety of holdings. _____

5. Our Sale's Department will relocate to the third floor. _____

6. Our editor's in chief office will remain on the second floor. _____

7. Michelle's and Caitlin's mom is going back to school. _____

8. You won't get far on a dollars worth of gas. _____

9. Because of her training, Katherine's salary is greater than Troys. _____

10. Giving two weeks notice is standard when leaving a job. _____

As writing authorities Strunk and White note in this quotation, nouns play significant roles in sentences. Being able to use nouns effectively will make you a better writer. Thus far you have studied four kinds of nouns (concrete, abstract, common, and proper), and you have learned how to make nouns plural. In this chapter you will learn how to use the apostrophe in making nouns possessive. Learning to make nouns possessive can be difficult, but don't give up!

LEVEL 1

Showing Possession With Apostrophes

Possession occurs when one noun (or pronoun) possesses another. Notice in the following phrases how possessive nouns show ownership, origin, authorship, or measurement:

James O'Keefe's idea (Ownership)

Cape Cod's beaches (Origin)

Steinbeck's novels (Authorship)

three years' time (Measurement)

Trivia Tidbit

Many languages do not use an apostrophe to show possession. For example, in the French language, possession is shown with prepositional phrases, such as *the fine wines of the vineyard* instead of *the vineyard's fine wines*.

1. companies' 2. students' 3. Brown's 4. Perrys' 5. Sales 6. editor in chief's 7. Michelle 8. dollar's 9. Troy's 10. weeks'

In expressing possession, speakers and writers have a choice. They may show possession with an apostrophe construction, or they may use a prepositional phrase with no apostrophe:

the ideas of James O'Keefe

the beaches of Cape Cod

the novels of Steinbeck

the time of three years

The use of a prepositional phrase to show ownership is more formal and tends to emphasize the ownership word. The use of the apostrophe construction to show ownership is more efficient and more natural, especially in conversation. In writing, however, deciding where to place the apostrophe can be perplexing. Here are three simple but effective steps that will help you write possessives correctly using the apostrophe.

Study Tip

Whenever you have any doubt about using an apostrophe, always put the expression into an *of* phrase. Doing this will help you immediately recognize the ownership word and see whether it ends in an *s*.

Three Steps in Using the Apostrophe Correctly

1. **Look for possessive construction.** Usually two nouns appear together. The first noun shows ownership of (or a special relationship to) the second noun.

   the woman['s] briefcase
   the witness['s] testimony
   the children['s] teacher
   both investors['] portfolios

2. **Reverse the nouns.** Use the second noun to begin a prepositional phrase to help you identify the ownership word. The object of the preposition is the ownership word.

   briefcase of the *woman*
   testimony of the *witness*
   teacher of the *children*
   portfolios of both *investors*

3. **Examine the ownership word.** To determine the correct placement of the apostrophe, you must know whether the ownership word is singular or plural and whether it ends in an *s*.

   a. **If the ownership word does NOT end in *s*, add an apostrophe and *s*, whether the noun is singular or plural.**

      the *woman's* briefcase (Ownership word is singular, does not end in *s*)
      the *children's* teacher (Ownership word is plural, does not end in *s*)

   b. **If the ownership word DOES end in *s* and is <u>singular</u>, add an apostrophe and *s*.**

      the *witness's* testimony (Ownership word is singular, ends in *s*)
      the *boss's* office (Ownership word is singular, ends in *s*)

   c. **If the ownership word DOES end in *s* and is <u>plural</u>, add an apostrophe only.**

      both *investors'* portfolios (Ownership word is plural, ends in *s*)
      the *students'* test scores (Ownership word is plural, ends in *s*)

Notice that an apostrophe and *s* is added to make all nouns possessive, unless the noun is plural and ends in *s*. In this case, add an apostrophe only.

In very rare situations you will make singular nouns ending in *s* possessive by adding just an apostrophe, but only when pronunciation of the extra syllable is difficult, as in the following sentence:

Arkansas' economy is strengthening. (Extra *s* would be difficult to pronounce; add apostrophe only)

Here is a brief summary showing the four possible scenarios of possession:

	Singular Ownership Word	Plural Ownership Word
Does not end in *s*	**Add an apostrophe and *s***	**Add an apostrophe and *s***
	child's room (one child)	children's games
	teacher's class (one teacher)	women's clothing
	doctor's office (one doctor)	geese's habitat
Ends in *s*	**Add an apostrophe and *s***	**Add an apostrophe only**
	waitress's tips (one waitress)	waitresses' uniforms (more than one waitress)
	witness's testimony (one witness)	teachers' meeting (more than one teacher)
	class's rules (one class)	doctors' convention (more than one doctor)
	boss's office (one boss)	bosses' meeting (more than one boss)

A word of caution: Do NOT use apostrophes for nouns that simply show more than one of something. In the sentence *These companies are opening new branches in the West*, no apostrophes are required. The words *companies* and *branches* are plural; they are not possessive. In addition, be careful to avoid changing the spelling of singular nouns when making them possessive. For example, the *secretary's* desk (meaning one secretary) is NOT spelled *secretaries'*.

The guides for possessive construction presented thus far cover the majority of possessives found in business and professional writing.

Now complete the reinforcement exercises for Level 1.

LEVEL 2

Additional Possessive Constructions

You can greatly improve your skill in using apostrophes by understanding the following additional possessive constructions.

Descriptive Versus Possessive Nouns

When nouns provide description or identification only, the possessive form is NOT used. Writers have the most problems with descriptive nouns ending in *s*,

such as *Human Resources* Department. No apostrophe is needed, just as none is necessary in *Legal* Department.

Human Resources Department (Not *Human Resources' Department*)

the electronics industry (Not *electronics' industry*)

Los Angeles Dodgers (Not *Los Angeles' Dodgers*)

United States Air Force (Not *United States' Air Force*)

Compound Nouns

Make compound nouns possessive by adding an apostrophe or *'s* to the end of the compound word.

mother-in-law's birthday (Singular)

editor in chief's office (Singular)

sisters-in-law's children (Plural, does not end in *s*)

several start-ups' financial reports (Plural, ends in *s*)

Names of Organizations

Organizations with possessives in their names may or may not use apostrophes. Follow the style used by the individual organization. Consult the organization's stationery, directory listing, or Web site if you are unsure.

Organization's Legal Name Contains Apostrophe	Organization's Legal Name Does Not Contain Apostrophe
McDonald's	Starbucks
Noah's Bagels	Sears
Domino's Pizza	Marshalls
Kinko's	Mrs. Fields
Macy's	Chevys Fresh Mex

Names of People

When making proper names possessive, follow the same rules for making other nouns possessive. Singular names are made possessive by adding an apostrophe and *s* to the end. Plural names will always end in *s*; to make the plural name possessive, simply add an apostrophe.

Singular Name	Singular Possessive	Plural Possessive
Ms. Leopold	Ms. Leopold's résumé	the Leopolds' vacation
Mr. Smythe	Mr. Smythe's car	the Smythes' children
Ms. Morris	Ms. Morris's daughter	the Morrises' party
Mr. Horowitz	Mr. Horowitz's job	the Horowitzes' business

Notice that you can use the apostrophe and *s* to make singular names possessive, even if the name ends in an *s* or an *s* sound. This **traditional style** is used by many writers, and it is the style we recommend. However, some writers prefer the **popular style**. When using the popular style, add an apostrophe alone to show possession when a singular name ends in *s* (*Ms. Morris' car,*

Mr. Horowitz' job). Whichever style you use, use it consistently in your writing. You can read more about these two styles in the FAQs About Business English section in this chapter.

Abbreviations

Make abbreviations possessive by following the three steps in using the apostrophe described in Level 1.

> the NBA's playoff game (Singular, does not end in *s*)
>
> CBS's fall schedule (Singular, ends in *s*)
>
> both CEOs' signatures (Plural, ends in *s*)
>
> Levi Strauss & Co.'s jeans (Notice that apostrophe and *s* come after period)

Awkward Possessives

When the addition of an apostrophe results in an awkward construction, show ownership by using a prepositional phrase.

> **Awkward:** my sister's attorney's advice
>
> **Improved:** advice of my sister's attorney
>
> **Awkward:** my company's conference room's equipment
>
> **Improved:** the equipment in my company's conference room
>
> **Awkward:** my speech professor, Laurie Lema's, office
>
> **Improved:** office of my speech professor, Laurie Lema

To avoid an awkward possessive, use an *of* phrase starting with the object owned, such as *advice of my sister's attorney.*

Now complete the reinforcement exercises for Level 2.

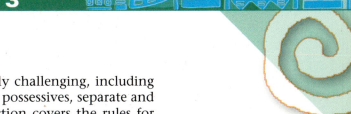

LEVEL 3

Challenging Possessive Constructions

A few situations related to possession can be extremely challenging, including showing possession with time and money, incomplete possessives, separate and combined ownership, and academic degrees. This section covers the rules for these challenging situations.

Showing Possession With Time and Money

Pay particular attention to the following possessive constructions, keeping in mind that time and money can show possession. The explanations and hints in parentheses will help you understand and remember these conventional expressions.

> a day's work (the work of one single day)
>
> three days' pay (the pay of three days)
>
> one year's salary (the salary of one year)
>
> five years' experience (the experience of five years)
>
> a dollar's worth (the worth of one single dollar)
>
> ten dollars' worth (the worth of ten dollars)

your money's worth (the worth of your money)

today's weather (only one today is possible)

tomorrow's work (only one tomorrow is possible)

Incomplete Possessives

When the second noun in a possessive noun construction is unstated, the first noun is nevertheless treated as a possessive. It can help to think about what implied noun is being possessed. The implied noun is shown in brackets in these examples.

I need to run by the doctor's [*office*] on the way home to pick up a prescription.

The team members will meet at Patrick's [*home*] after the game.

This year's sales are higher than last year's [*sales*].

Her test scores are higher than other students' [*test scores*].

Separate or Combined Ownership

When two nouns express **separate ownership**, make both nouns possessive. When two nouns express **combined ownership** (both nouns own an item jointly or together), make only the *second* noun possessive.

Study Tip

Look at the object owned (*rights, business*). If that object is singular, ownership is usually combined.

Separate Ownership

Both landlords' and tenants' rights will be considered during our talks.

Michelle's and Sam's cell phones both rang at the same time.

Combined Ownership

The husband and wife's business is thriving. (The husband and wife own one business.)

Michelle and Sam's apartment is near many restaurants and cafés. (Michelle and Sam own one apartment.)

Academic Degrees

When academic degrees are written in a generic sense, they should be written with possessive apostrophes. The apostrophe is necessary even if the word *degree* is implied. You will learn more about academic degrees, including when to capitalize them, in future chapters.

She earned her *associate's* degree before transferring to a four-year university.

A *bachelor's* degree can open many doors.

Jeff earned his *master's* before taking the certification exam.

But, Earning his *doctoral* degree was the proudest moment of his life. (No apostrophe)

Now complete the reinforcement exercises for Level 3.

Spot the BLOOPER

Using the skills you are learning in this class, try to identify why the following items are bloopers. Consult your textbook, dictionary, or reference manual as needed.

Blooper 1: Father's Day sign at a chocolate shop in San Francisco's North Beach neighborhood: "Dad's Love Candy."

Blooper 2: Headline in the *North County Times* [San Diego]: "Two Picasso's Stolen in Paris."

Blooper 3: From the cover of *Florida Today's TV Week*: "Tune in to see who will win this years [Indianapolis 500] trophy."

Blooper 4: From Lois and Selma DeBakey's collection of bad medical writing: "The receptionist called the patients names." (How does the missing apostrophe alter the meaning?)

Blooper 5: From an article in *The Telegraph* [Nashua, New Hampshire]: "According to the state police statement, Platte lived in the basement of his parent's ranch-style home, while his parent's Lawrence and Linda Platte lived on the second floor." [Can you spot two errors?]

Blooper 6: Announcement pasted on top of a Domino's pizza box: "We accept all competitors coupons."

Blooper 7: *The Cheyenne Edition* [Colorado Springs, Colorado] presented advice to moms on junk food: "Talk to your children's friend's mothers."

Blooper 8: Printed on a greeting card: "Happy Holidays from the Smith's."

Blooper 9: Large awning on a Philadelphia restaurant: "Steak's and Hoagie's"

Blooper 10: An article in *The Press* [Atlantic City, New Jersey] said that *American Idol's* Kelli Clarkson "remains the most successful alumnus by far."

Question	Answer

Q: How do I type the names *Macy★s* and *Wal★Mart*—when the stores actually use stars instead of apostrophes? I don't have a star on my keyboard. And what about Yahoo!, which has an exclamation mark at the end? What if a company writes its name in lowercase, such as *eBay*, and that company name comes at the beginning of a sentence?

A: Some companies (and individuals) seek distinction by displaying their names in lowercase or by including atypical symbols. You are under no obligation to reproduce such idiosyncrasies. We agree with outspoken copy editor Bill Walsh, who considers such usage exhibitionism and illiterate. Use only appropriate punctuation. Change the stars to appropriate punctuation (*Macy's, Wal-Mart*). Skip the exclamation mark for Yahoo, and capitalize organization names—regardless of the company's preferred style.

Q: I recently heard the expression *a stone's throw*? Should *stone* be possessive in this expression?

A: Some common expressions that refer to distance or geography use the possessive case. Here are a few examples: *at arm's length, for heaven's sake, in today's world,* and a *stone's throw.*

Q: In preparing an announcement for sales reps, our sales manager wrote about a *two months' training period.* I wanted to make it *a two-month training period.* Who is right?

A: Actually, you both are correct! The expression *two months' training period* is possessive (training period of two months). If the expression is *two-month training period*, it is descriptive and no apostrophe is required. Only a slight difference in wording distinguishes a descriptive phrase from a possessive phrase. Sometimes it is hard to tell them apart.

Q: Where should the apostrophe go in *employee's handbook*?

A: This is tricky. If the writer considers the handbook from one employee's point of view, the expression is singular: *employee's handbook.* This is also true of expressions such as *owner's manual.* If the writer is referring to a group, the references are plural: *employees' handbook* (a handbook for all employees), *owners' manuals* (the manuals of all owners). But you should also know that a few organizations prefer to use these terms as adjectives: *owner manual, employee handbook.*

Q: I am renewing my license to drive, and it occurred to me that I am not sure how to write this word correctly. Is it *driver's license, drivers' license,* or *driver license*?

A: That depends on the state in which you live. Some states, such as Kansas, Illinois, and Iowa, use *driver's license.* Most states, including California, New York, and Florida, have dropped the possession altogether, referring to it simply as *driver license.*

Question	Answer

Q: I work for the Supreme Court in Arizona, and I have a problem with the following sentence involving the restaurant chain Denny's: *The plaintiff was in fact fired ostensibly for violating Denny's alcoholic beverage service policy.* How do I make possessive a proper name that is already possessive?

A: As you suspected, you can't add another apostrophe. In the interests of clarity, we would consider the name descriptive, thus avoiding an additional *'s.* You would write *Denny's alcoholic beverage service policy.* By the same reasoning, you would not add another apostrophe to anything possessed by *McDonald's.*

Q: Why does *Martha's Vineyard* have an apostrophe whereas *Harpers Ferry* doesn't?

A: The federal government maintains a Board on Geographic Names in the United States. This board has a policy that "geographic names in the U.S. should not show ownership of a feature." British maps, says board secretary Roger Payne, are "littered with apostrophes." To avoid such clutter, the board allows no possessive on any federal maps or documents, unless previously dispensated. Only four geographic names have dispensations: Martha's Vineyard, (Massachusetts), Carlos Elmer's Joshua View (Arizona), Ike's Point (New Jersey), and John E.'s Pond (Rhode Island).

Q: Is there an apostrophe in *Veterans Day,* and if so, where does it go?

A: *Veterans Day* has no apostrophe, but *New Year's Day* does have one. Other holidays that are spelled with an apostrophe are *Valentine's Day, St. Patrick's Day, Mother's Day, Father's Day, President's Day,* and *April Fool's Day.*

Q: As the holiday season approaches, I am wondering whether the expression is *Season's Greetings* or *Seasons' Greetings.*

A: If you are referring to one season, it is *Season's Greetings.*

Q: I was reading a newspaper and noticed this sentence: *Mr. Morris' attorney made her opening statement.* Because this sentence refers to a singular proper noun (*Mr. Morris*), why isn't it written like this: *Mr. Morris's attorney?*

A: Traditionalists, as represented in *The Chicago Manual of Style* and *The Modern Language Association Style Manual,* prefer adding an apostrophe and *s* to singular proper nouns that end in *s* sounds, such as *Mr. Morris.* This is also the method we present in this chapter. On the other hand, writers of more popular literature, as represented in *The Associated Press Stylebook and Libel Manual,* prefer the simpler style of adding just an apostrophe to singular proper nouns that end in *s* sounds. You may apply either style, but be consistent. Please note that the style choice applies only to singular proper names ending in *s* sounds. Plural names are always made possessive with the addition of an apostrophe only.

5

Reinforcement Exercises

LEVEL 1

Online Homework Help! For immediate feedback on odd-numbered items, go to **www.meguffey.com.**

 A. **(Self-check)** Rewrite the following phrases avoiding the use of the apostrophe. Use a prepositional phrase. Does the ownership word end in an *s* sound?

	Revision	End in *s* Sound?
Example: the receptionist's schedule	schedule of the receptionist	No
1. the retailer's locations	_____	_____
2. a beginner's luck	_____	_____
3. two men's opinions	_____	_____
4. our company's policy	_____	_____
5. the two companies' agreement	_____	_____
6. the children's education	_____	_____
7. our customers' opinions	_____	_____
8. all candidates' speeches	_____	_____
9. this customer's e-mail message	_____	_____
10. her parents' wishes	_____	_____

Check your answers below.

 B. Using apostrophes, change the following prepositional phrases into possessive constructions. Ownership words are italicized.

Example: requirements of the *position*   the position's requirements _____

1. qualifications of the *job applicant*   _____

2. presentations of the *students*   _____

3. permit for a *seller*   _____

4. rights of *patients*   _____

5. addresses of *customers*   _____

6. Web site of the *organization*   _____

7. prices of *competitors*   _____

8. buying power of *Asians*   _____

9. offices of several *doctors*   _____

10. meeting of *stockholders*   _____

1. locations of the retailer, No 2. luck of a beginner, No 3. opinions of two men, No 4. policy of our company, No 5. agreement of the two companies, Yes 6. education of the children, No 7. opinions of our customers, Yes 8. speeches of all candidates, Yes 9. e-mail message of this customer, No 10. wishes of her parents, Yes

C. In the following sentences, make the word in parentheses possessive.

1. Some college (student) e-mail addresses are unprofessional. _____

2. Several (employee) suggestions were adopted by management. _____

3. The (company) annual report is available online. _____

4. The three (economists) theories created international news. _____

5. All (customers) personal information is stored on a secure server. _____

6. An (inventor) patent protects an invention for 17 years. _____

7. All (passengers) bags must be X-rayed, and some will be opened. _____

8. My (boss) husband retired last month. _____

9. When a bill receives the (governor) signature, it becomes law. _____

10. The (waitresses) uniforms make them look competent and professional. _____

D. Underline the errors in possessive construction in the following sentences. Each sentence contains one error. Write the correct form in the space provided.

Example: Several <u>students</u> scholarship applications were successful.   students' _____

1. City council members listened to all citizens complaints. _____

2. My bosses office is always such a mess! _____

3. One witness' testimony convinced the jury to convict. _____

4. Passenger's concerns about cell phone use on planes are justified. _____

5. Some companies are cutting expenses by requiring employee's, customers, and vendors to communicate by e-mail. _____

6. Several companies Web sites were recognized for being innovative. _____

7. Our waitresses personality is upbeat. _____

8. The profits of all company's are being affected by developing technologies and worldwide competition. _____

9. Many company's products and services are marketed globally. _____

10. Worldwide literacy rate's have increased sharply. _____

11. Nearly all management firms will tailor their services and charges to a clients needs. _____

12. Success depends on an individuals ability to adapt to change. _____

13. Several customers account information was stolen by hackers. _____

14. All depositor's qualify for free online bill paying. _____

15. The childrens' play area is open every day. _____

16. All taxpayers returns are checked by our computer. _____

17. America's first telephone directory was distributed to 50 subscriber's in New Haven, Connecticut, in 1878. _____

18. Many people think that athlete's earnings are too high. _____

19. Harvard is Americas richest university. _____

20. Many chef's work with organic products. _____

A. (Self-check) Underline the errors in possessive construction in the following sentences. Each sentence contains one error. Write the correct form in the space provided.

Example: The <u>FBIs</u> Web site features photos of wanted criminals.   FBI's _____

1. The Morris's son attends Middlebury College.   _____

2. The Los Angeles' Dodgers signed a star pitcher.   _____

3. Warren Buffetts wealth makes him one of America's richest citizens.   _____

4. Emily Dickinsons home is located in Amherst, Massachusetts.   _____

5. The first runner-ups prize of $500 went to Lynn Seaman.   _____

6. The SECs ruling in the securities fraud case is expected today.   _____

7. All teachers contribute to the State Teacher's Retirement System.   _____

8. Her brother's-in-law position was eliminated.   _____

9. Where can I find the editor in chiefs office?   _____

10. Our Human Resource's Department has several job listings.   _____

Check your answers below.

B. Underline the errors in possessive construction in the following sentences. Each sentence contains one error. Write the correct form in the space provided.

1. The United States' Treasury promotes economic growth and stability.   _____

2. Web graphic's must be designed with the audience's needs in mind.   _____

3. On the second floor is the chief of staffs office.   _____

4. Many of Ernest Hemingways books are considered classics.   _____

5. All beneficiaries names must be submitted when we issue policies.   _____

6. The IRSs goal is to simplify the language used on tax forms.   _____

7. Airline deregulation significantly affected the avionics' industry.   _____

8. NBCs fall schedule has not been finalized yet.   _____

9. Numerous employees personnel folders will be reviewed.   _____

10. You can download many new's releases promoting software programs.   _____

11. Chuck Norris films are enjoyed by fans of the martial arts.   _____

12. Most of this companys customers are concentrated nearby.   _____

13. Apple Incs. products have revolutionized the way we listen to music.   _____

14. Some air-freight lines and all bus lines are subject to the ICCs latest regulation.   _____

15. Licia Capone took Dr. Fox prescription to a pharmacy.   _____

16. Because of the gravity of the offense, the district attorneys staff is investigating. _____

17. Lucasfilm Ltd.s most popular films include *Star Wars* and *Indiana Jones*.   _____

19. They took their complaint to small claim's court.   _____

20. Tess e-mail message was forwarded to the entire staff.   _____

1. Morrises' 2. Los Angeles 3. Buffett's 4. Dickinson's 5. runner-up's 6. SEC's 7. Teachers'
8. brother-in-law's 9. chief's 10. Resources

C. Writing Exercise. Rewrite these sentences to remedy awkward or incorrect possessives.

Example: His company's accountant's suggestions are wise.

The suggestions of his company's accountant are wise.

(**Hint**: Start your sentence with the word that is owned.)

1. My sister's lawyer's hourly fee is high.

_____

2. Michael Jordan's father's support was instrumental to the athlete's success.

_____

3. Stephenie Meyer's latest book's success has been overwhelming.

_____

4. The engineer's assistant's computer held all the necessary equations.

_____

5. My supervisor's friend's motor home is always parked in the company lot.

_____

LEVEL 3

A. (Self-check) Select an acceptable possessive form.

1. Let's plan to meet at (a) Victorias, (b) Victoria's before going to the restaurant. _____

2. (a) Microsoft's and Mozilla's, (b) Microsoft and Mozilla's browsers support the latest animation technology. _____

3. (a) Lisa's and Greg's, (b) Lisa and Greg's daughter is applying to law schools. _____

4. Your totals for the last three columns are certainly different from (a) Kims, (b) Kim's, (c) Kim. _____

5. This year's new home sales are higher than last (a) year, (b) year's, (c) years'. _____

6. Max plans to earn his (a) master, (b) masters', (c) master's degree in engineering. _____

7. Grace has three (a) year's, (b) years', (c) years experience in early childhood education. _____

8. Please verify Ms. (a) Lopezes', (b) Lopez's work hours. _____

9. Have you noticed that the (a) Horowitzes, (b) Horowitzes' have a new car? _____

10. In one (a) days, (b) days', (c) day's time we will be on a plane to Hawaii! _____

Check your answers below.

B. Underline the errors in possessive construction in the following sentences. Each sentence contains one error. Write the correct form in the space provided.

1. Sue's and Bob's new home is located in South Beach. _____

2. This company's product line is superior to that companys. _____

3. At least a dozen buyers and sellers' finances were scrutinized. _____

4. We were all invited to the party at the Thomas. _____

1.b 2.a 3.b 4.b 5.b 6.c 7.c 8.b 9.b 10.c

5. Despite a weeks delay, the package finally arrived. _____

6. It took William two years to earn his masters degree. _____

7. A dollars worth of gas won't get you very far. _____

8. After seven years time the property reverts to state ownership. _____

9. I can find other peoples errors but not my own. _____

10. Attorney's salaries have increased significantly over the last decade. _____

C. Skill Maximizer. To offer extra help in areas that cause hesitation for business and professional writers, we provide Skill Maximizers. This exercise reviews all three levels of this chapter. Underline the errors in possessive construction in the following sentences. Each sentence contains one error. Write the correct form in the space provided.

1. Drivers for Dominos Pizza cover 9 million miles each week in the United States alone. _____

2. Brooke's goal is to earn her bachelors degree from Columbia University in New York City. _____

3. Several student's were awarded academic scholarships. _____

4. We were surprised when Allison married her bosses son. _____

5. The butler stood at the door and called the guests names as they arrived. _____

6. Many artists paintings will be on display at the museum's exhibit. _____

7. To validate the contract, both parties signatures are needed. _____

8. Our mens team placed 12th in the cross-country championship. _____

9. At the CPAs annual conference, we interviewed the graduates of many colleges and universities. _____

10. Does your company routinely monitor employees Web use? _____

11. Ryan decided to follow his father-in-law advice in seeking a job in the hospitality industry. _____

12. Barbara always wants to put her two cents worth in. _____

13. Although Jasons car was slightly damaged, the repair costs were high. _____

14. Only one HMOs doctors complained that they were restricted in the amount of time they could spend listening to patients' comments. _____

15. If our departments had been aware of each others needs, we could have shared our inventories. _____

16. The discovery of DNAs structure revealed a baby's 46 chromosomes arranged in pairs. _____

17. Many employee's are upset about the new policy. _____

18. When jury members heard the eyewitnesses stories, they were stunned. _____

19. One waitresses service was outstanding. _____

20. Charlie and Tom's bikes were stolen from their garages last night. _____

D. FAQs About Business English Review. In the space provided, write the correct answer choice.

1. She plans to apply for a job at (a) Macy's, (b) Macy*s, (c) Macys. _____

2. Lawmakers are keeping the idea at (a) arms, (b) arm's length for now. _____

3. Her office is a (a) stones, (b) stone's, (c) stones' throw from her home. _____

4. For (a) heavens, (b) heavens', (c) heaven's sake! You don't really believe that nonsense, do you? _____

5. All new service representatives will receive three (a) months, (b) month's, (c) months' training. _____

6. On (a) Veterans, (b) Veteran's, (c) Veterans' Day we honor those who served our country. _____

7. The office will be closed on (a) St. Patricks', (b) St. Patrick's, (c) St. Patricks Day. _____

8. At all of its restaurants, (a) Denny's, (b) Dennys', (c) Dennys's employees are trained to give good service. _____

9. Ms. (a) Morris's, (b) Morris' presentation was outstanding. (Traditional style) _____

10. Ms. (a) Morris's, (b) Morris' proposal was adopted by the board. (Popular style) _____

E. Writing Exercise. Compose original sentences illustrating the possessive forms of the words shown in parentheses.

Example: (two years) <u>You must have two years' experience to apply for the job.</u>

1. (Leonard) _____

_____

2. (contractor) _____

_____

3. (Milli and Robert) _____

_____

4. (Congress) _____

_____

5. (customers) _____

_____

6. (mother-in-law) _____

_____

Your boss is irritated by unwanted e-mail messages, such as "Earn Big Money Working at Home!" She asks you to use the Web to find a way to stop this misuse of her computer. You decide to use a well-known search engine, Google.

Goal: To learn to refine search terms.

1. With your Web browser on the screen, key the following URL in the location box or address bar: **http://www .google.com** and then press **Enter.**

2. On the Google opening page, locate the **Search** box. Key the search term *email* (Google seems to prefer this spelling). Press **Google Search** or **Enter.**

3. How many results did Google find? Millions? Look over the site titles presented. Do you see any relevant sites?

4. To reduce the number of "hits," you must refine your search term. Scroll back to the top of the screen and locate the **Search** box again. Key a new search term: *unwanted email.*

5. Scroll down to see the number of hits. This refined search term still brings millions of hits.

6. Scroll back to the **Search** box and insert a new search term. Include quotation marks: "*unwanted email*." This time Google will find only those sites that include *unwanted e-mail* as a unit.

7. Click a link that looks promising. Find an answer to this question: What can an e-mail user do about unwanted messages (**spam**)? (If nothing happens on your screen when you click a URL, look at the status line at the bottom of your screen. It tells you whether the site has been contacted. Some sites are slow to respond.)

8. Find and print one or two pages with advice on how to deal with unwanted e-mail.

9. End your session by clicking the **X** in the upper right corner of your browser. Turn in all printed copies or send your instructor an e-mail message summarizing what you learned.

▶▶ Chat About It

Your instructor may assign any of the following topics for you to discuss in class, in an online chat room, or on an online discussion board. Some of the discussion topics may require outside research. You may also be asked to read and respond to postings made by your classmates.

Discussion Topic 1: Practice making your own name possessive. Write four complete sentences showing your name in these formats: singular, singular possessive, plural, plural possessive. (Remember that you must add the word *the* before your last name to make it plural.) Share your sentences with your classmates. Be prepared to give them feedback on their sentences.

Discussion Topic 2: The apostrophe is one of the most frequently misused punctuation marks.

Find an example of a misused punctuation mark in a newspaper or magazine article, on a sign in your neighborhood, or online. Share the error with your classmates. Be sure to explain why the apostrophe has been misused, and provide a corrected version.

Discussion Topic 3: In this chapter you learned about Bill 101, which makes French the official language of Quebec. Do some research to find out more about this law, especially as it pertains to company names that contain apostrophes. Report your findings, in your own words, to your classmates. Remember to cite your sources by providing the names and Web site addresses.

Discussion Topic 4: In this chapter you learned that some languages, such as French, don't use the apostrophe to show possession. Choose a language other than French and English and find out how possession is shown in that language. Report your findings to your classmates.

Discussion Topic 5: Some individuals believe that the apostrophe should be abolished from the English language. Do a Google search using the search term *abolish apostrophe* to locate various Web sites and blog entries devoted to this topic. Review several sites and then decide how you feel about this issue. Should we abolish the apostrophe in English? Why or why not? Share your thoughts with your classmates, and be sure to defend your position.

Posttest

Underline any incorrect possessive forms. Write correct versions.

1. A major vote will take place at the stockholders meeting. _____

2. One witnesses attire was inappropriate for the courtroom. _____

3. Our Human Resource's Department is on the fifth floor. _____

4. My father's-in-law birthday is in November. _____

5. I stop by Starbuck's every day for a latte. _____

6. This month's sales figures were better than last month. _____

7. Ms. Johnsons secretary located all the accounts receivable. _____

8. In just two years time, your profits will likely double. _____

9. Sheila's and Mark's daughter will start school next year. _____

10. She will earn her bachelors degree next spring. _____

1. stockholders' 2. witness's 3. Resources 4. father-in-law's 5. Starbucks 6. last month's 7. Johnson's 8. years' 9. Sheila 10. bachelor's

POSSESSIVE NOUNS

"When something has been read without effort, great effort has gone into its writing."

—**Enrique Jardiel Poncela, Spanish playwright and novelist**

Chapter 6

Personal Pronouns

OBJECTIVES

When you have completed the materials in this chapter, you will be able to do the following:

LEVEL 1
- Use personal pronouns correctly as subjects and objects.
- Distinguish between personal possessive pronouns (such as *its*) and contractions (such as *it's*).

LEVEL 2
- Choose the correct pronoun in compound constructions, comparatives, and appositives.
- Use reflexive pronouns correctly.

LEVEL 3
- Use subjective-case pronouns as complements following linking verbs.
- Select the correct pronouns for use with the infinitive *to be*.

Underline the correct pronoun in each sentence.

1. Bruce and (I, me, myself) were promoted to management positions.

2. Please contact Allison or (I, me, myself) with any questions.

3. Send the signed contract to Dylan or (she, her) by June 1.

4. The CEO invited my husband and (I, me) to the benefit dinner.

5. (Us, We) employees will vote whether to approve the contract.

6. No one in the office deserved the award more than (her, she).

7. Are you sure it was (she, her) who called me yesterday morning?

8. Reliable managers like you and (he, him) are difficult to retain.

9. Inconsiderate people annoy my roommate as much as (I, me).

10. The interview team believed the best candidate to be (he, him).

One area of writing that will require great effort is deciding how to use pronouns properly. As you will remember from Chapter 2, **pronouns** are words that substitute for nouns and other pronouns. They enable us to speak and write without awkward repetition. Grammatically, pronouns may be divided into seven types (personal, relative, interrogative, demonstrative, indefinite, reflexive, and reciprocal). Rather than consider all seven pronoun types, this textbook will be concerned only with those pronouns that cause difficulty in use.

LEVEL 1

Guidelines for Using Personal Pronouns

Personal pronouns indicate the person speaking, the person spoken to, or the person or object spoken of. Notice in the following table that personal pronouns change their form (or **case**) depending on who is speaking (called the **person**), how many are speaking (the **number**), and the sex (or **gender**) of the speaker. For example, the third-person feminine singular objective case is *her*. Most personal pronoun errors by speakers and writers involve faulty usage of case forms. Study this table to avoid errors in personal pronoun use.

1. I 2. me 3. her 4. me 5. We 6. she 7. she 8. him 9. me 10. him

	Subjective Case*		Objective Case		Possessive Case	
	Sing.	**Plural**	**Sing.**	**Plural**	**Sing.**	**Plural**
First Person (person speaking)	I	we	me	us	my mine	our ours
Second Person (person spoken to)	you	you	you	you	your yours	your yours
Third Person (person or things spoken of)	he she it	they	him her it	them	his, her hers, its	their theirs

*Some authorities prefer the term nominative case.

Basic Use of the Subjective Case

Subjective-case pronouns are used primarily as the subjects of verbs. Every verb or verb phrase, regardless of its position in a sentence, has at least one subject. If that subject is a pronoun, it must be in the subjective case.

> *They* will attend the conference.
>
> *He* wonders whether *they* offer wireless access.

Basic Use of the Objective Case

Objective-case pronouns most commonly are used as objects of verbs or objects of prepositions.

Object of a Verb

As you learned in Chapter 3, objects of action verbs can be direct or indirect. A **direct object** is a noun or pronoun that answers the question *What?* or *Whom?* An **indirect object** is a noun or pronoun that answers the question *To whom?*, *To what?*, *For whom?*, or *For what?* When pronouns act as direct or indirect objects of verbs, they must be in the objective case.

> Please ask *her* where she would like to go for dinner.
>
> Can you meet *them* at the airport at 10 a.m.?
>
> The attorney sent *them* an important e-mail message.
>
> The network supervisor issued *her* a new password.

Object of a Preposition

As you learned in Chapter 2, a preposition is a word in a position *before* its object. The **object of a preposition** is a noun or pronoun. The objective case is used for pronouns that are objects of prepositions.

> Our team leader sent the final report to *us*.
>
> The photographer took a professional photo of *her*.
>
> Just between *you* and *me*, profits are slipping.

When the words *between, but, like,* and *except* are used as prepositions, errors in pronoun case are likely to occur. To avoid such errors, isolate the prepositional phrase, and then use an objective-case pronoun as the object of the preposition (*Every employee [but Weston and her] will work overtime this weekend*).

Basic Use of the Possessive Case

Possessive pronouns show ownership. Unlike possessive nouns, possessive pronouns never have apostrophes. Study these five common possessive pronouns: *hers, yours, ours, theirs, its*. Notice the absence of apostrophes.

Do not confuse possessive pronouns with contractions. **Contractions** are shortened (contracted) forms of subjects and verbs, such as *it's* (for *it is* or *it has*), *there's* (for *there is*), *they're* (for *they are*), and *you're* (for *you are*). In these examples the apostrophes indicate omitted letters.

Possessive Pronouns	Contractions
Those parking spots are *theirs*.	*There's* not a lot we can do.
To park the car, turn *its* wheel to the left.	*It's* difficult to parallel park.
Is this credit card *yours*?	*You're* the next speaker.
Hers was the best report.	**Note:** Never use *her's*.
That driveway is *ours*.	**Note:** Never use *our's*.

As you learned in Chapter 2, words such as *my, our, your, his, her, its,* and *their* function as adjectives when they describe nouns (*my cell phone, our retreat, your address, his car, her condo, its trunk, their vacation*). This concept will be further explained in Chapter 11.

Now complete the reinforcement exercises for Level 1.

LEVEL 2

Challenges in Using Personal Pronouns

Choosing the correct personal pronouns in compound constructions, comparatives, and appositives requires a good understanding of the following guidelines.

Compound Subjects and Objects

When a pronoun appears in combination with a noun or another pronoun, we must give special attention to case selection. Use this technique to help you choose the correct pronoun case: Ignore the extra noun or pronoun and its related conjunction, and consider separately the pronoun in question to determine what the case should be.

~~Meaghan and~~ he attended the conference. (Ignore *Meaghan and*.)
(Compound subject)

~~You and~~ I must write the report. (Ignore *You and*.)
(Compound subject)

Lindsay asked ~~you and~~ me for advice. (Ignore *you and*.)
(Compound object)

Would you like ~~Rasheed and~~ them to help you? (Ignore *Rasheed and*.)
(Compound object)

Notice in the first sentence, for example, that when *Meaghan and* is removed, the pronoun *he* must be selected because it functions as the subject of the verb. In the third sentence when *you and* is removed, the pronoun *me* must be selected because it functions as the object of a verb.

Comparatives

In statements of **comparison**, words are often implied but not actually stated. **Comparatives** are often introduced by words such as *than* or *as*. To determine pronoun case in only partially complete comparative statements introduced by *than* or *as*, always mentally finish the comparative by adding the implied missing words.

> Christina enjoys reading as much as *he*. (Christina enjoys reading as much as *he* [not *him*] enjoys reading.)
>
> Nader Sharkes is a better cook than *she*. (. . . better cook than *she* [not *her*] is.)
>
> Tardiness annoys Judy Sunayama-Foster as much as *me*. (. . . as much as it annoys *me* [not *I*].)

Appositives

Appositives are words or groups of words that explain or rename previously mentioned nouns or pronouns. When a pronoun has an appositive, it takes the same case as the appositive that follows it. To determine more easily what pronoun case to use for a pronoun in combination with an appositive, temporarily ignore the appositive.

> *We* ~~consumers~~ are protected by laws. (Ignore the appositive *consumers*.)
>
> Action must be taken by *us* ~~employees~~. (Ignore the appositive *employees*.)

Reflexive Pronouns

Reflexive pronouns that end in *-self* or *–selves* emphasize or reflect on their **antecedents** (the nouns or pronouns previously mentioned). Examples of reflexive pronouns include *myself, yourself, himself, herself, itself, ourselves, yourselves,* and *themselves*.

> *I* will prepare the proposal *myself*. (*Myself* reflects on *I*.)
>
> The president *himself* greeted each winner. (*Himself* emphasizes *president*.)

Errors result when we use reflexive pronouns instead of personal pronouns. If no previously mentioned noun or pronoun is stated in the same sentence, use a personal pronoun instead of a reflexive pronoun.

> Send your request to either James or *me*. (Not *myself*)
>
> Amy Beitel and *I* analyzed the research implications. (Not *myself*)

Please note that *hisself, themself,* and *theirselves* are not acceptable words.

> Now complete the reinforcement exercises for Level 2.

Advanced Uses of Subjective-Case Pronouns

Although the following applications appear infrequently, careful speakers and writers try to understand why certain pronouns are used.

Subject Complement

Study Tip

Whenever a pronoun follows a linking verb, that pronoun will be in the subjective case.

As we saw earlier in this chapter, subjective-case pronouns usually function as subjects of verbs. Less frequently, subjective-case pronouns also perform as subject complements. A pronoun that follows a linking verb and renames the subject must be in the subjective case. As you learned in Chapter 2, **linking verbs** express a state of being and generally link to the subject words that describe or rename them. Some linking verbs are *am, is, are, was, were, be, being,* and *been.* Other linking verbs express the senses: *feels, appears, tastes, sounds, seems, looks.*

> It *is he* who will make the final decision. (Not *him*)
>
> I am sure it *was she* who sent the instant message. (Not *her*)
>
> If you *were I*, what would you do? (Not *me*)

When a sentence includes a verb phrase, look at the final word of the verb phrase. If it is a linking verb, use a subjective pronoun.

> It *might have been they* who made reservations. (Not *them*)
>
> The driver *could have been he*. (Not *him*)
>
> If the manager *had been I*, your money would have been refunded. (Not *me*)

In conversation it is common to say, *It is me,* or more likely, *It's me.* Careful speakers and writers, though, normally use subjective-case pronouns after linking verbs. If the resulting constructions sound too formal, revise your sentences appropriately. For example, instead of *It is I who placed the order,* use *I placed the order.* When answering the telephone, careful speakers say, *This is she* or *This is he.*

Infinitive *to be* Without a Subject

An **infinitive** is the present tense of a verb preceded by the word *to*—for example, *to sit, to run,* and *to dream.* An important infinitive is *to be.* Subjective pronouns are used following the infinitive *to be* when the infinitive has no subject. In this instance the infinitive joins a complement (not an object) to the subject.

> Mikhail was mistakenly thought to be *I*. (The infinitive *to be* has no subject; *I* is the complement of the subject *Mikhail*.)
>
> Why would Jennifer want to be *she*? (The infinitive *to be* has no subject; *she* is the complement of the subject *Jennifer*.)

Infinitive *to be* With a Subject

When the **infinitive** *to be* has a subject, any pronoun following it will function as an object. Therefore, the pronoun following the infinitive will function as its object and must be in the objective case.

> The interviewer believed the best candidate to be *her*. (The subject of the infinitive *to be* is *the candidate*; therefore, the pronoun functions as an object.
>
> Try it another way: *The interviewer believed her to be the best candidate.* You would not say, *The interviewer believed she to be the best candidate.*)

Gary expected the caller to be *me*. (The subject of the infinitive *to be* is *caller*; therefore, the pronoun functions as an object.)

Simon judged the top five performers to be *them*. (The subject of the infinitive *to be* is *performers*; therefore, use the objective-case pronoun *them*.)

Whenever you have selected a pronoun for the infinitive *to be* and you want to test its correctness, try reversing the pronoun and its antecedent. For example, *We thought the winner to be her* (*We thought her* [not *she*] *to be the winner*).

Summary of Pronoun Cases

The following table summarizes the uses of subjective- and objective-case pronouns.

Subjective Case	
Subject of the verb	*They* are managers.
Subject complement	The top applicant is *he*.
Infinitive *to be* without a subject	Sharon pretended to be *she*.

Objective Case	
Direct or indirect object of the verb	Give *him* another chance.
Object of a preposition	Send the order to *him*.
Object of an infinitive	Ann hoped to call *us*.
Infinitive *to be* with subject	We thought the guests to be *them*.

Now complete the reinforcement exercises for Level 3.

Types of Pronouns

For those of you interested in a total view, here is a summary of the seven types of pronouns. This list is presented for your interest alone, not for potential testing.

- **Personal pronouns** replace nouns or other pronouns. Examples:

  Subjective Case: I, we, you, he, she, it, they

  Objective Case: me, us, you, him, her, it, them

  Possessive Case: my, mine, our, ours, your, yours, his, hers, its, their, theirs

- **Relative pronouns** join subordinate clauses to antecedents. Examples: *who, whose, whom, which, that, whoever, whomever, whichever, whatever.*
- **Interrogative pronouns** replace nouns in a question. Examples: *who, whose, whom, which, what.*
- **Demonstrative pronouns** designate specific persons or things. Examples: *this, these, that, those.*
- **Indefinite pronouns** replace nouns. Examples: *everyone, anyone, someone, each, everybody, anybody, one, none, some, all,* and so on.
- **Reflexive pronouns** emphasize or reflect on antecedents. Examples: *myself, yourself, himself, herself, itself, oneself,* and so on.
- **Reciprocal pronouns** indicate mutual relationship. Examples: *each other, one another.*

Spot the BLOOPER

Using the skills you are learning in this class, try to identify why the following items are bloopers. Consult your textbook, dictionary, or reference manual as needed.

Blooper 1: Pitcher Roger Clemens, testifying before Congress about steroid use in baseball, said, "In Andy and I's conversation, he obviously disremembers."

Blooper 2: AT&T sent this notice to its customers: "AT&T supports the human spirit through it's sponsorship of the US Paralympic Team."

Blooper 3: Headline on a flyer from the American Automobile Association offering a free U.S. road map to new members: "Your's free."

Blooper 4: United States Secretary of Education Arne Duncan said of a friend and mentor, "He gave my sister and I the opportunity to start a great school on the South Side of Chicago."

Blooper 5: In an *Entertainment Weekly* interview, Barack Obama was asked if he and Michelle argue about anything. He replied, "She likes *American Idol*, her and the girls, in a way that I don't entirely get."

Blooper 6: Tennis star Venus Williams, commenting at Wimbledon about her upcoming match against her sister Serena: "Now it's every Williams for themself."

Blooper 7: WSB-TV presented the results of Georgia's educational proficiency test that all students are required to take. The reporter, after talking with a student, said, "Her and most of her classmates flunked the test."

Blooper 8: Senator Charles Schumer in a letter to *The Wall Street Journal*: "Democrats like myself do not oppose all new domestic oil supplies."

Blooper 9: From an ad in the Winnetka [Illinois] *Talk*: "The Northbrook Community Nursery School held it's gala on May 7.... The school would like to thank all of it's donors."

Blooper 10: Paris Hilton wore a T-shirt that said "Thats Hot" on the front and "Your Not" on the back.

FAQs

Answered by Dr. Guffey and Professor Seefer

Dr. Guffey   Professor Seefer

Question	Answer
Q: My colleague insists that the word *his* is an adjective when it is used in an expression such as *his car*. I learned that *his* is a pronoun. Who is correct?	**A:** When words such as *my, our, your, his, her, its,* and *their* function as adjectives, they are classified as adjectives. Although most people consider them pronouns, when these words describe nouns they are actually functioning as adjectives. Your colleague is right.
Q: On the radio I recently heard a talk-show host say, *My producer and myself....* A little later that same host said, *Send any inquiries to the station or myself at this address.* This sounded half right and half wrong, but I would have trouble explaining the problem. Can you help?	**A:** The problem is a common one: use of a reflexive pronoun (*myself*) when it has no preceding noun on which to reflect. Correction: *My producer and I* and *Send inquiries to the station or me.* Reflexive pronouns like *myself* should be used only with obvious antecedents, such as *I, myself, will take the calls.* Individuals in the media often misuse reflexive pronouns, perhaps to avoid sounding egocentric with the overuse of *I* and *me*.
Q: My boss is ready to send out a letter that says, *I respectfully call you and your client's attention to....* What's wrong with this?	**A:** Your boss should have written *I respectfully call your and your client's attention to....* However, the best way to handle this awkward wording is to avoid using the possessive form. Instead, use a prepositional phrase (*I respectfully call to the attention of you and your client...*).
Q: My supervisor told me that when I answer the telephone, I should say *This is she.* However, this sounds unnatural to me. How can I answer the phone naturally but still sound professional?	**A:** To sound natural and professional, try saying *This is...*followed by your name.

Question	Answer
Q: I often catch myself using the response *me too* when I agree or have taken part in the same activity as someone else. For example, my friend will say, *I love that new sushi restaurant*, and I will respond, *Me too*. Is this a correct use of the pronoun *me*?	**A:** Although you will hear this response commonly used, grammatically it is incorrect. When you respond with these words, you are really saying, *Me love that new sushi restaurant too*. However, responding with *I too*, which is grammatically correct, would probably sound too stuffy. If you want to respond correctly but naturally, try saying something like *So do I* or *I do too*.
Q: Should a hyphen be used in the word *dissimilar*?	**A:** No. Prefixes such as *dis*, *pre*, *non*, and *un* do not require hyphens. Even when the final letter of the prefix is repeated in the initial letter of the root word, no hyphens are used: *disspirited*, *preenroll*, *nonnutritive*.
Q: I thought I knew the difference between *to* and *too*, but could you provide me with a quick review?	**A:** *To* may serve as a preposition (*I am going to the store*), and it may also serve as part of an infinitive construction (*to sign his name*). The adverb *too* may be used to mean "also" (*Andrea will attend too*). In addition, the word *too* may be used to indicate "to an excessive extent" (*the letter is too long*).
Q: Is there some rule about putting periods in organization names that are abbreviated? For example, does *IBM* have periods?	**A:** When the names of well-known business, educational, governmental, labor, and other organizations or agencies are abbreviated, periods are normally not used to separate the letters. Thus, no periods would appear in IBM, ITT, UCLA, AFL-CIO, YWCA, or AMA. The names of radio and television stations and networks are also written without periods: Station WJR, KNX-FM, PBS, WABC-TV. In addition, geographical abbreviations generally do not require periods: USA, UK, ROC. Finally, the two-letter state abbreviations recommended by the U.S. Postal Service require no periods: NY, OH, CA, MI, NJ, OR, MA, and so on.
Q: I just included this sentence in a letter to a customer: *We look forward to having you as apart of our celebration.* Did I do something wrong?	**A:** Yes, but your error is easy to fix. The word *apart* should be written as two words in your sentence (*a part*). Write *apart* as one word when used as an adverb meaning "at a distance" or "as a separate unit." (*This is my first year living apart from my family* or *It is hard to tell their twin daughters apart*.) Write *a part* as two words when you are using the article *a* followed by the noun *part*, as is the case in your sentence (*. . . having you as a part of our celebration*). Here is a trick: If you can remove the *a* and the sentence still makes sense, write *a part* as two words.
Q: Is the word *backup* written as one word or two? Or should I hyphenate it?	**A:** It depends on how the word is being used. When using *backup* as a noun (*We need a backup in case this plan doesn't work*) or as an adjective (*I keep my backup files on a flash drive*), write it as one word. When using *back up* as a verb (*We recommend that you back up your files every week*), write it as two words. Whether one word or two, don't hyphenate!

6

Reinforcement Exercises

LEVEL 1

Online Homework Help! For immediate feedback on odd-numbered items, go to **www.meguffey.com**.

A. (Self-check) Select the correct form.

1. Do you think (she, her) will apply for the position? _____
2. Everyone except (he, him) prefers to use instant messaging for internal communication. _____
3. Send the contract to (they, them) by Friday's deadline. _____
4. (They, Them), as well as some other employees, volunteered for the project. _____
5. We are not surprised that someone like (he, him) was nominated for the award. _____
6. I am having lunch today with Bethany Stewart and (she, her). _____
7. All the purchases made by (I, me) arrived on time. _____
8. We are very impressed with (your, you're) application. _____
9. Our student business club is having (its, it's) annual banquet in May. _____
10. Sean is certain that nobody but (he, him) can access these files. _____

Check your answers below.

B. Writing Exercise. In the spaces provided, list five personal pronouns that can be used as subjects of verbs and five that can be used as objects of verbs or objects of prepositions.

As subjects: 1. _____ 2. _____ 3. _____ 4. _____ 5. _____

As objects: 1. _____ 2. _____ 3. _____ 4. _____ 5. _____

C. In the spaces provided, write the correct letter to indicate how the italicized pronouns function in these sentences.

a = subject of a verb   b = object of a verb   c = object of a preposition

Example: Please tell *her* that the refund is being processed.   **b** ____

1. Now that her children are in school, *she* has decided to return to work. _____
2. We need more politicians like *her*. _____
3. *I* plan to attend the graduation ceremony in June. _____
4. The office received an announcement that *he* will be the keynote speaker. _____
5. After Jeff finished his presentation, the supervisor praised *him*. _____
6. Professor Sumrall asked *me* for my e-mail address. _____

1. she 2. him 3. them 4. They 5. him 6. her 7. me 8. your 9. its 10. him

7. The agreement between Lotus Cirilo and *him* will benefit the organization. _____

8. Please send the government rebate checks directly to *us*. _____

9. Everyone except *you* approved the terms of the new contract. _____

10. You should see *me* before going to the meeting. _____

11. The manager and *we* were impressed with the publicist's speaking skills. _____

12. Susan Kline asked whether the terms of the proposal were satisfactory to *them*. _____

13. To prepare for their study abroad trip, Antonia and *she* will take a conversational Italian class. _____

14. We learned that April Howell and *he* will be purchasing the franchise as a joint venture. _____

15. Everyone but *us* sends and receives text messages daily. _____

16. Please send Allan Lacayo and *me* information about Bluetooth technology. _____

17. William Dobrenen and *I* completed our project on time. _____

18. We will attend the fund-raising event with *her*. _____

19. When the product was introduced, other salespeople and *they* attended four training sessions. _____

20. Please forward *me* the e-mail message you received from the client. _____

D. Select the correct pronoun.

1. The cheetah is the only cat in the world that cannot retract (its, it's) claws. _____

2. Just between you and (I, me), I think Paul Bernhardt is most qualified. _____

3. Everyone except (she, her) took part in the Web conference. _____

4. Please have (he, him) notarize this document. _____

5. The city is proud that (it's, its) implemented a disaster preparedness training program. _____

6. Nobody but (I, me) has been authorized to use the equipment. _____

7. Are you sure that this apartment is (there's, theirs, their's)? _____

8. Tina Wenzel sent the documents to (they, them) for their signatures. _____

9. (Your, You're) new office is on the third floor. _____

10. (Ours, Our's) is the third building on the right. _____

LEVEL 2

A. (Self-check) Select the correct pronoun and write it in the space provided.

1. My colleague and (I, me) were surprised to learn that the word *ginormous* was added to the dictionary. _____

2. A flexible benefits plan was offered to (we, us) employees. _____

3. No one knows technical jargon better than Neal Skapura and (she, her). _____

4. Both programmers, Alicia and (he, him), are testing spam-blocking software. _____

5. (Us, We) delegates stayed at the Westin Hotel during the convention. _____

6. Ray Goralka and (myself, I, me) were singled out for commendation. _____

7. Proposals submitted by (her and me, she and I) were considered first. _____

8. No one but my friend and (I, me) spoke up during the discussion. _____

9. Your completed application form can be sent to Paula McDonald or (I, me, myself). _____

10. The announcement surprised Professor Kiledal as much as (she, her). _____

Check your answers below.

B. Select the correct pronoun and write it in the space provided.

1. The CEO's announcement surprised him as much as (I, me). _____

2. My colleague and (I, me) plan to expand our operations overseas. _____

3. Corey has been with the company six months longer than (I, me). _____

4. The office manager is in charge of (we, us) trainees. _____

5. Our CEO, Tamara Vesselovskaia, said that no other employees were quite like Anastasia and (he, him). _____

6. He has no one but (hisself, himself) to blame. _____

7. It is interesting that (us, we) accountants were audited this year. _____

8. Will you and (he, him) have time to meet with the delegate? _____

9. The copilots, Kyle and (he, him), requested permission to land. _____

10. An argument between Nikki and (he, himself, him) caused problems in the office. _____

11. Dr. Douglas Zlock and (I, me, myself) will make the announcement very soon. _____

12. Believe me, no one knows that problem better than (I, me). _____

13. News of the merger pleased President Reuben Ellis as much as (I, me). _____

14. All employees but Dan Galvin and (I, me) agreed to the economy measures. _____

15. Several of (we, us) candidates plan to visit local colleges. _____

16. Do you think Theresa can complete the work more quickly than (he, him)? _____

17. A proposed annual budget was sent to (we, us) homeowners prior to the vote. _____

18. The signatures on the letter appear to have been written by you and (she, her). _____

19. Contracts were sent to the authors, Pat Tallent and (she, her). _____

20. Everyone except two drivers and (he, him) has checked in with the dispatcher. _____

C. Skill Maximizer. To make sure you have mastered personal pronouns, read the following sentences and underline any faulty pronoun use. Each sentence contains one error. Write an improved form in the space provided.

1. CEO David Neeleman and him discussed how to improve public relations at JetBlue after passengers were stranded for hours on planes because of bad weather. _____

2. Please submit your expense claim to Ron or I by Friday afternoon. _____

3. If neither Matt nor I receive an e-mail confirmation of our itinerary, him and I cannot make the trip. _____

1. I 2. us 3. she 4. he 5. We 6. I 7. her and me 8. me 9. me 10. her

4. E-mail messages intended for she and him were accidently forwarded to the entire department. _____

5. Just between you and I, neither Kris nor he met the monthly quota. _____

6. Because of it's success, our organization's diversity program is being expanded. _____

7. Both owners, Mark Messenger and him, agreed to sign the lease agreement by 5 p.m. _____

8. It's surprising that us renters were not consulted about the remodeling. _____

9. Please send you're expense claim to Sue Trakas or me. _____

10. All students except Jake and she use laptops in class. _____

11. I think that failing to get to meetings on time is rude, and it angers the boss even more than I. _____

12. We are supposed to change our passwords monthly, but some employees don't change their's at all. _____

13. The yellow Toyota Prius in the employee parking lot is her's. _____

14. If you and her are selected for the training program, you will both have your tuition paid. _____

15. If the computer continues to give you trouble, check it's wiring. _____

16. I'm afraid its too late to apply for the grant. _____

17. Several academic scholarships were awarded to we students. _____

18. Your sure to enjoy our new interactive training program. _____

19. Her boyfriend loves Indian food as much as her. _____

20. Are you sure this lunch bag is your's? _____

   D. Writing Exercise. Write complete sentences that use the words shown.

Example: Kim Grantham and (pronoun)

   Kim Grantham and I agreed to market our invention. _____

1. My supervisor and (pronoun)

   _____

2. The two sales reps, Paul and (pronoun)

   _____

3. Just between you and (pronoun)

   _____

4. Except for Yumiko and (pronoun)

   _____

5. The manager expected Jeff and (pronoun)

   _____

6. its

   _____

7. ours

   _____

A. (Self-check) Select the correct pronoun and write it in the space provided.

1. Was it (they, them) who redesigned the company Web site? _____

2. It might have been (she, her) who recommended our new paralegal. _____

3. If you were (he, him), would you send personal e-mail during work hours? _____

4. President Eileen Ferris asked the team and (I, me) to write a proposal. _____

5. If I were (he, him), I would decline the nomination. _____

6. Hyong Than said that it was (he, him) who used the printer last. _____

7. We all assumed the new president would be (she, her). _____

8. The audience didn't discover that Marcelle was (she, her) until the final act. _____

9. They thought Marcelle to be (she, her). _____

10. I will forward the message to you and (they, them) immediately. _____

Check your answers below.

 B. Select the correct pronoun.

1. If you were (I, me), would you apply for additional financing? _____

2. When Marc answered the telephone, he said, "This is (he, him)." _____

3. The committee chair asked Emma and (I, me) to serve on a special task force. _____

4. Most committee members assumed that the chairperson would be (her, she). _____

5. Do you think it was (they, them) who left the door unlocked overnight? _____

6. We tried to contact (he and she, him and her) in Beijing. _____

7. Voter polls indicate that the new supervisor will be (he, him). _____

8. I am sure that it was (she, her) who called this morning. _____

9. The lifeguard credited with the rescue was thought to be (he, him). _____

10. If the renter hadn't been (he, him), the apartment might have been left in better shape. _____

11. Professor Laveda Pullens declared the scholarship recipient to be (her, she). _____

12. The student club invited David Casper and (she, her) to speak at a campus event. _____

13. Ratha and Zach were certain it was not (they, them) who caused the network to crash. _____

14. The intruder was taken to be (he, him). _____

15. When Christopher opened the door, he expected to see you and (he, him). _____

16. It must have been (they, them) who reported the missing funds. _____

17. We hope to obtain Hillary Clinton and (he, him) as keynote speakers. _____

18. If the caller is (he, him), please get his cell phone number. _____

19. The partners are confident that the new client will be (she, her). _____

20. Are you certain it was (she, her) who conducted the public speaking class? _____

1. they 2. she 3. he 4. me 5. he 6. he 7. she 8. she 9. her 10. them

C. Review. Underline any errors in possessive nouns or personal pronouns in the following sentences. For each sentence write a corrected form in the space provided. Each sentence contains one error.

1. Many attorney's, like Sang-Hee and me, never argue a case before a judge. _____

2. On the way to the airport, Jorge and I passed a white stretch limousine that was stalled at the side of the road with it's hood up. _____

3. The Accounting Department processed expense claims for Sally and me, but Sallie's claim was rejected. _____

4. Although I am sure it was him who sent the e-mail announcement, the CEO and she don't seem to remember it at all. _____

5. Our company's Web site describing our new graphic's capabilities stimulated many inquiries. _____

6. Just between you and me, I think your going to be promoted. _____

7. If chocolate could teach, Martha and me would now be extremely educated. _____

8. I hope you're able to attend the conference because its going to be very informative. _____

9. Theirs just one problem: neither Geoff nor I know the password. _____

10. The board has voted to give all employee's a retroactive pay increase. _____

11. Both the network administrator and me are concerned about the increase in personal Web use and its tendency to slow productivity. _____

12. Although Tonya and I agreed to pay two months rent in advance, the landlord would not rent to her and me. _____

13. No one knows the details of the contract better than me. _____

14. All of we accountants attended a seminar about the Sarbanes-Oxley Act. _____

15. After reviewing our insurance policy and the companys explanation, my wife and I are certain there is a mistake in the reimbursement amount. _____

16. The best manager's believe that recharging one's batteries away from the office really works wonders. _____

17. Us human resources administrators are concerned with safeguarding our employees' personal information. _____

18. If you were me, how would you intervene in the conflict between Shaun and her? _____

19. Please send all RSVP's to Tracy or me before December 1. _____

20. Although Neda Mehrabani protested, I am convinced it was her who sent the gift to Robert and me. _____

 D. FAQs About Business English Review. In the space provided, write the correct answer choice.

1. Please send the signed contract to _____ by December 31. _____
   a. I   b. me   c. myself

2. Because the office buildings are so _____, we cannot make exact comparisons. _____
   a. dis-similar   b. dissimilar   c. dis similar

3. The insurance doesn't cover _____ conditions. _____
   a. preexisting   b. pre-existing   c. pre existing

4. She is trying to eat more _____ foods.   _____
    a. non fattening   b. nonfattening   c. non-fattening

5. Her PowerPoint presentation was _____.   _____
    a. un imaginative   b. un-imaginative   c. unimaginative

6. She hung up after being on hold for _____ long.   _____
    a. to   b. too

7. Many performers wanted to be _____ of the inauguration festivities.   _____
    a. apart   b. a part

8. He hates to be _____ from his wife for too long.   _____
    a. apart   b. a part

9. I hope you made a _____ copy of your hard drive.   _____
    a. backup   b. back-up   c. back up

10. Be sure to _____ your files before going home tonight.   _____
    a. backup   b. back-up   c. back up

When you are working on your own computer, you will want to *bookmark* or save the URLs (uniform resource locators, or Web addresses) of your favorite Web pages.

Goal: To learn to bookmark favorite pages.

1. With your Web browser on the screen, locate the address bar. Key this URL: **http://www.libraryspot.com.**

2. Because you will likely want to return to this page, save the URL by clicking **Favorites** in the upper section of your browser. Click **Add to Favorites** (or whatever your browser says). Click **OK** (or first choose the folder in which to save the URL and then click **OK**).

3. Examine the main page of LibrarySpot, an award-winning library and reference site.

4. Click some of the LibrarySpot links that interest you. Return to the main page by clicking the **Back** button.

5. Gather information about interesting events on a specific date, for example, your birthday. Click **What happened on a particular day?** under the **You Asked For It** heading. Then click **Today in History**, click **AnyDay-in-History**, and select your birthday from the drop-down menu (month and day only). Press the **Show Events** button to

show a list of events that happened on your birthday throughout history. Make a list of the ten most interesting events you find. Print one page if possible.

6. Return to the address bar in your browser and key this URL: **http://www.bartleby.com/.**

7. Examine the main page of Bartleby.com Great Books Online, an excellent site where you can access a variety of books for free, including reference, poetry, fiction, and nonfiction. Search for topics, titles, or authors that interest you. Print one page of something interesting you find.

8. Return to the Bartleby.com main page. Bookmark this page or save it to your favorites.

9. Return to the LibrarySpot Web site by clicking **Favorites** and the appropriate link.

10. End your session. Turn in your list of interesting events and your printout(s). If your instructor prefers, send an e-mail summarizing what you learned.

▶▶ **Chat About It**

Your instructor may assign any of the following topics for you to discuss in class, in an online chat room, or on an online discussion board. Some of the discussion topics may require outside research. You may also be asked to read and respond to postings made by your classmates.

Discussion Topic 1: People frequently misuse pronouns. For example, they have trouble knowing whether to choose *I* or *me*, *he* or *him*, *she* or *her*, and so on. Why do you think pronouns are so troublesome? After reading Chapter 6, what did you discover about your pronoun use? What types of mistakes have you been making? How will your pronoun use change?

Discussion Topic 2: The pronoun is one of the most frequently misused parts of speech in the English language. Some people don't know the rules, but others misuse pronouns intentionally. For example, you might not be comfortable saying *This is she,* or you might think that *everyone except him and me* doesn't sound right. Have you ever misused pronouns intentionally? If so, why did you do it? Do you think your pronoun use will change after reading this chapter? Explain.

Discussion Topic 3: In this chapter you learned that Birmingham, England, has outlawed apostrophes on street signs. Do some research to find out more about this ban (hint: search for the words *Birmingham* and *apostrophes*). Report your findings, in your own words, to your classmates. Remember to cite your sources by providing the names and Web site addresses. How do you feel about this ban? Do you think the United States should do the same? Why or why not?

Discussion Topic 4: Do you think it is important to use pronouns correctly in the workplace? Why or why not?

Discussion Topic 5: Samuel Johnson, who wrote the first true English dictionary, said "What is written without effort is in general read without pleasure." What do you think he meant by this? What does this mean to you as a business communicator?

Posttest

Underline the correct pronoun in each sentence.

1. Do you know whether the new medical records clerk is (she, her)?

2. (We, Us) factory workers plan to negotiate for higher wages.

3. The layoff announcement surprised my colleagues as much as (I, me).

4. My staff and (I, me, myself) will be happy to help you.

5. An e-mail outlining the new procedure was sent to (we, us) employees.

6. I am convinced that no one will try harder than (she, her).

7. Daryl said it was (they, them) who picked up the order today.

8. Just between you and (I, me), I am not happy with the contract changes.

9. Alex believed the top candidate to be (he, him).

10. The top award winner was thought to be (she, her).

1. she 2. We 3. me 4. I 5. us 6. she 7. they 8. me 9. him 10. she

> *"Grammar is the logic of speech, even as logic
> is the grammar of reason."*
>
> **—Richard C. Trench,
> Anglican archbishop and poet**

Chapter 7

Pronouns and Antecedents

OBJECTIVES

When you have completed the materials in this chapter, you will be able to do the following:

LEVEL 1
- Make personal pronouns agree with their antecedents in number and gender.
- Understand the traditional use of common gender and be able to use its alternatives with sensitivity.

LEVEL 2
- Make personal pronouns agree with subjects joined by *or* or *nor*.
- Make personal pronouns agree with indefinite pronouns, collective nouns, organization names, and the antecedents *each* and *every*.

LEVEL 3
- Understand the functions of *who*, *whom*, *whoever*, and *whomever*, and follow a three-step procedure in using these words correctly.
- Use the possessive pronoun *whose* and the contraction *who's* correctly.

Underline the correct word in each sentence.

1. Every member of the men's basketball team had (his, their) own assigned locker.
2. Either Kathy or Stephanie left (her, their) jacket in the conference room.
3. The paralegals and legal assistants prepared (his, her, their) documents.
4. (Meteorologists, They) predict snow tonight.
5. A patient must show (his, their, his or her) proof of insurance upon arrival.
6. The office manager, along with her staff, submitted (her, their) time sheet.
7. The committee submitted (its, their) recommendation to the board.
8. Either of the branches may send (its, their) manager to the meeting.
9. (Who, Whom) did you select for the management trainee position?
10. Send the supplies to (whoever, whomever) placed the order.

In order for our grammar to be logical, we must use pronouns correctly. Pronouns enable us to communicate efficiently. They provide short forms that save us from the boredom of repetitious nouns. But they can also get us in trouble if the nouns to which they refer—their **antecedents**—are unclear. This chapter shows you how to avoid pronoun–antecedent problems. It also presents solutions to a major problem for sensitive communicators today—how to handle the *his/her* dilemma.

LEVEL 1

Fundamentals of Pronoun-Antecedent Agreement

When pronouns substitute for nouns, the pronouns must agree with their antecedents in number (singular or plural) and gender (masculine, feminine, or neuter). Here are suggestions for using pronouns effectively.

Making Pronoun References Clear

Do not use a pronoun if your listener or reader might not be able to identify the noun it represents.

1. his 2. her 3. their 4. Meteorologists 5. his or her 6. her 7. its 8. its 9. Whom 10. whoever

Trivia Tidbit

Ships have traditionally been referred to with feminine pronouns, even if the ship has a masculine name.

Unclear:	Matthew told Ron that he had been selected for the position.
Clear:	Matthew told Ron that Ron had been selected for the position.
Unclear:	In that ball park *they* do not allow *you* to smoke in the stands.
Clear:	The ball park management does not allow fans to smoke in the stands.
	Or: Smoking is not allowed in the ball park stands.
Unclear:	When Annette Jenkins followed Dawn O'Malley as president, many of *her* policies were reversed.
Clear:	When Annette Jenkins followed Dawn O'Malley as president, many of O'Malley's policies were reversed.

Making Pronouns Agree With Their Antecedents in Number

Pronouns must agree in number with the nouns they represent. For example, if a pronoun replaces a singular noun, that pronoun must be singular. If a pronoun replaces a plural noun, that pronoun must be plural.

Michelangelo felt that *he* was a failure. (Singular antecedent and pronoun)

Great *artists* often doubt *their* success. (Plural antecedent and pronoun)

If a pronoun refers to two nouns joined by *and*, the pronoun must be plural.

The *managers* and *union representatives* discussed *their* differences. (Plural antecedent and pronoun)

Max and *Sarah* need new passwords issued to *them* immediately. (Plural antecedent and pronoun)

Review the table of personal pronouns in Chapter 6 if needed.

Pronoun–antecedent agreement can be complicated when words or phrases come between the pronoun and the word to which it refers. Disregard phrases such as those introduced by *as well as*, *in addition to*, and *together with*. Find the true antecedent and make the pronoun agree with it.

The *president*, together with many cabinet members, is sending *his* personal thanks. (Singular antecedent and pronoun)

The *cabinet members*, along with the president, are sending *their* personal thanks. (Plural antecedent and pronoun)

A female *member* of the group of protesting employees demanded that *she* be treated equally. (Singular antecedent and pronoun)

Making Pronouns Agree With Their Antecedents in Gender

Pronouns exhibit one of three *genders*: masculine (male), feminine (female), or neuter (neither masculine nor feminine). Pronouns must agree with their antecedents in gender.

Warren Buffet discussed *his* investment strategies. (Masculine gender)

Kathy prepared for *her* trip to Beirut. (Feminine gender)

The suggestion has *its* strong points. (Neuter gender)

Choosing Alternatives to Common-Gender Antecedents

Trivia Tidbit

Despite efforts for the past 160 years, no one has yet come up with an acceptable multipurpose, unisex pronoun. Suggested replacements: *ne* (1850), *le* (1884), *se* (1938), *ve* (1970), *e* (1977), *ala* (1988), *pers* (1992), and *wun* (1995). What would you suggest to fill the void in our language?

Occasionally, writers and speakers face a problem in choosing pronouns of appropriate gender. Although first-person (*I*) and second-person (*you*) singular pronouns may be used to refer to either gender, third-person singular pronouns (*he, she*) refer to specific genders. English has no all-purpose third-person singular pronoun to represent indefinite nouns (such as *a student* or *an employee*).

For this reason writers and speakers have in the past used masculine pronouns to refer to nouns that might be either masculine or feminine. For example, in the sentence *An employee has his rights*, the pronoun *his* referred to its antecedent *employee*, which might name either a feminine or masculine person.

Communicators today, however, avoid masculine pronouns (*he, his*) when referring to indefinite nouns that could be masculine or feminine. Critics call these pronouns "sexist" or "gender biased" because they exclude women. To solve the problem, sensitive communicators rewrite those sentences requiring such pronouns. Although many alternatives exist, here are three options:

Gender-Biased: A *passenger* must show *his* passport before boarding.

Alternative No. 1: *Passengers* must show *their* passports before boarding. (Make the subject plural to avoid the need for a singular pronoun. Remember to make the object [*passports*] plural too.)

Alternative No. 2: A passenger must show *a* passport before boarding. (Use an article [*a*] to replace the pronoun. This alternative, however, is less emphatic.)

Alternative No. 3: A *passenger* must show *his* or *her* passport before boarding. (Use both masculine and feminine pronouns [*his* or *her*]. Because this construction is wordy and clumsy, avoid its frequent use.)

Wrong: A passenger must show *their* passport before boarding. (Substituting the plural pronoun *their* is incorrect because *their* does not agree with its singular antecedent, *passenger*.)

Now complete the reinforcement exercises for Level 1.

Special Pronoun/Antecedent Agreement Challenges

The following guidelines will help you avoid errors in pronoun–antecedent agreement in special cases. These special instances include sentences in which the antecedents (a) are joined by *or* or *nor*, (b) are indefinite pronouns, or (c) are collective nouns or company names.

Antecedents Joined by *or* or *nor*

When antecedents are joined by *or* or *nor*, the pronoun should agree with the closer antecedent. The closer antecedent will be the one that comes after the *or* or *nor*.

> Either April or *Gloria* left *her* message on the discussion board.

> Neither the employees nor the *supervisor* expects to see *his* salary increased this year.

> Neither the supervisor nor the *employees* expect to see *their* salaries increased this year. (Notice that salaries must also be made plural.)

You may be wondering why antecedents joined by *and* are treated differently from antecedents joined by *or* or *nor*. The conjunction *and* joins one plus one to make two antecedents; therefore, use a plural pronoun. The conjunctions *or* and *nor* require a choice between two antecedents. Always match the pronoun to the closer antecedent.

Indefinite Pronouns as Antecedents

Indefinite pronouns are pronouns such as *anyone*, *something*, and *everybody*. These pronouns are indefinite because they refer to no specific person or object. Some indefinite pronouns are always singular; others are always plural.

Always Singular		Always Plural
anybody	everything	both
anyone	neither	few
anything	nobody	many
each	no one	several
either	nothing	
everybody	somebody	
everyone	someone	

When an indefinite pronoun functions as an antecedent of a pronoun, make certain that the pronoun agrees with its antecedent. Do not let a prepositional phrase obscure the true antecedent.

> *Somebody* in the men's league left *his* car lights on. (Antecedent *Somebody* is singular and masculine.)

> *Everyone* in the women's choir selected *her* song choice. (Antecedent *Everyone* is singular and feminine.)

> *Each* of the corporations had *its* own home office. (Antecedent *Each* is singular and neutral.)

Few of our employees have *their* own private parking spaces. (Antecedent *Few* is plural. Notice that *spaces* is also plural.)

Several of our branches list *their* job openings on the company's intranet. (Antecedent *Several* is plural.)

The words *either* and *neither* can be confusing. When these words stand alone and function as sentence subjects, they are always considered singular. When they are joined with *or* or *nor* to form conjunctions, however, they may connect plural subjects. These plural subjects, then, may act as antecedents to plural pronouns.

 **Study Tip**

> *Either* of the women *is* able to see *her* personnel record. (*Either* is a singular pronoun and functions as the subject of the sentence. It controls the singular verb *is*. *Either* is also the antecedent of the pronoun *her*.)

When *either* or *neither* is followed by an *of* phrase, it is functioning as a singular pronoun (for example, *Either of the books is available*).

> *Either* the woman *or* her friends have left *their* packages. (*Either/or* is used as a conjunction to join the two subjects, *woman* and *friends*. The pronoun *their* agrees with its plural antecedent, *friends*.)

Collective Nouns as Antecedents

Collective nouns refer to a collection of people, animals, or objects. Examples are *jury, faculty, committee, staff, union, team, flock,* and *group*. Such words may be either singular or plural depending on the mode of operation of the collection to which they refer. When a collective noun operates as a unit, it is singular. When the elements of a collective noun operate separately, the collective noun is plural.

> Our *committee* released *its* status report. (*Committee* operating as one unit)

> The *jury* rendered *its* verdict. (*Jury* operating as one unit)

> The *jury* were divided in *their* opinions. (*Jury* operating as individuals)

Trivia Tidbit

However, if you want to use a collective noun in a plural sense, the sentence will seem less awkward if you add a plural noun. (*The jury members were divided in their opinions*).

In American English, companies and organizations are generally considered to be singular. In British English, companies and organizations are generally considered to be plural.

Company and Organization Names as Antecedents

Company and organization names, including names of sports teams and musical groups, are generally considered singular. Unless the actions of the organization are attributed to individual representatives of that organization, pronouns referring to organizations should be singular.

> Southwest Airlines is adding three new planes to *its* fleet.

> The United Nations, in addition to other organizations, is expanding *its* campaign to fight hunger.

> Downey, Felker & Torres, Inc., plans to move *its* corporate headquarters.

> The band *U2* is known throughout the world for *its* humanitarian efforts.

> The *Pittsburgh Steelers* won *its* sixth Super Bowl in 2009.

The Antecedents *each* and *every*

When *each* or *every* comes before a compound subject joined by *and*, the compound subject is considered singular.

Each female player and coach is expected to supply *her* own uniform. (Think *Each single female player and each single coach is expected to supply her own uniform.*)

Every father and son received *his* invitation separately. (Think *Every single father and every single son received his invitation separately.*)

Now complete the reinforcement exercises for Level 2.

LEVEL 3

Advanced Pronoun Use

The use of the pronouns *who* and *whom* presents a continuing dilemma for speakers and writers. In conversation the correct choice of *who* or *whom* is especially difficult because of the mental gymnastics necessary to locate subjects and objects. The following guidelines explain when to use *who* and *whom*.

The Challenge of *who* and *whom*

In conversation, speakers may have difficulty analyzing a sentence quickly enough to use the correct *who* or *whom* form. In writing, however, an author has ample time to scrutinize a sentence and make a correct choice—if the author understands the traditional functions of *who* and *whom*. *Who* is the subjective-case form. Like other subjective-case pronouns, *who* may function as the subject of a verb or as the subject complement of a noun following the linking verb. *Whom* is the objective-case form. It may function as the object of a verb or as the object of a preposition.

> *Who* do you think will be chosen for the job? (*Who* is the subject of the verb phrase *will be chosen.*)
>
> Allison asked me *who* my boss is. (*Who* is the complement of *boss.*)
>
> *Whom* should we recommend? (*Whom* is the object of the verb phrase *should recommend.*)
>
> Edmund is the one to *whom* I spoke. (*Whom* is the object of the preposition *to.*)

How to Choose Between *who* and *whom*

The choice between *who* and *whom* becomes easier if the sentence in question is approached using the following three steps:

1. Isolate the *who/whom* clause.
2. Invert the clause, if necessary, to restore normal subject–verb–object order.
3. Substitute the subjective pronoun *he* (*she* or *they*) for *who*. Substitute the objective pronoun *him* (*her* or *them*) for *whom*. If the sentence sounds correct with *him*, replace *him* with *whom*. If the sentence sounds correct with *he*, replace *he* with *who*.

Study the following sentences and notice how the choice of *who* or *whom* is made:

Here are the records of the man (who/whom) we have selected.

Isolate:	____ we have selected
Invert:	we have selected ____
Substitute:	we have selected <u>him</u>
Equate:	we have selected <u>whom</u>
Complete:	Here are the records of the man *whom* we have selected.

Do you know (who/whom) his doctor is?

Isolate: _____ his doctor is

Invert: his doctor is _____ (*or* _____ is his doctor)

Substitute: his doctor is <u>he</u> (*or* <u>he</u> is his doctor)

Equate: his doctor is <u>who</u> (*or* <u>who</u> is his doctor)

Complete: Do you know *who* his doctor is?

When looking at this example, remember from Chapter 6 that subjective-case pronouns follow linking verbs.

In choosing *who* or *whom,* ignore parenthetical expressions such as *I hope, we think, I believe, they said,* and *you know.*

Edward is the candidate (who/whom) we believe is best.

Isolate: _____ we believe is best

Ignore: _____ [we believe] is best

Substitute: <u>he</u> is best

Equate: <u>who</u> is best

Complete: Edward is the candidate *who* we believe is best.

Examples:

Whom do you think we should call? (Invert: You do think we should call him/*whom.*)

The person to *whom* we gave our evaluation was Roshanda. (Invert: The evaluation was given to him/*whom.*)

Do you know *who* the manager is? (Invert: The manager is he/*who.*)

Whom would you like to include in the acknowledgment? (Invert: You would like to include him/*whom* in the acknowledgment.)

The Use of *whoever* and *whomever*

As with *who* and *whom, whoever* is subjective and *whomever* is objective. The selection of the correct form is sometimes complicated when *whoever* or *whomever* appears in clauses. These clauses may act as objects of prepositions, objects of verbs, or subjects of verbs. Within the clauses, however, you must determine how *whoever* or *whomever* is functioning in order to choose the correct form. Study the following examples and explanations.

Issue a password to *whoever needs one.* (The clause *whoever needs one* is the object of the preposition *to.* Within the clause itself, *whoever* acts as the subject of *needs* and is therefore in the subjective case. Think: *he needs one.*)

A scholarship will be given to *whoever meets the criteria.* (The clause *whoever meets the criteria* is the object of the preposition *to.* Within the clause, *whoever* acts as the subject of *meets* and is therefore in the subjective case. Think: *he meets the criteria.*)

We will accept the name of *whomever they nominate.* (The clause *whomever they nominate* is the object of the preposition *of.* Within the clause, *whomever* is the object of *they nominate* and is therefore in the objective case. Think: *they nominate him.*)

The Use of *whose*

The pronoun *whose* functions as a possessive pronoun. Like other possessive pronouns, *whose* has no apostrophe. Do not confuse it with the contraction *who's,* which means "who is" or "who has."

> We haven't decided *whose* proposal will be accepted.
>
> *Whose* applications were submitted by the deadline?
>
> Please let me know *who's* on call this evening.
>
> Do you know *who's* scheduled to give the keynote address?

Now complete the reinforcement exercises for Level 3.

Spot the BLOOPER

Using the skills you are learning in this class, try to identify why the following items are bloopers. Consult your textbook, dictionary, or reference manual as needed.

Blooper 1: J. K. Rowling on her Web site before the final Harry Potter book was released: "I'd like to ask everyone who calls themselves a Potter fan to help preserve the secrecy of the plot for all those who are looking forward to reading the book at the same time on publication day."

Blooper 2: Sign at the entrance to a Groton, Massachusetts, middle school: "Education is the process of helping everyone discover their uniqueness."

Blooper 3: Barack Obama in an *Entertainment Weekly* interview, when asked about his daughters' interest in *American Idol*: "I think the girls did vote in last year's contest. I don't know who they voted for, but I recall that a vote was cast."

Blooper 4: Billboard for a Ford dealership seen on I-275 in Tampa, Florida: "Who's country are you supporting?"

Blooper 5: An article in *The Economist*: "In the past two years police have rescued 251 women whom they believe were trafficked to Britain."

Blooper 6: News anchor on Channel 11 in Minneapolis, Minnesota: "If you learned that your significant other was wanted for a crime, would you turn he or she in?"

Blooper 7: From a newspaper ad urging readers to call the Literacy Hot Line: "If you or someone you know wants to improve their reading skills, call the Literacy Hot Line."

Blooper 8: Sign in an Office Depot restroom: "Employees must wash your hands."

Blooper 9: From the *FEEA Helping Hand* newsletter under advice for scholarship applicants: "Carefully check your application and essay for spelling and grammar—it counts."

Blooper 10: From a letter to members of the National Council of Teachers of English: "It takes a special person to choose teaching as their life goal."

FAQs

Answered by Dr. Guffey and Professor Seefer

Dr. Guffey   Professor Seefer

Question	Answer

Q: I am disgusted with and infuriated at a New York University advertisement I just saw in our newspaper. It says, *It's not just who you know… .* why would a leading institution of learning use such poor grammar?

A: Because it sounds familiar. But familiarity doesn't make it correct. You are right in recognizing that the proper form is *whom* (isolate the clause *you know him* or *whom*). The complete adage—or more appropriately, cliché—correctly stated is: *It's not what you know but <u>whom</u> you know.*

Q: Please help me decide which *maybe* to use in this sentence: *He said that he (maybe, may be) able to help us.*

A: Use the two-word verb *may be*. Don't confuse it with the adverb *maybe*, which means "perhaps" (*Maybe she will call*).

Q: I don't seem to be able to hear the difference between *than* and *then*. Can you explain it to me?

A: The conjunction *than* is used to make comparisons (*your watch is more nearly accurate than mine*). The adverb *then* means "at that time" (*we must complete this task; then we will take our break*) or "as a consequence" (*if all the angles of the triangle are equal, then it must be equilateral as well*).

Q: What is the order of college degrees, and which ones are capitalized?

A: Two kinds of undergraduate degrees are commonly awarded: the associate's degree, a two-year degree; and the bachelor's degree, a four-year degree. A variety of graduate degrees exist. The most frequently awarded are the master's degree and the doctorate. Notice that these words (*associate's, bachelor's*, and *master's*) are written using the possessive case. In addition, Merriam-Webster dictionaries do not capitalize the names of degrees: *associate of arts degree, bachelor of science, master of arts, doctor of philosophy*. However, when used with an individual's name, the abbreviations for degrees are capitalized: *Craig Bjurstrom, MA; Rhianna Landini, PhD.*

Q: I am totally confused by job titles for women today. What do I call a woman who is a *fireman*, a *policeman*, a *chairman*, or a *spokesman*? And what about the word *mankind*?

A: As more and more women enter nontraditional careers, some previous designations are being replaced by neutral, inclusive titles. Here are some substitutes:

actor	for *actress*
firefighter	for *fireman*
mail carrier	for *mailman*
police officer	for *policeman*
flight attendant	for *steward* or *stewardess*
reporter or journalist	for *newsman*
server	for *waiter* or *waitress*

Words like *chairman, spokesman*, and *mankind* traditionally have been used to refer to both men and women. Today, though, sensitive writers strive to use more inclusive language. Possible substitutes are *chair, spokesperson*, and *humankind*.

Question	Answer
Q: Everyone says "consensus of opinion." Yet, I understand that there is some objection to this expression.	**A:** Yes, the expression is widely used. However, because *consensus* means "collective opinion," the addition of the word *opinion* results in a redundancy.
Q: Should *undercapitalized* be hyphenated? I can't find it in my dictionary.	**A:** The prefixes *under* and *over* are not followed by hyphens. These prefixes join the main word: *undercapitalized, underdeveloped, underbudgeted, overbuild, overhang, overjoyed,* and so forth.
Q: I can never seem to keep *your* and *you're* straight. How can I decide which to use in a sentence?	**A:** Remember that *your* is a possessive pronoun used to refer to something owned by *you* (*your hard work is appreciated*). On the other hand, *you're* is a contraction for *you are* (*we think you're going to love your new vehicle*).
Q: I am confused by indefinite pronouns such as *everyone, anyone, someone,* and so on. Is there a trick I can use to remember whether to write these as one word or two?	**A:** Yes, indefinite pronouns can be tricky! First of all, *someone* (*we need to hire someone new*) is always written as one word, and *no one* is always written as two (*no one has applied for the position yet*). If the word *of* follows *everyone* or *anyone*, write it as two words (*every one of the suggestions is valid; any one of our employees can answer your question*). If the word *of* does not follow, write these indefinite pronouns as one word (*everyone voted yes; I didn't see anyone at the door*).
Q: I am a woman who will be getting married next year. Do I refer to the man I am marrying as my *fiancé* or *fiancée*? What is the difference?	**A:** First of all, congratulations on your upcoming marriage! You should refer to the man you are going to marry as your *fiancé*, the word that describes a man who is engaged to be married. He will refer to you as his *fiancée*, which describes a woman engaged to be married.

7 Reinforcement Exercises

LEVEL 1

Online Homework Help! For immediate feedback on odd-numbered items, go to **www.meguffey.com**.

A. (Self-check) Select the correct word(s) to complete the following sentences.

1. Every nurse must perfect (his, her, his or her, their) bedside manner. _____

2. When an attorney shows up in court, (he, she, he or she, they) should dress professionally. _____

3. Every applicant must submit (his, her, his or her, their) résumé by e-mail. _____

4. The visiting scientist and our resident engineer had (his, her, his or her, their) problems finding the control center. _____

5. One of the members of the girls' cross-country team set (her, their) personal-best record. _____

6. (They, Researchers) report that the rate of deforestation in Brazil's Amazon rainforest has increased sharply. _____

7. One of the men asked whether (he, they) could use his cell phone during the meeting. _____

8. All flight attendants must have (her, his, his or her, their) uniforms cleaned regularly. _____

9. Robert, after consulting the production staff and others, made (his, their) pricing decision. _____

10. No employee must automatically retire when (he reaches, she reaches, he or she reaches, they reach) the age of 65. _____

Check your answers below.

B. Select the correct word(s) to complete the following sentences.

1. Some people are reluctant to enter (his, his or her, their) credit card information online. _____

2. A shift supervisor, as well as other members of management, must do (his, her, his or her, their) best to exhibit strong ethics. _____

3. A judge must deliver (his, her, his or her, their) jury instructions in plain English. _____

4. Both Dr. Awbrey and Dr. Freeman submitted (her, their) registration forms for the AMA convention. _____

5. Bob Eustes, one of our top chefs, entered (his, their) signature dish in the competition. _____

1. his or her 2. he or she 3. his or her 4. their 5. her 6. Researchers 7. he 8. their 9. his 10. he or she reaches

6. In some doctors' offices (you, patients) can pass the time by watching DIRECTV.

     _____

7. An employee should know what rights (he has, she has, he or she has, they have) in the workplace.

     _____

8. Mr. Petrino and Mr. Winterstein had already discussed the matter with (his, their) attorneys.

     _____

9. If the insured party causes an accident, (he, she, he or she, they) will be charged an additional fee in future premiums.

     _____

10. An accountant must double-check (his, her, his or her, their) financial statement figures for accuracy.

     _____

C. Writing Exercise. Rewrite the following sentences to avoid the use of gender-biased pronouns. Show three different versions of each sentence.

1. Every new teacher must have *her* lesson plans approved.

   a. _____

   b. _____

   c. _____

2. Be sure that each new employee has received *his* orientation packet.

   a. _____

   b. _____

   c. _____

3. A doctor must submit *his* insurance paperwork on time.

   a. _____

   b. _____

   c. _____

D. Writing Exercise. Rewrite these sentences to make the pronoun references clear.

1. The article reported that Google had acquired Image America and that it planned to use its aerial photography technology.

   _____

   _____

2. They make you wear a coat and tie in that restaurant.

   _____

3. Mr. Williams told Mr. Whitman that he needed to take a vacation.

   _____

4. Recruiters like to see job objectives on résumés; however, it may restrict their chances.

   _____

   _____

          PRONOUNS AND ANTECEDENTS

5. Ms. Hartman talked with Courtney about her telecommuting request, but she needed more information.

_____

_____

LEVEL 2

A. (Self-check) Select the correct word(s) to complete the following sentences.

1. Anyone in the department can share (his, her, his or her, their) suggestions for increasing sales. _____

2. Users were upset when Facebook changed (its, their) terms of service agreement. _____

3. Coldplay announced (its, their) summer concert calendar. _____

4. Someone in the women's choir lost (her, their) voice. _____

5. Every man, woman, and child in the club made (his, her, his or her, their) own contribution to the used clothing drive. _____

6. Either Laurie McDonough or Lorraine Love will present (her, their) research findings at the meeting. _____

7. Nobody in the boisterous crowd could hear (his, her, his or her, their) name when called. _____

8. The president asked for budget cuts, and Congress indicated (its, their) willingness to legislate some of them. _____

9. Neither of the men would admit (his, their) part in causing the accident. _____

10. The Green Bay Packers made (its, their) first-round draft picks. _____

Check your answers below.

B. Select the appropriate pronoun(s) to complete the following sentences.

1. No one can go home for the evening until the jury announces (its, their) verdict. _____

2. Every employee and manager was told when (his, her, his or her, their) annual performance review would be held. _____

3. Neither her dog nor her cat has had (their, its) annual shots. _____

4. Not one of the employees cast (his, her, his or her, their) vote to approve the new union contract. _____

5. Someone in this office reported that (his, her, his or her, their) computer had a virus. _____

6. The Supreme Court will announce (its, their) decision in October. _____

7. Every one of the bands started (its, their) set with an upbeat song. _____

8. The inspection team will give (its, their) recommendations by May 1. _____

9. Neither the glamour nor the excitement of the job had lost (its, their) appeal. _____

10. Any new subscriber may cancel (his, her, his or her, their) subscription within the first ten days. _____

11. Union members elected (its, their) officers by electronic ballot. _____

1. his or her 2. its 3. its 4. her 5. his or her 6. her 7. his or her 8. its 9. his 10. its

12. The Dallas Cowboys saw (its, their) possibility of going to the playoffs increase after the surprise win.

_____

13. McCormick & Kuleto's is proud of (its, their) fresh seafood.

_____

14. Every renter and homeowner should exercise (his, her, his or her, their) right to vote.

_____

15. If anyone needs assistance, Vonne Smilely will help (him, her, him or her, them).

_____

LEVEL 3

A. (Self-check) Select the correct word and write it in the space provided.

1. (Who, Whom) do you think we should hire for the data communications analyst position?

_____

2. We are not sure (who, whom) discovered the security breach.

_____

3. This is the applicant (who, whom) impressed the hiring team.

_____

4. The contract will be awarded to (whoever, whomever) submits the lowest bid.

_____

5. Lana Bunner is the investment counselor of (who, whom) I spoke.

_____

6. When I return the call, for (who, whom) should I ask?

_____

7. (Who, Whom) may I say is calling?

_____

8. Will you recommend an attorney (who, whom) can handle this case?

_____

9. Do you know (whose, who's) been invited to give the keynote address?

_____

10. (Whose, Who's) car is blocking the entry?

_____

Check your answers below.

B. Select the correct word and write it in the space provided.

1. Evelyn, (who, whom) left last week, was our most experienced automotive service technician.

_____

2. Jake will help (whoever, whomever) is next in line.

_____

3. He is the vocational counselor (who, whom) we believe has the most connections to local employers.

_____

4. Christine Groth, (who, whom) recently passed the bar exam, immediately hung out her shingle.

_____

5. (Who, Whom) have you asked to develop cutting-edge ads for our products?

_____

6. For (who, whom) does the bell toll?

_____

7. I have hotel recommendations for (whoever, whomever) plans to travel to the Caribbean this summer.

_____

8. The "Father of Accounting" to (who, whom) the professor referred is Luca Pacioli.

_____

9. James Franklin is the one (who, whom) launched the *New-England Courant* in 1721, which marks the birth of the American newspaper.

_____

10. Please tell us the name of (whoever, whomever) you recommend for the position.

_____

1. Whom 2. who (subject complement) 3. who 4. whoever 5. whom 6. whom 7. Who 8. who 9. who's 10. Whose

134 • CHAPTER 7   PRONOUNS AND ANTECEDENTS

11. Adam Smith, (who, whom) is known as the "Father of Capitalism," was born in 1723. _____

12. Do you know (who, whom) will be taking your place? _____

13. Please put the call through to (whoever, whomever) is in charge of the project. _____

14. I wonder (who, whom) the speaker is talking about. _____

15. In making introductions, who should be introduced to (who, whom)? _____

16. Twitter has an older base of individuals (who, whom) use its service than MySpace and Facebook. _____

17. Barack Obama sent text messages to millions of supporters to let them know (who, whom) he had selected as his running mate. _____

18. Jimmy Carter said, "As a superdelegate, I would not disclose (who, whom) I am rooting for, but I leave you to make that guess." _____

19. Female CEOs, (who, whom) make roughly 85 percent of what male CEOs make, took their case to the media. _____

20. A University of Illinois sociologist found that those (who, whom) have better social skills earn an average $3,200 more yearly than those with poorer social skills. _____

C. In the following sentences, determine whether to use *whose* or *who's*. Write the correct word in the space provided.

1. Rose Kessler was nominated by her students for the "(Whose, Who's) Who Among American Teachers" list. _____

2. While looking for volunteers, the office manager asked, "(Whose, Who's) it going to be?" _____

3. The committee chair asked, "(Whose, Who's) recommendation should we adopt?" _____

4. (Whose, Who's) had a chance to study the brief? _____

5. (Whose, Who's) opinion do you respect the most? _____

6. We are not sure (whose, who's) proposal will be adopted. _____

7. It is unclear (whose, who's) planning to take part in tomorrow's walkout. _____

8. A State University of New York psychologist found that someone (whose, who's) handshake is firm is more likely to be socially dominant. _____

9. (Whose, Who's) handshake demonstrated more confidence? _____

10. (Whose, Who's) on first? _____

D. Skill Maximizer. To make sure you have mastered chapter concepts in all three levels, read the following sentences and underline any faulty pronoun use. Write an improved form in the space provided. Each sentence contains one error.

1. The task force submitted their recommendation a week early. _____

2. The Boston Red Sox announced that their ticket prices would increase by $20 next season. _____

3. All Apple employees, except for Steve Jobs, received his or her free iPhones at the end of the year. _____

4. Anyone who grew up in the 1970s probably has some vinyl in their music collection. _____

CHAPTER 7 • 135

5. Each of the companies calculated their assets and liabilities before the merger. _____

6. *American Demographics* is known for their solid reputation among marketing executives. _____

7. Do you know who Troy is talking about? _____

8. Please direct my inquiry to whomever is in charge of quality control. _____

9. Neither the Cabinet members nor President Obama was ready for their decision to be revealed. _____

10. Who would you like to work with? _____

11. Each of the supermarkets featured their advertisements on Thursday. _____

12. Every one of the girls was pleased with their internship program. _____

13. Whose willing to serve as chair of the committee? _____

14. Our entire staff agreed that their response must be unified. _____

15. The instructor whom won the teaching award is Rhonda Wood. _____

16. An all-expense-paid trip to Florida will be given to whomever wins the sales contest. _____

17. General Motors reported that their sales increased in June. _____

18. The best CEO demonstrates transparency when communicating with his employees. _____

19. Researchers at Carnegie Mellon found that people are more likely to reveal his or her bad behavior when asked about it casually. _____

20. It's impossible to determine who's presentation was best. _____

E. FAQs About Business English Review. In the space provided, write the correct answer choice.

1. Is the newly hired person any better _____ the previous manager?
   a. than   b. then   _____

2. If all parties agree, _____the contract should be approved.
   a. than   b. then   _____

3. After completing her associate's degree, Sonia hopes to earn a _____ degree.
   a. Bachelor   b. Bachelor's   c. bachelor's   d. bachelors   _____

4. This _____ our most profitable year yet.
   a. maybe   b. may be   _____

5. _____ I will apply for that position after all.
   a. Maybe   b. May be   _____

6. Investigators reported that several of the company's buildings were _____.
   a. under-insured   b. underinsured   c. under insured   _____

7. All _____ must pass rigorous safety training.
   a. stewards   b. stewardesses   c. flight attendants   _____

8. A man engaged to be married is referred to as a
   a. fiancée   b. fiancé   _____

9. When _____ ready to order, let me know.
   a. you're   b. your   _____

10. _____ of the ideas was discussed thoroughly.
    a. Everyone   b. Every one   _____

▶▶ Learning Web Ways

As you become more familiar with the Web, you may begin to think that the Web is the perfect place for all research. Wrong! Information provided on the Web is not always useful and not always accurate. The following exercise helps you learn to think more critically about what you find on the Web.

Goal: To learn how to critically evaluate the information you find on the Web.

1. With your Web browser open, go to **http://www.lib.berkeley.edu/ TeachingLib/Guides/Internet/ Evaluate.html**.

2. Study this page, which is published by the UC Berkeley Library: **Evaluating Web Pages: Techniques to Apply & Questions to Ask.**

3. Read the five suggestions provided. Also read the section "WHY? Rationale for Evaluating What You Find on the Web."

4. Make a list of five or more questions that you might ask in deciding whether a Web site is reliable. When you finish, submit your list to your instructor or send it in an e-mail.

5. Now go to the University of Illinois library site: **http://www.uni.uiuc.edu/ library/computerlit/evaluatingsites .php**. Here you will find an exercise for evaluating Web sources.

6. Complete all five Web site evaluation exercises. Write your answers for each exercise and submit to your instructor.

7. End your session by clicking the **X** in the upper right corner.

▶▶ Chat About It

Your instructor may assign any of the following topics for you to discuss in class, in an online chat room, or on an online discussion board. Some of the discussion topics may require outside research. You may also be asked to read and respond to postings made by your classmates.

Discussion Topic 1: A magazine ad for BlackBerry wireless devices included the following headline: "Ask Someone Why They Love Their Blackberry." Similarly, a magazine ad for James Hardie International, a manufacturer of building projects, included this heading: "Because no one ever wished they'd spent more time painting their house." Both of these sentences include pronoun–antecedent disagreements, and similar disagreements appear in numerous print ads. Why do you think so many companies make these types of errors? How do errors like this make you feel about a company? What alternatives could these companies use to avoid these types of errors?

Discussion Topic 2: When George Bush (George W. Bush's father) ran for president against Bill Clinton in 1992, he used "trust" as a central theme of his campaign. Bumper stickers and posters were made saying "Who Do You Trust." When he made his nomination acceptance speech at the Republican National Convention in Houston, he included several sentences such as, "Who do you trust to make change work for you?" and "Who do you trust in this election?" In each case, he should have used *whom* instead of *who*. Why do you think he made these pronoun errors? Do you think it was intentional or accidental?

Discussion Topic 3: When Barack Obama held his first press conference after being elected in November 2008, he said this in response to a reporter's question: "Well, President Bush graciously invited Michelle and I to meet with him and first lady Laura Bush." Within minutes articles and blog entries began appearing online calling attention to Obama's grammatical error. What error did he make? Do you consider this an important or a minor error? Why? Why do you think the press was so quick to jump on this grammatical mistake? Does a president have an obligation to use proper grammar? Why or why not?

Discussion Topic 4: Select a language other than English and conduct research to find out how pronouns are used. Does the language have a common-gender third-person singular pronoun? If not, how does the language deal with gender issues when using pronouns? Report your findings to your classmates. Be sure to cite your sources, including Web site names and addresses.

Discussion Topic 5: Do you have any tricks for deciding what pronoun to use when writing and speaking? How do you decide quickly whether to use *who* or *whom*? Share your tricks and suggestions with your classmates.

Posttest

Underline the correct word in each sentence.

1. Did anyone on the women's softball team leave (her, their) glove on the bus?

2. On our college campus, (they, instructors) serve as advisors for student clubs.

3. A rider must show (his, his or her, their) ticket before boarding the bus.

4. Neither the professor nor her students thinks (her, their) college will host the event.

5. Everyone in the band played (his, his or her, their) best during the performance.

6. Macy's advertised (their, its) annual sale in today's newspaper.

7. The entire faculty voted to give (its, their) support to the president.

8. Neither of the companies could identify (its, their) equipment.

9. (Who, Whom) would you like to see as the next department manager?

10. (Whose, Who's) bid is most cost-effective?

Begin your review by rereading Chapters 4–7. Then test your comprehension of those chapters by filling in the blanks in the exercises that follow. Compare your responses with the key at the end of the book.

LEVEL 1

1. Several employees' (a) childs, (b) children, (c) childrens participated in this year's "Take Your Child to Work Day." _____

2. The Cape Cod National Seashore has some of the most spectacular (a) beachs, (b) beaches, (c) beach's on the East Coast. _____

3. The home of the (a) Ramirezes, (b) Ramirez's, (c) Ramirezes's is located near the bike path. _____

4. She made several (a) wishes, (b) wish's when she blew out the candles on her birthday cake. _____

5. We are giving careful consideration to each (a) company's, (b) companies', (c) companys stock. _____

6. Many of our (a) students', (b) students, (c) student's have difficulty with possessive constructions. _____

7. The committee completed (a) it's, (b) its work last week. _____

8. Let's keep this news between you and (a) me, (b) I. _____

9. All employees except Ryan and (a) he, (b) him agreed to the reorganization. _____

10. Ask both of the designers when (a) she, (b) he, (c) he or she, (d) they can give us estimates. _____

11. When a customer complains, (a) he, (b) she, (c) he or she, (d) they must be taken seriously. _____

12. The noun *pizza* is a(n) (a) abstract, (b) concrete noun. _____

13. The noun *loyalty* is (a) abstract, (b) concrete. _____

14. *I, he, she, we,* and *they* are (a) subjective-case, (b) objective-case pronouns. _____

LEVEL 2

15. Our Human (a) Resource's, (b) Resources, (c) Resources' Department posted six new positions. _____

16. Although he hired two (a) attorneys, (b) attornies, (c) attornies', (d) attorneys' to represent him, he did not win his case. _____

17. Pamela Hawkins consulted her three (a) sister-in-laws, (b) sister-in-law's, (c) sisters-in-law before making a decision. _____

18. We read an announcement that the (a) Millers, (b) Miller's, (c) Miller, (d) Millers' son won a scholarship. _____

19. Your (a) bosses, (b) boss's, (c) bosses' signature is required on this expense form.

     _____

20. Leonard Goodleman and (a) she, (b) her planned the high school reunion.

     _____

21. Both George W. Bush and Barack Obama served as president during the (a) 2000s, (b) 2000's, (c) 2000s'.

     _____

22. Insincerity irritates Dr. Loranjo as much as (a) I, (b) me.

     _____

23. Please mail the completed application to (a) I, (b) me, (c) myself.

     _____

24. Neither the foreman nor the jury members wanted (a) his name, (b) their names to be released by the media.

     _____

25. Every clerk and every administrative assistant elected to exercise (a) his, (b) her, (c) his or her, (d) their voting rights.

     _____

26. Hewlett-Packard was the first company to have (a) it's, (b) its own personalized postage.

     _____

27. (a) We, (b) Us college students take our education seriously.

     _____

28. Many (a) CPAs, (b) CPA's, (c) CPAs' complete tax forms for individuals.

     _____

LEVEL 3

29. (a) Greg and Patricia's, (b) Greg's and Patricia's new cabin is located on the shores of Lake Tahoe.

     _____

30. I certainly hope that today's weather is better than (a) yesterdays, (b) yesterday's, (c) yesterday.

     _____

31. In seven (a) days, (b) day's, (c) days' time, Maxwell will retire.

     _____

32. Following several financial (a) crisis, (b) crises, (c) crisises, the corporation was forced to declare bankruptcy.

     _____

33. Economics (a) is, (b) are Rachel's favorite academic subject.

     _____

34. The employee credited with the suggestion was thought to be (a) he, (b) him.

     _____

35. If I were (a) her, (b) she, I would decline the offer.

     _____

36. To (a) who, (b) whom did you send your application?

     _____

37. (a) Who, (b) Whom is available to work overtime this weekend?

     _____

38. Give the extra supplies to (a) whoever, (b) whomever needs them.

     _____

39. (a) Who, (b) Whom would you prefer to see in that job?

     _____

40. (a) Whose, (b) Who's lunch was left in the refrigerator over the weekend?

     _____

41. Do you know (a) whose, (b) who's going to speak at today's seminar?

     _____

42. He dreams of earning his (a) masters, (b) masters', (c) master's degree in chemical engineering.

     _____

FAQs About Business English Review

43. Professor Kartchner said it was (a) to, (b) too early to sign up for these classes.

     _____

44. Shorter, rather (a) then, (b) than longer, training sessions are preferable.

     _____

45. It can be difficult to get medical insurance if you have a (a) pre-existing, (b) pre existing, (c) preexisting condition.

46. Much desert land is (a) underdeveloped, (b) under developed, (c) under-developed.

47. Because our area code changed, we had to order new letterhead (a) stationary, (b) stationery.

48. You (a) maybe, (b) may be our most talented Web designer.

49. (a) Any one, (b) Anyone of these applicants could do the job.

50. You must submit (a) you're, (b) your application online.

Techniques for Effective Sentences

The basic unit in writing is the sentence. Sentences come in a variety of sizes, shapes, and structures. As business and professional communicators, we are most interested in functional sentences that say what we want to say correctly and concisely. In this workshop you will concentrate on two important elements: writing complete sentences and writing concise sentences.

Writing Complete Sentences

To be complete, a sentence must have a subject and a predicate and it must make sense. As you learned in Chapter 3, incomplete sentences are fragments. Let's consider four common fragment errors you will want to avoid.

1. The fragment contains a subject and a predicate, but it begins with a subordinate word (such as *because, as, although, since,* or *if*) and fails to introduce a complete clause. You can correct this problem by joining the fragment to a relevant main clause.

   Fragment: Because world markets and economies are becoming increasingly intermixed.

   Revision: Because world markets and economies are becoming increasingly intermixed, Americans will be doing more business with people from other cultures.

   Fragment: Although Americans tend to come to the point directly.

   Revision: Although Americans tend to come to the point directly, people from some other cultures prefer indirectness.

2. The fragment does not contain a subject and a predicate, but a nearby sentence completes its meaning.

   Fragment: In July and August every year in Europe. That's when many Europeans take vacations.

   Revision: In July and August every year, many Europeans take vacations.

3. The fragment starts with a relative pronoun such as *which, that,* or *who.* Join the fragment to a main clause to form a complete sentence.

   Fragment: Which is a precious item to North Americans and other Westerners.

   Revision: Concise business letters save time, which is a precious item to North Americans and other Westerners.

4. The fragment starts with a noun followed by a *who, that,* or *which* clause. Add a predicate to form a complete sentence.

   Fragment: The visiting Vietnamese executive who was struggling to express his idea in English.

   Revision: The visiting Vietnamese executive who was struggling to express his idea in English appreciated the patience of his listener.

Skill Check 2.1 Eliminating Sentence Fragments

Each of the following consists of a fragment and a sentence, not necessarily in that order. Use proofreading marks to eliminate the fragment.

Example:

Speak in short sentences and use common words if you want to be understood abroad.

1. Although you should not raise your voice. You should speak slowly and enunciate clearly.

2. A glazed expression or wandering eyes. These alert a speaker that the listener is lost.

3. In speaking with foreign businesspeople, be careful to avoid jargon. Which is special terminology that may confuse listeners.

4. Kevin Chambers, who is an international specialist and consultant. He said that much of the world wants to like us.

5. Graciously accept the blame for not making your meaning clear. If a misunderstanding results.

Skill Check 2.2 Making Sentences Complete

Expand the following fragments into complete sentences. Add your own ideas. Be ready to explain why each fragment is incomplete and what you did to remedy the problem.

Example: If we keep in mind that Americans abroad are often accused of talking too much.

Revision: If we keep in mind that Americans abroad are often accused of talking too much, we will become better listeners.

1. The businessperson who engages a translator for important contracts

   _____

2. Assuming that a nod, a yes, or a smile indicates agreement

   _____

3. If you learn greetings and a few phrases in the language of the country you are visiting

   _____

4. Although global business transactions are often conducted in English

   _____

5. Which is why Americans sometimes put words in the mouths of foreign friends struggling to express an idea

   _____

   _____

Writing Concise Sentences

Businesspeople and professionals value concise, economical writing. Wordy communication wastes the reader's time and sometimes causes confusion. You can make your sentences more concise by avoiding opening fillers, revising wordy phrases, and eliminating redundant words.

Avoiding Opening Fillers

Openers such as *there is, it is, you might be interested to learn that*, and *this is to inform you that* fill in sentences but generally add no meaning. Train yourself to question these constructions. About 75 percent can be eliminated, almost always resulting in more concise sentences.

Wordy: *There are* three students who volunteered to help.

Revised: Three students volunteered to help.

Wordy: *This is to inform you that* our offices will be closed on Monday.

Revised: Our offices will be closed on Monday.

Revising Wordy Phrases

Some of our most common and comfortable phrases are actually full of "word fat." When examined carefully, these phrases can be pared down considerably.

Wordy Phrases	Concise Substiutes
as per your suggestion	as you suggested
at this point in time	now
due to the fact that	because
for the purpose of	to
give consideration to	consider
in all probability	probably
in spite of the fact that	even though
in the amount of	for
in the event that	if
in the near future	soon
in the neighborhood of	about
in view of the fact that	since
with regard to	about

Notice how you can revise wordy sentences to make them more concise:

Wordy: *Due to the fact that* fire damaged our distribution center, we must delay some shipments.

Revised: *Because* fire damaged our distribution center, we must delay some shipments.

Wordy: We expected growth *in the neighborhood of* 25 percent.

Revised: We expected *about* 25 percent growth.

Eliminating Redundant Words

Words that are needlessly repetitive are said to be redundant. Writers must be alert to eliminating redundant words and phrases, such as the following:

advance warning	exactly identical	perfectly clear
alter or change	few in number	personal opinion
assemble together	free and clear	potential opportunity
basic fundamentals	grateful thanks	positively certain
collect together	great majority	proposed plan
consensus of opinion	integral part	reason why
contributing factor	last and final	refer back
dollar amount	midway between	true facts
each and every	new changes	very unique
end result	past history	visible to the eye

Wordy:	This paragraph is *exactly identical* to that one.
Revised:	This paragraph is *identical* to that one.
Wordy:	The *reason why* we are discussing the issue is to reach a *consensus of opinion.*
Revised:	The *reason* we are discussing the issue is to reach a *consensus.*

Skill Check 2.3 Writing Concise Sentences

In the space provided, rewrite the following sentences to make them more concise.

1. There is a free booklet that shows all the new changes in employee benefits.

_____

2. In view of the fact that health care benefits are being drastically altered, this is to inform you that an orientation meeting will be scheduled in the near future.

_____

_____

3. The reason why we are attending the protest is to make our opinions perfectly clear.

_____

4. In the event that McDonald's offers new menu items for the purpose of increasing sales, experts think that there is every reason to believe that the effort will be successful.

_____

5. There will be a special showing of the orientation training film scheduled at 10 a.m. due to the fact that there were so few in number who were able to attend the first showing.

_____

_____

6. This is to give you advance warning that we plan to alter or change the procedures for submitting travel expenses in the very near future.

_____

7. I am writing this e-mail message to let you know that each and every employee is invited to attend our holiday banquet.

_____

8. You might be interested to learn that accounting mistakes this past fiscal year were few in number.

_____

9. My personal opinion is that you understand the basic fundamentals of our operations.

_____

10. Please give consideration to the very unique skills I have to offer your organization.

_____

Writing Application 2.1

Assume you are Marcia Murphy and that you received the memo shown in Figure 2.1. Read the memo carefully, and then prepare a memo that responds to it. Show your appreciation to Jason Corzo for his advice. Explain that you are both excited and worried about your new assignment. Use your imagination to tell why. Describe how you expect to prepare for the new assignment. You might say that you plan to start learning the language, to read about the culture, and to talk with colleagues who have worked in Japan. Put this in your own words and elaborate. Make sure that your memo uses complete sentences and concise wording.

FIGURE 2.1
Interoffice Memo

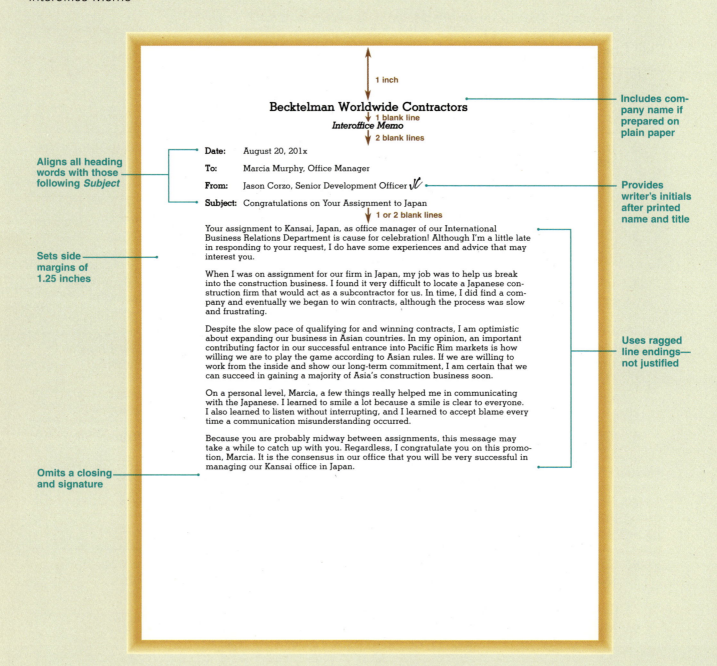

1 inch

Becktelman Worldwide Contractors
1 blank line
Interoffice Memo
2 blank lines

Includes company name if prepared on plain paper

Date: August 20, 201x

To: Marcia Murphy, Office Manager

From: Jason Corzo, Senior Development Officer *JC*

Provides writer's initials after printed name and title

Subject: Congratulations on Your Assignment to Japan
1 or 2 blank lines

Aligns all heading words with those following *Subject*

Your assignment to Kansai, Japan, as office manager of our International Business Relations Department is cause for celebration! Although I'm a little late in responding to your request, I do have some experiences and advice that may interest you.

When I was on assignment for our firm in Japan, my job was to help us break into the construction business. I found it very difficult to locate a Japanese construction firm that would act as a subcontractor for us. In time, I did find a company and eventually we began to win contracts, although the process was slow and frustrating.

Sets side margins of 1.25 inches

Despite the slow pace of qualifying for and winning contracts, I am optimistic about expanding our business in Asian countries. In my opinion, an important contributing factor in our successful entrance into Pacific Rim markets is how willing we are to play the game according to Asian rules. If we are willing to work from the inside and show our long-term commitment, I am certain that we can succeed in gaining a majority of Asia's construction business soon.

Uses ragged line endings— not justified

On a personal level, Marcia, a few things really helped me in communicating with the Japanese. I learned to smile a lot because a smile is clear to everyone. I also learned to listen without interrupting, and I learned to accept blame every time a communication misunderstanding occurred.

Because you are probably midway between assignments, this message may take a while to catch up with you. Regardless, I congratulate you on this promotion, Marcia. It is the consensus in our office that you will be very successful in managing our Kansai office in Japan.

Omits a closing and signature

Unit 3

Showing the Action

© Radius Images/Corbis

8 Verbs: Kinds, Voices, Moods, Verbals

© moodboard/Corbis

9 Verb Tenses and Parts

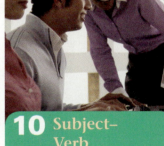

© Getty Images/Brand X Pictures/Jupiterimages

10 Subject–Verb Agreement

"One of the glories of English simplicity is the possibility of using the same word as noun and verb."

—Edward Sapir, linguist and anthropologist

Chapter 8

Verbs: Kinds, Voices, Moods, Verbals

OBJECTIVES

When you have completed the materials in this chapter, you will be able to do the following:

LEVEL 1
- Understand the three main kinds of verbs.
- Distinguish between transitive and intransitive verbs.

LEVEL 2
- Recognize the functions and specific uses of active- and passive-voice verbs.
- Understand and apply the subjunctive mood correctly.

LEVEL 3
- Use gerunds, infinitives, and participles correctly.
- Identify and remedy dangling verbal phrases and other misplaced modifiers.

Pretest

Underline the letter representing the correct answer.

1. In the sentence *Isabel listened to the message*, the verb *listened* is (a) transitive, (b) intransitive, (c) linking.

2. In the sentence *Hector seems excited about his upcoming vacation*, the verb *seems* is (a) transitive, (b) intransitive, (c) linking.

3. In the sentence *Geoffrey scheduled a Web conference*, the verb *scheduled* is (a) transitive, (b) intransitive, (c) linking.

4. In the sentence *The meeting was canceled*, the verb phrase *was canceled* is in the (a) active voice, (b) passive voice, (c) subjunctive mood.

5. In the sentence *Maria Lockhart taught the class*, the verb *taught* is in the (a) active voice, (b) passive voice, (c) subjunctive mood.

6. The sentence *Dylan wishes he were rich* is in the (a) indicative mood, (b) imperative mood, (c) subjunctive mood.

7. Emily acts as if she (a) was, (b) were the manager.

8. We appreciate (a) you, (b) your bringing the matter to our attention.

9. Jocelyn moved that the meeting (a) be, (b) is adjourned.

10. Try (a) and find, (b) to find an answer to my question.

You learned in Chapter 2 that many words in the English language can serve as more than one part of speech in sentences. As Edward Sapir pointed out, some words can be used as both nouns and verbs. Verbs are words that energize sentences. They tell what is happening, what happened, and what will happen. The verb is the most complex part of speech. A complete treatment of its forms and uses would require at least a volume. Our discussion of verbs will be limited to practical applications for businesspeople and professionals. In this chapter you will learn about kinds of verbs, verb voices, and verb moods. You will also learn about verbals, including gerunds, infinitives, and participles.

LEVEL 1

Kinds of Verbs

Verbs express an action, an occurrence, or a state of being.

> Alexandra <u>created</u> an innovative advertising campaign. (Action)
>
> The winter holidays <u>end</u> the fall semester. (Occurrence)
>
> Joe <u>is</u> the new technical writer. (State of being)

In relation to subjects, verbs generally tell what the subject is doing or what is being done to the subject. Verbs fall into three main categories:

Action Verbs:	Tell what a subject does, including physical and mental actions
Examples:	Naomi *walks* to work every day. Naomi *dreams* of buying a car.
Linking Verbs:	Tell a subject's state of being (*is, are, was, were, be, being, been, am, appear, seem, feel, taste, sound, look, smell*, etc.)
Examples:	The new employee *is* very responsible. The new employee *looks* very responsible.
Helping Verbs:	Are added to a main verb to create a verb phrase (*is, are, was, were, be, being, been, am, have, has, had, do, does, did, may, must, ought, can, might, could, should, would, shall, will*, etc.)
Examples:	Jonah *is working* late. Jonah *must be* tired.

Action Verbs

We will begin our discussion of verbs by focusing on verbs that express action. These verbs may be divided into two categories: transitive and intransitive. When a verb directs its action toward an object, it is *transitive*. When the action is complete in itself and requires no object, the verb is *intransitive*. Some verbs may be transitive or intransitive, depending on how they function in a sentence.

Transitive Verbs

A verb expressing an action directed toward a person or thing is said to be **transitive**. A transitive verb needs, in addition to its subject, a noun or pronoun to complete its meaning. This noun or pronoun functions as the **direct object** of the transitive verb. Notice in the following sentences that the verbs direct action toward objects.

> Employees made suggestions.
>
> Yesterday the president called her.
>
> Krispy Kreme sells doughnuts by the millions.

Objects usually answer the questions *What?* or *Whom?* In the first example, the employees made *what?* The object is *suggestions*. In the second example, the president called *whom?* The object is *her*. In the third example, Krispy Kreme sells *what?* The object is *doughnuts*.

Intransitive Verbs

An action verb that does not require an object to complete its action is said to be **intransitive**.

> Linda Robbins worked in our Payroll Department last summer.
>
> Stan dreams of opening his own business one day.
>
> Francesca listened carefully to the instructions.

Notice that the verbs in these sentences do not express actions directed toward persons or things. Prepositional phrases (*in our Payroll Department, of opening his own business, to the instructions*) and adverbs (*carefully*) do not receive the action expressed by the verbs. Therefore, prepositional phrases and adverbs do not function as objects of verbs.

Linking Verbs

You will recall that **linking verbs** *link* to the subject words that rename or describe the subject. A noun, pronoun, or adjective that renames or describes the subject is called a **complement** because it *completes* the meaning of the subject.

> Mohamed is the new researcher. (*Researcher* is a noun complement that completes the meaning of the sentence by renaming *Mohamed*.)
>
> His salary is excellent. (*Excellent* is an adjective complement that completes the meaning of *salary*.)
>
> The caller was she. (*She* is a pronoun complement that completes the meaning of *caller*.)

Notice in the preceding sentences that the noun, pronoun, or adjective complements following these linking verbs do not receive action from the verb; instead, the complements *complete* the meaning of the subject.

Many linking verbs are derived from the *to be* verb form: *am, is, are, was, were, be, being, been*. Other words that often serve as linking verbs are *feels, appears, tastes, seems, sounds, looks*, and *smells*. Notice that several of these words describe sense experiences. Verbs expressing sense experiences may be followed by complements just as the *to be* linking verbs often are.

> She feels bad about her behavior in the meeting. (*Bad* is an adjective complement following the linking verb *feel*. An adjective—not the adverb *badly*—is needed here to describe the senses.)
>
> Jay looks good in his interview suit. (*Good* is an adjective complement following the linking verb *looks*.)

The use of adjectives following such verbs will be discussed more completely in Chapter 11.

Helping Verbs

Helping verbs are added to main verbs, which can be action or linking, to form verb phrases. Helping verbs have no meaning on their own.

The primary helping verbs are forms of the verb *to be* (*am, is, are, was, were, be, being, been*), *to have* (*have, had, had*), and *to do* (*do, did, does*). Other helping verbs express necessity or possibility (*can, could, may, might, will, would, shall, should, must, ought to*).

> Alicia is scanning all incoming files for viruses. (The helping verb *is* is added to the main verb *scanning* to form a verb phrase.)
>
> Our company has been profitable for two years. (The helping verb *has* is added to the main verb *been* to form a verb phrase.)
>
> Mark can speak Chinese fluently. (The helping verb *can* is added to the main verb *speak* to create a verb phrase.)

Review of Verb Functions

The function of a verb in a sentence determines its classification. The verb *work*, for example, is intransitive when it has no object (*Kevin works for a large corporation*). The same verb is transitive when an object follows (*Kevin worked his*

Study Tip

Here's a mnemonic (memory) device to help you remember the verbs of the senses. Call them the FATS verbs, an acronym (word formed of initials) made from the first letters of *feel, appear, taste,* and *seem*.

Study Tip

If you find yourself saying "I feel badly," ask yourself this question: Would you ever say, "I feel goodly?" No! That means that you should always say "I feel bad (not badly)."

triceps on the weight bench). The verb *felt* is linking when it is used to connect a complement describing the subject (*Maria felt marvelous*). The same verb is transitive when it directs action to an object (*Maria felt the hot sand beneath her feet*). The verb *was* is linking when it is used to connect a complement describing the subject (*The calculation was accurate*). The same verb is a helping verb when it is added to a main verb to form a verb phrase (*Max was running to catch the bus*). To distinguish between classifications, study carefully the constructions in which the verbs appear.

To review briefly:

- Action verbs—two kinds:
  a. Transitive: need objects to complete their meaning
  b. Intransitive: do not need objects to complete their meaning
- Linking verbs: form a link to words that rename or describe the subject
- Helping verbs: added to main verbs to form verb phrases

Now complete the reinforcement exercises for Level 1.

LEVEL 2

Verb Voices

You will recall that an action verb expressing an action directed toward a person or thing is said to be transitive. Transitive verbs fall into two categories depending on the receiver of the action of the verbs.

Active Voice

When the verb expresses an action directed by the subject toward the object of the verb, the verb is said to be in the **active voice**.

> Angela <u>read</u> the text message. (Action directed to the object, *message*.)

Verbs in the active voice are direct and forceful; they clearly identify the doer of the action. For these reasons, writing that frequently uses the active voice is vigorous and effective. Writers of business and professional communications strive to use the active voice; in fact, it is called the **voice of business**.

Passive Voice

When the action in a verb is directed toward the subject, the verb is said to be in the **passive voice**. Study the following pairs:

Passive:	Our <u>computers</u> <u>are</u> <u>scanned</u> daily for viruses.
Active:	<u>We</u> <u>scan</u> our computers daily for viruses.
Passive:	The <u>lottery</u> <u>was</u> <u>won</u> by Veronica Cool.
Active:	Veronica Cool <u>won</u> the lottery.
Passive:	Three <u>errors</u> <u>were</u> <u>made</u> in the report.
Active:	The <u>accountant</u> <u>made</u> three errors in the report.

Because the passive voice can be used to avoid mentioning the performer of the action or to place less emphasis on the doer of the action, the passive voice is sometimes called the **voice of tact**. Notice how much more tactful the passive version of the last example shown above is. Although directness in

Study Tip

In the passive voice, verbs always require a *helping verb*, such as *is, are, was, were, being,* or *been.*

Study Tip

A clue to passive voice is a prepositional phrase beginning with *by.*

business writing is generally preferable, in certain instances the passive voice is used when indirectness is desired.

Verb Moods

Three verb moods are available to enable a speaker or writer to express an attitude toward a subject: (a) The **indicative mood** is used to express a fact (*We need the contract*); (b) the **imperative mood** is used to express a command (*Send the contract immediately*); (c) the **subjunctive mood** is used to express a doubt, a conjecture, or a suggestion (*If the contract were here, we would be pleased*). The subjunctive mood may cause speakers and writers difficulty and therefore demands special attention.

Subjunctive Mood

Careful speakers and writers use the subjunctive mood in the following constructions:

If and *wish* Clauses

When a statement that is doubtful or contrary to fact is introduced by *if, as if,* or *wish,* substitute the subjunctive form *were* for the indicative form *was.*

> If Laurie *were* prepared, we could proceed. (Laurie is *not* prepared.)
>
> She acts as if she *were* the boss. (She is *not* the boss.)
>
> José wishes he *were* able to snowboard. (José is *not* able to snowboard.)

But if the statement could possibly be true, use the indicative form.

> If Chris *was* in the audience, I missed him. (Chris might have been in the audience.)

That Clauses

When a *that* clause follows a verb expressing a command, recommendation, request, suggestion, or requirement, use the subjunctive verb form *be* for *to be* verbs. For third-person singular verbs, drop the *s* or *es.*

> The CEO required that all board members *be* [not *is*] present at the meeting.
>
> Our manager recommends that all reports *be* [not *are*] proofread twice.
>
> The Secret Service requires that everyone near the president *receive* [not *receives*] top security clearance.

Motions

When a motion is stated, a subjunctive verb form should be used in the following *that* clause.

> Manuel moved that a vote *be* [not *is*] taken.
>
> Jeremy seconded the motion that the meeting *be* [not *is*] adjourned.

Caution: In a sentence without *that* clauses, do not mix subjunctive and indicative verbs.

> **Correct:** If she *were skilled*, she *would receive* job offers. (Both verbs are subjunctive.)
>
> **Correct:** If she *is skilled*, she *will receive* job offers. (Both verbs are indicative.)
>
> **Incorrect:** If she *were skilled*, she *will receive* job offers. (One subjunctive verb and one indicative verb.)

Now complete the reinforcement exercises for Level 2.

Career Tip

To be an effective communicator, you will want to use the subjunctive mood correctly. A business or professional person would avoid saying *If I was you,* for example.

Verbals

As you learned earlier, English is a highly flexible language in which a given word may have more than one grammatical function. In this level you will study verbals. **Verbals** are words that function as nouns, adjectives, or adverbs. Three kinds of verbals are gerunds (verbal nouns), infinitives, and participles (verbal adjectives).

Gerunds

A **gerund** is a verb form ending in *ing* that is used as a noun. Gerunds often describe activities.

> *Marketing* our products on the Web is necessary. (Gerund used as the subject.)
>
> Amarjit enjoys *skiing*. (Gerund used as the direct object of a verb.)
>
> Travis insisted on *revealing* the code. (Gerund used as the object of a preposition.)

In using gerunds, follow this rule: Make any noun or pronoun modifying a gerund possessive, as in *Karen's procrastinating* or *Dale's computing*. Because we sometimes fail to recognize gerunds as nouns, we fail to make their modifiers possessive:

> **Incorrect:** The staff objects to *Curtis smoking*.
>
> **Correct:** The staff objects to *Curtis's smoking*.

Study Tip

To distinguish between *ing* forms used as nouns and those used as adjectives, try the *What?* question approach. In the sentence *I admired Sara's programming*, say to yourself, "I admired what?" Answer: "I admired Sara's *programming*, not Sara." Therefore, *programming* is the object and functions as an *ing* noun.

The staff does not object to Curtis, as the first version states; it objects to his smoking. If we substitute a more easily recognized noun for *smoking*, the possessive form seems more natural: *The staff objects to Curtis's behavior. Behavior* is a noun, just as *smoking* is a gerund; the noun or pronoun modifiers of both must be possessive.

> Stephanie resented *his calling* during lunch. (The gerund *calling* requires the possessive pronoun *his*, not the objective-case pronoun *him*.)
>
> The manager appreciated *your working* late. (Not *you working*.)

Not all verbs ending in *ing* are, of course, gerunds. Some are elements in verb phrases and some act as adjectives. Compare these three sentences:

> I saw Clay *driving*. (The word *driving* functions as an adjective describing Clay.)
>
> I admired Clay's *driving*. (As the object of the verb, *driving* acts as a gerund.)
>
> Clay is *driving*. (Here *is driving* is a verb phrase.)

Infinitives

When the present form of a verb is preceded by *to*, the most basic verb form results: the **infinitive**. The sign of the infinitive is the word *to*.

> Try *to call* when you arrive.
>
> *To write* clearly and concisely requires great skill.

In certain expressions infinitives may be misused. Observe the use of the word *to* in the following infinitive phrases. Do not substitute the conjunction *and* for the *to* of the infinitive.

Try *to call* when you arrive. (Not *try and call*)

Be sure *to speak* softly when you use your cell phone in public. (Not *be sure and speak*)

Check *to see* when the flight is due to arrive. (Not *check and see*)

When any word appears between *to* and the verb (*to carefully prepare*), an infinitive is said to be split. At one time split infinitives were considered great grammatical sins. Today most authorities agree that infinitives may be split if necessary for clarity and effect. Avoid, however, split infinitives that result in awkward sentences.

Awkward: Neal Skapura wanted *to*, if he could find time, *take* the online class.

Better: If he could find time, Neal Skapura wanted *to take* the online class.

Participles

A **participle** is a verb form that we use with helping verbs to form the present-participle and the past-participle tenses. You will learn about these tenses in Chapter 9. A participle can also serve as an adjective. As adjectives, participles modify nouns or pronouns, and they do not require helping verbs.

Avoid using participial phrases that sound awkward, such as these:

Awkward: Pam's having been promoted to office manager was cause for celebration.

Better: Pam's promotion to office manager was cause for celebration.

Awkward: Being as you live nearby, should we carpool?

Better: Because you live nearby, should we carpool?

Avoiding Misplaced Verbal Modifiers

Used correctly, verbal modifiers and phrases add clarity and description to your writing. Used incorrectly, they may seem humorous.

Introductory Verbal Phrases

Introductory verbal phrases must be followed by the words they can logically modify. Such phrases can create confusion or unintended humor when placed incorrectly in a sentence. Consider this sentence: *Sitting in the car, the mountains were breathtaking.* The introductory verbal phrase in this sentence is said to *dangle* because it is not followed immediately by a word it can logically modify. This sentence says the mountains are sitting in the car. The sentence could be improved by adding a logical subject: *Sitting in the car, we saw the breathtaking mountains.*

After reading an introductory verbal phrase, ask the question *Who?* The answer to that question must immediately follow the introductory phrase. For example, *To find a good job, who?* Answer: *To find a good job, Derek wrote to many companies.*

Observe how the following illogical sentences have been improved:

Illogical: Slipping on the stairs, his ankle was injured.

Logical: Slipping on the stairs, *he* injured his ankle.

Illogical: Turning on the fan, papers flew about the office.

Logical: Turning on the fan, *I* caused papers to fly about the office.

Illogical: After answering the telephone, the doorbell began to ring insistently.

Logical: After answering the telephone, Jeremy heard the doorbell ring insistently.

Illogical: Skilled with computers, the personnel director hired Ben Seaberry.

Logical: Skilled with computers, Ben Seaberry was hired by the personnel director.

But: To master a language, listen carefully to native speakers.
To master a language, (you) listen carefully to native speakers.
(In commands, the understood subject is *you*. Therefore, this sentence is correctly followed by the word to which it refers.)

Verbal Phrases in Other Positions

In other positions within sentences, verbal phrases must also be placed in logical relation to the words they modify.

Illogical: The missing purchase orders were found by Gordon Young's assistant lying in his top desk drawer.

Logical: Gordon Young's assistant found the missing purchase orders lying in his top desk drawer.

Illogical: Doctors discovered his wrist had been fractured in five places during surgery.

Logical: During surgery, doctors discovered his wrist had been fractured in five places.

Now complete the reinforcement exercises for Level 3.

Spot the BLOOPER

Using the skills you are learning in this class, try to identify why the following items are bloopers. Consult your textbook, dictionary, or reference manual as needed.

Blooper 1: From the book *A Thousand Days in Venice* by Marlena DeBlasi: "Plumped and tied up in cotton string, I braised the veal in butter and white wine."

Blooper 2: The manager of the Denver Nuggets quoted in the *Denver Post*: "I appreciate them giving it more time because Melo and us want everybody to know he's innocent." [Did you spot two bloopers?]

Blooper 3: In the University of St. Thomas *Daily Bulletin*: "Tim Scully's Videography class will present its world premier of music videos."

Blooper 4: Associated Press article appearing in *The Daily Sentinel* [Grand Junction, Colorado]: "In Rostock, Germany, more than 400 officers were injured as hooded protesters pelted police with rocks and bottles, 30 of whom were hospitalized with broken bones and cuts."

Blooper 5: From a *Los Angeles Daily News* story: "A screaming intruder made it onto the front lawn of the White House Sunday while President George W. Bush was at home before being apprehended by Secret Service officers."

Blooper 6: In an *Indianapolis Star* article about a search for Bigfoot by a man identified only as "Tom": "Allegedly covered in hair, standing more than 8 feet tall and reeking of a pungent odor, Tom believes the creature he saw in June to be Bigfoot."

Blooper 7: In a summons from Santa Clara County to potential jurors: "You might not qualify for a jury if you do not read, right, or understand the English language."

Blooper 8: From an advertisement for the Egyptian Tourist Authority appearing in *The Boston Globe*: "I wish I was in Egypt."

Blooper 9: In the *Atlanta Journal-Constitution*: ". . . [a University of Georgia player] apologized for an unspecified 'mistake' that led to him participating in the team's first practice of the season as a reserve."

Blooper 10: Headline from *The Urbana* [Ohio] *Daily Citizen*: "Volunteers Use Sandbags to Try and Save Water Plant."

FAQs

Answered by Dr. Guffey and Professor Seefer

Dr. Guffey   Professor Seefer

Question	Answer
Q: I learned that the verb *set* requires an object. If that is true, how can we say that the sun *sets* in the west?	**A:** Good question! The verb *set* generally requires an object, but it does have some standardized uses that do not require an object, such as the one you mention. Here's another: *Some concretes set quickly*. We doubt that anyone would be likely to substitute *sit* in either of these unusual situations. While we are on the subject, the verb *sit* also has some exceptions. Although generally the verb *sit* requires no object, *sit* has a few uses that require objects: *Sit yourself down* and *The waiter sat us at Table 1*.
Q: One of my favorite words is *hopefully*, but I understand that it is often used improperly. How should it be used?	**A:** Language purists insist that the word *hopefully* be used to modify a verb (*We looked at the door hopefully, expecting Mr. Guerrero to return momentarily*). The word *hopefully* should not be used as a substitute for *I hope that* or *We hope that*. Instead of saying *Hopefully, interest rates will decline*, one should say *I hope that interest rates will decline*.
Q: I saw this in an auction announcement for a Beverly Hills home: *Married to interior decorator Dusty Bartlett, their home saw many of the great Hollywood parties with friends such as Ingrid Bergman and Katharine Hepburn setting by the pool on weekends.* Am I just imagining, or does this sentence say that the home was married to the interior decorator?	**A:** Amazing, isn't it! But that's what the sentence says. This is a classic dangling modifier. An introductory verbal phrase must be immediately followed by words that the phrase can logically modify. This sentence doesn't give a clue. Did you see another problem? The verb *setting* should be *sitting*.
Q: I received a magazine advertisement recently that promised me a *free gift* and a *15 percent off discount* if I subscribed. What's wrong with this wording?	**A:** You have got a double winner here in the category of redundancies. The word *gift* suggests *free*; therefore, to say *free gift* is like *saying I am studying English English*. It would be better to say *special gift*. In the same way, *15 percent off discount* repeats itself. Omit *off*.
Q: When do you use *may* and when do you use *can*?	**A:** Traditionally, the verb *may* is used in asking or granting permission (*yes, you may use that desk*). *Can* is used to suggest ability (*you can succeed in business*). In informal writing, however, authorities today generally agree that *can* may be substituted for *may*.
Q: I just checked the dictionary and found that *cooperate* is now written as one word. It seems to me that years ago it was *co-operate* or *coöperate*. Has the spelling changed?	**A:** Yes, it has. And so has the spelling of many other words. As new words become more familiar, their spelling tends to become more simplified. For example, *per cent* and *good will* are now shown by most dictionaries as *percent* and *goodwill*. By the same token, many words formerly hyphenated are now written without hyphens: *strike-over* is now *strikeover*, *to-day* is *today*, *editor-in-chief* is *editor in chief*, *vice-president* is *vice president*, and *passer-by* is now *passerby*. Current dictionaries reflect these changes.

158   •   **CHAPTER 8**   VERBS: KINDS, VOICES, MOODS, VERBALS

Question	Answer

Q: On my computer I am using a program that checks the writer's style. My problem is that it flags every passive-voice verb and tells me to consider using an active-voice verb. Are passive-voice verbs totally forbidden in business and professional writing?

A: Of course not! Computer style-checkers capitalize on language areas that can be detected mechanically, and a passive-voice verb is easily identified by a computer. Although active-voice verbs are considered more forceful, passive-voice verbs have a genuine function in business and professional writing. Because they hide the subject and diffuse attention, passive verbs are useful in sensitive messages where indirect language can develop an impersonal, inconspicuous tone. For example, when a lower-level employee must write a persuasive and somewhat negative message to a manager, passive-voice verbs are quite useful.

Q: What's the correct verb in this sentence? *Tim recognized that, if his company (was or were) to prosper, it would require considerable capital.*

A: The verb should be *were* because the clause in which it functions is not true. Statements contrary to fact that are introduced by words such as *if* and *wish* require subjunctive-mood verbs.

Q: Are there two meanings for the word *discreet*?

A: You are probably confusing the two words *discreet* and *discrete*. *Discreet* means "showing good judgment" and "prudent" (*the witness gave a discreet answer, avoiding gossip and hearsay*). The word *discrete* means "separate" or "noncontinuous" (*Alpha, Inc., has installed discrete computers rather than a network computer system*). You might find it helpful to remember that the *e's* are separate in *discrete*.

Q: Is there a difference between the words *premier* and *premiere*? How can I decide which to use?

A: These words are the masculine (*premier*) and feminine (*premiere*) forms of "first" in the French language. However, they have different meanings in English. *Premier* can be used as an adjective meaning "first in position, rank, importance, or time" (*Google is one of the premier Web search tools*). As a noun *premier* refers to "the prime minister of a parliamentary government" (*The premier spoke to a large crowd*). The word *premiere* can serve as a noun or verb. As a noun *premiere* means "a first performance or exhibition" (*The Hollywood premiere was an exciting event*). As a verb *premiere* means "to give a first public performance" (*The film will premiere in New York City*) or "to appear for the first time as a performer" (*Johnny Depp made his acting premiere in the film* A Nightmare on Elm Street).

8 Reinforcement Exercises

LEVEL 1

Online Homework Help! For immediate feedback on odd-numbered items, go to **www.meguffey.com**.

 A. (Self-check) In the spaces provided, indicate whether the italicized verbs are transitive (*T*), intransitive (*I*), or linking (*L*).

Example: Kenisha *is* our office manager.   L

1. Social networking sites *appear* to be growing in popularity.   _____
2. The Sanchezes *auctioned* their car on eBay.   _____
3. Before the awards ceremony, the nominees *met* for a group photo.   _____
4. Claudia Eckelmann *is* the professor who won the award.   _____
5. Louisiana citizens *were* excited to meet Governor Jindal in person.   _____
6. Jan Williams *skied* down the slope before sunrise.   _____
7. The production manager *called* over four hours ago.   _____
8. Beverly Forsberg *felt* the rich leather of her new jacket.   _____
9. Well-written business letters *get* results.   _____
10. Personality *opens* doors, but only character keeps them open.   _____

Check your answers below.

B. Each of the following sentences contains an action verb that is either transitive or intransitive. If the verb is intransitive, underline it and write *I* in the space provided. If the verb is transitive, underline it, write *T* in the space provided, and also write its direct object.

Examples: After his presentation the manager <u>left</u>.   I

Employees <u>brought</u> their lunches.   T (lunches)

1. Rich Royka designed a Web site for his new business.   _____
2. Her cell phone rang during the movie.   _____
3. FedEx delivers packages seven days a week.   _____
4. Our suppliers raised their prices.   _____
5. Storm clouds gathered.   _____
6. Over the years our assets increased.   _____
7. Barack Obama sends many text messages.   _____

1. I 2. T 3. I 4. L 5. L 6. I 7. I 8. T 9. T 10. T

8. The employees protested. _____

9. Managers responded to their demands. _____

10. Jessica expects to pass the CPA exam. _____

C. Linking verbs are followed by complements that identify, rename, or describe the subjects. The most common linking verbs are the forms of *be* (*am, is, are, was,* and so on) and the verbs of the senses (*feels, appears, tastes, smells,* and so on). The following sentences all contain linking verbs. For each sentence underline the linking verb and write its complement in the space provided.

Examples: Leony <u>feels</u> confident in her abilities.   confident

Our current team leader <u>is</u> Joy DePover.   Joy DePover

1. Florence is famous for its Renaissance art. _____

2. His presentation was persuasive. _____

3. Those cookies smell fantastic! _____

4. Over the telephone his voice sounds resonant. _____

5. It was she who called you earlier. _____

6. LeRoy Haitz was our wedding photographer. _____

7. He feels comfortable buying items online. _____

8. Stacey appears knowledgeable about the improvement plan. _____

9. The plan sounds feasible. _____

10. It seems unusually cold in here today. _____

D. In the following sentences, selected verbs have been italicized. For each sentence indicate whether the italicized verb is transitive (*T*), intransitive (*I*), or linking (*L*). In addition, if the verb is transitive, write its object. If the verb is linking, write its complement. If the verb is helping, write the main verb in the verb phrase.

Examples: The new sales manager *is* Gary Smith.   L (Gary Smith)

Our Web site *generates* many hits each day.   T (hits)

1. The chair of our Curriculum Committee *is* Donna Holts. _____

2. A virtual keyboard *projects* the image of a full-sized computer keyboard onto any flat surface. _____

3. Virtual keyboards *work* best in rooms without bright lighting. _____

4. We *were* surprised when we saw Brad Pitt's new film. _____

5. It *was* she who sent the instant message. _____

6. Please *check* the links to make sure they are working. _____

7. Management *surveyed* employees to learn how they feel about flex time. _____

8. Her report *appears* accurate, but we must verify some data. _____

9. Todd *feels* marvelous about his recent promotion. _____

10. Producers *move* goods to market to meet seasonal demands. _____

11. We *appreciate* your generous donation. _____

12. The economy *seems* bright despite interest rate increases. _____

13. Joy DePover *is* the person whom you should call. _____

14. Researchers found that smoking *has* a detrimental effect on health. _____

15. Although consumers protested, the airline *ended* its meal service. _____

16. This software *identifies* almost any malware. _____

17. The physician *wrote* a prescription for allergy medicine. _____

18. We *listened* to the presentation with great interest. _____

19. All of us *feel* bad about her transfer. _____

20. Arthur *is* interested in running for office. _____

LEVEL 2

A. (Self-check) Transitive verbs in the following sentences have been italicized. For each sentence write *active* or *passive* to indicate the voice of the italicized verb.

Example: Several workplace safety infractions *were found* by inspectors. ___passive___

1. Leslie Mills *raised* additional funds for scholarships. _____

2. Additional funds for scholarships *were raised* by Leslie Mills. _____

3. Communication and computer skills *are required* by many hiring companies. _____

4. Many hiring companies *require* communication and computer skills. _____

5. Warren Buffett *owns* a number of shares in See's Candies. _____

Select the correct word and write it in the space provided.

6. If Jan Jones (was, were) our manager, morale would be much higher. _____

7. Mike Mixon recommended that the meeting (is, be) adjourned at 4:30 p.m. _____

8. If I (was, were) you, I would apply for the promotion. _____

9. Did your manager suggest that you (be, are) reimbursed for your educational expenses? _____

10. If Betty Pearman (was, were) at the opening session, we did not see her. _____

Check your answers below.

B. In the spaces provided, write *active* or *passive* to indicate the voice of the italicized verbs in the following sentences.

1. Steelcase Inc. *designed* a special office chair for collaboration and brainstorming sessions. _____

2. Our company *monitors* the Web activity of all employees. _____

3. The Web activity of all employees *is monitored* by our company. _____

1. active 2. passive 3. passive 4. active 5. active 6. were 7. be 8. were 9. be 10. was

4. You *withdrew* the funds in question on May 29. _____

5. Brad Eckhardt *was asked* to give the keynote address. _____

6. Workplaces *celebrate* National Boss's Day on October 16. _____

7. Researchers *found* a correlation between childhood obesity and asthma. _____

8. The White House Web site *was redesigned* to improve communication. _____

9. Barack Obama *is recognized* as the first truly "wired" president of the digital age. _____

10. Citizens often *apply* for government jobs online. _____

C. Writing Exercise. Careful writers use the active voice in business and professional communications when they want to identify the "doer" of the action. To give you practice, rewrite the following sentences changing their passive-voice verbs to active voice. Normally you can change a verb from passive to active voice by making the doer of the action—usually contained in a *by* phrase—the subject of the sentence.

Example: (Passive) Production costs must be reduced by manufacturers.

(Active) Manufacturers must reduce production costs. _____

1. Pollution was greatly reduced by General Motors when the company built its new plant. (**Hint:** *Who* greatly reduced pollution? Start your new sentence with that name.)

_____

2. A car with solar panels that will power the air conditioning system was designed by Toyota.

_____

3. Approximately one billion text messages are sent every day by Filipinos.

_____

4. Massive short-term financing is used by Nike to pay off its production costs during its slow season.

_____

5. Doctors are offered cash rewards by insurance companies for prescribing generic drugs.

_____

Some sentences with passive-voice verbs do not identify the doer of the action. Before these sentences can be converted to active voice, a subject must be provided.

Example: (Passive) New subscribers will be offered a bonus. (By whom?—let's say by *BusinessWeek*.)

(Active) *BusinessWeek* will offer new subscribers a bonus.

In each of the following sentences, first answer the question *By whom?* Then rewrite the sentence in the active voice, beginning with your answer as the subject.

6. The documents were carefully reviewed during the audit. (By whom?)

_____

7. Our Web site was recently redesigned to increase its attractiveness and effectiveness. (By whom?)

_____

8. Net income before taxes must be calculated carefully when you fill out your tax return. (By whom?)

_____

9. Only a few of the many errors and changes were detected during the first proofreading. (By whom?)

_____

10. A cell phone tower was constructed in their neighborhood. (By whom?)

_____

D. Underline any verbs that are used incorrectly in the following sentences. Each sentence contains one error. Write the correct forms in the spaces provided.

1. Chip wishes that he was able to retire by age fifty. _____

2. I move that Marcella is appointed chair of our Hiring Committee. _____

3. The CEO recommended that each employee is given one Friday off per month. _____

4. If a better employee benefit program was available, recruiting would be easier. _____

5. A stockholder moved that dividends are declared immediately. _____

6. If he was in my position, he would have made the same decision. _____

7. I wish that our server was working so that I could read my e-mail. _____

8. Jeanette Peavler, our IT manager, strongly advised that computer firewalls are installed. _____

9. Stevie said she wished that you was able to join her lunch today. _____

10. If Brenda Kanoy were in the office that day, I did not see her. _____

E. Writing Exercise. Complete the following sentences. Underline the verb needed to make the sentence correct.

1. I wish that I (was, were) _____

2. If my boss (was, were) _____

3. If you (was, were) in my position, _____

4. She acts as if she (was, were) _____

5. If he (was, were) at today's meeting, _____

LEVEL 3

A. (Self-check) In the following sentences, gerunds are italicized. Other *ing* words that are not italicized are not functioning as gerunds. Select appropriate modifiers.

1. We appreciate (you, your) *sending* us your résumé. _____

2. We noticed (Rachel, Rachel's) *driving* past the office. _____

3. The auditor questioned (his, him) *traveling* first-class. _____

4. Eric's hiring depends on (him, his) *making* a good impression in the interview. _____

5. The (person, person's) *picking* up the check gets to choose the restaurant. _____

From each of the sets of sentences that follow, select the sentence that is stated in the more logical manner. Write its letter in the space provided.

6. a. Police officers found the suspect hiding in the backyard with the help of a police dog.
b. With the help of a police dog, police officers found the suspect hiding in the backyard. _____

7. a. Served on a vintage silver platter, the Smiths admired the roasted Thanksgiving turkey.
b. Served on a vintage silver platter, the roasted Thanksgiving turkey was admired by the Smiths. _____

8. a. To complete the accounting equation, one must add liabilities to equity.
b. To complete the accounting equation, it is necessary to add liabilities to equity. _____

9. a. To graduate early, you must take classes during the summer semester.
b. To graduate early, classes must be taken during the summer semester. _____

10. a. Having completed 20 years of service, Peter Churchill was presented with a gold watch.
b. Having completed 20 years of service, a gold watch was presented to Peter Churchill. _____

Check your answers below.

B. Some of the italicized words in the following sentences function as gerunds; others do not. Select appropriate modifiers.

1. We noticed the (CEO, CEO's) brisk *walking* as she arrived at the press conference. _____

2. We appreciated (Sandra, Sandra's) *designing* the brochure for us. _____

3. The accuracy of the proposal resulted largely from (him, his) careful *editing*. _____

4. (You, Your) *developing* the new ad campaign made a big difference in this year's profits. _____

5. We appreciate (you, your) not *smoking* on the premises. _____

6. Did the boss recommend (them, their) *attending* the demonstration? _____

7. The (customer, customer's) *paying* his bill complimented the service. _____

8. We are incredulous at (them, their) *winning* the series. _____

9. The (player, player's) *winning* the final game takes the prize. _____

10. (Him, His) *being* on time for the appointment is very important. _____

C. From each of the pairs of sentences shown, select the more acceptable version and write its letter in the space provided.

1. a. He has to, as soon as he graduates, find a full-time job.
b. He has to find a full-time job as soon as he graduates. _____

2. a. Be sure to arrive at the interview on time.
b. Be sure and arrive at the interview on time. _____

3. a. She had to, as soon as possible, ask her boss for a day off.
b. She had to ask her boss for a day off as soon as possible. _____

VERBS: KINDS, VOICES, MOODS, VERBALS

4. a. Mary Anne Kayiatos needs to, if she can afford it, move to a larger apartment.
   b. Mary Anne Kayiatos needs to move to a larger apartment if she can afford it. _____

5. a. Try to find out when the meeting is scheduled.
   b. Try and find out when the meeting is scheduled. _____

6. a. We wondered about his ordering so few office supplies.
   b. We wondered about him ordering so few office supplies. _____

7. a. Our manager started to, as the deadline approached, check the names
      and addresses.
   b. As the deadline approached, our manager started to check the names
      and addresses. _____

8. a. I think their being present at the hearing is crucial.
   b. I think them being present at the hearing is crucial. _____

9. a. Since you understand the process, please explain it to the staff.
   b. Being as you understand the process, please explain it to the staff. _____

10. a. Ray Goralka's having been elected as president was expected by all employees.
   b. Ray Goralka's election as president was expected by all employees. _____

   D. Writing Exercise. Rewrite the following sentences to remedy any gerund, infinitive, or participle faults.

1. I would like to, when I have some free time, write a novel.

_____

2. Being as the company is doing well, I plan to buy some of its stock.

_____

3. We were surprised by Arianna's quitting so suddenly.

_____

4. I plan to, when my visa is issued, work in Japan for a year.

_____

5. Be sure to, if you haven't changed your mind, make your plane reservations.

_____

6. Please inform your two agents that I appreciate them booking my reservations.

_____

7. When you travel globally, try and ask good questions about the culture before you leave.

_____

8. Kent's having served on the board has led to many corporate innovations.

_____

9. Check and see whether the Web site is functioning properly.

_____

10. Serona Software requires employees to, every Friday, spend an hour networking on Facebook.

_____

E. Writing Exercise. Each of the following sentences has an illogical introductory verbal phrase. Rewrite each sentence using that introductory phrase so that it is followed by a word it can logically modify. You may need to add a subject. Keep the introductory verbal phrase at the beginning of the sentence.

Example: Cycling up Mount Diablo, the summit came into view.

Cycling up Mount Diablo, we saw the summit come into view.

1. Driving to the sales meeting, the radio was tuned to NPR.

2. To be binding, a consideration must support every contract.

3. As a baboon growing up in the jungle, I realized Kiki had special nutritional needs.

4. Selected as Employee of the Year, the CEO presented an award to Cecile Chang.

5. After breaking into the building, the police heard the alarm set off by the burglars.

The preceding sentences had misplaced introductory verbal phrases. The next sentences have misplaced verbal phrases in other positions. Rewrite these sentences so that the verbal phrases are close to the words they can logically modify.

6. An autopsy revealed the cause of death to be strangulation by the coroner.

7. A woman said someone stole a necklace from the safe in her closet, which was valued at $3,000.

8. The man pleaded guilty while standing before the judge facing five counts of first-degree murder.

9. His wallet was found by Dave Evola lying under the front seat of his car.

10. Geologists inspected the site where the boulders broke free from a helicopter.

VERBS: KINDS, VOICES, MOODS, VERBALS

F. FAQs About Business English Review. In the space provided, write the correct answer choice.

1. Many Web sites now promise _____ investigative services to locate old friends, competitive information, and deadbeat spouses.
   a. discreet   b. discrete   _____

2. The menu was divided into two _____ sections: vegetarian and nonvegetarian.
   a. discreet   b. discrete   _____

3. To celebrate the opening of their boutique, owners offered a _____ of designer fragrance.
   a. gift   b. free gift   _____

4. Our supervisor wants our _____ in adopting the new policy.
   a. co-operation   b. cooperation   _____

5. If I _____ in your shoes, I would be thrilled.
   a. were   b. was   _____

6. Our local gas station offers a _____ when you pay with cash.
   a. 10 percent discount   b. 10 percent off discount   _____

7. Many companies _____ offer online technical support.
   a. today   b. to-day   _____

8. The _____ issued a new style guide that outlined appropriate language usage.
   a. editor-in-chief   b. editor in chief   _____

9. The _____ of the film *The Rock* took place on Alcatraz Island.
   a. premier   b. premiere   _____

10. The product's _____ selling feature is its five-year warranty.
    a. premier   b. premiere   _____

Many colleges, universities, and organizations provide Web sites where you can access frequently asked questions (FAQs) about grammar. On many of these sites, you can enter your own questions and receive a response from a trained language specialist. Assume you have a question about business English and want to find a reputable site on which to find an answer.

Goal: To learn about Web sites that contain frequently asked questions (FAQs) about grammar.

1. In the address bar of your Web browser, enter the URL of your favorite search tool. (Do you have it bookmarked? We always try **http://www.google.com** first.)

2. With your search tool on the screen, enter *grammar FAQ* as your search term.

3. Click the listing for the **Frequently Asked Questions: Guide to Grammar and Writing** at Capital Community College (**http://grammar.ccc.commnet.edu/grammar/faq.htm**). (If you don't see this link, try another link for a college or university site.)

4. The opening FAQ page displays the questions that are asked by students and visitors most frequently. Scroll down to see the entire listing.

5. Find a question that you have and click its link. Read the response. Press the **Back** button in your browser to access more questions and answers.

6. End your session.

7. Write a summary of what you learned on the site and submit it to your instructor.

▶▶ Chat About It

Your instructor may assign any of the following topics for you to discuss in class, in an online chat room, or on an online discussion board. Some of the discussion topics may require outside research. You may also be asked to read and respond to postings made by your classmates.

Discussion Topic 1: As Edward Sapir said in the chapter's opening quote, "One of the glories of English simplicity is the possibility of using the same word as noun and verb." Think of three words that can be used as both a noun and a verb. Write two complete sentences for each word—one showing the word used as a noun and one showing the word used as a verb. Share your six sentences with your classmates. Be prepared to give feedback on your classmates' sentences.

Discussion Topic 2: Think of three things you enjoy doing. Write a complete sentence for each activity, using the activity as a gerund in each sentence. Share your three sentences with your classmates; then read and give feedback on their sentences. Did they use gerunds properly?

Discussion Topic 3: Why do you think the active voice is called the "voice of business"? Why should most writing be done using active-voice verbs? When would passive voice, or the "voice of tact," be more appropriate? Think of two specific workplace examples in which passive voice would be preferred, and share these examples with your classmates.

Discussion Topic 4: Prior to studying this chapter, had you ever heard of the subjunctive mood? Had you ever used it when speaking or writing? Now that you have learned about the subjunctive mood, will you start to use it? Why or why not?

Discussion Topic 5: Meg Whitman, former CEO of eBay, said, "When people use your brand name as a verb, that is remarkable." A classic example is the delivery company FedEx, which began its history as Federal Express. Over time the company's name became so synonymous with delivery that people began to use *FedEx* as a verb (*I will FedEx that package to you first thing tomorrow*). In order to capitalize on this phenomenon, the company officially changed its name to FedEx in 2000. Think of another company's name or brand that is now used as a verb. Share the company or brand name and a brief history with your classmates.

Posttest

Underline the letter representing the correct answer.

1. In the sentence *He tasted the cookies while they were still warm*, the verb *tasted* is (a) an action verb, (b) a linking verb, (c) a helping verb.

2. In the sentence *The cookies tasted delicious*, the verb *tasted* is (a) action, (b) linking, (c) helping.

3. In the sentence *Ruth Gregory forwarded the e-mail message*, the verb *forwarded* is (a) transitive, (b) intransitive, (c) subjunctive, (d) passive.

4. In the sentence *Elizabeth Costello inspected three properties*, the verb *inspected* is in the (a) active voice, (b) passive voice, (c) subjunctive mood.

5. In the sentence *Dan Galvin was given the award*, the verb phrase *was given* is in the (a) active voice, (b) passive voice, (c) subjunctive mood.

6. If Felix Etti (a) was, (b) were the instructor, the class would be full.

7. The doctor recommended that Ruth (a) take, (b) takes a long vacation.

8. Our team celebrated (a) our, (b) us being awarded the contract.

9. Be sure (a) to, (b) and stop by when you are in town.

10. (a) Being as, (b) Because you just received a raise, let's celebrate!

1.a 2.b 3.a 4.a 5.b 6.b 7.a 8.a 9.a 10.b

"Nostalgia is like a grammar lesson: you find the present tense, but the past perfect!"

—Owens Lee Pomeroy, poet

Chapter **9**

Verb Tenses and Parts

OBJECTIVES

When you have completed the materials in this chapter, you will be able to do the following:

LEVEL 1
- Write verbs in the present, past, and future tenses correctly.
- Understand challenges with using primary tenses.

LEVEL 2
- Recognize and use present and past participles.
- Write the correct forms of irregular verbs.

LEVEL 3
- Recognize verb forms in the progressive tenses.
- Recognize verb forms in the perfect tenses.

Pretest

Underline the letter representing the correct answer.

1. In the sentence *Sonya yearned for the good old days*, the verb *yearned* is in the (a) present, (b) past, (c) future tense.

2. In the sentence *The actor Heath Ledger will receive a posthumous award*, the verb *will receive* is in the (a) present, (b) past, (c) future tense.

3. In the sentence *Every employee needs to complete the training by Friday*, the verb *needs* is in the (a) present, (b) past, (c) future tense.

4. In the sentence *Brad is flying to Detroit next week*, *is flying* is (a) past participle, (b) present participle.

5. In the sentence *The board of directors has declared a stock dividend*, *has declared* is (a) past participle, (b) present participle.

6. Virginia Brunnell (a) brought, (b) brung a colleague to the seminar with her.

7. If we had (a) gone, (b) went to the training class, we might have learned something.

8. The year-end financial statements are (a) laying, (b) lying on your desk.

9. Because prices are (a) raising, (b) rising, we should look for an apartment immediately.

10. The partially completed building has (a) set, (b) sat there untouched for a year.

After studying this chapter, which discusses verb tenses and parts, the preceding quote will make much more sense to you. To begin, you must know that English verbs change **form (inflection)** to indicate four ideas: (1) number (singular or plural); (2) person (first, second, or third); (3) voice (active or passive); and (4) tense (time).

In contrast to languages such as French and German, English verbs today are no longer heavily inflected. That is, our verbs do not change form extensively to indicate number or person. To indicate precise time, however, English uses three rather complex sets of tenses: primary tenses, perfect tenses, and progressive tenses. Level 1 focuses on the primary tenses and helping verbs. Level 2 considers participles and irregular verbs. Level 3 treats the progressive and perfect tenses.

Study Tip

If you are an ESL (English as a Second Language) student, try searching the Web for *ESL verbs*. You will find many links to sites offering learning tips and helpful exercises.

1.b 2.c 3.a 4.b 5.a 6.a 7.a 8.b 9.b 10.b

Primary Tenses

We will begin our discussion of verbs with the **primary tenses** (also called **simple tenses**). These tenses are used to indicate the present, the past, and the future.

Present Tense

Verbs in the **present tense** express current or habitual action. Present-tense verbs may also be used in constructions showing future action.

> We *celebrate* employees' birthdays once a month.
> (Current or habitual action)
>
> She *travels* to Barcelona next week. (Future action)

Past Tense

Trivia Tidbit

Verbs in the **past tense** show action that has been completed. Regular verbs form the past tense with the addition of *d* or *ed*.

> The CPAs *audited* our firm last month.
>
> The report *focused* on changes in our department.

In British English some regular verbs are made past tense by adding *t* instead of *ed*. For example, we say *learned*, but in Great Britain they say *learnt*. Other examples include *burned/ burnt*, *dreamed/dreamt*, *leaned/leant*, *leaped/leapt*, and *spelled/spelt*.

Future Tense

Verbs in the **future tense** show actions that are expected to occur at a later time. Traditionally, the helper verbs *shall* and *will* have been joined with principal verbs to express future tense. In business and professional writing today, however, the verb *will* is generally used as the helper to express future tense. Careful writers continue to use *shall* in appropriate first-person constructions (*I/We shall attend the meeting*).

> Researchers *will study* the effects of cell phone use on brain cells.
>
> You *will receive* the contract before June 5.

Study Tip

Shall is relatively extinct in North America, Scotland, and Ireland. In England, however, *shall* enjoys regular usage. For an interesting historical account, see *Merriam-Webster's Dictionary of English Usage*.

Summary of Primary Tenses

The following table summarizes the various forms that express the primary tenses:

	Present Tense		Past Tense		Future Tense	
	Sing.	Plural	Sing.	Plural	Sing.	Plural
First Person:	I need	we need	I needed	we needed	I will need	we will need
Second Person:	you need	you need	you needed	you needed	you will need	you will need
Third Person:	he, she, it, needs	they need	he, she, it needed	they needed	he, she, it will need	they will need

Challenges Using Primary Tenses

Most adult speakers of our language have few problems using present, past, and future tenses. A few considerations, however, merit mention.

Using the -s Form Verbs

Note that third-person singular verbs require an -s ending (*he needs*). Therefore, whenever your subject is singular (other than *I* or *you*), you will add an *s* to the present-tense form of the verb. Add *es* if the verb ends in *s*, *sh*, *ch*, *x*, or *z*.

> She *works* for a large corporation. (Not *work*)
>
> This printer *breaks* down too often. (Not *break*)
>
> Barry *searches* his house for his missing car keys. (Not *search*)

Expressing "Timeless" Facts

Present-tense verbs are used to express "timeless" facts, even if these verbs occur in sentences with other past-tense verbs.

> What *is* the name of the customer who called yesterday? (Not *was*)
>
> Joan Brault's maiden name *is* Haitz. (Not *was*)
>
> What did you say his duties *are*? (Not *were*, if he continues to perform these duties)

Spelling Verbs That Change Form

Use a dictionary to verify spelling of verbs that change form. You must be particularly careful in spelling verbs ending in *y* (*hurry, hurries, hurried*) and verbs for which the final consonant is doubled (*occurred, expelled*).

> Now complete the reinforcement exercises for Level 1.

LEVEL 2

Present and Past Participles

To be able to use all the tenses of verbs correctly, you must understand the four principal parts of verbs: present, past, present participle, and past participle. You have already studied the present and past forms. Now, let's consider the participles.

Present Participle

The **present participle** of regular and irregular verbs is formed by adding *ing* to the present tense of the verb. The present participle must be preceded by one or more helping verbs, which are usually forms of *be* such as *am, is, are, was, were, be,* and *been*.

```
Helping verb   Present participle
       ↓          ↓
  Leanne is studying in South Africa.
```

```
Helping verb   Present participle
       ↓          ↓
  You are doing a fine job.
```

Past Participle

The **past participle** of a regular verb is formed by adding a *d* or *ed* to the present tense of the verb. (As you will learn in the next section, irregular verbs form their past participle differently.) Like present participles, past participles must combine with one or more helping verbs, which are usually forms of *to have,* such as *has, had,* or *have*:

Helping verb   Past participle
↓   ↓

Mark *has applied* for the scholarship.

Helping verbs   Past participle
↓   ↓

The figures *have been checked* by his supervisor.

Helping verb   Past participle
↓   ↓

The Iannuccis *have built* a cabin on the lake.

Irregular Verbs

Up to this point, we have considered only regular verbs. Regular verbs form the past tense by the addition of *d* or *ed* to the present tense form. **Irregular verbs**, however, form the past tense by varying the root vowel and, commonly, adding *en* to the past participle. A list of the more frequently used irregular verbs follows. Learn the forms of these verbs by practicing in patterns such as the following:

Present Tense:	Today I <u>drive</u>.
Past Tense:	Yesterday I <u>drove</u>.
Future Tense:	Tomorrow I <u>will drive</u>.
Past Participle:	In the past I have <u>driven</u>.
Present Participle:	Next week I <u>am driving</u>.

Frequently Used Irregular Verbs

Career Tip

In employment interviews, recruiters listen carefully to a candidate's spoken English. One quick way to be eliminated is to substitute a verb past tense for a past participle. INCORRECT: *He come over last night* or *I seen them.*

Present	Past	Past Participle	Present Participle
arise	arose	arisen	arising
be (am, is, are)	was, were	been	being
become	became	become	becoming
begin	began	begun	beginning
bite	bit	bitten	biting
blow	blew	blown	blowing
break	broke	broken	breaking
bring	brought	brought	bringing
build	built	built	building
burst	burst	burst	bursting
buy	bought	bought	buying
catch	caught	caught	catching
choose	chose	chosen	choosing
come	came	come	coming

Present	Past	Past Participle	Present Participle
dig	dug	dug	digging
do	did	done	doing
draw	drew	drawn	drawing
drink	drank	drunk	drinking
drive	drove	driven	driving
eat	ate	eaten	eating
fall	fell	fallen	falling
fight	fought	fought	fighting
fly	flew	flown	flying
forget	forgot	forgotten *or* forgot	forgetting
forgive	forgave	forgiven	forgiving
freeze	froze	frozen	freezing
get	got	gotten *or* got	getting
give	gave	given	giving
go	went	gone	going
grow	grew	grown	growing
hang (an object)	hung	hung	hanging
hang (a person)	hanged	hanged	hanging
hide	hid	hidden *or* hid	hiding
know	knew	known	knowing
lay (to place)	laid	laid	laying
lead	led	led	leading
leave	left	left	leaving
lend	lent	lent	lending
lie (to rest)	lay	lain	lying
lie (to tell a falsehood)	lied	lied	lying
lose	lost	lost	losing
make	made	made	making
pay	paid	paid	paying
prove	proved	proved *or* proven	proving
ride	rode	ridden	riding
ring	rang	rung	ringing
rise (to move up)	rose	risen	rising
run	ran	run	running
see	saw	seen	seeing
set (to place)	set	set	setting

Study Tip

When you look an irregular verb up in the dictionary, the dictionary will generally show its tenses in this order: past, past participle, present participle.

Present	Past	Past Participle	Present Participle
shake	shook	shaken	shaking
shrink	shrank	shrunk	shrinking
sing	sang	sung	singing
sink	sank	sunk	sinking
sit (to rest)	sat	sat	sitting
speak	spoke	spoken	speaking
spring	sprang	sprung	springing
steal	stole	stolen	stealing
strike	struck	struck *or* stricken	striking
swear	swore	sworn	swearing
swim	swam	swum	swimming
take	took	taken	taking
teach	taught	taught	teaching
tear	tore	torn	tearing
throw	threw	thrown	throwing
wake	woke	woken	waking
wear	wore	worn	wearing
write	wrote	written	writing

Three Pairs of Frequently Misused Irregular Verbs

Three pairs of verbs often cause confusion: *lie–lay, sit–set,* and *raise–rise.* The secret to using them correctly lies in (a) recognizing their tense forms and (b) knowing whether they are transitive or intransitive. Recall that transitive verbs require objects; intransitive verbs do not.

Lie–Lay

These two verbs are confusing because the past tense of *lie* is spelled in the same way that the present tense of *lay* is spelled. To be safe, memorize these verb forms:

	Present	Past	Past Participle	Present Participle
Intransitive:	lie (to rest)	lay	lain	lying
Transitive:	lay (to place)	laid (not *layed*)	laid	laying

The verb *lie* is intransitive; therefore, it requires no direct object to complete its meaning.

> I *lie* down for a nap every afternoon. (Present tense. Note that *down* is not a direct object.)

> "*Lie* down," Mark told his dog. (Commands are given in the present tense.)

Study Tip

Whenever you use *lay* in the sense of "placing" something, you must provide a receiver of the action: Try asking yourself "Lay what?" *Please lay the book down (lay what? the book).* If nothing receives the action, you probably want the verb *lie,* which means "resting."

Tomorrow I *will lie* down for a nap after lunch. (Future tense)

Yesterday I *lay* down for a nap. (Past tense)

The originals *have lain* in the copy machine for some time. (Past participle)

The contract *is lying* on the desk. (Present participle)

The verb *lay* is transitive and must have a direct object to complete its meaning. The objects in the following sentences have been underlined.

Watch me *lay* three <u>cards</u> down in this round. (Present tense)

Lay the <u>report</u> over there. (Command in the present tense)

We *will lay* new <u>tile</u> in the reception area. (Future tense)

He *laid* the <u>handouts</u> on the conference table. (Past tense)

He *has laid* <u>bricks</u> all his life. (Past participle)

The contractor *is laying* new <u>flooring</u> in the kitchen. (Present participle)

Sit–Set

Less troublesome than *lie–lay*, the combination of *sit–set* is nevertheless perplexing because the sounds of the verbs are similar. The intransitive verb *sit* (past tense, *sat;* past participle, *sat*) means "to rest" and requires no direct object.

I like to *sit* in the front row in class. (Present tense)

They *sat* in the theater through the closing credits. (Past tense)

Max *will sit* in Row 39 on Flight 880. (Future tense)

They *had sat* in the waiting room for two hours before they decided to leave. (Past participle)

Are you usually *sitting* here in the morning? (Present participle)

The transitive verb *set* (past tense, *set;* past participle, *set*) means "to place" and must have a direct object. The objects in the following sentences have been underlined.

Letty usually *sets* her coffee <u>mug</u> there. (Present tense)

We *set* a <u>vase</u> of flowers on the receptionist's desk. (Past tense)

We *will set* the <u>table</u> shortly before our guests arrive. (Future tense)

The CEO *had set* the <u>deadline</u> before conferring with his employees. (Past participle)

The committee *is setting* the ground <u>rules</u>. (Present participle)

Rise–Raise

The intransitive verb *rise* (past tense, *rose;* past participle, *risen*) means "to go up" or "to ascend" and requires no direct object.

The sun *rises* every morning in the east. (Present tense. *Every morning* is an adverbial phrase, not an object.)

The president *rose* from her chair to greet us. (Past tense)

The sun *will rise* tomorrow morning at 5:39 a.m. (Future tense)

The room temperature *has risen* steadily since the meeting began. (Past participle)

Our elevator *is rising* to the seventh floor. (Present participle)

Study Tip

To help you remember that these verbs are intransitive, look at the second letter of each:
l*i*e
s*i*t
r*i*se
Associate *i* with *i*ntransitive.

Trivia Tidbit

The English word with the most definitions is *set*. This word can be used as a noun, a verb, or an adjective.

The transitive verb *raise* (past tense, *raised;* past participle, *raised*) means "to lift up" or "to elevate" and must have a direct object. The objects in the following sentences have been underlined.

> Please *raise* the window. (Present tense)
>
> The nonprofit organization *raised* needed funds during its annual event. (Past tense)
>
> The restaurant *will raise* prices next month. (Future tense)
>
> Airlines *have raised* fares over the past year. (Past participle)
>
> AT&T *is raising* prices next month. (Present participle)

Now complete the reinforcement exercises for Level 2.

LEVEL 3

Progressive and Perfect Tenses

Thus far in this chapter, you have studied the primary tenses and irregular verbs. The remainder of this chapter focuses on two additional sets of verb tenses: the perfect and the progressive. Most native speakers and writers of English have little difficulty controlling these verb forms because they have frequently heard them used correctly. This largely descriptive section is thus presented for those who are not native speakers and for those who are eager to study the entire range of verb tenses.

Progressive Tenses

The **progressive tenses** are used to show continuous or repeated actions. The **present-progressive tense** describes ongoing actions that are happening presently. The **past-progressive tense** describes ongoing actions that occurred in the past, usually as another action was taking place. The **future-progressive tense** describes ongoing actions that will take place in the future. Form the progressive tenses by adding a form of *to be* to the present participle (*-ing*) form of a verb, as you can see in the following table.

Present-Progressive Tense		
First Person	**Second Person**	**Third Person**
I am hearing	you are hearing	he, she, it is hearing
we are hearing		they are hearing

Past-Progressive Tense		
First Person	**Second Person**	**Third Person**
I was hearing	you were hearing	he, she, it was hearing
we were hearing		they were hearing

Future-Progressive Tense		
First Person	**Second Person**	**Third Person**
I will be hearing	you will be hearing	he, she, it will be hearing
we will be hearing		they will be hearing

VERB TENSES AND PARTS

We *are importing* many of our products from China. (Present-progressive tense expresses action in progress.)

We *were sitting* down to dinner when we lost power. (Past-progressive tense indicates action that was begun in the past.)

They *will be receiving* the announcement shortly. (Future-progressive tense indicates action in the future.)

Perfect Tenses

The **perfect tenses** are used to show actions that are already completed, or *perfected*. The **present-perfect tense** describes actions that began in the past and have continued to the present. The **past-perfect tense** describes past actions that took place before other past actions. The **future-perfect tense** describes actions that will take place before other future actions. Form progressive tenses by adding a form of *to have* to the past participle form of a verb, as you can see in the following table.

Present-Perfect Tense		
First Person	**Second Person**	**Third Person**
I have heard	you have heard	he, she, it has heard
we have heard		they have heard

Past-Perfect Tense		
First Person	**Second Person**	**Third Person**
I had heard	you had heard	he, she, it had heard
we had heard		they had heard

Future-Perfect Tense		
First Person	**Second Person**	**Third Person**
I will have heard	you will have heard	he, she, it will have heard
we will have heard		

The national debt *has increased* substantially. (Present-perfect tense expresses action just completed, or *perfected*.)

The check *had cleared* the bank before I canceled payment. (Past-perfect tense shows an action finished before another action in the past.)

The polls *will have been closed* two hours when the results are telecast. (Future-perfect tense indicates action that will be completed before another future action.)

Now complete the reinforcement exercises for Level 3.

Spot the BLOOPER

Using the skills you are learning in this class, try to identify why the following items are bloopers. Consult your textbook, dictionary, or reference manual as needed.

Blooper 1: On the Fox Sports Web site, describing the competition for the Most Valuable Player trophy in the Pro Bowl: "The honor could have went to Terrell Owens, who caught two TD passes."

Blooper 2: An article in *The New York Times* reporting that the firing of Merrill Lynch's chair and CEO was partly because of the company's depressed stock price: "Last week, the stock sunk to as low as $59 a share."

Blooper 3: Headline in the *Cincinnati Enquirer*: "Europe lays low, hopes U.S. can mediate with Russia."

Blooper 4: Question asked in the Hartwell Sun [Georgia]: "How will possible layoffs effect the Hart County School System?"

Blooper 5: In the program for the Florida Center for the Books theatrical production of *Papa*, a play about Ernest Hemingway: "[the director] received her principle theatrical education at Yale University."

Blooper 6: In a job applicant's cover letter: "I had strong interpersonal and communication skills."

Blooper 7: From an article in the auto industry newspaper *AutoMotive*: "[The Ford F-150 pickup truck] is showing no signs of loosing its number one sales crown."

Blooper 8: From a *Parade* magazine cover: "She [Keira Knightley] shined in the hit films *Bend It Like Beckham* and *Pirates of the Caribbean*."

Blooper 9: From *The Arizona Republic*: "The great tree uprooted the back fence, causing it to raise 5 feet in the air."

Blooper 10: From an article in London's *Sunday Mail* about soccer great David Beckham, in which he discusses being baffled by his seven-year-old son's math homework: "It's done totally differently to what I was teached at school."

Question	**Answer**
Q: As a command, which is correct: *lay down* or *lie down*?	**A:** Commands are given in the present tense. You would never tell someone to *Closed the door* because commands are not given in the past tense. To say *Lay down* (which is the past-tense form of *lie*) is the same as saying *Closed the door*. Therefore, use the present tense: *Lie down*.
Q: We have a new e-mail program, and one of its functions is "messaging" people. When folks say, *I will message you*, it really grates on my nerves. Is this correct?	**A:** *Messaging* is certainly a popular term with the explosion of e-mail, instant messaging, and text messaging. As to its correctness, what we are seeing here is language in the act of evolving. A noun (*message*) has been converted to a verb. Converting nouns into verbs is common in English. It is called *verbing* (he *cornered* the market, we *tabled* the motion, I *penciled* it in on my calendar, the farmer *trucked* the vegetables to market). Actually, *message* was sometimes used as a verb over a century ago (in 1896 *the bill was messaged over from the house*). However, its recent use has been almost exclusively as a noun. Today, it is increasingly being used again as a verb. New uses of words usually become legitimate when the words fill a need and are immediately accepted. Some word uses, though, appear to be mere fads, such as *The homeless child could not language her fears*. Forcing the noun *language* to function as a verb is unnecessary since a good word already exists for the purpose: *express*. But other "nouns-made-verbs" have been in use long enough to sound reasonable: I *faxed* the document, he *videotaped* the program, she *keyed* the report.
Q: I'm embarrassed to ask this because I should know the answer—but I don't. Is there an apostrophe in this: *its relevance to our program?*	**A:** No. Use an apostrophe only for the contraction *it's*, meaning "it is" or "it has" (*it's a good plan; it's been nice knowing you*). The possessive pronoun *its*, as used in your example, has no apostrophe (*the car had its oil changed*).
Q: I thought I knew the difference between *principal* and *principle*, but now I'm not so sure. In a report from management, I saw this: *The principal findings of the market research are negative.* I thought *principal* always meant your "pal," the school principal.	**A:** You're partly right and partly wrong. *Principal* may be used as a noun meaning "chief" or "head person." In addition, it may be used as an adjective to mean "chief" or "main." This is the meaning most people forget, and this is the meaning of the word in your sentence. The word *principle* means a "law" or "rule." Perhaps it is easiest to remember *principle = rule*. All other uses require *principal*: the *principal* of the school, the *principal* of the loan, the *principal* reason.
Q: Even when I use a dictionary, I can't tell the difference between *affect* and *effect*. What should the word be in this sentence? *Changes in personnel (affected/effected) our production this month.*	**A:** No words generate more confusion than do *affect* and *effect*. In your sentence use *affected*. Let's see if we can resolve the *affect/effect* dilemma. *Affect* is a verb meaning "to influence" (*smoking affects health; government policies affect citizens*). *Affect* may also mean "to pretend or imitate" (*he affected a British accent*). *Effect* can be a noun or a verb. As a noun, it means "result" (*the effect of the law is slight*). As a verb (and here's the troublesome part) *effect* means "to produce a result" (*small cars effect gasoline savings; GM effected a new pricing policy*).

Question	Answer
Q: My son is studying a foreign language; and he asked me, an English teacher, why we capitalize the personal pronoun *I* in English when we don't capitalize other pronouns.	**A:** That's a fascinating topic, and a little research on the Web revealed that linguists ponder the same question. In a linguistic journal, linguists discussed some relevant theories. One linguist thought that perhaps the lowercase *i* was too easily confused with the number *1* or with similar looking *i*'s, *u*'s, and *v*'s in medieval handwriting. Another attributed the word's capital letter to our egocentric nature. Another suggested that because the pronoun *I* usually appeared as the first word in a sentence, it was capitalized for that reason. In earlier centuries, before the language was standardized, most nouns and pronouns were capitalized haphazardly. One linguist thought that a better question to ask would be why all of the other pronouns lost their capital letters and *I* retained its.
Q: Help! How do I write *fax*? Small letters? Capital letters? Periods? And is it proper to use it as a verb, such as *May we fax the material to you?*	**A:** The shortened form of *facsimile* is *fax*, written in small letters without periods. Yes, it may be used as a verb, as you did in your sentence.
Q: I'm confused. What is the correct spelling: *all together* or *altogether*? I can never remember whether it's one word or two.	**A:** It depends on how you're using the word. When spelled as one word, *altogether* means "completely or as a whole" (*Altogether we spent $400 on our vacation*). When spelled as two words, *all together* means "gathered in one location or all acting collectively" (*The committee members were all together in one room*).
Q: When should I write *cannot* as one word, and when should I write it as two words?	**A:** The word *cannot* is always written as one word.
Q: Can you help me? I just wrote this sentence: *She is suppose to place the order tomorrow.* Is there something wrong with it?	**A:** Yes, you should have used *supposed* instead of *suppose*. The verb *suppose* means to "lay down tentatively," or "to hold as an opinion" (*We suppose you might get a raise*). The adjective *supposed* means "something intended" (*I was supposed to call my mom today*). Here is a trick: If the word *to* follows this word, use *supposed*.

9

Reinforcement Exercises

LEVEL 1

Online Homework Help! For immediate feedback on odd-numbered items, go to **www.meguffey.com**.

A. (Self-check) Select the correct verb. Use your dictionary to verify spelling if necessary.

1. She (write, writes) dozens of e-mail messages daily.   _____

2. The bank (denyed, denied) our loan application.   _____

3. What (is, was) the name of eBay's former CEO?   _____

4. An increase in sales of vinyl record albums (occured, occurred) just as CD sales started to decrease.   _____

5. Alexandra knew that the distance between Atlanta and New Orleans (is, was) 470 miles.   _____

6. The researcher (tried, tryed) to get her findings published.   _____

7. What (is, was) your maiden name?   _____

8. Complaints are (refered, referred) to our Customer Service Department.   _____

9. An interviewer (need, needs) to treat job applicants with respect.   _____

10. The salespeople who called this morning said that they (be, are, were) with Taylor, Inc.   _____

Check your answers below.

B. Writing Exercise. In the following sentences, provide three tenses for each verb.

Example: He (arrive) at the office at 7:45 a.m.

            Past <u>arrived</u>   Present <u>arrives</u>   Future <u>will arrive</u>

1. A dental clinic (open) in our local supermarket.

    Past _____   Present _____   Future _____

2. Our supervisor (copy) us on every e-mail message related to the pending merger.

    Past _____   Present _____   Future _____

3. Samantha (hurry) to catch the early train.

    Past _____   Present _____   Future _____

4. Jason (try) to improve his writing skills.

    Past _____   Present _____   Future _____

5. Judy Reinman (cover) the same material in her class.

    Past _____   Present _____   Future _____

1. writes 2. denied 3. is 4. occurred 5. is 6. tried 7. is 8. referred 9. needs 10. are

6. Monsanto (label) its plastic soft-drink bottle.

Past _____   Present _____   Future _____

7. Courtney (plan) to major in finance.

Past _____   Present _____   Future _____

8. The local community college (invest) in child-care facilities for student parents.

Past _____   Present _____   Future _____

9. Interviewers (prefer) candidates with excellent communication skills.

Past _____   Present _____   Future _____

10. Questionnaires (sample) customers' reactions to our new product.

Past _____   Present _____   Future _____

    C. Writing Exercise. Compose sentences using the verbs shown.

1. (Present tense of *fly*) _____

2. (Past tense of *apply*) _____

3. (Future tense of *study*) _____

4. (Present tense of *learn*) _____

5. (Past tense of *cancel*) _____

6. (Future tense of *change*) _____

7. (Present tense of *buy*) _____

8. (Past tense of *trim*) _____

9. (Future tense of *enclose*) _____

10. (Past tense of *stir*) _____

LEVEL 2

    A. (Self-check) Write the correct verb. Do not add a helping verb.

Example: Mauricio should have (eat) before he left.   eaten _____

1. Darla Cullen has (teach) business courses for many years. _____

2. Have you (see) the new Clint Eastwood film? _____

3. They have (fly) over Kauai's Na Pali Coast in a helicopter. _____

4. Yesterday IBM (break) the news that it will lay off 4,600 employees. _____

5. Our e-mail and Web-use policy was (write) by Leslie Leong. _____

6. This morning's mild earthquake (shake) the windows in the conference room. _____

7. Over the past year, Dr. Deborah Kerlin (give) freely of her services. _____

8. Have you (speak) with the supervisor yet? _____

9. A person who shops in thrift stores is (know) as a "recessionista." _____

10. All employees should have (go) to the emergency procedures demonstration. _____

Check your answers below.

1. taught 2. seen 3. flown 4. broke 5. written 6. shook 7. gave 8. spoken 9. known 10. gone

B. In the spaces provided, indicate whether the italicized verbs are (*a*) present participle or (*b*) past participle.

Example: The federal government *is using* the Web to communicate with citizens. _____a_____

1. The government *has bypassed* the media to speak directly to the public. _____

2. Obama *is building* the largest online network ever seen in politics. _____

3. Experts *are watching* the White House Web site to ensure it doesn't become too political. _____

4. Many people *have indicated* that they like the changes. _____

5. Students *are preparing* for their freshman year at college. _____

6. Many students *have packed* the basics, including clothing, shower totes, and books. _____

7. Some students *are packing* flat-screen TVs, laptops with Wi-Fi, and espresso machines. _____

8. Investors from the U.S. *are benefiting* from Italy's emerging biotechnology sector. _____

9. Italy *has become* home to more than 220 biotechnology companies. _____

10. Many of Italy's biotechnology companies *have gone* public. _____

C. Underline any verb errors you find in the following sentences. Write the correct forms in the spaces provided. Do not add helping verbs or change the verb tense. Each sentence has one error. Write *C* if the sentence is correct as it stands.

Example: The witness <u>sweared</u> that he had seen the defendant the night of the robbery. _____swore_____

1. Ruth has chose to relocate to Chicago. _____

2. The world has shrank considerably as a result of new communication technologies. _____

3. Candace buyed a Vespa so that she could get around the city more easily. _____

4. Because stock prices had sank to an all-time low, many investors decided to purchase safe government bonds. _____

5. Blogs have became an important marketing tool for many businesses. _____

6. Some observers claim that Mark Zuckerberg stealed the idea for Facebook from his classmates. _____

7. Many people have took a course called "The Seven Principles of Public Speaking" to learn how to speak like Barack Obama. _____

8. We should have threw out that old printer long ago. _____

9. She payed a premium to get a copy of the book signed by the author. _____

10. The accounting fraud investigation leaded to several arrests. _____

11. In the late 1800s, women fighted for their right to vote. _____

12. The telephone has rang only twice in the past hour. _____

13. I can't believe Allison brang her dog to work. _____

14. Howling winds blowed all day, making outside work difficult. _____

15. The first pitch of the season was threw out by the president. _____

D. Lie–Lay. Write the correct forms of the verb.

Present	Past	Past Participle	Present Participle
lie (to rest):	lay	lain	lying
lay (to place):	laid	laid	laying

Select the correct verb.

1. If a book will not (lay, lie) flat, do not use force to open it further. _____

2. Norma had to (lay, lie) down until the dizziness passed. _____

3. Stacy (layed, laid) the mail on Ms. Tong's desk. _____

4. The contracts have been (lying, laying) in her in-box for some time. _____

5. In fact, they had (laid, lain) there for more than a week. _____

6. Newman told his dog to (lay, lie) down. _____

7. Please (lay, lie) your hand on the bible and take the oath. _____

8. Last night she (lay, laid) on the couch for hours watching old movies. _____

9. Some people risk getting skin cancer because they insist on (laying, lying) in the sun. _____

10. Shops in Broadway Plaza are (laying, lying) plans for the holiday season. _____

 E. Sit–Set; Rise–Raise. Write the correct forms of the verbs.

Present	Past	Past Participle	Present Participle
sit (to rest):	sat	sat	sitting
set (to place):	set	set	setting
rise (to go up):	rose	risen	rising
raise (to lift):	raised	raised	raising

Select the correct verb.

1. One important goal of the Susan G. Komen for the Cure organization is to (raise, rise) funds to fight breast cancer. _____

2. Alex always tries to (sit, set) next to the CEO during meetings. _____

3. Close the windows if you want to (raise, rise) the temperature in the room. _____

4. My temperature (raises, rises) when I exercise vigorously. _____

5. Have you been (sitting, setting) goals for your future? _____

6. Consumer prices are (rising, raising) faster than consumer income. _____

7. Brenda Woodward (raised, rose) the question of retroactive benefits. _____

8. Please (sit, set) your briefcase on the table for inspection. _____

9. Our office building (sits, sets) on the corner of Front and Pine. _____

10. The world literacy rate has (risen, raised) over the past few decades, especially for women. _____

F. Writing Exercise. Compose original sentences using the verbs shown. Add helping verbs as needed.

1. drawn _____

2. lent _____

3. sung _____

4. caught _____

5. blown _____

6. torn _____

7. drank _____

8. forgiven _____

9. driven _____

10. arose _____

LEVEL 3

A. (Self-check) Verbs in the following sentences have been italicized. In the space provided, indicate the tense of these verbs. Refer to the progressive- and perfect-tense tables in Level 3 to guide you.

Example: We *had recovered* your credit cards by the time you reported the loss.   past perfect _____

1. Our supervisor *will have made* a decision by the end of the month. _____

2. We are impressed by what we *are hearing*. _____

3. The media *will have reported* news of the layoffs before we are able to inform employees. _____

4. A design team *is modifying* our Web site to make it more accessible to the disabled. _____

5. Pierre Omidyar *had hired* Meg Whitman to revitalize eBay. _____

6. We *have* just *seen* the changes made to the Zappos Web site. _____

7. All employees *have followed* the manager's suggestions for increasing recycling. _____

8. We *will be seeing* increased security measures at the airport. _____

9. Gay Osterello *has worked* for John Muir Hospital for three decades. _____

10. We *are* now *experiencing* the effects of the last cutback. _____

Check your answers below.

_____ect 2. present progressive 3. future perfect 4. present progressive 5. past perfect 6. present · present perfect 8. future progressive 9. present perfect 10. present progressive

VERB TENSES AND PARTS   CHAP

B. Write the proper verb form.

Example: She (apply) with dozens of companies before finding the
perfect job. (Past perfect)   had applied

1. We (learn) that 11 percent of online adults use Twitter, Facebook, or
   other services to post status updates about their activities or thoughts.
   (Present perfect)   _____

2. We (anticipate) that this type of microblogging will continue to
   increase in the future. (Present progressive) _____

3. By the time the sun came up, William (do) four laps around the track.
   (Past perfect) _____

4. When her dean called, Glenda Flowers (get) ready for her next class.
   (Past progressive) _____

5. By the end of the year, Buffalo Wings and Rings (open) nine
   restaurants near college campuses. (Future perfect) _____

6. Our company (think) about offering on-site child care.
   (Present progressive) _____

7. Check to see whether they (receive) the signed contracts.
   (Present perfect) _____

8. By 5 p.m. we (finish) the contract and faxed it to our client.
   (Past perfect) _____

9. I (interview) with three companies next week. (Future progressive) _____

10. You (arrive) in Shanghai before I even board my flight. (Future perfect) _____

C. Review. These sentences review Chapters 1 through 9. In the space provided, write the
correct answer choice.

1. The number of spam messages has (a) rose, (b) risen, (c) raised steadily
   over the past few years. _____

2. Although Bill Gates dropped out of college, he has successfully (a) run,
   (b) ran a major corporation for years. _____

3. Jeff and (a) myself, (b) me, (c) I would have attended the conference
   if we had been reimbursed for travel expenses. _____

4. The company hid (a) its, (b) it's losses by inflating sales. _____

5. Every employee must name a beneficiary on (a) his, (b) his or her,
   (c) their life insurance forms. _____

6. During its first month of operation, the recycling program has (a) broken,
   (b) broke records for reducing waste. _____

7. Everyone except Helen Costigan and (a) myself, (b) me, (c) I was impressed
   by the month's recycling profits. _____

8. Many larger facilities can recycle at no net cost because (a) there, (b) they're, (c) their haulers are taking away less trash. _____

9. How long have you known that (a) your, (b) you're application was accepted? _____

10. Lorraine Ganz's contract, which is (a) laying, (b) lying, (c) lain on the desk, must be delivered immediately. _____

11. The joint meeting (a) began, (b) begun before the four CEOs arrived. _____

12. Not one of the job candidates whom we interviewed has (a) written, (b) wrote, (c) writed a thank-you letter. _____

13. Although I told James's dog to (a) lay, (b) lie down, it jumped up and knocked me over. _____

14. Maxwell has (a) wore, (b) worn the same suit to the last four interviews. _____

15. You should have (a) seen, (b) saw the e-mails sent to the manager and me. _____

16. The product's quality had (a) sank, (b) sunk so low in the eyes of consumers that it was removed from store shelves. _____

17. Research shows that U.S. employers will (a) lost, (b) loose, (c) lose about $994 billion to fraud this year. _____

18. (a) Us, (b) We employees need to work hard to make sure we don't miss this opportunity. _____

19. Cheryl said she (a) seen, (b) saw, (c) sawed you and him at Steven's party. _____

20. Because of an electrical malfunction, the temperature in the office had (a) risen, (b) raised to 95 degrees. _____

D. FAQs About Business English Review. In the space provided, write the correct answer choice.

1. The owners plan to sell the company and all of (a) its, (b) it's assets. _____

2. The (a) principle, (b) principal difference between a bear and a bull market is simple. _____

3. When stocks are falling, the end (a) effect, (b) affect is a "bear," or downward, market. _____

4. Rising stocks (a) effect, (b) affect a market differently; when stocks are increasing, it is a "bull" market. _____

5. We have an (a) all together, (b) altogether different situation here. _____

6. Because he is a person with high (a) principals, (b) principles, he refused the free trip to Hawaii. _____

7. We are (a) suppose, (b) supposed to earn a bonus at the end of the year. _____

8. We (a) cannot, (b) can not issue a cash refund for these returned items. _____

9. The employees were standing (a) all together, (b) altogether at the back of the auditorium. _____

10. You must (a) Fax, (b) fax a signed contract to close the deal. _____

▶▶ Learning Web Ways

Much of your communication on the job will involve e-mail; therefore, it is essential that you use e-mail effectively and professionally. This exercise will allow you to learn about Internet etiquette, or *netiquette*.

Goal: To learn about professional e-mail netiquette.

1. In the address bar of your Web browser, key the following URL: **http://www .albion.com/netiquette/**.

2. Read "The Core Rules of Netiquette" section. Use the **Next** link to move from rule to rule. When finished, return to the Netiquette home page by clicking **Netiquette** at the bottom of the page.

3. Test your netiquette knowledge by taking the Netiquette quiz.

4. Print the page showing your quiz results, end your session, and submit your printout to your instructor.

▶▶ Chat About It

Your instructor may assign any of the following topics for you to discuss in class, in an online chat room, or on an online discussion board. Some of the discussion topics may require outside research. You may also be asked to read and respond to postings made by your classmates.

Discussion Topic 1: Some people say that you will know you are fluent in a language when two things happen: (1) you start dreaming in it and (2) you are able to conjugate its verbs. To conjugate a verb means to make a systematic list of the various forms of a verb. Do you agree with this assertion about fluency? Why or why not? Share any experiences you have had learning a new language.

Discussion Topic 2: Bertha von Suttner, the first woman to win the Nobel Peace Prize, said, "After the verb *to love*, *to help* is the most beautiful verb in the world." What do you think is the most beautiful verb in the world and why? Share your thoughts with your classmates.

Discussion Topic 3: Select a language other than English and do research to find out how verbs are used. Does the language have regular and irregular verbs? How are various verb tenses formed? Share your findings with your classmates. Be sure to cite your sources.

Discussion Topic 4: William Safire, a columnist for *The New York Times* and a regular contributor to the "On Language" column in the *New York Times Magazine*, said, "Only in grammar can you be more than perfect." Now that you have studied Chapter 9, what does this statement mean to you? Share your thoughts with your classmates.

Discussion Topic 5: This chapter's opening quotation by the poet Owens Lee Pomeroy stated that "Nostalgia is like a grammar lesson: you find the present tense, but the past perfect!" Now that you have studied Chapter 9, what does this quote mean to you? Share your interpretation of this quote with your classmates.

Posttest

Underline the letter representing the correct answer.

1. In the sentence *Brett will apply for the medical clerk position*, the verb *will apply* is in the (a) present, (b) past, (c) future tense.

2. In the sentence *Melanie joined Toastmasters International to improve her speaking skills*, the verb *joined* is in the (a) present, (b) past, (c) future tense.

3. In the sentence *One quarter of Americans eat fast food every day*, the verb *eat* is in the (a) present, (b) past, (c) future tense.

4. In the sentence *One in eight Americans has worked at a fast-food restaurant, has worked* is (a) past participle, (b) present participle.

5. In the sentence *Sally is bringing home pizza for dinner tonight, is bringing* is (a) past participle, (b) present participle.

6. If you had (a) saw, (b) seen how professional she looked, you would have been impressed too.

7. Your telephone has (a) rung, (b) rang only twice while you were gone.

8. How long has this report been (a) laying, (b) lying on your desk?

9. Have you (a) payed, (b) paid the invoice yet?

10. Tony has (a) worn, (b) wore the same shirt every day this week.

1. c 2. b 3. a 4. a 5. b 6. b 7. a 8. b 9. b 10. a

"The beautiful part of writing is that you don't have to get it right the first time, unlike, say, a brain surgeon."

—Robert Cormier, writer

Chapter **10**

Subject–Verb Agreement

OBJECTIVES

When you have completed the materials in this chapter, you will be able to do the following:

LEVEL 1
- Locate the subjects of verbs despite prepositional phrases, intervening elements, and inverted sentence structure.
- Make verbs agree with subjects joined by *and*, with company and organization names, and with titles.

LEVEL 2
- Make verbs agree with subjects joined by *or* or *nor*.
- Select the correct verbs to agree with indefinite pronouns and collective nouns.

LEVEL 3
- Make verbs agree with *a number/the number*, quantities and measures, fractions and portions, and *who* and *that* clauses.
- Achieve subject–verb agreement with phrases and clauses as subjects and with subject complements.

Underline the letter representing the correct answer.

1. There (a) is, (b) are six items on today's agenda.

2. The professor and her students (a) is, (b) are visiting the Federal Reserve tomorrow.

3. McDonald's (a) has, (b) have seen an increase in sales.

4. One of the plant supervisors (a) plan (b) plans to implement a new safety program.

5. The head surgeon, along with her entire operating room team, (a) was, (b) were given training on the newest laser technology.

6. Neither the supervisor nor members of his team (a) is, (b) are satisfied with the level of service.

7. Neither the members of his team nor the supervisor (a) is, (b) are satisfied with the level of service.

8. Everyone (a) is, (b) are welcome to attend the grand-opening ceremony.

9. The team (a) has, (b) have developed a new marketing plan.

10. The number of e-mail messages (a) is, (b) are increasing daily.

Writing isn't brain surgery, but at times it can seem every bit as difficult. Fortunately, you have the ability to edit your writing. One important item to test for during editing is subject–verb agreement. Subjects must agree with verbs in number and person. Beginning a sentence with *He don't* damages the credibility and effectiveness of a writer or speaker.

If an error is made in subject–verb agreement, it can generally be attributed to one of three lapses: (a) failure to locate the subject, (b) failure to recognize the number (singular or plural) of the subject after locating it, or (c) failure to recognize the number of the verb. Suggestions for locating the true subject and determining the number of the subject and its verb follow.

Study Tip

This is one of the most important chapters in the book. Nothing reveals a person's education, or lack thereof, so quickly as verbs that don't agree with subjects. Study this chapter carefully to ensure that you sound educated and professional on the job.

LEVEL 1

Locating Subjects

All verbs have subjects. Locating these subjects can be difficult, particularly when (a) a prepositional phrase comes between the verb and its subject, (b) an intervening element separates the subject and verb, (c) sentences begin with *there* or *here*, and (d) sentences are inverted. You practiced locating subjects in Chapter 3, but because this is such an important skill, we provide additional instruction here.

1.b 2.b 3.a 4.b 5.a 6.b 7.a 8.a 9.a 10.a

Prepositional Phrases

Subjects of verbs are not found in prepositional phrases. Therefore, you must learn to ignore such phrases in identifying subjects of verbs. Some of the most common prepositions are *of, to, in, from, for, with, at,* and *by.* Notice in these sentences that the italicized prepositional phrases do not contain the subjects of the verbs.

> Each *of our employees* is trained to process returns. (The verb *is* agrees with its singular subject *Each.*)

> It appears that the invoice *for the two shipments* was lost. (The verb *was* agrees with its singular subject *invoice.*)

> The online version *of the magazine's college rankings* is available at its Web site. (The verb *is* agrees with its singular subject *version.*)

Some of the less easily recognized prepositions are *except, but, like,* and *between.* In the following sentences, distinguish the subjects from the italicized prepositional phrases.

> All managers *but Daniel* are attending the leadership workshop. (The verb *are* agrees with its plural subject *managers.*)

> Everyone *except the managers* is a member of the union. (The verb *is* agrees with its singular subject *everyone.*)

Intervening Elements

Groups of words introduced by expressions such as *along with, as well as, in addition to, such as, including, together with, plus,* and *other than* do NOT contain sentence subjects.

> Her favorite movie star, *as well as other local celebrities,* is scheduled to attend the fund-raiser.

In this sentence the writer has elected to emphasize the singular subject *star* and to de-emphasize *other local celebrities.* The writer could have given equal weight to these elements by writing *Her favorite movie star and other local celebrities are scheduled to attend the fund-raiser.* Notice that the number (singular or plural) of the verb changes when both *star* and *celebrities* are given equal emphasis. Study these additional examples:

> Our president, *together with her entire staff of employees,* agrees that the company will rebound. (The singular subject *president* agrees with the singular verb *agrees.*)

> Entrepreneurs *such as Debbi Fields* have started companies based on a single idea. (The plural subject *entrepreneurs* agrees with the plural verb *have.*)

> Our job application *plus three important employment documents* is available on our Web site. (The singular subject *application* agrees with the singular verb *is.*)

Sentences Beginning With *there* and *here*

In sentences beginning with *there* or *here,* look for the true subject AFTER the verb. The words *here* and *there* are function words that are not classified as subjects.

> There are several ways to contact our Customer Service Department. (The plural subject *ways* follows the verb *are.*)

> Here is the fuel oil consumption report. (The singular subject *report* follows the verb *is.*)

Be especially careful when using contractions. Remember that *here's* is the contraction for *here is*; therefore, it should be used only with singular subjects. Likewise, *there's* is the contraction for *there is* and should also be used only with singular subjects.

Incorrect: Here's the items you ordered. (The plural subject *items* does not agree with the verb *is*.)

Correct: Here are the items you ordered. (The plural subject *items* agrees with the verb *are*.)

Incorrect: There's three reasons you should hire me for the proofreader position. (The plural subject *reasons* does not agree with the verb *is*.)

Correct: There are three reasons you should hire me for the proofreader position. (The plural subject *reasons* agrees with the verb *are*.)

Inverted Sentence Order

Look for the subject after the verb in inverted sentences and in questions.

Related to everyday business are law and ethics. (Verb precedes plural subject.)

On the president's advisory team are several prominent economists. (Verb precedes plural subject.)

Have the product specifications been submitted? (Subject separates verb phrase.)

How important are salary, benefits, and job security? (Verb precedes subjects.)

Basic Rules for Subject–Verb Agreement

Once you have located the sentence subject, decide whether the subject is singular or plural and select a verb that agrees in number. Basic challenges occur when you have compound subjects joined by *and*, when your subject is a company or organization, and when your subject is a title of a publication or song.

Subjects Joined by *and*

When one subject is joined to another by the word *and*, the subject is generally plural and thus requires a plural verb.

Mark Zuckerberg and Tom Anderson are two influential people in the world of social networking.

The proposed law and its amendment are before the legislature.

Subjects joined by *and* are singular and thus take singular verbs in only two cases: (1) when the words are preceded by *each* or *every* and (2) when the words represent a single person or thing.

Each letter and memo requires a manager's signature. (Think *Each individual letter and each individual memo is . . .*)

Every man, woman, and child is eligible for a free birthday meal. (Think *Every single man, every single woman, and every single child is . . .*)

Macaroni and cheese is their daughter's favorite meal. (Words represent one dish.)

His wife and best friend is Christina. (Words represents one person.)

Study Tip

To help you select correct verbs, temporarily substitute *it* or *he* for singular subjects or *they* for plural subjects. Then you can more easily make verbs agree with their subjects.

Company and Organization Names

Even though they may appear to be plural, company and organization names, including names of sports teams and musical groups, are generally considered singular; therefore, they require singular verbs.

> US Airways <u>offers</u> the lowest fare to New York City.
>
> Richards, Bateman, and Richards, Inc., <u>is</u> offering the bond issue.
>
> The San Francisco 49ers <u>was recognized</u> for strong recruiting.
>
> Coldplay <u>has</u> just <u>announced</u> its summer concert calendar.

Titles

Titles of publications and of artistic works such as songs are singular; therefore, they require singular verbs.

> *Seven Secrets to Successful Investing* <u>was</u> an instant best seller.
>
> "Clocks" <u>is</u> one of Coldplay's most popular songs.

Now complete the reinforcement exercises for Level 1.

LEVEL 2

Special Rules for Subject–Verb Agreement

Making sure your subjects agree with your verbs sometimes requires the application of special rules. This is especially true when dealing with subjects joined by *or* or *nor*, indefinite pronouns as subjects, and collective nouns as subjects.

Subjects Joined by *or* or *nor*

Study Tip

Unlike subjects joined by *and*, subjects joined by *or* or *nor* require a choice between Subject No. 1 and Subject No. 2.

When two or more subjects are joined by *or* or *nor*, the verb should agree with the closer subject (the subject that follows *or* or *nor*).

> Neither the webmaster nor the clerks <u>know</u> the customer's password.
>
> Neither the clerks nor the webmaster <u>knows</u> the customer's password.
>
> Either Marcia or you <u>are</u> in charge of planning the event.
>
> Either you or Marcia <u>is</u> in charge of planning the event.

Indefinite Pronouns as Subjects

As you learned in Chapter 7, some indefinite pronouns are always singular, whereas other indefinite pronouns are always plural. In addition, some may be singular or plural depending on the words to which they refer.

Always Singular			Always Plural	Singular or Plural
anyone	every	nobody	both	all
anybody	everyone	nothing	few	more
anything	everybody	someone	many	most
each	everything	somebody	several	some
either	neither	something		any
				none

SUBJECT–VERB AGREEMENT

Singular indefinite pronouns require singular verbs. Ignore any prepositional phrases that follow the indefinite pronoun.

Either of the two ideas is acceptable.

Somebody on the committee has to take the minutes.

Each of our employees is eligible for promotion.

Everybody possesses the ability to succeed.

Plural indefinite pronouns require plural verbs.

Both of the candidates are qualified.

Few interviewees send thank-you notes after job interviews.

Many of our politicians are working hard to represent their constituents.

Several Web sites offer online technical support.

Some indefinite pronouns can be **singular** or **plural.** These indefinite pronouns, including *all, more, most, some, any*, and *none*, provide one of the few instances in which prepositional phrases become important in determining agreement. Although the prepositional phrase does not contain the subject of the sentence, it does contain the noun to which the indefinite pronoun refers. If that noun is singular, use a singular verb. If the noun is plural, use a plural verb.

Some of the report is controversial. (*Some* is singular because it refers to *report*.)

Some of the managers agree that the company needs reorganizing. (*Some* is plural because it refers to *managers*.)

Most of the work is completed. (*Most* is singular because it refers to *work*.)

Most of the applicants are women. (*Most* is plural because it refers to *women*.)

The indefinite pronouns *anyone* and *everyone* are spelled as two words when followed by *of* phrases.

Every one of us should attend the budget development meeting.

Any one of those Web sites can be used to book air and hotel reservations.

Collective Nouns as Subjects

Collective nouns such as *faculty, committee, team, audience, group, jury, crowd, class, board, flock*, and *council* may be singular or plural depending on how they are used in a sentence. When a collective noun operates as a single unit, its verb should be singular. When the elements of a collective noun operate separately, the verb should be plural.

The team has carefully studied the opponent's videos. (*Team* is operating as a single unit.)

The team were still dressing when the reporter entered the locker room. (*Team* members were acting separately. Although technically correct, the sentence would be less awkward if it read *The team members* were still dressing . . .)

Trivia Tidbit

In America collective nouns are almost always considered to be singular (*The staff is* . . .). In Britain, however, collective nouns are usually plural (*The staff are* . . .).

The city <u>council</u> <u>has</u> unanimously <u>approved</u> the parking fee increase. (*Council* is operating as a single unit.)

The city <u>council</u> <u>were</u> sharply divided over the increase in parking fees. (*Council* members were acting separately. Although technically correct, the sentence would be less awkward if it read *The city council <u>members</u> <u>were</u> sharply divided . . .*)

Now complete the reinforcement exercises for Level 2.

LEVEL 3

Additional Rules for Subject–Verb Agreement

In some instances it is difficult to know whether a subject is singular or plural. This is especially true when the word *number* is the subject of a sentence; when the subject is a quantity, measure, fraction, or portion; and when the subject is a phrase or clause. *Who* and *that* clauses and subject complements present additional challenges. Here are a few rules to guide you in selecting appropriate verbs for such subjects.

The Distinction Between *the number* and *a number*

When the word *number* is the subject of a sentence, its article (*the* or *a*) becomes significant. *The* is specific and therefore implies *singularity*; *a* is general and therefore implies *plurality*. This means that *the number* is singular and *a number* is plural. Ignore any prepositional phrases that follow.

The <u>number</u> of times you have been late to work <u>is</u> unacceptable. (Singular)

The <u>number</u> of requests for registered domain names <u>is</u> growing annually. (Singular)

A <u>number</u> of items <u>are</u> included on today's agenda. (Plural)

A <u>number</u> of stocks <u>are</u> traded daily. (Plural)

Quantities and Measures

When they refer to *total* amounts, quantities and measures are singular. If they refer to individual units that can be counted, quantities and measures are plural.

<u>Forty dollars</u> <u>is</u> all you will pay for monthly Internet access. (The quantity is expressed as a total amount.)

<u>Forty dollars</u> <u>were</u> <u>laid</u> out on the table during the demonstration. (The quantity is expressed as individual units. Although technically correct, the sentence would be less awkward if it read *Forty dollar bills* <u>were</u> <u>laid</u> out . . .)

<u>Three years</u> <u>is</u> the period of the loan. (The quantity is expressed as a total amount.)

<u>Three years</u> <u>are</u> needed to renovate the property totally. (The quantity is expressed as individual units.)

Fractions, Portions, and Percentages

Fractions, portions, and percentages may be singular or plural depending on the nouns to which they refer. To determine whether the subject is singular or plural, look at the prepositional phrase that follows.

One third of the contract was ratified. (The fraction *one third* is singular because it refers to *contract*.)

Only one third of voters approve of the new federal budget. (The fraction *one third* is plural because it refers to *voters*.)

A majority of the report discusses the pros and cons of the proposal. (The subject *majority* is singular because it refers to *report*.)

A majority of employees agree with the proposal. (The subject *majority* is plural because it refers to *employees*.)

A percentage of the budget is allocated to employee benefits. (The subject *percentage* is singular because it refers to *budget*.)

A percentage of the proceeds go to charity. (The subject *percentage* is plural because it refers to *proceeds*.)

Who and *That* Clauses

Verbs in *who* and *that* clauses (known as **relative pronoun clauses**) must agree in number and person with the nouns to which they refer. In *who* and *that* clauses introduced by *one of*, the verb is usually plural because it refers to a plural noun.

Susan Lamb is *one of* those managers who always get excellent results from their employees. (Read: Of those managers who always get excellent results from their employees, Susan Lamb is one. Note that the pronoun *their* also must agree with its antecedent.)

To Kill a Mockingbird is *one of* those books that have an influence on readers of all ages. [Read: Of those books that have an influence on readers of all ages, *To Kill a Mockingbird* is one.]

In *who* and *that* clauses introduced by *the only one of*, the verb is singular.

Maria is *the only one* of our employees who is certified to give CPR. (The adverb *only* makes the *who* clause singular.)

To Kill a Mockingbird is *the only one* of those books that is read in high school classes today. (The adverb *only* makes the *that* clause singular.)

Verbs must agree in person with the nouns or pronouns to which they refer. Identifying the subject can be even trickier when pronouns are combined with *who* clauses.

It is you who are responsible for booking our flights.

Could it be I who am to blame?

Was it you who were on the phone?

Phrases and Clauses as Subjects

Use a singular verb when the subject of a sentence is a phrase or clause.

Learning about different cultures is fascinating.

That verbs must agree with subjects is accepted.

Subject Complements

In Chapter 8 you learned that linking verbs are followed by complements. Although a complement may differ from the subject in number, the linking verb should always agree with the subject. To avoid awkwardness, reword sentences so that subjects and complements agree in number.

Awkward: The best part of the Web site is the graphics and video. (Although the singular subject *part* agrees with the singular verb *is*, it sounds awkward because of the plural complement *graphics and video*.)

Better: The best parts of the Web site are the graphics and video. (The plural subject agrees with the plural complement.)

Awkward: The reason for his bankruptcy was poor management and decision making.

Better: The reasons for his bankruptcy were poor management and decision making.

Now complete the reinforcement exercises for Level 3.

Spot the BLOOPER

Using the skills you are learning in this class, try to identify why the following items are bloopers. Consult your textbook, dictionary, or reference manual as needed.

Blooper 1: Tourism ad for Australia that appeared in the *San Francisco Chronicle*: "If you have just one spare hour, a tour of the world-famous [Sydney] Opera House are a must."

Blooper 2: Message printed on a Gap T-shirt: "The Days of This Society Is Numbered."

Blooper 3: Official banner welcoming Super Bowl fans to Tampa: "Welcome to Downtown Tampa: There's so many reasons to like it."

Blooper 4: Headline in the *Sun-Sentinel* [Fort Lauderdale]: "Plenty of Florida children needs homes."

Blooper 5: Letter to the editor in the *Atlanta Journal-Constitution*: "Why has the Atlanta Public Schools made steady progress?"

Blooper 6: From an Associated Press article: "Education and employer training is often the biggest need in an independently owned business."

Blooper 7: Headline from the Santa Barbara [California] *News-Press*: "Adding Rental Units Transform Home."

Blooper 8: Article about Meryl Streep in *Parade* magazine: "She's one of the few stars who hasn't nipped and tucked herself into an unrealistic image of youth."

Blooper 9: In an article in *The Times-Union* [Albany, New York], the interim superintendent of schools said: "A large number of students arrives without the basic skills we expect them to have."

Blooper 10: Headline in the *San Francisco Chronicle*: "One in 11 Have Trouble Speaking California's Official Language."

Question	Answer

Q: In a *New York Times* article about singer Michael Jackson and his fight with Sony Music Group, I saw this sentence: *Owning those rights are valuable because once Mr. Jackson owns them outright, he does not have to split royalty payments with Sony as he does now.* It seems to me the phrase *owning those rights* is singular and the verb should be *is.* Am I right?

A: Absolutely! When they act as sentence subjects, phrases and clauses are singular. You deserve a good grammar award!

Q: My uncle insists that *none* is singular. My English book says that it can be plural. Who's right?

A: Times are changing. Several years ago *none* was almost always used in a singular sense. Today, through usage, *none* may be singular or plural depending on what you wish to emphasize. For example, *None are more willing than we.* But, *None of the students is* (or *are* if you wish to suggest many students) *failing.*

Q: Please help me with this sentence that I am transcribing for a medical laboratory: *A copy of our analysis, along with our interpretation of its results, (has or have) been sent to you.*

A: The subject of your sentence is *copy*; thus the verb must be *has.* Don't let interrupting elements obscure the real sentence subject.

Q: I'm never sure how to handle words that are used to represent quantities and proportions in sentences. For example, what verb is correct in this sentence: *A large proportion of voters (was or were) against the measure.*

A: Words that represent fractional amounts (such as *proportion, fraction, minimum,* and *majority*) may be singular or plural depending on the words they represent. In your sentence *proportion* represents *voters*, which is plural. Therefore, use the plural verb *were.*

Q: What part of speech is *there* when it begins a sentence, such as *There are two vice presidents*?

A: The word *there* generally is classified as an adverb. But in this position, the word *there* functions as a pronoun. *Merriam-Webster's Collegiate Dictionary* calls *there* a "function" word when it replaces the grammatical sentence subject.

Q: In a recent *Wall Street Journal* article, I saw this sentence: *At issue is other tax breaks, especially Hope and Lifetime Learning education tax credits.* I don't usually question the *Journal,* but this sentence is weird. What is its problem?

A: Because the sentence order is inverted, the writer had trouble making the subject and verb agree. By moving the subject to the beginning, you can see that it is plural. And a plural subject always demands a plural verb: *Other tax breaks . . . are at issue.*

Q: I have a lot of trouble with verbs in sentences like this: *He is one of the 8 million Americans who (has or have) a drinking problem.*

A: You're not alone. Make your verb agree with the plural noun following *one of* (*Americans*). One easy way to work with sentences like this is to concentrate on the clause that contains the verb: *Of the 8 million Americans who have a drinking problem, he is one.*

Q: When writing e-mail messages, I often type in all capital letters. My boss just told me that I should stop this practice. Why?

A: Your boss is correct. Typing in all caps is often referred to as *shouting.* Because many people are offended by these types of messages, writing in all caps should be avoided. In addition, messages written in all caps or in all lowercase letters are difficult to read and look unprofessional. On the job, business communicators want their messages to be as professional and as easy to read as possible. Therefore, always use standard upper- and lowercase letters when writing your e-mail messages.

Q: I confuse *i.e.* and *e.g.* What's the difference?

A: The abbreviation *i.e.* stands for the Latin *id est,* meaning "that is" (*The package exceeds the weight limit, i.e., 5 pounds*). The abbreviation *e.g.* stands for the Latin *exempli gratia,* meaning "for the sake of example" or "for example" (*The manufacturer may offer a purchase incentive, e.g., a rebate or discount plan*). Notice the use of a comma after *i.e.* and *e.g.* Also notice that both abbreviations are written using lowercase letters and periods.

Q: I included this sentence in a job acceptance letter to my new employer: *I am anxious to begin my new position with Miller and Associates.* Is this sentence acceptable?

A: Have you mailed this letter yet? If not, you should change *anxious* to *eager* before doing so. *Anxious* is an adjective meaning "worried or apprehensive" (*Maggie is anxious about getting her biopsy results*). *Eager* is an adjective meaning "anticipating with enthusiasm" (*Stan is eager to get started on the new project*). Our guess is that you are eager to begin your new position!

10
Reinforcement Exercises
LEVEL 1

Online Homework Help! For immediate feedback on odd-numbered items, go to **www.meguffey.com**.

A. (Self-check) Select the correct word to complete each sentence below. Write the corresponding letter in the space provided.

1. Presenting today (a) is, (b) are two investment experts, Yukie Tokuyama and Eric Freidenreich. _____

2. The word *ginormous*, along with several other words, (a) was, (b) were added to the dictionary in 2009. _____

3. Here (a) is, (b) are three possibilities for improving employee morale. _____

4. One of the first computer viruses (a) was, (b) were the "elk cloner," which was written by a ninth-grade student in 1982. _____

5. Every man, woman, and child in the country (a) is, (b) are to be counted in the census. _____

6. There (a) is, (b) are three primary reasons to invest in foreign securities. _____

7. Addressing the conference (a) is, (b) are employees of the Federal Reserve. _____

8. Southwest Airlines (a) is, (b) are known for a fun culture that motivates employees. _____

9. A set of guidelines for protecting network security (a) was, (b) were developed. _____

10. *Freakonomics* by Steven D. Levitt and Stephen J. Dubner (a) appear, (b) appears to be one of the best-selling economics books of all time. _____

Check your answers below.

B. In the following sentences or groups of words, underline the simple subject(s).

Example: the <u>controller</u> and the <u>treasurer</u> of the county

1. A directory of e-mail addresses is on my computer.

2. the network administrator together with her staff

3. other services such as Web hosting and HTML coding

4. the production cost and the markup of each item

5. one of the many reasons for developing excellent communication skills

6. current emphasis on product safety and consumer protection

7. Farkas, Evans, & Everett, Inc., an executive placement service

8. the anger and frustration of the passengers

9. the lead actor, as well as those in supporting roles

10. the time and money involved in the project

 C. For each of the following sentences, circle the sentence subject. Then cross out any phrases that separate the verb from its subject. Choose the correct verb and write the corresponding letter in the space provided.

Examples: The (faculty advisor,) ~~along with club members~~, (a) is, (b) are here. _____a_____

Our (catalog) ~~of wireless devices~~ (a) is, (b) are being sent to you. _____a_____

1. Compensation, along with benefits and time off, (a) is, (b) are generally discussed after a job offer is made. _____

2. Now, just in time for the holidays, (a) comes, (b) come a variety of accessories made from recyclable materials. _____

3. The use of cell phones and pagers (a) is, (b) are not allowed during meetings. _____

4. A bachelor's degree from an accredited institution and three years of experience, (a) is, (b) are required for this position. _____

5. Everyone except temporary workers employed during the last year (a) has, (b) have become eligible for retroactive benefits. _____

6. The wingspan on each of Boeing's latest passenger planes (a) is, (b) are longer than the Wright brothers' first flight. _____

7. All cooperatives except the Lemon Growing Exchange (a) has, (b) have been able to show a profit for participating members. _____

8. Although the economy seems to be booming, only one of the major automobile manufacturers (a) has, (b) have been able to show profits. _____

9. Successful entrepreneurs such as Donald Trump (a) seem, (b) seems to possess enormous energy and passion. _____

10. The range of prices for these models (a) make, (b) makes it difficult to provide complete information online. _____

 D. Select the correct verb and write its letter in the space provided.

1. Bacon and eggs (a) is, (b) are the most popular breakfast item on the menu. _____

2. Each office and conference room (a) was, (b) were retrofitted for earthquake safety. _____

3. The book *EcoBarons* (a) discusses, (b) discuss business leaders who are working to save the planet from ecological destruction. _____

4. The New Orleans River Kings (a) was, (b) were a popular jazz band in the 1920s. _____

5. Here (a) is, (b) are a complete list of product features. _____

6. On the southern shore of Hawaii (a) is, (b) are numerous windmill farms. _____

7. Some managers think that grammar and punctuation (a) doesn't, (b) don't matter. _____

8. Janet (a) doesn't, (b) don't mind working extra hours this weekend. _____

9. Our governor, along with top congressional leaders, (a) is, (b) are protesting the budget cuts. _____

10. Sam and Lynne (a) is, (b) are both able to attend the meeting. _____

SUBJECT–VERB AGREEMENT

11. Cisco Systems (a) has, (b) have found a way to restructure its finances. _____

12. Lying on my desk (a) is, (b) are my itinerary and plane tickets. _____

13. Hunter, Knapp, and Huynh, Inc., a legal firm in Oklahoma City, (a) specializes, (b) specialize in patent law. _____

14. Considerable time and effort (a) was, (b) were spent on developing the plans. _____

15. How essential (a) is, (b) are experience and education in this field? _____

16. The Rolling Stones (a) have, (b) has been a popular rock band since 1962. _____

17. Biscuits and gravy (a) is, (b) are a popular dish in the South. _____

18. The New York Knicks (a) is, (b) are probably the most experienced team in the NBA. _____

19. Every online order and return (a) is, (b) are processed within one day. _____

20. Bruce Springsteen's "Streets of Philadelphia" (a) were, (b) was awarded an Oscar for Best Song in 1993. _____

LEVEL 2

A. (Self-check) Select the correct form or verb.

1. Everyone except a few employees (a) admit, (b) admits that the new CEO is doing a good job. _____

2. Either the AMC Pacer or the Yugo (a) is, (b) are considered to be the worst car of all time. _____

3. No one but the Human Resources director and a few managers ever (a) talk, (b) talks about balancing work and family issues. _____

4. Each of the research studies (a) concludes, (b) conclude that the U.S. workplace is safer than it has ever been. _____

5. The union (a) has, (b) have to vote on the proposed contract. _____

6. Every one of the new start-up companies (a) is, (b) are seeking venture capital. _____

7. Neither the employees nor their supervisor (a) think, (b) thinks the theft was an inside job. _____

8. (a) Everyone, (b) Every one of the sales reps made quota this month. _____

9. All that work (a) is, (b) are yet to be logged in. _____

10. Many surgeons, including Dr. Lisa Hudson, (a) listen, (b) listens to classical or rock music while operating. _____

Check your answers below.

B. Choose the correct answer.

1. The Department of Labor (a) report, (b) reports that unemployment is the highest it has been in decades. _____

2. Neither Brenda DeLee nor Robert Eustes (a) is, (b) are afraid of hard work. _____

3. (a) Everyone, (b) Every one of the résumés contained grammatical errors. _____

4. Several of the proposals (a) contains, (b) contain complex formulas. _____

5. Either the owner or her partners (a) is, (b) are responsible for the taxes. _____

6. Either the partners or the owner (a) was, (b) were contacted by the IRS. _____

7. The group of players, coaches, and fans (a) plan, (b) plans to charter a plane. _____

8. The group (a) is, (b) are taking their seats on the plane. _____

9. (a) Is, (b) Are either of the clients satisfied with our marketing campaign? _____

10. Something about these insurance claims (a) appear, (b) appears questionable. _____

11. An online version of *U.S. News & World Report*'s college rankings (a) is, (b) are now available. _____

12. The faculty (a) agrees, (b) agree that student learning is paramount. _____

13. The faculty (a) was, (b) were taking their seats when the dean entered the room. _____

14. Most of the adults using Twitter (a) accesses, (b) access the Internet wirelessly. _____

15. Most of the blog (a) is, (b) are dedicated to discussing online marketing strategies. _____

16. (a) Anyone, (b) Any one of these messages could be considered spam. _____

17. (a) Anyone (b) Any one can see that we need to hire more sales reps. _____

18. Everything about the contract clauses (a) seems, (b) seem debatable. _____

19. None of the passengers (a) is, (b) are upset with the new regulations. _____

20. None of the contract (a) deals, (b) deal with monetary issues. _____

C. **Writing Exercise.** Use your imagination in expanding the following sentences. When necessary, select the correct verb form first.

1. The staff is _____

_____

2. The staff are _____

_____

3. Our city council (has, have) _____

_____

4. Not one of the plans (was, were) _____

_____

5. Some of the jury members (believe, believes) _____

_____

6. Some of the proposal (need, needs) _____

_____

7. Somebody in the theater filled with patrons (was, were) _____

_____

8. Either Anne or you (is, are) _____

_____

9. Either you or Anne (was, were) _____

_____

10. Everything about the speeches (was, were) _____

_____

LEVEL 3

 A. (Self-check) For each sentence write the letter corresponding to the correct answer in the space provided.

1. The number of companies using Google to perform background checks on potential employees (a) is, (b) are growing. _____

2. A number of companies (a) is, (b) are also using social networking sites to investigate applicants. _____

3. Laury Fischer is one of those teachers who (a) has, (b) have earned the respect of their students. _____

4. Fifteen feet of pipe (a) is, (b) are exactly what was specified. _____

5. Didn't you know it is you who (a) has, (b) have been chosen for the promotion? _____

6. A large percentage of the donation (a) go, (b) goes to fight homelessness. _____

7. She is the only one of the service reps who (a) speak, (b) speaks three languages. _____

8. Whoever is named for the job (a) has, (b) have my approval. _____

9. To take online classes while working full-time (a) is, (b) are challenging. _____

10. The hardest part of the job (a) is, (b) are the bending and lifting. _____

Check your answers below.

 B. Select the correct verb.

1. Two hundred dollars (a) is, (b) are required as a down payment to hold the conference facility. _____

2. One hundred pennies (a) is, (b) are needed to make one dollar. _____

3. Our latest advertisements featuring the new digital media server (a) is, (b) are being broadcast on all major networks. _____

4. Is it he who (a) is, (b) are the new account representative? _____

5. Michael is the only one of the lab assistants who (a) was, (b) were able to repair the malfunctioning machine. _____

6. Michael is one of those lab assistants who (a) is, (b) are valued as employees. _____

7. "My Way" is one of those songs that (a) continues, (b) continue to sound fresh year after year. _____

8. Sixty days (a) is, (b) are the period of the loan. _____

9. Sixty days (a) is, (b) are reserved during the year for staff meetings. _____

10. At the rear of the building complex (a) is, (b) are the quality control lab and the science department. _____

11. Only a fraction of the conference delegates (a) was, (b) were unable to find accommodations at the Mandalay Bay resort. _____

12. Only a fraction of the conference room (a) was, (b) were set up by the time the meeting was scheduled to begin. _____

13. Keeping your skills up-to-date (a) is, (b) are important in today's economy. _____

1.a 2.b 3.b 4.a 5.b 6.b 7.b 8.a 9.a 10.a (Better: *The hardest parts of the job are . . .*)

SUBJECT–VERB AGREEMENT **CHAPTER 10** • 209

14. Over three fourths of the individuals attending the lecture series (a) is, (b) are college students. _____

15. Over three fourths of the contract (a) has, (b) have been ratified. _____

16. A number of women with MBAs (a) chooses, (b) choose to stay home to raise their children. _____

17. The number of women with MDs or law degrees who choose to stay home to raise a family (a) is, (b) are much lower. _____

18. Collaborating online with colleagues (a) is, (b) are easier than ever before. _____

19. A large percentage of younger employees (a) is, (b) are using social networks to collaborate and share knowledge in the workplace. _____

20. A large percentage of each day (a) is, (b) are spent online. _____

C. Writing Exercise. Some subject–verb constructions are grammatically correct but sound incorrect. Revise the following correct sentences so that they are not only correct but sound so. **Hint:** Make the subject and its complement agree in number.

Example: The best part of my job is meeting people and learning new things.

The best parts of my job are meeting people and learning new things.

1. The most important trait I have to offer an employer is energy and enthusiasm.

_____

2. The best part of my job is preparing and analyzing financial statements.

_____

3. The principal task in this office is abstracts and affidavits.

_____

4. The primary reason for his wealth is wise stock and other investment choices.

_____

5. The main objective this fiscal year is to increase sales and decrease expenses.

_____

For further practice in subject–verb agreement, write sentences using the following words as subjects of present-tense, present–progressive, or present–perfect verbs. See the tables in Chapter 9 if necessary. Your sentences should be complete.

Example: The number of voters is increasing rapidly as we approach the election date.

6. A number of businesses _____

_____

7. The number of businesses _____

_____

8. Every one of the students _____

_____

9. Some of the employees _____

_____

10. Some of the plan _____

_____

D. Skill Maximizer. To offer extra help in areas that cause hesitation for business and professional writers, this proficiency exercise reviews subject–verb agreement. Underline any subject–verb problem and write an improved form(s) in the space provided. Each sentence has one error.

1. There's many advantages to earning a college degree. _____

2. Corned beef and cabbage are a traditional Irish dish. _____

3. *Marvels of the Seven Seas* have numerous photographs depicting marine life in its natural habitat. _____

4. Persistent inflation and interest rate worries often causes stock prices to drop. _____

5. Was any of the members of the organization present for the final vote? _____

6. After several days of deliberation, the jury has announced their verdict. _____

7. Neither the defendant nor the plaintiffs was satisfied with the judgment. _____

8. Are either of the applicants available to interview on Friday? _____

9. Preparing the dinner for the annual banquet is gourmet chefs from around the world. _____

10. Globalization and the changing ethnic composition of America is causing many organizations to embrace diversity programs. _____

11. The use of UPC scanning devices, computer databases, and thermal-imaging receipts are everywhere in the retail industry. _____

12. One of the problems, in addition to those already mentioned, seem to be resistance to change. _____

13. Both a written proposal and an oral presentation is required for this project. _____

14. If the level of antioxidants in your diet are low, you may be susceptible to health problems. _____

15. A host of ethical issues surround business including economic justice, marketing irregularities, executive compensation, and whistle-blowing. _____

16. Dell Computers, along with many other technology companies, are outsourcing thousands of customer support jobs to India. _____

17. Any one of the stockholders have the right to delegate his or her proxy. _____

18. Mike is one of those accountants who strives for accurate and objective financial statements. _____

19. Kirsty is the only one of our accountants who have access to all financial data. _____

20. Everyone of the books she read last year discussed business concepts. _____

E. FAQs About Business English Review. In the space provided, write the correct answer choice.

1. Horns blow in different keys and tones; (a) e.g., (b) i.e., American car horns beep in the tone of F. _____

2. Mosquito sprays block the mosquito's sensors so that the mosquitoes don't know you are there; (a) e.g., (b) i.e., the sprays hide you. _____

3. We have (a) alot, (b) allot, (c) a lot of work to do before the end of the day. _____

4. Winning both Boeing contracts (a) is, (b) are important because the contracts will generate $57 million in revenues. _____

5. A group of photographers (a) was, (b) were waiting outside the building when we made the announcement. _____

6. None of the tourists (a) was, (b) were dressed appropriately to enter the temple. _____

7. None of the building (a) is, (b) are accessible to nonemployees. _____

8. There (a) was, (b) were a few team members still not in agreement. _____

9. Paul is (a) anxious, (b) eager for his upcoming vacation to Bermuda. _____

10. Marta is (a) anxious, (b) eager about the upcoming exam because she didn't study for it. _____

Today social networking is used for much more than just socializing. Companies have discovered that sites such as Facebook, MySpace, and LinkedIn can be powerful tools for marketing, recruiting, and communication. To become familiar with one of the most popular social networking areas, you will visit the Facebook site.

Goal: To learn about social networking.

1. In the address bar of your Web browser, enter the following URL: **http://www.facebook.com**.

2. Enter your name, e-mail address, password, gender, and birth date to create your account if necessary. Click **Sign Up**. If you already have a Facebook account, simply log on.

3. Take a few minutes to start getting your Facebook page set up. Upload a profile photo, enter some information about yourself, and set your security settings to ensure your privacy. If you need help at any time, click **Help** at the bottom of the page.

4. Use the **Search** tool at the top of the screen to search for people, groups, and fan pages. Any of the following may have Facebook pages you can join: your college, your employer, a college you would like to attend, a company you would like to work for, your sorority or fraternity, a student club you belong to, a professional organization you would like to join, a charitable organization, and so on.

5. Click the link for your name at the top of the page to return to your personal Facebook page. Print a copy of this page.

6. Log out of Facebook by clicking **Logout** at the top of the screen. Close your browser.

7. After logging out, write a brief summary (no more than one page) about how Facebook could be used for academic and professional purposes.

8. Submit your summary and your printout to your instructor.

Your instructor may assign any of the following topics for you to discuss in class, in an online chat room, or on an online discussion board. Some of the discussion topics may require outside research. You may also be asked to read and respond to postings made by your classmates.

Discussion Topic 1: A study tip in this chapter said the following: "Nothing reveals a person's education, or lack thereof, so quickly as verbs that don't agree with subjects." Do you agree with this statement? Why or why not?

Discussion Topic 2: What have you learned so far in this class that will help you sound educated and professional on the job? Why do you think it is important to sound this way in the workplace?

Discussion Topic 3: You learned in this chapter that American and British English rules treat collective nouns differently. Americans generally treat collective nouns as singular, whereas the English generally treat collective nouns as plural. What do you think accounts for this difference? What other differences have you noticed between American and British English?

Discussion Topic 4: In this chapter you learned that each year approximately 10,000 new words are introduced to the English language. Of those, about 1,000 are widely used, and roughly 200 of those words become a part of our permanent vocabulary. Why do you think so many words are added that never become a permanent part of our vocabulary?

Discussion Topic 5: American novelist Charlotte Perkins Gilman said, "Life is a verb." What do you think she meant by this? Do you agree? Why or why not? Share your opinions and thoughts with your classmates.

Posttest

Underline the letter representing the correct answer.

1. Banana leaves and coconut husks (a) is, (b) are being used as materials in carpets and seat cushions for cars.

2. Everyone except the president and other management members (a) is, (b) are eligible for early retirement.

3. The cost of supplies, along with service and equipment costs, (a) is, (b) are a major problem.

4. There (a) is, (b) are many ways we can use Facebook as a professional communication tool.

5. Appearing next on the program (a) was, (b) were Dr. Gwen Hester and Professor Michele Koci.

6. A number of surprising events (a) is, (b) are creating spikes in the stock market.

7. Starbucks (a) has, (b) have launched an "I'm In" campaign to encourage national service.

8. Neither the CFO nor members of his staff (a) are, (b) is surprised by the revenue declines.

9. The research team (a) has, (b) have determined that the number one feature women want in a vehicle is extra storage.

10. The number of union strikes in the United States (a) is, (b) are decreasing.

Reread Chapters 8–10. Then test your comprehension of those chapters by completing the exercises that follow. Check your answers at the end of the book.

LEVEL 1

In the blank provided, write the letter of the word or phrase that correctly completes each of the following sentences.

1. How important (a) is, (b) are seat comfort and legroom on flights? _____

2. In the sentence *An additive makes natural gas smell like rotten eggs,* the verb *smell* is (a) transitive, (b) intransitive, (c) linking, (d) helping. _____

3. In the sentence *We listened carefully to the president's address,* the verb *listened* is (a) transitive, (b) intransitive, (c) linking, (d) helping. _____

4. In the sentence *Tom Langlois is the consultant*, the word *consultant* is (a) an object, (b) a linking verb, (c) a complement. _____

5. In the sentence *Maggie booked her flight*, the word *booked* is (a) transitive, (b) intransitive, (c) linking, (d) helping. _____

6. In the sentence *Women comprise just 34 percent of Silicon Valley's technical workforce*, the verb *comprise* is (a) present tense, (b) past tense, (c) future tense. _____

7. Google, along with other U.S. Internet companies, (a) is, (b) are required to abide by China's laws. _____

8. Every employee and supervisor (a) attend, (b) attends a team-building retreat every year. _____

9. In the sentence *The global economy will become strong over the next decade,* the verb *will become* is (a) present tense, (b) past tense, (c) future tense. _____

10. Olsen, Leung, and Miller, Inc., (a) is, (b) are moving to a new location. _____

11. In the sentence *Hill International built some of the tallest skyscrapers in the world*, the verb *built* is (a) present tense, (b) past tense, (c) future tense. _____

12. There (a) is, (b) are many kind words we will be able to say about him at his retirement dinner. _____

13. The tone and wording of a business message (a) are, (b) is very important. _____

14. What (a) is, (b) was the name of the sales rep who offered the discount? _____

15. *Economics in One Lesson* (a) help, (b) helps readers learn the basics of economics quickly and easily. _____

Write the letter of the word or phrase that correctly completes each of the following sentences.

16. The (a) active voice, (b) passive voice is known as the "voice of business." _____

17. She suggested that everyone (a) meet, (b) meets at the café after work. _____

18. He acts as if he (a) was, (b) were the only employee who had to work overtime. _____

19. In the sentence *The contract was approved yesterday*, the verb is in the (a) active, (b) passive voice. _____

20. In the sentence *"Freegans" search through dumpsters to find usable items*, the verb is in the (a) active, (b) passive voice. _____

21. Freegans recommend that any discarded item (a) are, (b) be reused to reduce waste. _____

22. Many items have (a) laid, (b) lain, (c) lay in trash bins that are quite valuable. _____

23. If you had (a) rode, (b) ridden the subway to work, you would have been on time. _____

24. In the sentence *Some homeowners are wondering how the bailout will affect them*, the verb *are wondering* is (a) past participle, (b) present participle. _____

25. We think that (a) everyone, (b) every one of the candidates is qualified for the position. _____

26. The jury (a) need, (b) needs more time to make a decision. _____

27. If I (a) was, (b) were qualified, I would apply for that position. _____

28. Either the teenager or his parents (a) is, (b) are using the car right now. _____

29. Neither the parents nor the teenager (a) is, (b) are staying home tonight. _____

30. In the sentence *The deficit has grown over the past decade*, the verb *has grown* is (a) past participle, (b) present participle. _____

LEVEL 3

In the blank provided, write the letter that correctly completes each sentence.

31. Nearly everyone objected to (a) Sara, (b) Sara's using her BlackBerry during the meeting. _____

32. The number of taxpayers who file online (a) is, (b) are growing rapidly. _____

33. A large percentage of people (a) is, (b) are simplifying their lives. _____

34. It looks as if three fourths of the proposal (a) has, (b) have yet to be written. _____

35. She is one of those executives who always (a) tell, (b) tells the truth. _____

36. Try (a) and, (b) to be on time for work from now on. _____

For each of the following groups of sentences, select the one that is most logically written.

37. (a) To qualify for a full scholarship, applications must be submitted by January 1.
(b) To qualify for a full scholarship, submit your application by January 1. _____

38. (a) Skilled at troubleshooting Web security problems, Maria Lyan was hired instantly by the personnel manager.
(b) Skilled at troubleshooting Web security problems, the personnel manager hired Maria Lyan instantly. _____

39. (a) Using two search tools, I finally located the Web site.
(b) Using two search tools, the Web site was finally located. _____

40. (a) The waiter served a bowl of soup to the woman that was steaming hot.
(b) The waiter served a bowl of soup that was steaming hot to the woman. _____

FAQs About Business English Review

41. We value one trait in our employees above all others, (a) i.e., (b) e.g., integrity. _____

42. State budget cuts will certainly (a) affect, (b) effect education adversely. _____

43. Chemist Laura Burns announced her (a) principle, (b) principal findings in a journal article. _____

44. Both plaintiffs and defendants were (a) all together, (b) altogether pleased with the out-of-court settlement. _____

45. Typing an e-mail message in all capital letters is known as (a) preening, (b) shouting, (c) efficiency. _____

46. Chuck is (a) eager, (b) anxious to earn his MBA degree. _____

47. Many notable celebrities attended the movie (a) premier, (b) premiere. _____

48. We trusted that Shannon would be (a) discrete, (b) discreet during the negotiations. _____

49. If everyone will (a) co-operate, (b) co operate, (c) cooperate, our meeting might end on time. _____

50. The executives of AIG are (a) suppose, (b) supposed to eliminate benefits. _____

Techniques for Effective Paragraphs

As you learned in the Writer's Workshop for Unit 2, the basic unit in writing is the sentence. The next unit is the paragraph. Although no rule regulates the length of paragraphs, business writers recognize the value of short paragraphs. Paragraphs with fewer than eight printed lines look inviting and readable, whereas long, solid chunks of print appear formidable. In this workshop you will learn writing techniques for organizing sentences into readable, coherent, and clear paragraphs. The first important technique involves topic sentences.

Organizing Paragraphs Around Topic Sentences

A well-organized paragraph has two important characteristics. First, it covers just one subject. For example, if you are writing about your booth at the Las Vegas computer expo, you wouldn't throw in a sentence about trouble with the IRS. Keep all the sentences in a paragraph related to one topic. Second, a well-organized paragraph begins with a topic sentence that summarizes what the paragraph is about. A topic sentence helps readers by preparing them for what follows.

Consider the following scenario. Assume your company promotes an extensive schedule of team sports for employees after hours. One group enjoys weekend bicycling. You have been assigned the task of writing an e-mail message to the members of this group stating that they must wear helmets when cycling. One paragraph of your message covers statistics about cycling accidents and the incidence of brain injury for unhelmeted riders. Another paragraph discusses the protection offered by helmets:

> *Helmets protect the brain from injury.* They spread the force of a crash from the point of impact to a wider area. When an accident occurs, an unhelmeted head undergoes two collisions. The first occurs when the skull slams into the ground. The second occurs when the brain hits the inside of the skull. A helmet softens the second blow and acts as a shock absorber. Instead of crushing the brain, the impact crushes the foam core of the helmet, often preventing serious brain injury.

Notice how the preceding paragraph focuses on just one topic: how helmets protect the brain from injury. Every sentence relates to that topic. Notice, too, that the first sentence functions as a topic sentence, informing the reader of the subject of the paragraph.

The best way to write a good paragraph is to list all the ideas you may include. Following is a rough draft of ideas for the preceding paragraph. Notice that the fourth item doesn't relate to the topic sentence. By listing the ideas to be included in a paragraph, you can immediately see what belongs—and what doesn't. Once the list is made, you can easily write the topic sentence.

Paragraph Idea List

1. Helmets spread force of impact.
2. Crashes cause two collisions, the first when the skull hits the ground and the second when the brain hits the skull.
3. The foam core of the helmet absorbs the impact.
4. ~~The federal government has issued biking regulations requiring helmets.~~ [Cross out items that don't belong.]

Topic Sentence: Helmets protect the brain from injury.

Skill Check 3.1: Organizing a Paragraph

In a letter to the college president, the athletic director is arguing for a new stadium scoreboard. One paragraph will describe the old scoreboard and why it needs to be replaced. Study the following list of ideas for that paragraph.

1. The old scoreboard was originally constructed in the 1960s.

2. It is now hard to find replacement parts for it when something breaks.

3. The old scoreboard is not energy efficient.

4. Coca-Cola has offered to buy a new sports scoreboard in return for exclusive rights to sell soda on campus.

5. The old scoreboard should be replaced for many reasons.

6. It shows only scores for football games.

7. When we have soccer games or track meets, we are without any functioning scoreboard.

   a. Which sentence should be the topic sentence?
   b. Which sentence(s) should be developed in a different paragraph?
   c. Which sentences should follow the topic sentence?

Writing Coherent Paragraphs

Effective paragraphs are coherent; that is, they hold together. **Coherence** is a quality of good writing that doesn't happen accidentally. It is consciously achieved through effective organization and through skillful use of three devices. These writing devices are (a) repetition of key ideas or key words, (b) use of pronouns that refer clearly to their antecedents, and (c) use of transitional expressions.

Repetition of Key Ideas or Key Words. Repeating a key word or key thought from a preceding sentence helps guide a reader from one thought to the next. This redundancy is necessary to build cohesiveness into writing. Notice how the word *deal* is repeated in the second sentence.

> For the past six months, college administrators and Coca-Cola have been working on a *deal* in which the college would receive a new sports scoreboard. The *deal* would involve exclusive rights to sell soft drinks on the 12,000-student campus.

Use of Pronouns That Refer Clearly to Their Antecedents. Pronouns such as *this, that, they, these, those,* and *it* help connect thoughts in sentences. However, these pronouns are useful only when their antecedents are clear. Often it is better to make the pronoun into an adjective joined with its antecedent to ensure that the reference is absolutely clear. Notice how the pronoun *this* is clearer when it is joined to its antecedent *contract*.

Confusing: The Coca-Cola offer requires an exclusive contract committing the college for ten years without any provision preventing a price increase. *This* could be very costly to students, staff, and faculty.

Improved: The Coca-Cola offer requires an exclusive contract committing the college for ten years without any provision preventing a price increase. *This contract* could be very costly to students, staff, and faculty.

Avoid vague pronouns, such as *it* in the following example.

Confusing: Both Coca-Cola and PepsiCo offered to serve our campus, and we agreed to allow *it* to submit a bid.

Improved: Both Coca-Cola and PepsiCo offered to serve our campus, and we agreed to allow Coca-Cola to submit a bid.

Use of Transitional Expressions. One of the most effective ways to achieve paragraph coherence is through the use of transitional expressions. These expressions act as road signs. They indicate where the message is headed, and they help the reader anticipate what is coming. Some common transitional expressions follow:

although	furthermore	moreover
as a result	hence	nevertheless
consequently	however	of course
for example	in addition	on the other hand
for this reason	in this way	therefore

Other words that act as connectives are *first, second, finally, after, meanwhile, next, after all, instead, specifically, thus, also, likewise, as,* and *as if.*

The following paragraph achieves coherence through the use of all three techniques. (1) The key idea of *surprising battle* in the first sentence is echoed in the second sentence with repetition of the word *battle* coupled with *unexpected*, a synonym for *surprising*. (2) The use of a pronoun, *This*, in the second sentence connects the second sentence to the first. (3) The transitional words *however* and *as a result* in following sentences continue to build coherence.

A *surprising battle* between two global cola giants was recently fought in Venezuela. *This battle* was *unexpected* because Venezuelans had always been loyal Pepsi drinkers. *However*, when the nation's leading bottler sold half of its interest to Coca-Cola, everything changed. *As a result*, Coca-Cola turned the Pepsi-drinking nation of Venezuela into Coke drinkers almost overnight.

Skill Check 3.2: Improving Paragraph Coherence

In the following space or on a separate sheet of paper, use the information from Skill Check 3.1 to write a coherent paragraph about replacing the sports scoreboard. Remember that this paragraph is part of a letter from the athletic director to the college president. Include a topic sentence. Strive to illustrate all three techniques to achieve coherence.

_____

_____

_____

_____

_____

Developing Parallel Construction

Paragraph clarity can be improved by expressing similar ideas with similar grammatical structures. For example, if you are listing three ideas, do not use *ing* words for two of the ideas and a *to* verb with the third idea: *reading, eating, and studying* (not *to study*). Use adjectives with adjectives, verbs with verbs, phrases with phrases, and clauses with clauses. In the following list, use all verbs: *the machine sorted, stamped, and counted* (not *and had a counter*). For phrases, the wording for all parts of the list should be matched; *safety must be improved in the home, in the classroom, and on the job* (not *for office workers*).

Poor:	Ms. Tanaga is energetic, resourceful, and she can be relied on.
Improved:	Ms. Tanaga is energetic, resourceful, and reliable. (Matches adjectives.)
Poor:	The new shredder helped us save money, reduce pollution, and paper could be recycled.
Improved:	The new shredder helped us save money, reduce pollution, and recycle paper. (Matches verb–noun construction.)

Skill Check 3.3: Improving Parallel Construction

Revise each of the following sentences to improve parallel construction.

1. Some airlines offer frequent fliers free upgrades, priority boarding, and they can call special reservation numbers.

   _____

   _____

2. Your job is to research, design, and the implementation of a diversity program.

   _____

3. Few managers are able to write letters accurately, concisely, and with efficiency.

   _____

4. The new software totals all balances, gives weekly reports, and statements are printed.

   _____

5. Our objectives are to make our stock profitable, to operate efficiently, and developing good employee relations.

   _____

   _____

Writing Application 3.1

Revise the following paragraph. Add a topic sentence and improve the organization. Correct pronouns with unclear antecedents, wordiness, and misplaced verbal modifiers (which you learned about in Chapter 8). Add transitional expressions if appropriate.

You may be interested in applying for a new position within the company. The Human Resources Department has a number of jobs available immediately. The positions are at a high level. Current employees may apply immediately for open positions in production, for some in marketing, and jobs in administrative support are also available. To make application, these positions require immediate action. Come to the Human Resources Department. We have a list showing the open positions, what the qualifications are, and job descriptions are shown. Many of the jobs are now open. That's why we are sending this now. To be hired, an interview must be scheduled within the next two weeks.

Writing Application 3.2

Revise the following poorly written paragraph. Add a topic sentence and improve the organization. Correct misplaced modifiers, pronouns with unclear antecedents, wordiness, and any other writing faults. Add transitional expressions if appropriate.

> As you probably already know, this company (Lasertronics) will be installing new computer software shortly. There will be a demonstration April 18, which is a Tuesday. We felt this was necessary because this new software is so different from our previous software. It will be from 9 to 12 a.m. in the morning. This will show employees how the software programs work. They will learn about the operating system, and this should be helpful to nearly everyone. There will be information about the new word processing program, which should be helpful to administrative assistants and product managers. For all you people who work with payroll, there will be information about the new database program. We can't show everything the software will do at this one demo, but for these three areas there will be some help at the Tuesday demo. Oh yes, Paula Roddy will be presenting the demonstration. She is the representative from Quantum Software.

Writing Application 3.3

Assume you work in the Human Resources Department of Bank of America. You must write an e-mail announcement describing a special program of classes for your employees. Use the following information to write a well-organized paragraph announcement. This information is purposely disorganized; you must decide how to best organize it. Add any information needed for clarity.

Explain that Bank of America will reimburse any employee the full cost of tuition and books if that employee attends classes. Describe the plan. Skyline Community College, in cooperation with Bank of America, will offer a group of courses for college credit at very convenient locations for our employees. Actually, the classes will be offered at your downtown and East Bay branches. Tell employees that they should call Jean Fujimoto at Ext. 660 if they are interested. You'd better mention the tuition: $180 for a semester course. Explain that we (Bank of America) are willing to pay these fees because we value education highly. However, make it clear that employees must receive a grade of C or higher before they are eligible for reimbursement of course and book fees. It might be a good idea to attach a list of the courses and the times that they will be offered. Include a deadline date for calling Jean.

Use the e-mail message in Figure 3.1 as a model as you compose your e-mail announcement. You can refer to an attached list of courses and time, but you do not have to prepare the actual attachment.

FIGURE 3.1

E-Mail Message

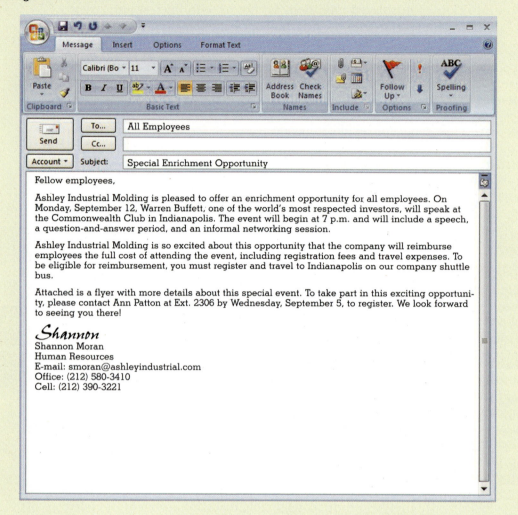

Unit 4

Modifying and Connecting Words

11 Modifiers: Adjectives and Adverbs

© Tetra Images/Jupiterimages

12 Prepositions

© Getty Images/Brand X Pictures/Jupiterimages

13 Conjunctions

© Jose Luis Pelaez, Inc./Blend Images/Corbis

> *"A man's character may be learned from the adjectives which he habitually uses in conversation."*
>
> **—Mark Twain, writer**

Chapter 11
Modifiers: Adjectives and Adverbs

OBJECTIVES

When you have completed the materials in this chapter, you will be able to do the following:

LEVEL 1
- Decide whether to use adjectives or adverbs in sentences.
- Form the comparative and superlative degrees of regular and irregular adjectives and adverbs.

LEVEL 2
- Use articles, demonstrative adjectives, possessive adjectives, compound adjectives, and independent adjectives correctly.
- Avoid double negatives.

LEVEL 3
- Master the correct usage of commonly confused adjectives and adverbs.
- Make comparisons within a group, and place adverbs and adjectives close to the words they modify.

Underline the letter representing the correct answer.

1. Of the two proposals, I like this one (a) better, (b) best.

2. When it is raining, people should drive (a) carefuller, (b) more carefully.

3. The (a) worse, (b) worst weather in London is in January.

4. (a) A, (b) An exceptional job was done on the Web site redesign.

5. (a) This, (b) These sorts of meetings can be very productive.

6. We (a) couldn't, (b) could hardly believe the news.

7. If you did (a) good, (b) well in the interview, you will be hired.

8. Our (a) six-year-old, (b) six year old lease must be renegotiated.

9. The (a) newly repaired, (b) newly-repaired copier seems to be working well.

10. Elizabeth took (a) less, (b) fewer sick days this year than she did last year.

You can use adjectives and adverbs to add character to your writing. Both adjectives and adverbs act as modifiers; that is, they describe or limit other words. Many of the forms and functions of adjectives and adverbs are similar. Because of this similarity, these two parts of speech may be confused. That is why we will treat adjectives and adverbs together in this chapter.

LEVEL 1

Basic Functions of Adjectives and Adverbs

Adjectives describe or limit nouns and pronouns. As you learned in Chapter 2, adjectives often answer the questions *What kind?*, *How many?*, or *Which one?* Adjectives in the following sentences are italicized.

> *Yellow* walls in homes and offices are *cheerful*. (Adjectives answer *What kind?*)
>
> *Small, independent* businesses are becoming *numerous*. (Adjectives answer *What kind?*)
>
> *Two government* grants were awarded to *the eight top* institutions. (Adjectives answer *How many?* and *What kind?*)
>
> *This* book discusses *economic* theory. (Adjectives answer *Which one?* and *What kind?*)

Adverbs usually describe or limit verbs, adjectives, or other adverbs. Adverbs may also modify pronouns, numerals, phrases, or entire sentences. Many adverbs are formed by adding *ly* to adjectives (*efficient, efficiently*). However, some of the most commonly used adverbs do not end in *ly*, including *here, there, tomorrow, today, always, later, never, now, often, seldom, sometimes, soon, still, when, indeed, much, not, so,* and *too.*

Career Tip

Good writers avoid vague and overworked adverbs and adjectives (such as *interesting, good, nice, great, very, really, so,* and *bad*). You should strive to use precise words that say exactly what you mean.

1.a 2.b 3.b 4.b 5.b 6.b 7.b 8.a 9.a 10.b

Adverbs often answer the questions *When?, How?, Where?,* or *To what extent?,* as you can see in these examples:

> *Today* we left work *early.* (Adverbs answer *When?* and *How?*)
>
> Please take a seat *there.* (Adverb answers *Where?*)
>
> Because we drove *so slowly,* we arrived *late* to the gathering. (Adverbs answer *To what extent?, How?,* and *When?*)
>
> The introductions were made *very quickly.* (Adverbs answer *To what extent?* and *How?*)

Deciding Whether to Use Adjectives or Adverbs

Because they are closely related, adjectives are sometimes confused with adverbs. Here are guidelines that will help you choose the appropriate adjective or adverb.

When to Use Adjectives

Use adjectives to modify or describe nouns and pronouns. Note particularly that adjectives (not adverbs) should follow linking verbs.

> The actors gave *incredible* performances.
>
> This pasta tastes *delicious.* (Not *deliciously*)
>
> I feel *bad* about the loss. (Not *badly*)
>
> She looks *good* in her business suit. (Not *well*)

When to Use Adverbs

Use adverbs to modify or describe verbs, adjectives, or other adverbs.

> The engine runs *smoothly.* (Not *smooth*)
>
> It runs *more smoothly* than before. (Not *smoother*)
>
> Listen *carefully* to the directions. (Not *careful*)

A few adverbs have two acceptable forms: *slow, slowly; quick, quickly; deep, deeply; direct, directly;* and *close, closely.*

> Drive *slowly.* (Or, less formally, *slow*)
>
> You may dial us *directly.* (Or, less formally, *direct*)
>
> Time passes *quickly.* (Not *quick*)

Comparative and Superlative Forms

Most adjectives and adverbs have three **forms,** or **degrees:** positive, comparative, and superlative. The **positive degree** of an adjective or an adverb is used in merely describing or in limiting another word. The **comparative degree** is used to compare two persons or things. The **superlative degree** is used in the comparison of three or more persons or things.

Regular Adjectives and Adverbs

Regular adjectives and **regular adverbs** form their comparative and superlative degrees similarly, which you will see in the following two sections.

Regular Adjectives

The **comparative degree** of most one-syllable and some two-syllable adjectives is formed by adding *r* or *er* (*nicer, quieter*). The **superlative degree** of short adjectives is formed by the addition of *st* or *est* (*warmest*). When a two-syllable adjective ends in *y*, change the *y* to *i* before adding *er* or *est* (*happier, heaviest*).

Long adjectives and those that are awkward or difficult to pronounce form the comparative and superlative degrees with the addition of *more* and *most* (*more careful, most beautiful*) or *less* and *least* (*less popular, least popular*). The following examples illustrate the comparative and superlative degrees of regular adjectives.

	Positive	Comparative	Superlative
One Syllable:	warm	warmer	warmest
Two Syllable:	quiet	quieter	quietest
Ending in ***y:***	pretty	prettier	prettiest
Two Syllable/ Awkward:	useful	more/less useful	most/least useful
Three or More Syllables:	excellent	more/less excellent	most/least excellent

The following sentences illustrate degrees of comparison for regular adjectives.

Sales are unusually *high*.	(Positive degree)
Sales are *higher* than ever before.	(Comparative degree)
Sales are the *highest* in years.	(Superlative degree)
The new process is *efficient*.	(Positive degree)
The new process is *more* (or *less*) *efficient* than our previous one.	(Comparative degree)
The new process is the *most* (or *least*) *efficient* one possible.	(Superlative degree)

Regular Adverbs

The **comparative degree** of some short adverbs (nearly all one-syllable) is formed by adding *r* or *er* (*faster*), and the **superlative degree** is formed by adding *st* or *est* (*fastest*). Most adverbs, however, form the comparative and superlative degrees with the addition of *more* and *most* (*more slowly, most beautifully*) or *less* and *least* (*less efficiently, least carefully*).

Trivia Tidbit

Nothing rhymes with the adjectives *orange, silver,* or *purple* or with the noun *month*.

	Positive	Comparative	Superlative
One Syllable:	fast	faster	fastest
Two or More Syllables:	neatly	more (or less) neatly	most (or least) neatly

The following examples illustrate how the comparative and superlative degrees of regular adverbs are formed.

He drives *carefully*.	(Positive degree)
He drives *more* (or *less*) *carefully* now.	(Comparative degree)
He drives *most* (or *least*) *carefully* at night.	(Superlative degree)

Do not create a double comparative form by using *more* and the suffix *er* together (such as *more neater*) or by using *most* and the suffix *est* together (such as *most fastest*).

Irregular Adjectives and Adverbs

A few adjectives and adverbs form the comparative and superlative degrees irregularly.

Study Tip

The comparative and superlative forms of irregular adjectives and adverbs appear in dictionaries. The comparative forms of regular adjectives and adverbs do not.

	Positive	Comparative	Superlative
Adjectives:	good, well	better	best
	bad	worse	worst
	far	farther, further	farthest, furthest
	little	littler, less	littlest, least
	many, much	more	most
Adverbs:	well	better	best
	many, much	more	most

Now complete the reinforcement exercises for Level 1.

LEVEL 2

Modifiers That Deserve Special Attention

A few adjectives and adverbs require special attention because they cause writers and speakers difficulty.

Articles

The **articles** *a, an,* and *the* make up a special category of adjectives, and these words must be used carefully. The **definite article** *the* is used to describe a specific person or thing, as in *the film* or *the films.* The definite article *the* can be used with singular or plural nouns.

When describing persons or things in general, use the **indefinite article** *a* or *an,* as in *a film* (meaning *any* film). Indefinite articles are used only with singular nouns. The choice of *a* or *an* is determined by the initial sound of the word modified. *A* is used before consonant sounds; *an* is used before vowel sounds.

Study Tip

The sound, not the spelling, of a word governs the choice between *a* and *an.* When the letter *u* sounds like a *y,* it is treated as a consonant: a *u*tility, a *u*sed car.

Before Vowel Sounds		Before Consonant Sounds	
an operator		a shop	
an executive		a plan	
an hour ⎱	*h* is not voiced;	a hook ⎱	
an honor ⎰	vowel is heard	a hole ⎰	*h* is voiced
an office ⎱	*o* sounds	a one-man show ⎱	*o* sounds like
an onion ⎰	like a vowel	a one-week trip ⎰	the consonant *w*

MODIFIERS: ADJECTIVES AND ADVERBS

Before Vowel Sounds		Before Consonant Sounds	
an understudy	*u* sounds	a union	*u* sounds like
an umbrella	like a vowel	a unit	the consonant *y*
an X-ray	*x* and *m* sound		
an M.D.	like vowels		

Demonstrative Adjectives

Demonstrative adjectives indicate whether a noun is plural or singular and whether it is located nearby or farther away. The demonstrative adjective *this*, and its plural form *these*, indicates something nearby. The demonstrative adjective *that*, and its plural form *those*, indicates something at a distance. Be careful to use the singular forms of these words with singular nouns and the plural forms with plural nouns: *this shoe, that road, these accounts, those records*. Pay special attention to the nouns *kind, type*, and *sort*. Match singular adjectives to the singular forms of these nouns and plural adjectives to the plural forms.

> **Incorrect:** Job interviewees should be prepared for these type of questions.
>
> **Correct:** Job interviewees should be prepared for this type of question.
>
> **Correct:** Job interviewees should be prepared for these types of questions.

Possessive Adjectives

As you learned in Chapters 2 and 6, some possessive pronouns serve as **possessive adjectives** when they describe nouns. Examples of these words include *my, our, your, his, her, its*, and *their*. You can tell that a pronoun is functioning as an adjective when it comes before the noun it is describing.

> *My job* has become demanding lately.
>
> Please visit *our offices* when you are in town.
>
> Please submit *your application* online.

Compound Adjectives

Writers may form their own adjectives by joining two or more words. When these words act as a single modifier preceding a noun, they are temporarily hyphenated. If these same words appear after a noun, they are generally not hyphenated.

Words Temporarily Hyphenated Before a Noun	Same Words Not Hyphenated After a Noun
never-say-die attitude	attitude of never say die
eight-story building	building of eight stories
state-sponsored program	program that is state sponsored
a case-by-case analysis	analysis that is case by case
follow-up appointment	an appointment to follow up
income-related expenses	expenses that are income related
four-year-old child	child who is four years old
home-based business	business that is home based

Compound adjectives shown in your dictionary with hyphens are considered permanently hyphenated. Regardless of whether the compound adjective appears before or after a noun, it retains the hyphens. Use a current dictionary or reference manual to determine what expressions are always hyphenated. Be sure that you find the dictionary entry that is marked *adjective*. Here are samples:

Permanent Hyphens Before Nouns	Permanent Hyphens After Nouns
first-class seats	seats that are first-class
up-to-date information	the information is up-to-date
old-fashioned attitude	attitude that is old-fashioned
short-term goals	goals that are short-term
well-known expert	expert who is well-known
full-time (part-time) employee	employee who is full-time (part-time)

Don't confuse adverbs ending in *ly* with compound adjectives: *newly decorated office* and *highly regarded architect* would not be hyphenated.

As compound adjectives become more familiar, they are often simplified and the hyphen is dropped. Some familiar compounds that are not hyphenated are *high school student, charge account balance, income tax return, home office equipment, word processing software, health care provider, human resources management, voice mail message*, and *data processing center*.

Hyphens are used even if part of the compound adjective is implied.

Several *three-* and *four-bedroom* homes are for sale.

High- and *low-priced* homes are selling quickly.

Independent Adjectives

Independent adjectives occur when two or more adjectives appearing before a noun independently modify the noun. Writers must separate independent adjectives with commas. Do not use a comma, however, when the first adjective modifies the combined idea of the second adjective and the noun.

Two Adjectives Independently Modifying a Noun	First Adjective Modifying a Second Adjective Plus a Noun
positive, reliable employee	efficient administrative assistant
economical, efficient car	graphite grey sports car
stimulating, provocative book	assistant deputy director

Double Negatives

When a negative adverb (*no, not, nothing, scarcely, hardly, barely*) is used in the same sentence with a negative verb (*didn't, don't, won't*), a substandard construction called a **double negative** results. Among professionals, such constructions are considered to be illogical and illiterate. In the following examples, notice that eliminating one negative corrects the double negative.

Incorrect: Calling her *won't* do *no* good.

Correct: Calling her will do no good.

Correct: Calling her won't do any good.

Study Tip

To determine whether successive adjectives are independent, mentally insert the word *and* between them. If the insertion makes sense, the adjectives are probably independent and require a comma.

Trivia Tidbit

At one time in the history of the English language, multiple negatives were used to emphasize an idea. (*Don't never say nothing wicked!*) But in the eighteenth century, grammarians adopted Latin logic and decreed that two negatives created a positive.

Incorrect:	We *couldn't hardly* believe the candidate's statement.
Correct:	We could hardly believe the candidate's statement.
Correct:	We couldn't believe the candidate's statement.

Incorrect:	Drivers *can't barely* see in the heavy fog.
Correct:	Drivers can barely see in the heavy fog.
Correct:	Drivers can't see in the heavy fog.

Incorrect:	He *didn't have nothing* to do with it.
Correct:	He had nothing to do with it.
Correct:	He didn't have anything to do with it.

Now complete the reinforcement exercises for Level 2.

LEVEL 3

Adjective and Adverb Challenges

In this section you will learn to use commonly confused adjectives and adverbs correctly. You will also learn how to make comparisons within a group and how to place adjectives and adverbs appropriately in sentences.

Commonly Confused Adjectives and Adverbs

The following adjectives and adverbs cause difficulty for some writers and speakers. With a little study, you can master their correct usage.

almost (adj.— nearly): *Almost* (not *Most*) everyone wants to work.

most (adj.— greatest in amount): *Most* managers are good leaders.

farther (adv.—actual distance): How much *farther* is the airport?

further (adv.—additionally): Let's discuss the issue *further*.

sure (adj.—certain): She is *sure* of her decision.

surely (adv.—undoubtedly): He will *surely* be victorious.

later (adv.—after expected time): The contract arrived *later* in the day.

latter (adj.—the second of two things): Of the two options, I prefer the *latter*.

fewer (adj.—refers to countable items): *Fewer* requests for tours were granted this year.

less (adj.—refers to amounts or quantities): *Less* time remains than we anticipated.

real (adj.—actual, genuine): The *real* power in the company lies with the board of directors.

really (adv.—actually, truly): Jan is *really* eager to take her vacation.

good (adj.—desirable): A number of *good* plans were submitted.

well $\begin{cases} \text{(adv.—satisfactorily): Amy did } \textit{well} \text{ on her performance evaluation.} \\ \text{(adj.—healthy): Jamal feels } \textit{well} \text{ enough to return to work.} \end{cases}$

Study Tip

Typically, *well* is an adverb. But Americans use it as an adjective when referring to health (*I feel well*). When referring to good spirits, use *good* (*I feel good*). By the way, the British do not make this distinction.

Comparisons Within a Group

When the word *than* is used to compare a person, place, or thing with other members of a group to which it belongs, be certain to include the words *other* or *else* in the comparison. This inclusion ensures that the person or thing being compared is separated from the group with which it is compared.

Illogical: Alaska is larger than any state in the United States. (This sentence suggests that Alaska is larger than itself.)

Logical: Alaska is larger than any *other* state in the United States.

Illogical: Our team had better results than any team in the company.

Logical: Our team had better results than any *other* team in the company.

Illogical: Alex works harder than anyone in the office.

Logical: Alex works harder than anyone *else* in the office.

Placing Adverbs and Adjectives

The position of an adverb or adjective can seriously affect the meaning of a sentence. Study these examples:

Only Cathi MacPherson can change the password. (No one else can change it.)

Cathi MacPherson can *only* change the password. (She can't do anything else.)

Cathi MacPherson can change *only* the password. (She can't change anything else.)

To avoid confusion, adverbs and adjectives should be placed close to the words they modify. In this regard, special attention should be given to the words *only, merely, first*, and *last*.

Confusing: He *merely* said that the report could be improved.

Clear: He said *merely* that the report could be improved.

Confusing: Seats in the five *first* rows have been reserved.

Clear: Seats in the *first* five rows have been reserved.

Now complete the reinforcement exercises for Level 3.

Spot the BLOOPER

Using the skills you are learning in this class, try to identify why the following items are bloopers. Consult your textbook, dictionary, or reference manual as needed.

Blooper 1: Headline in the Real Estate section of the *San Francisco Chronicle*: "A bit noisy but real nice."

Blooper 2: From a Citibank brochure: "Your Citibank card will only access your checking account for these type purchases." [Did you spot two errors?]

Blooper 3: From a full-page IBM advertisement: "Can you really buy a computer that makes someone feel differently about their job?"

Blooper 4: Headline in *The Daily Aztec*, the student newspaper at San Diego State University: "Juveniles Arrested for Attempted Parking Structure Theft."

Blooper 5: Steve Carell, playing the role of Michael Scott on *The Office*: "I think that I'm approachable as one of the guys, but maybe I need to be approachabler."

Blooper 6: From a radio advertisement for an Internet Service Provider (ISP): "With our Internet service you'll get less annoying pop-up ads."

Blooper 7: Headline from *The Atlanta Journal-Constitution*: "Braves Fans Owe Nothing to No One."

Blooper 8: From a radio commercial for The Club, a device to prevent auto theft: "The Club works where other cheap imitations fail." [Does this statement say that The Club is a cheap imitation?]

Blooper 9: From *The Naples* [Florida] *Daily News*: "We may publish more letters to the editor than any newspaper in America."

Blooper 10: Headline from *The Concord* [New Hampshire] *Monitor*: "How Can You Expect a Child Who Can't Tell Time to Only Get Sick During Office Hours?"

 # FAQs

Answered by Dr. Guffey and Professor Seefer

Dr. Guffey Professor Seefer

Question	Answer
Q: Is it necessary to hyphenate a *25 percent* discount?	**A:** No. Percents are not treated in the same way that numbers appearing in compound adjectives are treated. Thus, you would not hyphenate a *15 percent* loan, but you would hyphenate a *15-year* loan.
Q: Why does the sign above my grocery market's quick-check stand say *Ten or less items*? Shouldn't it read *Ten or fewer items*?	**A:** Right you are! *Fewer* refers to numbers or countable items, as in *fewer items*. *Less* refers to amounts or quantities, as in *less food*. Perhaps markets prefer *less* because it has fewer letters.

Question	Answer
Q: In my writing I want to use *firstly* and *secondly*. Are they acceptable?	**A:** Both words are acceptable, but most writers prefer *first* and *second* because they are more efficient and equally accurate.
Q: How many hyphens should I use in this sentence? *The three, four, and five year plans continue to be funded.*	**A:** Three hyphens are needed: *three-, four-, and five-year plans*. Hyphenate compound adjectives even when the parts of the compound are separated or suspended.
Q: Why can't I remember how to spell *already*? I want to use it in this sentence: *Your account has <u>already</u> been credited with your payment.*	**A:** You—and many others—have difficulty with *already* because two different words (and meanings) are expressed by essentially the same sounds. The adverb *already* means "previously" or "before this time," as in your sentence. The two-word combination *all ready* means "all prepared," as in *The club members are all ready to board the bus*. If you can logically insert the word *completely* between *all* and *ready*, you know the two-word combination is needed.
Q: I never know how to write *part time*. Is it always hyphenated?	**A:** The dictionary shows all of its uses to be hyphenated. *She was a part-time employee* (used as an adjective). *He worked part-time* (used as adverb). The adjective *full-time* also has permanent hyphenation.
Q: Here are some expressions that cause us trouble in our business letters. We want to hyphenate all of the following. Right? *Well-produced play, awareness-generation film, decision-making tables, one-paragraph note, swearing-in ceremony, point-by-point analysis, commonly-used book.*	**A:** All your hyphenated forms are correct except the last one. Don't use a hyphen with an *ly*-ending adverb.
Q: Is this a double negative? *We <u>can't</u> schedule the meeting because we have <u>no</u> room available.*	**A:** No, this is not regarded as a double negative. In grammar a double negative is created when two negative adverbs modify a verb, such as *can't hardly, won't barely*, or *can't help but*. Avoid such constructions.
Q: I can never seem to keep *desert* and *dessert* straight. When do I use each?	**A:** Yes, these two words can be tricky, especially because desert has several different meanings and two different pronunciations. As a noun, *desert* refers to arid land (*they were lost for days in the desert*). As an adjective, *desert* is used to describe something that is desolate or sparsely occupied (*a desert island*). These two forms have the same pronunciation, with the accent on the first syllabus. As a verb, *desert* means "to withdraw from or leave" (*the army will desert the village at noon*). The word *dessert* is a noun referring to a sweet course or dish (*my favorite part of the meal is dessert*). Both the verb *desert* and the noun *dessert* have the same pronunciation, with the accent on the second syllable.
Q: Is there a difference between *awhile* and *a while*?	**A:** Yes. Here's how to decide whether to write this as one word or two. *Awhile* as one word is an adverb meaning "for a period of time" (*we sat awhile to rest our feet*). As two words *a while* is a noun phrase with *a* serving as an article to describe the noun *while* (*I have been searching for a while for the perfect site*). A good trick to remember is that if this word follows the word *for*, write it as two words.

11 Reinforcement Exercises

LEVEL 1

Online Homework Help! For immediate feedback on odd-numbered items, go to **www.meguffey.com.**

 A. (Self-check) Select the correct answer.

1. This is the (a) worse, (b) worst the economy has been since the Great Depression. _____
2. The company's profits are (a) worse, (b) worst this quarter than last quarter. _____
3. Unless online orders can be processed (a) more efficient, (b) more efficiently, we lose business to our competitors. _____
4. Try to write (a) legible, (b) legibly on the application form. _____
5. Matthew felt (a) bad, (b) badly that he missed the meeting. _____
6. With (a) more careful, (b) carefuller planning, this problem could be avoided. _____
7. I can't think of a (a) better, (b) more better plan. _____
8. This is the (a) coldest, (b) most cold day we have had all year. _____
9. When giving your presentation, try to speak (a) natural, (b) naturally. _____
10. The outcome of the race between Connors and Morelli will determine the (a) faster, (b) fastest driver. _____

Check your answers below.

 B. Select the correct answer.

1. Politicians have discovered that social networking sites work (a) beautiful, (b) beautifully for campaigning. _____
2. Wal-Mart is the (a) more, (b) most generous of all corporate donors. _____
3. Chad looked (a) longing, (b) longingly at the freshly baked cookies. _____
4. The cookies smelled (a) delicious, (b) deliciously. _____
5. Since its tune-up, the engine runs (a) smoother, (b) more smoothly. _____
6. Please don't take her comments during the meeting (a) personal, (b) personally. _____
7. Leslie looked (a) calm, (b) calmly as she approached the podium. _____
8. This vendor offers (a) faster, (b) more fast delivery. _____
9. Michigan State was beaten (a) bad, (b) badly in the tournament. _____
10. Having prepared for months, we won the bid (a) easy, (b) easily. _____
11. To reduce legal costs, they wanted to reach a settlement (a) quick, (b) quickly. _____

1.b 2.a 3.b 4.b 5.a 6.a 7.a 8.a 9.b 10.a

12. Reaching a (a) quick, (b) quickly settlement could save the firm millions. _____

13. Our new ergonomically designed office furniture should keep employees working (a) comfortable, (b) comfortably. _____

14. Of the two proposals, this one is (a) more, (b) most persuasive. _____

15. If you had been (a) more diligent, (b) diligenter, you would have completed the report on time. _____

16. Between Tom and Max, Tom's credentials are (a) stronger, (b) strongest. _____

17. Sarah is the (a) friendlyest, (b) friendliest person in our office. _____

18. San Francisco is (a) more close, (b) closer to Hawaii than Los Angeles is. _____

19. Please let employees know if you would like them to dress (a) nicer, (b) more nicely for business meetings. _____

20. We watched the demonstration (a) careful, (b) carefully. _____

> **C. Writing Exercise.** In the space provided, write the correct comparative or superlative form of the adjective shown in parentheses.

Example: Of the two wireless plans, which is (good)?   better _____

1. Ian is the (creative) member of the team. _____

2. She did (well) on the certification exam than she expected. _____

3. Please send me the (current) figures you can find. _____

4. The new accounting software is (easy) to master than the software we were using. _____

5. Hotel rooms on upper floors are (quiet) than rooms on lower floors. _____

6. Of all the employees, Richard is the (little) talkative. _____

7. This candidate is (professional) than the previous interviewee. _____

8. Have you ever met a (kind) individual than Lien Phuong Pham? _____

9. This is the (bad) winter we have had in years. _____

10. Which is the (interesting) of the two novels? _____

LEVEL 2

A. (Self-check) Select the correct answer.

1. The candidate for governor appears to be (a) a, (b) an honest person. _____

2. Hospital workers are trying to form (a) a, (b) an union. _____

3. (a) This, (b) These kind of poor report worried management. _____

4. We (a) can, (b) can't hardly expect employees to feel good about the layoffs. _____

5. We don't have (a) nothing, (b) anything we can offer our guests. _____

6. (a) This, (b) These types of computer viruses can be difficult to detect. _____

7. A CEO must be concerned with the (a) day to day, (b) day-to-day operations of the organization. _____

8. We prefer to meet with you (a) face-to-face, (b) face to face to finalize the contract. _____

9. Some small businesses barely exist from (a) year-to-year, (b) year to year. _____

10. In the sentence *Her vacation must be postponed*, the word *Her* is a (a) possessive adjective, (b) possessive pronoun. _____

Check your answers below.

B. Select the correct answer.

1. Upgrading our computer equipment will be (a) a, (b) an large undertaking. _____

2. The wealthy financier left everything to (a) a, (b) an heir he had never met. _____

3. Our (a) five-year-old, (b) five year old contract must be renegotiated. _____

4. It is hard to believe that our company is already (a) five-years-old, (b) five years old. _____

5. Zappos.com received (a) a (b) an "A" grade for customer service. _____

6. (a) This kind, (b) These kinds of rumors can cause stock prices to plunge. _____

7. We can have your order delivered in about (a) a, (b) an hour. _____

8. The mortgage company (a) don't have no, (b) doesn't have any reason to deny the loan. _____

9. (a) This, (b) These types of errors can be caught by proofreading carefully. _____

10. After paying his taxes, Mark complained that he (a) has, (b) hasn't barely a dollar left. _____

11. The biotechnology industry is growing at (a) a, (b) an unusually fast pace. _____

12. Susan said she couldn't see (a) no, (b) any other way to install the program. _____

13. The company knew that it couldn't give (a) nothing, (b) anything to its favorite charity this year. _____

14. It is wise to keep your résumé (a) up-to-date, (b) up to date at all times. _____

15. We are having difficulty selling our (a) high priced, (b) high-priced merchandise. _____

16. Consumers are looking for quality merchandise that is (a) low priced, (b) low-priced. _____

17. I (a) can, (b) can't hardly believe that more than 6 million people use the microblogging service Twitter. _____

18. The rescue squad arrived quickly to help the (a) dog bite, (b) dog-bite victim. _____

19. In the sentence *The last piece of pizza is all yours*, the word *yours* is a (a) possessive adjective, (b) possessive pronoun. _____

20. In the sentence *Your raise has been approved*, the word *Your* is a (a) possessive adjective, (b) possessive pronoun. _____

1. b   2. a   3. a   4. a   5. b   6. b   7. b   8. b   9. b   10. a

C. Supply the proper article (*a* or *an*) for the following words.

Example: _an_ adjustment

1. ____ budget
2. ____ honor
3. ____ inventory
4. ____ usual occurrence
5. ____ Hawaiian

6. ____ warehouse
7. ____ F grade
8. ____ hour
9. ____ idea
10. ____ utility

11. ____ insult
12. ____ X-ray
13. ____ illegible letter
14. ____ one-year lease
15. ____ eight-year lease

D. Select the correct group of words below. Write its letter in the space provided. Use your dictionary if needed to determine whether compound adjectives have permanent hyphenation.

1. a. state of the art technology
   b. state-of-the-art technology _____

2. a. well-documented report
   b. well documented report _____

3. a. child who is ten-years-old
   b. child who is ten years old _____

4. a. ten-year-old child
   b. ten year old child _____

5. a. fully certified nurse
   b. fully-certified nurse _____

6. a. salary of $50,000 a year
   b. salary of $50,000-a-year _____

7. a. $50,000 a year salary
   b. $50,000-a-year salary _____

8. a. full-time job
   b. full time job _____

9. a. job that is full-time
   b. job that is full time _____

10. a. word processing program
    b. word-processing program _____

11. a. first-class accommodations
    b. first class accommodations _____

12. a. voice-mail message
    b. voice mail message _____

13. a. high school diploma
    b. high-school diploma _____

14. a. last-minute preparations
    b. last minute preparations _____

15. a. widely-acclaimed cure
    b. widely acclaimed cure _____

16. a. well known writer
    b. well-known writer _____

17. a. actor who is well known
    b. actor who is well-known _____

18. a. health care provider
    b. health-care provider _____

19. a. figures that are up-to-date
    b. figures that are up to date _____

20. a. no fault insurance
    b. no-fault insurance _____

E. Place commas where needed in the following groups of words.

1. yellow sports car
2. honest fair appraisal
3. concise courteous e-mail message
4. innovative software program
5. direct practical approach

6. snug cheerful apartment
7. imaginative daring designer
8. skilled financial analyst
9. impractical budget item
10. rising stock prices

MODIFIERS: ADJECTIVES AND ADVERBS

F. **Writing Exercise.** Compose sentences using the compound adjectives shown. Be sure that compound adjectives precede nouns. Add hyphens as needed.

Example: (up to the minute)

Your up-to-the-minute report arrived today.

1. (health care)

_____

2. (first class)

_____

3. (part time)

_____

4. (two year old)

_____

5. (once in a lifetime)

_____

6. (month by month)

_____

7. (work related)

_____

8. (state of the art)

_____

9. (voice mail)

_____

10. (day care)

_____

LEVEL 3

A. **(Self-check)** Select the correct answer.

Example: (a) Almost, (b) Most accountants are honest.   _b_

1. Sandra performed (a) good, (b) well on the CPA exam.   _____

2. Of credit card fraud and auction fraud, the (a) later, (b) latter makes up the largest percentage of complaints to the Federal Trade Commission.   _____

3. Patricia Franzoia was (a) real, (b) really surprised to learn that her performance review would be delivered online.   _____

4. Companies have reported (a) fewer, (b) less security breaches this year.   _____

5. The airport was (a) farther, (b) further away than it appeared on our map.   _____

6. My business professor Rose Kessler is more intelligent than (a) any teacher, (b) any other teacher I have ever had.   _____

7. We were told to answer the (a) ten last questions, (b) last ten questions. _____

8. We are concerned (a) with only, (b) only with your welfare and happiness. _____

9. The ballot measure will (a) sure, (b) surely pass. _____

10. New York City is more cosmopolitan than (a) any city, (b) any other city in the United States. _____

Check your answers below.

B. Select the correct answer.

1. Luis feels (a) good, (b) well about his presentation to the board. _____

2. Your new suit certainly fits you (a) good, (b) well. _____

3. The new suit looks very (a) good, (b) well on you. _____

4. Apples and brie cheese taste (a) good, (b) well on pizza. _____

5. Christopher thought that he did (a) good, (b) well in his interview. _____

6. We had (a) fewer, (b) less time to conduct the research than expected. _____

7. Rick feels (a) sure, (b) surely that part-time salaries will improve. _____

8. Fixed-line phones will (a) sure, (b) surely be replaced by mobile phones. _____

9. She wanted to debate the question (a) further, (b) farther. _____

10. Scroll down a little (a) further, (b) farther on the Web page to find the link. _____

11. In an effort to reduce expenses, New Tech will offer employees (a) fewer, (b) less benefit options next year. _____

12. Lavonda wasn't (a) real, (b) really sure she could attend the meeting. _____

13. Her (a) three last, (b) last three books have been best sellers. _____

14. Colonel Bauer asserted that the U.S. Army was safer for women than (a) any other, (b) any organization in America. _____

15. I (a) only have, (b) have only one idea for solving the security problem. _____

16. Of the two films we saw, I prefer the (a) later, (b) latter. _____

17. Houston is larger than (a) any other, (b) any city in Texas. _____

18. That version of software is (a) only sold, (b) sold only on Symantec's Web site. _____

19. The (a) first two, (b) two first applicants presented excellent résumés. _____

20. (a) Less, (b) Fewer money was spent on corporate holiday parties this year. _____

C. Writing Exercise. Compose sentences using the following words.

1. (farther) _____

_____

2. (further) _____

_____

1.b 2.b 3.b 4.a 5.a 6.b 7.b 8.a 9.a 10.b

MODIFIERS: ADJECTIVES AND ADVERBS

3. (latter) _____

_____

4. (fewer) _____

_____

5. (less) _____

_____

D. Skill Maximizer. The following sentences review Levels 1, 2, and 3. Select the correct answers.

1. Radio Shack announced employee layoffs in (a) a, (b) an e-mail message. _____

2. Which of the two marketing campaigns do you like (a) better, (b) best? _____

3. Sandy said that she (a) could, (b) couldn't barely hear you on your cell phone. _____

4. Because of excessive costs, designer Donna Karan made (a) less, (b) fewer trips to the Far East and Africa in search of "creative inspiration." _____

5. Mr. Wu interviewed a Canadian official and (a) a, (b) an European diplomat concerning the proposed two-year trade program. _____

6. Their daughter, who is (a) three years old, (b) three-years-old, is already reading. _____

7. Justin felt that he had done (a) good, (b) well answering difficult questions during his job interview. _____

8. I like this job better than (a) any other, (b) any job I have ever had. _____

9. You shouldn't have spoken so (a) rude, (b) rudely during the meeting. _____

10. Julie Perzel's only task was to make a (a) point by point, (b) point-by-point comparison of the programs. _____

E. FAQs About Business English Review. In the space provided, write the correct answer choice.

1. If you sign the contract today, we will give you a (a) 15 percent, (b) 15-percent discount. _____

2. She is looking for a (a) part time, (b) part-time job for the summer. _____

3. Do you prefer a (a) 24, 36, or 48 month, (b) 24-, 36-, or 48-month loan? _____

4. Jeff was (a) all ready, (b) already to purchase a new car when his loan fell through. _____

5. He had (a) all ready, (b) already selected the model and all of its accessories. _____

6. I believe we should offer this discount (a) awhile, (b) a while longer. _____

7. After using our wireless service for (a) awhile, (b) a while, you will begin to appreciate our quality. _____

8. My favorite (a) desert, (b) dessert is anything made with chocolate. _____

9. She promised to never (a) desert, (b) dessert us. _____

10. Driving across a (a) desert, (b) dessert can be dangerous. _____

You will be giving a presentation during an awards ceremony and would like to include inspirational quotations in your introduction and conclusion. You decide to search for relevant, business-related quotations on the Web.

Goal: To locate quotations online.

1. In the address bar of your Web browser, go to **http://www.quoteland.com**.

2. Click **Quotations by Topic**.

3. Scroll through the list of topics, and click on topics that sound appropriate for a business presentation. Select five quotations that you could include in your presentation, and copy them into a Word document. Be sure to copy both the quotation and the name of the person who is responsible for the quote.

4. To look at another source for business-related quotations, key this URL: **http://www .woopidoo.com**. Click **Quotes**. This will take you to a list of quotations organized by subject and by author. (**Hint:** Click **A to Z Inspirational Quote Subjects** or **A to Z Business Leaders** to access all quotes.)

5. Find five more quotations that you like, and copy them into your Word document.

6. End your session and submit your list of quotations to your instructor.

▶▶ **Chat About It**

Your instructor may assign any of the following topics for you to discuss in class, in an online chat room, or on an online discussion board. Some of the discussion topics may require outside research. You may also be asked to read and respond to postings made by your classmates.

Discussion Topic 1: Assume you are asked the following question during a job interview: *What is your greatest strength?* How would you answer? Come up with ONE adjective that describes your greatest strength (e.g., *dependable, flexible, conscientious*) and write a success story that proves you have this strength. Then share your success story with your classmates, beginning with this statement: *My greatest strength is that I am _____. For example....*

Discussion Topic 2: Think of your favorite published piece; it might be a novel, poem, song, essay, or article. Now, find a paragraph, passage, or stanza that is highly descriptive. The piece you select should make excellent use of adjectives and adverbs. Share your selection with your classmates. Be sure to tell them the name of the author and the title of the publication. Also tell them why you selected this piece of work.

Discussion Topic 3: Mark Twain once said the following: "Substitute 'damn' every time you're inclined to write 'very'; your editor will delete it and the writing will be just as it should be." What does he mean by this? How can you apply this technique to your own writing? Should all adverbs such as *very* be avoided when writing? Why or why not?

Discussion Topic 4: Thousands of adjectives exist in the English language that can be used to describe someone's personality. What TEN adjectives would you use to best describe yourself? Share these adjectives with your classmates.

Discussion Topic 5: Assume that you are selling an item on eBay. Choose the item; then write a one-paragraph description for it that will make it sound attractive. Be sure to use appropriate modifiers. Share your description with your classmates.

Posttest Underline the letter representing the correct answer.

1. Orders are processed (a) smoother, (b) more smoothly using this new software.

2. Steve feels (a) badly, (b) bad about having to reduce employee benefits.

3. (a) This kind, (b) These kinds of employees help make a company successful.

4. Gelato has (a) fewer, (b) less calories than ice cream.

5. It would be (a) a, (b) an honor to meet the author.

6. Tony felt he had done (a) good, (b) well on his certification exam.

7. Cassie completed a (a) page by page, (b) page-by-page review of the document.

8. Employees liked their (a) completely-redecorated, (b) completely redecorated office.

9. We must travel a little (a) farther, (b) further before stopping for the night.

10. We (a) could, (b) couldn't hardly believe the change in her personality.

1. b 2. b 3. b 4. a 5. b 6. b 7. b 8. b 9. a 10. a

"This is the sort of English up with which I will not put."

**—Winston Churchill, prime minister,
United Kingdom (1940–1945, 1951–1955)**

Chapter **12**

Prepositions

OBJECTIVES

When you have completed the materials in this chapter, you will be able to do the following:

LEVEL 1 ● Use objective-case pronouns as objects of prepositions.
● Avoid using prepositions in place of verbs and adverbs.

LEVEL 2 ● Use challenging prepositions correctly.
● Retain necessary prepositions, omit unnecessary ones, and construct formal sentences that avoid terminal prepositions.

LEVEL 3 ● Recognize idioms and idiomatic constructions.
● Use idioms involving prepositions correctly.

Underline the letter representing the correct answer.

1. Leaders like Jack Welch and (a) she, (b) her are admired.

2. Please send your order to my supervisor or (a) I, (b) me.

3. Please plan to sit (a) beside, (b) besides the CEO at the banquet.

4. Lydia is frustrated because she receives (a) to, (b) too much spam.

5. She feels (a) as if, (b) like these spam messages are affecting her productivity.

6. Divide the work evenly (a) between, (b) among the four secretaries.

7. Please turn your form (a) in to, (b) into your supervisor by Friday.

8. Do you plan (a) on taking, (b) to take a two-week vacation?

9. Management and workers alike agreed (a) to, (b) with the contract.

10. This plan is different (a) from, (b) than the one I suggested.

Legend has it that Winston Churchill said these words after an editor rearranged one of his sentences to avoid having it end with a preposition. Whether this story is true has long been debated, but it does illustrate how grammar rules can change over time. At one time it was considered unacceptable to end sentences with prepositions; however, this rule has changed, as you will learn later in this chapter.

Prepositions are connecting words. They show the relationship of a noun or pronoun to other words in a sentence. Chapter 12 reviews the use of objective-case pronouns following prepositions. This chapter also focuses on common problems that communicators have with troublesome prepositions. Finally, this chapter presents many idiomatic expressions in our language that require specific prepositions to sound correct.

LEVEL 1

Common Uses of Prepositions

This list contains the most commonly used prepositions. Notice that prepositions may consist of one word or more than one word.

about	below	in addition to	outside
above	beside	in spite of	over
according to	between	inside	through
after	but	into	to
along with	by	like	toward
alongside	down	near	under

1.b 2.b 3.a 4.b 5.a 6.b 7.a 8.b 9.a 10.a

among	during	of	until
around	except	off	up
at	for	on	upon
before	from	on account of	with
behind	in	opposite	within/without

A preposition often appears in a **prepositional phrase**, which consists of the preposition followed by the object of the preposition. The **object of a preposition** is a noun or pronoun. As you learned in Chapter 2, prepositions in phrases show a relationship between the object of the preposition and another word (or words) in the sentence. In the following sentences, prepositional phrases are italicized. Notice that a sentence can contain more than one prepositional phrase.

> Some *of our greatest innovations* were launched *during tough times.*
>
> The most important ideas *in business* were developed *over the past 100 years.*
>
> The assembly line, created *in 1910 by Henry Ford*, had a positive effect *on the economy.*

Objective Case Following Prepositions

As you learned in Chapter 6, pronouns that are objects of prepositions in prepositional phrases must be in the objective case. Objective-case pronouns include *me, us, you, him, her, it,* and *them.*

> We received comments *from him* and *her* about their dining experience.
>
> The disagreement is with the distributor, not *with you* and *me.*
>
> Give the account balances *to them.*

Less frequently used prepositions are *like, between, except,* and *but* (meaning "except"). These prepositions may lead to confusion in determining pronoun case. Consider the following examples.

> Just *between you and me*, I think this is a good investment.
> (Not *between you and I*)
>
> Volunteers *like Mr. Sheldon and him* are rare. (Not *like Mr. Sheldon and he*)
>
> Applications from everyone *but them* have arrived. (Not *but they*)

Typical Problems With Prepositions

In even the most casual speech or writing, the following misuses of prepositions should be avoided.

Of for *have*

The verb phrases *should have, would have,* and *could have* should never be written as *should of, would of,* or *could of.* The word *of* is a preposition and cannot be used in verb phrases.

> Investors *should have* done more research. (Not *should of*)
>
> I *would have* covered for you if I had been available. (Not *would of*)
>
> Alicia *could have* done better in the interview, but she wasn't prepared.
> (Not *could of*)

Off for *from*

The preposition *from* should never be replaced by *off* or *off of*.

> Kevin borrowed a flash drive *from* Jeff. (Not *off of*)
>
> Shannon said she got the information *from* you. (Not *off* or *off of*)

To for *too*

The preposition *to* means "in a direction toward." Do not use the word *to* in place of the adverb *too*, which means "additionally," "also," or "excessively." The word *to* may also be part of an infinitive construction.

> The 1965 Voting Rights Act is a monument *to* civil rights. (*To* meaning "in a direction toward")
>
> Profits were *too* small to declare dividends. (*Too* meaning "excessively")
>
> We would like to be included in the program *too*. (*Too* meaning "also")
>
> She is learning *to* program in HTML and Java. (*To* as part of the infinitive *to program*)

Now complete the reinforcement exercises for Level 1.

LEVEL 2

Challenging Prepositions

Use special caution with the following prepositions.

Among, between

Among means "in or through the midst of" or "surrounded by." It is usually used to speak of three or more persons or things; *between* means "shared by" and is usually used for two persons or things.

> A merger agreement was made *between* Oracle and PeopleSoft.
>
> Profits were distributed *among* the four partners.

Beside, besides

Beside means "next to"; *besides* means "in addition to."

> The woman sitting *beside* me on the plane was Anne Mulcahy, CEO of Xerox.
>
> *Besides* a résumé, you should bring a list of your references to the interview.

Except

The preposition *except*, meaning "excluding" or "but," is sometimes confused with the verb *accept*, which means "to receive."

> Everyone *except* Paula and him attended the training session.
>
> Did you *accept* the job offer from Starbucks?

In, into, in to

In indicates a position or location. *Into* can mean several things, including (a) entering something, (b) changing form, or (c) making contact. Some constructions may employ *in* as an adverb preceding an infinitive:

> The meeting was held *in* the conference room. (Preposition *in* indicates location.)
>
> We will move *into* our new facilities on May 1. (Preposition *into* indicates entering something.)

Trivia Tidbit

Prepositions are especially challenging when one is learning a new language. For example, in English we live "*on* a street." In other languages, such as Italian, we live "*in* a street."

Their son has grown *into* a fine young man. (Preposition *into* indicates changing form.)

I ran *into* Stan on the way to the meeting. (Preposition *into* indicates making contact with someone.)

They went *in* to see the manager. (Adverb *in* precedes infinitive *to see.*)

Like

The preposition *like* should be used to introduce a noun or pronoun. Do not use *like* to introduce a clause (a group of words with a subject and a predicate). To introduce clauses, use *as, as if,* or *as though.*

She looks *like* Reese Witherspoon. (*Like* used as a preposition to introduce the object *Reese Witherspoon.*)

He looks *as if* (not *like*) he is prepared. (Do not use *like* to introduce the clause *he is prepared.*)

As (not *Like*) I said in my e-mail message, the production deadline has changed. (Do not use *like* to introduce the clause *I said in my e-mail message.*)

Necessary Prepositions

Don't omit those prepositions necessary to clarify a relationship. Be particularly careful when two prepositions modify a single object.

Our appreciation *for* and interest *in* your ideas remain strong. (Do not omit *for.*)

What type *of* employee are you looking for? (Do not omit *of.*)

Don Foster is unsure *of* how to approach the problem. (Do not omit *of.*)

Benefits for exempt employees seem to be higher than *for* nonexempt employees. (Do not omit *for.*)

When did you graduate *from* high school? (Do not omit *from.*)

Unnecessary Prepositions

Omit unnecessary prepositions that clutter sentences.

Leave the shipment *outside* the door. (Better than *outside of*)

Both candidates are qualified. (Better than *both of the candidates*)

I am not sure when the delivery is scheduled. (Better than *is scheduled for*)

Where is the meeting? (Better than *meeting at*)

She could not help laughing. (Better than *help from laughing*)

Keep the paper near the printer. (Better than *near to*)

My cousin's office is opposite mine. (Better than *opposite to* or *opposite of*)

He met with the new manager at lunch. (Better than *met up with*)

Did I wake you? (Better than *Did I wake you up?*)

Ending a Sentence With a Preposition

In the past, language authorities warned against ending a sentence (or a clause) with a preposition. In formal writing today some careful authors continue to avoid ending sentences with prepositions. In conversation and informal writing, however, terminal prepositions are acceptable.

Informal:	What organization is he a member *of*?
Formal:	*Of* what organization is he a member?
Informal:	What is this tool used *for*?
Formal:	*For* what is this tool used?
Informal:	We missed the television news program he appeared on.
Formal:	We missed the television news program on which he appeared.
Informal:	When you called, whom did you speak to?
Formal:	When you called, *to* whom did you speak?

Now complete the reinforcement exercises for Level 2.

Trivia Tidbit

Some of the greatest writers have routinely ended sentences with prepositions. For example, Shakespeare included the following sentences in his plays: "We are such stuff as dreams are made on" (*The Tempest*); "I will wear my heart upon my sleeve for daws to peck at" (*Othello*); and "It is not enough to help the feeble up, but to support him after" (*The Complete Works of William Shakespeare*).

LEVEL 3

Idiomatic Use of Prepositions

Every language has **idioms**, which are word combinations that are unique to that language. These combinations have developed over time through usage and often cannot be explained rationally. A native speaker usually is unaware of idiom usage until a violation jars his or her ear, such as "He is capable *from* (rather than *of*) violence."

The following list shows words that require specific prepositions to denote precise meanings. This group is just a sampling of the large number of English idioms. Consult a dictionary when you are unsure of the correct preposition to use with a particular word.

acquainted with	Are you *acquainted with* the new CEO?
addicted to	Cathy is *addicted to* chocolate.
adept in	Are you *adept in* negotiation tactics?
adhere to	All employees must *adhere* to certain Web-use policies.
agree on (or upon) (mutual ideas)	Our team members *agree on* (or *upon*) nearly everything.
agree to (a proposal or to undertake an action)	Did they *agree to* reduced benefits? We *agree to* supporting our CEO.
agree with (a person or his or her idea)	I *agree with* you on this issue. We *agree with* her suggestion.
all of (when followed by a pronoun)	All *of us* contributed. (For efficiency omit *of* when *all* is followed by a noun, as *All members contributed.*)
angry about (a situation or condition)	Employees are *angry about* the reduction in benefits.
angry at (a thing)	Troy is *angry at* his car for breaking down this morning.
angry with (a person)	Are you *angry with* me for being late?
appreciation for	She has an *appreciation for* organic products.

both of (when followed by a pronoun)	Both *of them* were hired. (For efficiency omit *of* when *both* is followed by a noun, as *Both men were hired*.)
buy from	You may *buy from* any one of our approved vendors.
capable of	She is *capable of* remarkable accomplishments.
comply with	We must *comply with* governmental regulations.
conform to	Your products do not *conform to* our specifications.
contrast with	The angles *contrast with* the curves in that logotype.
convenient to (a location)	The office building is *convenient to* public transportation.
convenient for (a person)	We make returns *convenient for* our customers.
correspond to (a thing)	A company's success *corresponds to* its leadership.
correspond with (a person in writing)	We *correspond with* our clients regularly.
differ from (things)	Debit cards *differ from* credit cards.
differ with (person)	I *differ with* you in small points only.
different from (not *than*)	This product is *different from* the one I ordered.
disagree with	Do you *disagree with* him?
expert in	Dr. Rand is an *expert in* electronics.
guard against	We must *guard against* complacency.
identical with (not *to*)	Our strategy is *identical with* our competitor's.
independent of	Living alone, the young man was *independent of* his parents.
infer from	I *infer from* your remark that you are dissatisfied.
interest in	Matt has a great *interest in* the bond market.
negligent of	Pat was *negligent of* the important duties of his position.
oblivious of or to	He is often *oblivious of* (or *to*) what goes on around him.
plan to (not *on*)	We *plan to* expand our target market.
prefer to	Do you *prefer to* work a four-day week?
reason with	We tried to *reason with* the unhappy customer.
reconcile with (match)	Checkbook figures must be *reconciled with* bank figures.
reconcile to (accept)	He has never become *reconciled to* retirement.
respect for	He has great *respect for* his hardworking colleagues.
responsible for	William is *responsible for* locking the building.
retroactive to (not *from*)	The salary increase is *retroactive to* last July 1.
sensitive to	He is unusually *sensitive to* his employees' needs.
similar to	Your proposal topic is *similar to* mine.
standing in (not *on*) line	How long have you been *standing in* line?
talk to (tell something)	The speaker *talked to* the large group.
talk with (exchange remarks)	Let's *talk with* Theresa about our mutual goals.

Now complete the reinforcement exercises for Level 3.

Trivia Tidbit

An idiom can also be a phrase in which the words together have a different meaning from the dictionary definitions of the individual words, such as *ace in the hole, face value, seed money,* and *melting pot.* What do these idioms mean?

Spot the BLOOPER

Using the skills you are learning in this class, try to identify why the following items are bloopers. Consult your textbook, dictionary, or reference manual as needed.

Blooper 1: In a *Sacramento Bee* article about the growing popularity of social networking: "It seems, all of a sudden, like everyone is on Facebook."

Blooper 2: Bill Maher to John Kerry on Maher's MSNBC show: "You could of went to New Hampshire and killed two birds with one stone." [Did you notice two bloopers?]

Blooper 3: From a national ad for Amtrak: "We plan your vacation. You plan on having a great time."

Blooper 4: From a job applicant's résumé: "Education: Bachelor of engineering. Passed out in top 2 percent."

Blooper 5: From *The Atlanta Journal-Constitution*: A teacher accused of stealing drugs "resigned from his two-year job at Lanier Middle School before turning himself into authorities."

Blooper 6: Colorado Springs traffic sign: "Following to close."

Blooper 7: Sign at an Arby's restaurant in West St. Paul, Minnesota: "We now except checks!"

Blooper 8: Former Congressman Newt Gingrich on Fox News: "There's a phenomena out there that makes Senator Obama different than almost any other politician." [Did you spot two bloopers?]

Blooper 9: From the *Chicago Tribune*: "Sammy Sosa's late arrival at the Cubs' training camp turned into a hug-in between he and manager Don Baylor."

Blooper 10: From a job applicant's cover letter: "I would be prepared to meet with you at your earliest convenience to discuss what I can do to your company."

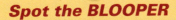 FAQs

Answered by Dr. Guffey and Professor Seefer

 Dr. Guffey Professor Seefer

Question	Answer
Q: What's wrong with saying *Lisa graduated college last year*?	**A:** The preposition *from* must be inserted for syntactical fluency. Two constructions are permissible: *Lisa graduated from college* or *Lisa was graduated from college*. The first version is more popular; the second is preferred by traditional grammarians.
Q: I have a sentence that begins *Beside(s) providing financial aid....* Is there any real difference between *beside* and *besides*?	**A:** Yes, indeed! *Beside* is a preposition meaning "by the side of" (*come sit beside me*). *Besides* is an adverb meaning "in addition to" (*besides paper we must order cartridges*). In your sentence use *besides*.

PREPOSITIONS

Question	Answer

Q: I'm writing a sentence that reads *Please proceed to the podium….* Is this correct, or should I use *precede* instead of *proceed*?

A: You're correct to use *proceed*, which means "to go forward or continue," in this sentence. The word *precede* means "to go before" (*A discussion will precede the final vote*).

Q: I was always taught that you should never end a sentence with a preposition. But sometimes following this rule sounds so stuffy and unnatural, such as saying *From where are you?* instead of *Where are you from?* Is it ever acceptable to end a sentence with a preposition?

A: In the past, language authorities warned against ending a sentence (or a clause) with a preposition. In formal writing today some careful authors continue to avoid terminal prepositions. In conversation and informal writing, however, terminal prepositions are acceptable.

Q: Can you tell me what sounds strange in this sentence and why? *The building looks like it was redesigned.*

A: The word *like* should not be used as a conjunction, as has been done in your sentence. Substitute *as if* (*the building looks as if it was redesigned*).

Q: Should *sometime* be one or two words in the following sentence? *Can you come over (some time) soon?*

A: In this sentence you should use the one-word form. *Sometime* means "an indefinite time" (*the convention is sometime in December*). The two-word combination means "a period of time" (*we have some time to spare*).

Q: I saw this printed recently: *Some of the personal functions being reviewed are job descriptions, job specifications, and job evaluation.* Is *personal* used correctly here?

A: Indeed not! The word *personal* means "private" or "individual" (*your personal letters are being forwarded to you*). The word *personnel* refers to employees (*all company personnel are cordially invited*). The sentence you quote requires *personnel*.

Q: Is there any difference between *proved* and *proven*?

A: As a past participle, the verb form *proved* is preferred (*he has proved his point*). However, the word *proven* is preferred as an adjective form (*that company has a proven record*). *Proven* is also commonly used in the expression *not proven*.

Q: How should I write *industry wide*? It's not in my dictionary.

A: A word with the suffix *wide* is usually written solid: *industrywide, nationwide, countrywide, statewide, worldwide.*

Q: Should the word *onto* be written as one word or two in this sentence? *I think we're really onto something.*

A: You are correct to write *onto* as one word in this sentence. As one word, *onto* is a preposition meaning "in or into a state of awareness about" or "to a position on" (*He turned onto Main Street*). Write *on to* as two words when neither of these definitions apply (*I moved on to the next chapter of my book. I passed the information on to my colleague*). Here is another trick to help you decide: if you can remove the word *on* and the sentence still makes sense, write *on to* as two words.

12 Reinforcement Exercises

LEVEL 1

 A. (Self-check) Select the letter corresponding to the correct answer.

1. All residents in our neighborhood except (a) they, (b) them have installed security systems. _____

2. Bill Gates (a) could of, (b) could have kept his fortune, but he chose to give much of it to a charitable foundation. _____

3. Many believe that corporate annual reports are (a) too, (b) to cryptic to understand. _____

4. Everyone seems to agree to the plan but (a) I, (b) me. _____

5. We were able to get her e-mail address (a) off of, (b) from Zachary. _____

6. Will invitations be sent to Jonathan and (a) her, (b) she? _____

7. Government has (a) to, (b) too consider the effects of inflation. _____

8. (a) To, (b) Too many people have lost money in the stock market. _____

9. With more experience, Alex (a) would of, (b) would have qualified for the position. _____

10. Let's keep this news between you and (a) I, (b) me. _____

Check your answers below.

 B. Select the correct answer.

1. In addition to Bill Gates, Warren Buffett and Carlos Slim donate large amounts to charity (a) to, (b) too. _____

2. (a) To, (b) Too save money, many people are taking "staycations," which means they are staying home instead of traveling. _____

3. Suggestions from everyone but (a) they, (b) them have been received. _____

4. Everyone in the office except (a) her, (b) she has a BlackBerry. _____

5. Our supervisor (a) would of, (b) would have published our performance reviews online if he had his choice. _____

6. I am going to try to get the price quote (a) off of, (b) from Richard. _____

7. You should make an appointment with Dr. Rosen or (a) she, (b) her. _____

8. Our union said that management's offer was "too little and (a) too, (b) to late." _____

9. Many small business owners think that the federal budget (a) should have, (b) should of included more tax breaks. _____

10. It is (a) to, (b) too soon to tell whether video phones will become standard. _____

1.b 2.b 3.a 4.b 5.b 6.a 7.a 8.b 9.b 10.b

11. Janet Robinson, CEO of *The New York Times*, spoke with the reporters and (a) I, (b) me about declining subscription figures.

12. Just between you and (a) me, (b) I, the difference between a job and a career is the difference between 40 and 60 hours a week.

13. You (a) could of, (b) could have gotten that promotion if you had worked a little harder.

14. Our manager, together with Tanya and (a) he, (b) him, helped to close the sale.

15. Last year we tried to order supplies (a) from, (b) off of them too.

16. You can always rely on coworkers like Michelle and (a) she, (b) her when you need extra help to meet a deadline.

17. Everyone except him and (a) I, (b) me received the announcement too late to respond.

18. To address the letter properly, you must use information (a) off of, (b) from their stationery.

19. Women were first given the right (a) to, (b) too vote in the Pitcairn Islands in 1838.

20. In 1920 women in the United States were finally given the right to vote (a) to, (b) too.

LEVEL 2

A. (Self-check) Select the correct answer.

1. The operating expenses will be divided equally (a) between, (b) among the six departments.

2. Web 2.0 technology is making its way (a) in, (b) into corporate offices.

3. We engrave identification serial numbers (a) inside, (b) inside of all new equipment.

4. The office (a) besides, (b) beside ours has become a victim of cybercrime.

5. It looks (a) like, (b) as if our firm will get the government contract.

6. Have you decided whether you will (a) except, (b) accept the position?

7. With his increased salary and new title, Tony feels (a) like, (b) as a king.

8. Differences (a) between, (b) among the two brothers affected their management styles.

9. When the door was opened, the contracts blew (a) off, (b) off of the desk.

10. What states (a) beside, (b) besides California are in financial trouble?

Check your answers below.

B. Writing Exercise. Rewrite the following sentences to omit unnecessary prepositions and include necessary ones.

Examples: What type network security is needed?
What type of network security is needed?
_____

Where are you going to?
Where are you going?
_____

1. Where should I send the application form to?

_____

2. A new café is opening opposite to the park.

_____

3. Special printing jobs must be done outside of the office.

_____

4. Charles had great respect and interest in the stock market.

_____

5. Who can tell me what time the meeting is scheduled for?

_____

6. What style clothes is recommended for the formal dinner?

_____

7. Leah couldn't help from laughing when Noah spilled his latte as he walked into the conference room.

_____

_____

8. Where shall we move the extra desks and chairs to?

_____

9. Lee Montgomery graduated college with a degree in graphic design.

_____

10. What type return policy does Zappos.com have?

_____

11. Please write up her performance appraisal quickly.

_____

12. Our appreciation and interest in the program remain strong.

_____

13. When did you graduate college?

_____

14. Where do you live at?

_____

15. I didn't mean to wake you up.

_____

C. Select the correct answer.

1. (a) Between, (b) Among Virgin America and JetBlue, which company provides the most on-board amenities? _____

2. All sites (a) accept, (b) except ours offers real-time technical support. _____

3. She hopes to go (a) in to, (b) into the accounting field. _____

4. The police chief likes to park (a) near to, (b) near the station. _____

5. Relief funds were divided (a) among, (b) between all hurricane victims. _____

6. (a) As, (b) Like we mentioned yesterday, Friday will be a half day. _____

7. The new research specialist will move into the office (a) beside, (b) besides mine. _____

8. He ran (a) in to, (b) into an old college buddy at the airport. _____

9. Your laptop computer looks just (a) like, (b) as mine. _____

10. The advertising campaign looks (a) like, (b) as if it will be quite successful. _____

11. Has anyone been (a) in to, (b) into see me this morning? _____

12. You are going to have to (a) accept, (b) except the changes. _____

13. Employees are required to turn expense reports (a) in to, (b) into their supervisors within one week. _____

14. If he (a) accepts, (b) excepts the position, he will have to move to Boise, Idaho. _____

15. (a) Beside, (b) Besides Zoe Stone and Jason Scogna, whom have you invited? _____

16. It looks (a) like, (b) as if Christina Orr-Cahall will be the next CEO of the Experience Music Project in Seattle. _____

17. Carly Fiorina, former CEO of Hewlett-Packard, has turned (a) in to, (b) into an important political leader. _____

18. She (a) met up with, (b) met with her new boss this morning. _____

19. Bill Gates never (a) graduated from, (b) graduated college. _____

20. Her political views are (a) opposite from, (b) opposite mine. _____

D. Writing Exercise. The following sentences end in prepositions. Rewrite the sentences to avoid terminal prepositions.

Example: Here is the information you asked about.

Here is the information about which you asked.

1. Whom did you send payment to?

_____

2. Please locate the file you put the contract in.

_____

3. What companies did you apply with?

_____

4. We have a number of loyal members we can rely upon.

_____

5. What company did you purchase these supplies from?

_____

LEVEL 3

A. (Self-check) Select the word that forms the correct idiomatic expression.

1. Some people are exceptionally adept (a) at, (b) in delivering bad news tactfully. _____
2. Public companies must comply (a) with, (b) to Sarbanes-Oxley requirements. _____
3. In a televised address, the president will talk (a) to, (b) with the nation at 6 p.m. _____
4. Many people plan (a) to simplify, (b) on simplifying their lives. _____
5. His management philosophy is quite different (a) than, (b) from mine. _____
6. Are you angry (a) with, (b) at me for disagreeing with you during the meeting? _____
7. How can they reconcile this new business venture (a) to, (b) with their recent bankruptcy? _____
8. Jordan is an expert (a) at, (b) in bioengineering. _____
9. Your work ethic is similar (a) with, (b) to mine. _____
10. Citizens must adhere (a) to, (b) with all state and federal laws. _____

Check your answers below.

B. Select the word that forms the correct idiomatic expression.

1. Julia is addicted (a) with, (b) to updating her status on Twitter. _____
2. I differ (a) with, (b) from you on the key points of this plan. _____
3. Our new office building is convenient (a) to, (b) with many restaurants and cafés. _____
4. We will make the salary increase retroactive (a) from, (b) to January 1. _____
5. I am very sensitive (a) to, (b) with your feelings. _____
6. How does common stock differ (a) with, (b) from preferred stock? _____
7. It was a pleasure talking (a) to, (b) with you yesterday during the interview. _____
8. The company plans (a) on developing, (b) to develop a new interactive Web site. _____
9. Customers were upset after standing (a) in, (b) on line for an hour. _____
10. Have you become acquainted (a) with, (b) to the new intern yet? _____
11. That film is much different (a) than, (b) from the book. _____
12. Your success on the job will correspond (a) to, (b) with your ability to adapt to change. _____
13. The light background on the Web page contrasts (a) to, (b) with the font color. _____

1.b 2.a 3.a 4.a 5.b 6.a 7.b 8.b 9.b 10.a

14. Do you hire an interpreter when your company corresponds (a) to, (b) with Chinese customers?

15. A firewall will help guard (a) against, (b) from unauthorized access to our intranet. _____

16. We infer (a) from, (b) about your statement that you will be running for city supervisor.

17. Your ethics do not conform (a) with, (b) to our expectations. _____

18. Christina has a great appreciation (a) for, (b) in contemporary art? _____

19. Employees reached their decision independent (a) from, (b) of the influence of union organizers. _____

20. Liz has an interest (a) in, (b) for increasing recycling in the workplace. _____

C. Writing Exercise. Write complete sentences using the expressions shown in parentheses.

1. (oblivious to)

_____

2. (reconcile with)

_____

3. (reconciled to)

_____

4. (plan to)

_____

5. (different from)

_____

D. FAQs About Business English Review. In the space provided, write the correct answer choice.

1. Josh said that he hopes to (a) graduate from, (b) graduate college within two years. _____

2. Diandra will take her vacation (a) some time, (b) sometime in August. _____

3. All (a) personal, (b) personnel matters are now handled by our Human Resources Department. _____

4. If you have (a) some time, (b) sometime to spare on Saturday, please drop by to help us. _____

5. Employees are not allowed to send (a) personal, (b) personnel e-mail messages during work hours. _____

6. New (a) industry wide, (b) industry-wide, (c) industrywide standards should make it easier to distribute our products internationally. _____

7. She moved (a) on to, (b) onto the next step in the process. _____

8. To reach our offices, turn left (a) on to, (b) onto Columbus Avenue. _____

9. Amazon.com has a (a) proved, (b) proven record of providing excellent customer service. _____

10. (a) Besides, (b) Beside Amazon.com, what other companies provide excellent customer service? _____

Your company is thinking about using blogs for research and marketing purposes, and you want to learn more about this communication tool.

Goal: To learn about weblogs (blogs).

1. In the address bar of your Web browser, type **http://en.wikipedia.org/wiki/Blog**.

2. Read the Wikipedia article to learn the following about blogs: history, types, and uses. Take notes on any interesting facts you learn about blogs.

3. Now go to Google Blog Search at **http://blogsearch.google.com/** to find a blog related to your major, profession, or hobby. Type a relevant search term in the search box and click **Search Blogs**.

4. Once you find a blog that interests you, read some of the most recent entries. List three interesting facts or opinions that you learned from these entries. How do blogs differ from other communication tools you have used?

5. Print one page from the blog.

6. End your session by clicking the **X** in the upper right corner of your browser. Turn in all printed pages and your answers to the questions.

▶▶ Chat About It

Your instructor may assign any of the following topics for you to discuss in class, in an online chat room, or on an online discussion board. Some of the discussion topics may require outside research. You may also be asked to read and respond to postings made by your classmates.

Discussion Topic 1: The opening quote to this chapter, widely attributed to Winston Churchill, states "This is the sort of English up with which I will not put." In this quote he is mocking the traditional rule that says a sentence should not end with a preposition. As you learned, this traditional rule has changed, and in most cases it is acceptable to end a sentence with a preposition. Why do you think grammar rules change over time? How can you keep up with current rules?

Discussion Topic 2: A U.S. gymnast said the following during an Associated Press interview: "All the girls were like, 'You can do it, it's fine.' I was like, 'C'mon, guys. I'm fine.' I'm like, 'OK, I've done this routine so many times.'" Do you or anyone you know use the word *like* in this way? Why do you think this use is so common today? Is this type of language appropriate in the workplace? Explain.

Discussion Topic 3: You learned in this chapter that idioms are word combinations that are unique to a language. Some idioms involve prepositions, such as *angry with* and *different from*. Other idioms are common expressions such as *above board* and *loose cannon*. Perform an Internet search for other English-language idioms that you find interesting, and share TEN idiomatic expressions with your classmates. Also share your thoughts about whether idiomatic expressions in the latter category should be used in business writing. Why or why not?

Discussion Topic 4: In this chapter you were introduced to some English idiomatic expressions such as *seed money* and *melting pot*. Choose another language and do Internet research to find five idiomatic expressions from that language. Share them with your classmates.

Discussion Topic 5: Marilyn vos Savant, an American writer and magazine columnist, said, "Although spoken English doesn't obey the rules of written language, a person who doesn't know the rules thoroughly is at a great disadvantage." What do you think she means by this? Do you agree with this statement? Why or why not?

Posttest Underline the letter representing the correct answer.

1. Between you and (a) I, (b) me, what do you think of the new CEO?

2. No one (a) except, (b) accept our controller was aware of the accounting discrepancies.

3. Please turn your uniform (a) into, (b) in to your supervisor on your last day.

4. Her presentation is still three minutes (a) to, (b) too long.

5. It looks (a) like, (b) as if we will be able to avoid layoffs.

6. Is it necessary for all documents to comply (a) to, (b) with the new guidelines?

7. Dividends will be distributed (a) between, (b) among stockholders.

8. (a) Beside, (b) Besides Jeffrey, who is able to work Saturday?

9. WebVan (a) could of, (b) could have survived with better management.

10. Employees have respect (a) for, (b) in leaders who exhibit ethical behavior.

1.b 2.a 3.b 4.b 5.b 6.b 7.b 8.b 9.b 10.a

PREPOSITIONS

"The American constitutions were to liberty, what a grammar is to language: they define its parts of speech, and practically construct them into syntax."

—**Thomas Paine,**
British revolutionary and intellectual

Chapter **13**

Conjunctions

OBJECTIVES

When you have completed the materials in this chapter, you will be able to do the following:

LEVEL 1
- Punctuate compound sentences using coordinating conjunctions such as *and, or, nor*, and *but*.
- Punctuate compound sentences using conjunctive adverbs such as *therefore, however*, and *consequently*.

LEVEL 2
- Punctuate introductory and terminal dependent clauses.
- Punctuate parenthetical, essential, and nonessential dependent clauses.

LEVEL 3
- Recognize correlative conjunctions such as *either . . . or, not only . . . but also*, and *neither . . . nor*.
- Convert simple sentences into a variety of more complex patterns.

263

In each pair of sentences, underline the letter of the one that is punctuated or written properly.

1. (a) Access the site and click the link.
   (b) Access the site, and click the link.

2. (a) Luke Wilkinson prefers to remain in New York City but Puya Soltani is considering the Albany area.
   (b) Luke Wilkinson prefers to remain in New York City, but Puya Soltani is considering the Albany area.

3. (a) Michael Paez attended the Phi Beta Lambda competition in Houston and brought home several awards.
   (b) Michael Paez attended the Phi Beta Lambda competition in Houston, and brought home several awards.

4. (a) All employees must be able to communicate effectively; therefore, we evaluate communication skills during employment interviews.
   (b) All employees must be able to communicate effectively, therefore, we evaluate communication skills during employment interviews.

5. (a) Performance reviews, therefore, will include discussion about employees' communication skills.
   (b) Performance reviews; therefore, will include discussion about employees' communication skills.

6. (a) When you receive an e-mail attachment, be sure to check it for a virus.
   (b) When you receive an e-mail attachment be sure to check it for a virus.

7. (a) Please let me know, when you receive the signed contract.
   (b) Please let me know when you receive the signed contract.

8. (a) Sherilyn said that Travis Garcia who works in our Marketing Department will be leaving next month.
   (b) Sherilyn said that Travis Garcia, who works in our Marketing Department, will be leaving next month.

9. (a) Employees who work in our Marketing Department are eligible for bonuses.
   (b) Employees, who work in our Marketing Department, are eligible for bonuses.

10. (a) Not only is this wireless service more reliable but it also is cheaper than the other.
    (b) This wireless service is not only more reliable but also cheaper than the other.

Study Tip

Understanding the differences among different types of conjunctions will help you use proper sentence structure and punctuate correctly.

This chapter covers a very important part of speech: conjunctions. **Conjunctions** are connecting words. They may be separated into two major groups: those that join grammatically equal words or word groups and those that join grammatically unequal words or word groups. Recognizing conjunctions and understanding their patterns of usage will, among other things, enable you to use commas and semicolons more appropriately.

1. a 2. b 3. a 4. a 5. a 6. a 7. b 8. b 9. a 10. b

Coordinating Conjunctions

Coordinating conjunctions connect words, phrases, and clauses of equal grammatical value or rank. The most common coordinating conjunctions are *and, or, but*, and *nor*. Notice in these sentences that coordinating conjunctions join grammatically equal elements.

> The qualities I admire most are *honesty, integrity*, and *reliability*. (Here the word *and* joins equal words.)
>
> Open your mind *to new challenges* and *to new ideas*. (Here *and* joins equal phrases.)
>
> You will find job listings *on our Web site* or *in our weekly newsletter*. (Here *or* joins equal phrases.)
>
> *Gasoline prices are falling*, but *college tuition costs are rising*. (Here *but* joins equal clauses.)

Three other coordinating conjunctions should also be mentioned: *yet, for*, and *so*. The words *yet* and *for* may function as coordinating conjunctions, although they are infrequently used as such.

> We use e-mail extensively, *yet* we still prefer personal contact with our customers.
>
> The weary traveler was gaunt and ill, *for* his journey had been long and arduous.

Study Tip

An easy way to remember the seven coordinating conjunctions is to think of the acronym ***FANBOYS***. Each letter stands for one of the coordinating conjunctions: *for, and, nor, but, or, yet*, and *so*.

The word *so* is sometimes informally used as a coordinating conjunction. In more formal contexts, the conjunctive adverbs *therefore* and *consequently* should be substituted for the conjunction *so*. You will study conjunctive adverbs later in this chapter.

> **Informal:**   The plane leaves at 2:15, *so* you still have time to pack.
>
> **Improved:**   The plane leaves at 2:15; *therefore*, you still have time to pack.

To avoid using *so* as a conjunction, try starting your sentence with *because* or *although*.

> **Informal:**   Driving while talking on a cell phone can be dangerous, so some states have made this practice illegal.
>
> **Improved:**   Because driving while talking on a cell phone can be dangerous, this practice is illegal in some states.

Punctuating Compound Sentences Using Coordinating Conjunctions

As you learned in Chapter 3, a **simple sentence** has one **independent clause**, that is, a clause that can stand alone. A **compound sentence** has two or more independent clauses. When coordinating conjunctions (*and, or, but, nor, for, yet*, and *so*) join independent clauses in compound sentences, place a comma before the coordinating conjunction.

> We can handle our invoice processing internally, *or* we can outsource it to a reputable firm. (Use a comma before *or* to join two independent clauses.)
>
> You can check your account balances online, *and* you can pay your bills electronically. (Use a comma before *and* to join two independent clauses.)

<u>Analyze</u> all your possible property risks, *and* <u>protect</u> yourself with our comprehensive homeowners' insurance. (Use a comma before *and* to join two independent clauses; the subject of each clause is understood to be *you*.)

However, when the coordinating conjunction *and* is used to connect short compound sentences, you may omit the comma. Consider a sentence short when the entire sentence contains up to 13 words.

Stephanie received a text message *and* she responded immediately.

Marcie sent an e-mail but Adam didn't answer.

Do not use commas when coordinating conjunctions join compound verbs, objects, or phrases.

<u>You</u> <u>can check</u> your account balances online *and* <u>pay</u> your bills electronically. (No comma needed because *and* joins the compound verbs of a single independent clause.)

<u>Our CEO</u> <u>said</u> that employees should not have to choose between working overtime *and* spending time with their families. (No comma needed because *and* joins the compound objects of a prepositional phrase.)

<u>Stockholders</u> <u>are expected</u> to attend the meeting *or* to send their proxies. (No comma needed because *or* joins two infinitive phrases.)

Conjunctive Adverbs

Conjunctive adverbs may also be used to connect equal sentence elements. Because conjunctive adverbs are used to effect a transition from one thought to another and because they may consist of more than one word, they have also been called **transitional expressions** or **transitional conjunctions**. The most common conjunctive adverbs follow:

accordingly	in fact	on the contrary
also	in other words	on the other hand
anyway	in the meantime	otherwise
consequently	indeed	that is
furthermore	likewise	then
hence	moreover	therefore
however	nevertheless	thus

In the following compound sentences, observe that conjunctive adverbs join clauses of equal grammatical value. Note that semicolons (NOT commas) are used before conjunctive adverbs that join independent clauses. Commas should immediately follow conjunctive adverbs of two or more syllables. Note also that the word following a semicolon is not capitalized—unless, of course, it is a proper noun.

Some companies oppose the use of social networking; *however,* other companies find that it encourages team collaboration and knowledge sharing.

Sarah did her best; *nevertheless,* she did not pass her CPA exam the first time.

Equipment expenditures are great this quarter; *on the other hand,* new equipment will reduce labor costs.

Generally, no comma is used after one-syllable conjunctive adverbs such as *hence, thus,* and *then* (unless a strong pause is desired).

> The first entertainment on planes began in 1928 when Transcontinental began distributing playing cards; *then* TWA installed radios in 1939.

> The growing use of handheld phones in cars endangers safety; thus several communities are giving away free bumper stickers that say "Drive Now, Talk Later."

Distinguishing Conjunctive Adverbs From Parenthetical Adverbs

Study Tip

Use a semicolon ONLY when you are joining two complete sentences.

Many words that function as conjunctive adverbs may also serve as parenthetical adverbs. **Parenthetical adverbs,** such as *however, therefore,* and *consequently,* are used to effect transitions from one thought to another in independent clauses. Use semicolons *only* with conjunctive adverbs that join two independent clauses. Use commas to set off parenthetical adverbs that interrupt the flow of one independent clause. Notice the differences in these examples:

> We believe, *however,* that cellular phone sales will continue to grow. (An adverb is used parenthetically.)

> We agree that cell phones are convenient; *however,* they must be used responsibly. (A conjunctive adverb is used to join two clauses.)

> The Federal Reserve System, *therefore,* is a vital force in maintaining a sound banking system and a stable economy. (An adverb is used parenthetically.)

> The Federal Reserve System is a vital force in maintaining a sound banking system; *therefore,* it is instrumental in creating a stable economy. (A conjunctive adverb joins two clauses.)

Now complete the reinforcement exercises for Level 1.

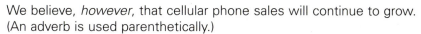

LEVEL 2

Subordinating Conjunctions

To join unequal sentence elements, such as independent and dependent clauses, use **subordinating conjunctions.** As you learned in Chapter 3, **dependent clauses** depend for their meaning on independent clauses. Dependent clauses are often introduced by subordinating conjunctions such as *if, when, because,* and *as.* A list of the most common subordinating conjunctions follows:

after	because	provided	until
although	before	since	when
as	even though	so that	where
as if	if	that	whether
as though	in order that	unless	while

Study Tip

Some experts call subordinating conjunctions **dependent conjunctions.** This term may help you remember that these conjunctions make clauses dependent on independent clauses for their meaning.

You should become familiar with this list of conjunctions. However, don't feel that you need to memorize them. Generally, you can recognize a subordinating conjunction by the way it limits, or subordinates, the clause it introduces. In the clause *because he wants to go to graduate school,* the subordinating conjunction *because* limits the meaning of the clause it introduces. The clause is incomplete and could not stand alone as a sentence.

Punctuation of Sentences With Dependent Clauses

Business and professional writers are especially concerned with clarity and accuracy. A misplaced or omitted punctuation mark can confuse a reader by altering the meaning of a sentence. The following guidelines for using commas help ensure clarity and consistency in writing. Some professional writers, however, take liberties with accepted conventions of punctuation, particularly in regard to comma usage. These experienced writers may omit a comma when they feel that such an omission will not affect the reader's understanding of a sentence. Beginning writers, though, are well advised to first develop skill in punctuating sentences by following traditional guidelines.

Introductory Dependent Clauses

Use a comma after a dependent (subordinate) clause that precedes an independent clause.

> *If* you are looking for an exciting career, think about becoming a forensic accountant.
>
> *Even though* Philo Farnsworth invented the television in 1927, he was never able to personally introduce it to consumers.
>
> *Because* President Franklin D. Roosevelt passed a series of securities laws in the 1930s, he helped create the Securities and Exchange Commission (SEC) to enforce them.

Use a comma after an introductory dependent clause even though the subject and verb may not be stated.

> *As* [it was] expected, the company was forced to lay off workers.
>
> *If* [it is] possible, send a replacement immediately.
>
> *When* [they are] printed, your brochures will be distributed.

Terminal Dependent Clauses

Generally, a dependent clause introduced by a subordinating conjunction does not require a comma when the dependent clause is **terminal**, meaning that it falls at the end of a sentence.

> Please call me *if* you have any questions.
>
> We must complete our research *before* we write the report.
>
> Many people are experiencing negative equity *because* their homes are worth less than what they owe on their mortgage loans.

If, however, the dependent clause at the end of a sentence interrupts the flow of the sentence, provides nonessential information, or sounds as if it were an afterthought, a comma should be used.

> I am sure I paid the bill, *although* I cannot find my receipt. (Dependent clause adds unnecessary information.)
>
> We will ship the goods within the week, *if* that is satisfactory with you. (Dependent clause sounds like an afterthought.)

Parenthetical Clauses

A **parenthetical clause** adds additional information to a sentence. Within sentences, dependent parenthetical clauses that interrupt the flow and are unnecessary for the grammatical completeness of the sentence are set off by commas.

The motion, *unless* you want further discussion, will be tabled until our next meeting.

At our next meeting, *provided* we have a quorum, the motion will be reconsidered.

Relative Clauses

The **relative pronouns** *who, whom, whose, which,* and *that* function as conjunctions when they introduce dependent clauses. *Who, whom,* and *whose* are used to refer to persons. These pronouns may introduce essential or nonessential clauses. *That* refers to animals or things and should be used to introduce essential clauses. *Which* refers to animals or things and introduces nonessential clauses. The tricky part is deciding whether a clause is essential or nonessential. In some cases, only the writer knows whether a clause is intended to be essential or nonessential.

An **essential (restrictive) clause** is needed to identify the noun to which it refers; therefore, no commas should separate this clause from its antecedent.

Any employee *who wants an August vacation* must apply soon. (The relative pronoun *who* refers to people, and it introduces an essential clause. The dependent clause is essential because it is needed to identify which employees must apply soon. No commas are needed.)

Any applicant *whom we contact* must complete our online application. (The relative pronoun *whom* refers to a person, and it introduces an essential clause. The dependent clause is essential because it is needed to identify which applicants must complete the online application. No commas are needed.)

Any student *whose GPA is above 3.0* qualifies for the scholarship. (The relative pronoun *whose* refers to a person, and it introduces an essential clause. The dependent clause is essential because it is needed to identify which students qualify for the scholarship. No commas are needed.)

A company *that* (not *who* or *which*) values its employees is likely to succeed. (The relative pronoun *that* introduces an essential clause. The dependent clause is essential because it is needed to identify which company is likely to succeed. No commas are needed.)

A **nonessential (nonrestrictive) clause** contains information that the reader does not need to know. The main clause is understandable without this extra information. Careful writers use *which* (not *that*) to introduce nonessential clauses. If the clause is nonessential, it should be set off from the rest of the sentence by commas. Notice that *two* commas are used to set off internal nonessential dependent clauses.

Jamie Langelier, *who* has excellent recommendations, is applying for a position in our department. (The relative pronoun *who* introduces a nonessential clause that is set off by commas. The antecedent of the dependent clause, *Jamie Langelier*, is clearly identified.)

Douglas Engelbert, *whom* few people have heard of, gave the first demonstration of a computer mouse in 1968. (The relative pronoun *whom* introduces a nonessential clause that is set off by commas. The antecedent of the dependent clause, *Douglas Engelbert*, is clearly identified.)

Bruce R. Bent, *whose* career was in finance, launched the first U.S. money market fund in 1970. (The relative pronoun *whose* introduces

Study Tip

Careful writers use the word *that* for essential clauses and the word *which* for nonessential clauses. Remember that dependent clauses introduced by *which* require commas.

a nonessential clause that is set off by commas. The antecedent of the dependent clause, *Bruce R. Bent*, is clearly identified.)

Software giant Microsoft, *which* is headquartered in Redmond, has many other offices in the state of Washington. (The relative pronoun *which* introduces a nonessential clause that is set off by commas. The antecedent of the dependent clause, *Microsoft*, is clearly identified.)

Punctuation Review

The following three common sentence patterns are very important for you to study and understand. Notice particularly how the sentences are punctuated.

Independent clause$_{()}$ + $\left\{\begin{array}{l}\text{and}\\\text{or}\\\text{nor}\\\text{but}\end{array}\right\}$ + Independent clause.   (Comma used when a coordinating conjunction joins independent clauses.)

Independent clause$_{()}$ + $\left\{\begin{array}{l}\text{therefore,}\\\text{consequently,}\\\text{however,}\\\text{nevertheless,}\end{array}\right\}$ + Independent clause.   (Semicolon used when a conjunctive adverb joins independent clauses.)

$\left\{\begin{array}{l}\text{Because}\\\text{If}\\\text{As}\\\text{When}\end{array}\right\}$ Dependent clause$_{()}$ + Independent clause.   (Comma used after a dependent clause introduced by a subordinate conjunction.)

Independent clause + $\left\{\begin{array}{l}\text{because}\\\text{if}\\\text{as}\\\text{when}\end{array}\right\}$ + Dependent clause.   (No comma used with terminal dependent clauses.)

Now complete the reinforcement exercises for Level 2.

LEVEL 3

Correlative Conjunctions

Correlative conjunctions, like coordinating conjunctions and conjunctive adverbs, join grammatically equal sentence elements. Correlative conjunctions are always used in pairs: *both . . . and, not only . . . but (also), either . . . or,* and *neither . . . nor.* When greater emphasis is desired, these paired conjunctions are used instead of coordinating conjunctions. Notice the difference in these examples when correlative conjunctions are used:

Zappos offers excellent customer service and a lenient return policy.

Zappos offers not only excellent customer service but also a lenient return policy. (More emphatic)

Your best chances for advancement are in the marketing department *or* in the sales department.

Your best chances for advancement are *either* in the marketing department *or* in the sales department. (More emphatic)

In using correlative conjunctions, place them so that the words, phrases, or clauses being joined are parallel in construction.

Study Tip

When using correlative conjunctions, concentrate on the words immediately following each conjunction. These words must be arranged in the same grammatical construction.

Not Parallel:	*Either* Michelle was flying into Oakland *or* to San Jose.
Parallel:	Michelle was flying *either* into Oakland *or* into San Jose.
Not Parallel:	I *neither* have the time *nor* the energy for this.
Parallel:	I have *neither* the time *nor* the energy for this.
Not Parallel:	He was *not only* talented, *but* he was *also* intelligent.
Parallel:	He was *not only* talented *but also* intelligent.

Sentence Variety

To make messages more interesting, good writers strive for variety in sentence structure. Notice the monotony and choppiness of a paragraph made up entirely of simple sentences:

> Leila Peters founded her own dessert business. She specialized in molded containers made of French chocolate. Her 350 designs were unique. She copyrighted them. Another chocolatier copied her spiral chocolate seashell. Leila sued. She won.

Compare the following version of this paragraph, which uses dependent clauses and other structures to achieve greater sentence variety:

> Leila Peters, who founded her own dessert business, specialized in molded containers made of French chocolate. Because her 350 designs were unique, she copyrighted them. When another chocolatier copied her spiral chocolate seashell, Leila sued and won.

Recognizing the kinds of sentence structures available to writers and speakers is an important step in achieving effective expression. Here is a review of four kinds of sentences you studied in Chapter 3.

Trivia Tidbit

The average American has a vocabulary of about 10,000 words. Compare this vocabulary to William Shakespeare's, whom many consider to be the greatest writer in the English language. He had a vocabulary of roughly 29,000 words.

Kind of Sentence	Minimum Requirement	Example
Simple	One independent clause	Leila Peters founded her own dessert business.
Compound	Two independent clauses	Leila founded her own dessert business, and she specialized in molded containers of French chocolate.
Complex	One independent clause and one dependent clause	Since Leila Peters founded her own dessert business, she has specialized in molded containers of French chocolate.
Compound-complex	Two independent clauses and one dependent clause	Leila's chocolate designs were copyrighted; therefore, when another chocolatier copied one, she sued and won.

Developing the ability to use a variety of sentence structures to facilitate effective communication takes practice and writing experience.

Now complete the reinforcement exercises for Level 3.

Spot the BLOOPER

Using the skills you are learning in this class, try to identify why the following items are bloopers. Consult your textbook, dictionary, or reference manual as needed.

Blooper 1: Sign on a snack cart in New York City, located near the carriage-ride terminal in Central Park: "Filly Cheese Steak."

Blooper 2: In a newsletter of the Friends of Music at Guilford [Vermont]: "The lunch was delicious and folks munched away merrily on folding chairs."

Blooper 3: In a *Newsweek* article about an incident that occurred during the Clinton presidency: "Neither Hillary nor the president mention it in their memoirs."

Blooper 4: From a column in *The Miami Herald*: "But the famous are not like you and I."

Blooper 5: Professionally made sign attached to an overhead bin on an Alaska Airlines plane: "THIS BINS FOR YOU."

Blooper 6: From a New York sport columnist: "While checking my bags at the counter, Magic Johnson arrived in a stretch limo."

Blooper 7: From the *Patriot-Ledger* [Quincy, Massachusetts]: "Clemens is able to come off the disabled list Sunday, but tests by Dr. Arthur Pappas led to the conclusion that Clemens' groin is still too weak to pitch in a game."

Blooper 8: Advice from a Canadian telephone company booklet: "Hang up if the caller doesn't say anything, or if the caller doesn't identify themself to your satisfaction." [Did you spot two bloopers?]

Blooper 9: From a Fox News ad about Donald Trump's new book: "Read my new book or your fired."

Blooper 10: From *The Atlanta Journal-Constitution*: "A Clayton County man, whom authorities say stole two cars, opened fire on several people and led police on a chase."

Question	Answer
Q: A friend of mine gets upset when I say something like, *I was so surprised by her remark.* She thinks I'm misusing *so.* Am I?	**A:** Your friend is right, if we are talking about formal expression. The intensifier *so* requires a clause to complete its meaning. For example, *I was so surprised by her remark that I immediately protested.* When one hears *so* as a modifier without a qualifying clause, the sentence sounds incomplete. *He was so funny.* So funny that what? *He was so funny that he became a stand-up comedian.*
Q: My English-teacher aunt says that I should say, *My cell phone is not so clear as yours* instead of *My cell phone is not as clear as yours.* Is she right?	**A:** As a matter of style in negative comparisons, some people prefer to use *not so . . . as.* However, it is just as acceptable to say *not as . . . as* (for example, *Price is not as (or so) important as location*).
Q: I don't think I'll ever be able to tell the difference between *that* and *which.* They sound alike to me. Any advice for keeping them straight?	**A:** The problem usually is the substitution of *which* for *that.* Whenever you're tempted to use *which,* remember that it requires a comma. Think *which + comma.* If the sentence doesn't sound right with a comma, then you know you need *that.* One eminent language specialist, William Strunk, advised careful writers to go *which*-hunting and remove all defining *whiches.* Examples: *The contract that we sent in June was just returned* (defines which one). *The Wilson contract, which we sent in June, was just returned* (adds a fact about the only contract in question).
Q: Can the word *that* be omitted from sentences? For example, *She said [that] she would come.*	**A:** The relative pronoun *that* is frequently omitted in conversation and casual writing. For absolute clarity, however, skilled writers include it.
Q: Does *Ms.* have a period after it? Should I use this title for all women in business today?	**A:** *Ms.* is probably a blend of *Miss* and *Mrs.* It is written with a period following it. Some women in business prefer to use *Ms.,* presumably because it is a title equal to *Mr.* Neither title reveals one's marital status. It is always wise, if possible, to determine the preference of the individual. However, when in doubt, use the personal title *Ms.* in business correspondence.
Q: Another employee and I are collaborating on a report. I wanted to write this: *Money was lost due to poor attendance.* She says the sentence should read: *Money was lost because of poor attendance.* My version is more concise. Which of us is right?	**A:** Most language authorities agree with your coauthor. *Due to* is acceptable when it introduces an adjective phrase, as in *Success was due to proper timing.* In this sense, *due to* is synonymous with *attributable to.* However, *because of* should introduce adverbial phrases and should modify verbs: *Money was lost because of poor attendance. Because of* modifies the verb phrase *was lost.*

Question	Answer
Q: I'm not sure which word to use in this sentence: *They have used all (they're, their, there) resources in combating the disease.*	**A:** Use *their*, which is the possessive form of *they*. The adverb *there* means "at that place" or "at that point" (*we have been there before*). *There* is also used as an expletive or filler preceding a linking verb (*there are numerous explanations*). *They're* is a contraction of *they* and *are* (*they're coming this afternoon*).
Q: Can you help me with the words *averse* and *adverse*? I have never been able to straighten them out in my mind.	**A:** *Averse* is an adjective meaning "disinclined" and generally is used with the preposition *to* (*The little boy was averse to bathing*). *Adverse* is also an adjective, but it means "hostile" or "unfavorable" (*Adverse economic conditions halted the company's growth*). In distinguishing between these two similar words, it might help you to know that the word *averse* is usually used to describe animate (living) objects.
Q: Should *reevaluate* be hyphenated?	**A:** No. It is not necessary to use a hyphen after the prefix *re* unless the resulting word may be confused with another word (*to re-mark the sales ticket, to re-cover the chair*).
Q: I plan to use this sentence in a letter I am writing to my references: *You will be receiving a call from one of my perspective employers.* Is this correct?	**A:** Before you send the letter, change *perspective* to *prospective*. *Perspective* is a noun that means "a mental picture or outlook" (*She has a new perspective of the company after reading the article*). *Prospective* is an adjective that means "likely to become" (*We have a prospective buyer for the building*).

13 Reinforcement Exercises

LEVEL 1

Online Homework Help! For immediate feedback on odd-numbered items, go to **www.meguffey.com**.

 A. (Self-check) Select *a, b,* or *c* to identify the following sentences.

   a. A comma correctly punctuates a compound sentence.
   b. The sentence is not compound; thus the comma should be omitted.
   c. Although the sentence is compound, the clauses are too short to require a comma.

Example: In 1908 the Model T went into production in Detroit, and Robert Peary also began his conquest of the North Pole. _____a_____

1. Glide Memorial Church will auction off a lunch with Warren Buffett, and bidding will start at $25,000. _____

2. A New York restaurant received so many complaints about cell phone users that it set up a cell phone lounge, and banished their use elsewhere. _____

3. E-mail your resume, or fax it. _____

4. Listen well, and look carefully. _____

5. Albert Einstein was four years old before he could speak, and seven years old before he could read. _____

In each pair of sentences, select the one that is punctuated or written properly.

Example: (a) Bill Gates believes in giving back, therefore, he created the Bill & Melinda Gates Foundation.
   (b) Bill Gates believes in giving back; therefore, he created the Bill & Melinda Gates Foundation. _____b_____

6. (a) Mother Teresa was best known for her work in Calcutta; however, she also founded facilities for the poor in the United States.
   (b) Mother Teresa was best known for her work in Calcutta, however, she also founded facilities for the poor in the United States. _____

7. (a) Karla read that the best time to ask for a raise is at 9 a.m. or 1 p.m. midweek, thus, she made an appointment to see her boss.
   (b) Karla read that the best time to ask for a raise is at 9 a.m. or 1 p.m. midweek; thus, she made an appointment to see her boss.
   (c) Karla read that the best time to ask for a raise is at 9 a.m. or 1 p.m. midweek; thus she made an appointment to see her boss. _____

8. (a) She was disappointed; however, when her boss was unavailable until Friday.
   (b) She was disappointed, however, when her boss was unavailable until Friday. _____

9. (a) Women live an average of seven years longer than men, consequently, three in four women are single when they die.
   (b) Women live an average of seven years longer than men; consequently, three in four women are single when they die. _____

10. (a) Women must, consequently, plan carefully for retirement.
(b) Women must; consequently, plan carefully for retirement.   _____

Check your answers below.

B. In each pair of sentences, select the one that is punctuated properly.

1. (a) Some small business owners are unhappy with the tax increases and plan to protest.
(b) Some small business owners are unhappy with the tax increases, and plan to protest.   _____

2. (a) Some small business owners are unhappy with the tax increases and they plan to protest.
(b) Some small business owners are unhappy with the tax increases, and they plan to protest.   _____

3. (a) Ariel wrote the letter, and Samantha proofread it.
(b) Ariel wrote the letter and Samantha proofread it.   _____

4. (a) The city of Vallejo has declared bankruptcy yet it remains optimistic that it will bounce back.
(b) The city of Vallejo has declared bankruptcy, yet it remains optimistic that it will bounce back.   _____

5. (a) The city of Vallejo has declared bankruptcy yet remains optimistic that it will bounce back.
(b) The city of Vallejo has declared bankruptcy, yet remains optimistic that it will bounce back.   _____

6. (a) You can send me a text message when you get the results, or you can e-mail me.
(b) You can send me a text message when you get the results or you can e-mail me.   _____

7. (a) Research the target company, then decide what to wear to the interview.
(b) Research the target company; then decide what to wear to the interview.   _____

8. (a) Some companies require employees to carry wireless devices with location-tracking software; however, many employees find this practice intrusive.
(b) Some companies require employees to carry wireless devices with location-tracking software, however, many employees find this practice intrusive.   _____

9. (a) The companies; however, say that they have the right to monitor their employees' whereabouts.
(b) The companies, however, say that they have the right to monitor their employees' whereabouts.   _____

10. (a) Many patients seek luxury amenities in hospitals, in fact, some even demand gourmet meals and flat-screen TVs.
(b) Many patients seek luxury amenities in hospitals; in fact, some even demand gourmet meals and flat-screen TVs.   _____

C. Writing Exercise. Rewrite the following sentences, inserting all necessary punctuation. If no additional punctuation is needed, write *Correct*.

Example: Kevin came to work ten minutes late on Monday and he was absent on Tuesday.

Kevin came to work ten minutes late on Monday, and he was absent on Tuesday.

Example: Some loans must be secured therefore the borrower must supply collateral.

Some loans must be secured; therefore, the borrower must supply collateral.

1.a 2.b 3.c 4.c 5.b 6.a 7.c 8.b 9.b 10.a

276   •   **CHAPTER 13**   CONJUNCTIONS

1. Some employees think their e-mail should be confidential but courts generally uphold an employer's right to monitor messages.

   _____

   _____

2. Women are outpacing men on college campuses and now earn the majority of diplomas in fields once dominated by men.

   _____

   _____

3. Periods of stock market growth are called *bull markets* and periods of stock market decline are known as *bear markets*.

   _____

   _____

4. Please make your decision and let me know immediately.

   _____

   _____

5. Several companies have been forced to lay off employees yet they are retaining their older, more experienced workers.

   _____

   _____

6. Many people fear becoming victims of identity theft however identity theft rarely results in actual financial loss for consumers.

   _____

   _____

7. Some people are surprised to learn however that most identify theft occurs through "dumpster diving."

   _____

   _____

8. Our company is faced nevertheless with unusually expensive communication costs.

   _____

   _____

9. Click fraud has become a huge problem thus a number of companies are no longer advertising on Web sites such as Google.

   _____

   _____

10. The Equal Pay for Equal Work Act was passed in 1963 consequently women's wages became more equitable.

    _____

    _____

D. Writing Exercise. Write sentences using the conjunctions as described below. Be sure to punctuate each sentence correctly.

1. Write a complete sentence using *and* as a coordinating conjunction between two independent clauses.

   _____

   _____

2. Write a complete sentence using *and* as a coordinating conjunction separating equal words.

   _____

   _____

3. Write a complete sentence using *or* as a coordinating conjunction between two phrases.

   _____

   _____

4. Write a complete sentence using *consequently* as a conjunctive adverb.

   _____

   _____

5. Write a complete sentence using *consequently* as a parenthetical adverb.

   _____

   _____

6. Write a complete sentence using *but* as a coordinating conjunction.

   _____

   _____

7. Write a complete sentence using *nevertheless* as a conjunctive adverb.

   _____

   _____

8. Write a complete sentence using *nevertheless* as a parenthetical adverb.

   _____

   _____

9. Write a complete sentence using *then* as a parenthetical adverb.

   _____

   _____

10. Write a complete sentence using *however* as a parenthetical adverb.

   _____

   _____

A. (Self-check) In each of the following pairs, select the properly punctuated sentence.

1. (a) Before we make an investment decision we should do some research.
   (b) Before we make an investment decision, we should do some research. _____

2. (a) We should do some research, before we make an investment decision.
   (b) We should do some research before we make an investment decision. _____

3. (a) Procter and Gamble, which made a fortune with Ivory soap, discovered the formula by accident.
   (b) Procter and Gamble which made a fortune with Ivory soap discovered the formula by accident. _____

4. (a) The company, that made a fortune with Ivory soap, discovered the formula by accident.
   (b) The company that made a fortune with Ivory soap discovered the formula by accident. _____

5. (a) As predicted interest rates will climb during any period of inflation.
   (b) As predicted, interest rates will climb during any period of inflation. _____

6. (a) A magazine that features the 100 best places to work is now on the newsstands.
   (b) A magazine, that features the 100 best places to work, is now on the newsstands. _____

7. (a) Victoria Lintelman, who was the top salesperson in the country, received a Porsche convertible as a bonus.
   (b) Victoria Lintelman who was the top salesperson in the country, received a Porsche convertible as a bonus. _____

8. (a) Any salesperson who sells more than the weekly quota will receive a bonus.
   (b) Any salesperson, who sells more than the weekly quota, will receive a bonus. _____

9. (a) Please contact me immediately if you would like to apply for the position.
   (b) Please contact me immediately, if you would like to apply for the position. _____

10. (a) If you would like to apply for the position please contact me immediately.
    (b) If you would like to apply for the position, please contact me immediately. _____

Check your answers below.

 B. After each sentence write the letter representing the correct word in the space provided. Remember that the relative pronoun *which* should be used only to introduce nonessential clauses and, as such, requires commas. Also remember that *who*, *whom*, and *whose* are used to refer to persons. *That* and *which* refers to animals or things.

1. Companies (a) who, (b) that, (c) which offer good benefits packages attract more job applicants. _____

2. Microsoft, (a) who, (b) that, (c) which offers excellent benefits, attracts numerous job applicants. _____

3. We seek applicants (a) who, (b) that, (c) whom are certified project managers. _____

4. The city council needs to come up with a plan (a) which, (b) that will satisfy all residents. _____

5. Are you the one (a) who, (b) that, (c) which handles employee grievances? _____

1.b 2.b 3.a 4.b 5.b 6.a 7.a 8.a 9.a 10.b

6. The IRS, (a) who, (b) that, (c) which audits only 2 percent of all income tax returns, is choked with paperwork. _____

7. Amazon.com is known as an organization (a) who, (b) that, (c) which emphasizes innovation and customer service. _____

8. Employers are looking for workers (a) who, (b) that, (c) whom demonstrate excellent communication skills, professionalism, and etiquette. _____

9. Interviewees (a) who, (b) that, (c) which demonstrate professionalism are more likely to be hired. _____

10. A book (a) that, (b) which has greatly influenced the business world is *Servant Leadership*. _____

C. Sort this group of words into three lists and write them under the following headings: *and, however, if, but, yet, moreover, although, nor, because, consequently, or, thus, since, then, when.*

Coordinating Conjunctions	Conjunctive Adverbs	Subordinating Conjunctions
_____	_____	_____
_____	_____	_____
_____	_____	_____
_____	_____	_____
_____	_____	_____

D. In each pair of sentences, select the one that is punctuated or written properly.

1. (a) Philip Knight who was the cofounder and former CEO of Nike was tattooed with the company's "swoosh" logo.
    (b) Philip Knight, who was the cofounder and former CEO of Nike, was tattooed with the company's "swoosh" logo. _____

2. (a) The man who was the cofounder and former CEO of Nike was tattooed with the company's "swoosh" logo.
    (b) The man, who was the cofounder and former CEO of Nike, was tattooed with the company's "swoosh" logo. _____

3. (a) If you have any questions about our proposal, please e-mail them to Kris Bertrand.
    (b) If you have any questions about our proposal please e-mail them to Kris Bertrand. _____

4. (a) Please e-mail Kris Bertrand, if you have any questions.
    (b) Please e-mail Kris Bertrand if you have any questions. _____

5. (a) We were notified that the network would be down for six hours, although we were not told why.
    (b) We were notified that the network would be down for six hours; although we were not told why. _____

6. (a) When completed the newly created Web site will enable customers to track shipments.
    (b) When completed, the newly created Web site will enable customers to track shipments. _____

7. (a) The warranty that you refer to in your recent letter covers only merchandise brought to our shop for repair.
(b) The warranty, that you refer to in your recent letter, covers only merchandise brought to our shop for repair. _____

8. (a) Your home warranty which covers earthquake damage expires in two years.
(b) Your home warranty, which covers earthquake damage, expires in two years. _____

9. (a) John Halamka, who serves as Harvard Medical School's chief information officer, was among the first to have a radio-frequency chip put into his arm to help doctors locate his medical records in an emergency.
(b) John Halamka who serves as Harvard Medical School's chief information officer was among the first to have a radio-frequency chip put into his arm to help doctors locate his medical records in an emergency. _____

10. (a) The person, who serves as Harvard Medical School's chief information officer, was among the first to have a radio-frequency chip put into his arm to help doctors locate his medical records in an emergency.
(b) The person who serves as Harvard Medical School's chief information officer was among the first to have a radio-frequency chip put into his arm to help doctors locate his medical records in an emergency. _____

11. (a) A secretary who joined our staff only two months ago received this month's merit award.
(b) A secretary, who joined our staff only two months ago, received this month's merit award. _____

12. (a) Tracey Barry who joined our staff only two months ago received this month's merit award.
(b) Tracey Barry, who joined our staff only two months ago, received this month's merit award. _____

13. (a) Zone Improvement Program codes, which are better known as zip codes, are designed to expedite the sorting and delivery of mail.
(b) Zone Improvement Program codes which are better known as zip codes are designed to expedite the sorting and delivery of mail. _____

14. (a) The Senate will surely, when it convenes in its regular session, discuss defense spending.
(b) The Senate will surely when it convenes in its regular session discuss defense spending. _____

15. (a) Marketers, who develop advertising targeted at heavy users, are attempting to build brand loyalty.
(b) Marketers who develop advertising targeted at heavy users are attempting to build brand loyalty. _____

16. (a) Because of the recession rents have decreased in many housing markets.
(b) Because of the recession, rents have decreased in many housing markets. _____

17. (a) Rents have decreased in many housing markets because of the recession.
(b) Rents have decreased in many housing markets, because of the recession. _____

18. (a) If desired you can have custom appliances installed in your kitchen.
(b) If desired, you can have custom appliances installed in your kitchen. _____

19. (a) Companies that retain experienced workers are generally more successful.
(b) Companies which retain experienced workers are generally more successful. _____

20. (a) We are looking for an accountant that demonstrates highly ethical behavior.
(b) We are looking for an accountant who demonstrates highly ethical behavior. _____

E. Writing Exercise. Use your imagination to write the following complete sentences. Remember that clauses must contain subjects and verbs. Each sentence must be punctuated properly.

1. A sentence using *if* in an introductory dependent clause.

   _____

   _____

2. A sentence using *if* in a terminal dependent clause.

   _____

   _____

3. A sentence using *because* in an introductory dependent clause.

   _____

   _____

4. A sentence using *because* in a terminal dependent clause.

   _____

   _____

5. A sentence using *although* in an introductory dependent clause.

   _____

   _____

6. A sentence using *after* in an introductory dependent clause.

   _____

   _____

7. A sentence using *who* to introduce an essential clause.

   _____

   _____

8. A sentence using *who* to introduce a nonessential clause.

   _____

   _____

9. A sentence using *that* to introduce an essential clause.

   _____

   _____

10. A sentence using *which* to introduce a nonessential clause.

   _____

   _____

A. (Self-check) Select the more effective version of each of the following pairs of sentences. Write its letter in the space provided.

1. (a) Either she will go to law school or to medical school.
   (b) She will go either to law school or to medical school. _____

2. (a) Lisa Gores did not attend the meeting, and neither did James O'Malley.
   (b) Neither Lisa Gores nor James O'Malley attended the meeting. _____

3. (a) Our investing objectives are both to get a decent return and to protect our assets.
   (b) Our investing objectives are both to get a decent return and protecting our assets. _____

4. (a) Be sure to either book our tickets in first- or business-class seats.
   (b) Be sure to book our tickets in either first- or business-class seats. _____

5. (a) The new network is not only faster but also more efficient.
   (b) Not only is the new network faster, but it is also more efficient. _____

Indicate the structure of the following sentences by writing the appropriate letter in the spaces provided.

a = simple sentence   c = complex sentence
b = compound sentence   d = compound-complex sentence

Example: Because some business owners want to avoid Sarbanes-Oxley requirements, they are securing funding using creative methods. _____c_____

6. Netscape's initial public offering (IPO) in 1995 was the catalyst for the Internet stock explosion of the late 1990s. _____

7. Because the needs of today's luxury travelers are changing, Ritz-Carlton is retraining its employees. _____

8. U.S. airlines reduced services and cut jobs, but they continued to lose money. _____

9. We have no working backup system, and other departments face a similar problem. _____

10. Bruce was offered a sales position in Des Moines; therefore, he eagerly made plans to travel to Iowa, where he looked forward to beginning his sales career. _____

Check your answers below.

 B. Which sentence in each sentence pair below is more effective?

1. (a) The pilot has decades of experience not only flying planes but also teaching others how to fly them more safely.
   (b) The pilot not only has decades of experience flying planes but teaches others how to fly them more safely. _____

2. (a) Neither Ed nor Trish was familiar with the details of the contract.
   (b) Neither Ed was familiar, nor was Trish, of the details of the contract. _____

3. (a) The couple will either honeymoon in Brazil or Peru.
   (b) The couple will honeymoon in either Brazil or Peru. _____

1.b 2.b 3.a 4.b 5.a 6.a 7.c 8.b 9.b 10.d

4. (a) Either bankruptcy can be declared by the debtor or it can be requested by the creditors.

(b) Bankruptcy can be either declared by the debtor or requested by the creditors. _____

5. (a) Our travel counselor will both plan your trip and make your reservations.

(b) Our travel counselor will both plan your trip and reservations will be made. _____

6. (a) Either send the proposal to Kathy Overby or to me.

(b) Send the proposal either to Kathy Overby or to me. _____

7. (a) Not only do banks use computers to sort checks, but they also use computers for disbursing cash automatically.

(b) Banks use computers not only to sort checks but also to disburse cash automatically. _____

8. (a) Neither the employees nor the managers were happy with the proposed cutbacks in benefits.

(b) Neither the employees were happy with the proposed cutbacks in benefits, and nor were the managers. _____

9. (a) Our customer service rep will process your return, and she will ship out replacements too.

(b) Our customer service rep will both process your return and ship out replacements. _____

10. (a) FotoNation not only patented red-eye detection for cameras but also software that detects smiles.

(b) FotoNation patented not only red-eye detection for cameras but also software that detects smiles. _____

C. Writing Exercise. Rewrite the following sentences to make them more effective.

1. Either stocks can be purchased online or they can be purchased from a broker.

_____

_____

2. Neither the staff was happy with the proposed cutbacks in class offerings, and nor were the students.

_____

_____

3. Not only does the Small Business Administration (SBA) provide training, but it also guarantees loans.

_____

_____

4. Users of cell phones are often guilty of rude behavior, so many restaurants and other public places have imposed bans.

_____

_____

_____

5. Old computer hardware creates hazardous dump sites, so computer manufacturers are starting recycling programs.

_____

_____

_____

D. Writing Exercise. Rewrite the following groups of simple sentences into _one_ sentence for each group. Add coordinating conjunctions, conjunctive adverbs, and subordinating conjunctions as needed to create more effective complex, compound, and compound-complex sentences.

Example: Sybase needed an executive assistant. It advertised online. It finally hired a recent graduate. The graduate had excellent skills.

After advertising for an executive assistant online, Sybase finally hired a

recent graduate who had excellent skills.

1. Rusty was recently hired as a transportation engineer. She will work for Werner Enterprises. Werner Enterprises is located in Omaha, Nebraska.

_____

_____

2. Marlon Lodge is a British linguist and musician. He taught English to German employees of HSBC. He discovered that his students caught on more quickly when he set new vocabulary to music.

_____

_____

_____

3. Cows will respond to beeps. Some Japanese ranchers learned of this phenomenon and equipped their cattle with pagers. Now they herd cattle with beepers. These ranchers need fewer workers as a result.

_____

_____

4. Skilled writers save time for themselves. They also save it for their readers. They organize their ideas into logical patterns. They do this before sitting down at their computers.

_____

_____

5. Nancy Burnett is a single parent. She has merchandising experience. Nancy started a mall-based chain of stores. These stores sell fashionable, durable clothing for children.

_____

_____

E. FAQs About Business English Review. In the space provided, write the correct answer choice.

1. Do you know whether (a) their, (b) they're, (c) there planning to attend Friday's symposium. _____

2. Please wait right over (a) their, (b) they're, (c) there until the interviewer is ready. _____

3. (a) Their, (b) They're, (c) There airline tickets will be issued electronically. _____

4. Because of (a) adverse, (b) averse weather conditions, several airlines had to delay flights. _____

5. Management is (a) adverse, (b) averse to any decrease in employee health benefits. _____

6. Which is preferable for business and professional writing?
   a. Everyone thought the new Web design was so beautiful.
   b. Everyone thought the new Web design was beautiful. _____

7. We will need to (a) re-write, (b) rewrite the entire contract. _____

8. The order (a) that, (b) which arrived today contained several damaged items. _____

9. Because of his position, he has an excellent (a) perspective, (b) prospective on the problem. _____

10. I sent my résumé to a (a) perspective, (b) prospective employer. _____

You have heard that spyware is dangerous and can be used to gather sensitive information from your computer. You decide to find out more.

Goal: To learn about spyware.

1. With your Web browser on the screen, go to the **Security at Home** page of the Microsoft site at **http://www.microsoft.com/protect**.

2. Click **Spyware** in the "Computer Security" menu to read articles about spyware. Read the following sections: **What is spyware?, Signs of spyware: Are you being watched?, How to help prevent spyware**, and **How to get rid of spyware**. Print at least two pages from these sections.

3. What is spyware? How can you tell whether you have it on your computer? What are five things you can do to protect your computer against spyware?

4. End your session by clicking the **X** in the upper right corner of your browser. Turn in all printed pages and your answers.

 ▶▶ **Chat About It**

Your instructor may assign any of the following topics for you to discuss in class, in an online chat room, or on an online discussion board. Some of the discussion topics may require outside research. You may also be asked to read and respond to postings made by your classmates.

Discussion Topic 1: How does the coordinating conjunction *but* affect you psychologically? Consider these two sentences: *Your interview went well, but we would like to invite you to come back* versus *Your interview went well, and we would like to invite you to come back*. How does the conjunction change the meaning in these two sentences? When you hear the word *but*, do you feel that bad news is coming? What can you do in your own communication to avoid the "*but* syndrome"?

Discussion Topic 2: Chapter 13 concludes our discussion of the parts of speech. What are the most important things that you have learned about the parts of speech in Chapters 4 through 13? Write four complete sentences that describe what you have learned. Each sentence should contain a different type of conjunction: coordinating conjunction, conjunctive adverb, subordinating conjunction, and correlative conjunction. Share your sentences with your classmates.

Discussion Topic 3: E-mail is used extensively to communicate in the business world; therefore, it is important to use this communication tool effectively and professionally. What is the most important advice you have for using e-mail in the workplace? Share your advice with your classmates. Be as detailed as possible.

Discussion Topic 4: As you learned in the Learning Web Ways exercise, spyware can be dangerous for computer users. Many other threats exist, including worms, viruses, adware, crimeware, rootkits, trojan horses, malware, phishing, pharming, spam, identity theft, and so on. Choose a specific threat and conduct research on it. Share your findings with your classmates. What is the threat? How can you determine whether you have been affected by it? How can you avoid the threat?

Discussion Topic 5: The American writer Wallace Stegner said, "Hard writing makes easy reading." What does he mean by this? Do you agree? How can you apply this quote to your business writing? Explain.

Posttest

In each pair of sentences, underline the letter representing the sentence that is punctuated correctly.

1. (a) Technology is changing rapidly, therefore, most employees need regular retraining.
   (b) Technology is changing rapidly; therefore, most employees need regular retraining.

2. (a) Sandy filled the order, and Benjamin prepared the invoice.
   (b) Sandy filled the order and Benjamin prepared the invoice.

3. (a) We are not sure, however, whether the order will arrive on time.
   (b) We are not sure; however, whether the order will arrive on time.

4. (a) Try instant messaging if your organization requires real-time communication.
   (b) Try instant messaging, if your organization requires real-time communication.

5. (a) If your organization requires real-time communication try instant messaging.
   (b) If your organization requires real-time communication, try instant messaging.

6. (a) We are posting the job announcement online, and we are also asking for employee referrals.
   (b) We are posting the job announcement online and we are also asking for employee referrals.

7. (a) The software demonstration by Paul Iatomasi who represents Cisco Systems will be Friday.
   (b) The software demonstration by Paul Iatomasi, who represents Cisco Systems, will be Friday.

8. (a) The individual who represents Cisco Systems will give the software demonstration.
   (b) The individual, who represents Cisco Systems, will give the software demonstration.

Select the sentence that is more effective.

9. (a) Neither can we ship the printer nor the computer until April 1.
   (b) We can ship neither the printer nor the computer until April 1.

10. (a) Malware not only includes viruses but also spyware.
    (b) Malware includes not only viruses but also spyware.

1.b 2.b 3.a 4.a 5.b 6.a 7.b 8.a 9.b 10.b

NAME_____

Begin your review by rereading Chapters 11–13. Then test your comprehension with the following exercises. Compare your responses with those provided at the end of the book.

LEVEL 1

Write the letter of the correct answer choice.

1. I have never read a (a) worst, (b) worse legal brief. _____

2. In comparing the three shipping companies, we decided that DHL is (a) fastest, (b) faster. _____

3. The board members (a) should have, (b) should of voted to adopt the proposal. _____

4. The service contract is (a) to, (b) too expensive. _____

5. We are fortunate to have exceptional employees like William and (a) him, (b) he. _____

6. Josh feels (a) bad, (b) badly about his performance during the job interview. _____

7. The engine runs (a) smoother, (b) more smoother, (c) more smoothly after the tune-up. _____

8. Can I borrow some change (a) from, (b) off of you? _____

9. Just between you and (a) I, (b) me, I'm afraid that Sal is going to be let go. _____

10. (a) Gina first took a job in Knoxville and later decided to move to Charlotte.
    (b) Gina first took a job in Knoxville, and later decided to move to Charlotte. _____

11. (a) Hai Nguyen might be assigned to work in our legal office or he might be assigned to our administrative headquarters.
    (b) Hai Nguyen might be assigned to work in our legal office, or he might be assigned to our administrative headquarters. _____

12. (a) Amy's payroll service was a huge success, consequently, she is opening a second office.
    (b) Amy's payroll service was a huge success; consequently, she is opening a second office. _____

13. (a) Kristin wrote a chronological résumé, but Cameron preferred a functional strategy for his résumé.
    (b) Kristin wrote a chronological résumé but Cameron preferred a functional strategy for his résumé. _____

Write the letter of the correct answer choice.

14. If you need (a) a, (b) an example of her work, take a look at her e-portfolio. _____

15. (a) This, (b) These kinds of behavior are unacceptable in the workplace. _____

16. We will hear complaints on a (a) case by case, (b) case-by-case basis. _____

17. The company is (a) five years old, (b) five-years old. _____

18. No one (a) accept, (b) except the CEO has the override password. _____

19. Power in our government is balanced (a) among, (b) between its three branches. _____

20. You must turn your paperwork (a) into, (b) in to me by Monday. _____

21. Does anyone (a) beside, (b) besides you know the password? _____

22. The plan (a) that, (b) which we adopted will save the company thousands of dollars annually. _____

23. (a) Alice Waters, who owns Chez Panisse in Berkeley, is a champion of locally grown organic food.
    (b) Alice Waters who owns Chez Panisse in Berkeley is a champion of locally grown organic food. _____

24. (a) Before sending her résumé Holly made sure it was flawless.
    (b) Before sending her résumé, Holly made sure it was flawless. _____

25. (a) We are looking for an affordable, efficient heating system.
    (b) We are looking for an affordable efficient heating system. _____

26. (a) Send all checks to Gretchen Scotvold, who is in charge of contributions.
    (b) Send all checks to Gretchen Scotvold who is in charge of contributions. _____

LEVEL 3

Write the correct answer choice.

27. Morgan had a (a) real, (b) really productive morning. _____

28. Esteban performed (a) good, (b) well on his certification exam. _____

29. Let's discuss these ideas (a) further, (b) farther over lunch. _____

30. If you have (a) less, (b) fewer than ten items, you may use the quick-check lane. _____

31. Jacksonville is larger than (a) any other city, (b) any city in Florida. _____

32. Examine carefully the (a) 50 first, (b) first 50 pages of the booklet. _____

33. Air France (a) plans to fly, (b) plans on flying to China. _____

34. The approved contract is not very different (a) than, (b) from the first version. _____

35. We asked that our salary increase be retroactive (a) to, (b) from the first of the year. _____

36. Facebook will (a) surely, (b) sure start selling stock soon. _____

37. It was a pleasure talking (a) to, (b) with you during the interview yesterday. _____

38. (a) You can either be transferred to Pittsburgh or to Providence.
    (b) You can be transferred either to Pittsburgh or to Providence. _____

39. (a) He is not only qualified but also fully certified.
    (b) He is not only qualified but he is also fully certified too. _____

FAQs About Business English Review

40. She has (a) all ready, (b) already handled the customer inquiry. _____

41. (a) Adverse, (b) Averse working conditions caused many employees to resign. _____

42. When you visit New York, be sure to spend (a) sometime, (b) some time at the Metropolitan Museum of Art. _____

43. All (a) personnel, (b) personal matters are now handled in our Human Resources Department. _____

44. Microsoft Office (a) maybe, (b) may be facing some tough competition from Google. _____

45. I feel as if our supervisor will (a) dessert, (b) desert us if things go badly. _____

46. After a day of flying, we slept (a) awhile, (b) a while before going to dinner. _____

47. I would like my item to (a) proceed, (b) precede yours on the agenda. _____

48. I passed the information (a) onto, (b) on to my supervisor. _____

49. The senator called for a (a) nation-wide, (b) nation wide, (c) nationwide ban on phosphates. _____

50. This document must be (a) rewritten, (b) re-written. _____

E-Mail Messages and Memos

E-mail messages and memos are increasingly important forms of internal communication for most companies today. Organizations are downsizing, flattening chains of command, forming work teams, and empowering rank-and-file employees. Given more power in making decisions, employees find that they need more information. They must collect, exchange, and evaluate information about the products and services they offer. Management also needs input from employees to respond rapidly to local and global market actions. This growing demand for information results in an increasing use of memos and especially e-mail. That is why anyone entering a business or profession today should know how to write good e-mail messages and memos.

Characteristics of E-Mail Messages and Memos

E-mail messages and memos have a number of characteristics in common:

- They begin with the headings *To, From, Date,* and *Subject.*
- They generally cover just one topic.
- They are informal.
- They are concise.

E-mail messages and memos use efficient standard formats, such as you see in Figure 4.1. So that they can be acted on separately, e-mail messages and memos should discuss only one topic. Let's say you send your supervisor an e-mail message requesting a copier repair. You also add a comment about an article you want to appear in the company newsletter. The supervisor may act on one item and overlook the other. He might also want to forward your request for a copier repair directly to the operations manager, but he has to edit or rekey the message because of the second topic. Thus, e-mail messages and memos are most helpful when they cover just one subject.

Because they replace conversation, these messages tend to be informal. They may include first-person pronouns, such as *I* and *me,* as well as occasional contractions, such as *can't* or *haven't.* The tone, however, should not become familiar or unprofessional. Moreover, memos and e-mail messages should not be wordy. Concise messages save time and often are more easily understood than longer documents.

Writing Plan

For most informational and procedural messages, follow a **direct writing plan** that reveals the most important information first. Here are specific tips for writing the subject line, first sentence, body, and closing of e-mail messages and memos.

Subject Line. In the subject line, summarize the message. Although brief, a subject line must make sense and should capture the reader's interest. Instead of *Meeting,* for example, try *Meeting to Discuss Hiring Two New Employees.* A subject line is like a newspaper headline. It should snag attention, create a clear picture, and present an accurate summary. It should not be a complete sentence and should rarely occupy more than one line. When writing a subject line, capitalize the first letter of all major words to make the subject line look important and professional.

FIGURE 4.1
Comparing E-mail Messages and Memos

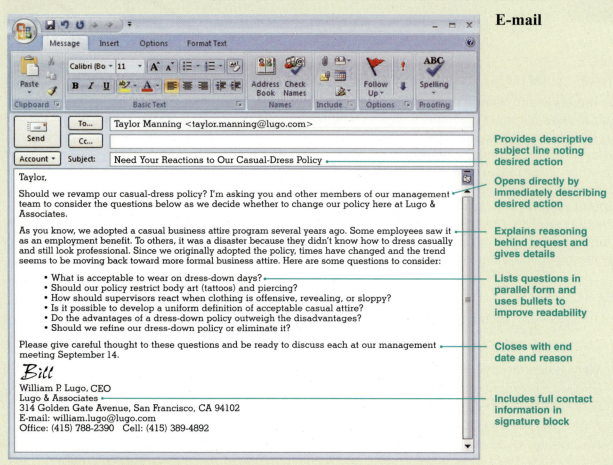

E-mail

Message | Insert | Options | Format Text

Calibri (Bo ▾ 11 ▾ | A⁺ A⁻ | ☰ ▾ ☰ ▾ | Paste | Address Book | Check Names | Follow Up ▾ | ! | ABC Spelling
Clipboard | Basic Text | Names | Include | Options | Proofing

To... Taylor Manning <taylor.manning@lugo.com>

Cc...

Subject: Need Your Reactions to Our Casual-Dress Policy

— **Provides descriptive subject line noting desired action**

Taylor,

Should we revamp our casual-dress policy? I'm asking you and other members of our management team to consider the questions below as we decide whether to change our policy here at Lugo & Associates.

— **Opens directly by immediately describing desired action**

As you know, we adopted a casual business attire program several years ago. Some employees saw it as an employment benefit. To others, it was a disaster because they didn't know how to dress casually and still look professional. Since we originally adopted the policy, times have changed and the trend seems to be moving back toward more formal business attire. Here are some questions to consider:

— **Explains reasoning behind request and gives details**

- What is acceptable to wear on dress-down days?
- Should our policy restrict body art (tattoos) and piercing?
- How should supervisors react when clothing is offensive, revealing, or sloppy?
- Is it possible to develop a uniform definition of acceptable casual attire?
- Do the advantages of a dress-down policy outweigh the disadvantages?
- Should we refine our dress-down policy or eliminate it?

— **Lists questions in parallel form and uses bullets to improve readability**

Please give careful thought to these questions and be ready to discuss each at our management meeting September 14.

— **Closes with end date and reason**

Bill
William P. Lugo, CEO
Lugo & Associates
314 Golden Gate Avenue, San Francisco, CA 94102
E-mail: william.lugo@lugo.com
Office: (415) 788-2390   Cell: (415) 389-4892

— **Includes full contact information in signature block**

Memo

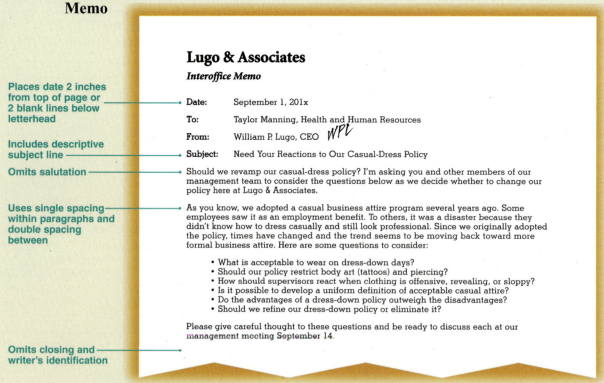

Places date 2 inches from top of page or 2 blank lines below letterhead

Includes descriptive subject line

Omits salutation

Uses single spacing within paragraphs and double spacing between

Omits closing and writer's identification

Lugo & Associates
Interoffice Memo

Date: September 1, 201x

To: Taylor Manning, Health and Human Resources

From: William P. Lugo, CEO *WPL*

Subject: Need Your Reactions to Our Casual-Dress Policy

Should we revamp our casual-dress policy? I'm asking you and other members of our management team to consider the questions below as we decide whether to change our policy here at Lugo & Associates.

As you know, we adopted a casual business attire program several years ago. Some employees saw it as an employment benefit. To others, it was a disaster because they didn't know how to dress casually and still look professional. Since we originally adopted the policy, times have changed and the trend seems to be moving back toward more formal business attire. Here are some questions to consider:

- What is acceptable to wear on dress-down days?
- Should our policy restrict body art (tattoos) and piercing?
- How should supervisors react when clothing is offensive, revealing, or sloppy?
- Is it possible to develop a uniform definition of acceptable casual attire?
- Do the advantages of a dress-down policy outweigh the disadvantages?
- Should we refine our dress-down policy or eliminate it?

Please give careful thought to these questions and be ready to discuss each at our management meeting September 14.

First Sentence. Although an explanation occasionally may precede the main idea, the first sentence usually tells the primary idea of the message. For example, an appropriate first sentence in an e-mail message announcing a new vacation procedure follows:

> Here are new guidelines for employees taking two- or three-week vacations between June and September.

The opening of the message may issue a polite command (*Please answer the following questions about . . .*), make a request (*Please begin research on a summer internship program*), or ask a question (*Can your department complete the printing of a . . .*). Try not to begin with a lengthy explanation. Get to the point as quickly as possible.

Skill Check 4.1 Openings for E-Mail Messages and Memos

Which subject line is better for an e-mail or memo? Circle its letter.

1. a. SUBJECT: Inventory
   b. SUBJECT: Annual Pharmacy Inventory Scheduled for June 2

2. a. SUBJECT: This E-Mail Message Announces Revised Procedures for Applying for Dental Benefits
   b. SUBJECT: Revised Procedures for Dental Benefits Applications

Which opening sentence is better for an e-mail or memo?

3. a. Employees interested in learning about new communication technologies are invited to a workshop on January 31.
   b. For some time now we have been thinking about the possibility of holding a workshop about new communication technologies for some of our employees.

4. a. We have noticed recently a gradual but steady decline in the number of customers purchasing items from our Web site.
   b. Please conduct a study and make recommendations regarding the gradual but steady decline of online customer purchases.

5. Write a subject line for a memo that describes the possibility of a new sports scoreboard sponsored by Coca-Cola, a topic to be discussed at the next management council meeting.

_____

_____

6. Write a subject line for an e-mail or memo announcing a demonstration of new software for all employees to be given November 16.

_____

_____

Body of Message. Provide details of the message in the body. If you are asking for information, arrange your questions in a logical order. If you are providing information, group similar information together. Think about using side headings in bold print, such as you see in these paragraphs. They help readers understand, locate, and reference information quickly. You can also improve the readability of any message by listing items with numbers or bullets. Compare the two sets of instructions that follow:

Hard to Read
The instructions for operating our copy machine include inserting your meter in the slot, loading paper in the upper tray, and then copies are fed through the feed chute.

Improved

Here are instructions for using the copy machine:

- Insert your meter in the slot.
- Load paper in the upper tray.
- Feed copies through the feed chute.

Notice that all the items in the preceding bulleted list are parallel in construction. That means that each item uses the same grammatical form. All begin with verbs. This kind of balanced writing helps readers anticipate and understand information more readily.

Skill Check 4.2 Listing Information

In the space provided, revise the following paragraph so that it includes an introductory sentence and a list of four items.

> We are trying to improve budget planning, and we would also like to control costs. To accomplish these goals, we must change our procedures for submitting requests in the future for outside printing jobs. The new procedures include first determining your exact printing specifications for a particular job. Then we want you to obtain two estimates for the job. These estimates should be submitted in writing to Kelly. Finally, you may place the outside print order—but only after receiving approval.

_____

_____

_____

_____

_____

_____

Closing an E-Mail Message or Memo. E-mail messages and memos frequently end with (a) a request for action, (b) a summary of the message, or (c) a closing thought. If action on the part of the reader is sought, be sure to spell out that action clearly. A vague request such as *Drop by to see this customer sometime* is ineffective because the reader may not understand exactly what is to be done. A better request might be worded as follows: *Please make an appointment to see Rebecca Johnson before June 2 so that we can complete the contract by June 15*. Notice that an **end date** is given. This technique, particularly when coupled with a valid reason, is effective in prompting people to act.

Another way to close an internal message is by summarizing its major points. A closing summary is helpful if the message is complicated. When no action request is made and a closing summary is unnecessary, the writer may prefer to end the memo with a simple closing thought, such as *I appreciate your assistance, What do you think of this proposal?*, or *Call me if I may answer questions*. Avoid tired, mechanical phrases such as *Please don't hesitate to call on me*, or *Thank you in advance for your cooperation*. If you wish to express these thoughts, find a fresh way to say them.

Figure 4.1 shows how the four parts of a writing plan (subject line, first sentence, body, closing) combine to create a readable, efficient e-mail message. For more information on memo and e-mail formats, see Appendix C.

Special Tips for Sending E-Mail Messages

Instead of using paper to send memos, increasing numbers of businesspeople are turning to e-mail to send messages. To make the best use of e-mail, implement the following suggestions:

- **Compose offline.** Instead of dashing off hasty messages online, take the time to compose offline. Consider using your word processing program and then cutting and pasting your message to the e-mail compose box. This avoids "self-destructing" online (losing all your writing through some glitch or pressing the wrong key).

- **Get the address right.** E-mail addresses are sometimes complex, often illogical, and always unforgiving. Omit one character or misread the letter *l* for the number *1,* and your message bounces. Solution: Use your electronic address book for people you write to frequently. And double-check every address that you key in manually. Also be sure that you don't reply to a group of receivers when you intend to answer only one.

- **Keep lines, paragraphs, and messages short.** Try to keep your lines under 65 characters in length and your paragraphs no longer than eight lines. Above all, keep your message short. If it requires more than three screens, consider sending it in hard-copy form.

- **Care about correctness.** Senders and receivers of e-mail tend to be casual about spelling, grammar, and usage. However, people are still judged by their writing; and you never know how far your message will travel. Read and edit any message before hitting the **Send** button!

- **Don't send anything you wouldn't want published**. Because e-mail seems like a telephone call or a person-to-person conversation, writers sometimes send sensitive, confidential, inflammatory, or potentially embarrassing messages. Beware! E-mail creates a permanent record that often does not go away even when deleted. And every message is a corporate communication that can be used against you or your employer. Don't write anything that you wouldn't want your boss, your family, or a judge to read.

- **Type your name at the bottom of your messages**. You should type your name at the bottom of all e-mail messages to personalize them. Depending on the receiver, you may also want to add contact information after your name.

Special Tips for Replying to E-Mail Messages

Before replying to an e-mail message, think about some of the suggestions provided here. You can save yourself time and heartache by developing good reply procedures.

- **Scan all messages in your inbox before replying to each individually.** Because subsequent messages often affect the way you respond, read them all first (especially all those from the same individual).

- **Don't automatically return the sender's message.** When replying, cut and paste the relevant parts. Avoid irritating your recipients by returning the entire "thread" (sequence of messages) on a topic.

- **Revise the subject line if the topic changes.** When replying or continuing an e-mail exchange, revise the subject line as the topic changes.

- **Never respond when you are angry.** Always allow some time to cool off before shooting off a response to an upsetting message. You often come up with different and better alternatives after thinking about what was said. If possible, iron out differences in person.

Finally, remember that office computers are meant for work-related communication. Unless your company specifically allows it, never use your employer's computers for personal messages, personal shopping, or entertainment. Assume that all e-mail is monitored. Employers legally have the right to eavesdrop on employee e-mail messages, and many do.

Writing Application 4.1

Revise the following poorly written message. It suffers from wordiness, indirectness, and confusing instructions. Include a numbered list in your revision, and be sure to improve the subject line. Prepare this as an e-mail message or as an internal memo.

TO: All Staff Members
FROM: Roy Minami, Manager
DATE: July 11, 201x
SUBJECT: COPIER RULES

Some of you missed the demonstration of the operation of our new Turbo X copier last week. I thought you might appreciate receiving this list of suggestions from the salesperson when she gave the demonstration. This list might also be helpful to other employees who saw the demo but didn't take notes and perhaps can't remember all these pointers. It's sometimes hard to remember how to operate a machine when you do it infrequently. Here's what she told us to do. There are two paper loading trays. Load 8 1/2-x-11-inch or 8 1/2-x-14-inch paper in the two loading trays. The paper should curve upward in the tray. You should take your copy and feed it into the machine face up. However, if you have small sheets or book pages or cut-and-pasted copy, lift the copier door and place your copy face down on the glass.

Before you begin, select the number of copies to be made by pressing the touch selector panel. Don't push too hard. If copies become jammed, open the front door and see where the paper got stuck in the feed path. Remove jammed paper. Oh yes, your meter must be inserted before the machine will operate. We urge you, of course, to make only as many copies as you really need. Keep this list to use again.

Don't hesitate to call on me if you need a private demonstration.

Writing Application 4.2

As the manager of Reprographic Services, write an e-mail message to Kevin Suzuki, manager, Technical Services. You are very worried that one of the computers of your operators may be infected with a virus. The computer belongs to Jackie Jimenez. Jackie says that each time she opens a previously stored document in her Word program, the contents of the document are immediately deleted. Fortunately, because Jackie has backup files, she hasn't lost anything yet. But obviously she can't go on using this computer. You plan to assign Jackie some temporary tasks for the rest of the day; however, she must have her computer up and running by tomorrow. You want a technician to inspect her machine before 5 p.m. today. You know that Kevin likes to learn as much about a computer problem as possible before he sends a technician, so include sufficient details to help him identify the problem.

Writing Application 4.3

As the manager of the Customer Services Division, Milwaukee Breweries, write an e-mail message to Melissa Miller, supervisor, Customer Services. Ask Melissa to draft a form letter that can be sent to groups requesting plant tours. In your e-mail message, explain that the brewery has always encouraged tour groups to see your home plant brewery. However, you cannot sponsor tours at this time because of extensive remodeling. You are also installing a new computer-controlled bottling system. Tours are expected to resume in September. You need a form letter that can be sent to all groups but that can be personalized for individual responses. You want the letter draft by Monday, April 6. The letter should build good customer relations, a primary goal of your tour policy. The letter might enclose a free product coupon and a brochure picturing your operations. Tell Melissa to add any information that she feels would improve the letter.

Unit 5

Punctuating Sentences

14 Commas

© Brand X Pictures/Jupiterimages

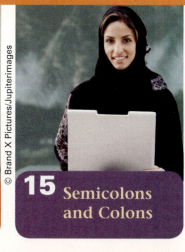

15 Semicolons and Colons

© BananaStock/Jupiterimages

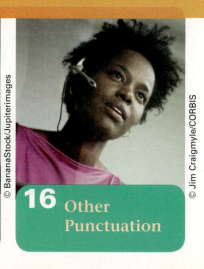

16 Other Punctuation

© Jim Craigmyle/CORBIS

"Think of punctuation marks as the traffic signs of writing. Just as traffic signs guide drivers, so punctuation marks guide readers and writers."

**—Marie Rackham,
retired English teacher**

Chapter 14

Commas

OBJECTIVES

When you have completed the materials in this chapter, you will be able to do the following:

LEVEL 1
- Use commas correctly in series, direct address, and parenthetical expressions.
- Use commas correctly in punctuating dates, time zones, addresses, geographical items, and appositives.

LEVEL 2
- Use commas correctly in punctuating independent adjectives, verbal phrases, and prepositional phrases.
- Use commas correctly in punctuating independent, introductory, terminal, and nonessential clauses.

LEVEL 3
- Use commas correctly in punctuating degrees, abbreviations, and numerals.
- Use commas correctly to indicate omitted words and contrasting statements, for clarity, and with short quotations.

Pretest   Insert appropriate commas in the following sentences.

1. The couple will travel to London Paris and Munich this summer.

2. Jeanie Dewhurst PhD sent an important notice to her staff.

3. After a long search Kathy Sarnie found a charming historic apartment in downtown Boston.

4. Your interview Ms. Diaz will take place on Tuesday June 9 at 10 a.m.

5. Zappos ships its shoes from Shepherdsville Kentucky to U.S. addresses only.

6. The attorney had reason to believe by the way that the judge was not impartial and might even be biased against this case.

7. America's interstate highway system began in 1956 and it has given birth to many new industries.

8. Although tired employees preferred the evening not the morning in-service training programs.

9. Patricia T. O'Conner said "When a tiny word gives you a big headache it's probably a pronoun."

10. Thomas Edison the inventor of the electric light and the phonograph has 1093 patents to his name.

Trivia Tidbit

Some writers in other languages envy English. Our systematic use of commas and other punctuation makes it easy to signal pauses, to emphasize ideas, and to enhance readability.

When you talk with a friend, you are probably unaware of the "invisible" commas, periods, and other punctuation marks that you are using. In conversation your pauses and voice inflections punctuate your thoughts and clarify your meaning. In writing, however, you must use a conventional set of symbols, punctuation marks, to help your reader understand your meaning, just as traffic signs help to guide drivers.

Over the years we have gradually developed a standardized pattern of usage for all punctuation marks. This usage has been codified (set down) in rules that are observed by writers who wish to make their writing as precise as possible. As noted earlier, some professional writers may deviate from conventional punctuation practices. In addition, some organizations, particularly newspapers and publishing houses, maintain their own style manuals to establish a consistent "in-house" style.

The punctuation guidelines presented in this book represent a consensus about punctuation styles that are acceptable in business and professional writing. Following these guidelines will enable you to write with clarity, consistency, and accuracy.

1. London, Paris,   2. Dewhurst, PhD,   3. search, charming,   4. interview, Diaz, Tuesday, June 9,   5. Shepherdsville, Kentucky,   6. believe, way,   7. 1956,   8. tired, evening, morning,   9. said, headache,   10. Edison, phonograph, 1,093

Basic Guidelines for Using Commas

The most used and misused punctuation mark, the **comma**, indicates a pause in the flow of a sentence. *Not all sentence pauses, however, require commas.* It is important for you to learn the standard rules for the use of commas so that you will not be tempted to clutter your sentences with needless, distracting commas. Here are the guidelines for basic comma usage.

Series

Commas are used to separate three or more equally ranked elements (words, phrases, or short clauses) in a series. Remember to place a comma (called a **serial comma**) before the final conjunction in a series. A comma before the conjunction ensures separation of the last two items. Some writers omit the comma before the conjunction in a series. Business writers, however, are encouraged to use this comma to ensure clarity and ease of reading. No commas are used when conjunctions join all the items in a series.

> Only in June, July, and August is our favorite beachside restaurant open. (Series of words. Notice that a comma precedes *and*, but no comma follows the last item, *August*.)

> Wireless technology enables you to respond to customers' requests, change sales forecasts, and manage suppliers while you are away from the office. (Series of phrases)

> Denise Morita is the owner, Chuck Risby is the marketing manager, and Cheryl Summers is the executive assistant. (Series of clauses)

> We need wireless access to e-mail and Web sites and the company intranet. (No commas needed when conjunctions are repeated.)

Direct Address

Direct address occurs when a person is being addressed or spoken to directly, rather than being spoken about. Words and phrases of direct address, including names, affiliations, and titles, are set off with commas.

> *Sonya*, do you plan to attend Monday's sales meeting? (At beginning of sentence)

> Are you, *members of the class of 2011*, ready to go out and take on the world? (In middle of sentence)

> We are happy to confirm your reservation, *sir*. (At end of sentence)

Parenthetical Expressions

Parenthetical words, phrases, and clauses may be used to create transitions between thoughts. These expressions interrupt the flow of a sentence and are unessential to its grammatical completeness. These commonly used expressions, some of which are listed below, are considered nonessential because they do not answer specifically questions such as *When?, Where?, Why?,* or *How?* Set off these expressions with commas when they are used parenthetically.

after all	at the same time	finally
as a matter of fact	by the way	for example
as a result	consequently	fortunately

Study Tip

As you begin to learn about commas, try to name a rule or guideline for every comma you insert. For example, *comma/series, comma/parenthetical,* and so forth.

Trivia Tidbit

Serial commas have actually played roles in court cases. For example, the will of a deceased man left everything to *John, Phil and Mary.* John's attorneys argued that John received half and Phil and Mary had to share the other half. What do you think?

furthermore	in summary	otherwise
however	in the first place	that is
in addition	in the meantime	then
in conclusion	needless to say	therefore
incidentally	nevertheless	too
in fact	no	under the circumstances
in general	no doubt	unfortunately
in my opinion	of course	without a doubt
in other words	on the other hand	yes

No, I won't be able to attend the symposium. (At beginning of sentence)

We know, *without a doubt*, that our customer service is outstanding. (In middle of sentence)

You have checked your résumé for accuracy, *no doubt*. (At end of sentence)

The words in question are set off by commas only when they are used parenthetically and actually interrupt the flow of a sentence.

However the vote goes, we will abide by the result. (No comma is needed after *however*.)

We have *no doubt* that you will be able to fulfill the duties of this position. (No commas are needed to set off *no doubt*.)

Don't confuse short introductory essential prepositional phrases for parenthetical expressions. Notice that the following phrases are essential and therefore require no commas. Punctuating with prepositional phrases will be discussed later in this chapter.

In the fall many students begin college. (No comma is needed because the short prepositional phrase answers the question *When?*)

For that reason our competitors are lowering their prices. (No comma is needed because the short prepositional phrase answers the question *Why?*)

With your help our production team can meet its goal. (No comma is needed because the short prepositional phrase answers the question *How?*)

Dates and Time Zones

Commas are used to set off elements of dates and time zones in sentences.

Dates

Dates can be made up of various elements, including weekday, calendar date, and year. When dates contain more than one element, the second and succeeding elements are normally set off by commas. Study the following examples:

On January 19 we opened for business. (No comma needed for one element.)

On January 19, 2009, we opened for business. (Two commas set off second element.)

On Monday, January 19, 2009, we opened for business. (Commas set off second and third elements.)

In January 2009 Barack Obama was inaugurated as president of the United States. (Commas are not used with the month and year only.)

Study Tip

How important are commas? Notice how commas change the meaning of this sentence. Version 1: *The actress Nicole Kidman says Halle Berry is the best actress in films.* Version 2: *The actress Nicole Kidman, says Halle Berry, is the best actress in films.*

Study Tip

Phrases are essential (no commas) when they answer the questions *When?, Where?, Why?,* or *How?*

Study Tip

In separating dates and years, many writers remember the initial comma but forget the final one (*On January 10, 2012, the new fiscal year begins*).

Time Zones

Commas also set off time zones used with clock times.

> Our flight leaves Atlanta at 10:50 a.m., EST, and arrives in Salt Lake City at 12:15 p.m., MST.
>
> He placed his online bid at 6:38 p.m., PST, which was two minutes before the auction closed.

Addresses and Geographical Items

When dates, addresses, and geographical items contain more than one element, the second and following elements should be set off by commas.

Addresses

When addresses are written in sentence form, separate the parts of the address with commas. Do not, however, place a comma between the city and zip code.

> Please send a copy of your passport to Barbara Briggs, Classic Journeys, 7855 Ivanhoe Avenue, Suite 220, La Jolla, California 92037, before your trip. (Commas are used between all elements except the state and zip code, which are considered a single unit.)

Geographical Items

Use commas to set off a state when it follows the name of a city. Commas are also used to set off the name of a country when it follows the name of a city.

> He moved from Bangor, Maine, to Lexington, Kentucky. (Two commas set off the state unless it appears at the end of the sentence.)
>
> Our flight from Shanghai, China, to Moscow, Russia, will take 13 hours. (Two commas set off the country unless it appears at the end of the sentence.)

Appositives

You will recall that **appositives** rename, describe, or explain preceding nouns or pronouns. An appositive that provides information not essential to the identification of its antecedent should be set off by commas.

> Nancy Deason, *the Nantucket Catering Company representative*, is here. (The appositive adds nonessential information; commas set it off.)
>
> You may pick up your order from the location closest to your home, *our Southlake branch*.

When an appositive is needed to identify the noun or pronoun referred to earlier in the sentence, do not set it off with commas.

> The catering company representative *Nancy Deason* is here to see you. (The appositive is needed to identify which sales representative has arrived; therefore, no commas are used.)
>
> The book *The Whuffie Factor* explains how businesses can use social networking effectively. (The appositive is needed to identify the specific book; therefore, no commas are used.)

Closely related one-word appositives do not require commas.

> My supervisor *Doug* sometimes uses my computer.

Now complete the reinforcement exercises for Level 1.

Study Tip

When separating cities and states, remember to include the comma after the state if the sentence continues (*my friend from Wheeling, West Virginia, called*). ∧

Special Guidelines for Using Commas

At this level we will review comma usage guidelines that you studied in previous chapters, and we will add one new guideline.

Independent Adjectives

Separate two or more adjectives that equally modify or describe a noun (see Chapter 11).

> Online customers can conduct *secure, real-time* banking transactions.
>
> We are looking for an *industrious, ambitious* person to hire.

Study Tip

When trying to decide whether to place a comma between adjectives, read the sentence with the conjunction *and* between the conjunctions. If the sentence makes sense, place a comma between the adjectives.

Introductory Verbal Phrases

Verbal phrases (see Chapter 8) that precede main clauses should be followed by commas. Prepositional phrases containing verb forms are also followed by commas.

> *To apply for the position*, you must visit our Web site. (Infinitive verbal phrase)
>
> *Working overtime*, we completed the project before the deadline. (Participial verbal phrase with verb form ending in *ing*)
>
> *Intrigued by the idea*, Emily researched study abroad opportunities. (Participial verbal phrase with verb form ending in *ed*)
>
> *By enrolling early*, you will receive our special discount. (Prepositional phrase with a verb form)

Prepositional Phrases

One or more introductory prepositional phrases (see Chapter 12) totaling four or more words should be followed by a comma.

> *On the first Tuesday of each month*, museum admission is free.
>
> *During the summer months*, rentals usually increase.

Introductory prepositional phrases of fewer than four words require *no* commas.

> *In 2012* Wal-Mart will celebrate its fiftieth anniversary.
>
> *On September 30* we expect a major announcement.

Prepositional phrases in other positions do not require commas when they are essential and do not interrupt the flow of the sentence.

> We have installed *in our Chicago office* a centralized telecommunications system. (No commas are needed around the prepositional phrase because it answers the question *Where?* and does not interrupt the flow of the sentence.)
>
> The announcement *about our fall promotion* will be made next week. (No commas are needed because the prepositional phrase answers the question *Which one?* and does not interrupt the flow of the sentence.)

Independent Clauses

When a coordinating conjunction (see Chapter 13) joins independent clauses, use a comma before the coordinating conjunction. When using the coordinating conjunction *and*, you can omit the comma when the entire sentence is short (up to 13 words).

> In Japan the wireless Internet has become wildly successful, and companies are pushing for even more sophisticated services.

> Joshua ordered pasta and Isabella ordered lobster. (No comma is needed because the entire sentence is short.)

Introductory Clauses

Dependent clauses that precede independent clauses are followed by commas. Remember that dependent clauses usually begin with subordinating conjunctions (see Chapter 13).

> *When you have finished*, please turn out the lights and lock the door.

> *If you have any questions*, please call me at Ext. 2306.

> *Because we rely on e-mail*, we have cut back on voice mail.

Terminal Dependent Clauses

Whether to use a comma to separate a dependent clause at the end of a sentence depends on whether the added information is essential. Generally, terminal dependent clauses add information that answers questions such as *When?, Why?,* and *How?* Such information is essential; thus no comma is necessary. Only when a terminal clause adds unnecessary information or an afterthought should a comma be used.

> Please turn out the lights and lock the door *when you have finished.* (No comma is needed because the terminal clause provides essential information and answers the question *When?*)

> Please call me at Ext. 2306 *if you have any questions.* (No comma is needed because the terminal clause provides essential information and answers the question *Why?*)

> We have cut back on faxing *because we rely on e-mail.* (No comma is needed because the terminal clause provides essential information and answers the question *Why?*)

> I plan to leave at 3:30, *although I could stay if you need me.* (A comma is needed because the terminal clause provides additional unnecessary information.)

Nonessential Clauses

Use commas to set off **nonrestrictive clauses**. These types of clauses are used parenthetically or supply information unneeded for the grammatical completeness of a sentence.

> Employee layoffs, *as you will surely agree*, must be avoided if at all possible. (Commas are needed because the italicized clause adds unnecessary information.)

> We received a phone call from Vice President Joseph Biden, *who will be speaking to our organization next week.* (Commas are necessary because the italicized clause adds unnecessary information.)

The culprit behind the spam, which advertised everything from cable descramblers to herbal remedies, was finally apprehended. (Commas are necessary because the italicized clause adds unneeded information. The relative pronoun *which* is a clue that the clause is unnecessary.)

Do NOT use commas to set off clauses that contain essential information. You might want to review this topic in Chapter 13.

An executive *who is preparing proposals* certainly needs an up-to-date reference manual. (No commas are necessary because the italicized clause is essential; it tells what executive needs an up-to-date reference manual.)

Now complete the reinforcement exercises for Level 2.

LEVEL 3

Additional Guidelines for Using Commas

The last guidelines for commas include suggestions for punctuating degrees, abbreviations, numerals, omitted words, contrasting statements, and short quotations.

Degrees and Abbreviations

The abbreviations *Jr.* and *Sr.* and Roman numerals added to a person's name are not set off by commas unless the person chooses to include them. When in doubt, ask the person or look at his or her business card.

John T. O'Dell Jr. is frequently confused with John T. O'Dell Sr.

Stafford Elahi III received his master's degree last year.

Degrees, personal titles, and professional designations following individuals' names are set off by commas.

Norman Rosen, MD, uses telemedicine connections to keep in touch with his patients.

Cathy Formusa, PhD, believes in using holistic methods in her practice.

We have retained Lissa Godbey, Esq., to represent us.

Company abbreviations such as *Inc.* and *Ltd.* are set off by commas only if the company's legal name includes the commas.

Despair, Inc., provides motivational products and posters for pessimists and underachievers. (The company's legal name includes a comma.)

Lucasfilm Ltd. is probably best known for its *Star Wars* films. (The legal name does not include a comma before *Ltd.*)

Numerals

Unrelated figures appearing side by side should be separated by commas.

By 2014, 258 million people will access mobile broadband services wirelessly through their laptops.

On page 10, two illustrations show the wiring diagram.

Study Tip

In America the term *Esq.* may be used as a courtesy title by attorneys addressing each other. If used, no other title is written (*Don Smith, Esq.*).

Trivia Tidbit

A variety of abbreviations are used in company names in the United States to designate the type of business. For example, *Inc.* ("incorporated") identifies a corporation; *Ltd.* ("limited") identifies a limited liability company; *LLP* identifies a limited liability corporation; and *PC* identifies a professional corporation.

Numbers of more than three digits require commas when expressed in U.S. format.

| 1,760 | 47,950 | 6,500,000 |

However, calendar years and zip codes are written without commas within the numerals.

| **Calendar Years:** | 1776 | 1945 | 2012 |
| **Zip Codes:** | 02116 | 45327 | 90265 |

Telephone and fax numbers, house numbers, decimals, page numbers, serial numbers, metric numbers, social security numbers, policy numbers, and contract numbers are also written without commas within the numerals.

Telephone/Fax Number:	(415) 937-5594
House Number:	5411 Redfield Circle
Decimal Number:	.98651, .0050
Page Number:	Page 1036
Serial Number:	36-5710-1693285763
Contract Number:	NO. 359063420

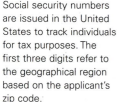

Omitted Words

A comma is used to show the omission of words that are understood.

> Last summer we hired 12 interns; this summer, only 3 interns.
> (Comma shows omission of *we hired* after *summer*.)

Contrasting Statements

Commas are used to set off contrasting or opposing expressions. These expressions are often introduced by such words as *not, never, but,* and *yet*.

> We chose Tommaso's, not Steps of Rome, to cater our World Cup celebration party. (Two commas set off a contrasting statement that appears in the middle of a sentence.)

> The riskier the investment, the greater the potential return. (One comma sets off a contrasting statement that appears at the end of a sentence.)

> The more he protests, the less we believe him. (One comma sets off a contrasting statement that appears at the end of a sentence.)

Clarity

Commas are used to separate words repeated for emphasis and words that may be misread if not separated.

> It will be a very, very long time before Kendra is able to return to South Asia.

> Whoever goes, goes at his or her own expense.

> No matter what, you know you have our support.

> In business, time is money.

Short Quotations

A comma is used to separate a short quotation from the rest of a sentence. If the quotation is divided into two parts, two commas are used.

> Alice Beasley said, "The first product to use a bar code was Wrigley's gum."

> "The first product to use a bar code," said Alice Beasley, "was Wrigley's gum."

Now complete the reinforcement exercises for Level 3.

Spot the BLOOPER

Using the skills you are learning in this class, try to identify why the following items are bloopers. Consult your textbook, dictionary, or reference manual as needed.

Blooper 1: Sentence printed in a British newspaper: "The defendant said his barrister had a history of drug abuse." [How could two commas have changed the meaning of this sentence?]

Blooper 2: A large portable sign located near Soperton, Georgia: "We sell crack and shell pecans." [How would the addition of commas change the meaning of this sentence?]

Blooper 3: Poster for a university departmental event: "Door prizes will include lab equipment, books written by members of the biology department and a fruitcake."

Blooper 4: Sign outside a restaurant in Grenada, Mississippi: "LETS EAT SENIOR CITIZENS." [Did you spot two bloopers?]

Blooper 5: From *The Union-Leader* [Manchester, New Hampshire]: "Prince Louis Ferdinand of Prussia, a grandson of Germany's last emperor who worked in a Detroit auto plant in the 1930s and later opposed Nazi dictator Adolf Hitler, has died at age 86." [Could a comma help clarify who worked in the auto plant?]

Blooper 6: From *The Pacifica Tribune* [Pacifica, California]: "The land was eventually sold to Andy Oddstad who built homes and also became the site of Linda Mar Shopping Center."

Blooper 7: From an AP story about a lawsuit filed by a woman who said she was burned by a pickle that fell out of her McDonald's burger: "While attempting to eat the hamburger, the pickle dropped from the hamburger onto her chin."

Blooper 8: From *The Boston Globe*: "Then her hair caught fire while sitting in a front seat during a fireworks display."

Blooper 9: Banner at an educational task force meeting in Raleigh, North Carolina: "Excellance in Secondary Education."

Blooper 10: Photo caption in the *Cherokee Ledger-News* [Canton, Georgia]: "Gordon Wilson points out places where his unit operated during World War II in his Woodstock home."

FAQs

Answered by Dr. Guffey and Professor Seefer

Dr. Guffey   Professor Seefer

Question	Answer

Q: I remember when company names with *Inc.* and *Ltd.* always had commas around these abbreviations. Has this changed?

A: Today's practice is to use commas only if the official company name includes the commas. For example, the following company names are written without commas: Gap Inc., Apple Inc., Phizer Inc., Caterpillar Inc. However, other companies include the commas: Canon U.S.A., Inc.; Motorola, Inc.; Novell, Inc.; Cisco Systems, Inc. One way to check on the official name is to search for the company's Web site and look at it there.

Q: When the company name *Sun Microsystems, Inc.,* appears in the middle of a sentence, is there a comma following *Inc.*?

A: Current authorities recommend the following practice in punctuating *Inc.*: If the legal company name includes a comma preceding *Inc.*, then a comma should follow *Inc.* if it is used in the middle of a sentence (*we learned that Sun Microsystems, Inc., has an education software program*).

Q: My boss always leaves out the comma before the word *and* when it precedes the final word in a series of words. Should the comma be used?

A: Although some writers omit that comma, which is called a serial comma, careful writers favor its use so that the last two items in the series cannot be misread as one item. For example, *The departments participating are Engineering, Accounting, Marketing, and Advertising*. Without that final comma, the last two items might be confused as one item.

Q: Should I use a comma after the year in this sentence? *In 2010 we began operations.*

A: No. Commas are not required after short introductory prepositional phrases (fewer than four words) unless confusion might result without them. If two numbers, for example, appear consecutively, a comma would be necessary to prevent confusion: *In 2010, 156 companies used our services.*

Q: Are these three words interchangeable: *assure, ensure,* and *insure?*

A: Good question! Although all three words mean "to make secure or certain," they are not interchangeable. *Assure* refers to persons and may suggest setting someone's mind at rest (*let me assure you that we are making every effort to locate it*). *Ensure* and *insure* both mean "to make secure from loss," but only *insure* is now used in the sense of protecting or indemnifying against loss (*the building and its contents are insured*). Use *ensure* to mean "to make certain" (*the company has ensured the safety of all workers*).

Q: It seems to me that the word *explanation* should be spelled as *explain* is spelled. Isn't this unusual?

A: Many words derived from root words change their grammatical form and spelling. Consider these: *disaster, disastrous; maintain, maintenance; repeat, repetition; despair, desperate, desperation; pronounce, pronunciation.*

Q: Is *appraise* used correctly in this sentence? *We will appraise stockholders of the potential loss.*

A: No, it's not. Your sentence requires *apprise*, which means "to inform or notify." The word *appraise* means "to estimate" (*he will appraise your home before you set its selling price*).

Question	Answer
Q: Which word is correct in this sentence? *The officer (cited, sited, sighted) me for speeding.*	**A:** Your sentence requires *cited*, which means "to summon" or "to quote." *Site* means "a location," as in *a building site* or *a Web site*. *Sight* means "a view" or "to take aim," as in *the building was in sight*. The word *sight* also refers to "the ability to see."
Q: When the word *too* appears at the end of a sentence, should it be preceded by a comma?	**A:** When the adverb *too* (meaning "also") appears at the end of a clause, it requires no comma (*His friend is coming too*). However, when *too* appears in the middle of the sentence, particularly between the subject and the verb, it requires two commas to set it off (*His friend, too, is coming*). When *too* means "to an excessive extent," it requires no commas (*The speech was too long*).
Q: I just moved to the United States from Croatia. Did I *emigrate* or *immigrate*?	**A:** To *emigrate* means "to move from a country," so you emigrated from Croatia. To *immigrate* means "to move to a country," so you immigrated to the United States.

14

Reinforcement Exercises

LEVEL 1

Online Homework Help! For immediate feedback on odd-numbered items, go to **www.meguffey.com.**

A. (Self-check) Insert necessary commas. In the space provided, indicate briefly the reason for the comma (for example, *series, parenthetical, direct address, date, address, essential appositive*, and so forth). Write *C* if the sentence is correct.

Example: Do you think‚in the meantime‚that we should discuss the
terms of the contract?   parenthetical _____

1. Tuesday September 11 2001 is a day that many Americans will
   never forget.   _____

2. Hong Kong is on the other hand one of the most densely populated
   areas in the world.   _____

3. Bronte Tennyson Athens Florence London Paris and Tarzan are
   all towns in the state of Texas.   _____

4. Herb Kelleher grew up in Haddon Heights New Jersey before he
   moved to Dallas Texas to start Southwest Airlines in 1971.   _____

5. Clarence Darrow the famous trial lawyer defended John Scopes
   in the evolution trial.   _____

6. The famous journalist H. L. Mencken covered the Scopes Trial.   _____

7. The plane landed in Seattle at 10:54 a.m. PST in stormy weather. _____

8. Your refund Mr. Takeda was issued yesterday.   _____

9. We have no doubt that such practices are widespread.   _____

10. Please send the order to Alison Spence 34 Wildwood Drive Chatham
    Massachusetts 02633.   _____

Check your answers below.

B. Insert necessary commas. In the space provided, indicate briefly the reason(s) for the comma (for example, *series, parenthetical, direct address, date, time zone, address, essential appositive*, and so forth). Write *C* if the sentence is correct.

1. The first ball dropped in Times Square in New York City on January 1 1908
   at 12 a.m. EST.   _____

2. In 1908 the Model T also went into production in Henry Ford's plant
   in Detroit Michigan.   _____

1. Tuesday, September 11, 2001, (date)   2. Hong Kong is, hand, (parenthetical)   3. Bronte, Tennyson, Athens, Florence, London, Paris, (series)   4. Haddon Heights, New Jersey, Dallas, Texas, (geographical items)   5. Darrow, lawyer, (nonessential appositive)   6. C (essential appositive)   7. 10:54 a.m., PST, (time zone)   8. refund, Mr. Takeda, (direct address)   9. C   10. Spence, Drive, Chatham, (address)

3. The American explorer Admiral Robert Peary set out for the North Pole in July 1908. _____

4. Everything that happened in 1908 was bigger better faster and stranger than anything that had happened before. _____

5. Some people say consequently that modern life in the United States began in 1908. _____

6. Please tell us Mr. Trump what it's like to produce and star in _The Apprentice_. _____

7. _The Apprentice_ has had contestants work for such companies as Gillette Norwegian Cruise Line Arby's and General Motors. _____

8. As a matter of fact celebrity contestants even compete to raise money for their favorite charities. _____

9. Applications for _The Apprentice_ should be sent to the Casting Department 149 South Barrington Avenue Los Angeles CA 90049 by the deadline. _____

10. Sam Walton the founder of Wal-Mart started out running a small store in Arkansas. _____

11. Wal-Mart opened its first store in Shanghai on July 28 2005 in the Pudong area. _____

12. This store in China opened of course 13 years after Sam Walton's death. _____

13. Nevertheless his family has continued to run the business with great success. _____

14. Popular places for destination weddings include Hawaii Mexico and the Caribbean because of their warm weather. _____

15. My sister Susan and her husband Gary traveled to Barbados in the Caribbean for the wedding of friends. _____

16. Phone cable and Internet companies are all becoming involved in the on-demand video business. _____

17. Strict rules are needed however to make sure that companies don't start charging for access to public information. _____

18. In February 1935 Parker Brothers started selling the board game _Monopoly_. _____

19. Charles B. Darrow who was a heater salesman in Pennsylvania was the first to patent the board game _Monopoly_. _____

20. The National Monopoly Championship will be aired on ESPN at 8 p.m. EST. _____

C. Insert necessary commas. In the space provided for each sentence, write the number of commas that you inserted. If the sentence is correct, write _C_. Be prepared to explain each comma.

1. Matt Susan and Aidan arrived in Dubai on November 2. _____

2. Matt a journalist for a U.S. newspaper was assigned to cover a story in Dubai. _____

3. His wife Susan was happy to come along on the trip. _____

4. Dubai has banned dancing loud music kissing holding hands and hugging in public. _____

5. You can also get in trouble in Dubai for wearing skimpy clothing or swearing or displaying rude gestures. _____

6. I hope Mark that you will accept the position in Hannibal Missouri as soon as possible. _____

7. The author Mark Twain was born in the town of Florida Missouri on Sunday November 30 1835 and was raised in Hannibal. _____

8. Mark Twain was a printer's apprentice he was a licensed riverboat pilot and he was a newspaper reporter. _____

9. Damon Washington the chief security officer responded to a disturbance that awoke nearly everyone in the building at 1:30 a.m. PST. _____

10. We have no doubt that we will complete the project by Friday April 9. _____

11. Send your application to Cathy Verrett 160 East Tolman Drive Philadelphia Pennsylvania 19106 before August 4. _____

12. Our next sales letter of course must target key decision makers. _____

13. In the meantime our sales letter must include more than facts testimonials and guarantees. _____

14. Incidentally we have shipped your wood sample to our designers in Dallas Texas and Charleston South Carolina for their inspection. _____

15. Members may choose from many martial arts Pilates aqua fitness and salsa classes offered at Bally Total Fitness. _____

16. Western Air Express a former U.S. airline served the first food on planes in 1928. _____

17. Our analysis Mr. and Mrs. Parker shows that you owe additional taxes for 2008 2009 and 2010. _____

18. Most people by the way don't like the idea of passengers using cell phones while flying on planes. _____

19. The Small Business Administration which celebrated its fiftieth anniversary in 2003 helps entrepreneurs start manage and finance small companies. _____

20. The famous investor Warren Buffett agreed to give $37 billion to charity. _____

LEVEL 2

A. **(Self-check)** Insert necessary commas. In the space provided, indicate briefly the reason for the comma (for example, *independent adjectives, introductory verbal phrase, independent clauses,* and so forth). Write *C* if the sentence is correct.

Example: Madison read several enlightening, educational articles.   independent adjectives

1. To succeed in life find a career that you are passionate about. _____

2. At the beginning of each fiscal year we prepare an opening trial balance. _____

3. In April we will launch a satellite office in Fort Lauderdale. _____

4. It takes 43 facial muscles to frown but it takes only 17 muscles to smile. _____

5. If your computer seems to be working more slowly lately you
may be the victim of malware.

_____

6. You may be the victim of malware if your computer seems to
be working more slowly lately.

_____

7. The work in this office is strictly confidential as I am sure you are
well aware.

_____

8. The person who designed your Web site is talented.

_____

9. Dr. Marialice Kern who studies how exercise can be used to control
diabetes will speak at the conference in Oxford.

_____

10. We expect honest thorough answers during the interview process.

_____

Check your answers below.

B. Insert necessary commas. In the space provided, indicate briefly the reason for the comma
or its absence (for example, _independent adjectives, introductory verbal phrase, introductory
clause_, and so forth). Write _C_ if the sentence is correct.

1. In 1927 Herbert Hoover placed the first videoconference call from
Washington to the president of AT&T in New York.

_____

2. The "picturephone" was demonstrated at the 1964 World's Fair
but the device never became popular with consumers.

_____

3. PictureTel a subsidiary of IBM released the first PC-based
videoconferencing system in 1991.

_____

4. In 2001 doctors conducted the first transatlantic tele-surgery.

_____

5. Digital camera users are looking for reliable long-lasting batteries.

_____

6. Agreeing to serve as our leader Frances Sheppard worked with
students and faculty to devise an online learning program.

_____

7. If I were you I would invest in real estate.

_____

8. When you look up the meaning of "wiki" in an online dictionary
you learn that it is a type of Web site that allows users to quickly
add and edit information.

_____

9. Dan Bricklin who created the first spreadsheet has now developed
a multiuser wiki spreadsheet program.

_____

10. The man who created the first spreadsheet has now developed a
multiuser wiki spreadsheet program.

_____

11. Because today's college graduates owe an average of $30,000 each in
student loans some refer to these graduates as "Generation Broke."

_____

12. Many of these college graduates are moving back home because
they can't afford to live on their own.

_____

13. Only college graduates will be considered and only those with
technical skills will be hired.

_____

14. Any increase in salaries as you might have expected is presently impossible because of declining profits. _____

15. For a period of at least six months we cannot increase salaries. _____

16. In 2006 the letter *W* was officially added to the Swedish dictionary. _____

17. Clearing the papers from his desk he finally located the contract. _____

18. The sportswriter charged that professional football players are overpaid overprivileged athletes. _____

19. Ben Cohen the cofounder of Ben & Jerry's visited Google headquarters to sign copies of his book for employees. _____

20. Beginning in the fall of 2005 Google has hosted authors for weekly book-signing events. _____

C. Insert necessary commas. For each sentence write, in the space provided the number of commas that you inserted. If the sentence is correct, write *C*. Be prepared to explain each comma.

1. Companies should make the return of merchandise a seamless painless process. _____

2. ATMs around the world hand out an estimated $26 billion daily which might surprise some people. _____

3. The first ATM was placed outside a bank in Enfield a north London suburb in June 1967. _____

4. If scientists are correct the earth's surface is composed of a number of shifting plates that move a few inches each year. _____

5. Our current liability insurance in view of the new law that went into effect April 1 needs to be increased. _____

6. The happy carefree students celebrated the completion of their examinations although many had to leave immediately for their jobs. _____

7. Agreeing to serve as our chair Patrick Leong made valuable contributions to our committee. _____

8. She wants a peppy sporty Mini Cooper for her fortieth birthday. _____

9. By the spring of next year we hope to have upgraded our wireless network. _____

10. Antonio Perez who is chief executive officer of Eastman Kodak said that Kodak needs more change if it hopes to survive the advent of digital imaging. _____

11. Some companies have excellent voice mail systems but others use impersonal systems that frustrate and irritate callers. _____

12. In 2009 an estimated 200 billion e-mail spam messages were sent each day. _____

13. Although it represents a small share of our total sales the loss of the Portland territory would negatively affect our profits. _____

14. We do not at this time see any reason for continuing this inefficient profitless practice. _____

15. When you send an e-mail message remember that it may be forwarded to someone else. _____

16. As Professor Brunton predicted the resourceful well-trained graduate was hired immediately. _____

17. We hope that the new year will be prosperous for you and that we may have many more opportunities to serve you. _____

18. You were probably concerned about your increased insurance rates but you didn't know where to find adequate economical coverage. _____

19. Many teenage accidents are related to speeding and the impact of teen-related car crashes amounts to $40 billion annually. _____

20. Safeco a Seattle-based insurance company introduced Teensurance which uses a device under the dashboard that alerts parents by e-mail if their child is speeding. _____

LEVEL 3

A. (Self-check) Insert necessary commas. In the space provided, indicate briefly the reason for the comma (for example *omitted words, contrasting statement, clarity, short quotation*, and so forth).

1. What it is is a matter of principle. _____

2. Most employees arrived to work at 7 a.m.; the rest at 8 a.m. _____

3. "Those who cannot remember the past" said George Santayana "are condemned to repeat it." _____

4. In the fall we will open a branch in Peoria; in the spring in Wichita. _____

5. Andy Kivel PhD specializes in information management. _____

6. In April 2009 34 heads of state and government met in Trinidad for the Summit of the Americas. _____

7. Boeing announced that it will cut over 10000 jobs this year. _____

8. We were expecting Ms. Weber not Mr. Allen to conduct the audit. _____

9. "A résumé is a balance sheet without any liabilities" said personnel specialist Robert Half. _____

10. The octogenarians had known each other for a long long time. _____

Check your answers below.

B. Insert necessary commas. In the space provided, indicate briefly the reason(s) for the comma (for example, *omitted words, contrasting statement, clarity, short quotation*, and so forth). Write *C* if the sentence is correct.

1. "A lie can travel halfway around the world" said Mark Twain "while the truth is putting on its shoes." _____

2. You can find the answer on page 1034 of the textbook. _____

3. It is good to be confident, not arrogant. _____

4. "Nothing you can't spell will ever work" said humorist Will Rogers. _____

5. In February 2009 7500 people in Australia were left homeless because of brushfires. _____

6. On January 1 your Policy No. 8643219 will expire. _____

7. Lynn Craig LVN and Shaun Parrisher RN work at St. Elizabeth's. _____

1. is, (clarity)   2. rest, (omitted words)   3. past," Santayana, (short quotation)   4. spring, (omitted words)   [**Note:** Do not use a comma after a short introductory prepositional phrase.]   5. Kivel, PhD, (abbreviation)   6. 2009, (adjacent numerals)   7. 10,000 (numerals)   8. Weber, Allen, (contrasting statement)   9. liabilities," (short quotation)   10. long, (clarity)

8. On paper diets often sound deceptively simple. _____

9. The better we treat our customers the more loyal they will be to our company. _____

10. Major responsibility for the loan lies with the signer; secondary responsibility with the cosigner. _____

11. We are looking for stable not risky stocks in which to invest. _____

12. Motion-picture producer Samuel Goldwyn said "A verbal contract isn't worth the paper it's written on." _____

13. In short employees must be more considerate of others. _____

14. Donna Meyer PhD and Victor Massaglia MD spoke at the opening session. _____

15. In 2008 1040000 total vehicles were recalled in the United States. _____

16. It was General Motors Corp. not Ford Motor Co. that had the most recalls. _____

17. General Motors Corp. recalled 1.8 million vehicles; Ford Motor Co. 1.6 million. _____

18. What it was was an international power struggle. _____

19. "Be fearful when others are greedy" said Warren Buffett "and greedy when others are fearful." _____

20. The White House is located at 1600 Pennsylvania Avenue. _____

C. **Writing Exercise.** Select five comma rules that you think are most important. Name the rule; then write an original sentence illustrating that rule.

Comma Rule	Sentence Illustration
1. _____	_____
2. _____	_____
3. _____	_____
4. _____	_____
5. _____	_____

D. **Skill Maximizer.** To make sure you have mastered the use of commas, try your skill on these challenging sentences that cover all levels. Insert needed commas and write the number that you added in the space provided. Write *C* if the sentence is correct. Be prepared to discuss the rule for each comma you add.

1. Do you think Dr. Simanek that I should start exercising more? _____

2. The flight to Chicago Illinois will depart at 6:05 p.m. EST. _____

3. You can cancel your reservation by writing to Royal Caribbean International 1050 Caribbean Way Miami Florida 33132. _____

4. On October 24 1901 Annie Taylor at the age of 64 became the first person to go over Niagara Falls in a barrel. _____

5. John D. Rockefeller who founded Standard Oil was known as a driven determined and philanthropic man.

6. Rockefeller by the way was born in Richland New York in July 1938.

7. Denise Minor who was our first team leader moved to Worcester Massachusetts.

8. The person who became our next team leader was from Cambridge Massachusetts.

9. At a recent meeting of our team we decided that members should at their convenience complete an online training module.

10. Although *National Geographic* prints only about 30 photographs for each article the photographer takes about 14,000 images.

11. If you work in an office with open cubicles it is rude to listen to Web radio any kind of streaming audio or your iPod without headphones.

12. Renouncing her wealthy social background Florence Nightingale became a nurse and is considered the founder of modern nursing.

13. The Glass-Steagall Act of 1933 banned banks from investing in stocks but was repealed in 1999.

14. Although bored employees managed to stay awake during the CEO's speech.

15. Whatever it is it is not very amusing.

16. Our yearly budget was over $2000000 for equipment supplies and utilities.

17. Cooperation not competition is what is needed at this time.

18. "There is no such thing" said Tom Peters "as a minor lapse in integrity."

19. My cousin Rich lives in Slingerlands New York.

20. In 2008 an extra leap second was added to the end of the year.

E. FAQs About Business English Review. In the space provided, write the correct answer choice.

1. The Rileys could not (a) ensure, (b) insure, (c) assure their home because they live in the potential path of hurricanes.

2. Mrs. Riley tried to (a) ensure, (b) insure, (c) assure the agent that their house was stable and secure.

3. To (a) ensure, (b) insure, (c) assure your timely arrival, please leave an hour early.

4. A realtor should (a) apprise, (b) appraise your property before you list it for sale.

5. Our insurance agent (a) apprises, (b) appraises all clients of the limitations of home ownership policies.

6. Luckily, the officer did not (a) sight, (b) cite, (c) site him for speeding.

7. Have you checked out their new Web (a) sight, (b) cite, (c) site?

8. The singer Andrea Bocelli was visually challenged from birth and completely lost his (a) sight, (b) cite, (c) site at age twelve.

9. Be sure to use correct (a) pronounciation, (b) pronunciation during your job interview.

10. Drazan (a) emigrated, (b) immigrated from his homeland of Croatia in 2008.

▶▶ Learning Web Ways

Soon you will be looking for a job. You decide to learn as much as possible about wages and trends in your career area.

Goal: To gather job-search and career information.

1. With your Web browser on the screen, go to **http://www.salary.com**.

2. Click **All titles** in the "Salary Wizard" section. Then choose your job category from the drop-down menu. Enter your zip code and press **Search**.

3. Study the list of job titles. Select one by clicking **Base Salary Range** below it. For this job title, what is the median salary in your geographic area? What are the high and low salary figures listed?

4. At the top of the graph, click **Benefits**. What benefits does someone in this position generally receive? What is the dollar value of these benefits? (**Hint:** Subtract the base salary from the total amount.)

5. Select your education level from the drop-down menu and click **Next** to find out how much your education is worth. What educational level have most individuals in this job title achieved?

6. End your session and submit your answers.

▶▶ Chat About It

Your instructor may assign any of the following topics for you to discuss in class, in an online chat room, or on an online discussion board. Some of the discussion topics may require outside research. You may also be asked to read and respond to postings made by your classmates.

Discussion Topic 1: As you learned in this chapter, punctuation in written documents sometimes plays a role in court cases. The punctuation used helps the court interpret the meanings of these documents. Do research to find an example of a court case that involved punctuation. Share your findings with the class.

Discussion Topic 2: Patricia T. O'Conner wrote a book called *Woe Is I: The Grammarphobe's Guide to Better English in Plain English*. Find a copy of the book at your college or local library and select one chapter to read. Summarize the chapter and share your summary with your classmates. Include your personal comments about what you read.

Discussion Topic 3: The actor Matthew McConaughey said, "Life is a series of commas, not periods." What do you think he meant by this? Share your interpretation with your classmates.

Discussion Topic 4: In this chapter you learned that various abbreviations such as *Inc.* and *Ltd.* are used to identify businesses in the United States. Different such abbreviations are used throughout the world. Choose a country and find out what company abbreviations are used. Share your findings with your class.

Discussion Topic 5: In the beginning of this chapter, you read this quote by Marie Rackham: "Think of punctuation marks as the traffic signs of writing. Just as traffic signs guide drivers, so punctuation marks guide readers and writers." Do you agree with this analogy? Share your thoughts about punctuation with your classmates. What analogy would you use to describe punctuation?

Posttest

Insert appropriate commas in the following sentences. Write *C* if the sentence is correct.

1. Successful entrepreneurs must have vision creativity and drive.

2. Fortunately America tends to survive economic downturns which gives us all hope.

3. Rick Skrenta who created the first computer virus wrote the malicious code in 1982 as a harmless prank.

4. In 1999 we experienced the first computer virus that was spread over e-mail.

5. Please let us know Ms. Knox what we can do to ensure a pleasant smooth transition.

6. The manager thinks on the other hand that all service calls must receive prior authorization and that current service contracts must be honored.

7. Connie Jo Clark PhD and Tim Murphy CPA have been asked to speak at our Scottsdale Arizona conference.

8. When trained all employees in this company should be able to offer logical effective advice to customers.

9. To meet the deadline make sure your application fee is received by January 25 2012 at 5 p.m. PST.

10. Michelle attended an eye-gazing party in New York City and in two minutes she had met her soul mate.

1. vision, creativity. 2. Fortunately, downturns, 3. Skrenta, virus, 4. C 5. know, Ms. Knox, pleasant, 6. thinks, hand, 7. Clark, PhD, Murphy, CPA, Scottsdale, Arizona. 8. trained, logical, 9. deadline, January 25, 2012, 5 p.m., 10. City,

"But the thermals that benignly waft our sentences to new altitudes—that allow us to coast on air, and loop-the-loop, suspending the laws of gravity—well, they are the colons and semicolons."

—Lynne Truss, *Eats, Shoots & Leaves*

Chapter 15

Semicolons and Colons

OBJECTIVES

When you have completed the materials in this chapter, you will be able to do the following:

LEVEL 1
- Use semicolons correctly in punctuating compound sentences.
- Use semicolons when necessary to separate items in a series.

LEVEL 2
- Learn the proper and improper use of colons to introduce listed items.
- Correctly use colons to introduce quotations and explanatory sentences.

LEVEL 3
- Distinguish between the use of commas and semicolons preceding expressions such as *namely, that is,* and *for instance* as well as when separating certain independent clauses joined by *and, or, nor,* or *but.*
- Use colons appropriately and be able to capitalize words following colons when necessary.

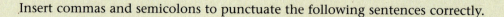

Insert commas and semicolons to punctuate the following sentences correctly.

1. "Green" technologies are gaining a strong following consequently many industries are beginning to produce green products and recycling programs.

2. The Ford Edsel was one of the most famous failures in history Coca-Cola's New Coke was another well-known disappointment.

3. We are not sure however that instant messaging is right for everyone.

4. Three of the world's most innovative companies are Apple Google and Toyota.

5. Apple earns most of its revenue from Macs iPods and iPhones.

6. The following experts were invited to speak Janet Black College of San Mateo Lanny Hertzberg Cosumnes River College and Bob Duxbury Santa Rosa Junior College.

7. Although the committee had many cities from which to choose it decided to focus on the following namely Tampa Des Moines and Little Rock.

8. Denis Waitley said "The secret to productive goal setting is in establishing clearly defined goals, writing them down and then focusing on them several times a day with words, pictures and emotions as if we've already achieved them."

9. John Moe has one major educational goal he wants to earn his law degree.

10. The meeting will begin promptly at 10 45 a.m.

This chapter introduces semicolons and colons, which can be two powerful punctuation marks in business writing. Skilled writers use semicolons and colons to signal readers about the ideas that will follow. You can improve your writing and look more professional if you know how to use semicolons and colons correctly. In this chapter you will learn basic uses and advanced applications of these two important punctuation marks.

1. following; consequently, 2. history; 3. sure, however, 4. Apple, Google, 5. Macs, iPods, 6. speak: Black, Mateo; Hertzberg, College; Duxbury, 7. choose, following; namely, Tampa, Moines, 8. said: 9. goal: 10. 10:45

Basic Uses of the Semicolon

Semicolons tell readers that two closely related ideas should be thought of together. The semicolon is a stronger punctuation mark than a comma, which signifies a pause; but the semicolon is not as strong as a period, which signifies a complete stop. Understanding the use of semicolons will help you avoid fundamental writing errors, such as the comma splice and the run-on sentence. The most basic use of the semicolon occurs in compound sentences. Many business and professional communicators use a comma when they should be using a semicolon. Study the following examples to make sure you don't make this error.

Independent Clauses Separated by Conjunctive Adverbs

Semicolons are used primarily when two independent clauses are separated by a conjunctive adverb or a transitional expression. Common conjunctive adverbs include *therefore, however, consequently*, and *then*. You studied this basic semicolon use in Chapter 13. Here are some review examples:

Study Tip

Remember that a comma is used only after a two-syllable conjunctive adverb. And don't capitalize the word following a semicolon unless it is a proper noun.

> Kevin Powell wanted to improve his presentation skills; *consequently*, he joined Toastmasters International. (Semicolon separates two independent clauses joined by the conjunctive adverb *consequently*.)

> Kevin learned a lot from his Toastmasters experience; *therefore*, he started a student chapter on campus. (Semicolon separates two independent clauses joined by the conjunctive adverb *therefore*.)

> Manuel Gonzales worked for the university for over 20 years; *thus* he had witnessed many changes. (Semicolon separates two independent clauses joined by the conjunctive adverb *thus*.)

Remember that words that function as conjunctive adverbs may also serve as parenthetical adverbs. As you learned in Chapter 13, use semicolons only with conjunctive adverbs that join two independent clauses. Use commas to set off parenthetical adverbs that interrupt the flow of one independent clause.

> We are sure, consequently, that our revenues will increase.

> We hope, therefore, that you will consider exchanging the item instead.

Independent Clauses Without Coordinating Conjunctions or Conjunctive Adverbs

Two or more closely related independent clauses not separated by a conjunctive adverb or a coordinating conjunction (*and, or, nor, but, so, yet, for*) require a semicolon.

> Sales meetings during prosperous times were lavish productions that focused on entertainment; meetings today focus on training and motivation.

> Not all job openings are found in classified ads or in job databases; the "hidden" job market accounts for as many as two thirds of all available positions.

Series Containing Internal Commas or Complete Thoughts

Semicolons are used to separate items in a series when one or more of the items in the series contain internal commas. Using a semicolon in this way will make your sentences clearer to your readers.

> The three U.S. cities with the largest populations are New York City, New York; Los Angeles, California; and Chicago, Illinois.

> Speaking at the symposium will be Carlos Slim, chair, TelMex; Katsuaki Watanabe, president, Toyota Motor Corporation; and Irene Rosenfeld, CEO, Kraft Foods.

Semicolons are also used to separate three or more independent clauses that appear in a series.

> The first step consists of surveying all available information related to the company objective so that an understanding of all problems can be reached; the second step involves interviewing consumers, wholesalers, and retailers; and the third step consists of developing a research design in which the actual methods and procedures to be used are indicated.

A series of short independent clauses, however, may be separated by commas.

> Amazon.com was founded in 1994, it unveiled its Web site in 1995, and it went public in 1997.

Now complete the reinforcement exercises for Level 1.

LEVEL 2

Basic Uses of the Colon

Although it has a variety of functions, the **colon** is most often used to introduce lists, quotations, and explanatory sentences.

Formally Listed Items

Use a colon after an independent clause that introduces one item, two items, or a list of items. A list may be shown vertically or horizontally in sentence form and is usually introduced by such words as *the following, as follows, these,* or *thus.* A colon is also used when words like these are implied but not stated.

> The best leaders possess *one* important trait: integrity. (An independent clause introduces a single item.)

> Text messages are now used to deliver *the following* types of information: medical, financial, educational, and political. (Formal list with introductory expression stated)

> Several of the world's tallest buildings are located in Abu Dhabi: Etihad Towers, Sky Tower, Tameer Towers, and Nation Towers. (Formal list with introductory expression only implied)

> These are some of the financial services the Federal Reserve provides to member banks:
> 1. Collecting checks, payments, and other credit instruments
> 2. Electronically transferring funds
> 3. Distributing and receiving cash and coins (Formal list shown vertically)

Do not use a colon unless the list is introduced by an independent clause. Lists often function as sentence complements or objects. When this is the case and the statement introducing the list is incomplete, no colon should be used. It might be easiest to remember that lists introduced by verbs or prepositions require no colons (because the introductory statement is incomplete). Therefore, generally do not place a colon after a verb or a preposition.

> Four countries that have high literacy rates are Norway, Canada, Bermuda, and Switzerland. (No colon is used because the introductory statement is not complete; the list is introduced by the verb *are*.)

> Three requirements for this position are a master's degree, computer knowledge, and five years' experience in systems analysis. (No colon is used because the introductory statement is not complete; the list is introduced by a *to be* verb and functions as a complement to the sentence.)

> Awards of merit were presented to Professor Laham, Mr. Langlois, and Dr. Pieroni. (No colon is used because the introductory statement is not an independent clause; the list functions as an object of the preposition *to*.)

Do not use a colon when an intervening sentence falls between the introductory statement and the list.

> According to a recent survey, these are the best companies to work for. The survey was conducted by *Fortune*.
>
> NetApp   Boston Consulting Group
> Edward Jones   Google

Long Quotations

Use a colon to introduce long one-sentence quotations and quotations of two or more sentences. Remember to enclose the quotation in quotation marks.

> Michael Gerber said: "My experience has shown me that the people who are exceptionally good in business aren't so because of what they know but because of their insatiable need to know more."

Longer quotations that contain two or more sentences (and will take up more than three lines) are placed in a separate paragraph without quotation marks. Indent the left and right margins to set the quote apart from its introductory sentence and any sentence that follows.

> Patricia T. O'Connor, editor at *The New York Times Book Review*, explains why grammar is so difficult for many people:
>
> > We all come from the factory wired for language. By the time we know what it is, we've got it. Toddlers don't think about language; they just talk. Grammar is a later addition, an ever-evolving set of rules for using words in ways that we can all agree upon. But the laws of grammar come and go. English today isn't what it was a hundred years ago, and it's not what it will be a hundred years from now.

Incomplete quotations not interrupting the flow of a sentence require no colon, no comma, and no initial capital letter.

> The River Walk area of San Antonio is sometimes described as "the Venice of the Southwest."

Explanatory Sentences

Use a colon to separate two independent clauses if the second clause explains, illustrates, or supplements the first.

> The company's new directors faced a perplexing dilemma: they had to choose between declaring bankruptcy and investing more funds to recoup previous losses.

> To succeed in this job, you must remember one thing: you are here to serve the customer.

Now complete the reinforcement exercises for Level 2.

LEVEL 3

Special Uses of Semicolons

You have just studied the basic uses for semicolons. Occasionally, though, semicolons are used in circumstances demanding special attention.

Trivia Tidbit

The first printed semicolon appeared in the work of Aldus Manutius in 1494. Manutius was a famous Italian printer and publisher.

Study Tip

Some of these introductory expressions have abbreviations. Instead of *for example*, you can use the abbreviation *e.g.* Instead of *that is*, you can use the abbreviation *i.e.* And instead of *namely*, you can use the abbreviation *viz.* Punctuate these abbreviations in the same way you would the full word.

Introductory Expressions Such as *namely, for instance,* and *that is*

When introductory expressions (such as *namely, for instance, that is,* and *for example*) immediately follow independent clauses, they may be preceded by either commas or semicolons. Generally, if the words following the introductory expression form a series or an independent clause, use a semicolon before the introductory expression and a comma after.

> Google offers unique benefits to its employees; *for instance*, an on-site hair stylist, meals prepared by gourmet chefs, financial planning classes, shuttle service, and an outdoor volleyball court. (A semicolon is used because *for instance* introduces a series.)

> Several books give tips for starting your own business; *for example*, Pamela Slim and Guy Kawasaki's *Escape From Cubicle Nation* is an excellent resource. (A semicolon is used because *for example* introduces an independent clause.)

If the list or explanation that follows the introductory expression is not a series or an independent clause, use commas before and after the introductory expression.

> We are proposing many new additions to the health care package, *for example*, holistic medicine and chiropractic benefits. (A comma is used because *for example* introduces neither a series nor an independent clause.)

> We value one trait in our employees above all others, i.e., integrity. (A comma is used because *i.e.* introduces neither a series nor an independent clause.)

These same introductory expressions may introduce parenthetical words within sentences. Commas usually punctuate individual items introduced parenthetically within sentences. If the introductory expression introduces several items punctuated by internal commas, then use dashes or parentheses. Dashes and parentheses will be treated in detail in Chapter 16.

The biggest health problem facing employees, *namely*, work-related stress, costs a large employer about $3.5 million annually. (Commas are used because the introductory expression *namely* introduces a single item.)

Basic employee rights—*for instance*, minimum wage, overtime, and child labor protection—were first mandated in 1938 with the passage of the Fair Labor Standards Act. (Dashes are used because the introductory expression *for instance* introduces several items punctuated with internal commas.)

Special Uses of Colons

Colons also have other uses that are common in business writing.

Business Letter Salutations

Colons are placed after the salutation of a business letter when mixed punctuation is used.

Dear Dr. Kerlin: Dear Customer Service: Dear Anastasia:

When using mixed punctuation in a business letter, place a colon after the salutation and a comma after the complimentary close. When using open punctuation, omit the semicolon and comma.

Time

In expressions of time, use a colon to separate hours from minutes.

11:30 a.m.   6:15 p.m.   17:40 (24-hour clock)

Publication Titles

Place a colon between titles and subtitles of books, articles, and other publications.

Training Camp: What the Best Do Better Than Everyone Else (Book title)

"Cash for Keys: LA's Go-To Guy on Foreclosures" (Article title)

Capitalization Following Colons

When a colon is used to introduce a series in sentence format, do not capitalize the first word after the colon unless it is a proper noun.

The six Cs of effective business communication are the following: clarity, courtesy, conciseness, completeness, correctness, and confidence.

These Montana cities will receive heavy promotional advertising: Butte, Great Falls, Helena, and Whitefish.

When a colon is used to introduce a series in a vertical list, capitalize the first letter of each item in the list.

To be legally enforceable, a contract must include at least three elements:
1. Mutual assent of competent parties
2. A consideration
3. A lawful purpose

Study Tip

Use end punctuation in a vertical list only when the items are complete sentences.

Do not capitalize the first letter of an independent clause following a colon if that clause explains or supplements the first one (unless, of course, the first word is a proper noun).

Special Olympics has one overriding mission: through the power of sport, Special Olympics strives to create a better world by fostering the acceptance and inclusion of all people.

The graduates have something special to look forward to: Bill Gates will be delivering their commencement address.

SEMICOLONS AND COLONS

CHAPTER 15 • 329

Capitalize the first letter of an independent clause following a colon if that clause states a formal rule or principle as a complete sentence.

In business the Golden Rule is often stated in the following way: He with the gold rules.

For a quotation following a colon, capitalize the first letter of the quotation.

Samuel Smiles, a Scottish author and reformer, once said: "Lost wealth may be replaced by industry, lost knowledge by study, lost health by temperance or medicine, but lost time is gone forever."

A Final Word

Semicolons are excellent punctuation marks when used carefully and knowingly. After reading this chapter, though, some students are guilty of semicolon overkill. They begin to string together two—and sometimes even three—independent clauses with semicolons. Remember to use semicolons in compound sentences *only* when two ideas are better presented together.

Now complete the reinforcement exercises for Level 3.

Spot the BLOOPER

Using the skills you are learning in this class, try to identify why the following items are bloopers. Consult your textbook, dictionary, or reference manual as needed.

Blooper 1: Advertisement for a car wash: "We do not scratch your paint finish with machinery, we do it by hand." [Did you notice two errors?]

Blooper 2: From a student paper: "The three kinds of blood vessels are: arteries, vanes, and caterpillars." [How many errors did you notice?]

Blooper 3: From a bad-news letter to a client: "We apologize for any incontinence this delay has caused."

Blooper 4: From the Web site for the National Steinbeck Center, announcing the annual Steinbeck Festival: "The focus this year will be on the many awards Steinbeck received during his career and the affect awards and fame have on a writer's literary career and personal life."

Blooper 5: From *The Wall Street Journal*: "The casino has hired a former French waiter to ride a three-wheeled bicycle through the lobby with fresh bread baked by French bakers in the bike basket."

Blooper 6: Story on radio station KCBS about a ship that ran into the San Francisco Bay Bridge: "Pilot pleaded guilty to dumping oil and killing birds in a San Francisco courtroom."

Blooper 7: Statement by Lawrence Bunin, general manager of the SAT college entrance exams: "Less kids are taking the SAT, threatening the viability of the program itself."

Blooper 8: From a column in *The New York Times:* "Is their a price to be paid for demolition-derby politics?"

Blooper 9: Billboard for McDonald's: "Get your 4 dollar's worth."

Blooper 10: Sign in a public park: "Dog's allowed on leash's with scooper's."

Question

Q: My partner and I are preparing an announcement describing our new Web business. We don't agree on how to punctuate this sentence: *We offer a wide array of network services; such as design, support, troubleshooting, and consulting, etc.*

Answer

A: First, drop the semicolon before *such as*. No comma or semicolon is necessary before a list introduced by *such as*. Second, do not use *etc.* at the end of a series. If you have other services to offer, name them. Tacking on *etc.* suggests that you have more items but for some reason you are not listing them.

Q: When I list items vertically, should I use a comma or semicolon after each item? Should a period be used after the final item? For example,
Please inspect the following rooms and equipment:
1. *The control room*
2. *The power transformer and its standby*
3. *The auxiliary switchover equipment*

A: Do not use commas or semicolons after items listed vertically, and do not use a period after the last item in such a list. However, if the listed items are complete sentences, periods should be used after each item.

Q: Which word should I use in this sentence? *Our department will (disburse or disperse) the funds shortly.*

A: Use *disburse*. *Disperse* means "to scatter" (*Police dispersed the unruly crowd*) or "to distribute" (*Information will be dispersed to all divisions*). *Disburse* means "to pay out." Perhaps this memory device will help you keep them straight: associate the *b* in *disburse* with *bank* (*Banks disburse money*).

Q: I've been told that I should spell *judgment* without the *e*. Why, then, do I sometimes see this word spelled *judgement*? Are both spellings acceptable?

A: Most dictionaries will give both the preferred and any alternate spellings of a word. The preferred spelling will always be listed first. Although *judgement* is included in many dictionaries as an alternate spelling, it should not be used in business or any other type of writing because most people would identify it as being misspelled. If you use this spelling in Word, it will be flagged as being misspelled. In addition, if you look this word up in any law dictionary using this spelling, you won't find it because *judgment* is the only accepted spelling in the legal field.

Question	Answer

Q: I can never keep the words *capital* and *capitol* straight. Which one would I use in the sentence *He invested $150,000 of his own (capital, capitol) in his new business?*

A: This sentence requires the noun *capital*, which means "the wealth of an individual or firm." The noun *capital* also refers to a city serving as the seat of government (*Montpelier is the capital of Vermont*). As an adjective, *capital* describes (a) an uppercase letter (*capital letter*), (b) something punishable by death (*capital punishment*), or (c) something excellent (*a capital idea*). The noun *capitol* is used to describe a building used by the U.S. Congress (always capitalized) or a building where a state legislature meets (capitalized only to describe the full building name). *They visited the United States Capitol on their recent trip to Washington, DC. They had visited their state capitol building many times before their trip.*

Q: A memo from our vice president said, *The new benefits package is equally as good as the previous package.* Is *equally as* correct English?

A: Writers should use *equally* or *as* but not both together. *The new benefits package is as good as the previous package* OR *The new benefits package equals the previous package* OR *The new benefits package and the previous package are equally good.*

Q: The other day I said, *Do you think he meant to infer that employees might be laid off?* A coworker corrected me. What's wrong with what I said?

A: You should have used *imply* in your sentence. The word *imply* means "to suggest without stating." The word *infer* means to read a conclusion (*From the survey results, we inferred that customers want live online customer support*).

Q: I work in an office where we frequently send letters addressed to people on a first-name basis. Should I use a comma or a colon after a salutation like *Dear Antonio?*

A: The content of the letter, not the salutation (greeting), determines the punctuation after the salutation. If the letter is a business letter, always use a colon. If the letter is totally personal, a comma may be used, although a colon would also be appropriate.

Q: Should I space once or twice after a colon?

A: You can space once or twice after a colon that introduces a list, a long quotation, or an explanatory sentence. Spacing twice after a colon increases clarity in business documents. Do not space after a colon used in time, and space just once after a colon used in a publication title.

Q: I've just signed a contract to rent an apartment. Am I the *lessee* or the *lessor?*

A: You are the *lessee*, and your landlord is the *lessor*.

15 Reinforcement Exercises

LEVEL 1

Online Homework Help! For immediate feedback on odd-numbered items, go to **www.meguffey.com**.

 A. (Self-check) For each of the following sentences, underline any errors in punctuation. Then in the space provided, write the correct punctuation mark plus the word preceding it. Write *C* if the sentence is correct.

Example: The price of gas has been steadily increasing, therefore, people are starting to drive less.   increasing;

1. Our virus software is not current, updates must be downloaded and installed first.   _____

2. Texting is a leap backward in the science of communication, in fact, it is similar to Morse Code.   _____

3. Mark Zuckerberg worked for years to build Facebook, it was years before the company made a profit.   _____

4. Investors' expectations were high consequently, competitive bidding for the new IPO was brisk.   _____

5. E-business has always been a risky undertaking, online companies seem to disappear as quickly as they appear.   _____

6. According to Red Herring, four of the top European entertainment companies are Double Fusion, Jerusalem, Israel; Echovox, Geneva, Switzerland; IceMobile, Amsterdam, The Netherlands; and Mobix Interactive, London, United Kingdom.   _____

7. The United Kingdom has the most companies on the list; and France and Israel tie for second place.   _____

8. Communications is the largest sector on the list Internet services make up the second-largest sector.   _____

9. One of the hottest areas is mobile communications, a number of companies offer chipsets and software to manage the downloading of video and other rich media to handsets and mobile phones.   _____

10. Consumers are also looking for alternative sources of power, thus some companies are offering such products as paper-thin batteries for compact devices.   _____

Check your answers below.

1. current; 2. communication; 3. Facebook; 4. high; 5. undertaking; 6. C 7. list; 8. list; 9. communications; 10. power;

B. Add any necessary commas or semicolons to the following sentences. (Do not add periods.) In the spaces provided, write the number of punctuation marks you inserted. Write *C* if a sentence is correct as written.

Example: Check 21 went into effect in October 2004, however, many consumers still don't understand this law.   2

1. Check 21 allows checks to be processed electronically consequently checks clear much more quickly.   _____

2. Maxwell arrived he clocked in and he began waiting on customers.   _____

3. German shoppers generally bring their own plastic or cloth bags for groceries therefore they were unaccustomed to Wal-Mart's bagging techniques.   _____

4. Greenland is the largest island in the world it is about ten times the size of Great Britain.   _____

5. Five cities expected to bid on the 2020 Summer Olympics are Cape Town South Africa Busan South Korea Istanbul Turkey Lima Peru and Birmingham Alabama USA.   _____

6. The city to host the 2016 Summer Olympics will be announced soon the 2016 Summer Paralympics will be held in the same city.   _____

7. The shortest recorded reign of any monarch was that of Louis XIX of France it lasted only 15 minutes.   _____

8. Toyota wants to expand beyond automobiles hence the company has moved into consulting, prefab houses, advertising, health care support, and sweet potatoes.   _____

9. Dave identified the problem Jessica offered suggestions and Mallory critiqued each idea.   _____

10. Web advertising attempts to reach large international audiences television advertising is aimed at national or local audiences.   _____

11. New York was chosen as the city where people would most like to live and work San Diego came in second.   _____

12. Computer hackers can easily decode short passwords thus passwords should be at least six characters long and be a mix of letters and numerals.   _____

13. We have hired "white hat" hackers their job is to test how well our computer systems withstand assaults by real hackers.   _____

14. Smart companies assume their computer networks will be broken into consequently they develop computer-use policies to limit the damage.   _____

15. Among the oddly named towns in the United States are Boring, Maryland; Truth or Consequences, New Mexico; Rough and Ready, California; and Slap Out, Alabama.   _____

16. Recent speakers at the Commonwealth Club include Jack Welch former CEO General Electric Arthur Frommer Founder Frommer Travel Guides and Ellen Tauscher congresswoman 10th District of California.   _____

17. Consumers expect anytime anywhere access to businesses therefore wireless cell phone use is growing.   _____

18. Women now earn the majority of bachelor's degrees in business, biological sciences, social sciences and history in addition women outpace men in degrees in education and psychology.   _____

19. If you want to tie all actions at a cash register to an individual install fingerprint scanners as a result you will experience fewer instances of theft. _____

20. Some of the most famous product failures in history, along with the companies responsible, have included the Hula Burger McDonald's the Betamax Sony and Breakfast Mates Kellogg's. _____

LEVEL 2

A. (Self-check) For each of the following sentences, underline any errors in punctuation. Then in the space provided, write the correct punctuation plus the preceding word. If a colon should be omitted, write *Omit colon*. Write *C* if the sentence is correct.

Example: Business model patents were awarded to: Netflix, TiVo, and Priceline. **Omit colon**

1. In order to be awarded a business model patent, the idea must be: concrete, useful, new, and unique. _____

2. *Fortune* selected the following companies as the most socially responsible: Vodaphone, General Electric, HSBC Holdings, France Télécom, and HBOS. _____

3. Other socially responsible companies include the following: Please check the *Fortune* Web site for the complete list.
Nokia   Électricité de France   GDF Suez. _____

4. Andrew Carnegie said; "Think of yourself as on the threshold of unparalleled success. A whole clear, glorious life lies before you. Achieve! Achieve!" _____

5. The head of the computer security firm admitted one big problem: it is difficult finding good people without criminal records. _____

6. Five of the worst computer passwords are: your first name, your last name, the Enter key, *Password*, and the name of a sports team. _____

7. We have requests for information from three local companies: Sterling Laboratories, Putnam Brothers, and Big Dog, Inc. _____

8. The computer virus scheduled to hit April 1 was called: "Conficker." _____

9. The most commonly observed holidays are the following: Thanksgiving, Labor Day, Christmas, July Fourth, and New Year's Day. _____

10. Shane proposed a solution to our day-care problem: open a home office and share child-care duties. _____

Check your answers below.

B. For the following sentences, add any necessary but missing punctuation marks. For each sentence indicate in the space provided the number of additions you have made. Mark *C* if the sentence is correct as it stands.

Example: According to the Federal Trade Commission (FTC),the following scams are most likely to arrive in your e-mail box,business opportunities,chain letters,work-at-home schemes,and investment opportunities.   5

1. Gavin Newsom declared his campaign for California governor simultaneously on Facebook, Twitter, and YouTube. _____

1. Omit colon 2. C 3. following. 4. said: 5. C 6. Omit colon 7. C 8. Omit colon 9. C 10. C

2. Political expert Simon Rosenberg said "We're seeing a reinventing of politics; and in a state as wired as California, and a campaign as expensive as this one will be, the candidates who can figure out how to tap into the power and passion of their supporters will have an advantage." _____

3. Newsom cited one important reason for announcing his candidacy this way he wants to attract young voters. _____

4. Three similar types of tropical storms with different names are cyclones typhoons and hurricanes. _____

5. American Apparel, maker of trendy clothing, unveiled its latest, hippest retail outlet a computer-generated boutique operating as a simulation game. _____

6. Polygraph examinations generally consist of four elements a preexamination interview, a demonstration, questioning of the examinee, and a postexamination interview. _____

7. Babe Ruth, former American League baseball player, once said "The way a team plays as a whole determines its success. You may have the greatest bunch of individual stars in the world, but if they don't play together, the club won't be worth a dime." _____

8. Experts suggest the following tips for choosing a business name
    1. Avoid generic names.
    2. Keep it brief.
    3. Don't be too narrow or too literal. _____

9. Each balance sheet is a statement of assets liabilities and owner's equity. _____

10. Google offers many services in addition to its Web-search tool including the following Google Maps Google Finance Google News Gmail Google Health and Google Earth. _____

11. Google has also acquired these popular online products YouTube Blogger and Picasa. _____

12. For graduation you must complete courses in mathematics, accounting, English, management, and business communication. _____

13. The law of supply and demand can function only under the following condition: producers must know what consumers want. _____

14. Professor Marilyn Simonson asked that research reports contain the following sections introduction body summary and bibliography. _____

15. Additional costs in selling the house are title examination, title insurance, transfer tax, preparation of documents, and closing fee. _____

16. Henry Ford said "If money is your hope for independence, you will never have it. The only real security that a man can have in this world is a reserve of knowledge, experience, and ability." _____

17. Of all the discoveries and inventions in human history, the four greatest are said to be these speech, fire, agriculture, and the wheel. _____

18. Ritz employees follow these four rules build strong relationships with guests, create memorable experiences for guests, seek opportunities to innovate, and continuously learn and grow. _____

19. Many young employees today are making one big mistake they are sharing too much information about their personal lives online. _____

20. BJ Fogg, director of Stanford University's Persuasive Technology Lab, said "Finding the right balance will take time, if it is ever achieved. Unlike face-to-face conversations, there's really no good way yet for people to let one another know that they are being too revealing." _____

C. Writing Exercise. Write original sentences to illustrate the following. For example: *I generally use the Internet for e-mail; however, I plan to get better at using it for research.*

1. (Semicolon with conjunctive adverb) _____

   _____

2. (Semicolon without coordinating conjunction or conjunctive adverb) _____

   _____

3. (Semicolon with series containing internal commas) _____

   _____

4. (Colon with listed items) _____

   _____

5. (Colon with an explanatory sentence) _____

   _____

LEVEL 3

A. **(Self-check)** Insert necessary punctuation. In the space provided, write the number of punctuation marks that you inserted. Write *C* if the sentence is correct.

1. Five companies have been selected as the most admired in the world; namely, Apple, Berkshire Hathaway, Toyota Motor, Google, and Johnson & Johnson. _____

2. Many airlines, including Delta and American, now charge for items like headphones, playing cards, and food; JetBlue, which is trying to reduce its expenses, even charges for pillows and blankets. _____

3. Many new words have been added to the dictionary; for example, *webinar, subprime, malware,* and *edamame.* _____

4. The meeting started promptly at 1:15 p.m. and ended at 3:45 p.m. _____

5. "Smart kitchens" are now offered in many new homes for example some smart kitchens come with ovens that can cook food on demand via a cell phone. _____

6. All employees are urged to observe the following rule: When in doubt, consult the company style manual. _____

7. The writer of a research report should include a variety of references; for example, books, periodicals, government publications, and newspapers. _____

8. A must-read book for retail managers is *Why We Buy The Science of Shopping.* _____

9. You may pay your invoice using any of the following methods: credit card, check, or online payment. _____

10. For the opening session of the women's leadership conference, the keynote speaker will be Angela Braly, president and CEO of WellPoint; the afternoon keynote speaker will be Lynn Elsenhans, president and CEO of Sunoco. _____

Check your answers below.

1. C 2. C 3. C 4. C 5. 2 6. C 7. C 8. 1 9. C 10. C

B. For the following sentences, add necessary punctuation. For each sentence indicate the number of additions you made.

Example: If she completes the proposal‸Sharon Allen will fly to Washington on Tuesday‸if not‸she will leave on Thursday.   ___3___

1. We are looking for many traits in our new sales associate for example good communication skills outgoing personality and patience.   _____

2. Because of her computer expertise Leslie Leong was chosen as our network administrator because of his people skills Bruce Koller was chosen as trainer.   _____

3. The book group will discuss Stacy Perman's *In-N-Out Burger A Behind-the-Counter Look at the Fast-Food Chain That Breaks All the Rules* at next week's meeting.   _____

4. Companies that plan to expand in China should be aware of several important factors for example regulatory environment cultural differences and technologies in use.   _____

5. Large and small companies have an important reason for expanding in China that is by 2025 China is predicted to become the world's largest economy.   _____

6. Three times have been designated for the interviews Thursday at 6 30 p.m. Friday at 3 30 p.m. and Monday at 10 a.m.   _____

7. An author, composer, or photographer may protect his or her product with a government-approved monopoly namely a copyright.   _____

8. Ben Bernanke, the chair of the Federal Reserve, promised to use plain English in his communications however many complain that he is using "Fedspeak" instead.   _____

9. Invitations were sent to Richard Anderson CEO Delta Air Lines Keith Wandell CEO Harley Davidson and Constance Lau CEO Hawaiian Electric Industries.   _____

10. AT&T plans to provide the following to low-income families computer equipment Internet access and training.   _____

C. FAQs About Business English Review. In the space provided, write the correct answer choice.

1. We admired the architecture on the (a) capital, (b) capitol building in Providence, Rhode Island.   _____

2. Carson City is the (a) capital, (b) capitol of Nevada.   _____

3. We will invest in (a) capital, (b) capitol so that we can expand our business.   _____

4. Reimbursements will be (a) disbursed, (b) dispersed to employees on Friday.   _____

5. Some cities use fogging machines to (a) disburse, (b) disperse mosquito-control pesticides.   _____

6. Information about the new procedure will be (a) disbursed, (b) dispersed to employees by e-mail.   _____

7. We (a) inferred, (b) implied from our research study that customers prefer the new taste.   _____

8. Did her comment (a) infer, (b) imply that she is looking for another job?   _____

9. Each month Brandi must write a rent check to her (a) lessor, (b) lessee.   _____

10. Because Brandi is renting the apartment, she is the (a) lessor, (b) lessee.   _____

You are now ready to hunt for a job, and you decide to learn what you can to make your job search a success.

Goal: To find valuable career information on the Web.

1. With your Web browser on the screen, go to the Quintessential Careers site: **http://www.quintcareers.com**.

2. At the Quintessential Careers site, click **Open Our Career Toolkit**.

3. On the Career Resources Toolkit for Job-Seekers site, click **Career, College, and Job-Related Articles**. Click **Job Hunting Do's and Don'ts Articles**.

4. Scroll down to read the article titles, and click the article of your choice.

5. Read and print the article.

6. Use the **Back** button to repeat the process for another article. Choose a second article to read and print.

7. To explore more of this career site, press the **Back** button to return to the main page, or reenter **http://wwwquintcareers.com**.

8. End your session and submit two printed pages with the articles you read.

▶▶ **Chat About It**

Your instructor may assign any of the following topics for you to discuss in class, in an online chat room, or on an online discussion board. Some of the discussion topics may require outside research. You may also be asked to read and respond to postings made by your classmates.

Discussion Topic 1: Do you use semicolons when writing? Why or why not? Do you think your habits will change now that you have studied this chapter? Explain.

Discussion Topic 2: Lewis Thomas wrote about the semicolon in *The Medusa and the Snail*:

> The semicolon tells you that there is still some question about the preceding full sentence; something that needs to be added. The period tells you that that is that; if you didn't get all the meaning you wanted or expected, anyway you got all the writer intended to parcel out and now you have to move along. But with the semicolon there you get a pleasant feeling of expectancy; there is more to come; read on; it will get clearer.

Is this how the semicolon makes you feel when you see it in print? How do you think a semicolon differs from a comma or a period in the way it makes a reader feel?

Discussion Topic 3: Search an online bookseller or your local bookshop to find an interesting book that uses a colon in its title. Share the title, author, and a brief summary of the book with your classmates. The summary should be in your own words.

Discussion Topic 4: In this chapter you learned that business letter salutations (*Dear Ms. Lawrence*) are followed by colons (when using mixed punctuation), not commas. Commas are used in salutations in personal correspondence. Why do you think there are differences in punctuation for salutations depending on whether the letter is professional or personal?

Discussion Topic 5: In the beginning of this chapter, you read this quote by Lynne Truss: "But the thermals that benignly waft our sentences to new altitudes—that allow us to coast on air, and loop-the-loop, suspending the laws of gravity—well, they are the colons and semicolons." What do you think she means by this? Share your interpretation of this quote with your classmates.

Posttest

Add appropriate semicolons, colons, and commas. Write *C* if the sentence is correct.

1. Nostalgia sells in uncertain times that is why companies like Dunkin' Donuts and Nationwide Insurance are resurrecting old advertising campaigns.

2. Other companies that are reviving old advertising campaigns are Bumble Bee Foods, Eight O'Clock Coffee, and Carl's Jr.

3. Nick Hahn, managing consultant, said "Placing the product in the past is comforting to consumers. It grounds them in a time when things were better."

4. Dunkin' Donuts recently tried pushing coffee drinks and bagels now it is returning its focus to donuts.

5. Companies must have one goal when using nostalgia in advertising campaigns they must evoke a brand's heritage in a contemporary way.

6. Gas prices are rising dramatically therefore more people are walking and riding their bikes to work.

7. The following instructors have been chosen to represent their schools at the professional meeting Jessica Stoudenmire El Camino College Sandra Farrar Louisiana Technical College and Sandra Ostheimer Southwest Wisconsin Technical College.

8. All morning sessions begin at 930 a.m. all afternoon sessions begin at 145 p.m.

9. The Allen & Company conference which is one of the most high-profile get-togethers in the country is attended by 300 billionaires for example, Bill Gates, Warren Buffett, Rupert Murdoch, and Steve Jobs.

10. Have you read Robert K. Greenleaf's book *Servant Leadership A Journey Into the Nature of Legitimate Power and Greatness*?

1. times;   2. C   3. said: 4. bagels;   5. campaigns: 6. dramatically; therefore,   7. meeting: Stoudenmire, El Camino College; Farrar, Louisiana Technical College; Ostheimer,   8. 9:30 a.m.; 1:45   9. conference, country, billionaires; 10. *Leadership:*

"Punctuation isn't some subtle, arcane concept that's difficult to manage and probably won't make much of a difference one way or another. It's not subtle, it's not difficult, and it can make all the difference in the world."

—Patricia T. O'Conner, *Woe Is I*

Chapter 16

Other Punctuation

OBJECTIVES

When you have completed the materials in this chapter, you will be able to do the following:

LEVEL 1
- Use periods to correctly punctuate statements, commands, indirect questions, polite requests, abbreviations, initials, and numerals.
- Use question marks and exclamation marks correctly.

LEVEL 2
- Use hyphens correctly.
- Recognize acceptable applications for dashes and parentheses, and correctly punctuate material set off by parentheses and dashes.

LEVEL 3
- Use double and single quotation marks properly, and correctly place other punctuation marks in relation to quotation marks.
- Use italics, brackets, and apostrophes appropriately.

Pretest

Use proofreading marks to insert appropriate punctuation in the following sentences. See the inside back cover for a list of proofreading symbols.

1. Would you please send me your e-mail address

2. Wow What a show

3. Three industries pipelines construction and petroleum refining are experiencing the most growth

4. Please invite Radene Schroeder PhD and M L Vasquez

5. Dr Liz Stanier Ms Teresa Ling and Mr Juan Ramirez have been appointed to the SEC

6. The chapter titled How Companies Cope was the best one in the book *The World Is Flat* by Thomas L Friedman

7. I wonder whether all candidates for the CEO position completed MBA degrees

8. Did Dr Phil say If you want more you have to require more from yourself

9. My ex boss may reconsider and hire me back

10. The 50s brought us beatniks Elvis Presley and James Dean

As you have already learned, punctuation really can make all the difference in your writing. This chapter continues our discussion of punctuation by teaching you how to use periods, question marks, and exclamation marks correctly. It also includes suggestions for punctuating with hyphens, dashes, parentheses, quotation marks, brackets, italics, and apostrophes.

LEVEL 1

Uses for the Period

The period can be used to punctuate sentences, abbreviations, initials, and numerals. Guidelines for each use are covered in this section.

To Punctuate Statements, Commands, and Indirect Questions

Use a period at the end of a statement, a command, or an indirect question.

Study Tip

If the last word in a sentence is an abbreviation that ends with a period, do not add an extra period to end the sentence. Only one period is necessary.

In 1809 Mary Kies became the first woman to be issued a U.S. patent. (Statement)

Please tell FedEx to deliver the package before 5 p.m. (Command)

Our supervisor asked whether we had received the package yet. (Indirect question)

1. address. 2. Wow! show! 3. industries—pipelines, construction, refining—growth. 4. Schroeder, PhD, M. L. Vasquez. 5. Dr. Stanier, Ms. Ling, Mr. SEC. 6. "How Companies Cope" L. Friedman. 7. degrees. 8. Dr. say, "If more, yourself?" 9. ex-boss back. 10. '50s beatniks, Presley, Dean.

To Punctuate Polite Requests

Use a period, not a question mark, to punctuate a polite request. A **polite request** is a command or suggestion phrased as a request. Such a request asks the reader to perform a specific action instead of responding with a *yes* or *no*.

> Could you please turn your cell phone off during the meeting. (Polite request)
>
> May I suggest that you submit your application online. (Polite request)
>
> Will you be sure to tell the customer that his return will be processed soon. (Polite request)

If you are uncomfortable using a period at the end of a polite request, rephrase the sentence so that it is a statement:

> Please turn your cell phone off during the meeting. (Polite request rephrased as a statement)
>
> You should submit your application online. (Polite request rephrases as a statement)
>
> Be sure to tell the customer that his return will be processed soon. (Polite request rephrased as a statement)

To Punctuate Abbreviations

Abbreviations are shortened versions of words. Because of their inconsistencies, abbreviations present problems to writers. The following suggestions will help you organize certain groups of abbreviations and provide many models. In studying these models, note the spacing, capitalization, and use of periods. For a more thorough list of acceptable abbreviations, consult an up-to-date reference manual or dictionary.

Lowercase Abbreviations

Use periods after most abbreviations beginning with lowercase letters. Notice that the internal periods are not followed by spaces.

a.m. (ante meridiem)	i.e. (that is)	etc. (et cetera)
p.m. (post meridiem)	e.g. (for example)	ft. (foot or feet)
misc. (miscellaneous)	yd. (yard or yards)	in. (inch or inches)

Exceptions: mph (miles per hour), wpm (words per minute), mm (millimeter), and kg (kilogram).

Upper- and Lowercase Abbreviations

Use periods for most abbreviations containing capital and lowercase letters.

Dr. (Doctor)	Esq. (Esquire)	Mr. (Mister)
Ms. (blend of Miss and Mrs.)	No. (number)	Sat. (Saturday)

Exceptions: Academic degrees such as AA (associate of arts), BS (bachelor of science), MBA (master of business administration), PhD (doctor of philosophy) and EdD (doctor of education)

Uppercase Abbreviations

Use all capital letters without periods or internal spaces for the abbreviations of many business and nonprofit organizations, educational institutions, government agencies, radio and television stations, professional organizations, sports associations, job titles, professional designations, stock symbols, airport codes, and business and technology terms.

Trivia Tidbit

Did you ever wonder what the dot over the lowercase letters *i* and *j* is called? This dot is called a *tittle*.

Study Tip

Use abbreviations only when you know that your reader will understand what they stand for. If necessary, define an abbreviation the first time you use it in a document.

Study Tip

Most a[...]
fall in th[...]
capitali[...]
periods[...]

GMC (General Motors Corporation)	ARF (Animal Rescue Foundation)
UGA (University of Georgia)	BYU (Brigham Young University)
CIA (Central Intelligence Agency)	SBA (Small Business Administration)
NPR (National Public Radio)	PBS (Public Broadcasting Service)
AMA (American Marketing Association)	IIA (Institute of Internal Auditors)
MLB (Major League Baseball)	NCAA (National Collegiate Athletic Association)
CEO (chief executive officer)	CFO (chief financial officer)
RN (registered nurse)	CPA (certified public accountant)
GOOG (Google NASDAQ stock symbol)	LUV (Southwest Airlines NYSE stock symbol)
MCO (Orlando International airport code)	CNX (Chiang Mai International airport code)
VAT (value-added tax)	IPO (initial public offering)
PDF (portable document format)	URL (uniform resource locator)

Study Tip

Remember that abbreviations (*FBI, NFL*) are pronounced letter by letter; acronyms (*PIN, radar*) are pronounced as words. When acronyms are formed with all uppercase letters, they are also written without periods or spaces.

Exceptions: Periods and spaces are included when initials are used for a person's first and middle names (*Mr. J. A. Jones*). In addition, some abbreviations have two forms (*c.o.d., COD* [collect on delivery], *f.o.b., FOB* [free on board]).

Geographic Abbreviations

Use all capital letters without periods or internal spaces for the abbreviations of geographical areas, two-letter state abbreviations, and Canadian province abbreviations. For a complete list of two-letter state and Canadian province abbreviations, consult Figure C.5 in Appendix C.

USA (United States of America)	UK (United Kingdom)
AR (Arkansas)	HI (Hawaii)
NS (Nova Scotia)	BC (British Columbia)

Exception: In business writing use periods when using the abbreviation for *United States* as an adjective (*U.S. Postal Service, U.S. currency*).

To Punctuate Numerals

For a monetary sum, use a period (decimal point) to separate dollars from cents.

> Payments of $13.92 and $28.67 were made from our petty cash fund.

Use a period (decimal point) to mark a decimal fraction.

> Approximately 67.8 percent of eligible voters voted in Tuesday's election.

Spacing After Periods

When typewriters and printers used monospaced fonts, typists were taught to leave two spaces after a period at the end of a sentence. Two spaces provided a strong visual break so that the end of the sentence was apparent. With modern proportional fonts, however, this added visual break is unnecessary. Most typists leave only one space after terminal periods today. A two-space break is equally acceptable, especially when misreading may occur. For example, when abbreviations appear at the end of one sentence and the beginning of the next, two spaces prevent confusion (*Your appointment is at 2 p.m. Dr. Wiley will see you then.*) The same spacing guidelines you use for periods will apply to other end punctuation (question marks and exclamation marks), which will be discussed in the next two sections.

Uses for the Question Mark

The question mark punctuates direct questions and questions added to statements.

To Punctuate Direct Questions

Use a question mark at the end of a direct question. A **direct question** requires an answer.

> What can we do to increase our sales revenue?
>
> Has the music industry been successful in stopping illegal file sharers?

To Punctuate Questions Added to Statements

Place a question mark after a question that is added to the end of a statement. Use a comma to separate the statement from the question.

> Many airports offer wireless Internet access, don't they?
>
> This order should be sent by e-mail, don't you think?

To Indicate Doubt

A question mark within parentheses may be used to indicate a degree of doubt about some aspect of a statement.

> Each application should be accompanied by two (?) letters of recommendation.
>
> After Google went public (2004?), its stock price increased dramatically.

Uses for the Exclamation Mark

Because the exclamation mark expresses strong emotion, business and professional writers use it sparingly.

To Express Strong Emotion

After a word, phrase, clause, or sentence expressing strong emotion, use an exclamation mark.

> Wow! I never expected her to say something like that.
>
> How incredible! Our sales increased almost 50 percent this quarter.
>
> What a work of art!

Do not use an exclamation mark after mild interjections, such as *oh* and *well*.

> Oh, now I see what you mean.
>
> Well, I guess we will have to wait for an answer.

Now complete the reinforcement exercises for Level 1.

Trivia Tidbit

American author F. Scott Fitzgerald once said, "Cut out all the exclamation points. An exclamation point is like laughing at your own joke."

Uses for the Hyphen

Hyphens are used to form compound words, words with prefixes, and compound numbers. The hyphen can also be used to divide a word over two lines.

Study Tip

As you learned in Chapter 11, do not hyphenate compound adjectives that come after the nouns they are describing unless they have permanent hyphenation.

To Form Compound Words

Use the hyphen to form compound nouns, verbs, and adjectives.

> The *air-conditioning* in our building works well during the summer. (Compound noun)
>
> The attorney will *cross-examine* the witness. (Compound verb)
>
> She is hoping to get a *full-time* job. (Compound adjective with permanent hyphenation)
>
> We will be trying out a *voice-activated* input system. (Compound adjective with temporary hyphenation)
>
> Please print these announcements on *8 ½- by 11-inch* bond paper. (Compound adjective with common ending *inch*)

To Form Words With Prefixes

Use hyphens in words with prefixes such as *ex, self,* or *quasi.*

> The keynote speaker was *ex-President* Bush.
>
> She has been working hard to improve her *self-esteem.*
>
> Mariet is our *quasi-official* leader.

Do not hyphenate most words that begin with prefixes such as *anti, bi, co, extra, inter, micro, mini, multi, mid, non, over, under, post, pre, re, semi,* or *un* unless the unhyphenated word could be confused with another word. Also use a hyphen when the prefix is added to a word that starts with a capital (*anti-American, non-European*).

> It is *unnerving* that so many of our projects are *underfunded.*
>
> My *coworkers* have *reexamined* our *interoffice* communication practices.
>
> More *nondiscriminatory* laws should be passed.
>
> When her employment contract expires, Brenda plans to *re-sign.* (Hyphenate to avoid confusing with *resign.*)

When writing family titles, hyphenate words that contain *ex, great,* or *in-law.* Do not hyphenate words that contain *step, half,* or *grand.*

> His *ex-wife* still keeps in touch with his *grandparents.*
>
> Your *mother-in-law* looks just like her *great-aunt.*
>
> Is he your *stepbrother* or your *half brother?*

To Form Compound Numbers

Use the hyphen to form compound numbers between twenty-one and ninety-nine when written in word form. Number expression will be covered in detail in Chapter 18.

> *Eighty-six* applicants passed the entry exam.

To Divide a Word Over Two Lines

Use a hyphen when you must divide a word over two lines. However, because divided words can be confusing, use this technique sparingly.

> We hope to get a response by late tomorrow from Dan Knox, super-
> intendent of the school district.

Uses for the Dash

Do not confuse the hyphen with the dash. The dash is often used to show emphasis. As an emphatic punctuation mark, however, the dash loses effectiveness when it is overused. With a word processor, you create a dash by typing two hyphens with no space before, between, or after the hyphens. In printed or desktop publishing–generated material, a dash appears as a solid line that is longer than a hyphen (an *em* dash). Most word processors will automatically convert two hyphens to an *em* dash. Study the following suggestions for and illustrations of appropriate uses of the dash.

Study Tip

The dash tends to be overused in writing today. To make your writing look more professional, use the dash only when necessary, and never use more than two dashes in a sentence.

To Set Off Parenthetical Elements and Appositives

Within a sentence, parenthetical elements and appositives are usually set off by commas. If, however, the parenthetical element or appositive itself contains internal commas, use dashes (or parentheses) to set it off.

> Sources of raw materials—farming, mining, fishing, and forestry—are
> all dependent on energy.

> Four legal assistants—Priscilla Alvarez, Vicki Evans, Yoshiki Ono, and
> Edward Botsko—received cash bonuses for outstanding service.

You can place any parenthetical element between dashes instead of commas. However, remember that doing so will emphasize the parenthetical element.

> All employees—and that includes Ann Patterson—must work over-
> time this weekend.

To Indicate an Interruption or Afterthought

An interruption or abrupt change of thought or afterthought may be separated from the rest of a sentence by a dash. However, sentences with abrupt changes of thought or with appended afterthoughts can usually be improved through rewriting.

> We will refund your money—no questions asked—if you are not
> completely satisfied. (Interruption of thought)

> You can submit your report on Friday—no, we must have it by
> Thursday at the latest. (Abrupt change of thought)

To Set Off a Summarizing Statement

Use a dash (not a colon) to separate an introductory list from a summarizing statement.

> Flexibility, initiative, intelligence—these are the qualities we seek in
> all employees.

> Facebook, Twitter, YouTube—these are some of the most frequently
> used social networking tools.

To Attribute a Quotation

Place a dash between a quotation and its source.

> "Live as if you were to die tomorrow. Learn as if you were to live forever."—Mahatma Gandhi

> "Never, never, never, never give up."—Winston Churchill

Uses for Parentheses

Parentheses are generally used in pairs. Parentheses can be used to enclose a complete sentence or to enclose a word or expression within a sentence. This section covers guidelines for using parentheses correctly.

To Set Off Nonessential Sentence Elements

Generally, nonessential sentence elements may be punctuated as follows: (a) with commas, to make the lightest possible break in the normal flow of a sentence; (b) with dashes, to emphasize the enclosed material; and (c) with parentheses, to de-emphasize the enclosed material.

> Figure 17, which appears on page 9, clearly illustrates the process. (Normal punctuation)

> Figure 17—which appears on page 9—clearly illustrates the process. (Dashes emphasize enclosed material.)

> Figure 17 (which appears on page 9) clearly illustrates the process. (Parentheses de-emphasize enclosed material.)

Explanations, references, and directions are often enclosed in parentheses.

> Our café's current hours (7 a.m. to 3 p.m.) will be extended soon (to 6 p.m.).

> A small studio apartment in Florence, Italy, rents for about 1.100 euros ($1,385) per month.

> I recommend that we direct more funds (see the budget on page 14) to research and development.

To Show Numerals and Enclose Enumerated Items

In legal documents and contracts, numerals may appear in both word and figure form. Parentheses enclose the figures. However, business writers are encouraged not to use this wordy technique for most messages.

> Your contract states that the final installment payment is due in ninety (90) days.

When using numbers or letters to enumerate lists within sentences, enclose the numbers or letters in parentheses. Use letters for items that have no particular order. Use numbers for items that suggest a sequence.

> The Federal Trade Commission (FTC) has initiated several programs to protect individual privacy, including (a) the National Do Not Call Registry, (b) the Fair Credit Reporting Act, and (c) an identity theft Web site.

> To pay your bill online, (1) log onto our secure Web site, (2) click the **Pay Bill** link, (3) select the bill you want to pay, (4) input the amount you want to pay, (5) select the date on which you want to make payment, (6) click the **Pay** button, and (7) click the **Confirm** button.

Punctuating Around Parentheses

If the material enclosed by parentheses is embedded within another sentence, a question mark or exclamation mark may be used where normally expected. Do not, however, use a period after a statement embedded within another sentence.

> We checked fares for several airlines on the Sidestep Web site (have you seen it?) last night.
>
> Photoshop's "hints palette" feature (see Chapter 5) provides helpful illustrations and tips.

If the material enclosed by parentheses is not embedded in another sentence, use whatever punctuation is required.

> Report writers must document all references. (See Appendix A for a guide to current documentation formats.)

In sentences involving expressions within parentheses, a comma, semicolon, or colon that would normally occupy the position occupied by the second parenthesis is then placed after that parenthesis.

> When we finalize the contract (on March 3), we can begin the remodel. (Comma follows the closing parenthesis.)
>
> Your tax return was received before the deadline (April 15); however, you did not include your payment. (Semicolon follows the closing parenthesis.)

Now complete the reinforcement exercises for Level 2.

LEVEL 3

Uses for Quotation Marks

Guidelines for using quotation marks to enclose direct quotations, quotations within quotations, short expressions, definitions, and literary titles are covered in this section. You will also learn how to place other punctuation in relation to quotation marks.

To Enclose Direct Quotations

Double quotation marks are used to enclose direct quotations. Unless the exact words of a writer or speaker are being repeated, however, do not use quotation marks.

> "Honesty pays dividends both in dollars and in peace of mind," said B. C. Forbes. (Direct quotation enclosed)
>
> Abraham Lincoln said that we cannot escape tomorrow's responsibility by evading it today. (Indirect quotation requires no quotation marks.)

Capitalize only the first word of a direct quotation.

> "The human race has only one really effective weapon," said Mark Twain, "and that is laughter." (Do not capitalize *and*.)

Single quotation marks (apostrophes on most keyboards) are used to enclose quoted passages cited within quoted passages.

> Delores Tomlin remarked, "In business writing I totally agree with Aristotle, who said, 'A good style must, first of all, be clear.'" (Single quotation marks within double quotation marks)

Study Tip

Be careful that you don't overuse quotation marks. Enclose words in quotation marks only when you have a valid reason for doing so.

To Enclose Short Expressions

Slang, jargon, words used in a special sense such as humor or irony, and words following *stamped* or *marked* are often enclosed within quotation marks.

> You deserve "props" for coming up with this great idea. (Slang)
>
> Computer criminals are often called "hackers." (Jargon)
>
> Orrin claimed he was "too ill" to come to work yesterday. (Irony)
>
> The package was stamped "Handle with Care." (Words following *stamped*)

Quotation marks are used to enclose specific definitions of words or expressions. The word or expression being defined is italicized.

> The term *malware* refers to "software developed for the purpose of causing harm to a computer system."
>
> Businesspeople use the term *working capital* to indicate an "excess of current assets over current debts."

To Enclose Titles

Quotation marks are used to enclose the titles of subdivisions of literary and artistic works, such as magazine and newspaper articles, short stories, chapters of books, episodes of television shows, poems, lectures, paintings, sculptures, and songs. However, italics (or underscores) are used to enclose the titles of complete works, such as the names of books, magazines, pamphlets, movies, television series, music albums, and newspapers (see next section).

> I loved the *Wall Street Journal* article titled "Why Does 'Everybody' Now Put 'Everything' in Quotation Marks?"
>
> In the episode of *The Office* titled "Diversity Day," the boss, played by Steve Carell, managed to offend everyone.

Punctuating Around Quotation Marks

Periods and commas are always placed inside closing quotation marks, whether single or double.

> Katie Wheeler said, "Be sure to mark the envelope 'Confidential.'"
>
> The article is titled "Corporate Espionage," but I don't have a copy.

Semicolons and colons are, on the other hand, always placed outside closing quotation marks.

> Our contract stipulated that "both parties must accept arbitration as binding"; therefore, the decision reached by the arbitrators is final.
>
> Three dates have been scheduled for the seminar called "Successful E-Business": April 1, May 3, and June 5.

Question marks and exclamation marks may go inside or outside closing quotation marks, as determined by the form of the quotation.

> Chris Stefanetti asked, "How will you vote on this issue?" (Quotation is a question.)
>
> "The next time your cell phone rings," fumed the CEO, "we will ask you to leave!" (Quotation is an exclamation.)
>
> Do you know who it was who said, "You've got to love what you do to really make things happen"? (Incorporating sentence asks question; quotation does not.)
>
> I can't believe that the check was stamped "Insufficient Funds"! (Incorporating sentence is an exclamation; quotation is not.)

When did the supervisor say, "Who is able to work overtime this weekend?" (Both incorporating sentence and quotation are questions. Use only one question mark inside the quotation marks.)

Uses for Italics

Italics (or underscore if italics are not accessible) are normally used for titles of books, magazines, pamphlets, newspapers, movies, television shows, music albums, plays, musicals, and other complete published or artistic works that contain subdivisions. In addition, words under discussion in the sentence and used as nouns are italicized.

> *Bank on Yourself*, a book by author Pamela G. Yellen, was favorably reviewed in *The Wall Street Journal*.
>
> Two of the most frequently misspelled words are *definitely* and *separate*. (Words used as nouns)

Italic type was invented in the 15th century in Italy for use in courts.

Uses for Brackets

Within quotations, brackets are used by writers to enclose their own inserted remarks. Such remarks may be corrective, illustrative, or explanatory. Brackets are also used within quotations to enclose the word *sic*, which means "thus" or "so." This Latin form is used to emphasize the fact that an error obvious to all actually appears thus in the quoted material.

> "A nautical mile," reported Chris Day, "is equal to 6,080 feet [1,853,184 meters]."
>
> "The company's reorganization program," wrote President Theodore Bailey, "will have its greatest affect [*sic*] on our immediate sales."

What we call *parentheses* in America are called *round brackets* in Great Britain.

Uses for Apostrophes

As you have already learned, the apostrophe is used to form possessives and contractions. The apostrophe can also be used to take the place of omitted letters and as a symbol for *feet*. The guidelines for these uses are covered in this section.

To Form Noun Possessives

In Chapter 5 you learned that the apostrophe can be used to make common and proper nouns possessive. Do not use the apostrophe to make nouns plural.

> She didn't understand her *boss's* instructions.
>
> *Today's* software requires more processing power.
>
> The *Harrises'* small consulting firm is thriving.
>
> The *companies'* attorneys are evaluating the merger agreement. (Notice that *companies'* is a plural word showing possession, whereas *attorneys* is merely plural.)

Some last names, such as *O'Malley* and *D'Angelo*, contain apostrophes. Most last names with apostrophes have Irish, French, Italian, and African roots.

To Form Contractions

Chapter 6 illustrated how to use the apostrophe to form contractions, which are shortened forms of subjects and verbs. Don't confuse contractions with pronouns.

> *It's* too early to determine if *we'll* make a profit this year. (*It's* represents *it is; we'll* represents *we will*.)
>
> *You're* invited to show us your portfolio next week. (*You're* represents *you are*.)

I've no way of knowing if *there's* a solution to this problem. (*I've* represents *I have*; *there's* represents *there is*.)

You'd be happier if you *didn't* complain so much. (*You'd* represents *You would*; *didn't* represents *did not*.)

To Take the Place of Omitted Letters or Figures

The apostrophe can be used to take the place of omitted letters or figures. This is especially common when expressing a year.

Music, films, and fashions of the *'70s* are suddenly popular again.

Job prospects for the class of *'12* look promising.

He stops by *Dunkin' Donuts* on his way to work every morning.

To Serve as the Symbol for *feet*

In technical documents the apostrophe can be used as the symbol for *feet*. (A quotation mark is used as the symbol for inches.)

The conference room is 14' × 16'. (14 feet by 16 feet)

She is only 5' 1", but she can overpower a room. (5 feet 1 inch)

Now complete the reinforcement exercises for Level 3.

Spot the BLOOPER

Using the skills you are learning in this class, try to identify why the following items are bloopers. Consult your textbook, dictionary, or reference manual as needed.

Blooper 1: From *Titanic: The Artifact Exhibit*: "The iceberg's stone-hard spur punctures Titanic's hull in six of it's forward compartments."

Blooper 2: Ad for Saks Fifth Avenue published in *The New York Times* that features a T-shirt with this slogan: "Saks is a girls best friend."

Blooper 3: A gardening article about the dwarf amaryllis, published in *Florida Today*: "They are an ideal compliment to the larger blooming amaryllis or can be stunning as a mass planting of their own."

Blooper 4: At the bottom of all four pages of the menu at PizzaGram Plus in Guilderland, New York: "Our food is cooked to order. We appreciate your patients."

Blooper 5: From *The Times & Record News* [Wichita Falls, Texas]: "Do not sweep an area where there have been rodents with a broom."

Blooper 6: State director of the Obama presidential campaign, as quoted in an Atlanta newsletter: "We have massive amounts of volunteers coming in everyday making phone calls. We're just so excited." [Did you spot two errors?]

Blooper 7: In the *ABA* [American Bar Association] *Journal*: "A witness testified is was him, not Mousawi, on the video."

Blooper 8: Street sign located in neighborhoods throughout Cape Cod: "Slow Children At Play." [How could punctuation change the meaning of this sign?]

Blooper 9: Sign in a high school in California intended to honor its mascot: "We are the Scots who could be prouder." [Could proper punctuation have changed this message?]

Blooper 10: From a sales brochure for New Life Health Center: "We have every day low prices on hundreds of products. Here's a few to peak your interest!" [Can you spot three errors?]

Question	Answer
Q: My team and I are writing a proposal in which we say that *some of the current dot coms are undervalued.* We can't agree on how to write *dot coms*.	**A:** This playful reference to Internet companies is a little slangy, but it has become part of our common language. The standard way to write this expression is with a hyphen (*dot-com*).
Q: Should a period go inside or outside quotation marks? At the end of a sentence, I have typed the title "Positive vs. Negative Values." The author of the document wants the period outside because she says the title does not have a period in it.	**A:** In the United States typists and printers have adopted a uniform style: when a period or comma falls at the same place quotation marks would normally fall, the period or comma is always placed inside the quotation marks—regardless of the content of the quotation. In Britain a different style is observed.
Q: I have a phone extension at work, and I often want to tell people to call me at this extension. Can I abbreviate the word *extension*? If so, what is the proper abbreviation?	**A:** The abbreviation for *extension* is *Ext.* Notice that the abbreviation is capitalized and ends with a period. When you use this abbreviation in conjunction with a phone number, place a comma before and after (*To reserve your spot, please call me at 685-1230, Ext. 2306, before November 30.*)
Q: We are having an argument in our office about abbreviations. Can *department* be abbreviated *dep't*? How about *manufacturing* as *mf'g*?	**A:** In informal writing or when space is limited, words may be contracted or abbreviated. If a conventional abbreviation for a word exists, use it instead of a contracted form. Abbreviations are simpler to write and easier to read. For example, use *dept.* instead of *dep't*; use *natl.* instead of *nat'l*; use *cont.* instead of *cont'd*. Other accepted abbreviations are *ins.* for *insurance*; *mfg.* for *manufacturing*; *mgr.* for *manager*; and *mdse.* for *merchandise*. Notice that all abbreviations made up of lowercase letters end with periods.
Q: Where should the word *sic* be placed when it is used?	**A:** *Sic* means "thus" or "so stated," and it is properly placed immediately following the word or phrase to which it refers. For example, *The kidnappers placed a newspaper advertisement that read "Call Monna [sic] Lisa." Sic* is used within a quotation to indicate that a quoted word or phrase, though inaccurately spelled or used, appeared thus in the original. *Sic* is italicized and placed within brackets.
Q: I've looked in the dictionary but I'm still unsure about whether to hyphenate *copilot*.	**A:** The hyphen is no longer used in most words beginning with the prefix *co* (*coauthor, cocounsel, codesign, cofeature, cohead, copilot, costar, cowrite*). Only a few words retain the hyphen (*co-official, co-owner, co-organizer*). Check your dictionary for usage. In reading your dictionary, notice that centered periods are used to indicate syllables (*co•work•er*); hyphens are used to show hyphenated syllables (*co-own*).

Question	Answer

Q: I sometimes see three periods in a row in documents I'm reading and in book and film reviews. Does this use of periods have a name? When is this type of punctuation used?

A: A series of three periods, with spaces before, between, and after each period, is called an *ellipsis* (. . .). Ellipses are usually used to show that information has been left out of quoted material. (*Roger Ebert's review of* Chicago *includes these words:* "By filming it in its own spirit, by making it frankly a stagy song-and-dance revue . . . the movie is big, brassy fun.") The ellipsis shows that this is not Roger Ebert's complete quote and that words have been omitted between *revue* and *the*.

Q: I recently received an invitation to my high school reunion that used the apostrophe like this: *the class of '99*. Is this a correct use of the apostrophe?

A: Yes. In addition to forming noun possession and contractions, the apostrophe has several other uses. It can be used to take the place of omitted letters or figures (*He stops by Dunkin' Donuts every morning on his way to work*). This is especially common when expressing a year (*The '60s were a time of protest and change*). In technical documents the apostrophe can be used as the symbol for *feet*. A quotation mark is used as the symbol for *inches* (*At only 5' 4", Tony is shorter than many women he dates*).

Q: Should I use *complimentary* or *complementary* to describe free tickets?

A: Use *complimentary*, which can mean "containing a compliment, favorable, or free" (*the dinner came with complimentary wine; he made a complimentary remark*). *Complementary* means "completing or making perfect" (*The online edition of* The Wall Street Journal *is the perfect complement to your print subscription. The complementary colors enhanced the room*). An easy way to remember *compliment* is by thinking "*I* like to receive a compl*i*ment."

Q: Years ago I was taught to always space twice after period. Has this rule changed?

A: The rule requiring that one space twice after end punctuation dates back to the days of typewriters, which used monospacing. This meant that each letter or character took up the same amount of space on the page. The extra space was needed to make it easier for readers to determine when a new sentence began. When word processors came out, introducing proportional spacing (which means that letters and characters take up different amounts of space on the page, depending on their actual size and width), the need to space twice after end punctuation was eliminated. However, habits die hard! Many people still insist on spacing twice after end punctuation, and there's really nothing wrong with doing so. What we recommend is to choose one spacing style and to be consistent.

16 Reinforcement Exercises

LEVEL 1

Online Homework Help! For immediate feedback on odd-numbered items, go to **www.meguffey.com**.

 A. (Self-check) In the spaces provided after each sentence, indicate whether a period, question mark, or exclamation mark is needed as end punctuation. Write the correct end punctuation mark in the space provided. If no additional punctuation is required, write *C*.

Example: Could you please check these figures for accuracy   ___.___

1. Will you be sure to log off before you leave _____

2. What an amazing idea _____

3. The meeting is at 2 p.m., isn't it _____

4. Has anyone checked the FedEx Web site to see whether our package was delivered _____

5. The NYSE stock symbol for Berkshire Hathaway is BRK _____

6. Wow! How inspirational _____

7. Warren asked whether our company will start using the smart cards manufactured by Fargo Electronics, Inc _____

8. Did Tracy mail the test results when she left at 5 p.m. _____

9. I wonder whether he has checked with the three credit reporting bureaus to find out whether his credit card has been used fraudulently _____

10. Dr. Helen C. Haitz and Emile Brault, PhD, will appear on TV at 2 p.m., EST. _____

Check your answers below.

 B. Write the letter of the correctly punctuated sentence.

1. a. The L.V.N. exam will take place on Friday at 8 am.
   b. The LVN exam will take place on Friday at 8 a.m.
   c. The LVN exam will take place on Friday at 8 AM. _____

2. a. Can you please forward the e-mail message to me?
   b. Can you, please, forward the e-mail message to me?
   c. Can you please forward the e-mail message to me. _____

3. a. Wyatt asked whether Google's original name was Googol.
   b. Wyatt asked whether Google's original name was Googol?
   c. Wyatt asked, whether Google's original name was Googol. _____

4. a. Did our CEO interview Ms. E. W. Rasheen for the C.P.A. position?
   b. Did our C.E.O. interview Ms. E. W. Rasheen for the C.P.A. position?
   c. Did our CEO interview Ms. E. W. Rasheen for the CPA position? _____

1. leave. 2. idea! 3. it? 4. delivered? 5. BRK. 6. inspirational! 7. Inc. 8. 5 p.m. 9. fraudulently? 10. C.

5. a. Many more MBA programs are available in the USA than in the UK.
    b. Many more M.B.A. programs are available in the U.S.A. than in the U.K.
    c. Many more M.B.A. programs are available in the USA than in the UK.   _____

6. a. Advertisements will air on the following radio stations: KFOG, KGO,
      and KCSM.
    b. Advertisements will air on the following radio stations: K.F.O.G., K.G.O.,
      and K.C.S.M..
    c. Advertisements will air on the following radio stations; KFOG, KGO,
      and KCSM.   _____

7. a. The No. 1 official at the E.P.A. has a BA from MSU Mankato.
    b. The No. 1 official at the EPA has a BA from MSU Mankato.
    c. The No 1 official at the EPA has a B.A. from MSU Mankato.   _____

8. a. The recipient's address is 5 Sierra Drive, Rochester, N.Y. 14616.
    b. The recipient's address is 5 Sierra Drive, Rochester, NY 14616.
    c. The recipient's address is 5 Sierra Drive, Rochester, Ny. 14616.   _____

9. a. Shondra wondered whether the organic produce was worth the extra cost?
    b. Shondra wondered whether the organic produce was worth the extra cost.
    c. Shondra wondered, whether the organic produce was worth the extra cost?   _____

10. a. Have you ever wondered why LUV is the stock symbol for Southwest Airlines?
    b. Have you ever wondered why LUV is the stock symbol for Southwest Airlines.
    c. Have you ever wondered why L.U.V. is the stock symbol for Southwest Airlines?   _____

C. In the following sentences, all punctuation has been omitted. Insert commas, periods, question marks, colons, and exclamation marks. Some words have extra spaces between them so that punctuation may be inserted; however, a space does not mean that punctuation is necessary. Use a caret (∧) to indicate each insertion. In the space at the right, indicate the number of punctuation marks you inserted. Consult a reference manual or a dictionary for abbreviation style if necessary.

Example: Virginia asked whether Murray J∘Demo was hired as C F O at Dolby
      Laboratories, Inc∘   ∧   2
           ∧

1. Will you please meet Susan B Smith Ph D at S E C headquarters in Washington D C   _____

2. The H T M L workshop will be held from 9 a m until 4 p m   _____

3. Dr Jacqueline A Young will travel from the U S A to the R O C in 2014   _____

4. You did change your P I N as the bank requested didn't you   _____

5. Reece Soltani M S was recognized for her work with the F D A   _____

6. What a dilemma the latest F C C regulations have created   _____

7. Stop Don't eat that apple   _____

8. Deliver the signed contracts to Ms C M Gigliotti before 6 p m E S T   _____

9. If G M A C offers commercial financing at low rates we would be interested   _____

10. What a great game we saw on E S P N   _____

11. Dan wondered whether he had earned enough units for his A A degree   _____

12. After completing his B A degree at U C L A Ben Lindsay transferred to
    M I T and began working on his M B A   _____

13. Ms J S Novak has been appointed consultant for educational services to the
    A F L - C I O   _____

14. Does he often use the abbreviations e g and i e in his e-mail messages   _____

15. Since the funds were earned in the U K I must consult my C P A about paying taxes in the U S A   _____

16. Some users wonder whether the F A Q s on the U S P S Web site are current   _____

17. Has the erroneous charge of $45 95 been removed from my account   _____

18. The guest list includes the following individuals Dr Lyn Clark Ms Frances Hendricks and Professor Jean Sturgill   _____

19. Lt Gen Maxwell asked whether the U S Census Bureau office will be open until 6 p m   _____

20. Well we did a fantastic job didn't we   _____

LEVEL 2

A. (Self-check) Write the letter of the correctly punctuated sentence in the space provided. Use a dictionary or reference manual as needed.

1.
a. Forty five companies have reserved booths at the USA International Eco Green Trade Show.
b. Forty-five companies have reserved booths at the USA International Eco Green Trade Show.
c. Forty five companies have reserved booths at the U.S.A. International Eco Green Trade Show.   _____

2.
a. Many of my coworkers are bilingual, and some can even speak three languages.
b. Many of my co-workers are bi-lingual, and some can even speak three languages.
c. Many of my coworkers are bi-lingual, and some can even speak three languages   _____

3.
a. Paul Pogranichny scored a perfect 800 (can you believe it) on the GMAT.
b. Paul Pogranichny scored a perfect 800 (can you believe it?) on the GMAT.
c. Paul Pogranichny scored a perfect 800 (can you believe it) on the G.M.A.T.?   _____

4.
a. Mission statement, management bios, product description, operating budget: these should all appear in a company's business plan.
b. Mission statement, management bios, product description, operating budget—these should all appear in a company's business plan.
c. Mission statement, management bios, product description, operating budget; these should all appear in a company's business plan.   _____

5.
a. "The greatest glory in living lies not in never falling, but in rising every time we fall." —Nelson Mandela
b. "The greatest glory in living lies not in never falling, but in rising every time we fall," Nelson Mandela
c. "The greatest glory in living lies not in never falling, but in rising every time we fall": Nelson Mandela   _____

6. (Emphasize parenthetical element.)
a. Currently our basic operating costs: rent, utilities, and wages, are 10 percent higher than last year.
b. Currently our basic operating costs (rent, utilities, and wages) are 10 percent higher than last year.
c. Currently our basic operating costs—rent, utilities, and wages—are 10 percent higher than last year.   _____

7. a. Our operating revenue for 2011 (see Appendix A) exceeded our expectations.
b. Our operating revenue for 2011, see Appendix A, exceeded our expectations.
c. Our operating revenue for 2011: see Appendix A, exceeded our expectations. _____

8. a. Recently you applied for a position (executive assistant); however, you did not indicate for which branch your application is intended.
b. Recently you applied for a position; (executive assistant) however, you did not indicate for which branch your application is intended.
c. Recently you applied for a position (executive assistant;) however, you did not indicate for which branch your application is intended. _____

9. (Emphasize.)
a. Sales, sales, and more sales: that's what we need to succeed.
b. Sales, sales, and more sales—that's what we need to succeed.
c. Sales, sales, and more sales; that's what we need to succeed. _____

10. (De-emphasize.)
a. Four features—camera, text messaging, Web access, and voice mail—are what Americans want most on their cell phones.
b. Four features, camera, text messaging, Web access, and voice mail, are what Americans want most on their cell phones.
c. Four features (camera, text messaging, Web access, and voice mail) are what Americans want most on their cell phones. _____

Check your answers below.

B. Select the correctly hyphenated word from each pair below. Write its letter in the space provided. Use your dictionary or reference manual if needed to determine whether a word should be hyphenated.

1. a. ex mayor b. ex-mayor	_____	**11.** a. semiannual b. semi-annual	_____
2. a. self-confidence b. self confidence	_____	**12.** a. bi-weekly b. biweekly	_____
3. a. quasi public b. quasi-public	_____	**13.** a. pre-existing b. preexisting	_____
4. a. stepson b. step-son	_____	**14.** a. rewrite b. re-write	_____
5. a. great-grandfather b. great grandfather	_____	**15.** a. co-chair b. cochair	_____
6. a. half sister b. half-sister	_____	**16.** a. coownership b. co-ownership	_____
7. a. anti-smoking b. antismoking	_____	**17.** a. under-funded b. underfunded	_____
8. a. extracurricular b. extra-curricular	_____	**18.** a. nonacademic b. non-academic	_____
9. a. intergenerational b inter-generational	_____	**19.** a. non-American b. nonAmerican	_____
10. a. multitalented b. multi-talented	_____	**20.** a. post-industrial b. postindustrial	_____

1. b 2. a 3. b 4. b 5. a 6. c 7. a 8. a 9. b 10. c

C. Insert dashes or parentheses in the following sentences. In the space provided after each sentence, write the number of punctuation marks you inserted. Count each parenthesis and each dash as a single mark.

Example: (Emphasize.) Three S&P corporations—GE, Verizon, and Cisco—hold more cash assets than any other large corporation.   __2__

1. (De-emphasize.) The Tony-award-winning production of *The 39 Steps* have you seen the reviews? will be opening here shortly.   _____

2. "Web 2.0 is the business revolution in the computer industry caused by the move to the Internet as a platform, and an attempt to understand the rules for success on that new platform." Tim O'Reilly.   _____

3. Social networking, video sharing, blogs, and wikis these are all features you will find on Web 2.0.   _____

4. (De-emphasize.) Five start-up companies Digg, Last.fm, Newsvine, Tagworld, and YouTube are expected to play major roles in developing the social media content for Web 2.0.   _____

5. (Emphasize.) Three of the biggest problems with Web 2.0 privacy, overuse, and etiquette will be discussed at the Web 2.0 Summit in San Francisco.   _____

6. (De-emphasize.) As soon as you are able to make an appointment try to do so before December 30, we will process your passport application.   _____

7. Funds for the project will be released on the following dates see Section 12.3 of the original grant: January 1, March 14, and June 30.   _____

8. Health Vitals Tracker, Stormchaser, iRovr, MapCrawl these are just some of the many apps available for the iPhone.   _____

9. (De-emphasize.) Editors of *Condé Nast Traveler* selected five cruise ships Carnival Dream, Celebrity Equinox, Oasis of the Seas, Seabourn Odyssey, and Viking Legend that provide the best amenities to passengers.   _____

10. The BlackBerry warranty contract is limited to sixty 60 days.   _____

    D. Writing Exercise. Using three different forms of punctuation, correctly punctuate the following sentence. In the space provided, explain how the three methods you have employed differ.

1. Numerous appeals all of which came from concerned parents prompted us to rethink the school closure.

2. Numerous appeals all of which came from concerned parents prompted us to rethink the school closure.

3. Numerous appeals all of which came from concerned parents prompted us to rethink the school closure.

    Explanation: _____

_____

A. (Self-check) Indicate whether the following statements are true (*T*) or false (*F*).

1. Double quotation marks are used to enclose the exact words of a writer or speaker. _____

2. Names of books, magazines, television series, movies, and newspapers should be italicized. _____

3. Periods and commas are always placed after closing quotation marks. _____

4. Brackets are used by writers to enclose their own remarks inserted into a quotation. _____

5. A quotation within a quotation is shown with single quotation marks. _____

6. Semicolons and colons are always placed before closing quotation marks. _____

7. Titles of articles, book chapters, poems, and songs should be enclosed in quotation marks. _____

8. If both a quotation and its introductory sentence are questions, use a question mark before the closing quotation marks. _____

9. The word *sic* is used to show that a quotation is free of errors. _____

10. Use the apostrophe to take the place of omitted letters or figures. _____

Check your answers below.

 B. Insert all necessary punctuation in the following sentences. Be especially alert for direct quotations. Underlines may be used for words that might be italicized in print.

Example: The term *preferred stock* means "stock having priority over common stock in the distribution of dividends."

1. The graduating class of 99 held its ten year reunion on a cruise ship

2. (De-emphasize.) In three countries Ukraine, Russia, and Indonesia over 60 percent of men smoke cigarettes

3. Smoking is still allowed in Russias trains, clubs, and restaurants

4. Louis Camilleri, CEO of Philip Morris, said Were being very socially responsible in a rather controversial industry

5. Whether you think you can or think you can't, said Henry Ford, you're right

6. The word *mashup* is a technology term that is defined as a Web site that uses content from more than one source to create a completely new service

7. Kym Anderson's chapter titled Subsidies and Trade Barriers appears in the book *How to Spend $50 Billion to Make the World a Better Place*

8. Did Donald Trump really say Anyone who thinks my story is anywhere near over is sadly mistaken

9. In his speech the software billionaire said Our goal is to link the world irregardless [*sic*] of national boundaries and restrictions

10. Oprah Winfrey said that the best jobs are those we'd do even if we didn't get paid

1. T 2. T 3. F 4. T 5. T 6. F 7. T 8. T 9. F 10. T

11. Garth said he was stoked about his upcoming vacation to Mexico

12. The postal worker said Shall I stamp your package Fragile

13. Did you see the article titled Why Jobs Are Going Unfilled Amid Layoffs in *BusinessWeek*

14. The French expression *répondez s'il vous plaît* means respond if you please

15. Would you please send a current catalog to Globex, Inc

16. (Direct quotation.) "The man who does not read good books said Mark Twain has no advantage over the man who cannot read them

17. (Emphasize.) Three of the largest manufacturers Dell, IBM, and Hewlett-Packard submitted bids

18. In *Forbes* I saw an article titled Are There Any Rules in the Bailout Game

19. (De-emphasize.) Albert Einstein once said that only two things the universe and human stupidity are infinite

20. (Emphasize.) Albert Einstein once said that only two things the universe and human stupidity are infinite

C. **Writing Exercise.** On a separate sheet write a paragraph describing your ideal job. Try to include as many of the punctuation marks you have studied as possible. Include commas, semicolons, colons, periods, question marks, exclamation marks, hyphens, dashes, parentheses, quotation marks, italics, apostrophes, and possibly even brackets. Include a quotation from your boss. Make up the name of a book or article that you could publish about this job.

 D. **FAQs About Business English Review.** In the space provided, write the correct answer choice.

1. When the economy slowed, many (a) dot.coms, (b) dot-coms, (c) dot coms went out of business. _____

2. Which sentence is punctuated correctly?
   a. Have you read the article titled "In-Flight Internet: Is It Secure"?
   b. Have you read the article titled "In-Flight Internet: Is It Secure?"
   c. Have you read the article titled "In-Flight Internet: Is It Secure?"? _____

3. One of the best ways to motivate employees is to _____ their work.
   a. compliment   b. complement _____

4. This white wine is the perfect (a) compliment, (b) complement to this grilled fish. _____

5. Companies often make acquisitions in order to acquire _____ products.
   a. complimentary   b. complementary _____

6. Your comments about your neighbor's garden were very (a) complimentary, (b) complementary. _____

7. He gets along well with his (a) co-workers, (b) co workers, (c) coworkers. _____

8. This document outlines our (a) co-ownership, (b) coownership, (c) co ownership agreement. _____

9. Brooke Shields was in the class of (a) '87, (b) 87', (c) 87 at Princeton University. _____

10. Many people are surprised to learn that Tom Cruise is only (a) 5"7', (b) 5 7, (c) 5' 7". _____

►► Learning Web Ways

You want to conduct business research on the Web, but you want to make sure that the sites you visit are credible. You just found out that the American Library Association (ALA) has put together a list of reputable business sites, and you want to learn more.

Goal: To locate some of the best business-related sites on the Web.

1. With your Web browser on the screen, go to the American Library Association's *Best of the Best Business Web sites* site (**http://www .ala.org/rusa/brass/besthome.cfm**).

2. In the **Subject Index** section, click your major or business area of interest.

3. Read the description for each related Web site. Click the link for the site that sounds most interesting or relevant. (**Note:** The site will open in a separate browser window.)

4. Find two or three facts on the site that will help you in your studies or career. Write down what you learn and explain how it will help you in your studies or in your career.

5. Print two pages from this Web site. End your session. Submit your printouts and answers to the questions posed here.

►► Chat About It

Your instructor may assign any of the following topics for you to discuss in class, in an online chat room, or on an online discussion board. Some of the discussion topics may require outside research. You may also be asked to read and respond to postings made by your classmates.

Discussion Topic 1: You learned many punctuation rules in Chapters 14, 15, and 16. What tips and tricks do you have for remembering these rules? Share your techniques with your classmates.

Discussion Topic 2: One of the most misused punctuation marks is the quotation mark. For example, a restaurant in Walnut Creek, California, had a sign that read *Our customers are "special."* Stop-n-Shop advertised *"All Natural" Jumbo Sea Scallops.* And a sign in a New York health club locker room said *Thank you for keeping your "health" club as clean as possible.* What do these misused quotation marks communicate to readers? Why do you think this misuse occurs so often? Share your thoughts with your classmates. If possible, find an example of misused quotation marks to include.

Discussion Topic 3: Do you or someone you know have a name that contains an apostrophe (*O'Leary, D'Artagnans*), a hyphen (*Al-Kurd, Boutros-Ghali*), or a space (*von Trapp, van der Heiden*)? Names like these can cause problems when using a computer to make appointments,

book reservations, or fill out an online form. Why? Because many computer programs don't know how to handle names that contain punctuation or spaces. Some programs block names like these; others mistake the punctuation for programming code; and some simply drop a portion of the name or close up the space. If you have a name like this, have you ever experienced problems? Share your experiences with your classmates. If you had a name like this, what would you do? Share your ideas.

Discussion Topic 4: Does proper punctuation matter in business? Should you use proper punctuation in all documents or just formal documents? What about using proper punctuation in e-mail messages? Share your opinions with your classmates.

Discussion Topic 5: Yes, there really is a National Punctuation Day! It takes place every year in September. Visit the site **http://www .nationalpunctuationday.com** and explore the contents of the site. Share at least three interesting items you found on the site with your classmates.

Posttest

Use proofreading marks to insert necessary punctuation.

1. The C F O wondered whether the rise in G D P would affect his company's stock price

2. You can have four family phone lines for just $8999 a month

3. Our ex C E O returned to the company for the awards ceremony

4. Will you please send me a copy of the article titled Winning Negotiation Strategies

5. When did we receive this package marked Confidential

6. The only guests who have not sent RSVPs are Miss Mendoza Mrs Gold and Mr Sims

7. Taking pictures, surfing Web sites, watching TV shows these are just some of the things people do with their cell phones.

8. Did Dr Simanek say "I'd like to put you on an exercise program"

9. (De-emphasize) Of the three best places to retire as selected by Fortune Hudson Heights, Tudor City, and Chicago the top two are in New York

10. (Emphasize) The three most powerful women in business Indra Nooyi, Anne Mulcahy, and Meg Whitman are all in their 50s

1. price. 2. $89.99 month. 3. ex-CEO ceremony. 4. "Winning Negotiation Strategies." 5. "Confidential"? 6. Mendoza, Mrs. Gold, and Mr. Sims. 8. Dr. say, "I'd program"? 9. (Hudson Heights, Tudor City, and Chicago), New York. 10. —Indra Nooyi, Anne Mulcahy, and Meg Whitman— 50s.

First, review Chapters 14–16. Then, test your comprehension of those chapters by completing the exercises that follow and comparing your responses with those shown at the end of the book.

LEVEL 1

Insert necessary punctuation in the following sentences. In the space at the right, indicate the number of punctuation marks you inserted. Write *C* if the sentence is correct.

1. Because employers want to hire the right people many conduct Web searches to discover more about candidates. _____

2. However employers conduct these Web searches they may find information that will eliminate a candidate. _____

3. Professor how can I clean up my "digital dirt" before I look for a job _____

4. A career workshop will be held on Monday May 2 on the college campus. _____

5. Using a technology called "telesensing" cell phones can be used to take someone's pulse check on sick relatives and warn police about criminals hiding behind walls. _____

6. Tod Sizer a researcher at Bell Labs is developing ways to read cell phone signals bounced off the body. _____

7. A jogger who has a phone with a telesensing chip will be able to monitor heart and respiration rates. _____

8. Nearby mobile phones however can cause interference with telesensing. _____

Select a, b, or c to indicate the correctly punctuated sentence.

9. a. Unethical behavior that results in personal gain is reprimanded unethical behavior that results in corporate gain is also reprimanded.
   b. Unethical behavior that results in personal gain is reprimanded, unethical behavior that results in corporate gain is also reprimanded.
   c. Unethical behavior that results in personal gain is reprimanded; unethical behavior that results in corporate gain is also reprimanded. _____

10. a. Reports have arrived from our offices in Geneva, Switzerland, Munich, Germany, and Vienna, Austria.
    b. Reports have arrived from our offices in Geneva, Switzerland; Munich, Germany; and Vienna, Austria.
    c. Reports have arrived from our offices in: Geneva, Switzerland; Munich, Germany; and Vienna, Austria. _____

11. a. Small businesses can benefit from having a logo; therefore, we recommend working with a logo development company.

b. Small businesses can benefit from having a logo, therefore, we recommend working with a logo development company.

c. Small businesses can benefit from having a logo; therefore we recommend working with a logo development company.

_____

12. a. Would you please check the IRS Web site.

b. Would you please check the I.R.S. Web site.

c. Would you please check the IRS Web site?

_____

13. a. We are astonished needless to say about the misstatement of profits.

b. We are astonished, needless to say, about the misstatement of profits.

c. We are astonished, needless to say; about the misstatement of profits.

_____

14. a. She said she held AA and BS degrees didn't she?

b. She said she held A.A. and B.S. degrees, didn't she?

c. She said she held AA and BS degrees, didn't she?

_____

LEVEL 2

Select a, b, or c to indicate the correctly punctuated sentence.

15. a. Wow! A total of 89.9 percent of the voters approved!

b. Wow, a total of 89 point 9 percent of the voters approved!

c. Wow. A total of 89.9 percent of the voters approved!

_____

16. a. *Forbes* reported that the three best American towns in which to live are: Plymouth, Minnesota, Fort Collins, Colorado, and Naperville, Illinois.

b. *Forbes* reported that the three best American towns in which to live are: Plymouth, Minnesota; Fort Collins, Colorado; and Naperville, Illinois.

c. *Forbes* reported that the three best American towns in which to live are Plymouth, Minnesota; Fort Collins, Colorado; and Naperville, Illinois.

_____

17. a. In addition, the list included the following towns: Irvine, Norman, and Fishers.

b. In addition, the list included the following towns, Irvine, Norman, and Fishers.

c. In addition, the list included the following towns; Irvine, Norman, and Fishers.

_____

18. a. Jack Welch said, "I've learned that mistakes can often be as good a teacher as success."

b. Jack Welch said: "I've learned that mistakes can often be as good a teacher as success."

c. Jack Welch said; "I've learned that mistakes can often be as good a teacher as success."

_____

19. a. Three of the best U.S. cities for singles: Cambridge, Somerville, and Boston, are located in Massachusetts.

b. Three of the best U.S. cities for singles—Cambridge, Somerville, and Boston—are located in Massachusetts.

c. Three of the best U.S. cities for singles, Cambridge, Somerville, and Boston, are located in Massachusetts.

_____

20.
  a. Wal-Mart, Exxon Mobile, Royal Dutch Shell, BP, and Toyota Motor—these are the five largest companies in the world.
  b. Wal-Mart, Exxon Mobil, Royal Dutch Shell, BP, and Toyota Motor: these are the five largest companies in the world.
  c. Wal-Mart, Exxon Mobil, Royal Dutch Shell, BP, and Toyota Motor, these are the five largest companies in the world.   _____

21. (Emphasize.)
  a. Three airlines, Southwest Airlines, Continental Airlines, and Alaska Air, were ranked by *Fortune* as the most admired by experts in the industry.
  b. Three airlines: Southwest Airlines, Continental Airlines, and Alaska Air, were ranked by *Fortune* as the most admired by experts in the industry.
  c. Three airlines—Southwest Airlines, Continental Airlines, and Alaska Air— were ranked by *Fortune* as the most admired by experts in the industry.   _____

22.
  a. The largest U.S. charities are United Way, Salvation Army, and Feed the Children.
  b. The largest U.S. charities are: United Way, Salvation Army, and Feed the Children.
  c. The largest U.S. charities are—United Way, Salvation Army, and Feed the Children.   _____

23. (De-emphasize.)
  a. A pilot project—refer to page 6 of the report—may help us justify the new system.
  b. A pilot project, refer to page 6 of the report, may help us justify the new system.
  c. A pilot project (refer to page 6 of the report) may help us justify the new system.   _____

24.
  a. In 2009, the Oasis of the Seas, the world's largest cruise ship, made her maiden voyage.
  b. In 2009 the Oasis of the Seas, the world's largest cruise ship, made her maiden voyage.
  c. In 2009, the Oasis of the Seas, the world's largest cruise ship; made her maiden voyage.   _____

25.
  a. If you would like to sail on the Oasis of the Seas, contact Royal Caribbean Cruises directly.
  b. If you would like to sail on the Oasis of the Seas contact Royal Caribbean Cruises directly.
  c. If you would like to sail on the Oasis of the Seas; contact Royal Caribbean Cruises, directly.   _____

26.
  a. The Oasis of the Seas is an architectural nautical marvel.
  b. The Oasis of the Seas is an architectural, nautical marvel.
  c. The Oasis of the Seas, is an architectural nautical marvel.   _____

27.
  a. Please re-write these instructions to make them more understandable.
  b. Please re write these instructions to make them more understandable.
  c. Please rewrite these instructions to make them more understandable.   _____

28.
  a. I work hard to increase the self-esteem of my coworkers.
  b. I work hard to increase the self-esteem of my co-workers.
  c. I work hard to increase the selfesteem of my coworkers.   _____

Select a, b, or c to indicate the correctly punctuated sentence.

29.
a. Incidentally "telematics" enables a car to wirelessly exchange data with external sources such as cell phones, MP3 players, and navigation systems.
b. Incidentally—"telematics" enables a car to wirelessly exchange data with external sources such as cell phones, MP3 players, and navigation systems.
c. Incidentally, "telematics" enables a car to wirelessly exchange data with external sources such as cell phones, MP3 players, and navigation systems.

_____

30.
a. Our goal is to encourage, not hamper, good communication.
b. Our goal is to encourage—not hamper, good communication.
c. Our goal is to encourage, not hamper good communication.

_____

31.
a. One American company is going to try to sell Mexican food in Mexico, namely Taco Bell.
b. One American company is going to try to sell Mexican food in Mexico, namely, Taco Bell.
c. One American company is going to try to sell Mexican food in Mexico: namely, Taco Bell.

_____

32.
a. Four companies offer the best benefits for new college graduates, namely, Electronic Arts, Pricewaterhouse Coopers, Randstad, and Pacific Northwest National Laboratory.
b. Four companies offer the best benefits for new college graduates; namely, Electronic Arts, Pricewaterhouse Coopers, Randstad, and Pacific Northwest National Laboratory.
c. Four companies offer the best benefits for new college graduates; namely Electronic Arts, Pricewaterhouse Coopers, Randstad, and Pacific Northwest National Laboratory.

_____

33.
a. The computer was producing "garbage," that is, the screen showed gibberish.
b. The computer was producing "garbage"; that is, the screen showed gibberish.
c. The computer was producing "garbage;" that is, the screen showed gibberish.

_____

34.
a. Boston is often called "Beantown" and "The Hub of the Universe".
b. Boston is often called 'Beantown' and 'The Hub of the Universe.'
c. Boston is often called "Beantown" and "The Hub of the Universe."

_____

35.
a. The Economist, a British magazine, featured an article called "Off Their Trollies: American Consumers Struggle With Their Debts."
b. *The Economist*, a British magazine, featured an article called "Off Their Trollies: American Consumers Struggle With Their Debts."
c. "The Economist," a British magazine, featured an article called *Off Their Trollies: American Consumers Struggle With Their Debts*.

_____

36.
a. "It has been my observation, said Henry Ford, that most people get ahead during the time that others waste time."
b. "It has been my observation," said Henry Ford, "That most people get ahead during the time that others waste time."
c. "It has been my observation," said Henry Ford, "that most people get ahead during the time that others waste time."

_____

37. a. Who was it who said, "If I'm going to do something, I do it spectacularly or I don't do it at all."?
b. Who was it who said, "If I'm going to do something, I do it spectacularly or I don't do it at all?"
c. Who was it who said, "If I'm going to do something, I do it spectacularly or I don't do it at all"?   _____

38. a. Did the office manager really say, "Stamp this package 'Confidential'?"
b. Did the office manager really say, "Stamp this package 'Confidential'"?
c. Did the office manager really say, "Stamp this package "Confidential"?   _____

39. a. Rudy Giuliani said, "When you confront a problem, you begin to solve it."
b. Rudy Giuliani said; "When you confront a problem, you begin to solve it."
c. Rudy Giuliani said, "When you confront a problem you begin to solve it".   _____

40. a. The graduating class of 09' faced bleak job prospects.
b. The graduating class of 09 faced bleak job prospects.
c. The graduating class of '09 faced bleak job prospects.   _____

FAQs About Business English Review

Write the letter of the word or phrase that correctly completes each sentence.

41. Every measure has been taken to (a) insure, (b) ensure your safety.   _____

42. Because few stockholders were (a) appraised, (b) apprised of the CEO's total salary package, no complaints were heard.   _____

43. Have you ever been (a) cited, (b) sited, (c) sighted for a speeding violation?   _____

44. You can request a refund by visiting our Web (a) cite, (b) site, (c) sight.   _____

45. We offer (a) complimentary, (b) complementary shipping for all purchases.   _____

46. Paul invested $20,000 as (a) capitol, (b) capital to start a new business.   _____

47. Cheyenne is the (a) capital, (b) capitol of Wyoming.   _____

48. All rebates will be (a) dispersed, (b) disbursed next month.   _____

49. John Muir, who founded the Sierra Club, (a) emigrated, (b) immigrated from Sweden when he was eleven years old.   _____

50. Janice was late giving her rent check to her (a) lessee, (b) lessor.   _____

Professional Business Letters

Business letters are important forms of external communication. That is, they deliver information to individuals outside an organization. Although e-mail has become incredibly successful for both internal and external communication, many important messages still require written letters. Business letters are necessary when a permanent record is required, when formality is significant, and when a message is sensitive and requires an organized, well-considered presentation. Business letters may request information, respond to requests, make claims, seek adjustments, order goods and services, sell goods and services, recommend individuals, develop goodwill, apply for jobs, or achieve many other goals. All business and professional people have to write business letters of various kinds, but a majority of those letters will be informational.

Characteristics of Business Letters

Writers of good business letters—whether the messages are informational, persuasive, or negative—are guided by the six Cs: conciseness, clarity, correctness, courtesy, completeness, and confidence. In earlier Writing Workshops, you learned techniques for making your writing concise and clear. You have also studied many guidelines for correct grammar and usage throughout this textbook. At this point we will review some of these techniques briefly as they relate to business letters.

Conciseness. Concise letters save the reader's time by presenting information directly. You can make your letters concise by avoiding these writing faults: (a) wordy phrases (such as *in addition to the above* and *in view of the fact that*), (b) excessive use of expletives (such as *There are four reasons that explain . . .* or *It is a good plan*), (c) long lead-ins (such as *This message is to inform you that* or *I am writing this letter to*), (d) needless adverbs (such as *very, definitely, quite, extremely,* and *really*), and (e) old-fashioned expressions (such as *attached please find* and *pursuant to your request*).

Clarity. Business letters are clear when they are logically organized and when they present enough information for the reader to understand what the writer intended. Informational letters are usually organized directly with the main idea first. Clarity can be enhanced by including all the necessary information. Some authorities estimate that one third of all business letters are written to clarify previous correspondence. To ensure that your letters are clear, put yourself in the reader's position and analyze what you have written. What questions may the reader ask? Does your information proceed logically from one point to another? Are your sentences and paragraphs coherent?

Correctness. Two aspects of correctness are accuracy of facts and accuracy of form. In regard to facts, good writers prepare to write by gathering relevant information. They collect supporting documents (previous letters, memos, e-mail messages, and reports), they make inquiries, they jot down facts, and they outline the message. Correct letters require thorough preparation. In the same manner, correct letters require careful proofreading and attention to form. Typographical errors, spelling irregularities, and grammatical faults distract the reader and damage the credibility of the writer. Correct business letters also follow one of the conventional formats, such as block or modified block, shown in Appendix C.

Courtesy. You develop courtesy in business letters by putting yourself in the place of the reader. Imagine how you would like to be treated, and show the same consideration and respect for the individual receiving your message. The ideas you express and the words used to convey those ideas create an impression on the reader. Be alert to words that may create a negative feeling such as *you claim, unfortunately, you neglected, you forgot*, and *your complaint*.

Completeness. In order for a letter to be complete, it should answer all questions your reader might have. When formulating your message, consider the who, what, when, where, why, and how. The goal in writing complete letters is to avoid unnecessary follow-up. You don't want to waste your reader's time or your own.

Confidence. Employers want employees who are confident in themselves and in what they do. Therefore, avoid using words that make you sound weak such as *I think, I feel*, and *I believe*. Just come right out and say it with confidence!

Skill Check 5.1 Reviewing the Six Cs

1. Which of the following is *most* concise?
   a. Due to the fact that we had a warehouse fire, your shipment is delayed.
   b. This is to inform you that your shipment will be delayed.
   c. Because of a warehouse fire, your shipment is delayed.
   d. There was a warehouse fire, which explains why your shipment is delayed. _____

2. Which of the following is clear and logical?
   a. If the strike is not settled quickly, it may last a while.
   b. Flying over the rain forests of Indonesia, the trees form a solid and menacing green carpet.
   c. This is not to suggest that Salt Lake, Denver, and Houston are not the most affordable areas for housing.
   d. Prince Charles complained that the citizens of Britain speak and write their language poorly. _____

3. Which of the following is grammatically correct?
   a. We hope that you and he will be in town for our next seminar.
   b. A host of ethical issues involve business, including e-mail privacy, whistleblowing, and mission statements.
   c. We must develop a policy on returning merchandise. So that they know about it before they are made.
   d. Jeffrey has 20 years experience in the software industry. _____

4. Which of the following is *most* courteous?
   a. During your interview, I informed you that if we were not successful in finding a suitable candidate, I would contact you.
   b. We appreciate receiving your letter describing your treatment by our store security personnel.
   c. In your letter of June 1, you claim that you were harassed by our store security personnel.
   d. Unfortunately, we are unable to complete your entire order because you neglected to provide a shirt size. _____

5. Which of the following sounds *most* conversational?
   a. Attached herewith is the form you requested.
   b. Pursuant to your request, we are forwarding the form you requested.
   c. Under separate cover we are sending the form you requested.
   d. You will receive the form you requested in a separate mailing. _____

6. Which of the following sounds *most* confident?
 a. I hope to hear from you soon about the available position.
 b. Our committee thinks that this is the best way to handle the problem.
 c. I look forward to speaking with you about my proposal.
 d. We believe that our product will best meet your needs.

Writing Plan

Most business letters have three parts: opening, body, and closing. This three-part writing plan will help you organize the majority of your business messages quickly and effectively.

Opening. The opening of a business letter may include a subject line that refers to previous correspondence or summarizes the content of the message. If you decide to include a subject line, it should make sense but should not be a complete sentence; it is not followed by a period.

The first sentence of a business letter that requests or delivers information should begin directly with the main idea. If you are asking for information, use one of two approaches. Ask the most important question first, such as *Do you have a two-bedroom cottage on Devil's Lake available for the week of July 8–15?* A second approach involves beginning with a summary statement, such as *Please answer the following questions regarding. . . .* If the letter delivers information, begin with the most important information first, such as *Yes, we have a two-bedroom cottage on Devil's Lake available for. . . .* or *Here is the information you requested regarding. . . .* Most informational business letters should NOT begin with an explanation of why the letter is being written.

Body. The body of the letter provides explanations and additional information to clarify the first sentence. Use a separate paragraph for each new idea, being careful to strive for concise writing. If the message lends itself to enumeration, express the items in a bulleted or numbered list. Be certain, of course, to construct the list so that each item is parallel.

Think about the individual reading your message. Will that person understand what you are saying? Have you included enough information? What may seem clear to you may not be so evident to your reader. In responding to requests, don't hesitate to include more information than was requested—if you feel it would be helpful. Maintain a friendly, conversational, and positive tone.

Closing. Business letters that demand action should conclude with a specific request, including end dating if appropriate. That is, tell the reader when you would like the request complied with, and, if possible, provide a reason (for example, *Please send me this information by June 1 so that I can arrange my vacation*).

Letters that provide information may end with a summary statement or a pleasant, forward-looking thought (for example, *We are happy to provide this information to help you plan your summer vacation*). Business organizations may also use the closing to promote products or services. Avoid ending your letters with mechanical phrases such as *If I can be of further service, don't hesitate to call on me,* or *Thanks for any information you can provide.* Find a fresh way to express your desire to be of service or to show appreciation.

Figure 5.1 illustrates the application of the writing plan to an information request. Notice that the subject line summarizes the main topic of the letter, while the first paragraph provides more information about the reason for writing. The body of the letter explains the main idea and includes a list of questions so that the reader can see quickly what information is being requested. The closing includes an end date with a reason.

Figure 5.1
Information Request

GraphicPros

264 South Halsted Street
Chicago Heights, IL 60412
FAX (708) 345-2210   VOICE (708) 345-8329   WEB: http://www.graphicpros.com

March 5, 201x

Ms. Kesha Scott
Micro Supplies and Software
P. O. Box 800
Fort Atkinson, WI 53538-2900

Dear Ms. Scott:

Subject: Availability and Price of Equipment Security Devices ● —————— **Summarizes main idea**

Please provide information and recommendations regarding security equipment ● —————— **Introduces purpose immediately**
to prevent the theft of office computers, keyboards, monitors, faxes, and printers.

Our office now has 18 computer workstations and 6 printers that we must secure ● —————— **Explains need for information**
to desks or counters. Answers to the following questions will help us select the
best devices for our purpose.

1. What device would you recommend that can secure a workstation con-
    sisting of a computer, monitor, and keyboard?

2. What expertise and equipment are required to install and remove the   **Groups open-ended**
    security device?   **questions into list for**
                                                                               quick comprehension
3. How much is each device? Do you offer quantity discounts, and, if so,   **and best feedback**
    how much?

Because our insurance rates will be increased if the security devices are not ● —————— **Courteously provides an**
installed before May 12, we would appreciate your response by March 20.   **end date and reason**

Sincerely

Brent R. Barnwell
Brent R. Barnwell
Office Manager

Skill Check 5.2 Reviewing the Writing Plan

In the space provided, write *a, b,* or *c* to identify the letter part where each of the
following might logically be found.

a. Opening   b. Body   c. Closing

1. Explanation and details   _____

2. Subject line that summarizes main idea   _____

3. End date with reason   _____

4. Numbered or bulleted list   _____

5. Main idea   _____

6. Summary statement or forward-looking thought   _____

Writing Application 5.1

Revise the following poorly written letter. Use block style (every line starts at the left margin) and mixed punctuation. This is a personal business letter; follow the format shown in Appendix C. Remember that the following letter is poorly written. Improve it!

1435 Sunrise Circle
Upland, CA 91786
Current date

Ms. Barbara L. Hernandez
Manager, Rainbow Resort
1102 West Brannan Island Road
Isleton, CA 95641-1102

Dear Ms. Hernandez:

I saw an advertisement recently in *Sunset* magazine where Rainbow Resort rents houseboats. My family and I (there are three kids and my wife and me) would like to take a vacation on a houseboat from July 17 through July 24 in the California Delta area. We have never done this before, but it sounds interesting.

Please send me any information you may have. I will have to make my vacation plans soon.

I have no idea how much this might cost. If we rent a houseboat, we want to know do you provide bedding, dishes, pots and pans, and the like? I am wondering about navigating a houseboat. Will we have to take a course or training on how to operate it? It may be too difficult for us to operate. How far can we travel in the Delta area in one of your houseboats? What if we decide to stay on more than one week? I actually have two weeks of vacation, but we may want to travel in our RV part of the time. Does insurance come with the rental fee? Our kids want to know if it has TV.

Yours,

Leslie E. Childers

Writing Application 5.2

Assume you are Barbara Hernandez. Write a response to Mr. Childers' letter. Use block style and mixed punctuation. Tell Mr. Childers that the rental fee, which is $175 per day or $1,000 per week, does include insurance. You have a houseboat available for July 17–24, but definite reservations must be made for that time and for the week following, if Mr. Childers decides to stay two weeks. Your houseboats can travel about 100 miles on the inland waterways of the Delta. Rainbow Resort provides bedding, dishes, and kitchenware. Yes, each houseboat has a TV set. You also provide an AM/FM radio and a CD player. Your houseboats accommodate four to ten people, and you require a deposit of $500 for a one-week reservation. Reservations must be received by June 1 to ensure a July vacation. Your houseboats are easy to operate. No special training is required, but you do give each operator about 30 minutes of instruction. Send Mr. Childers a brochure describing Rainbow Resort and the memorable holiday he and his family can enjoy. The scenery and attractions are good.

Writing Application 5.3

Write a personal business letter in response to the following problem. For your home office you ordered a VoIP phone system called the Plantronics Calisto Pro Series DECT 6.0. This hands-free system comes with a Bluetooth headset that allows you to answer your landline, mobile, and VoIP phone calls with one device. It had many other attractive features, and you were eager to try it. When the system arrived, however, you followed all installation instructions and discovered that an irritating static sound interfered with every telephone call you made or received. You don't know what is causing the static, but the product description promised the following: "Thanks to the system's superior noise-canceling Bluetooth headset with extended mouthpiece, you will always sound professional. The Calisto Pro phone operates on DECT 6.0 frequency, which means that call clarity is not affected by Wi-Fi networks or home appliances, such as the microwave, and you can roam up to 300 feet from the base without suffering any degradation in sound quality."

Because you need a clear signal for your business, you returned the VoIP phone system January 15 by UPS Next Business Day shipping service to ElectroWare, Inc., the Web-based supplier from whom you purchased the system. You still have a copy of the invoice, which states that merchandise may be returned for any reason within 30 days after purchase. You also have the UPS receipt proving that you returned it. However, your Visa statement (No. 5390-3390-2219-0002) has not shown a credit for the return. Your last two statements show no credit for $249.95. You are wondering what happened. Did ElectroWare receive the returned VoIP phone system? Why hasn't your account been credited? If ElectroWare did not receive the shipment, you want UPS to trace it. Write to ElectroWare, Inc., 22121 Crystal Creek Boulevard, Bothell, Washington 98201-2212. You have complied with their instructions regarding returning merchandise, and you want them to credit your account. You do not want another VoIP phone system from ElectroWare. Be sure to open your letter with a direct request for the action you want taken.

Unit 6

Writing With Style

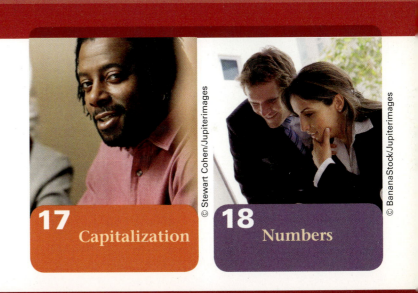

"There is no rule on how to write. Sometimes it comes easily and perfectly; sometimes it's like drilling rock and then blasting it out with charges."

**—Ernest Hemingway,
American writer**

Chapter 17

Capitalization

OBJECTIVES

When you have completed the materials in this chapter, you will be able to do the following:

LEVEL 1
- Properly capitalize sentence beginnings, the pronoun *I*, proper nouns, and proper adjectives.
- Determine when to capitalize geographic locations, organization names, academic courses and degrees, and seasons.

LEVEL 2
- Understand how to capitalize business correspondence components and personal titles.
- Correctly capitalize numbered and lettered items; points of the compass; departments, divisions, offices, agencies, and committees; government terms; product names; and published and artistic titles.

LEVEL 3
- Capitalize beginning words; celestial bodies; ethnic, cultural, language, and religious references; and words following *marked* and *stamped*.
- Apply special rules in capitalizing personal titles and terms.

Pretest

Use proofreading marks to show any letters that should be capitalized in the following sentences. See the inside back cover for a list of proofreading symbols.

1. Did you receive the spanish translation of the book *the panic of 1907* that i sent you?

2. Subject: sales meeting next thursday

3. the week before mother's day is the busiest time for the united states postal service.

4. The securities and exchange commission will meet at trump tower in new york city on april 29 to discuss requirements for using plain english in proxy statements.

5. Last spring father traveled to the midwest to visit his mother in des moines, iowa.

6. After receiving a master's degree from the university of rhode island, cerise became director of the merchant services department in the corporate offices of bank of america.

7. Our company president and vice president met with several supervisors on the west coast to discuss how to compete against google's new online offerings.

8. The internal revenue service requires corporations to complete form 1120 before the april 15 deadline.

9. Jim Baldwin will fly to the east coast on united airlines so that he can run in the boston marathon.

10. Tennessee is called the volunteer state because of the record number of volunteers the state provided during the war of 1812 and the mexican war.

One difficult thing about writing is learning the rules that will help you write with style. In this chapter you will learn the rules of capitalization. Rules governing capitalization reflect conventional practices; that is, they have been established by custom and usage. By following these conventions, a writer tells a reader, among other things, what words are important. In earlier times writers capitalized most nouns and many adjectives at will; few conventions of capitalization or punctuation were consistently observed. Today most capitalization follows definite rules that are fully accepted and practiced at all times. Dictionaries are helpful in determining capitalization practices, but they do not show all capitalized words. To develop skill in controlling capitals, study the rules and examples in this chapter.

Trivia Tidbit

Some languages don't have capital letters, including Hebrew, Arabic, Korean, Thai, Japanese, and Chinese.

1. Spanish *The Panic* I 2. Sales Meeting Next Thursday 3. The Mother's Day United States Postal Service 4. Securities Exchange Commission Trump Tower New York City April English 5. Father Midwest Des Moines Iowa 6. University Rhode Island Cerise Merchant Services Department Bank America 7. West Coast Google's 8. Internal Revenue Service Form April 9. East Coast United Airlines Boston Marathon 10. The Volunteer State War Mexican War

Basic Rules of Capitalization

Beginning of a Sentence

Capitalize the first letter of a word beginning a sentence.

> Since it was founded in 1910, the Boy Scouts of America has taught more than 10 million members how to be conservation minded.

> Boy Scout troops around the country collect recyclables and e-waste, build trails, restore streams, and plant trees.

The Pronoun *I*

Capitalize the pronoun *I*, no matter where it appears or how it is used in a sentence.

> If *I* were you, *I'd* continue my education.

> If you give me a chance, *I'm* sure *I* could change your mind.

Proper Nouns

Capitalize proper nouns, including the *specific* names of persons, places, schools, streets, parks, buildings, holidays, events, months, days, nicknames, agreements, Web sites, software programs, historical periods, and so forth. Do *not* capitalize common nouns that make *general* reference.

Proper Nouns	Common Nouns
Barbara Walters	the first female news anchor
Mexico, Canada	neighboring countries of the United States
University of Virginia, Northgate High School	a university and a high school
Abbey Road, Baker Street	famous streets in London
Fenway Park, Wrigley Field	legendary baseball parks
Chrysler Building, Empire State Building	famous buildings in New York City
Veterans Day, New Year's Day	two holidays
Boston Marathon, World Series, World Cup	well-known sporting events
January, February, March	first three months of the year
Saturday, Sunday	weekend days
the Big Apple, the Peach State	city and state nicknames
European Union	an agreement among several countries
Wikipedia, Google, Facebook	popular Web sites
PowerPoint, QuickBooks, Photoshop	software programs
Great Depression, Digital Age	periods of time
U.S. Postal Service	a trip to the post office

Trivia Tidbit

English is the only language in which the first-person singular pronoun (*I*) is capitalized. For example, in Italian (*io*) and French (*je*), the first-person pronoun is capitalized only if it appears at the beginning of a sentence. In some languages, such as German, the second-person pronoun *you* is capitalized.

Career Tip

Many large companies publish style manuals showing their preferred capitalization and the spelling of frequently used terms. One of the first tasks of a new employee is becoming familiar with the company style manual.

Trivia Tidbit

Months and days of the week are not capitalized in all languages. These are some of the languages that do not capitalize months or days: Dutch, Finnish, French, Hungarian, Italian, Polish, Russian, Spanish, Swedish, and Vietnamese.

Redwood Room, Clift Hotel	a room in the hotel
Golden Gate Bridge, Brooklyn Bridge	bridges over bodies of water
Supreme Court, Senate	components of government

Proper Adjectives

Capitalize most adjectives that are derived from proper nouns.

American politics	Swiss watch
Renaissance art	British rock
Freudian slip	Jamaican dollar
Keynesian economics	Internet access

Study Tip

Most proper nouns retain their capital letters when they become adjectives—for example, French toast, Russian roulette, Persian cat, Spanish moss, Italian marble, and Swedish massage.

Do not capitalize those adjectives originally derived from proper nouns that have become common adjectives (without capitals) through usage. Consult your dictionary when in doubt.

plaster of paris	venetian blinds
french fries	china dishes
chauvinist	diesel engine
monarch butterfly	roman numerals

Geographic Locations

Capitalize the names of *specific* places such as continents, countries, states, cities, counties, mountains, valleys, lakes, rivers, seas, oceans, geographic regions, and neighborhoods. Capitalize *county* and *state* when they follow proper nouns.

South America, Asia, Europe	Lake Louise, Lake Tahoe
Chile, Taiwan, Hungary	Snake River, Mississippi River
Maine, Arizona, New York State	Sea of Cortez, Mediterranean Sea
Bangor, Phoenix, Syracuse	Arctic Ocean, Pacific Ocean
Broward County, Cook County	Pacific Northwest, Texas Panhandle
Mount Everest, Rocky Mountains	European Community (EC)
Yosemite Valley, Shenandoah Valley	Upper West Side, Chinatown

Do not capitalize the words *city, state,* or *county* when they precede geographic locations unless they are part of the official geographical name or unless they are used by a governing body as part of an official name.

I spent two weeks in the *city* of Chicago. (*City* is not part of geographical name.)

In the *City of Industry* is a McDonald's restaurant that is used strictly for filming movies and commercials. (*City* is part of geographical name.)

Monica plans to attend college in the *state* of Wisconsin. (*State* is used generically.)

The Web site for the *State* of Wisconsin lists statewide job openings. (*State* is used by a governing body as part of its official name.)

Organization Names

Capitalize the principal words in the names of all business, civic, educational, government, labor, military, philanthropic, political, professional, religious, sports, and social organizations. Capitalize *the* only when it is part of an organization's official name (such as *The Coca-Cola Company* and *The World Bank*). In organization names, articles (*a, an, the*), short conjunctions (*and, but, or, nor*), prepositions that have two or three letters (*of, in, on, for, to*), the word *to* in infinitives, and the word *as* are not capitalized unless they are the first or last word in the organization name.

Genentech	Chamber of Commerce
Pepperdine University	Securities and Exchange Commission
United Farm Workers of America	United States Marine Corps
Habitat for Humanity	Green Party
American Medical Association	Knights of Columbus
National Football League	Alpha Omicron Pi

Generally, do NOT capitalize *committee, company, association, board,* and other shortened name forms when they are used to replace full organization names. If these shortened names, however, are preceded by the word *the* and are used in formal or legal documents (contracts, bylaws, minutes), they may be capitalized.

Does the *company* offer tuition reimbursement benefits? (Informal document)

The Treasurer of the *Association* is herein authorized to disburse funds. (Formal document)

Academic Courses and Degrees

Study Tip

Course titles with numbers are capitalized (*Marketing 101*) because they refer to specific courses. Those without numbers usually are not capitalized (*marketing*).

Capitalize the names of numbered courses and specific course titles. Do not capitalize the names of academic subject areas unless they contain a proper noun.

Marina took Accounting 186, English 122, and Management 120 last semester.

Marina excelled in her accounting, English, and business management courses last semester.

All finance majors must take business English and business law courses.

Capitalize abbreviations of academic degrees whether they stand alone or follow individuals' names. Do not capitalize general references to degrees unless they are used after and in conjunction with an individual's name.

Jan Sophianopoulos earned AA, BA, and MS degrees before her thirtieth birthday. (Associate of Arts, Bachelor of Arts, and Master of Science degrees)

Patrick Couglin, JD, gave his opening statement in court this morning. (Juris Doctor)

Matthew hopes to earn bachelor's and master's degrees in business administration. (General reference to degrees and major)

Elizabeth Wyman, Doctor of Engineering, served as a consultant on the project.

Seasons

Do not capitalize seasons unless they are combined with a year.

> Our annual sales meeting is held each spring.
>
> Lynn Spiesel will begin working on her master's degree during the Fall 2011 semester.

Now complete the reinforcement exercises for Level 1.

LEVEL 2

Special Rules of Capitalization
Business Correspondence Components

Capitalize the first word of certain business correspondence components that are included in letters, memos, and e-mail messages. In subject lines do NOT capitalize articles (*a, an, the*), conjunctions (*and, but, or, nor*), and prepositions with three or fewer letters (*in, to, by, for*) unless they appear at the beginning or end of the subject line.

Study Tip

Capitalize only the first word in a salutation (*My dear Ms. Jones*) or in a complimentary close (*Very truly yours*).

> **SUBJECT:** Monthly Sales Meeting on June 9 (Capitalize the first letter of all primary words in a subject line; an alternative is to type the subject line in all capital letters.)
>
> Dear Mr. Hemingway: (Capitalize the first word and all nouns in a *salutation*.)
>
> Sincerely, (Capitalize the first word of a *complimentary close*.)

Titles of People

Many rules exist for capitalizing personal and professional titles of people.

Titles Preceding Names

Capitalize courtesy titles (such as *Mr., Mrs., Ms., Miss,* and *Dr.*) when they precede names. Also capitalize titles representing a person's profession, company position, military rank, religious station, political office, family relationship, or nobility when the title precedes the name and replaces a courtesy title.

Career Tip

Find a job you love, and you will never have to work a day in your life.

> The staff greeted *Mr. and Mrs.* Gary Smith. (Courtesy titles)
>
> Speakers included *Professor* Franco Guidone and *Dr.* Rebecca Alex. (Professional titles)
>
> Sales figures were submitted by *Budget Director* Magee and *Vice President* Anderson. (Company titles)
>
> Will *Major General* Donald M. Franklin assume command? (Military titles)
>
> Discussing the issue are *Rabbi* Isaac Elchanan, *Archbishop* Jean-Pierre Ricard, and *Reverend* Cecil Williams. (Religious titles)
>
> We expect *President* Barack Obama to meet with *Prime Minister* Gordon Brown. (Political titles)
>
> Only *Aunt* Brenda and *Uncle* Skip had been to Alaska. (Family relationship)
>
> Onlookers waited for *Prince* Charles and *Queen* Elizabeth to arrive. (Nobility)

Titles Followed by Appositives

Do not capitalize a person's title—professional, business, military, religious, political, family, or one related to nobility—when the title is followed by the person's name used as an appositive. You will recall that **appositives** rename or explain previously mentioned nouns or pronouns.

> Only one *professor*, Judith Myers, was available to serve as club advisor.
>
> University employees asked their *president*, Judy Walters, to help raise funds.
>
> Reva Hillman discovered that her *uncle*, Paul M. Hillman, had named her as his heir.

Titles or Offices Following Names

Do not capitalize titles or offices following names unless they appear in a displayed list.

> Stewart Butterfield, *president* of Flickr.com, met with Mary Williams, *vice president* of Research and Development, to discuss new photo-sharing technology.
>
> After repeated requests, Kay Carver, *supervisor*, Document Services, announced extended hours.
>
> Barack Obama, *president* of the United States, conferred with Hillary Clinton, *secretary of state*.
>
> John Roberts, *chief justice* of the U.S. Supreme Court, promised a ruling in October.
>
> The following *employees* will represent Sun Microsystems at this year's Emerging Technology Conference (ETech):
>
> > Peter Norvig, *Director of Research*
> >
> > Radia Perlman, *Software Designer*
> >
> > Tim Bray, *Director of Web Technologies*

Titles or Offices Replacing Names

Generally, do not capitalize a title or office that replaces a person's name. However, if using a title in direct address (speaking directly to a person), capitalize the title if it replaces the name.

> Neither the *president* nor the *general counsel* of the company could be reached for comment.
>
> An ambitious five-year plan was developed by the *director of marketing* and the *sales manager*.
>
> The *president* conferred with the *joint chiefs of staff* and the *secretary of defense*.
>
> At the reception the *mayor* of Providence spoke with the *governor* of Alaska.
>
> What do you think I can do, *Professor*, to improve my grade? (Direct address)

Titles in Business Correspondence

Capitalize titles in addresses and closing lines of business correspondence.

> Ms. Chrisanne Knox
> Director of Marketing and Communications
> Diablo Valley College
> 321 Golf Club Road
> Pleasant Hill, CA 94523

> Very sincerely yours,
>
> Stephen Finton
> Comptroller

Family Titles

Do not capitalize family titles used with possessive pronouns or possessive nouns.

> We are meeting my *sister* and Victoria's *mom* for lunch at The Cheesecake Factory.

> Did you hear that his *father* met Adam's *cousin* at the sales conference?

But do capitalize titles of close relatives when they are used without pronouns.

> Please call *Father* and *Uncle* Joe immediately.

> What do you think about my decision, *Mom?*

Numbered and Lettered Items

Capitalize nouns followed by numbers or letters except in *page, paragraph, line, size, verse,* and *vitamin* references.

> United Flight 0889 to Beijing will depart from Gate B32.

> Take Exit 12 off State Highway 5 and follow the signs to Building I-63-B.

> Volume II, Appendix A, contains a copy of Medicare Form 72T. Instructions are on page 6, line 12.

> Taking vitamin C daily can help protect against immune system deficiencies and cardiovascular disease.

Points of the Compass

Capitalize *north, south, east, west,* and other points of a compass when they represent *specific* regions.

Study Tip

A clue to the capitalization of a region is the use of *the* preceding it: *the East Coast, the West, the Pacific Northwest.*

the Middle East, the Far East	the Midwest, the Southeast
the East Coast, the West Coast	the Pacific Northwest
Northern and Southern Hemispheres	Easterners, Southerners

Do not capitalize the points of the compass when they are used in directions or in general references.

> To find the conference facility, drive *south* on Highway 1 and turn *east* on Roswell Road.

> Mickey Todd will cover the territory consisting of all states *west* of the Mississippi River.

> The *southern* part of California is prone to wildfires.

Departments, Divisions, Offices, Agencies, and Committees

Capitalize the principal words in the official names of divisions, departments, offices, government agencies, and committees. Also capitalize the main words in the names of schools or colleges within universities. When a department or division is referred to by its function because the official name is unknown, do not capitalize this reference. Outside your organization capitalize only *specific* department, division, or committee names.

Contact our Client Support Department for more information. (Specific department)

Miguel Zuliani works with the International Division of Apple. (Specific division)

The Office of Thrift Supervision regulates the savings and loan industry. (Specific office)

The nation's unemployment rate is calculated by the Bureau of Labor Statistics. (Specific government agency)

Howard Berman chairs the Committee on Foreign Affairs. (Specific committee)

The Marshall School of Business at the University of Southern California offers a virtual electronic library. (School within a university)

I will be sending my résumé to the human resources departments of several companies. (Unofficial or unknown department name)

A steering committee has not yet been named. (Unofficial or unknown name)

Government Terms

Do not capitalize the words *federal, government, nation,* or *state* unless they are part of a specific title.

Neither the state government nor the federal government would fund the proposal.

The Department of Labor administers a variety of federal labor laws that apply to employees in all the states.

The president should do everything possible to uphold our nation's values.

Product Names

Capitalize product names only when they represent specific brand names or trademarks of products. Except in advertising, common names following manufacturers' names are not capitalized. Also note that all words capitalized in the list below are protected trademarks and should, therefore, not be used generically.

Coca-Cola	ChapStick lip balm	Band-Aid
Kleenex tissues	Dumpster waste receptacle	Saran Wrap
Jet Ski	Post-It notes	Scotch tape
Gap jeans	Styrofoam cup	Starbucks coffee
Xerox copier	Apple computer	Chrysler Jeep
Q-tip swab	Ace bandage	Excel spreadsheet

Published and Artistic Titles

Capitalize the main words in the titles of books, magazines, newspapers, articles, movies, plays, albums, songs, poems, Web sites, and reports. Do *not* capitalize articles (*a, an, the*), conjunctions (*and, but, or, nor*), and prepositions with three or fewer letters (*in, to, by, for*) unless they begin or end the title. The word *to* in infinitives (*to run, to say, to write*) and the word *as* are also not capitalized unless they appear as the first word of a title or subtitle.

Remember that the titles of published works that contain subdivisions (such as books, magazines, pamphlets, newspapers, TV series, plays, albums, and musicals) are italicized or underscored. Titles of literary or artistic works without subdivisions (such as chapters, newspaper articles, magazine articles, songs, poems, and episodes in a TV series) are placed in quotation marks.

> Roger Fisher's *Getting to Yes: Negotiating Agreement Without Giving In* (Book)
>
> "China Looms Large in India's Election" appearing in *BusinessWeek* (Article in magazine)
>
> *The Wall Street Journal* (Newspaper)
>
> *Late Night With David Letterman* (TV series)
>
> *Life Is Beautiful* (Movie)
>
> Bob Dylan's "When the Ship Comes In" on *The Times They Are A-Changin'* (Song and album)
>
> "Ask the Career Doctor," a link at Quintessential Careers (Link at a Web site)

Now complete the reinforcement exercises for Level 2.

LEVEL 3

Additional Rules of Capitalization

Beginning Words

In addition to capitalizing the first word of a complete sentence, capitalize the first words in quoted sentences, independent phrases, enumerated items, and formal rules or principles following colons.

> Dale Carnegie said, "Most of the important things in the world have been accomplished by people who have kept on trying when there seemed to be no hope at all." (Quoted sentence)
>
> No, not at the present time. (Independent phrase)
>
> Follow these steps to apply for a student visa:
>
> 1. Complete the visa application for the appropriate country.
> 2. Gather required information and arrange for application fee.
> 3. Submit your application in person prior to traveling to the country. (Enumerated items)
>
> Our office manager repeated his favorite rule: Treat the customer as you would like to be treated. (Rule following colon)

Celestial Bodies

Capitalize the names of **celestial bodies** including planets, planet satellites, stars, constellations, and asteroids. Do not capitalize the terms *earth, sun*, or *moon* unless they are used as the names of specific bodies in the solar system.

> Why on earth did you vote against the resolution?
>
> The planets closest to the Sun are Mercury, Mars, and Earth.
>
> It is best to avoid extended exposure to the sun.

Ethnic, Cultural, Language, and Religious References

Terms that relate to a particular culture, language, race, or religion are capitalized.

> In Hawaii, Asian and Western cultures merge.
>
> Both English and Hebrew are spoken by Jews in Israel.
>
> Native Americans and Latinos turned out to support their candidates.

Hyphenate terms such as *African-American* and *French-Canadian* when they are used as adjectives (*African-American collection* or *French-Canadian citizens*). Do not hyphenate these terms when they are nouns.

> Asian-American communities can be found in almost every major U.S. city.
>
> Many Asian Americans place great value on higher education.

Words Following *marked* and *stamped*

Capitalize words that follow the words *marked* and *stamped*.

> Although the package was stamped "Fragile," the postal carrier threw it into the back of the truck.
>
> The check came back marked "Insufficient Funds."

Special Uses of Personal Titles and Terms

Generally, titles are capitalized according to the specifications set forth earlier. However, when a title of an official appears in that organization's minutes, bylaws, or other official documents, it is capitalized.

> The Controller will have authority over departmental budgets. (Title appearing in bylaws)
>
> By vote of the stockholders, the President is empowered to declare a stock dividend. (Title appearing in annual report)

When the terms *ex, elect, late,* and *former* are used with capitalized titles, they are not capitalized.

> We went to hear ex-President Carter and Mayor-elect Brown speak at the symposium.
>
> The late President Kennedy has been honored with a library and museum in Boston.
>
> We just learned that former President Bush will speak on campus next month.

Now complete the reinforcement exercises for Level 3.

Spot the BLOOPER

Using the skills you are learning in this class, try to identify why the following items are bloopers. Consult your textbook, dictionary, or reference manual as needed.

Blooper 1: From the *Miami Herald*: "[The cable industry's] reputation proceeds them and it has for years."

Blooper 2: From an advertisement in *The New Yorker*: "Safer than any car Volvo's ever built."

Blooper 3: From a Wendy's International poster: "Be Cool in School! Good Grades Has Its Rewards!"

Blooper 4: Billboard outside a Niagara Falls fast-food restaurant: "We have men in black toys." [Would capital letters have changed the meaning of this sentence?]

Blooper 5: From the *Minnesota Daily*: "The *Daily* is having it's annual Spring Awards Banquet, in order to attend you must purchase tickets through our web link." [Did you spot three errors?]

Blooper 6: ABC News anchor Charlie Gibson: "What makes a presidential candidate lose their cool?"

Blooper 7: From an Associated Press (AP) article: "It would take a person spending $1 million per day, everyday, the next 169 years to spend as much money as AIG lost during the fourth quarter, which lasted just 92 days."

Blooper 8: Headline in *The Washington Times*: "Threat of espionage hinder Paris air show."

Blooper 9: Photo caption in the *Los Angeles Times*: "Presidential hopeful John Edwards unveils his plan to regulate coal-burning power plants while in San Francisco."

Blooper 10: From a gossip column in the *Atlanta Journal-Constitution*: "While in town, Demi Moore and Ashton Kutcher were over scene at the Falcons-Saints game Sunday."

FAQs

Answered by Dr. Guffey and Professor Seefer

Dr. Guffey   Professor Seefer

Question	Answer
Q: I'm having trouble not capitalizing *president* when it refers to the president of the United States. It used to be capitalized. Why isn't it now?	**A:** For some time the trend has been away from "upstyle" capitalization. Fewer words are capitalized. Our two principal authorities (*Merriam-Webster's Collegiate Dictionary* and *The Chicago Manual of Style*) both recommend lowercase for *president of the United States*. In addition, many publications, including *The New York Times*, capitalize the word *president* only when it's used as a title with a last name (*President Obama*). However, other authorities maintain that the term should always be capitalized because of high regard for the office.
Q: I don't know how to describe the copies made from our copy machine. Should I call them *Xerox* copies or something else?	**A:** They are *Xerox* copies only if made on a Xerox copier. Copies made on other machines may be called *xerographic* copies, *machine* copies, *photocopies,* or *copies*.
Q: In the doctor's office where I work, I see the word *medicine* capitalized, as in *the field of Medicine*. Is this correct?	**A:** No. General references should not be capitalized. If it were part of a title, as in the Northwestern College of *Medicine*, it would be capitalized.
Q: I'm writing a paper for my biology class on *in vitro fertilization*. Since this is a medical term, shouldn't I capitalize it?	**A:** Don't capitalize medical procedures or diseases unless they are named after individuals (*Tourette's syndrome*). *In vitro* means "outside the living body." Specialists in the field use the abbreviation *IVF* after the first introduction of the term.
Q: I work for a state agency, and I'm not sure what to capitalize or hyphenate in this sentence: *State agencies must make forms available to non-English-speaking applicants*.	**A:** Words with the prefix *non* are usually not hyphenated (*nonexistent, nontoxic*). But when *non* is joined to a word that must be capitalized, it is followed by a hyphen. Because the word *speaking* combines with *English* to form a single-unit adjective, it should be hyphenated. Thus, the expression should be typed *non-English-speaking applicants*.
Q: When we use a person's title, such as *business manager*, in place of a person's name, shouldn't the title always be capitalized?	**A:** No. Business titles are capitalized only when they precede an individual's name, as in *Business Manager Smith*. Do not capitalize titles when they replace an individual's name: *Our business manager will direct the transaction*.

Question	Answer

Q: How do you spell *marshal*, as used in *the Grand Marshal of the Rose Parade*?

A: The preferred spelling is with a single *l*: *marshal*. In addition to describing an individual who directs a ceremony, the noun *marshal* refers to a high military officer or a city law officer who carries out court orders (*the marshal served papers on the defendant*). As a verb, *marshal* means "to bring together" or "to order in an effective way" (*the attorney marshaled convincing arguments*). The similar-sounding word *martial* is an adjective and means "warlike" or "military" (*martial law was declared after the riot*). You'll probably need a dictionary to keep those words straight!

Q: My boss has just placed me in charge of editing a new company newsletter, which will be published bimonthly. I hate to admit it, but I was afraid to ask my boss what *bimonthly* means. Does this mean that the newsletter will come out twice a month? That's a lot of work!

A: You can relax! *Bimonthly* means that your company newsletter will be published every other month. If your boss had said the newsletter would be published *semimonthly*, you would have been editing two newsletters every month. The same applies to the words *biweekly* (every other week) and *semiweekly* (twice a week).

Q: How can I keep the words *advice* and *advise* straight? I can never decide which one to use.

A: It's best to remember that *advice* is a noun meaning "a suggestion or recommendation" (*She went to her attorney for tax advice*). The word *advise* is a verb meaning "to counsel or recommend" (*Her attorney advised her to open an IRA*).

Q: Lately I've noticed odd capitalization in some company and product names. For example, is the online auction site written as *EBay*, *eBay*, or *Ebay*? How can I ever keep these company names straight?

A: The correct way to write this company name is *eBay*. And you're absolutely right that it can be difficult to keep company and product names straight when they use unusual capitalization. Other examples include PowerPoint, QuickBooks, iPhone, iPod, BlackBerry, TurboCAD, ConocoPhillips, DuPont, FedEx, ExxonMobil, FreeWave Technologies, PayPal, iRobot, MasterCard, NetZero, PeopleSoft, i-flex Solutions, PepsiCo, SkyWest Airlines, TheStreet.com, MySpace, and UTStarcom. To make things even more confusing, just because a company or product sounds like two separate words, don't assume that each word is capitalized. For example, these products and companies capitalize the first letter only: Photoshop, Lucasfilm, Amtrak, Autodesk, Citigroup, Ecolab, Facebook, Kmart Corporation, Craigslist, and Sun Microsystems. To ensure that you are writing product and company names correctly, check the official Web site for the company or product.

17

Reinforcement Exercises

LEVEL 1

Online Homework Help! For immediate feedback on odd-numbered items, go to **www.meguffey.com.**

 A. (Self-check) In the following sentences, use standard proofreading marks to correct errors you find in capitalization. Use three short lines (≡) under a lowercase letter to indicate that it is to be changed to a capital letter. Draw a diagonal (/) through a capital letter you wish to change to a lowercase letter. Indicate at the right the total number of changes you have made in each sentence.

Example: The Bandit Henry McCarthy was also known as Billy the kid.   2

1. The entire Staff is invited to attend a special Seminar on monday, june 4. _____

2. Born in new jersey, herb kelleher, former CEO of southwest airlines, grew up in the State of texas. _____

3. Starbucks ensures high standards by training its Baristas in Coffee preparation techniques and Customer Service. _____

4. In the Fall i plan to begin my Master's Degree in Marketing at golden gate university. _____

5. Sondra uses comcast for her internet access at home. _____

6. Pelee island is located on the canadian side of lake erie. _____

7. Regulations of the sarbanes-oxley act of 2002 resulted in costly expenses for our Company. _____

8. Salt lake city, in the State of Utah, was founded by Brigham Young and a small Party of Mormons in 1847. _____

9. To this day, AT&T remains a dominant force in the Telecommunications industry. _____

10. The boston marathon is an annual Sporting Event hosted by the City of Boston, Massachusetts, on patriot's day, the third Monday of April. _____

Check your answers below.

 B. Use proofreading marks to correct any capitalization errors in these sentences. Indicate the total number of changes at the right. If no changes are needed, write *0*.

1. Do you think i should apologize for the freudian slip i made during today's Meeting? _____

2. The Post Office doesn't deliver mail to Steven Stark's home in the City of Santa Maria, California, anymore. _____

3. Stark, who owns an internet company, now gets all his mail delivered Online. _____

1. (4) staff seminar Monday June 2. (8) New Jersey Herb Kelleher Southwest Airlines state Texas 3. (4) baristas coffee customer service 4. (8) fall I master's degree marketing Golden Gate University 5. (2) Comcast Internet 6. (4) Island Canadian Lake Erie 7. (4) Sarbanes-Oxley Act company 8. (4) Lake City state party 9. (1) telecommunications 10. (7) Boston Marathon sporting event city Patriot's Day

4. A company in beaverton, oregon, called earth class mail has developed Technology that makes digital mail possible. _____

5. People who receive digital mail worry about Mail Fraud and Identity Theft. _____

6. The united states postal service says that it isn't worried about the increasing popularity of Digital Mail. _____

7. The Jackson Family visited Florida during the Winter and soon learned why it is known as the sunshine state. _____

8. Kendra Hawkins was sent to our Kansas city branch office for the Months of april and may, but she hopes to return by Summer. _____

9. Our Company encourages Employees to earn Associate's and Bachelor's Degrees at nearby Colleges and Universities. _____

10. Nontraditional Students face the challenge of juggling full-time jobs while working on their Degrees. _____

11. All company representatives gathered in kansas city in the chouteau room of the hyatt regency crown center for the annual Spring sales meeting. _____

12. Work schedules will have to be adjusted in november for veterans day. _____

13. Last Fall Tish Young took out a policy with the prudential life insurance company. (The word *the* is part of the company name.) _____

14. The green bay packers won the first super bowl in 1967. _____

15. Professor Solis employed the socratic method of questioning students to elicit answers about Business Management. _____

16. After driving through New York state, we stayed in New York city and visited the Empire State building. _____

17. Matthew Simmons completed the requirements for a Master's Degree at ucla. _____

18. Members of the sierra club work hard to make sure that the endangered species act protects the Gray Wolf, which makes its home in the northern rockies. _____

19. His report on diesel engines contained many greek symbols in the Engineering equations. _____

20. The Hip-Hop Music mogul's customized lincoln navigator sported big wheels, satellite radio, three dvd players, six tv screens, a sony playstation 3, and vibrating front seats. _____

LEVEL 2

A. **(Self-check)** Use proofreading marks to correct errors you find in capitalization. Indicate at the right the total number of changes you make. If no changes are needed, write *0*.

Example: Project manager Karen O'Brien was promoted to Vice President. __3__

1. Martin Cooper, a General Manager of Motorola, created the first true Cell Phone. _____

2. General manager Cooper made his first call to his Rivals in AT&T's research and development department. (Assume this is the official name of this department.) _____

3. Mary Minnick, former Executive Vice President of the Coca-Cola company, also served as President of the Company's Marketing, Strategy, and Innovation Department. _____

4. Additional information on the features of our new Security Software is available on Page 41 in appendix B.

5. Both my Mother and my Sister purchased Dell Laptops as christmas gifts to themselves.

6. The Fishing Industry in the Pacific northwest is reeling from the impact of recent Federal regulations.

7. Our business manager and our executive vice president recently attended an e-business seminar in southern California.

8. My Uncle recommended that I read the article titled "The 100 best companies to work for."

9. Please send the order to Ms. Milagros Ojermark, manager, customer services, Atlas Fitness Equipment inc., 213 Summit Drive, Spokane, Washington 99201.

10. SUBJECT: new payroll processing procedure

Check your answers below.

B. Use proofreading marks to correct errors in the following sentences. Indicate the number of changes you make for each sentence.

1. A Federal Judge in san francisco ruled that Businesses must make their web sites accessible to the Blind.

2. All Government Agencies must also make their Sites accessible.

3. U.S. district judge Marilyn Hall Patel authorized a Class-Action Lawsuit against Target corporation for failure to make its site accessible.

4. Health minister Anbumani Ramadoss announced that India will become the first Country to ban images of smoking in all tv shows and new films.

5. My uncle Eduardo recently purchased a ford escape to use for his trip to the west coast this Summer.

6. Because brazil, australia, and argentina are located in the southern hemisphere, their Summers and Winters are the opposite of ours.

7. When the president, the secretary of state, and the secretary of labor traveled to minnesota, stringent security measures were put into place.

8. To locate the exact amount of Federal funding, look on Line 7, Page 6 of supplement no. 4.

9. Steve Chen, one of the Founders of YouTube, hurried to gate 16 to catch flight 263 to north Carolina.

10. My Father suggested that I read the book *The Seven Habits Of Highly Successful People.*

11. Send all inquiries in writing to Tom Fitzgerald, CEO, Lucky Brand Jeans corporation, 5233 Alcoa avenue, vernon, california 90058.

12. SUBJECT: new regulation in effect immediately.

13. Google was originally named googol; however, an Angel Investor made a check out to "Google, inc.," and this typo became the Company's name.

1. (4) general manager cell phone 2. (5) Manager rivals Research and Development Department 3. (6) executive vice president Company president company's 4. (4) security software page Appendix 5. (4) mother sister laptops Christmas 6. (4) fishing industry Northwest federal 7. (1) Southern 8. (5) uncle Best Companies to Work For 9. (4) manager Customer Services Inc. 10. (4) New Payroll Processing Procedure

14. Memorial Day is a Federal Holiday; therefore, Banks will be closed. _____

15. Franklin became an assistant to the administrator of the Governor Bacon Health center, which is operated by the department of health and social services in Delaware. _____

16. Many Cybercriminals use a fraudulent scheme known as "Phishing" to obtain personal information from Victims. _____

17. For lunch Ahmal ordered a big mac, french fries, and a coca-cola. _____

18. A midwesterner who enjoys sunshine, Mr. Franco travels South each Winter to vacation in Georgia. _____

19. Illy, a company founded in the Northern part of Italy during World war I, produces coffee made from pure arabica beans. _____

20. Please contact our customer service department to discuss a refund for your Apple Computer. _____

LEVEL 3

A. (Self-check) Use standard proofreading marks to indicate necessary changes. Write the total number of changes at the right.

Example: Mercury, venus, earth, and mars are dense and solid.　　3

1. Because the package was marked "fragile," the Mail Carrier handled it gently. _____

2. The guiding principle of capitalization is this: capitalize *specific* names and references, but do not capitalize *general* references. _____

3. In South America most Brazilians speak portuguese, most Surinamese speak dutch, and most Guyanese speak english. _____

4. The Late President Franklin D. Roosevelt, who served in Office during the great depression, is remembered for his policies aiding the recovery of the american economy. _____

5. The most common lies job seekers make on their Résumés are the following:
   1. inflated job titles
   2. false employment dates
   3. fake academic credentials _____

6. How on Earth do these job seekers think they will get away with it? _____

7. Money traders watched carefully the relation of the american dollar to the chinese yuan, the european euro, and the japanese yen. _____

8. The library of congress featured a collection of african-american writers. _____

9. David Crystal said, "texting may be using a new technology, but its linguistic processes are centuries old." _____

10. Our Organization's bylaws state the following: "The Secretary of the Association will submit an agenda two weeks before each meeting." _____

Check your answers below.

1. (3) "Fragile" mail carrier 2. (1) Capitalize 3. (3) Portuguese Dutch English 4. (5) late office Great Depression American 5. (4) résumé Inflated False Fake 6. (1) earth 7. (4) American Chinese European Japanese 8. (4) Library Congress African-American 9. (1) Texting 10. (1) organization's

B. Use proofreading marks to indicate necessary changes. Write the number of changes at the right.

1. Long considered the ninth Planet, pluto lost this classification in 2006. _____

2. Craig Merrigan said about the new ThinkPad, which is covered in hand-tooled leather, "it's the first computer that smells good." _____

3. As the Sun beat down on the crowd, Former vice president Dick Cheney continued his Graduation Address to the students of brigham young university in Utah. _____

4. Would you like a ride home? yes, thank you very much. _____

5. Warren Buffett, one of the World's greatest investors, says that everyday investors should follow this rule: never lose the money. _____

6. Terry noticed that the english spoken by asians in hong kong sounded more british than american. _____

7. Our accounting department should mark this Invoice "paid." _____

8. The Minutes of our last meeting contained the following statement: "the vice president acted on behalf of the president, who was attending a conference in the far East." _____

9. Our Office Manager always uses "Best Regards" as his complimentary close. _____

10. Futurists predict that these career fields will offer excellent opportunities in the next decade and beyond:
    1. cybersecurity
    2. forensic science
    3. genetic counseling
    4. geriatric care management
    5. health care technology
    6. homeland security
    7. life care planning _____

C. Review. Select *a* or *b* to indicate correct capitalization. Assume that each group of words is part of a complete sentence.

1. a. my physical therapist	b. my Physical Therapist	_____
2. a. the Golden Gate bridge	b. the Golden Gate Bridge	_____
3. a. awarded a Bachelor's degree	b. awarded a bachelor's degree	_____
4. a. courses in Farsi and anatomy	b. courses in farsi and anatomy	_____
5. a. the Redwood Room at the Clift Hotel	b. the redwood room at the Clift Hotel	_____
6. a. French fries and a pepsi-cola	b. french fries and a Pepsi-Cola	_____
7. a. a file marked "urgent"	b. a file marked "Urgent"	_____
8. a. a summer vacation	b. a Summer vacation	_____
9. a. the president's speech	b. the President's speech	_____
10. a. a Television show on PBS	b. a television show on PBS	_____
11. a. she and i will attend	b. she and I will attend	_____
12. a. Euclid Avenue in Cleveland	b. Euclid avenue in Cleveland	_____
13. a. on a Friday in July	b. on a friday in july	_____
14. a. conduct a google search	b. conduct a Google search	_____

15. a. SUBJECT: 2011 Annual Report Available   b. SUBJECT: 2011 annual report available   _____

16. a. a british rock band   b. a British rock band   _____

17. a. talking with my Mom and Dad   b. talking with my mom and dad   _____

18. a. visiting the City of Chicago   b. visiting the city of Chicago   _____

19. a. in the southern part of town   b. in the Southern part of town   _____

20. a. Starbucks Coffee   b. Starbucks coffee   _____

D. Writing Exercise. On a separate sheet write one or two paragraphs summarizing an article from a local newspaper. Choose an article with as many capital letters as possible. Apply the rules of capitalization you learned in this chapter.

E. FAQs About Business English Review. In the space provided, write the correct answer choice.

1. Please make a (a) xerox, (b) photocopy of the contract to send to Washington.   _____

2. We have made provisions for any (a) nonEnglish-speaking, (b) non-English-speaking candidate.   _____

3. He plans to pursue a career in the field of (a) economics, (b) Economics.   _____

4. Many people get a (a) Flu, (b) flu shot each year.   _____

5. The fire (a) marshal, (b) martial suspected that arson was involved in the fire.   _____

6. To prevent looting after the earthquake, officials declared (a) marshal, (b) martial law.   _____

7. Our e-mail newsletter is sent to customers (a) bimonthly, (b) semimonthly on the 15th and the last day of the month.   _____

8. Employees are paid (a) biweekly, (b) semiweekly, which means they get 26 paychecks a year.   _____

9. Brooke's counselor gave her good (a) advice, (b) advise about what courses to take.   _____

10. Our network administrator will (a) advice, (b) advise you about how often to change your password.   _____

Even if you read your local paper daily, breaking news happens all the time. As a business student, you should know how to keep up with the latest happenings. You know that many Web sites offer up-to-the-minute business news.

Goal: To keep up with business news online.

1. With your Web browser on the screen, go to Reuters, a highly respected global information company, at **http://www .reuters.com**. Click **BUSINESS & FINANCE** in the menu to the left of your screen.

2. Click on the link for a business news story that interests you.

3. Click **Print This Article** to print a copy of the article from this Web site; then read the article.

4. In a paragraph of three or four sentences, summarize the story. What did you learn about business from the story?

5. End your session. Submit your printouts and answers to the questions posed here.

▶▶ **Chat About It**

Your instructor may assign any of the following topics for you to discuss in class, in an online chat room, or on an online discussion board. Some of the discussion topics may require outside research. You may also be asked to read and respond to postings made by your classmates.

Discussion Topic 1: In this chapter you learned that the first-person singular pronoun *I* is capitalized; however, in other languages such as French and Italian, this same pronoun is not capitalized. Why do you think we capitalize this pronoun in English? Try doing research to find an answer. Share your thoughts and findings with your classmates.

Discussion Topic 2: The word *capitalize* comes from *capital*, meaning "head." The word *capital*, in all its uses (capital of a state or country, capital punishment, capitalism, capital letter), is associated with some sort of importance. Why do you think some words are capitalized in English and others are not? What do capitalized words communicate in our writing? Why do you think it is important to follow standard capitalization rules? Share your thoughts with your classmates.

Discussion Topic 3: Choose a language other than English and conduct research to find out what capitalization rules are used. What words are commonly capitalized? What pronouns are capitalized, if any? Does the language use capital letters at all? Share your findings with your classmates.

Discussion Topic 4: Many countries, especially in Europe, have a system similar to U.S. trademarks based on **geographical indications (GIs)**. Certain products can be identified only if they originate from a particular area. For example, Gorgonzola cheese, Kalamata olives, and Champagne can be labeled as such only if they come from the designated region of Italy, Greece, or France. Choose a specific country and do research on its use of geographical indication. What specific products are covered by GIs in this country? Share your findings with your classmates.

Discussion Topic 5: In this chapter you learned that some company and product names contain unconventional capitalization; for example, eBay, PeopleSoft, PowerPoint, and QuickBooks. If you were writing to these companies, would it be important to get the capitalization right? Why or why not? What if you were including these software packages on a résumé? Would it matter whether you capitalized them properly? Share your opinions with your classmates.

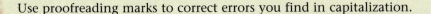

Use proofreading marks to correct errors you find in capitalization.

1. Do you think i should try to earn an MBA Degree?

2. SUBJECT: employee retreat this friday

3. I really enjoyed the book *The Snowball: Warren Buffett And The Business Of Life.*

4. My Mom is trying to become fluent in spanish before her trip this Summer to the Southern part of Spain.

5. Blanca studied english literature, Accounting, and psychology at central wyoming college.

6. The Engineers will meet in the san marino room of the red lion inn next thursday.

7. Applicants must have a Master's Degree to be considered for the Controller position.

8. My Father attended a Training Session on Dragon Naturally Speaking, a Voice-Recognition Software program, in the midwest.

9. Alvin Toffler, an American Writer and Futurist, once said, "it is better to err on the side of daring than the side of caution."

10. At a town hall meeting in Georgia, president Obama said he was embarrassed that he didn't speak a Foreign language.

"Not everything that can be counted counts, and not everything that counts can be counted."

—Albert Einstein, theoretical physicist

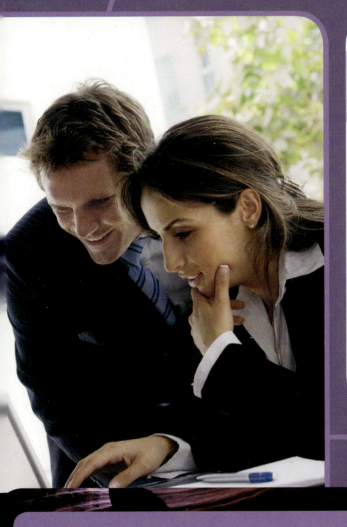

Chapter 18

Numbers

OBJECTIVES

When you have completed the materials in this chapter, you will be able to do the following:

LEVEL 1
- Correctly choose between figure and word forms to express general numbers and numbers beginning sentences; and properly place hyphens and commas in numbers as needed.
- Express money, dates, clock time, addresses, and telephone and fax numbers appropriately.

LEVEL 2
- Use the correct form in writing related numbers, consecutive numbers, periods of time, ages, anniversaries, and round numbers.
- Use the correct form in expressing numbers used with words, abbreviations, and symbols.

LEVEL 3
- Express correctly weights, measurements, and fractions.
- Use the correct form in expressing percentages, decimals, and ordinals.

Pretest

Underline any incorrect expression of numbers, and write an improved form in the blank provided (for example, *$10* rather than *ten dollars*).

1. Panasonic asked 10000 managers to spend at least $1050 on its products by July thirty-first.

_____

2. 2/3 of teens admit that emoticons and other informal writing styles have crept into their school writing assignments.

_____

3. In addition, 38% of teens said they use text message abbreviations such as LOL in their school assignments.

_____

4. Please plan to attend the 1st informational meeting on September 18th at ten a.m.

_____

5. When Megan reached 17 years of age, she applied to 3 colleges in 2 states.

_____

6. Please take twenty-two dollars to pick up 50 forty-four-cent stamps at the post office.

_____

7. Of the thirty-four students who took the notary public class on November 23rd, only two didn't pass the test.

_____

8. The art treasure measures only nine inches by twelve inches, but it is said to be worth nearly two million dollars.

_____

9. Our main office is located at 1 Broadway Lane.

_____

10. By 2015 U.S. Internet advertising is expected to increase 27% to $29,600,000,000.

_____

Just as capitalization is governed by convention, so is the expression of numbers. Usage and custom determine whether numbers are to be expressed in the form of a figure (for example, *5*) or in the form of a word (for example, *five*). Numbers expressed as figures are shorter and more easily comprehended, yet numbers used as words are necessary in certain instances. The following guidelines are observed in expressing numbers that appear in written *sentences*. Numbers that appear in business documents such as invoices, statements, and purchase orders are always expressed as figures.

LEVEL 1

Basic Guidelines for Expressing Numbers

In this level you will learn the general rules for expressing numbers. You will also learn how to correctly express items that appear frequently in business correspondence, including monetary amounts, dates, clock time, addresses, and telephone and fax numbers.

1. 10,000 $1,050 July 31   2. Two thirds   3. 38 percent   4. first 18 10 a.m.   5. seventeen three two
6. $22 fifty 44-cent   7. 34 November 23   8. 9 by 12 inches $2 million   9. One   10. 27 percent $29.6 billion

NUMBERS

General Rules

Writing Numbers in Word or Figure Form

The numbers *one* through *ten* are generally written as words. Numbers above *ten* are written as figures.

> Our office building has *nine* private offices and *two* conference rooms.
>
> Of the *32* IPOs backed by private-equity firms, only *13* resulted in a positive return to investors.

Study Tip

To remember it better, some people call this the "Rule of Ten": Words for one through ten; figures for 11 and above.

Numbers That Begin Sentences

Numbers that begin sentences are written as words. If a number involves more than two words, however, the sentence should be rewritten so that the number no longer falls at the beginning.

> *Eighty-four* homes in the city are listed at below-market prices.
>
> A total of *320* distributors will market our product. (Not *Three hundred twenty* distributors will market our product.)

Placing Commas in Numbers

When expressing numbers in figure form, separate groups of three digits by commas to improve clarity. This rule does not apply, however, when writing some numbers, including years, house numbers, telephone and fax numbers, zip codes, account numbers, and page numbers.

> In 1987 American Airlines saved *$40,000* by eliminating one olive from each salad served.
>
> *BusinessWeek* asked *2,000* executives for their predictions about the workplace of the future.

Hyphenating Numbers

Compound numbers from *21* through *99* are hyphenated when they are written in word form.

> *Thirty-nine* people applied for the forensic science technician position.
>
> *Fifty-six* stocks performed below expectations last month.

Money

Trivia Tidbit

The dollar sign ($) first appeared in business correspondence among the British, Americans, Canadians, and Mexicans in the 1770s.

Sums of money $1 or greater are expressed as figures. If a sum is a whole dollar amount, most writers omit the decimal and zeros (even if the amount appears with fractional dollar amounts). Always include commas in monetary figures $1,000 or greater. Use the dollar sign ($) instead of the word *dollars*, and do not add a space between the currency symbol and the figure.

> The service charge for changing airline tickets has risen from *$50* to *$150* on most airlines.
>
> This statement shows purchases of *$7.13, $10, $43.50, $90*, and *$262.78*.
>
> A ticket for a first-class parlor suite on the Titanic cost *$4,350* (about *$69,600* today).

Sums less than $1 are written as figures that are followed by the word *cents*. If they are part of related sums greater than $1, use a dollar sign and a decimal instead of the word *cents*. However, if a sentence contains unrelated amount of money, treat each amount separately.

Jack needed *75 cents* to buy the morning newspaper.

Our monthly petty cash statement showed purchases of *$7.13*, *$.99*, *$2.80*, *$1*, and *$.40*. (Related numbers)

For every *$10* you spend in our restaurant, we will donate *50 cents* to Special Olympics. (Unrelated numbers)

Dates

In dates, numbers that appear after the name of the month are written in **cardinal figures** (*1, 2, 3*, etc.). Those that stand alone or appear before the name of a month are written in **ordinal figures** (*1st, 2nd, 3rd*, etc.).

The New York Stock Exchange was formed on *May 17, 1792*.

On the *8th* of June and again on the *23rd*, Seattle experienced record rainfall.

Most American communicators express dates in the following form: month, day, year. A comma is used to separate the day and the year. An alternative form, used primarily in military and international correspondence, uses this order without a comma: day, month, year. Some business organizations, especially those doing business globally, prefer the international date style for its clarity.

On *July 17, 1861,* the first paper money, known as *greenbacks*, was issued by the United States government. (General date format)

An international antismoking treaty took effect on *24 February 2005*. (Military and international date format)

Clock Time

Figures are used when clock time is expressed with *a.m., p.m., noon*, or *midnight*. Omit the colon and zeros with even clock hours (those without minutes), even if they appear with times that contain hours and minutes.

The first shift starts at *8 a.m.*; the second, at *3:30 p.m.*

The silent auction opens at *6:30 p.m.*, and bids may be placed until *12 midnight*.

As an alternative, even clock hours can be used with the word *o'clock*. When using this format, either figures or words may be used. Note that phrases such as *in the afternoon* or *in the morning* may follow clock time expressed with *o'clock* but not with time expressed with *a.m.* and *p.m.*

Department mail is usually distributed at *ten* (or *10*) *o'clock* in the morning.

In the United States we use a 12-hour clock to express most time, which requires the use of *a.m.* or *p.m.* for clarity. However, much of the world uses a 24-hour clock format, which is known as **international time**. In the United States, we use this 24-hour clock in the military and in other applications such as international flight schedules and online auctions.

Your flight leaves Las Vegas, Nevada, at *15:47* and arrives in Vancouver, British Columbia, at *21:05*. (Military and international time format; 15:47 is equivalent to 3:47 p.m., and 21:05 is equivalent to 9:05 p.m.)

Addresses

Except for the number *One*, house numbers are expressed as figures. Apartment numbers, suite numbers, box numbers, and route numbers are also written in figure form. Do not use commas to separate digits in house numbers.

```
5 Sierra Drive                      27321 Van Nuys Boulevard
One Peachtree Plaza, Suite 900      1762 Cone Street, Apt. 2B
P.O. Box 8935                       Rural Route 19
```

Street names that are numbered *ten* or below are written as ordinal words (*First, Second, Third*). In street names involving numbers greater than *ten*, the numeral portion is written in ordinal figure form (*11th, 22nd, 33rd, 41st*).

```
201 Third Street                    1190 54th Street
2320 West 22nd Street               3261 South 103rd Avenue
```

Study Tip

Ordinal figures are formed by adding *st, nd, rd,* or *th* to the figure.

Telephone and Fax Numbers

Telephone and fax numbers are expressed with figures. When used, the area code is placed in parentheses before the telephone number. Be sure to include a space after the closing parenthesis. As an alternate form, you may separate the area code from the telephone number with a hyphen. A third format that has gained acceptance is to separate the parts of the number with periods. When you include an extension, separate it from the phone number with a comma.

Please call us at *555-1101* to place your order.

You may reach me at *(801) 643-3267, Ext. 244*, after 9:30 a.m.

Call our toll-free number at *800-340-3281* for the latest stock quotes.

Please fax your order to *415.937.5594*.

Now complete the reinforcement exercises for Level 1.

LEVEL 2

Special Guidelines for Expressing Numbers

Special guidelines exist for expressing related and consecutive numbers. In this level you will also learn how to use numbers to express periods of time, ages and anniversaries, numbers used in conventional phrases, numbers used with abbreviations and symbols, and round numbers.

Career Tip

If your company has a style manual, check it for number preferences. Larger companies may prescribe the figure or word form they prefer for often-used numbers.

Related Numbers

Related numbers are those used similarly in the same document. They should be expressed as the largest number is expressed. Thus, if the largest number is greater than *ten*, all the numbers should be expressed as figures.

Only *2* orders out of *459* could not be filled on time.

Of the *98* e-mail documents Casey received today, *19* were marked "Urgent" and *7* were marked "Confidential."

We ordered *15* pizzas, *12* salads, and *4* cakes for the employee luncheon. (Note that items appearing in a series are always considered to be related.)

Unrelated numbers within the same reference are written as words or figures according to the general guidelines presented earlier in this chapter.

Study Tip

Remember that numbers included in a series (three or more items) are ALWAYS considered related.

Twenty-three contract changes will be discussed by *89* employees working in *eight* departments.

During the *four* peak traffic hours, *three* bridges carry at least *20,000* cars.

Consecutive Numbers

With consecutive numbers, remember that the second number is ALWAYS a figure. The first number is usually a word, unless it requires three or more words (*120 5-year-old* children.)

Consecutive numbers occur when two numbers appear one after the other, both modifying a following noun (such as *ten 44-cent stamps*). Express the first number in words and the second in figures. If, however, the first number cannot be expressed in *one or two words*, place it in figures also (*120 44-cent* stamps). Do not use commas to separate the figures.

Kelsey purchased *two 16GB* flash drives. (Use word form for the first number and figure form for the second.)

Historians divided the era into *four 25-year* periods. (Use word form for the first number and figure form for the second.)

Did you request *twenty 100-watt* bulbs? (Use word form for the first number and figure form for the second.)

We will need at least *150 100-watt* bulbs. (Use figure form for the first number since it requires more than two words.)

Periods of Time

Periods of time (seconds, minutes, hours, days, weeks, months, and years) are treated as any other general number. That is, numbers ten and below are written in word form. Numbers above ten are written in figure form.

A customer can finalize an order on our Web site within *two to three* minutes.

After a *183*-day strike, workers returned to their jobs.

Congress has regulated minimum wages for over *72* years.

Figures are easier to understand and remember than words are. That's why business terms, even for numbers under ten, are generally written as figures.

Figures are used to achieve special emphasis in expressing business concepts such as discount rates, interest rates, contracts, warranty periods, credit terms, loan periods, and payment terms.

Pay your invoice within *10 days* and receive a *2 percent* discount.

Your loan must be repaid within *60 days* in accordance with its terms.

Higher interest rates are offered on *6-* to *9-month* certificates of deposit.

Ages and Anniversaries

Ages and anniversaries that can be expressed in one or two words are generally written in word form. Those that require more than two words are written in figures. Figures are also used when an age (a) appears immediately after a person's name; (b) is expressed in exact years, months, and sometimes days; or (c) is used in a legal or technical sense.

When he was *fifty-five*, Ernest Hemingway was awarded the Nobel Prize in Literature. (Use word form for age expressed in two or fewer words.)

January 28, 2010, marked the *twenty-fifth* anniversary of the recording of "We Are the World." (Use word form for an anniversary expressed in two or fewer words.)

Katharine Ralph, *63*, plans to retire in two years. (Use figure form for age appearing immediately after a name.)

The child was adopted when he was *3 years 8 months and 24 days* old. (Use figure form for age expressed in terms of exact years and months. Notice that commas are not used to separate age expressions.)

Although the legal voting age is *18*, young people must be *21* to purchase alcohol. (Use figure form for age used in a legal sense.)

Round Numbers

Round numbers are approximations. They may be expressed in word or figure form, although figure form is shorter and easier to comprehend.

Approximately *200* (or *two hundred*) people showed up for the grand opening.

We have received about *20* (or *twenty*) reservations for the wine tasting.

For ease of reading, round numbers in the millions or billions should be expressed with a combination of figures and words. If *one million* is used as an approximation, use all word form; otherwise, write this number using figures and words (*1 million*). Use a combination of figures and words for all other numbers.

The U.S. national debt is about *$11.3 trillion*.

The world population is approximately *6.7 billion,* and the U.S. Census Bureau expects this figure to grow to around *9.2 billion* by 2050.

U.S. cell phone users receive nearly *1.5 million* spam text messages every year.

Numbers Used With Words, Abbreviations, and Symbols

Numbers used with words are expressed as figures. Remember to apply the capitalization rules that you learned in Chapter 17. Notice, too, that no commas are used in serial, account, and policy numbers.

page 28	Policy 04-168315	Area Code 213
Room 232	Volume 5	Highway 101
Option 3	Form 1040	Public Law 96-221

Numbers used with abbreviations are also expressed as figures.

Apt. 23	Serial No. 265188440	Nos. 199 and 202
Ext. 3206	Account No. 08166-05741	Social Security No. 535-52-2016

Notice that the word *number* is capitalized and abbreviated when it precedes a number. However, if the word *number* begins a sentence, do not abbreviate it.

Number 348 submitted the winning bid.

Symbols (such as #, %, ¢) are usually avoided in contextual business writing (sentences). In other business documents where space is limited, however, symbols are frequently used. Numbers appearing with symbols are expressed as figures.

45%	39¢	#2 can	2/10, n/60

Now complete the reinforcement exercises for Level 2.

Additional Guidelines for Expressing Numbers

The following guidelines will help you use appropriate forms for weights and measurements, fractions, percentages, decimals, and ordinals.

Weights and Measurements

Study Tip

When writing temperatures, specify whether the temperature is Fahrenheit or Celsius. Notice that these two common temperature measurement scales are capitalized.

Weights and measurements, including temperatures, are expressed as figures. When one weight or measure consists of several words treated as a single unit (*3 feet 4 inches*), do not use a comma to separate the units.

> My new iPhone measures only *4.5 by 2.4 by 0.43 inches* and weighs just *4.8 ounces*.
>
> Your flight from St. Louis to Las Vegas will take *4 hours 45 minutes*.
>
> The truck required *21 gallons* of gasoline and *2 quarts* of oil to travel *250 miles*.
>
> The highest temperature ever recorded was *136 degrees Fahrenheit* in 1922 in El Azizia, Libya.

In messages that contain sentences, spell out nouns following numerals in weights and measurements (*21 gallons* instead of *21 gal.*). In business forms or in statistical presentations, however, you may abbreviate weights and measurements.

8′ × 10′	#10	7 oz.	3,500 sq. ft.	2 lb.	12 qt.

Fractions

Study Tip

A fraction immediately followed by an *of* phrase usually functions as a noun (*one third of the cars*). Therefore, it is not hyphenated.

Simple fractions are fractions in which both the numerator and denominator are whole numbers. If the simple fraction can be expressed in two words, use word form. If a fraction functions as a noun, no hyphen is used. If it functions as an adjective, a hyphen separates its parts.

> Linguists predict that as many as *one half* of the world's 6,800 languages could disappear over the next century. (The fraction is used as a noun.)
>
> A *two-thirds* majority is needed to carry the measure. (The fraction is used as an adjective.)

Long or awkward fractions appearing in sentences may be written either as figures or as a combination of figures and words.

> Scientists have determined that the polio virus measures *1 millionth* of an inch. (A combination of words and figures is easier to comprehend.)
>
> Flight records revealed that the emergency system was activated *13/200* of a second after the pilot was notified. (Figure form is easier to comprehend.)

Mixed fractions, which are whole numbers combined with fractions, are always expressed with figures.

> Her carry-on bag measures *21¼ inches* by *13½ inches* by *8¾ inches*.

Use the extended character set of your word processing program to insert fractions that are written in figures. Fractions written in figures that are not found in extended character sets of word processing programs are formed by using the diagonal to separate the two parts. When fractions that are constructed with diagonals appear with key fractions, be consistent by using the diagonal construction for all the fractions involved.

Study Tip

Use figures to express metric measurements. When including metric measurements in a sentence, spell out the units of measure (*5 kilometers, 1.75 liters*)

The shelves were supposed to be *36 5/8* inches wide, not *26 3/8* inches. (Notice that fractions that must be constructed with diagonals are separated from their related whole numbers.)

Percentages and Decimals

Percentages are expressed with figures followed by the word *percent*. The percent sign (%) is used only on business forms or in statistical presentations.

U.S. unemployment rates have been as high as *14.4 percent* and as low as *1.9 percent*.

The number of Facebook visitors over age thirty-five has increased by *113 percent*.

Decimals are expressed with figures. If a decimal does not contain a whole number (an integer), a zero should be placed before the decimal. Notice that commas are not used in the decimal portion of a number, no matter how many digits it has.

Lance Armstrong had the highest average speed in the Tour de France when he maintained an average speed of *25.882* miles per hour in 2005. (The decimal contains a whole number.)

The smallest winged insect is the Tanzanian parasitic wasp, which has a wingspan of *0.2* millimeters. (Place a zero before a decimal that does not contain a whole number.)

Ordinals

Ordinal numbers are used to show the position in an ordered sequence. Although ordinal numbers are generally expressed in word form (*first, second, third*), three exceptions should be noted: (a) Figure form is used for dates appearing before a month or appearing alone; (b) figure form is used for street names involving numbers greater than *ten*; and (c) figure form is used when the ordinal would require more than two words.

Most Ordinals

City Lights Books recently celebrated its *fiftieth anniversary*.

Before the *eighteenth century*, spelling was not standardized.

Of the 215 cities analyzed worldwide, Vienna, Austria, ranks *first* in quality of living.

Ciro D. Rodriguez represents the *Twenty-third Congressional District* in Texas.

Dates

Please respond by the *20th* so that I can make our reservation.

Paychecks are issued on the *1st* and the *15th* of each month.

Streets

Forbes magazine ranked *Fifth Avenue* in New York City as the most expensive street in the world.

Our headquarters will move to 3589 *23rd Street* on the 6th of September.

Larger Ordinals

Peter Buck of Subway ranks *301st* on *Forbes* list of the 400 richest Americans.

First Federal Bank ranks *103rd* in terms of capital investments.

Some word processing programs automatically set ordinal suffixes (*st, nd, rd, th*) superscript. If you dislike this program feature, you may turn it off.

Now complete the reinforcement exercises for Level 3.

Spot the BLOOPER

Using the skills you are learning in this class, try to identify why the following items are bloopers. Consult your textbook, dictionary, or reference manual as needed.

Blooper 1: A photo in *People* magazine showed people holding signs in support of Susan Boyle, the British amateur singing sensation. On one sign a fan had written: "Susan Your a Super STAR in our EYE's."

Blooper 2: From *The Denver Post*: "The Allied Jewish Federation, which overseas the fund drive, hopes to raise $5.5 million."

Blooper 3: From an advertisement for CNN: "The average computer has 110 keys. We say you only need three."

Blooper 4: From *The Suburban & Wayne Times* [Wayne, Pennsylvania]: "Cases of Lyme disease, which is transmitted by deer carrying ticks, are on the rise."

Blooper 5: From *The Journal-American* [Bellevue, Washington]: "Youths caught breaking the law or their parents could face a $250 fine or community service."

Blooper 6: Sign in front of a restaurant: "Open seven days a week and weekends"

Blooper 7: Classified advertisement: "For Sale. 8 puppies from a German Shepherd and an Alaskan Hussy."

Blooper 8: *The Times Union* [Albany, New York] featured an advertisement with the following 2-inch headline: "On Thursday morning, I found the car of my dreams in my pajamas."

Blooper 9: A column in *The Charlotte Observer* mentioned the wealth of Sam Walton's widow and daughter. "Forbes estimates that each are worth $16 billion."

Blooper 10: Large banner displayed prominently behind Hillary Clinton as she spoke during a gathering of Silicon Valley CEOs about the importance in today's economy of training skilled workers: "New Jobs for Tommorrow."

Question	Answer
Q: I recently saw the following format used by a business to publish its telephone number on its stationery and business cards: 212.582.0903. Is it now an option to use periods in telephone numbers?	**A:** Yes, this is now an acceptable option for writing telephone and fax numbers that perhaps reflects European influences. To some, the style is upscale and chic; to others, it's just confusing. Telephone and fax numbers written in the traditional formats are most readily recognized. That's why it's probably safer to stick with hyphens or parentheses: 212-582-0903 or (212) 582-0903.
Q: My manager is preparing an advertisement for a charity event. She has written this: *Donors who give $100 dollars or more receive plaques.* I know this is not right, but I can't exactly put my finger on the problem.	**A:** The problem is in *$100 dollars.* That is like saying *dollars dollars.* Drop the word *dollars* and use only the dollar sign: *Donors who give $100 or more. . . .*
Q: I'm never sure when to hyphenate numbers, such as *thirty-one.* Is there some rule to follow?	**A:** When written in word form, the numbers *twenty-one* through *ninety-nine* are hyphenated. Numbers are also hyphenated when they form compound adjectives and precede nouns (*ten-year-old* child, *16-story* building, *four-year* term, *30-day* lease).
Q: A fellow team member wants to show dollar amounts in two forms, such as the following: *The consultant charges two hundred dollars ($200) an hour.* I think this is overkill. Do we have to show figures in two forms?	**A:** In formal legal documents, amounts of money may be expressed in words followed by figures in parentheses. However, business writers do not follow this practice because it is unnecessary, wordy, and pretentious. In fact, some readers are insulted because the practice suggests they are not bright enough to comprehend just one set of figures.
Q: Should I put quotation marks around figures to emphasize them? For example, *Your account has a balance of "$2,136.18."*	**A:** Certainly not! Quotation marks are properly used to indicate an exact quotation, or they may be used to enclose the definition of a word. They should not be used as a mechanical device for added emphasis.

Question	Answer

Q: What should I write: *You are our No. 1 account*, or *You are our number one account*? Should anything be hyphenated?

A: Either is correct, but we prefer *No. 1* because it is more easily recognizable. No hyphen is required.

Q: How should I spell the word *lose* in this sentence: *The employee tripped over a (lose or loose) cord*?

A: In your sentence use the adjective *loose*, which means "not fastened," "not tight," or "having freedom of movement." Perhaps you can remember it by thinking of the common expression *loose change*, which suggests unattached, free coins jingling in your pocket. If you *lose* (*mislay*) some of those coins, you have less money and fewer *o's*.

Q: I'm having trouble telling the difference between these two words: *aid* and *aide*. Can they be used interchangeably?

A: Absolutely not! The word *aid* is a verb meaning "to help or assist" (*Ben & Jerry's aids many environmental organizations*). *Aid* is also a noun meaning "assistance" (*The United States plans to send foreign aid to several African countries*). The word *aide* is also a noun but refers to "a person who acts as an assistant" (*The student aide assisted her professor with grading*).

Q: The following three sentences appeared in an assignment my daughter received from her fifth grade teacher: *It's going to be interesting! For each state list it's geographical region. On your map identify each state and note its' capital.* I always have trouble myself with *its* and *it's*, but it seems as if something is wrong here.

A: You're right! Even teachers have trouble with *its* and *it's*. In the first sentence, *it's*, a contraction for *it is*, has been used correctly (*It is going to be interesting!*). In the last two sentences, the teacher should have used the possessive form of *it*, which is *its*, to show possession. In fact, the word *its'* does not exist. Now your only decision is whether you should point out these errors to your daughter's teacher!

Q: I thought the past tense of *spell* is *spelled*. One of my colleagues, however, uses the past tense *spelt*. Are both forms acceptable?

A: Your colleague is probably from Great Britain, where the past tense of *spell* is indeed *spelt*. However, the American past-tense form is *spelled*, just as you thought. In fact, many words are spelled differently in American and British English. For example, in America we spell *organization* with a *z*; in Great Britain this word is spelled *organisation*. When writing for American audiences, always use the American spelling of words.

18 Reinforcement Exercises

LEVEL 1

Online Homework Help! For immediate feedback on odd-numbered items, go to **www.meguffey.com.**

 A. (Self-check) Choose (a) or (b) to complete the following sentences.

1. All (a) eleven, (b) 11 restaurant managers said they had problems with employees clocking in for other employees. _____

2. (a) 23, (b) Twenty three (c) Twenty-three call centers in India announced that they will be switching from customer service to mortgage processing. _____

3. On the (a) 13th, (b) thirteenth of April, two Domino's employees posted a prank video on YouTube that made the company look bad. _____

4. It took the management of Domino's (a) 2, (b) two days to respond publicly to the prank. _____

5. Domino's offered customers (a) $5.00, (b) $5 off every pizza to encourage them to return. _____

6. The new Emporis buildings are located at (a) Three, (b) 3 Peachtree Pointe in Atlanta. _____

7. Financial institutions are clustered on (a) Seventh, (b) 7th Avenue in New York City. _____

8. Send the letter to (a) 320 27th Street, (b) 320 27 Street. _____

9. Organizers expect (a) 38000, (b) 38,000 to attend the Macworld Conference & Expo. _____

10. We plan to meet again at (a) 9:00 a.m., (b) 9 a.m. Tuesday. _____

Check your answers below.

 B. Assume that the following phrases appear within sentences (unless otherwise noted) in business correspondence. Write the preferred forms in the spaces provided. If a phrase is correct as shown, write *C*.

Example: 1135 54 Street   1135 54th Street _____

1. seventeen new status updates   _____

2. on Fourth Street   _____

3. charged $.10 per copy   _____

4. received 4 e-mail messages   _____

5. on April ninth   _____

6. located on 1st Street   _____

1.b 2.c 3.a 4.b 5.b 6.b 7.a 8.a 9.b 10.b

7. charges of $3.68, 79 cents, and $40.00 _____

8. on the eleventh of May _____

9. meeting at 11:00 a.m. _____

10. arrived at 10 p.m. in the evening _____

11. a total of seventy-nine orders _____

12. on August 31st _____

13. moved to 12655 32nd Street _____

14. costs $49 dollars _____

15. (Beginning of sentence) 27 interviewees _____

16. 1319 people visited _____

17. the address is 7 Hampton Square _____

18. the address is 1 Hampton Square _____

19. has sixty-six rooms _____

20. (International style) at 6 p.m. _____

21. (International style) on April 15, 2009 _____

22. located at 2742 8th Street _____

23. at five thirty p.m. _____

24. call (800)123-4567 _____

25. for one hundred dollars _____

26. costs exactly 90¢ _____

27. at 18307 Eleventh Street _____

28. call 800/598-3459 _____

29. all 50 states _____

30. bought 2 lattes _____

C. **Writing Exercise.** Rewrite these sentences correcting any errors you note.

1. 259 identity theft complaints were filed with the FTC on November 2nd alone.

   _____

2. Please call me at 925/685/1230 Ext. 309.

   _____

3. On April 15th Alicia submitted the following petty cash disbursements: $2.80, 95 cents, $5.00, and 25 cents.

   _____

4. Erika Rothschild moved from 1,716 Sunset Drive to 1 Bellingham Court.

   _____

5. 24 different wireless packages are available from our 3 local dealers.

_____

6. On the 18 of March, I sent you 3 e-mail messages about restricting Internet use.

_____

7. Although McDonald's advertised a sandwich that cost only ninety-nine cents, most customers found that lunch cost between three dollars and three dollars and ninety-nine cents.

_____

_____

8. Regular work breaks are scheduled at 10:00 a.m. in the morning and again at 3:30 p.m. in the afternoon.

_____

9. We want to continue operations through the thirtieth, but we may be forced to close by the twenty-second.

_____

10. The United States experienced 20000 job cuts between April first and April thirtieth.

_____

LEVEL 2

A. (Self-check) Select (a) or (b) to complete each of the following sentences.

1. Laura Lorraine prepared (a) 2 40-page, (b) two 40-page business proposals. _____

2. People have been receiving spam in their e-mail boxes for over (a) thirty, (b) 30 years. _____

3. Your flight will depart from (a) Gate Nine, (b) Gate 9. _____

4. Of the 235 e-mail messages sent, only (a) 7, (b) seven bounced back. _____

5. Although she is only (a) 25, (b) twenty-five, Gillian Martin owns her own restaurant in Las Vegas. _____

6. AIG lost (a) $62 billion, (b) $62,000,000,000 in just 92 days. _____

7. Have you completed your IRS Form (a) Ten Forty, (b) 1040? _____

8. San Francisco observed the (a) 100th, (b) one hundredth anniversary of the great earthquake in 2006. _____

9. Your short-term loan covers a period of (a) 60, (b) sixty days. _____

10. The serial number on my monitor is (a) 85056170, (b) 85,056,170. _____

Check your answers below.

1.b 2.b 3.b 4.a 5.b 6.a 7.b 8.b 9.a 10.a

B. For the following sentences underscore any numbers or words that are expressed inappropriately and write the correct forms in the spaces provided. If a sentence is correct as written, write *C*.

Example: The documentation group has prepared <u>4 twenty-page</u> reports.   four 20-page

1. At Amherst College in Massachusetts, just five of 1680 students have landline phones.   _____

2. No. 4 on the agenda will take about twenty-five minutes to discuss.   _____

3. Our board of directors is composed of 15 members, of whom three are doctors, four are nurses, and eight are other health care professionals.   _____

4. We plan to order five six-month subscriptions for our employees.   _____

5. After a period of sixteen years, ownership reverts to the state.   _____

6. One New York spammer sent more than 825,000,000 unsolicited e-mail messages.   _____

7. The following policy Nos. are listed for Lisa Orta: No. 1355801 and No. 1355802.   _____

8. Model 8,400 costs $10,000 and can be leased for $275 a month.   _____

9. Over 53,000,000 Chinese visit online forums regularly.   _____

10. Of the 385 manuscript pages, ten pages require minor revisions and eight pages demand heavy revision.   _____

11. John Bologni, forty-one, and Sarah Flores, thirty-three, were interviewed for the two executive positions.   _____

12. On page forty-four of Volume two, you will see that absenteeism costs American corporations $74,000,000,000 annually.   _____

13. Warranties on all GPS devices are limited to ninety days.   _____

14. The total book club membership of eight hundred thousand received the four bonus books.   _____

15. Only two of the 78 staff members took a sick day last month.   _____

16. Rich Snyder became president of In-N-Out Burger when he was just 24 years old.   _____

17. When the child was two years six months old, his parents established a trust fund for $1.6 million.   _____

18. Bill Gates' mansion on Lake Washington features a wall of twenty-four video screens, parking for twenty cars, and a reception hall for one hundred people.   _____

19. Taking 7 years to construct, the 40,000-square-foot home reportedly cost more than fifty million dollars.   _____

20. Volkswagen has sold more than 21,500,000 Beetles since 1934, making it the most successful car ever built.   _____

 C. Assume that the following phrases appear in business or professional correspondence. Write the preferred forms in the spaces provided. If a phrase is correct as shown, write *C*.

1. sold for $1,500,000   _____

2. one hundred seven five-page essays   _____

3. a law that is one year two months and five days old

_____

4. nine offices with eleven computers and fifteen desks

_____

5. three seventy-five pound weights

_____

6. loan period of sixty days

_____

7. Joan Brault, seventy-four, and Frank Brault, seventy-two

_____

8. Account No. 362,486,012

_____

9. five point eight billion dollars

_____

10. Highway Twenty-nine

_____

11. you are Number 25

_____

12. fifty-nine employee suggestions

_____

13. about three hundred voters

_____

14. four point four million people

_____

15. Section three point two

_____

16. 9 three-bedroom apartments

_____

17. warranty period of two years

_____

18. insurance for 15 computers, 12 printers, and 3 scanners

_____

19. selected Numbers 305 and 409

_____

20. took out a nine-month CD

_____

LEVEL 3

A. (Self-check) Choose (a) or (b) to complete the following sentences.

1. More than (a) one half, (b) one-half, (c) 1/2 of drivers are driving less to keep gas costs down. _____

2. Today more than (a) 29 percent, (b) twenty-nine percent of all car owners drive a hybrid vehicle. _____

3. The size of carry-on baggage should not exceed (a) 22" × 14" × 9", (b) 22 by 14 by 9 inches. _____

4. Most airlines do not allow carry-on baggage that weighs more than (a) 40, (b) forty pounds. _____

5. Darrell Issa represents the (a) 49th, (b) Forty-ninth Congressional District. _____

6. Surprising pollsters, Senator Williams received a (a) two-thirds, (b) two thirds majority. _____

7. This copier can make copies up to (a) 11 by 17 inches, (b) eleven by seventeen inches. _____

8. Maintenance costs are only (a) 0.5, (b) .5 percent above last year's. _____

9. One builder is offering houses in Los Angeles that are only (a) eight hundred eighty, (b) 880 square feet. _____

10. Did you know that many office buildings have no (a) 13th, (b) thirteenth floor? _____

Check your answers below.

B. Writing Exercise. Rewrite the following sentences with special attention to appropriate number usage.

1. "Kingda Ka," which claims to be the world's fastest and tallest roller coaster, travels one hundred twenty eight miles per hour and is four hundred fifty six feet high.

   _____

   _____

2. When the ride first opened on May 21st, 2005, nearly 1/3 of the visitors to Six Flags Great Adventure in New Jersey lined up for a high-speed joyride on four eighteen-passenger rail cars.

   _____

   _____

3. Swiss engineers used precise instruments to ensure that Kingda Ka's three thousand one hundred eighteen feet of steel track were within 0.05 inches of specifications.

   _____

   _____

4. To ride Kingda Ka, you must be at least fifty-four inches but less than 6' 5" tall.

   _____

5. Only the Kingda Ka ride can reach speeds of one hundred twenty-eight mph in three point three seconds, achieving a negative gravity force with 6.5 seconds of weightlessness at the top before taking a forty-one-story plunge.

   _____

   _____

6. Located in the 4th Congressional District, Six Flags Great Adventure is seventy-four miles from New York City and attracts over three million visitors each summer.

   _____

   _____

7. The square mileage of Washington, DC, is 68 point 2; and its population is about 550 thousand.

   _____

8. Although Washington, DC, has a population of 591833, its population during the week grows to approximately 1,000,000 because of commuters.

_____

_____

9. African Americans make up approximately fifty-five point six percent of the population in Washington, DC.

_____

10. Almost 2/3 of eligible Americans voted in the last presidential election.

_____

C. **Writing Exercise.** In your local newspaper, find ten sentences with numbers. Write those sentences on a separate sheet. After each one, explain what rule the number style represents. Strive to find examples illustrating a variety of rules.

D. **FAQs About Business English Review.** In the space provided, write the correct answer choice.

1. Your contribution of (a) $100, (b) 100 dollars, (c) $100 dollars to the Animal Rescue Foundation is greatly appreciated. _____

2. (a) Twenty-one, (b) 21 interns were hired for the summer. _____

3. The United States sent foreign (a) aide, (b) aid to tsunami victims in Indonesia. _____

4. Lyle is training to become an (a) aide, (b) aid in a psychiatric facility. _____

5. Investors were afraid that they would (a) loose, (b) lose money on junk bonds. _____

6. Sharon hunted for (a) loose, (b) lose change for the parking meter. _____

7. You are our (a) No. 1, (b) number-one choice for the position. _____

8. (a) It's, (b) Its', (c) Its been a pleasure working with you on this project. _____

9. The company lost (a) it's, (b) its', (c) its funding. _____

10. She (a) spelt, (b) spelled the word incorrectly. _____

You have heard a lot about Internet fraud and want to learn how to avoid becoming a victim yourself.

Goal: To learn how to avoid being a victim of Internet fraud.

1. With your Web browser on the screen, go to the U.S. Department of Justice Internet Fraud site at **http://www.usdoj.gov/ criminal/fraud/internet/**. Click **What Is Internet Fraud?**

2. Read the description of Internet fraud. Next scroll down to learn about major types of Internet fraud. Finally, read what the U.S. Department of Justice is doing to combat Internet fraud and how you can deal with Internet fraud.

3. Copy the information you found most helpful into a Word document and print it.

4. On a separate sheet, list five strategies that could help you avoid becoming a victim of Internet fraud.

5. End your session. Submit your printouts and answers.

▶▶ Chat About It

Your instructor may assign any of the following topics for you to discuss in class, in an online chat room, or on an online discussion board. Some of the discussion topics may require outside research. You may also be asked to read and respond to postings made by your classmates.

Discussion Topic 1: Many errors have been made in business because people didn't proofread numbers carefully enough. For example, Royal Caribbean Cruise Line listed a $1,399 cabin online for $139. Starwood Hotels left a zero off a price, thereby offering a $850 bungalow for just $85. United Airlines accidentally listed a $2,500 ticket for just 25 cents. And Texas Women's University transposed two numbers in a phone number; instead of reaching the TWU Admissions Department, students called a sex hotline instead! Why do you think it is important to proofread numbers carefully for accuracy? Why do you think errors like these are made? Share your thoughts with your classmates. If you have any related personal experiences, share those too.

Discussion Topic 2: The currency of the United States is the dollar, represented by the dollar sign ($). Other countries use different currencies represented by different symbols. Choose a country and do research to determine the name of the country's currency and its currency symbol. Report your findings to your classmates.

Discussion Topic 3: In this chapter you learned that the United States uses date and time formats that are different from those used in much of the world. Choose a country and research its accepted date and time formats. Share your findings with your classmates. In addition, discuss what problems can result from the use of different date and time formats around the world.

Discussion Topic 4: In his book *On Writing*, the author Stephen King wrote, "One of the really bad things you can do to your writing is to dress up the vocabulary, looking for long words because you're maybe a little bit ashamed of your short ones." What do you think Stephen

King means by this? How can you apply this advice to your own professional writing? Share your thoughts with your classmates.

Discussion Topic 5: The American writer Mark Twain once said, "I have always tried hard and faithfully to improve my English and never to degrade it. I always try to use the best English to describe what I think and what I feel, or what I don't feel and don't think." Why do you think Mark Twain believed so strongly in using English properly? Do you agree? How has this class changed the way you will use English in your personal and professional lives? Share your thoughts with your classmates.

Posttest

Underline numbers that are expressed inappropriately. Write corrected forms in the spaces provided.

1. 58 restaurants will compete in the cooking competition. _____

2. We can offer you Internet access for just $30 dollars a month. _____

3. The author Julia Flynn Silar tries to post at least 4 140-character updates on Twitter every day. _____

4. If you save only five hundred dollars annually, you will have fifty-four thousand dollars after twenty-five years if it earns an average of 10%. _____

5. Approximately 7,500,000 people in the United States control about 11 trillion dollars in assets. _____

6. By the June 30th application deadline, we received ninety-eight applications for a job that pays $10.00 an hour. _____

7. Please call our office, located at 3549 6th Avenue, at 585/663-0785, to schedule an appointment. _____

8. Flight thirty-seven will depart from Gate five at 5:00 p.m. _____

9. On the ninth of August, 3500 computer programmers will attend a convention in the city of Baltimore. _____

10. The coldest temperature ever recorded was minus eighty-nine point two degrees Celsius in 1983 in Antarctica. _____

1. Fifty-eight 2. $30 3. four 140-character 4. $500, $54,000, 25, 10 percent 5. 7.5 million, $11 trillion 6. June 30, 98, $10 7. 3549 Sixth Avenue, (585) 663-0785 8. Flight 37, Gate 5, 5 p.m. 9. 9th 3,500 10. -89.2 degrees

First, review Chapters 17 and 18. Then test your comprehension of those chapters by completing the exercises that follow. Compare your responses with those shown at the end of the book.

LEVEL 1

Select the letter of the group of words that is more acceptably expressed.

1. a. courses in Management, Farsi, and Biology   b. courses in management, Farsi, and biology   _____

2. a. living in Madison county   b. living in Madison County   _____

3. a. the State of North Dakota   b. the state of North Dakota   _____

4. a. a fall promotional event   b. a Fall promotional event   _____

5. a. French Fries   b. french fries   _____

6. a. the 17th of May   b. the seventeenth of May   _____

7. a. forty-five dollars   b. $45   _____

8. a. on 16th Avenue   b. on Sixteenth Avenue   _____

9. a. on July 4th   b. on July 4   _____

10. a. May i join you?   b. May I join you?   _____

11. a. 35 Graduate Students   b. 35 graduate students   _____

12. a. sold for $100   b. sold for $100 dollars   _____

13. a. e-mail message to the president   b. E-mail message to the President   _____

14. a. i plan to attend   b. I plan to attend   _____

15. a. 300000 homes in the Suburbs   b. 300,000 homes in the suburbs   _____

LEVEL 2

Select the letter of the group of words that is more acceptably expressed.

16. a. my Grandma and Grandpa   b. my grandma and grandpa   _____

17. a. travel west on Highway 20   b. travel West on Highway 20   _____

18. a. our manager, Jean Hunnicutt   b. our Manager, Jean Hunnicutt   _____

19. a. our Legal Department   b. our legal department   _____

20. a. a message from Alyssa Mendes, Sales Manager   b. a message from Alyssa Mendes, sales manager   _____

21. a. a message from Sales Manager Mendes   b. a message from sales manager Mendes   _____

22. a. for the past four years   b. for the past 4 years   _____

23. a. 4 twenty-story buildings   b. four 20-story buildings   _____

24. a. nine paralegals assigned to 14 cases   b. 9 paralegals assigned to 14 cases   _____

25. a. SUBJECT: Payroll Data Due Today   b. SUBJECT: payroll data due today   _____

26. a. cost three dollars and seventy five cents   b. cost $3.75   _____

27. a. traveled south on Highway 85   b. traveled South on Highway 85   _____

28. a. my Father recommended a good Book   b. my father recommended a good book   _____

29. a. Henry Ford said, "the greatest thing in life is to keep your mind young."   b. Henry Ford said, "The greatest thing in life is to keep your mind young."   _____

LEVEL 3

Select the correct group of words and write its letter in the space provided.

30. a. a world of possibilities   b. a World of possibilities   _____

31. a. Mayor-Elect Bailey   b. Mayor-elect Bailey   _____

32. a. an e-mail marked "urgent"   b. an e-mail marked "Urgent"   _____

33. a. 2/3 of voters   b. two thirds of voters   _____

34. a. less than 0.3 percent   b. less than .3 percent   _____

35. a. 89 degrees Fahrenheit   b. eighty-nine degrees fahrenheit   _____

36. a. 80% of the votes   b. 80 percent of the votes   _____

37. a. a one third interest   b. a one-third interest   _____

38. a. a Catholic wedding   b. a catholic wedding   _____

39. a. italian and greek cultures   b. Italian and Greek cultures   _____

40. a. 3rd place   b. third place   _____

FAQs About Business English Review

Write the letter of the word or phrase that correctly completes each sentence.

41. Do you have any (a) advise, (b) advice you can give me about graduate programs?   _____

42. Our newsletter comes out (a) bimonthly, (b) semimonthly on the 1st and the 15th of each month.   _____

43. The Red Cross immediately sent (a) aid, (b) aide following the hurricane.   _____

44. The guard will (a) mashal, (b) martial top-seeded runners to the start line.   _____

45. Ramona doesn't want to (a) loose, (b) lose her opportunity to travel abroad.   _____

46. (a) Its, (b) It's, (c) Its' going to take a lot of work to secure this contract.   _____

47. This scholarship is open to (a) nonEnglish-speaking (b) non-English-speaking students.

48. On Friday Bob is scheduled to have a (a) biopsy, (b) Biopsy.

49. Colette dreams of pursuing a career in the field of (a) medicine, (b) Medicine.

50. Our (a) organisation, (b) organization is hosting a fund-raiser for Special Olympics.

Short Reports

Reports are a fact of life in the business world today. They are important because they convey needed information, and they help decision makers solve problems. Organizing information into a meaningful report is an important skill you will want to acquire if your field is business.

Characteristics of Reports

As an introduction to report writing, this workshop focuses on the most important characteristics of reports. You will learn valuable tips about the format, data, headings, and writing plan for short business reports and internal proposals.

Format. How should a business report look? Three formats are commonly used. *Letter format* is appropriate for short reports prepared by one organization for another. A letter report, as illustrated in Figure 6.1, is like a letter except that it is more carefully organized. It includes side headings and lists where appropriate. *Memo format* is common for reports written within an organization. These internal reports look like memos—with the addition of side headings. *Report format* is used for longer, more formal reports. Printed on plain paper (instead of letterhead or memo forms), these reports begin with a title followed by carefully displayed headings and subheadings.

Data. Where do you find the data for a business report? Many business reports begin with personal observation and experience. If you were writing a report on implementing flextime for employees, you might begin by observing current work schedules and by asking what schedules employees prefer. Other sources of data for business reports include company records, surveys, questionnaires, and interviews. If you want to see how others have solved a problem or collect background data on a topic, you can consult magazines, journals, and books. Much information is available electronically through online library indexes or from searching databases and the Web.

Headings. Good headings in a report highlight major ideas and categories. They guide the reader through a report. In longer reports they divide the text into inviting chunks, and they provide resting places for the eyes. Short reports often use *functional headings* (such as *Problem, Summary,* and *Recommendations*). Longer reports may employ *talking headings* (such as *Short-Term Parking Solutions*) because they provide more information to the reader. Whether your headings are functional or talking, be sure they are clear and parallel. For example, use *Visible Costs* and *Invisible Costs* rather than *Visible Costs* and *Costs That Don't Show*. Don't enclose headings in quotation marks, and avoid using headings as antecedents for pronouns. For example, if your heading is *Laser Printers*, don't begin the next sentence with *These produce high-quality output.* . . .

Skill Check 6.1 Reviewing the Characteristics of Short Reports

Select a letter to indicate the best format for the report described.
a. Memo format   b. Letter format   c. Report format

1. A short report to a company from an outside consultant   _____

2. A short report from a product manager to her boss   _____

3. A long report describing a company's diversity program   _____

4. If you were writing a report to persuade management to purchase more computers, the best way to begin collecting data would be to
a. observe current use
b. consult books and journals
c. search the Internet   _____

5. Which combination of report headings is best?
a. Delivery Costs, Suppliers
b. Reduction of Delivery Costs, Recommendations
c. "Delivery Costs," "Supply Costs"
d. Reducing Delivery Costs, Finding New Suppliers   _____

Writing Plan for a Short Report

Short reports often have three parts: introduction, findings, and recommendations. If the report is purely informational, a summary may be made instead of recommendations.

Introduction. This part of a report may also be called *Background*. In this section you will want to explain why you are writing. You may also (a) describe what methods and sources you used to gather information and why they are credible, (b) provide any special background information that may be necessary, and (c) offer a preview of your findings.

Findings. This section may also be called *Observations, Facts, Results,* or *Discussion.* Important points to consider in this section are organization and display. You may wish to organize the findings (a) chronologically (for example, to describe the history of a problem), (b) alphabetically (if you were, for example, evaluating candidates for a position), (c) topically (for example, discussing sales by regions), or (d) from most to least important (such as listing criteria for evaluating equipment). To display the findings effectively, you could (a) use side headings, (b) number each finding, (c) underline or boldface the key words, or (d) merely indent the paragraphs.

Summary or Recommendations. Some reports just offer information. Such reports may conclude with an impartial summary. Other reports are more analytical, and they generally conclude with recommendations. These recommendations tell readers how to solve the problem and may even suggest ways to implement the necessary actions. To display recommendations, number each one and place it on a separate line.

Notice that the letter report in Figure 6.1 includes an introduction, findings and analyses, and recommendations.

Writing Plan for an Internal Proposal

Both managers and employees must occasionally write reports that justify or recommend something such as buying equipment, changing a procedure, hiring an employee, consolidating departments, or investing funds. Here is a writing plan for an internal proposal that recommends a course of action.

Introduction. In this section, identify the problem briefly. Use specific examples, supporting statistics, and authoritative quotes to lend credibility to the seriousness of the problem. If you think your audience will be receptive, announce your recommendation, solution, or action immediately and concisely. If you think your audience will

FIGURE 6.1
Short Report - Letter Format

Liberty Environmental, Inc.

2593 North Globe Road
Arlington, VA 22207   (804) 356-1094   www.lei.com

October 9, 201x

Ms. Sharon J. Goode
Richmond Realty, Inc.
3390 Chesterfield Avenue
Richmond, VA 22368

Dear Ms. Goode:

At the request of Richmond Realty, I have completed a preliminary investigation of its •──── **Explains purpose, outlines sources of information, and previews findings**
Mountain Park property listing regarding the possibility of environmental liabilities. The
following findings and recommendations are based on my physical inspection of the site,
official records, and interviews of officials and persons knowledgeable about the site.

Findings and Analyses

My preliminary assessment of the Mountain Park listing and its immediate vicinity revealed
rooms with damaged floor tiles on the first and second floors of 2539 Mountain View
Drive. Apparently, in recent remodeling efforts, these tiles had been cracked and broken. •──── **Describes findings and explains their significance**
Examination of the ceiling and attic revealed possible contamination from asbestos.

Located on the property is Mountain Technology, a possible hazardous waste generator.
Although I could not examine its interior, this company has the potential for producing
hazardous material contamination.

Recommendations ───── **Concludes with recommendations for solving the problem**

To reduce its potential environmental liability, Richmond Realty should take the following
steps in regard to its Mountain Park listing:

• Conduct an immediate asbestos survey at the site, including inspection of ceiling •──── **Uses bulleted list to improve readability and comprehension**
   insulation material, floor tiles, and insulation around a gas-fired heater vent pipe at
   2539 Mountain View Drive.

• Prepare an environmental audit of the generators of hazardous waste currently operat- •──── **Begins each recommendation with a verb for consistency**
   ing at the site, including Mountain Technology.

• Obtain lids for the dumpsters situated in the parking areas and ensure that the lids
   are kept closed.

If you would like to discuss the findings or recommendations in this report, please call
me and I will be glad to answer your questions.

Sincerely,

Scott R. Evans

Scott R. Evans

---

need to be persuaded or educated, do not announce your solution until after you
have explained its advantages.

Body. In writing the body of an internal proposal, you may want to include all or
some of the following elements. Explain more fully the benefits of the recommendations or steps to be taken to solve the problem. Include a discussion of pros, cons,
and costs. If appropriate, describe the factual and ethical negative consequences of
the current situation. For example, if your internal proposal recommends purchasing
new equipment, explain how much time, effort, money, and morale are being lost
by continuing to use outdated equipment that needs constant repairs. Quantification
through accurate facts and examples builds credibility and persuasive appeal. Explain

the benefits of your proposal. A bulleted list improves readability and emphasis. Anticipate objections to your proposal and discuss ways to counter those objections. The body should also provide a plan and schedule for implementing your proposal. If many people will be included in implementing the proposal, prepare a staffing section. Describe who will be doing what. You may also describe alternative solutions and show how they will not work as well as your proposal.

Conclusion. In the conclusion summarize your recommendation. Describe the specific action to be taken. Ask for authorization to proceed. To motivate the reader, you might include a date for the action to take place and a reason for the deadline.

An internal proposal is generally formatted as a memo such as the one shown in Figure 6.2. In this memo report the writer expects the reader to be receptive to the

FIGURE 6.2
Internal Proposal – Memo Format

Date:	September 20, 201x
To:	Kevin Castro, Vice President
From:	James Worthington, Operations Manager JW
Subject:	PILOT TESTING SMART TIRES

Next to fuel, truck tires are our biggest operating cost. Last year we spent $211,000 replacing and retreading tires for 495 trucks. This year the costs will be greater because prices have jumped at least 12 percent and because we've increased our fleet to 550 trucks. Truck tires are an additional burden since they require labor-intensive paperwork to track their warranties, wear, and retread histories. To reduce our long-term costs and to improve our tire tracking system, I recommend that we do the following:
(Introduces problem briefly but with concrete facts)

- Purchase 24 Goodyear smart tires.
- Begin a one-year pilot test on six trucks.
(Presents recommendations immediately)

How Smart Tires Work

Smart tires have an embedded computer chip that monitors wear, performance, and durability. The chip also creates an electronic fingerprint for positive identification of a tire. By passing a handheld sensor next to the tire, we can learn where and when a tire was made (for warranty and identification), how much tread it had originally, and its serial number.
(Justifies recommendations by explaining proposal and benefits)

How Smart Tire Could Benefit Us

Although smart tires are initially more expensive than other tires, they could help us improve our operations and save us money in four ways:
(Offers counterargument to possible objection)

1. **Retreads.** Goodyear believes that the wear data is so accurate that we should be able to retread every tire three times, instead of our current two times. If that's true, in one year we could save at least $27,000 in new tire costs.
2. **Safety.** Accurate and accessible wear data should reduce the danger of blowouts and flat tires. Last year, drivers reported six blowouts.
3. **Record keeping and maintenance.** Smart tires could reduce our maintenance costs by digitizing the numbers needed to meet safety regulations.
4. **Theft protection.** The chip can be used to monitor each tire as it leaves or enters the warehouse or yard, thus discouraging theft.

Summary and Action

Specifically, I recommend that you do the following:
(Explains recommendation in more detail)

- Authorize the special purchase of 24 Goodyear smart tires at $450 each, plus one electronic sensor at $1,200.
- Approve a one-year pilot test in our Atlanta territory that equips six trucks with smart tires and tracks their performance.
(Specifies action to be taken)

Please let me have your authorization by September 30 so that I can begin the pilot test before the winter driving season is upon us.
(Concludes with deadline and reason)

recommendation of pilot testing smart tires. Thus, the proposal begins directly with the recommendations announced immediately. The body discusses how the recommendation would work, and it itemizes benefits. It anticipates objections and counters them. The closing summarizes what action is to be taken and presents a deadline.

Writing Application 6.1

Organize the following information into a short letter report. As Cynthia M. Chavez, president, Chavez and Associates, you have been hired as a consultant to advise the St. Petersburg, Florida, City Council. The City Council has asked you and your associates to investigate a problem with Pinellas Park Beachway.

In 1979 St. Petersburg constructed a 12-foot pathway, now called the Pinellas Park Beachway. It was meant originally for bicycle riders, but today it has become very popular for joggers, walkers, bikers, in-line skaters, skateboarders, sightseers, and people walking their dogs. In fact, it has become so popular that it is dangerous. Last year the St. Petersburg Police Department reported an amazing 65 collisions in the area. And this doesn't count the close calls and minor accidents that no one reported. The City Council wants your organization to identify the problem and come up with some workable recommendations for improving safety.

As you look into the matter, you immediately decide that the council is right. A problem definitely exists! In addition to the many pedestrians and riders, you see that families with rented pedal-powered surreys clog the beachway. Sometimes they even operate these vehicles on the wrong side. Your investigation further reveals that bicyclists with rental bikes do not always have bells to alert walkers. And poor lighting makes nighttime use extremely dangerous. You have noticed that conditions seem to be worst on Sundays. This congestion results from nearby art and crafts fairs and sales, attracting even more people to the crowded area.

Your investigation confirms that the beachway is dangerous. But what to do about it? In a brainstorming session, your associates make a number of suggestions for reducing the dangers to users. By the way, the council is particularly interested in lessening the threat of liability to the city. One of your associates thinks that the beachway should be made 15 or more feet wide. Another suggests that the beachway be lighted at night. Someone thinks that a new path should be built, on the beach side of the existing beachway; this path would be for pedestrians only. Educating users about safety rules and etiquette would certainly be wise for everyone. One suggestion involves better striping or applying colors to designate different uses for the beachway. And why not require that all rental bicycles be equipped with bells? One of the best recommendations involved hiring uniformed "beach hosts" who would monitor the beachway, give advice, offer directions, and generally patrol the area.

In a short report, outline the problem and list your recommendations. Naturally, you would be happy to discuss your findings and recommendations with the St. Petersburg City Council.

Writing Application 6.2

Assume that your office needs a piece of equipment such as a photocopier, fax, scanner, digital camera, computer, printer, or the like. Do the research necessary to write a convincing internal proposal to your boss. Because you feel that your boss will be receptive to your request, you can use the direct approach.

Developing Spelling Skills

Why Is English Spelling So Difficult?

No one would dispute the complaint that many English words are difficult to spell. Why is spelling in our language so perplexing? For one thing, our language has borrowed many of its words from other languages. English has a Germanic base on which a superstructure of words borrowed from French, Latin, Greek, and other languages of the world has been erected. For this reason, its words are not always formed by regular patterns of letter combinations. In addition, spelling is made difficult because the pronunciation of English words is constantly changing. Today's spelling was standardized nearly 300 years ago, but many words are pronounced differently today than they were then. Therefore, pronunciation often provides little help in spelling. Consider, for example, the words *sew* and *dough.*

Study Tip

You can improve your spelling by using Spell Right at **www.meguffey .com.** Test your skills with a self-checked pretest, midterm, and final exam.

What Can Be Done to Improve One's Spelling?

Spelling is a skill that can be developed, just as arithmetic, keyboarding, and other skills can be developed. Because the ability to spell is a prerequisite for success in business and in most other activities, effort expended to acquire this skill is effort well spent.

Three traditional approaches to improving spelling have met with varying degrees of success.

1. Rules or Guidelines
The spelling of English words is consistent enough to justify the formulation of a few spelling rules, perhaps more appropriately called **guidelines** since the generalizations in question are not invariably applicable. Such guidelines are, in other words, helpful but not infallible.

2. Mnemonics
Another approach to improving one's ability to spell involves the use of mnemonics or memory devices. For example, the word *principle* might be associated with the word *rule,* to form in the mind of the speller a link between the meaning and the spelling of *principle.* To spell *capitol,* one might think of the *dome* of the capitol building and focus on the *o*'s in both words. The use of mnemonics can be an effective device for the improvement of spelling only if the speller makes a real effort to develop the necessary memory hooks.

3. Rote Learning
A third approach to the improvement of spelling centers on memorization. The word is studied by the speller until it can be readily reproduced in the mind's eye.

The 1-2-3 Spelling Plan

Proficiency in spelling is not attained without concentrated effort. Here's a plan to follow in mastering the 400 commonly misspelled words included in this appendix. For each word, try this 1-2-3 approach.

1. Is a spelling guideline applicable? If so, select the appropriate guideline and study the word in relation to that guideline.
2. If no guideline applies, can a memory device be created to aid in the recall of the word?
3. If neither a guideline nor a memory device will work, the word must be memorized. Look at the word carefully. Pronounce it. Write it or repeat it until you can visualize all its letters in your mind's eye.

Before you try the 1-2-3 plan, become familiar with the six spelling guidelines that follow. These spelling guidelines are not intended to represent all the possible spelling rules appearing in the various available spelling books. These six guidelines are, however, among the most effective and helpful of the recognized spelling rules.

Guideline 1: Words Containing *ie* or *ei*

Although there are exceptions to it, the following familiar rhyme can be helpful.

   (a) Write *i* before *e*
   (b) Except after *c,*
   (c) Or when sounded like *a*
       As in *neighbor* and *weigh.*

Study these words illustrating the three parts of the rhyme.

(a) *i* Before *e*		(b) Except After *c*	(c) or When Sounded Like *a*
achieve	grief	ceiling	beige
belief	ingredient	conceive	eight
believe	mischief	deceive	freight
brief	niece	perceive	heir
cashier	piece	receipt	neighbor
chief	shield	receive	reign
convenient	sufficient		their
field	view		vein
friend	yield		weight

Exceptions: These exceptional *ei* and *ie* words must be learned by rote or with the use of a mnemonic device.

caffeine	height	seize
either	leisure	sheik
financier	neither	sleight
foreigner	protein	weird

Guideline 2: Words Ending in *e*

For most words ending in an *e,* the final *e* is dropped when the word is joined to a suffix beginning with a vowel (such as *ing, able,* or *al*). The final *e* is retained when a suffix beginning with a consonant (such as *ment, less, ly,* or *ful*) is joined to such a word.

Final *e* Dropped	Final *e* Retained
believe, believing	arrange, arrangement
care, caring	require, requirement
hope, hoping	hope, hopeless
receive, receiving	care, careless
desire, desirable	like, likely
cure, curable	approximate, approximately
move, movable	definite, definitely
value, valuable	sincere, sincerely
disperse, dispersal	use, useful
arrive, arrival	hope, hopeful

Exceptions: The few exceptions to this spelling guideline are among the most frequently misspelled words. As such, they deserve special attention. Notice that they all involve a dropped final *e*.

acknowledgment	ninth
argument	truly
judgment	wholly

Guideline 3: Words Ending in *ce* or *ge*
When *able* or *ous* is added to words ending in *ce* or *ge*, the final *e* is retained if the *c* or *g* is pronounced softly (as in *change* or *peace*).

advantage, advantageous	change, changeable
courage, courageous	service, serviceable
outrage, outrageous	manage, manageable

Guideline 4: Words Ending in *y*
Words ending in a *y* that is preceded by a consonant normally change the *y* to *i* before all suffixes except those beginning with an *i*.

Change *y* to *i* Because *y* Is Preceded by a Consonant	Do Not Change *y* to *i* Because *y* Is Preceded by a Vowel
accompany, accompaniment	employ, employer
study, studied, studious	annoy, annoying, annoyance
duty, dutiful	stay, staying, stayed
industry, industrious	attorney, attorneys
carry, carriage	valley, valleys
apply, appliance	

Change *y* to *i* Because *y* Is Preceded by a Consonant	Do Not Change *y* to *i* When Adding *ing*
try, tried	accompany, accompanying
empty, emptiness	apply, applying
forty, fortieth	study, studying

secretary, secretaries	satisfy, satisfying
company, companies	try, trying
hurry, hurries	

Exceptions: day, daily; dry, dried; mislay, mislaid; pay, paid; shy, shyly; gay, gaily.

Guideline 5: Doubling a Final Consonant

If one-syllable words or two-syllable words accented on the second syllable end in a single consonant preceded by a single vowel, the final consonant is doubled before the addition of a suffix beginning with a vowel.

Although complex, this spelling guideline is extremely useful and therefore well worth mastering. Many spelling errors can be avoided by applying this guideline.

One-Syllable Words	Two-Syllable Words
can, canned	acquit, acquitting, acquittal
drop, dropped	admit, admitted, admitting
fit, fitted	begin, beginner, beginning
get, getting	commit, committed, committing
man, manned	control, controller, controlling
plan, planned	defer, deferred (but deference*)
run, running	excel, excelled, excelling
shut, shutting	occur, occurrence, occurring
slip, slipped	prefer, preferring (but preference*)
swim, swimming	recur, recurred, recurrence
ton, tonnage	refer, referring (but reference*)

Because the accent shifts to the first syllable, the final consonant is not doubled.

Here is a summary of conditions necessary for application of this guideline.

1. The word must end in a single consonant.
2. The final consonant must be preceded by a single vowel.
3. The word must be accented on the second syllable (if it has two syllables).

Words derived from *cancel, offer, differ, equal, suffer,* and *benefit* are not governed by this guideline because they are accented on the first syllable.

Guideline 6: Prefixes and Suffixes

For words in which the letter that ends the prefix is the same as the letter that begins the main word (such as in *dissimilar*), both letters must be included. For words in which a suffix begins with the same letter that ends the main word (such as in *coolly*), both letters must also be included.

Prefix	Main Word	Main Word	Suffix
dis	satisfied	accidental	ly
ir	responsible	incidental	ly
il	literate	clean	ness
mis	spell	cool	ly
mis	state	even	ness
un	necessary	mean	ness

On the other hand, do not supply additional letters when adding prefixes to main words.

Prefix	Main Word
dis	appoint (*not* dissappoint)
dis	appearance
mis	take

Perhaps the most important guideline one can follow in spelling correctly is to use the dictionary whenever in doubt.

400 Most Frequently Misspelled Words* (Divided into 20 Lists of 20 Words Each)

List 1

1. absence
2. acceptance
3. accessible
4. accidentally
5. accommodate
6. accompaniment
7. accurately
8. accustom
9. achievement
10. acknowledgment
11. acquaintance
12. acquire
13. across
14. actually
15. adequately
16. admitted
17. adolescence
18. advantageous
19. advertising
20. advice, advise

List 2

21. afraid
22. against
23. aggressive
24. all right
25. almost
26. alphabetical
27. already, all ready
28. although
29. amateur
30. among
31. amount
32. analysis
33. analyze
34. angel, angle
35. annoyance
36. annual
37. answer
38. apologized
39. apparent
40. appliance

List 3

41. applying
42. approaches
43. appropriate
44. approximately
45. arguing
46. argument
47. arrangement
48. article
49. athlete
50. attack
51. attendance, attendants
52. attitude
53. attorneys
54. auxiliary
55. basically
56. beautiful
57. before
58. beginning
59. believing
60. benefited

Compiled from lists of words most frequently misspelled by students and businesspeople.

List 4

61. biggest
62. breath, breathe
63. brief
64. business
65. calendar
66. capital, capitol
67. career
68. careless
69. carrying
70. cashier
71. ceiling
72. certain
73. challenge
74. changeable
75. chief
76. choose, chose
77. cloths, clothes
78. column
79. coming
80. committee

List 5

81. companies
82. competition
83. completely
84. conceive
85. conscience
86. conscientious
87. conscious
88. considerably
89. consistent
90. continuous
91. controlling
92. controversial
93. convenience
94. council, counsel
95. cylinder
96. daily
97. deceive
98. decision
99. define, definitely
100. dependent

List 6

101. description
102. desirable
103. destroy
104. development
105. difference
106. dining
107. disappearance
108. disappoint
109. disastrous
110. discipline
111. discussion
112. disease
113. dissatisfied
114. distinction
115. divide
116. doesn't
117. dominant
118. dropped
119. due
120. during

List 7

121. efficient
122. eligible
123. embarrass
124. encourage
125. enough
126. environment
127. equipped
128. especially
129. exaggerate
130. excellence
131. except, accept
132. exercise
133. existence
134. experience
135. explanation
136. extremely
137. familiar
138. families
139. fascinate
140. favorite

List 8

141. February
142. fictitious
143. field
144. finally
145. financially
146. foreigner
147. fortieth
148. forty, fourth, forth
149. forward, foreword
150. freight
151. friend
152. fulfill
153. fundamentally
154. further, farther
155. generally
156. government
157. governor
158. grammar
159. grateful
160. guard

List 9

161. happiness
162. hear, here
163. height
164. heroes
165. hopeless
166. hoping
167. huge
168. humorous
169. hungry
170. ignorance
171. imaginary
172. imagine
173. immediately
174. immense
175. importance
176. incidentally
177. independent, independently
178. indispensable
179. industrious
180. inevitable

List 10

181. influential
182. ingredient
183. initiative
184. intelligence
185. interest
186. interference
187. interpretation
188. interrupt
189. involve
190. irrelevant
191. irresponsible
192. island
193. jealous
194. judgment
195. kindergarten
196. knowledge
197. laboratory
198. laborer
199. laid
200. led, lead

List 11

201. leisurely
202. library
203. license
204. likely
205. literature
206. lives
207. loneliness
208. loose, lose
209. losing
210. luxury
211. magazine
212. magnificence
213. maintenance
214. manageable
215. maneuver
216. manner
217. manufacturer
218. marriage
219. mathematics
220. meant

List 12

221. mechanics
222. medicine
223. medieval
224. mere
225. miniature
226. minutes
227. mischief

228. misspell
229. mistake
230. muscle
231. mysterious
232. naturally
233. necessary
234. neighbor

235. neither
236. nervous
237. nickel
238. niece
239. ninety
240. ninth

List 13

241. noticeable
242. numerous
243. obstacle
244. occasionally
245. occurrence
246. off
247. offered

248. official
249. omitted, omit
250. operate
251. opinion
252. opportunity
253. opposite
254. organization

255. origin
256. original
257. paid
258. pamphlet
259. parallel
260. particular

List 14

261. passed, past
262. pastime
263. peaceable
264. peculiar
265. perceive
266. performance
267. permanent

268. permitted
269. persistent
270. personal, personnel
271. persuading
272. phase, faze
273. philosophy

274. physical
275. piece
276. planned
277. pleasant
278. poison
279. political
280. possession

List 15

281. possible
282. practical
283. precede
284. preferred
285. prejudice
286. preparation
287. prevalent

288. principal, principle
289. privilege
290. probably
291. proceed
292. professor
293. prominent

294. proving
295. psychology
296. pursuing
297. quantity
298. quiet, quite
299. really
300. receipt

List 16

301. receiving, receive
302. recognize
303. recommend
304. reference
305. referring, refer
306. regard
307. relative
308. relieving
309. religious
310. reminiscent
311. repetition
312. representative
313. requirement
314. resistance
315. responsible
316. restaurant
317. rhythm
318. ridiculous
319. sacrifice
320. safety

List 17

321. satisfying
322. scenery
323. schedule
324. science
325. secretaries
326. seize
327. sense, since
328. sentence
329. separate, separately
330. sergeant
331. serviceable
332. several
333. shining
334. shoulder
335. significance
336. similar
337. simply
338. sincerely
339. site, cite, sight
340. source

List 18

341. speak, speech
342. specimen
343. stationary, stationery
344. stopped
345. stories
346. straight, strait
347. strenuous
348. stretch
349. strict
350. studying
351. substantial
352. subtle
353. succeed
354. success
355. sufficient
356. summary
357. suppose
358. surprise
359. suspense
360. swimming

List 19

361. syllable
362. symbol
363. symmetrical
364. synonymous
365. technique
366. temperament
367. temperature
368. tendency
369. than, then
370. their, there, they're
371. themselves
372. theories
373. therefore
374. thorough
375. though
376. through
377. together
378. tomorrow
379. tragedies
380. transferred

List 20

381. tremendous
382. tried
383. truly
384. undoubtedly
385. unnecessary
386. until
387. unusual

388. useful
389. using
390. vacuum
391. valuable
392. varies
393. vegetable
394. view

395. weather, whether
396. weird
397. were, where
398. wholly, holy
399. writing
400. yield

Developing Vocabulary Skills

If you understand the meanings of many words, you can be said to have a "good vocabulary." Words are the basis of thought. We think with words, we understand with words, and we communicate with words.

A large working vocabulary is a significant asset. It allows us to use precise words that say exactly what we intend. In addition, we understand more effectively what we hear and read. A large vocabulary also enables us to score well on employment and intelligence tests. Lewis M. Terman, who developed the Stanford-Binet IQ tests, believes that vocabulary is the best single indicator of intelligence.

In the business world, where precise communication is extremely important, surveys show a definite correlation between vocabulary size and job performance. Skilled workers, in the majority of cases, have larger vocabularies than unskilled workers. Supervisors know the meanings of more words than the workers they direct, and executives have larger vocabularies than employees working for them.

Having a good vocabulary at our command doesn't necessarily ensure our success in life, but it certainly gives us an advantage. Improving your vocabulary will help you expand your options in an increasingly complex world.

Vocabulary can be acquired in three ways: accidentally, incidentally, and intentionally. Setting out intentionally to expand your word power is, of course, the most efficient vocabulary-building method. One of the best means of increasing your vocabulary involves using 3-by-5 cards. When you encounter an unfamiliar word, write it on a card and put the definition of the word on the reverse side. Just five to ten minutes of practice each day with such cards can significantly increase your vocabulary.

Your campaign to increase your vocabulary can begin with the 18 lists of selected business terms and words of general interest included in this appendix. You may already know partial definitions for some of these words. Take this opportunity to develop more precise definitions for them. Follow these steps in using the word lists:

1. Record the word on a 3-by-5 card.
2. Look up the word in your dictionary. Compare the dictionary definitions of the word with the definition alternatives shown after the word in your copy of *Business English*. Select the correct definition, and write its letter in the space provided in your textbook. (The definitions provided in your textbook are quite concise but should help you remember the word's most common meaning.)
3. On the reverse side of your card, write the phonetic spelling of the word and the word's part of speech. Then write its definition using as much of the dictionary definition as you find helpful. Try also to add a phrase or sentence illustrating the word.
4. Study your 3-by-5 cards often.
5. Try to find ways to use your vocabulary words in your speech and writing.

List 1

1. adjacent = (a) previous, (b) similar, (c) overdue, (d) nearby _____

2. ambivalence = having (a) uncertainty, (b) ambition, (c) compassion, (d) intelligence _____

3. belligerent = (a) overweight, (b) quarrelsome, (c) likable, (d) believable _____

4. contingent = (a) conditional, (b) allowable, (c) hopeless, (d) impractical _____

5. decadent = in a state of (a) repair, (b) happiness, (c) decline, (d) extreme patriotism _____

6. entitlement = (a) label, (b) tax refund, (c) screen credit, (d) legal right _____

7. equivalent = (a) subsequent, (b) identical, (c) self-controlled, (d) plentiful _____

8. paramount = (a) foremost, (b) high mountain, (c) film company, (d) insignificant _____

9. plausible = (a) quiet, (b) acceptable, (c) notorious, (d) negative _____

10. unilateral = (a) powerful, (b) harmonious, (c) one-sided, (d) indelible _____

List 2

1. affluent = (a) rich, (b) slippery, (c) persistent, (d) rebellious _____

2. autocrat = one who (a) owns many cars, (b) is self-centered, (c) has power, (d) collects signatures _____

3. benevolent = for the purpose of (a) religion, (b) doing good, (c) healing, (d) violence _____

4. entrepreneur = (a) business owner, (b) traveler, (c) salesperson, (d) gambler _____

5. impertinent = (a) stationary, (b) bound to happen, (c) obsolete, (d) rude and irreverent _____

6. imprudent = (a) unwise, (b) crude, (c) vulnerable, (d) lifeless _____

7. mediator = one who seeks (a) overseas trade, (b) profits, (c) safe investment, (d) peaceful settlement _____

8. preponderance = (a) thoughtful, (b) exclusive right, (c) superiority, (d) forethought _____

9. recipient = (a) receiver, (b) respondent, (c) voter, (d) giver _____

10. reprehensible = (a) obedient, (b) independent, (c) blameworthy, (d) following _____

List 3

1. affable = (a) cheap, (b) pleasant, (c) strange, (d) competent _____

2. consensus = (a) population count, (b) attendance, (c) tabulation, (d) agreement _____

3. criterion = (a) standard, (b) command, (c) pardon, (d) law _____

4. diligent = (a) gentle, (b) industrious, (c) prominent, (d) intelligent _____

5. hydraulic = operated by means of (a) air, (b) gasoline, (c) liquid, (d) mechanical parts _____

6. hypothesis = (a) triangle, (b) promulgate, (c) highest point, (d) theory _____

7. phenomenon = (a) imagination, (b) rare event, (c) appointment, (d) clever saying _____

8. reticent = (a) silent, (b) strong-willed, (c) inflexible, (d) disagreeable   _____

9. sanctuary = a place of (a) healing, (b) refuge, (c) rest, (d) learning   _____

10. stimulus = something that causes (a) response, (b) light, (c) pain, (d) movement   _____

List 4

1. beneficiary = one who (a) receives a license, (b) creates goodwill, (c) receives proceeds, (d) makes friends   _____

2. constrain = (a) restrict, (b) filter, (c) use, (d) inform   _____

3. corroborate = (a) contradict, (b) recall, (c) erode, (d) confirm   _____

4. dun (n) = a demand for (a) legal action, (b) payment, (c) credit information, (d) dividends   _____

5. equitable = (a) fair, (b) profitable, (c) similar, (d) clear   _____

6. fluctuate = (a) rinse out, (b) magnetic field, (c) pricing schedule, (d) swing back and forth   _____

7. indolent = (a) self-indulgent, (b) lazy, (c) pampered, (d) uncertain   _____

8. nullify = (a) disappear, (b) imitate, (c) invalidate, (d) enhance   _____

9. obsolete = (a) ugly, (b) outmoded, (c) audible, (d) scant   _____

10. stabilize = to make (a) pleasant, (b) congenial, (c) traditional, (d) firm   _____

List 5

1. arbitrate = (a) decide, (b) construct, (c) conquer, (d) ratify   _____

2. coalition = (a) deliberation, (b) allegiance, (c) adherence, (d) alliance   _____

3. collate = (a) assemble, (b) denounce, (c) supersede, (d) uninformed   _____

4. conglomerate = combination of (a) executives, (b) companies, (c) investments, (d) countries   _____

5. franchise = (a) fictitious reason, (b) right, (c) obligation, (d) official announcement   _____

6. logistics = (a) speculations, (b) analytic philosophy, (c) reasonable outcome, (d) details of operation   _____

7. proxy = authority to (a) act for another, (b) write checks, (c) submit nominations, (d) explain   _____

8. subsidiary = (a) below expectations, (b) country dominated by another, (c) company controlled by another, (d) depressed financial condition   _____

9. termination = (a) end, (b) inception, (c) identification, (d) evasive action   _____

10. virtually = (a) absolutely, (b) precisely, (c) almost entirely, (d) strictly   _____

List 6

1. affiliate = (a) trust, (b) attract, (c) effect, (d) join   _____

2. alter = (a) table for religious ceremony, (b) solitary, (c) attribute, (d) modify   _____

3. boisterous   = (a) vociferous, (b) masculine, (c) cheerful, (d) brusque   _____

4. configuration   = (a) stratagem, (b) foreign currency, (c) form, (d) comprehension   _____

5. conveyance   = (a) vehicle, (b) transformation, (c) baggage, (d) consortium   _____

6. infringe   = (a) ravel, (b) decorative border, (c) encroach, (d) frivolous   _____

7. jurisdiction   = (a) science of law, (b) enunciation, (c) justice, (d) authority   _____

8. nonpartisan   = (a) unbiased, (b) antisocial, (c) ineffective, (d) untenable   _____

9. parity   = (a) price index, (b) justice under law, (c) plenitude, (d) equality of purchasing power   _____

10. usury   = (a) method of operation, (b) implementation, (c) illegal interest, (d) customary   _____

List 7

1. anonymous   = (a) multiplex, (b) powerless, (c) vexing, (d) nameless   _____

2. cartel   = (a) combination to fix prices, (b) ammunition belt, (c) partnership to promote competition, (d) placard   _____

3. conjecture   = (a) coagulation, (b) gesticulation, (c) guesswork, (d) connection   _____

4. disparity   = (a) unlikeness, (b) separation, (c) lacking emotion, (d) repudiation   _____

5. environment   = (a) urban area, (b) zenith, (c) surroundings, (d) latitude   _____

6. impetus   = (a) oversight, (b) stimulus, (c) hindrance, (d) imminent   _____

7. portfolio   = a list of (a) books, (b) security analysts, (c) corporations, (d) investments   _____

8. quiescent   = (a) presumptuous, (b) latent, (c) immoderate, (d) volatile   _____

9. surrogate   = (a) substitute, (b) accused, (c) authenticate, (d) suspend   _____

10. tariff   = (a) marsupial, (b) announcement, (c) ship, (d) duty   _____

List 8

1. accrue   = (a) conform, (b) accumulate, (c) diminish, (d) multiply   _____

2. amortize   = (a) pay off, (b) reduce, (c) romance, (d) kill   _____

3. commensurate   = (a) infinitesimal, (b) erroneous, (c) reliable, (d) proportional   _____

4. consortium   = (a) configuration, (b) partnership or association, (c) royal offspring, (d) rental property   _____

5. discernible   = (a) perceptive, (b) pretentious, (c) recognizable, (d) dissident   _____

6. frugal   = (a) thrifty, (b) wasteful, (c) judicious, (d) profligate   _____

7. pecuniary   = (a) rudimentary, (b) eccentric, (c) financial, (d) distinctive   _____

8. retract   = (a) disavow, (b) reorganize, (c) reciprocate, (d) hide   _____

9. scrutinize   = (a) cheerfully admit, (b) baffle, (c) persist, (d) examine carefully   _____

10. tenacious   = (a) falling apart, (b) holding on, (c) immobile, (d) chagrined   _____

List 9

1. amiable	= (a) contumacious, (b) impetuous, (c) feasible, (d) congenial	_____
2. credible	= (a) plausible, (b) deceitful, (c) religious, (d) tolerant	_____
3. defendant	= one who (a) sues, (b) answers suit, (c) judges, (d) protects	_____
4. dissipate	= (a) accumulate, (b) partition, (c) liquify, (d) scatter or waste	_____
5. incentive	= (a) impediment, (b) support, (c) motive, (d) remuneration	_____
6. innocuous	= (a) harmless, (b) injection, (c) facetious, (d) frightening	_____
7. oust	= (a) install, (b) instigate, (c) shout, (d) expel	_____
8. pittance	= (a) tiny amount, (b) tithe, (c) abyss, (d) pestilence	_____
9. plaintiff	= one who (a) defends, (b) is sad, (c) sues, (d) responds	_____
10. superfluous	= (a) extraordinary, (b) very slippery, (c) shallow, (d) oversupplied	_____

List 10

1. adroit	= (a) ideal, (b) resilient, (c) witty, (d) skillful	_____
2. derogatory	= (a) minimal, (b) degrading, (c) originating from, (d) devious	_____
3. escrow	= (a) international treaty, (b) public registration, (c) licensed by state, (d) type of deposit	_____
4. facsimile	= (a) principle, (b) prototype, (c) exact copy, (d) counterfeit	_____
5. inordinate	= (a) unwholesome, (b) excessive, (c) unimportant, (d) treacherous	_____
6. logical	= (a) reasoned, (b) irrelevant, (c) lofty, (d) intricate	_____
7. malfeasance	= (a) prevaricate, (b) injurious, (c) superstitious, (d) misconduct	_____
8. noxious	= (a) pernicious, (b) unusual, (c) pleasant, (d) inconsequential	_____
9. résumé	= (a) budget report, (b) minutes of meeting, (c) photo album, (d) summary of qualifications	_____
10. spasmodic	= (a) paralyzing, (b) intermittent or fitful, (c) internal, (d) painful	_____

List 11

1. animosity	= (a) happiness, (b) deep sadness, (c) hatred, (d) study of animals	_____
2. caveat	= (a) headwear, (b) warning, (c) neckwear, (d) prerogative	_____
3. conscientious	= (a) meticulous, (b) productive, (c) cognizant, (d) sophisticated	_____
4. cosmopolitan	= (a) provincial, (b) multicolored, (c) heavenly, (d) worldly	_____
5. decipher	= (a) preclude, (b) decode, (c) demise, (d) reproach	_____
6. euphemism	= (a) religious discourse, (b) facial expression, (c) figurative speech, (d) inoffensive term	_____
7. fraudulent	= (a) loquacious, (b) candid, (c) deceitful, (d) despotic	_____
8. peripheral	= (a) supplementary, (b) imaginary, (c) visionary, (d) supernatural	_____
9. pungent	= (a) knowledgeable, (b) wise religious man, (c) acrid, (d) vulnerable	_____
10. requisite	= (a) essential, (b) demand, (c) skillful, (d) discreet	_____

List 12

1. ad valorem	= (a) esteemed, (b) genuine, (c) recompense, (d) proportional	_____
2. carte blanche	= (a) white carriage, (b) credit terms, (c) full permission, (d) geographical expression	_____
3. de facto	= (a) prejudicial, (b) actual, (c) valid, (d) unlawful	_____
4. esprit de corps	= (a) group enthusiasm, (b) strong coffee, (c) central authority, (d) government overturn	_____
5. modus operandi	= (a) method of procedure, (b) practical compromise, (c) business transaction, (d) flexible arbitration	_____
6. per capita	= per unit of (a) income, (b) population, (c) birth, (d) household	_____
7. per diem	= (a) daily, (b) weekly, (c) yearly, (d) taxable	_____
8. prima facie	= (a) self-taught, (b) apparent, (c) principal, (d) artificial effect	_____
9. status quo	= (a) haughty demeanor, (b) steadfast opinion, (c) position of importance, (d) existing condition	_____
10. tort	= (a) rich cake, (b) extended dream, (c) wrongful act, (d) lawful remedy	_____

List 13

1. acquit	= (a) discharge, (b) pursue, (c) interfere, (d) impede	_____
2. annuity	= (a) yearly report, (b) insurance premium, (c) tuition refund, (d) annual payment	_____
3. complacent	= (a) appealing, (b) self-satisfied, (c) sympathetic, (d) scrupulous	_____
4. contraband	= (a) discrepancy, (b) opposing opinion, (c) smuggled goods, (d) ammunition	_____
5. insolvent	= (a) uncleanable, (b) unexplainable, (c) bankrupt, (d) unjustifiable	_____
6. malicious	= marked by (a) good humor, (b) ill will, (c) great pleasure, (d) injurious tumor	_____
7. negligent	= (a) careless, (b) fraudulent, (c) unlawful, (d) weak	_____
8. nominal	= (a) enumerated, (b) beneficial, (c) extravagant, (d) insignificant	_____
9. rescind	= (a) consign, (b) oppose, (c) repeal, (d) censure	_____
10. stringent	= (a) rigid, (b) expedient, (c) compliant, (d) resilient	_____

List 14

1. affirm	= (a) business organization, (b) validate, (c) elevate, (d) encircle	_____
2. exonerate	= (a) commend, (b) declare blameless, (c) banish, (d) emigrate	_____
3. expedite	= (a) elucidate, (b) get rid of, (c) amplify, (d) rush	_____
4. hamper (v)	= (a) impede, (b) delineate, (c) release, (d) assuage	_____
5. implement (v)	= (a) suppress, (b) ameliorate, (c) carry out, (d) attribute	_____
6. induce	= (a) teach, (b) construe, (c) persuade, (d) copy	_____
7. obliterate	= (a) obstruct, (b) prevent, (c) minimize, (d) erase	_____

8. quandary = a state of (a) doubt, (b) certainty, (c) depression, (d) apprehension _____

9. surmount = (a) hike, (b) overcome, (c) interpret, (d) specify _____

10. veracity = (a) truthfulness, (b) swiftness, (c) efficiency, (d) persistence _____

List 15

1. aggregate = constituting a (a) hostile crowd, (b) word combination, (c) total group, (d) sticky mass _____

2. ambiguous = (a) peripatetic, (b) uncertain, (c) enterprising, (d) deceptive _____

3. amend = (a) alter, (b) pray, (c) praise, (d) utter _____

4. apportion = (a) sanction, (b) ratify, (c) estimate, (d) divide _____

5. collaborate = (a) scrutinize, (b) cooperate, (c) surrender, (d) accumulate _____

6. ingenuity = (a) innocence, (b) torpor, (c) cleverness, (d) self-composure _____

7. irretrievable = not capable of being (a) sold, (b) identified, (c) explained, (d) recovered _____

8. lenient = (a) liberal, (b) crooked, (c) benevolent, (d) explicit _____

9. retrench = (a) dig repeatedly, (b) curtail, (c) reiterate, (d) enlighten _____

10. trivial = (a) composed of three parts, (b) momentous, (c) paltry, (d) economical _____

List 16

1. audit = (a) examine, (b) speak, (c) exchange, (d) expunge _____

2. arrears = (a) old-fashioned, (b) gratuity, (c) overdue debt, (d) option _____

3. curtail = (a) obstruct, (b) restore, (c) rejuvenate, (d) shorten _____

4. encumber = (a) grow, (b) substantiate, (c) burden, (d) illustrate _____

5. exemplify = (a) segregate, (b) divulge, (c) illustrate, (d) condone _____

6. extension = (a) unusual request, (b) prolonged journey, (c) haphazard results, (d) extra time _____

7. fortuitous = (a) accidental, (b) courageous, (c) radical, (d) assiduous _____

8. innovation = (a) reorganization, (b) occupancy, (c) introduction, (d) solution _____

9. syndicate = (a) union of writers, (b) council of lawmakers, (c) group of symptoms, (d) association of people _____

10. venture = (a) speculative business transaction, (b) unsecured loan, (c) stock split, (d) gambling debt _____

List 17

1. acquiesce = (a) gain possession of, (b) confront, (c) implore, (d) comply _____

2. enumerate = (a) articulate, (b) list, (c) enunciate, (d) see clearly _____

3. erratic = (a) pleasurable, (b) wandering, (c) exotic, (d) serene _____

4. expedient = serving to promote (a) fellowship, (b) one's self-interests, (c) good of others, (d) speedy delivery _____

5. feasible   = (a) auspicious, (b) profuse, (c) reasonable, (d) extraneous   _____

6. literal   = (a) exact, (b) devout, (c) apropos, (d) noticeable   _____

7. lucrative   = (a) providential, (b) swift, (c) pleasant, (d) profitable   _____

8. negotiable   = (a) essential, (b) adequate, (c) open to discussion, (d) economical   _____

9. nonchalant   = (a) dull, (b) cool, (c) unintelligent, (d) sagacious   _____

10. reconcile   = (a) resolve differences, (b) calculate, (c) modify, (d) remunerate   _____

List 18

1. apprehensive   = (a) knowledgeable, (b) fearful, (c) reticent, (d) autonomous   _____

2. circumspect   = (a) cautious, (b) uncertain, (c) cooperative, (d) frugal   _____

3. collateral   = (a) revenue, (b) secret agreement, (c) book value, (d) security for a loan   _____

4. insinuation   = (a) disagreeable proposal, (b) indirect suggestion, (c) elucidating glimpse, (d) flagrant insult   _____

5. liaison   = (a) legal obligation, (b) treaty, (c) connection between groups, (d) quarantine   _____

6. procrastinate   = (a) predict, (b) reproduce, (c) postpone, (d) advance   _____

7. ratification   = the act of (a) confirming, (b) reviewing, (c) evaluating, (d) inscribing   _____

8. renovate   = (a) renegotiate, (b) restore, (c) supply, (d) deliver   _____

9. saturate   = to fill (a) slowly, (b) dangerously, (c) as expected, (d) to excess   _____

10. vendor   = (a) seller, (b) manufacturer, (c) tradesman, (d) coin collector   _____

Document Format Guide

Business communicators produce numerous documents that have standardized formats. Becoming familiar with these formats is important because business documents actually carry two kinds of messages. Verbal messages are conveyed by the words chosen to express the writer's ideas. Nonverbal messages are conveyed largely by the appearance of a document and its adherence to recognized formats. To ensure that your documents carry favorable nonverbal messages about you and your organization, you should give special attention to the appearance and formatting of your e-mail messages, letters, envelopes, résumés, and fax cover sheets.

E-Mail Messages

E-mail messages are sent by computers through networks. After reading e-mail messages, receivers may print, store, or delete them. E-mail is an appropriate channel for *short* messages. E-mail should not replace business letters or memos for messages that are lengthy, require permanent records, or transmit confidential or sensitive information. This section provides information on formats and usage. The following suggestions, illustrated in Figure C.1 and also in Figure 4.1 of the Unit 4 Writer's Workshop on page 294, may guide you in setting up the parts of any e-mail message. Always check, however, with your organization so that you can follow its practices.

To Line

Include the receiver's e-mail address after *To*. If the receiver's address is recorded in your address book, you just have to click on it. Be sure to enter all addresses very carefully since one mistyped letter prevents delivery.

From Line

Most mail programs automatically include your name and e-mail address after *From*.

Cc and *Bcc*

Insert the e-mail address of anyone who is to receive a copy of the message. *Cc* stands for "carbon copy" or "courtesy copy." Don't be tempted, though, to send needless copies just because it is easy. *Bcc* stands for "blind carbon copy." Some writers use *bcc* to send a copy of the message without the addressee's knowledge. Writers also use the *bcc* line for mailing lists. When a message is sent to a number of people and their e-mail addresses should not be revealed, the *bcc* line works well to conceal the names and addresses of all receivers. In the Microsoft Outlook e-mail program, the *bcc* notation appears only when a writer chooses to use it.

Subject

Identify the subject of the e-mail message with a brief but descriptive summary of the topic. Be sure to include enough information to be clear and compelling.

FIGURE C.1
E-Mail Message

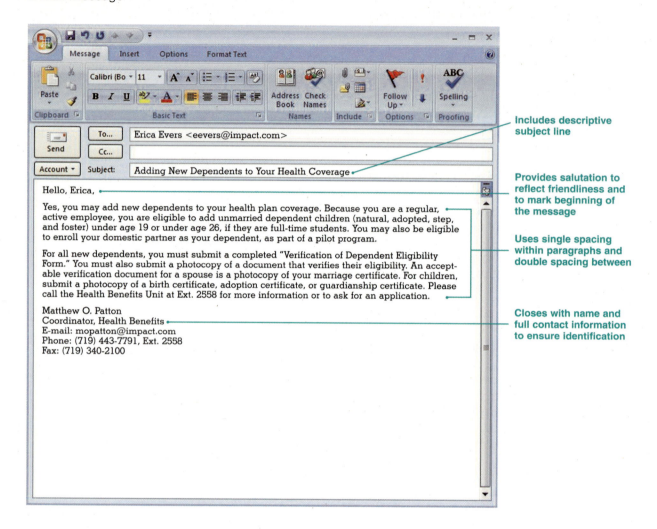

Includes descriptive
subject line

Provides salutation to
reflect friendliness and
to mark beginning of
the message

Uses single spacing
within paragraphs and
double spacing between

Closes with name and
full contact information
to ensure identification

Capitalize the initial letters of main words. Main words are all words except (a) the articles *a, an,* and *the*; (b) prepositions containing two or three letters (such as *at, to, on, by, for*); (c) the word *to* in an infinitive (*to work, to write*); and (d) the word *as*—unless any of these words are the first or last word in the subject line.

Salutation
Include a brief greeting, if you like. Some writers use a salutation such as *Dear Erica* followed by a comma or a colon. Others are more informal with *Hi, Erica; Hello, Erica; Good morning;* or *Greetings*.

Message
Cover just one topic in your message, and try to keep your total message under three screens in length. Single-space and be sure to use both upper- and lower-case letters. Double-space between paragraphs.

Closing
Conclude an e-mail message, if you like, with *Cheers, Best wishes,* or *Warm regards,* followed by your name and complete contact information. Some people omit their e-mail address because they think it is provided automatically. However, some programs and routers do not transmit the address automatically. Therefore, always include it along with other identifying information in the closing.

Attachment

Use the attachment window or button to select the path and file name of any file you wish to send with your e-mail message. You can also attach a Web page to your message.

Business Letters

Business communicators write business letters primarily to correspond with people outside the organization. Letters may go to customers, vendors, other businesses, and the government. The following information will help you format your letters following conventional guidelines.

Spacing and Punctuation

For some time typists left two spaces after end punctuation (periods, question marks, and so forth). This practice was necessary, it was thought, because typewriters did not have proportional spacing and sentences were easier to read if two spaces separated them. Professional typesetters, however, never followed this practice because they used proportional spacing, and readability was not a problem. Influenced by the look of typeset publications, many writers now leave only one space after end punctuation. As a practical matter, however, it is not wrong to use two spaces.

Letter Placement and Line Endings

The easiest way to place letters on the page is to use the defaults of your word processing program. In Microsoft Word 2003, default side margins are set at 1.25 inches; in Word 2007 they are set at 1 inch. Many companies today find these margins acceptable. If you want to adjust your margins to better balance shorter letters, use the following chart:

Words in Body of Letter	Margin Settings	Blank Lines After Date
Under 200	1.5 inches	4 to 10
Over 200	1 inch	2 to 3

Experts say that a "ragged" right margin is easier to read than a justified (even) margin. You might want to turn off the justification feature of your word processing program if it automatically justifies the right margin.

Business Letter Parts

Professional-looking business letters are arranged in a conventional sequence with standard parts. Following is a discussion of how to use these letter parts properly. Figure C.2 illustrates the parts of a letter formatted in block style. See Figure 1.1 on page 60 in Chapter 3 for an example of a personal business letter.

Letterhead

Most business organizations use 8½ × 11-inch paper printed with a letterhead displaying their official name, street address, Web address, e-mail address, and telephone and fax numbers. The letterhead may also include a logo and an advertising message.

Dateline

On letterhead paper you should place the date one blank line below the last line of the letterhead or 2 inches from the top edge of the paper (line 13). On plain paper place the date immediately below your return address. Because the date goes on line 13, start the return address an appropriate number of lines above it. The most

FIGURE C.2
Block and Modified Block Letter Styles

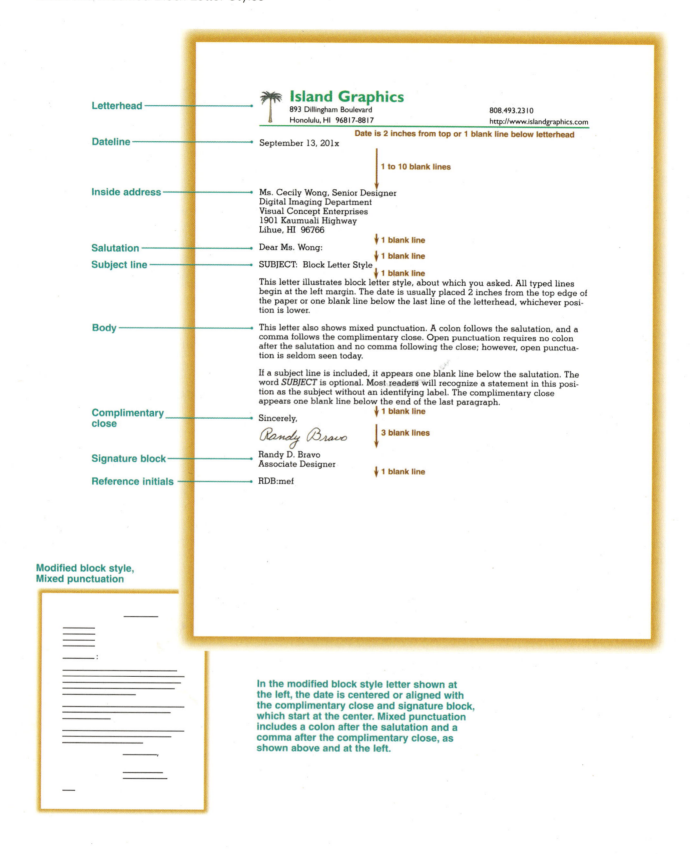

Letterhead

Dateline

Inside address

Salutation

Subject line

Body

Complimentary close

Signature block

Reference initials

Island Graphics
893 Dillingham Boulevard
Honolulu, HI 96817-8817

808.493.2310
http://www.islandgraphics.com

Date is 2 inches from top or 1 blank line below letterhead

September 13, 201x

1 to 10 blank lines

Ms. Cecily Wong, Senior Designer
Digital Imaging Department
Visual Concept Enterprises
1901 Kaumuali Highway
Lihue, HI 96766

1 blank line

Dear Ms. Wong:

1 blank line

SUBJECT: Block Letter Style

1 blank line

This letter illustrates block letter style, about which you asked. All typed lines begin at the left margin. The date is usually placed 2 inches from the top edge of the paper or one blank line below the last line of the letterhead, whichever position is lower.

This letter also shows mixed punctuation. A colon follows the salutation, and a comma follows the complimentary close. Open punctuation requires no colon after the salutation and no comma following the close; however, open punctuation is seldom seen today.

If a subject line is included, it appears one blank line below the salutation. The word *SUBJECT* is optional. Most readers will recognize a statement in this position as the subject without an identifying label. The complimentary close appears one blank line below the end of the last paragraph.

1 blank line

Sincerely,

Randy Bravo

3 blank lines

Randy D. Bravo
Associate Designer

1 blank line

RDB:mef

**Modified block style,
Mixed punctuation**

In the modified block style letter shown at the left, the date is centered or aligned with the complimentary close and signature block, which start at the center. Mixed punctuation includes a colon after the salutation and a comma after the complimentary close, as shown above and at the left.

common dateline format is as follows: *June 9, 2010.* Don't use *th* (or *rd, nd,* or *st*) when the date is written this way. For European or military correspondence, use the following dateline format: *9 June 2010.* Notice that no commas are used.

Addressee and Delivery Notations

Delivery notations such as *FAX TRANSMISSION, FEDERAL EXPRESS, MESSENGER DELIVERY, CONFIDENTIAL,* and *CERTIFIED MAIL* are typed in all capital letters two blank lines above the inside address.

Inside Address

Type the inside address—that is, the address of the organization or person receiving the letter—single-spaced, starting at the left margin. The number of lines between the dateline and the inside address depends on the size of the letter body, the type size (point or pitch size), and the length of the typing lines. Generally, one to ten blank lines are appropriate.

Be careful to duplicate the exact wording and spelling of the recipient's name and address on your documents. Usually, you can copy this information from the letterhead of the correspondence you are answering. If, for example, you are responding to *Jackson & Perkins Company,* do not address your letter to *Jackson and Perkins Corp.*

Always be sure to include a courtesy title such as *Mr., Ms., Mrs., Dr.,* or *Professor* before a person's name in the inside address—on both the letter and the envelope. Although many women in business today favor *Ms.,* you should use whatever title the addressee prefers.

In general, avoid abbreviations such as *Ave.* or *Co.* unless they appear in the printed letterhead of the document you are answering.

Attention Line

An attention line allows you to send your message officially to an organization but to direct it to a specific individual, officer, or department. However, if you know an individual's complete name, it is always better to use it as the first line of the inside address and avoid an attention line. Here are two common formats for attention lines:

The MultiMedia Company
931 Calkins Avenue
Rochester, NY 14301

The MultiMedia Company
Attention: Marketing Director
931 Calkins Avenue
Rochester, NY 14301

ATTENTION MARKETING DIRECTOR

Attention lines may be typed in all caps or with upper- and lowercase letters. The colon following *Attention* is optional. Notice that an attention line may be placed two lines below the address block or printed as the second line of the inside address. Use the latter format so that you may copy the address block to the envelope and the attention line will not interfere with the last-line placement of the zip code. Mail can be sorted more easily if the zip code appears in the last line of a typed address. Whenever possible, use a person's name as the first line of an address instead of putting that name in an attention line.

Salutation

For most letter styles, place the letter greeting, or salutation, one blank line below the last line of the inside address or the attention line (if used). If the letter is addressed to an individual, use that person's courtesy title and last name (*Dear Mr. Lanham*). Even if you are on a first-name basis (*Dear Leslie*), be sure to add a colon (not a comma or a semicolon) after the salutation. Do not use an individual's full name in the salutation (not *Dear Mr. Leslie Lanham*) unless you are unsure of gender (*Dear Leslie Lanham*).

For letters with attention lines or those addressed to organizations, the selection of an appropriate salutation has become more difficult. Formerly, writers used *Gentlemen* generically for all organizations. With increasing numbers of women in business management today, however, *Gentlemen* is problematic. Because no universally acceptable salutation has emerged as yet, you could use *Ladies and Gentlemen* or *Gentlemen and Ladies*.

Subject and Reference Lines

Although experts suggest placing the subject line one blank line below the salutation, many businesses actually place it above the salutation. Use whatever style your organization prefers. Reference lines often show policy or file numbers; they generally appear one blank line above the salutation. Use initial capital letters for the main words or all capital letters.

Body

Most business letters and memorandums are single-spaced, with double-spacing between paragraphs. Very short messages may be double-spaced with indented paragraphs.

Complimentary Close

Typed one blank line below the last line of the letter, the complimentary close may be formal (*Very truly yours*) or informal (*Sincerely* or *Cordially*).

Signature Block

In most letter styles the writer's typed name and optional identification appear three or four blank lines below the complimentary close. The combination of name, title, and organization information should be arranged to achieve a balanced look. The name and title may appear on the same line or on separate lines, depending on the length of each. Use commas to separate categories within the same line, but not to conclude a line.

Sincerely yours,	Cordially yours,
Jeremy M. Wood	*Casandra Baker-Murillo*
Jeremy M. Wood, Manager	Casandra Baker-Murillo
Technical Sales and Services	Executive Vice President

Courtesy titles (*Ms., Mrs.,* or *Miss*) should be used before names that are not readily distinguishable as male or female. They should also be used before names containing only initials and international names. The title is usually placed in parentheses, but it may appear without them.

Yours truly,	Sincerely,
Ms. K. C. Tripton	*Mr. Leslie Hill*
(Ms.) K. C. Tripton	(Mr.) Leslie Hill
Project Manager	Public Policy Department

Some organizations include their names in the signature block. In such cases the organization name appears in all caps one blank line below the complimentary close, as shown here:

Cordially,

LIPTON COMPUTER SERVICES

Shelina A. Simpson

Shelina A. Simpson
Executive Assistant

Reference Initials

If used, the initials of the typist and writer are typed one blank line below the writer's name and title. Generally, the writer's initials are capitalized and the typist's are lowercased, but this format varies.

Enclosure Notation

When an enclosure or attachment accompanies a document, a notation to that effect appears one blank line below the reference initials. This notation reminds the typist to insert the enclosure in the envelope, and it reminds the recipient to look for the enclosure or attachment. The notation may be spelled out (*Enclosure, Attachment*), or it may be abbreviated (*Enc., Att.*). It may indicate the number of enclosures or attachments, and it may also identify a specific enclosure (*Enclosure: Form 1099*).

Copy Notation

If you make copies of correspondence for other individuals, you may use *cc* to indicate carbon copy, *pc* to indicate photocopy, or merely *c* for any kind of copy. A colon following the initial(s) is optional.

Second-Page Heading

When a letter extends beyond one page, use plain paper of the same quality and color as the first page. Identify the second and succeeding pages with a heading consisting of the name of the addressee, the page number, and the date. Use the following format or the one shown in Figure C.3:

Ms. Sara Hendricks   2   May 3, 2010

Both headings appear six blank lines (1 inch) from the top edge of the paper followed by two blank lines to separate them from the continuing text. Avoid using a second page if you have only one line or the complimentary close and signature block to fill that page.

Plain-Paper Return Address

If you prepare a personal or business letter on plain paper, place your address immediately above the date. Do not include your name; you will type (and sign) your name at the end of your letter. If your return address contains two lines, begin typing so that the date appears 2 inches from the top. Avoid abbreviations except for a two-letter state abbreviation.

> 580 East Leffels Street
> Springfield, OH 45501
> December 14, 2010

> Ms. Ellen Siemens
> Escrow Department
> TransOhio First Federal
> 1220 Wooster Boulevard
> Columbus, OH 43218-2900

> Dear Ms. Siemens:

For letters in the block style, type the return address at the left margin. For modified block style letters, start the return address at the center to align with the complimentary close.

Letter and Punctuation Styles

Most business letters today are prepared in either block or modified block style, and they generally use mixed punctuation.

FIGURE C.3
Second-Page Heading

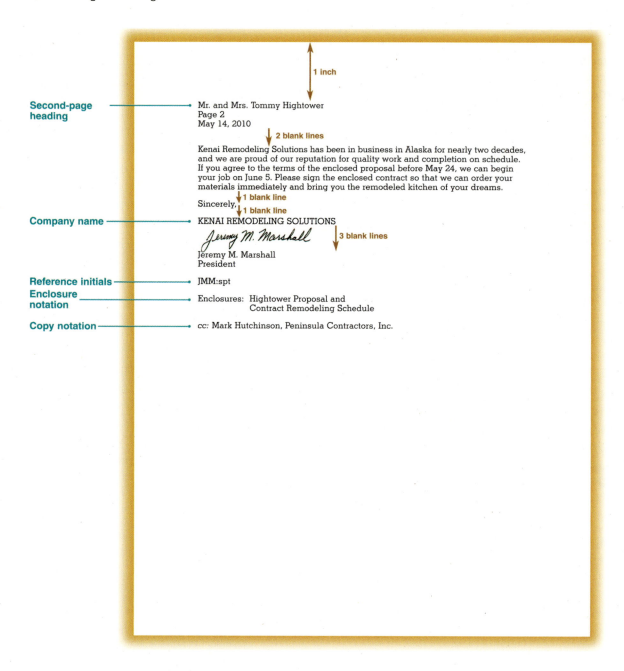

Block Style

In the block style, shown in Figure C.2, all lines begin at the left margin. This style is a favorite because it is easy to format.

Modified Block Style

The modified block style differs from block style in that the date and closing lines appear in the center, as shown at the bottom of Figure C.2. The date may be (a) centered, (b) begun at the center of the page (to align with the closing lines), or (c) backspaced from the right margin. The signature block—including the complimentary close, writer's name and title, or organization identification—begins at the center. The first line of each paragraph may begin at the left margin or may be indented five or ten spaces. All other lines begin at the left margin.

Mixed Punctuation Style

Most businesses today use mixed punctuation, shown in Figure C.2. It requires a colon after the salutation and a comma after the complimentary close. Even when the salutation is a first name, a colon is appropriate.

Envelopes

An envelope should be of the same quality and color of stationery as the letter it carries. Because the envelope introduces your message and makes the first impression, you need to be especially careful in addressing it. Moreover, how you fold the letter is important.

Return Address

The return address is usually printed in the upper left corner of an envelope, as shown in Figure C.4. In large companies some form of identification (the writer's initials, name, or location) may be typed above the company name and address. This identification helps return the letter to the sender in case of nondelivery.

On an envelope without a printed return address, single-space the return address in the upper left corner. Beginning on line 3 on the fourth space (½ inch) from the left edge, type the writer's name, title, company, and mailing address. On a word processor, select the appropriate envelope size and make adjustments to approximate this return address location.

Mailing Address

On legal-sized No. 10 envelopes (4⅛ × 9½ inches), begin the address on line 13 about 4 ¼ inches from the left edge, as shown in Figure C.4. For small envelopes (3⅝ × 6½ inches), begin typing on line 12 about 2½ inches from the left edge.

FIGURE C.4
Envelope Formats

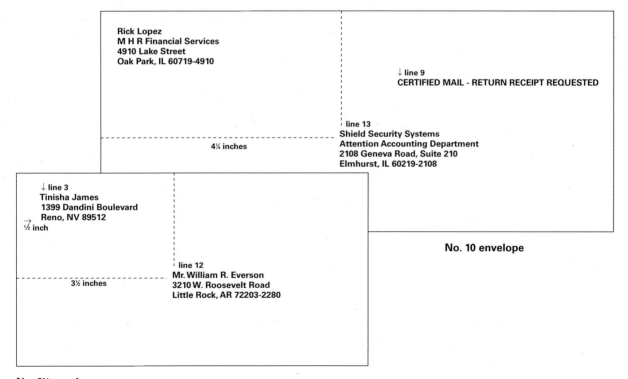

On a word processor, select the correct envelope size and check to be sure your address falls in the desired location.

The U.S. Postal Service recommends that addresses be typed in all caps without any punctuation. This Postal Service style, shown in the small envelope in Figure C.4, was originally developed to facilitate scanning by optical character readers. Today's OCRs, however, are so sophisticated that they scan upper- and lowercase letters easily. Many companies today do not follow the Postal Service format because they prefer to use the same format for the envelope as for the inside address. If the same format is used, writers can take advantage of word processing programs to copy the inside address to the envelope, thus saving keystrokes and reducing errors. Having the same format on both the inside address and the envelope also looks more professional and consistent. For those reasons you may choose to use the familiar upper- and lowercase combination format. But you will want to check with your organization to learn its preference.

In addressing your envelopes for delivery in this country or in Canada, use the two-letter state and province abbreviations shown in Figure C.5. Notice that these abbreviations are in capital letters without periods.

Folding

The way a letter is folded and inserted into an envelope sends additional nonverbal messages about a writer's professionalism and carefulness. Most businesspeople follow the procedures shown here, which produce the least number of creases to distract readers.

For large No. 10 envelopes, begin with the letter face up. Fold slightly less than one third of the sheet toward the top, as shown in the following diagram. Then fold down the top third to within ⅓ inch of the bottom fold. Insert the letter into the envelope with the last fold toward the bottom of the envelope.

For small No. 6¾ envelopes, begin by folding the bottom up to within ⅓ inch of the top edge. Then fold the right third over to the left. Fold the left third to within ⅓ inch of the last fold. Insert the last fold into the envelope first.

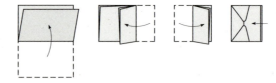

Memorandums

Memorandums deliver messages within organizations, although e-mail is quickly replacing the use of printed memos. Some offices use memo forms imprinted with the organization name and, optionally, the department or division names. The design and arrangement of memo forms vary; however, they usually include the basic elements of *TO, FROM, DATE,* and *SUBJECT.* Large organizations may include other identifying headings, such as *FILE NUMBER, FLOOR, EXTENSION, LOCATION,* and *DISTRIBUTION.*

FIGURE C.5

Abbreviations of States, Territories, and Provinces

State or Territory	Two-Letter Abbreviation	State or Territory	Two-Letter Abbreviation
Alabama	AL	North Dakota	ND
Alaska	AK	Ohio	OH
Arizona	AZ	Oklahoma	OK
Arkansas	AR	Oregon	OR
California	CA	Pennsylvania	PA
Canal Zone	CZ	Puerto Rico	PR
Colorado	CO	Rhode Island	RI
Connecticut	CT	South Carolina	SC
Delaware	DE	South Dakota	SD
District of Columbia	DC	Tennessee	TN
Florida	FL	Texas	TX
Georgia	GA	Utah	UT
Guam	GU	Vermont	VT
Hawaii	HI	Virgin Islands	VI
Idaho	ID	Virginia	VA
Illinois	IL	Washington	WA
Indiana	IN	West Virginia	WV
Iowa	IA	Wisconsin	WI
Kansas	KS	Wyoming	WY
Kentucky	KY		
Louisiana	LA	**Canadian Province**	**Two-Letter Abbreviation**
Maine	ME		
Maryland	MD	Alberta	AB
Massachusetts	MA	British Columbia	BC
Michigan	MI	Labrador	LB
Minnesota	MN	Manitoba	MB
Mississippi	MS	New Brunswick	NB
Missouri	MO	Newfoundland	NF
Montana	MT	Northwest Territories	NT
Nebraska	NE	Nova Scotia	NS
Nevada	NV	Ontario	ON
New Hampshire	NH	Prince Edward Island	PE
New Jersey	NJ	Quebec	PQ
New Mexico	NM	Saskatchewan	SK
New York	NY	Yukon Territory	YT
North Carolina	NC		

Because of the difficulty of aligning computer printers with preprinted forms, many business writers use a standardized memo template (sometimes called a "wizard"). This template automatically provides attractive headings with appropriate spacing and formatting. Other writers store their own preferred memo formats.

If no printed or stored computer forms are available, memos may be keyed on company letterhead or plain paper, as shown in Figure C.6. On a full sheet of paper, leave a 1.5-inch top margin. Double-space and type in all caps the guide words: *TO:, FROM:, DATE:, SUBJECT*. Align all the fill-in information two spaces after the longest guide word (*SUBJECT:*). Leave two blank lines after the last line of the heading, and begin typing the body of the memo. Like business letters, memos are single-spaced.

Memos are generally formatted with side margins of 1.25 inches, or they may conform to the printed memo form.

FIGURE C.6
Memo on Plain Paper

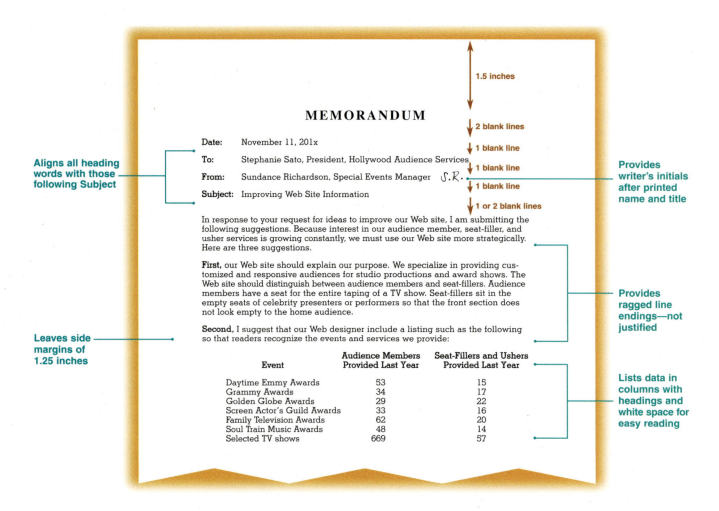

Aligns all heading words with those following Subject

Leaves side margins of 1.25 inches

1.5 inches

2 blank lines

1 blank line

1 blank line

1 blank line

1 or 2 blank lines

Provides writer's initials after printed name and title

Provides ragged line endings—not justified

Lists data in columns with headings and white space for easy reading

MEMORANDUM

Date: November 11, 201x

To: Stephanie Sato, President, Hollywood Audience Services

From: Sundance Richardson, Special Events Manager   S.R.

Subject: Improving Web Site Information

In response to your request for ideas to improve our Web site, I am submitting the following suggestions. Because interest in our audience member, seat-filler, and usher services is growing constantly, we must use our Web site more strategically. Here are three suggestions.

First, our Web site should explain our purpose. We specialize in providing customized and responsive audiences for studio productions and award shows. The Web site should distinguish between audience members and seat-fillers. Audience members have a seat for the entire taping of a TV show. Seat-fillers sit in the empty seats of celebrity presenters or performers so that the front section does not look empty to the home audience.

Second, I suggest that our Web designer include a listing such as the following so that readers recognize the events and services we provide:

Event	Audience Members Provided Last Year	Seat-Fillers and Ushers Provided Last Year
Daytime Emmy Awards	53	15
Grammy Awards	34	17
Golden Globe Awards	29	22
Screen Actor's Guild Awards	33	16
Family Television Awards	62	20
Soul Train Music Awards	48	14
Selected TV shows	669	57

Fax Cover Sheets

Documents transmitted by fax are usually introduced by a cover sheet, such as that shown in Figure C.7. As with memos, the format varies considerably. Important items to include are (a) the name and fax number of the receiver, (b) the name and fax number of the sender, (c) the number of pages being sent, and (d) the name and telephone number of the person to notify in case of unsatisfactory transmission.

When the document being transmitted requires little explanation, you may prefer to attach an adhesive note (such as a Post-it fax note) instead of a full cover sheet. These notes carry essentially the same information as shown in our printed fax cover sheet. They are perfectly acceptable in most business organizations and can save considerable paper and transmission costs.

Résumés

A résumé is a carefully prepared document that summarizes your education, experience, and other qualifications for a job. The goal of a résumé is obtaining an interview. The résumé format most preferred by recruiters is the chronological résumé,

FIGURE C.7
Fax Cover Sheet

FAX TRANSMISSION

DATE: _____

TO: _____   **FAX NUMBER:** _____

           _____

           _____

FROM: _____   **FAX NUMBER:** _____

           _____

           _____

NUMBER OF PAGES TRANSMITTED INCLUDING THIS COVER SHEET: ___

MESSAGE:

If any part of this fax transmission is missing or not clearly received, please call:

NAME: _____

PHONE: _____

---

shown in Figure C.8. It focuses on experience and arranges jobs in reverse chronological order. A functional résumé focuses on a candidate's skills rather than on past employment. Résumés have various formats and organization plans, but most include a main heading, career objective, summary of qualifications, education, work experience, capabilities and skills, and awards.

Main Heading
Whether chronological or functional, your résumé should always begin with your name. Add your middle initial for an even more professional look. Following your name, list your contact information, including your complete address, area code and phone number, and e-mail address. Be sure your e-mail address sounds professional.

Career Objective
Include a well-written career objective that is customized for each position you seek. Change the objective for different applications—for example, to apply for an advertised position in an attorney's office: *Career Objective: To obtain a position as an administrative assistant in an attorney's office.*

Summary of Qualifications
At the top of a résumé, the summary of qualifications lists the skills and experience most appealing to the hiring company. It should include three to eight bulleted statements that prove you are the ideal candidate for the position. Consider your experience, your education, your unique skills, awards you have won, certifications, and any other accomplishments that you want to highlight.

FIGURE C.8
Chronological Résumé

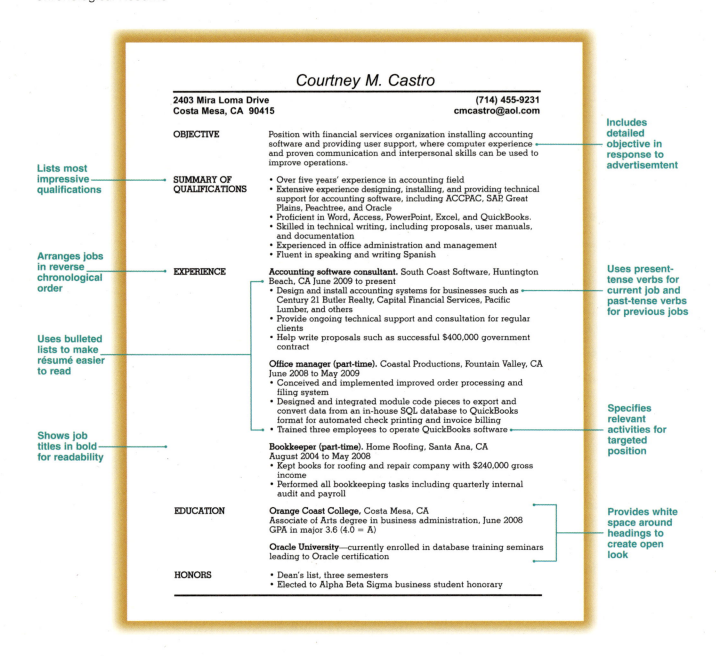

Lists most impressive qualifications

Arranges jobs in reverse chronological order

Uses bulleted lists to make résumé easier to read

Shows job titles in bold for readability

Courtney M. Castro

2403 Mira Loma Drive   **(714) 455-9231**
Costa Mesa, CA 90415   **cmcastro@aol.com**

OBJECTIVE — Position with financial services organization installing accounting software and providing user support, where computer experience and proven communication and interpersonal skills can be used to improve operations.

SUMMARY OF QUALIFICATIONS
- Over five years' experience in accounting field
- Extensive experience designing, installing, and providing technical support for accounting software, including ACCPAC, SAP, Great Plains, Peachtree, and Oracle
- Proficient in Word, Access, PowerPoint, Excel, and QuickBooks.
- Skilled in technical writing, including proposals, user manuals, and documentation
- Experienced in office administration and management
- Fluent in speaking and writing Spanish

EXPERIENCE
Accounting software consultant. South Coast Software, Huntington Beach, CA June 2009 to present
- Design and install accounting systems for businesses such as Century 21 Butler Realty, Capital Financial Services, Pacific Lumber, and others
- Provide ongoing technical support and consultation for regular clients
- Help write proposals such as successful $400,000 government contract

Office manager (part-time). Coastal Productions, Fountain Valley, CA June 2008 to May 2009
- Conceived and implemented improved order processing and filing system
- Designed and integrated module code pieces to export and convert data from an in-house SQL database to QuickBooks format for automated check printing and invoice billing
- Trained three employees to operate QuickBooks software

Bookkeeper (part-time). Home Roofing, Santa Ana, CA August 2004 to May 2008
- Kept books for roofing and repair company with $240,000 gross income
- Performed all bookkeeping tasks including quarterly internal audit and payroll

EDUCATION
Orange Coast College, Costa Mesa, CA
Associate of Arts degree in business administration, June 2008
GPA in major 3.6 (4.0 = A)

Oracle University—currently enrolled in database training seminars leading to Oracle certification

HONORS
- Dean's list, three semesters
- Elected to Alpha Beta Sigma business student honorary

Includes detailed objective in response to advertisemtent

Uses present-tense verbs for current job and past-tense verbs for previous jobs

Specifies relevant activities for targeted position

Provides white space around headings to create open look

Education

Include your education next—if it is more noteworthy than your work experience. Include the name and location of schools, dates of attendance, major fields of study, and degrees received. Once you have attended college, don't bother to list high school information. Grade-point averages are important to potential employers. One way to enhance your GPA is to calculate it in your major courses only. Do not list all the courses you have taken. Refer to specific courses only if you can relate them to the position sought.

Work Experience

When your work experience is significant and relevant to the position sought, this information should appear before education. List your employment in reverse chronological order, with the most recent employment first. Include only those jobs you think will help you win the targeted position. Include (a) employer's name, city, and state; (b) dates of employment (month and year); (c) most important job title; and (d) significant duties, activities, accomplishments, and promotions. In a bulleted list, describe your employment achievements concisely but concretely.

Capabilities and Skills

Recruiters want to know specifically what you can do for their companies. List your special skills, such as your ability to use software programs, office equipment, and communication technology tools. If you speak a foreign language or use sign language, include it on your résumé. Describe proficiencies you have acquired through training and experience. If you are preparing a functional résumé, you will place more focus on skills than on any other section.

Awards, Honors, and Activities

If you have three or more awards or honors, highlight them by listing them under a separate heading. If not, put them in the education or work experience section. Include awards, scholarships, (financial and other), fellowships, dean's list, honors, recognition, commendations, and certificates.

Personal Data

Today's résumés generally omit personal data, such as birth date, marital status, height, weight, national origin, health, and religious affiliation. Such information doesn't relate to genuine occupational qualifications, and recruiters are legally barred from asking for such information. Some job seekers do, however, include hobbies or interests (such as skiing or photography) that might grab the recruiter's attention or serve as conversation starters.

References

Most applicants do not list references on their résumés. They take up valuable space and are not normally instrumental in securing an interview. You should, however, have them listed on a separate sheet and be ready to distribute them when asked.

Self-Help Exercises

Self-Help Exercises
Reference Skills

NAME _____

Nearly every student who takes this English course says, "I wish I had more exercises to try my skills on." Because of the many requests, we provide this set of self-help exercises for extra reinforcement. Immediate feedback is an important ingredient in successful learning. Therefore, a key to these exercises begins on page 532. Don't check the key, of course, until you have completed each exercise.

Use a current dictionary to complete the following exercise.

1. In grammar the word *neuter* means
   a. asexual
   b. neutral
   c. neither feminine nor masculine
   d. both feminine and masculine
   _____

2. An *autocrat* is one who enjoys
   a. owning many cars
   b. ruling by himself or herself
   c. democratic relationships
   d. racing automobiles
   _____

3. The words *in so much as* should be written
   a. in so much as
   b. in somuchas
   c. insomuch as
   d. in somuch as
   _____

4. The abbreviation *MST* stands for
   a. master in statistical technology
   b. Mountain Standard Time
   c. manual or standard transmission
   d. master
   _____

5. *Amanuensis* originally meant
   a. deterioration of sight
   b. coarse herbs including pigweeds
   c. a slave with secretarial duties
   d. a female warrior
   _____

6. The word *(non)productive* should be written
   a. non-productive
   b. nonproductive
   c. non productive
   d. non-Productive
   _____

7. When the word *notwithstanding* is used to mean "nevertheless," it functions as what part of speech?
   a. conjunction
   b. adverb
   c. preposition
   d. adjective
   _____

8. The plural of the word *proxy* is
   a. proxies'
   b. proxys
   c. proxy's
   d. proxies
   _____

9. The word *filibuster* comes from a _____ word meaning "freebooter."
   a. French
   b. Spanish
   c. Italian
   d. Russian
   _____

10. *Foggy Bottom* is the site of
    a. a cathedral in London
    b. the U.S. Department of State
    c. a famous Irish castle
    d. a San Francisco nightclub
    _____

Self-Help Exercises
Parts of Speech

2

Worksheet 1

A. This exercise is designed to help you develop a better understanding of the parts of speech. Using Chapter 2, write a brief definition or description of the eight parts of speech listed here. Then list three words as examples of each part of speech.

	Brief Definition	**Three Examples**		
1. noun	Names person, place, thing, quality, feeling, concept, activity, measure	Anthony	paper	truth
2. pronoun	_____	_____	_____	_____
3. verb	_____	_____	_____	_____
4. adjective	_____	_____	_____	_____
5. adverb	_____	_____	_____	_____
6. preposition	_____	_____	_____	_____
7. conjunction	_____	_____	_____	_____
8. interjection	_____	_____	_____	_____

B. Fill in the parts of speech for all the words in these sentences. Use a dictionary if necessary.

We sent an e-mail message to Jennifer, but she was very busy.

1. We _____

2. sent _____

3. an _____

4. e-mail _____

5. message _____

6. to _____

7. Jennifer _____

8. but _____

9. she _____

10. was _____

11. very _____

12. busy _____

Gosh, the computer and printer processed this lengthy report in 20 seconds.

13. Gosh _____

14. the _____

15. computer _____

16. and _____

17. printer _____

18. processed _____

19. this _____

20. lengthy _____

21. report _____

22. in _____

23. 20 _____

24. seconds _____

We arrived promptly, but the committee meeting started late.

25. We _____

26. arrived _____

27. promptly _____

28. but _____

29. the _____

30. committee _____

31. meeting _____

32. started _____

33. late _____

Worksheet 2

Fill in the parts of speech for all the words in these sentences. Use a dictionary if necessary.

I sold property in Fresno, but one transaction may not clear escrow.

1. I _____
2. sold _____
3. property _____
4. in _____

5. Fresno _____
6. but _____
7. one _____
8. transaction _____

9. may _____
10. not _____
11. clear _____
12. escrow _____

Oh, did Lee really think he could change that method of operation?

13. Oh _____
14. did _____
15. Lee _____
16. really _____

17. think _____
18. he _____
19. could _____
20. change _____

21. that _____
22. method _____
23. of _____
24. operation _____

The old accounting system was neither accurate nor efficient, but one company had used it faithfully for the past 40 years.

25. The _____
26. old _____
27. accounting _____
28. system _____
29. was _____
30. neither _____
31. accurate _____

32. nor _____
33. efficient _____
34. but _____
35. one _____
36. company _____
37. had _____
38. used _____

39. it _____
40. faithfully _____
41. for _____
42. the _____
43. past _____
44. 40 _____
45. years _____

Kerry quietly slipped into an empty seat during the long class film.

46. Kerry _____
47. quietly _____
48. slipped _____
49. into _____

50. an _____
51. empty _____
52. seat _____
53. during _____

54. the _____
55. long _____
56. class _____
57. film _____

E-mail has completely changed the way we communicate with our customers.

58. E-mail _____
59. has _____
60. completely _____
61. changed _____

62. the _____
63. way _____
64. we _____
65. communicate _____

66. with _____
67. our _____
68. customers _____

Self-Help Exercises
Sentences: Elements, Varieties, Patterns, Types, Faults

3

Worksheet 1

Locating Subjects and Verbs

Action verbs tell what the subject is doing or what is being done to the subject. For each of the following sentences, locate the action verb and underline it twice. Then locate the subject of the verb and underline it once. To locate the subject, use the verb preceded by *Who?* or *What?* In the example the verb is *answered*. To help you find the subject, ask, *Who answered?*

Example: A <u>group</u> of applicants <u>answered</u> the advertisement.

1. The applicant with the best qualifications received the first interview.
2. In the afternoon session, the speaker made a dynamic presentation.
3. During the sales campaign, our telephones rang constantly.
4. In the winter we will hire four new employees for this department.
5. Our management team built a strong program of sales and service.
6. The most successful salespeople received trips to Hawaii.
7. In the meantime, our human resources manager will send you an application form.
8. Last week we released our new line of upscale, stylish cell phones.
9. One of the vice presidents was given a promotion recently.
10. Today's computers require managers to think with new clarity and precision.
11. The printout with all the customers' names and addresses was accurate.
12. One of our top salespeople sold $2 million worth of life insurance.
13. A list of restaurants with low-priced meals is available in the lobby.
14. Everything except labor and parts is covered by your warranty.
15. A committee consisting of 11 employees plus the manager was appointed to investigate.

Linking verbs (such as *am, is, are, was, were, be, being,* and *been*) often join to the sentence words that describe or rename the subject. In the following sentences, underline the linking verbs twice and the subjects once.

Examples: E. J. <u>Todd</u> <u>was</u> president of the organization last year.
In the morning the <u>air</u> <u>is</u> cool.

16. Mr. Thomas is the office manager for Ryerson Metals Corporation.
17. The new copiers are very dependable.
18. Ms. Seymour is the person for the job.
19. Mr. Torres has been office manager for nine years.
20. Our new offices are much brighter than our previous ones.

Worksheet 2

Sentence Variety

From the following list, select the letter that accurately describes what type each sentence is.

a = simple   c = complex

b = compound   d = compound-complex

1. Raul applied with five companies, but he interviewed with only two. _____

2. Raul applied with five companies but interviewed with only two. _____

3. Although Raul applied with five companies, he interviewed with only two. _____

4. Raul, who is applying for jobs, sent résumés to five companies; however, he interviewed with only two. _____

5. He brought a list of references, a notebook, and a nice pen to the interview with him. _____

6. If he is invited to a second interview, he will contact his references. _____

7. Raul answered all of the questions confidently; therefore, he feels as if he did well during the interview. _____

8. When answering the questions, Raul used proper grammar and an enthusiastic tone. _____

9. He focused on his most impressive traits, told success stories, and kept his answers focused on the needs of the employer. _____

10. Because he was properly prepared, both employers were extremely impressed. _____

Sentence Patterns

Finish the following sentences in the patterns indicated.

SUBJECT–VERB

Example: Cell phones ___ring___ .

11. Stockholders _____.
12. Stock prices _____.
13. Employees _____.
14. The security alarm _____.
15. In 1945 World War II _____.
16. Last year's sales _____.

SUBJECT–ACTION VERB–OBJECT

Example: The sales director made a ___call___ .

17. Our salesperson sold a _____.
18. The network was infected with a _____.
19. Ricky mailed the _____.
20. I telephoned _____.
21. Someone locked _____.
22. The clerk filed all the _____.

SUBJECT–LINKING VERB–COMPLEMENT

Examples: She is very <u>friendly</u>.

Eric could have been the <u>manager</u>.

23. Sales have been _____.

24. Susan is the new _____.

25. Last year the owner was _____.

26. I am _____.

27. The writer could have been _____.

28. The caller was _____.

Compose original sentences in the following patterns.

29. (Subject–verb) _____

30. (Subject–verb) _____

31. (Subject–action verb–object) _____

32. (Subject–action verb–object) _____

33. (Subject–linking verb–complement) _____

Worksheet 3

Sentence Types

From the following list select the letter that accurately describes each of the following groups of words. Add end punctuation marks to all complete sentences.

a = fragment d = question
b = statement e = exclamation
c = command

1. The management of a multinational corporation with branch offices in several cities _____
2. Send me a brochure describing your latest workout equipment _____
3. Will you be working next weekend or during the week _____
4. The work schedule is usually posted late in the week _____
5. What an amazing presentation _____
6. If you have an opportunity to be promoted to a managerial position _____
7. For a generous return on your funds, invest in second trust deeds _____
8. In all levels of business, written and spoken English is extremely important in achieving success _____
9. Because it is difficult to improve your language skills on your own _____

Sentence Faults

From the following list select the letter that accurately describes each of the following groups of words.

a = correctly punctuated sentence c = comma splice
b = fragment d = run-on sentence

10. I will have the answer soon, first I must make a telephone call. _____
11. If you consider all the pros and cons before you make a decision. _____
12. We have no idea what to order only Ms. Sanchez can do that. _____
13. Your entire department is entitled to overtime compensation. _____
14. You check the current address list, and I will check the old one. _____
15. You check the current address list, I will check the old one. _____
16. You check the current address list I will check the old one. _____
17. Although we have complete confidence in our products and prices. _____
18. When you return from the conference, please submit a brief report describing the information you learned. _____
19. We must focus our charitable contributions on areas that directly relate to our business, therefore, we are unable to send a check this year. _____
20. If you agree that this memo accurately reflects our conversation. _____

Self-Help Exercises
Nouns

4

LEVEL 1

Write the preferred plural forms of the nouns shown below. Use a dictionary if necessary.

1. giraffe _____
2. foot _____
3. switch _____
4. Bush _____
5. box _____
6. language _____
7. fax _____
8. sandwich _____
9. income tax _____
10. child _____
11. success _____
12. value _____
13. dress _____
14. branch _____
15. recommendation _____
16. woman _____
17. mismatch _____
18. taxi _____
19. loaf (of bread) _____
20. annex _____
21. belief _____
22. Ross _____
23. storm _____
24. ranch _____
25. Jones _____
26. Chavez _____
27. letter _____
28. business _____
29. computer _____
30. wish _____

Write the preferred plural forms of the nouns shown below. Use a dictionary if necessary.

1. wharf
2. chief of police
3. 2010
4. Wolf
5. embargo
6. LVN
7. size 10
8. amt.
9. faculty
10. by-product
11. entry
12. looker-on
13. company
14. knife
15. court-martial
16. A
17. Sherman
18. memo
19. valley
20. zero
21. life
22. yr.
23. Murphy
24. runner-up
25. oz.
26. journey
27. MBA
28. wolf
29. Kelly
30. minority

Write the preferred plural forms of the nouns shown below. Use a dictionary if necessary.

1. datum _____

2. thesis _____

3. bacterium _____

4. Chinese _____

5. parenthesis _____

6. headquarters _____

7. alumna _____

8. millennium _____

9. genus _____

10. news _____

11. sheep _____

12. alumnus _____

13. larva _____

14. basis _____

15. memorandum _____

Select the correct word in parentheses and complete the sentences in your own words.

16. The goods produced in that factory (is, are) _____

_____

17. Mathematics (is, are) _____

_____

18. Several (formula, formulas) _____

_____

19. Four separate (analysis, analyses) _____

_____

20. In the business curriculum, economics (is, are) _____

_____

5 Self-Help Exercises
Possessive Nouns

LEVEL 1

Worksheet 1

Before you begin this exercise, review the three-step plan for placing apostrophes:

1. Look for possessive construction. (Usually two nouns appear together.)

2. Reverse the nouns. (Use a prepositional phrase, such as *employees of the company*.)

3. Examine ownership word. (Does it end in an *s* sound?)
   a. If the ownership word does NOT end in an *s* sound, add an apostrophe and *s*.
   b. If the ownership word DOES end in *s* and is singular, add an apostrophe and *s*.
   c. If the ownership word DOES end in *s* and is plural, add an apostrophe only.

Using apostrophes, change the following prepositional phrases into possessive constructions.

Example: home of the couple   the couple's home _____

1. passwords of all employees   _____
2. office of this company   _____
3. uniforms of the women   _____
4. signature of an employee   _____
5. e-mail message of the supervisor   _____
6. opinions of all members   _____
7. the landing of the pilot   _____
8. agreement of both partners   _____
9. notebook of Jeffrey   _____
10. strengths of the department   _____
11. grades of the students   _____
12. customs of those people   _____
13. presentation of a student   _____
14. credit from the bank   _____
15. savings of citizens   _____
16. mountains of Canada   _____
17. requirements of the employer   _____
18. résumés of all candidates   _____
19. policies of the government   _____
20. fees of both attorneys   _____

Worksheet 2

Write the correct possessive form of the word in parentheses in the space provided.

1. He managed to get the (author) signature on the title page of the book. _____

2. Several (drivers) inquiries prompted the posting of a better sign. _____

3. We found the (carpenter) tools after he left the building. _____

4. The electronics store installed a hidden video camera to observe a suspected (thief) activities. _____

5. The (company) ethics statement is posted on its Web site. _____

6. Several (employees) passwords must be reset. _____

7. Only the (CEO) car may be parked in the special zone. _____

8. Most (readers) letters supported the magazine's editorial position. _____

9. Where is the (caller) message? _____

10. All (authors) rights are protected by copyright law. _____

Correct any errors in the following sentences by underlining the errors and writing the correct forms in the spaces provided. Each sentence contains one error.

11. Like its clothing, the Gaps corporate offices are simple, clean, and comfortable. _____

12. The names of these customers' are not alphabetized. _____

13. Some of the countrys biggest manufacturers are being investigated. _____

14. All employee's suggestions are confidential. _____

15. Your organizations voice mail system is excellent. _____

16. The vice presidents resignation left a vital position unfilled. _____

17. Are you researching your familys genealogy? _____

18. My attorneys name is William Glass. _____

19. Several employee's plan to take Friday off. _____

20. Not a single farmers crop was undamaged by the storm. _____

21. A citizens committee was formed to address parking problems. _____

22. Several company's relocated to our city last year. _____

23. Each customers complimentary game tickets were mailed today. _____

24. Childrens clothing is on the first floor. _____

25. The announcement of new benefits for employees was made in the supervisors memo, which she sent out yesterday. _____

Correct any errors in the following sentences by underlining the errors and writing the correct form in the spaces provided. Each sentence contains one error.

1. The document required the notary publics signature and his seal. _____

2. Lee Ross office is on the south side of the campus. _____

3. At least one companies' records are computerized. _____

4. My uncle's lawyer's suggestions in this matter were excellent. _____

5. The editor's in chief office is on the fifth floor. _____

6. Beth Browns home is farther away than anyone else's. _____

7. All RN's uniforms must now be identical. _____

8. The president's assistant's telephone number has been changed. _____

9. Have you called the new sales' representative? _____

10. My brother's-in-law beard is neat and well trimmed. _____

11. We spent our vacation enjoying New Englands' historical towns. _____

12. CBSs' report on the vote was better than any other station's. _____

13. The bank is reconsidering the Rodriguez's loan application. _____

14. I have no idea where Weses car is parked. _____

15. The Los Angeles' symphony planned an evening of Beethoven. _____

16. Did you hear that the Horowitz's are moving? _____

17. Have you visited the Morris's vacation home? _____

18. The two architects licenses were issued together. _____

19. Who is James partner for the team project? _____

20. All FBI agent's must pass rigorous security investigations. _____

21. Professor Braults lecture was well organized and informative. _____

22. The Caldwell's are building a new patio in their backyard. _____

23. Visitors at Graceland swore they saw Elvis ghost. _____

24. Fans of the Dallas's Cowboys cheered their team. _____

25. The CEO answered all the reporters questions carefully. _____

Correct any errors in the following sentences by underlining the errors and writing the correct forms in the spaces provided. Each sentence contains one error.

1. Clark's and Clark's reference manual is outstanding. _____

2. We borrowed my aunt's and uncle's motor home for the weekend. _____

3. Workers said they expected to be paid for an honest days work. _____

4. Robin's and John's new car came with a five-year warranty. _____

5. Diana's and Jason's marriage license was lost. _____

6. He earned his associates degree last spring. _____

7. Our sales this year are greater than last years. _____

8. The union meeting will be held at Larrys. _____

9. I'm going over to Jennifers to pick her up. _____

10. Debbie and Julie's iPods have similar song lists. _____

11. During lunch Juan stopped at the stationers for supplies. _____

12. She will earn her bachelors degree from UCLA. _____

13. This month's expenses are somewhat less than last months. _____

14. Applicants will have at least a years wait for an apartment. _____

15. The days news is summarized every hour on WABC. _____

16. This account has been credited with four months interest. _____

17. One day Stan hopes to earn his masters degree. _____

18. In three years time, the software paid for itself. _____

19. One years interest on the account amounted to $120. _____

20. I see that someone else books got wet also. _____

21. Both class test results were misplaced. _____

22. The other three boss desks are rather neat. _____

23. A dollars worth of gas should get us home. _____

24. Tomorrows meeting has been canceled. _____

25. I hope that tomorrow's sales are as strong as todays. _____

6 Self-Help Exercises
Personal Pronouns

LEVEL 1

Worksheet 1

List seven pronouns that could be used as <u>subjects</u> of verbs.

1. _____   3. _____   5. _____   7. _____

2. _____   4. _____   6. _____

List seven pronouns that could be used as <u>objects</u> of verbs or <u>objects</u> of prepositions.

8. _____   10. _____   12. _____   14. _____

9. _____   11. _____   13. _____

Pronouns as Subjects

Select the correct pronoun to complete each of the following sentences. All the omitted pronouns function as subjects of verbs.

15. Ms. Georges and (I, me) submitted purchase requisitions. _____

16. In the afternoon training session, the manager and (she, her) will make presentations. _____

17. Will you and (he, him) be going to the sales meeting? _____

18. Mr. North and (they, them) expect to see you Saturday. _____

19. It is difficult to explain why Matt and (her, she) decided to move. _____

20. Of all the applicants, only (we, us) agreed to be tested now. _____

21. Ramon and (she, her) deserve raises because of their hard work. _____

22. After Ms. Cortez and (he, him) had returned, customers were handled more rapidly. _____

23. Only you and (her, she) will participate in the demonstration. _____

24. After the spring sales campaign ends, the marketing manager and (he, him) will be promoted. _____

25. Because we are most familiar with the project, you and (I, me) must complete the report. _____

Worksheet 2

Personal Pronouns as Objects

Select the correct pronoun to complete each of the following sentences. All the omitted pronouns function as objects of verbs or prepositions. Prepositions have been underlined to help you identify them.

1. Just <u>between</u> you and (I, me), our branch won the sales trophy. _____

2. Michelle said that she had seen you and (he, him) at the airport. _____

3. We hope to show (they, them) the billing procedure this afternoon. _____

4. Everybody <u>but</u> (I, me) is ready to leave. _____

5. Have you talked <u>with</u> Brad and (her, she) about this change? _____

6. We need more workers <u>like</u> Maria and (him, he) to finish the job. _____

7. All supervisors <u>except</u> Mrs. Young and (her, she) approved the plan. _____

8. This insurance program provides you and (they, them) with equal benefits. _____

9. Terms of the settlement were satisfactory <u>to</u> (we, us). _____

10. Every operator <u>but</u> Maddie and (I, me) had an opportunity for overtime. _____

Possessive-Case Pronouns

Remember that possessive-case pronouns (*yours*, *his*, *hers*, *its*, *whose*, and *theirs*) do not contain apostrophes. Do not confuse these pronouns with the following contractions: *it's* (it is), *there's* (there is), *who's* (who is), and *you're* (you are). In the following sentences, select the correct word.

11. Do you think (its, it's) necessary for us to sign in? _____

12. Is (theirs, their's) the white house at the end of the street? _____

13. The contract and all (its, it's) provisions must be examined. _____

14. (There's, Theirs) a set of guidelines for us to follow. _____

15. Jack's car and (hers, her's) are the only ones left in the lot. _____

16. The check is good only if (its, it's) signed. _____

17. I was told that Sue's and (yours, your's) were the best departments. _____

18. (Who's, Whose) umbrella is that lying in the corner? _____

19. Most car registrations were sent April 1, but (our's, ours) was delayed. _____

20. (You're, Your) taking Courtney's place, aren't you? _____

Select the correct pronoun to complete these sentences.

1. Do you expect Mr. Jefferson and (they, them) to meet you? _____
2. No one could regret the error more than (I, me, myself). _____
3. These photocopies were prepared by Charles and (she, her). _____
4. (We, Us) policyholders are entitled to group discounts. _____
5. Procrastination disturbs Steven as much as (I, me, myself). _____
6. For the summer only, Universal Parcel is hiring James and (I, me, myself). _____
7. Have you corresponded with the authors, Dr. Lee and (she, her)? _____
8. On that project no one works as hard as (he, him, himself). _____
9. Everyone but Mr. Foster and (he, him) can help customers if necessary. _____
10. Do you know whether Gary and (I, me, myself) signed it? _____
11. Only Erik (himself, hisself) knows what is best for him. _____
12. We asked two women, Denise and (she, her), to come along. _____
13. The proceeds are to be divided among Mr. Shelby, Ms. Huerra, and (she, her). _____
14. Ms. Greerson thinks that Mr. Cardillo is a better salesperson than (she, her). _____
15. All property claims must be submitted to my lawyer or (I, me, myself) before April 15. _____
16. The new contract was acceptable to both management and (us, we). _____
17. When reconciling bank statements, no one is more accurate than (she, her). _____
18. The best time for you and (he, him) to enroll is in January. _____
19. The president and (I, me, myself) will inspect the facility. _____
20. Everyone except Kevin and (I, me, myself) was able to join the program. _____
21. Send an application to Human Resources or (I, me, myself) immediately. _____
22. (She and I, Her and me, Her and I) are among the best-qualified candidates. _____
23. Have you invited Jon and (she, her, herself) to our picnic? _____
24. Most of the e-mail messages sent to (us, we) employees are considered spam. _____
25. Only Rasheed and (I, me, myself) were given cell phones by the company. _____

Worksheet 1

Remember that pronouns that rename the subject and that follow linking verbs must be in the subjective case: (*It was he who placed the order*). When the infinitive *to be* has no subject (and that subject must immediately precede the infinitive *to be*), the pronoun that follows must be in the subjective case (*My sister is often taken to be I*).

In the following sentences, select the correct word.

1. It must have been (her, she) who called this morning.   _____

2. I certainly would not like to be (he, him).   _____

3. Do you think that it was (they, them) who complained?   _____

4. Tram answered the telephone by saying, "This is (her, she)."   _____

5. Ms. Richards thought the salesperson to be (he, him).   _____

6. If you were (she, her), would you take the job?   _____

7. Cecile is sometimes taken to be (her, she).   _____

8. Jim said that yesterday's driver could have been (he, him).   _____

9. Ms. Soriano asked Frank and (I, me) to help her.   _____

10. Was it (they, them) who made the contribution?   _____

11. The most accurate proofreader seems to be (he, him).   _____

12. Producer Edwards would not allow me to be (he, him) in the production.   _____

13. Mr. Fox wants to assign you and (her, she) the project.   _____

14. Are you sure it was (I, me) who was called to the phone?   _____

15. The visitor was thought to be (she, her).   _____

16. If it had not been (she, her) who made the announcement, I would not have believed it.   _____

17. How could anyone have thought that Courtney was (I, me)?   _____

18. I do not wish to discourage either you or (he, him).   _____

19. If anyone is disappointed, it will be (I, me).   _____

20. What makes Joan wish to be (she, her)?   _____

21. Do you think it was (he, him) who made the large contribution?   _____

22. Mr. Rivera selected you and (he, him) because of his confidence in your abilities.   _____

23. If it had been (she, her), we would have recognized her immediately.   _____

24. Everyone thought the new manager would be (she, her).   _____

25. Because the president is to be (he, him), Mr. Thomas will act as CEO.   _____

Worksheet 2

Select the correct word to complete the following sentences.

1. Only the president and (he, him) can grant leaves of absence. _____

2. The manager mistook Danielle to be (I, me). _____

3. The body of the manuscript is followed by (its, it's) endnotes. _____

4. Our staff agreed that you and (she, her) should represent us. _____

5. How can you believe (us, we) to be guilty? _____

6. I'm not sure (theirs, there's) enough time left. _____

7. Everyone thought the new manager would be (he, him). _____

8. My friend and (I, me) looked for jobs together. _____

9. This matter will be kept strictly between you and (I, me). _____

10. Good employees like you and (she, her) are always on time. _____

11. Judge Waxman is fully supported by (we, us) consumers. _____

12. We agree that (your, you're) the best person for the job. _____

13. Send the announcement to Ms. Nguyen and (she, her) today. _____

14. All employees except Kim and (he, him) will be evaluated. _____

15. Many locker combinations are listed, but (your's, yours) is missing. _____

16. Apparently the message was intended for you and (I, me, myself). _____

17. Was it (he, him, himself) who sent the mystery e-mail message? _____

18. The bank is closed, but (it's, its) ATM is open. _____

19. Please submit the report to (him or me, he or I) before May 1. _____

20. (There's, Theirs) only one path for us to follow. _____

21. For you and (he, him), I would suggest careers in marketing. _____

22. These personnel changes affect you and (I, me, myself) directly. _____

23. My friend and (I, me, myself) are thinking of a trip to Hawaii. _____

24. Only two branches plan to expand (they're, their) display rooms. _____

25. The operator thought it was (she, her) calling for assistance. _____

26. Because you are a member of the audit review team, you have a better overall picture of the operations than (I, me, myself). _____

27. Though you may not agree with our decision, I hope you will support Todd and (I, me) in our effort to get the job done. _____

28. Some of the recent decisions made by (us, we) supervisors will be reviewed by the management council when it meets in January. _____

29. I wonder if it was (she, her) who was reprimanded for excessive e-mail use. _____

30. Do you think (theirs, their's, there's) any real reason to change our computer passwords every month? _____

Self-Help Exercises
Pronouns and Antecedents

7

LEVEL 1

Pronouns must agree with the words for which they substitute. Don't let words and phrases that come between a pronoun and its antecedent confuse you.

Examples: Every one of the women had *her* forms ready. (Not *their*)
Our supervisor Bob, along with four assistants, offered *his* support. (Not *their*)

Select the correct word(s) to complete these sentences.

1. Ms. Kennedy, in addition to many other members of the staff, sent (her, their) best wishes. _____

2. Every employee must have (his, her, his or her, their) physical examination completed by December 31. _____

3. After a job well done, everyone appreciates (his, her, his or her, their) share of credit. _____

4. Several office workers, along with the manager, announced (his or her, their) intention to vote for the settlement. _____

5. Individuals like Mr. Herndon can always be depended on to do (her, his, his or her, their) best in all assignments. _____

6. If a policyholder has a legitimate claim, (he, she, he or she, they) should contact us immediately. _____

7. Every one of the employees brought (her or his lunch, their lunches) to the outdoor event. _____

8. When a customer walks into our store, treat (him, her, him or her, them) as you would an honored guest in your home. _____

9. Carolyn Davis, along with several other company representatives, volunteered to demonstrate (her, his, his or her, their) equipment. _____

10. A few of the members of the touring group, in addition to their guide, wanted (his or her picture, their pictures) taken. _____

11. Any female member of the project could arrange (her, their) own accommodations if desired. _____

12. Every player on the men's ball team complained about (his, their) uniform. _____

Rewrite this sentence to avoid the use of gender-biased pronoun. Show three versions.

Every employee must obtain his parking permit in the supervisor's office.

13. _____

14. _____

15. _____

Underline any pronoun–antecedent errors in the following sentences. Then write a corrected form in the space provided.

1. Last Friday either Ms. Monahan or Ms. Chavez left their computer on. _____

2. The Federal Drug Administration has not yet granted it's approval for the drug. _____

3. Every clerk, every manager, and every executive will be expected to do their part in making the carpooling program a success. _____

4. Somebody left his cell phone in the tray at the airport security check. _____

5. Neither one of the men wanted to have their remarks quoted. _____

6. Every one of the delegates to the women's conference was wearing their name tag. _____

7. The vice president and the marketing director had already made his reservations. _____

8. Each of the pieces of equipment came with their own software. _____

9. The firm of Higgins, Thomas & Keene, Inc., is moving their offices to Warner Plaza. _____

10. Every manager expects the employees who report to them to be willing to earn their salaries. _____

11. Neither of the women had their driver's license in the car. _____

12. We hoped that someone in the office could find their copy of the program. _____

13. Either the first telephone caller or the second one did not leave their number. _____

14. If everybody will please take their seats, we can get started. _____

15. The faculty agreed to publicize their position on budget cuts. _____

16. We saw that HomeCo reduced their prices on lawn mowers. _____

17. Few of the color printers had the sale price marked on it. _____

18. Every one of the male employees agreed to be more careful in protecting their computer password. _____

19. Each bridesmaid will pay for their own gown. _____

20. All managers and employees know that she or he must boost productivity. _____

Worksheet 1

In selecting *who* or *whom* to complete the following sentences, follow these three steps:

1. Isolate the *who/whom* clause.

   Example: (*who, whom*) the contract names

2. Invert to normal subject–verb order.

   Example: the contract names (*who, whom*)

3. Substitute the subjective pronoun *he* (*she* or *they*) for *who*. Substitute the objective pronoun *him* (*her* or *them*) for *whom*. If the sentence sounds correct with *him*, replace *him* with *whom*. If the sentence sounds correct with *he*, replace *he* with *who*.

   Example: the contract names *him* equates to the contract names *whom*

   Complete: We do not know *whom* the contract names.

   Example: We do not know (who, whom) the contract names.   whom _____

1. (Who, Whom) will you invite to your party?   _____

2. Rick Nash is the employee (who, whom) the CEO asked to present to the board.   _____

3. Do you know (who, whom) will be taking your place?   _____

4. To (who, whom) did she refer in her letter?   _____

5. Did Mr. Glade say (who, whom) he wanted to see?   _____

6. Dr. Truong is a man (who, whom) everyone respects.   _____

7. (Who, Whom) was president of your organization last year?   _____

8. (Who, Whom) do you want to work with?   _____

9. (Who, Whom) has the best chance to be elected?   _____

10. I know of no one else (who, whom) plays so well.   _____

In choosing *who* or *whom* to complete these sentences, ignore parenthetical phrases such as *I think, we know, you feel,* and *I believe.*

11. Julie is a person (who, whom) I know will be successful on the job.   _____

12. The human resources director hired an individual (who, whom) he thought would be the best performer.   _____

13. Is Ms. Hastings the dealer (who, whom) you think I should call?   _____

14. Major Kirby, (who, whom) I think will be elected, is running in the next election.   _____

15. (Who, Whom) do you believe will be given the job?   _____

Worksheet 2

In the following sentences, selecting *who, whom, whoever,* or *whomever* first requires isolating the clause within which the pronoun appears. Then, *within the clause,* determine whether a nominative-case (*who, whoever*) or objective-case (*whom, whomever*) pronoun is required.

Example: Give the package to (whoever, whomever) opens the door.
(*He* or *she* opens the door = *whoever* opens the door.)   whoever _____

1. A bonus will be given to (whoever, whomever) brings in the most new clients. _____

2. Discuss the problem with (whoever, whomever) is in charge of the program. _____

3. We will interview (whoever, whomever) you recommend. _____

4. You may give the tickets to (whoever, whomever) you wish. _____

5. Johnson said to give the parking pass to (whoever, whomever) asked for it. _____

6. The committee members have promised to cooperate with (whoever, whomever) is selected to chair the committee. _____

7. Please call (whoever, whomever) you believe can repair the machine. _____

8. (Whoever, Whomever) is nominated for the position must be approved by the full membership. _____

9. Reservations have been made for (whoever, whomever) requested them in advance. _____

10. (Whoever, Whomever) is chosen to lead the delegation will command attention at the caucus. _____

In choosing *who* or *whom* to complete these sentences, be especially alert to pronouns following the linking verbs. Remember that the nominative *who* is required as a subject complement.

Example: Was it (who, whom) I thought it was? (It was *he* = *who.*)   who _____

11. (Who, Whom) is the customer who wanted a replacement? _____

12. The visitor who asked for me was (who, whom)? _____

13. Was the new CEO (who, whom) we thought it would be? _____

14. The winner will be (whoever, whomever) is the top salesperson. _____

15. For (who, whom) was this new printer ordered? _____

Worksheet 3

In the following sentences, select the correct word.

1. (Who, Whom) did you call for assistance? _____

2. Mr. Lincoln, (who, whom) we thought would never be hired, did well in his first assignment. _____

3. By (who, whom) are you currently employed? _____

4. You should hire (whoever, whomever) you feel has the best qualifications. _____

5. Did the caller say (who, whom) he wanted to see? _____

6. The man (who, whom) I saw yesterday walked by today. _____

7. (Whoever, Whomever) is first on the list will be called next. _____

8. The sales rep sent notices to customers (who, whom) she felt should be notified. _____

9. Is the manager (who, whom) we thought it would be? _____

10. The manager praised the clerk (who, whom) worked late. _____

11. She is the one (who, whom) Kevin helped yesterday. _____

12. Many of us thought Mr. Alison was a nice person with (who, whom) to work. _____

13. (Who, Whom) is Stacy often mistaken to be? _____

14. (Who, Whom) did you say to call for reservations? _____

15. Please make an appointment with (whoever, whomever) you consider to be the best internist. _____

16. Here is a list of satisfied customers (who, whom) you may wish to contact. _____

17. (Whoever, Whomever) is suggested by Mr. Arthur must be interviewed. _____

18. The candidate (who, whom) the party supports will win. _____

19. Marcia is one on (who, whom) I have come to depend. _____

20. For (who, whom) are these contracts? _____

21. Do you know (whose, who's) jacket this is? _____

22. Do you know (whose, who's) working overtime tonight? _____

23. We are not sure (whose, who's) signed up for Friday's seminar. _____

24. It doesn't matter (whose, who's) comments those are. _____

25. You will never guess (whose, who's) running for president! _____

8 Self-Help Exercises
Verbs: Kinds, Voices, Moods, Verbals

Fill in the answers to the following questions with information found in your text.

1. What kind of action verbs direct action toward a person or thing (transitive or intransitive)? _____

2. What kind of action verbs do not require an object to complete their action (transitive or intransitive)? _____

3. What kind of verbs link to the subject words that rename or describe the subject (action, linking, or helping)? _____

4. What do we call the nouns, pronouns, and adjectives used with linking verbs that complete the meaning of a sentence by renaming or describing the subject? _____

5. What kind of verbs are added to main verbs, which can be action or linking, to form verb phrases? _____

In each of the following sentences, indicate whether the underlined verb is transitive (*T*), intransitive (*I*), or linking (*L*). In addition, if the verb is transitive, write its object. If the verb is linking, write its complement. The first two sentences are followed by explanations to assist you.

6. Jeff <u>ran</u> along the dirt path back to his home. (The verb *ran* is intransitive. It has no object to complete its meaning. The phrase *along the dirt path* tells where Jeff ran; it does not receive the action of the verb.) _____

7. It <u>might have been</u> Jessica who called yesterday. (The verb phrase ends with the linking verb *been*. The complement is *Jessica*, which renames the subject *it*.) _____

8. Juan <u>input</u> the addresses of our most recent customers. _____

9. Customers <u>crowded</u> into the store at the beginning of the sale. _____

10. Sherry <u>was</u> a consultant on the software conversion project. _____

11. Levi Strauss first <u>sold</u> pants to miners in San Francisco in the 1800s. _____

12. The bank <u>faxed</u> you the loan application. _____

13. Chocolate fudge ice cream <u>tastes</u> better than chocolate mint. _____

14. Do you think it <u>was</u> he who suggested the improvement? _____

15. We <u>walked</u> around the shopping mall on our lunch hour. _____

16. Our company recruiter <u>asks</u> the same questions of every candidate. _____

17. Many corporations <u>give</u> gifts to important foreign clients. _____

18. All employees <u>listened</u> intently as the CEO discussed annual profits. _____

19. Ellen <u>feels</u> justified in asking for a raise. _____

20. Customers <u>have</u> high expectations from most advertised products. _____

Worksheet 1

Transitive verbs that direct action toward an object are in the active voice. Transitive verbs that direct action toward a subject are in the passive voice. Writing that incorporates active-voice verbs is more vigorous and more efficient than writing that contains many passive-voice verbs. To convert a passive-voice verb to the active voice, look for the doer of the action. (Generally the doer of the action is contained in a *by* phrase.) In the active voice the agent becomes the subject.

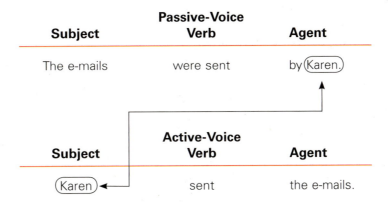

For each of the following sentences, underline the doer of the action. Write that word in the space provided. Then rewrite the sentence changing the passive-voice verbs to active voice. Your rewritten version should begin with the word (and its modifiers) that you identified as the doer of the action.

Agent

1. The text message was not received by Mark until Monday morning. _____

   _____

   _____

2. Our order was shipped last week by Dell. _____

   _____

   _____

3. Withdrawals must be authorized by Sherri Bradford beginning next week. _____

   _____

   _____

4. Wyatt was asked by Mr. Stern to be responsible for turning out the lights at the end of the day. _____

   _____

   _____

5. Employees who travel a great deal were forced by management to surrender their frequent-flier mileage awards. _____

   _____

   _____

Worksheet 2

Some sentences with passive-voice verbs do not identify the doer of the action. Before these sentences can be converted, a subject must be provided. Use your imagination to supply subjects.

Passive: Interest will be paid on all deposits. (*By whom?* By First Federal.)

Active: First Federal will pay interest on all deposits.

By Whom?

1. Our departmental report must be completed before 5 p.m. _____

   _____

   _____

2. Checks were written on an account with insufficient funds. _____

   _____

   _____

3. Decisions are made in the courts that affect the daily lives of all Americans. _____

   _____

   _____

4. Employees working with computers were warned to change their passwords frequently. _____

   _____

   _____

5. Our accounting records were scrutinized during the audit. _____

   _____

   _____

Worksheet 3

Write the correct answers in the spaces provided.

1. If I (was, were) you, I would complete my degree first.

   _____

2. If Mr. Greer (was, were) in the office yesterday, he did not sign the checks.

   _____

3. One of the stockholders moved that a committee (be, is) constituted to study the problem immediately.

   _____

4. If the manager were here, he (will, would) sign the work order and we could proceed.

   _____

5. Government officials recommend that all homes (are, be) stocked with an emergency supply of food and water.

   _____

6. Dr. Washington suggested that the patient (rest, rests) for the next two days.

   _____

7. Angela wished that she (was, were) able to fly to Phoenix to visit her sister.

   _____

8. Under the circumstances, even if the voter registration drive (was, were) successful, we might lose the election.

   _____

9. After consulting management, our manager suggested that all employees (are, be) given three-week vacations.

   _____

10. It has been moved and seconded that the meeting (is, be) adjourned.

   _____

Worksheet 1

A verb form ending in *ing* and used as a noun is a gerund.

> *Passing* the examination is important. (Gerund used as subject.)

A noun or pronoun modifying a gerund should be possessive.

> *Your* passing the examination is important.

Don't confuse verbals acting as nouns with those acting as adjectives.

> The man *passing* the test received his license. (*Passing* functions as an adjective describing *man*.)

> The man's *passing* the test is important. (Verbal noun *passing* functions as the subject of the verb *is*.)

In the following sentences, underline any gerunds and write their modifiers in the space provided. If a sentence contains no gerund, write *None*.

Example: It is your <u>smoking</u> that disturbs the others.   your _____

1. This job offer is contingent on your passing our physical examination.   _____
2. Our office certainly did not approve of his investing in high-risk securities.   _____
3. It was Mr. Cortina's gambling that caused him to lose his job.   _____

Some of the remaining sentences contain gerunds. If any error appears in the modifier, underline the error and write the correct form in the space provided. If the sentence is correct, write *C*.

Example: Jamie Salazar was instrumental in <u>us</u> acquiring the Collins' account.   our _____

4. The individual receiving the award could not be present to accept it.   _____
5. Do you think you criticizing the manager had anything to do with your transfer?   _____
6. We deeply appreciate you calling us to give us this news at this time.   _____
7. An employee taking a message must write clearly.   _____
8. Ms. Fackler said that me working overtime was unnecessary this weekend.   _____

Worksheet 2

From the sets of sentences that follow, select the sentence that is the more logically stated. Write its letter in the space provided.

1. a. Try and come to lunch with us on Friday.
b. Try to come to lunch with us on Friday. _____

2. a. To get to the meeting quickly, a shortcut was taken by Mike.
b. To get to the meeting quickly, Mike took a shortcut. _____

3. a. When investing money in the stock market, one must expect risks.
b. When investing money in the stock market, risks must be expected. _____

4. a. After filling out an application, the human resources manager gave me an interview.
b. After filling out an application, I was given an interview by the human resources manager. _____

5. a. Driving erratically down the street, the driver was stopped by the officer.
b. Driving erratically down the street, the officer stopped the driver. _____

Check your answers to the preceding five questions. Using the better versions of the sentence sets as models, rewrite the following sentences to make them logical. Add words as necessary, but retain the verbal expressions as sentence openers.

6. Completing the examination in only 20 minutes, a perfect score was earned by Maria.

_____

_____

_____

7. To locate the members' names and addresses, the current directory was used.

_____

_____

_____

8. Driving through the desert, the highway seemed endless.

_____

_____

_____

9. Addressing an audience for the first time, my knees shook and my voice wavered.

_____

_____

_____

9 Self-Help Exercises
Verb Tenses and Parts

LEVEL 1

Select the correct verb.

1. Did you tell me that the caller's name (is, was) Scott? _____

2. A bad accident (occured, occurred) late last evening. _____

3. Mr. Anderson says that the car you are driving (is, was) red. _____

4. Are you sure that her maiden name (is, was) Spitnale? _____

5. We were taught that an ounce of prevention (is, was) worth a pound of cure. _____

In the space provided, write the verb form indicated in parentheses.

Example: Joan (carry) a heavy workload every day. (present tense)   carries _____

6. The software company (plan) to expand its markets abroad. (present tense) _____

7. A Kentucky Fried Chicken franchise (sell) American-style fast food in Japan. (future tense) _____

8. The giant Mitsubishi conglomerate (supply) the Colonel with chicken in Japan. (past tense) _____

9. The marketing director (study) possible sales sites in foreign countries. (present tense) _____

10. We (analyze) such factors as real estate, construction costs, and local attitudes toward fast food. (future tense) _____

11. Management (apply) a complex formula to forecast the profitability of the new business. (past tense) _____

12. We (consider) the vast differences between the two cultures. (past tense) _____

13. A local franchise (vary) the side dishes to accommodate cultural preferences. (present tense) _____

14. Kentucky Fried Chicken (insist) on retaining its original recipe in foreign stores. (present tense) _____

15. Kentucky Fried Chicken products (appeal) to the average customer in Japan. (future tense) _____

16. Doing business in Japan (require) an appreciation of rituals and formalities. (present tense) _____

17. When you visit East Asia, the presentation of business cards (demand) special attention to ceremony. (future tense) _____

18. Western businesspeople (try) to observe local customs. (past tense) _____

Worksheet 1

Select the correct verb.

1. If her cell phone had (rang, rung), she would have heard it. _____
2. Ice (froze, freezed) in the pipes last night. _____
3. Before leaving on her vacation, Ms. Stanton (hid, hide) her silver and other valuables. _____
4. Have you (chose, chosen) a location for the new equipment? _____
5. Three new homes were recently (builded, built) on Fairfax Avenue. _____
6. He had already (drank, drunk) two bottles of water when he asked for more. _____
7. We (hung, hanged) a new painting in the reception area. _____
8. Are you sure you have (gave, given) him the correct combination? _____
9. Andre and the others had (went, gone) on the hike earlier. _____
10. The smaller dog was (bit, bitten) by a larger neighborhood dog. _____

Underline any errors in the following sentences. Write the correct form in the space provided. Do not add helping verbs, and do not delete any helping verbs that already appear in these sentences.

Example: After we run out of food, we had to return to camp headquarters. ran_____

11. We had ate a small snack before we ordered dinner. _____
12. The TV commercial was sang by an actress whose lips did not match the sound track. _____
13. I can't believe he sweared during the meeting. _____
14. Hundreds of mushrooms sprung up after the rain. _____
15. Many people were shook by the minor earthquake yesterday. _____
16. Tracy had wore her stylish new boots only twice. _____
17. Fortunately, he had wrote most of his report before his computer crashed. _____
18. Their car was stole from its parking place overnight. _____
19. Because of a threatening storm, she should have took a cab. _____
20. If we had went to the movie premier, we would have seen the stars. _____

Worksheet 2

Lie–Lay

Use the following chart to help you select the correct form of *lie* or *lay* in these sentences.

Present	Past	Past Participle	Present Participle
lie (rest)	lay (rested)	lain (have, has, or had rested)	lying (resting)
lay (place)	laid (placed)	laid (have, has, or had placed)	laying (placing)

Example: This afternoon I must (rest) down before dinner.   lie _____

1. I am sure that I (placed) the book on the desk yesterday.   _____

2. Andrea angrily told her dog to (rest) down.   _____

3. This month's bills have been (resting) in the drawer for weeks.   _____

4. Kim has (placed) her books on the desk near the entrance.   _____

5. The worker was (placing) concrete blocks for the foundation.   _____

6. This evening I must (rest) down before we leave.   _____

7. Yesterday I (rested) in my room, worrying about today's exam.   _____

8. (Place) the papers in a stack over there.   _____

9. That old candy has (rested) on the shelf for several weeks.   _____

10. Let the fabric (rest) there for several hours until it dries.   _____

Now try these sentences to test your skill in using the forms of *lie* and *lay*.

11. Will you be able to (lie, lay) down before dinner?   _____

12. How long have these papers been (laying, lying) here?   _____

13. Please tell your very friendly dog to (lay, lie) down.   _____

14. Will the mason (lay, lie) bricks over the concrete patio?   _____

15. The contract has (laid, lain) on his desk for over two weeks.   _____

16. Yesterday I (laid, lay) down in the afternoon.   _____

17. Mothers complain about clothes that are left (laying, lying) around.   _____

18. Returned books (lie, lay) in a pile at the library until the staff can return them to the stacks.   _____

19. I'm sure I (laid, layed, lied) my keys on this counter.   _____

20. When you were (lying, laying) the groceries down, did you see my keys?   _____

Use Chapter 9 to look up the verb tenses required in the following sentences.

Example: By June 1 you (work) here one full year. (future perfect)   <u>will have worked</u>

1. McDonald's (open) many restaurants in foreign countries.
   (present perfect)   _____

2. McDonald's (plan) to launch a franchise program. (present progressive)   _____

3. We (call) for service at least three times before a technician arrived.
   (past perfect)   _____

4. She (work) on that project for the past six months. (present perfect)   _____

5. We (see) the very first screening of the documentary. (past progressive)   _____

6. The mayor (sign) the proclamation at this afternoon's public ceremony.
   (future progressive)   _____

7. The bulldozer working on street repairs (broke) the water main. (past perfect)   _____

8. I (see) two good movies recently. (present perfect)   _____

9. We (consider) the installation of a new e-mail system. (present progressive)   _____

10. Americans across the country (hear) the president's message in four time zones.
    (past progressive)   _____

The next sentences review Level 2.

11. The alarm had (rang, rung) three times before we responded.   _____

12. Yesterday we (drank, drunk) many glasses of water because of the heat.   _____

13. You must (chose, choose) a new Internet service provider.   _____

14. The car has been (drove, driven) many miles.   _____

15. Steve claims he (saw, seen) the report yesterday.   _____

16. If Rasheed had (went, gone) earlier, he would have told us.   _____

17. Daphne said she (seen, saw) an accident on her way to work.   _____

18. The tour guide checked to see whether everyone had (ate, eaten) before
    we left the lunch stop.   _____

19. Rodney had (wrote, written) four e-mail messages before he realized they were
    not being received.   _____

20. The price of our stocks (raised, rose) again yesterday.   _____

21. Witnesses had (swear, swore, sworn) to tell the truth during the trial.   _____

22. Stock prices (sank, sunk) so low that investors were sitting on their cash.   _____

23. Because it was washed in hot water, the cashmere sweater (shrank, shrunk).   _____

24. If we had (began, begun) the report earlier, we could have met the deadline.   _____

25. Employees had been (forbade, forbidden) to use company computers
    for games or shopping.   _____

10 Self-Help Exercises
Subject–Verb Agreement

Worksheet 1

For each of the following sentences, cross out any phrase that comes between a verb and its subject. Then select the correct verb and write it in the space provided.

Example: One ~~of the most interesting books on all the lists~~ (is, are) *Becoming a Millionaire at 21.*   is

1. Many Web sites on the government's prohibited list (provide, provides) games or amusement that employees may not access.   _____

2. The supervisor, together with two technicians, (is, are) working on the faulty circuit.   _____

3. This company's supply of raw materials (come, comes) from South America.   _____

4. A good many workers in addition to Jennifer (think, thinks) the work shifts should be rearranged.   _____

5. Everyone except you and John (is, are) to repeat the test.   _____

6. The table as well as two chairs (was, were) damaged.   _____

7. A list with all the customers' names and addresses (is, are) being sent.   _____

8. Other equipment such as our terminals and printers (need, needs) to be reevaluated.   _____

9. One of the online shopping sites (has, have) a section devoted to clearance items.   _____

10. Several copies of the report (is, are) being prepared for distribution.   _____

11. The furniture, as well as all the equipment including computers, (is, are) for sale.   _____

12. Effects of the disease (is, are) not known immediately.   _____

13. Three salespeople, in addition to their district sales manager, (has, have) voiced the same suggestion.   _____

14. Profits from his home business (is, are) surprising.   _____

15. Every one of the potential businesses that you mention (sounds, sound) good.   _____

16. A shipment of 8,000 drill sets (was, were) sent to four warehouses.   _____

17. Everyone except the evening employees (is, are) coming.   _____

18. We learned that two subsidiaries of the corporation (is, are) successful.   _____

19. Officials in several levels of government (has, have) to be consulted.   _____

20. A letter together with several enclosures (was, were) mailed yesterday.   _____

Worksheet 2

For each of the following sentences, underline the subject. Then select the correct verb and write it in the space provided.

Example: Here (is, are) a <u>copy</u> of the findings for your files. **is**

Suggestion: If you know that a subject is singular, temporarily substitute *he, she,* or *it* to help you select the proper verb. If you know that a subject is plural, temporarily substitute *they* for the subject.

1. The flow of industrial goods (travel, travels) through different distribution channels from the flow of consumer goods. _____

2. Here (is, are) the newspaper and magazines you ordered. _____

3. Coleman, Harris & Juarez, Inc., one of the leading management consultant firms, (is, are) able to accept our business. _____

4. The books on the open shelves of our company's library (is, are) available to all employees. _____

5. There (appear, appears) to be significant points omitted from the report. _____

6. The various stages in the life cycle of a product (is, are) instrumental in determining profits for that product. _____

7. No one except the Cunninghams (was, were) able to volunteer. _____

8. A member of the organization of painters and plasterers (is, are) unhappy about the recent settlement. _____

9. The size and design of its container (is, are) influential in the appeal of a product. _____

10. Just one governmental unit from the local, state, or national levels (is, are) all we need to initiate the project. _____

11. American Airlines (has, have) improved service while cutting costs. _____

12. Only two seasons of the year (provide, provides) weather that is suitable for gliding. _____

13. (Has, Have) the moving van of the Wongs arrived yet? _____

14. At present the condition of the company's finances (is, are) extremely strong as a result of the recent bond sale. _____

15. Incoming luggage from three flights (is, are) now being sorted. _____

16. The salary of Maria Chavez, along with the earnings of several other employees, (has, have) been increased. _____

17. One of the best designs (appear, appears) to have been submitted by your student. _____

18. Trying to improve relations between doctors and patients, the American Medical Association, along with several dozen medical societies, (is, are) helping doctors embrace online consultations. _____

19. Certainly the ease and convenience of shopping at any hour of the day or night—and getting fast delivery without ever leaving home—(is, are) very appealing. _____

20. Aggressiveness and delinquency in boys (is, are) linked to high levels of lead in their bones, according to a recent study. _____

For each of the following sentences, underline the subject. Then select the correct word and write it in the space provided.

1. Most of the salary compensation to which he referred (is, are) beyond basic pay schedules. _____

2. The Committee on Youth Activities (has, have) enlisted the aid of several well-known athletes. _____

3. Each of the young men and women (deserve, deserves) an opportunity to participate in local athletics. _____

4. Either your company or one of your two competitors (is, are) going to win the government contract. _____

5. All the work for our Special Products Division (is, are) yet to be assigned. _____

6. Either of the two small businesses (is, are) able to secure a loan. _____

7. City council members (was, were) sharply divided along partisan lines. _____

8. Neither the packing list nor the two invoices (mention, mentions) the missing ottoman. _____

9. Every one of your suggestions (merit, merits) consideration. _____

10. Our survey shows that (everyone, every one) of the owner-managed businesses was turning a profit. _____

11. Either Steven or you (is, are) expected to return the call. _____

12. Each of the machines (has, have) capabilities that are suitable for our needs. _____

13. Mrs. Roberts said that most of the credit for our increased sales (belong, belongs) to you. _____

14. First on the program (is, are) the group of Indo-European folk dancers. _____

15. Some of the enthusiasm (is, are) due to the coming holiday. _____

16. After 10 p.m. the staff (has, have) to use the front entrance only. _____

17. (Was, Were) any of the supervisors absent after the holiday? _____

18. The union (has, have) made an agreement with management. _____

19. We were informed that neither management nor the employees (has, have) special privileges. _____

20. Most of the work that was delivered to us four days ago (is, are) completed. _____

In the following sentences, select the correct word.

1. Reed says that 75 feet of plastic pipe (has, have) been ordered. _____

2. The number of women in the labor force (is, are) steadily increasing. _____

3. Phillip said that he is one of those individuals who (enjoy, enjoys) a real challenge. _____

4. Over two thirds of the stock issue (was, were) sold immediately after it was released. _____

5. Gerald is the only one of the four applicants who (was, were) prepared to complete the application form during the interview. _____

6. That most offices are closed on weekends (is, are) a factor that totally escaped Mr. Brotherton. _____

7. The majority of the employees (favor, favors) the reorganization plan. _____

8. Telephones (is, are) one item that we must install immediately. _____

9. At least four fifths of the women in the audience (is, are) willing to participate in the show. _____

10. How could it be I who (am, is) responsible, when I had no knowledge of the agreement until yesterday? _____

11. Let it be recorded that on the second vote the number of members in favor of the proposal (is, are) less than on the first vote. _____

12. Only half of the box of highlighters (is, are) left in the supply cabinet. _____

13. Are you one of those people who (like, likes) to sleep late? _____

14. I'm sure that it is you who (is, are) next on the list. _____

15. It looks as if 20 inches of extra cord (is, are) what we need. _____

16. Our office manager reports that a number of printers (need, needs) repair. _____

17. At least one third of the desserts purchased for the party (was, were) uneaten. _____

18. Hiking in Europe and sailing to Scandinavia (is, are) what I plan for my future vacations. _____

19. Sherry Lansing is one of our e-mail users who (complain, complains) about the system. _____

20. Whoever submitted an application earliest (has, have) the right to be interviewed first. _____

11 Self-Help Exercises
Modifiers: Adjectives and Adverbs

LEVEL 1

Write the correct comparative or superlative form of the adjective shown in parentheses.

Example: Carmen is (neat) than her sister.   neater _____

1.   We hope that the new procedures prove to be (effective)
     than previous procedures.   _____

2.   Of all the suggestions made, Mr. Bradley's suggestion is the (bad).   _____

3.   Mrs. Schrillo's daughter is certainly (friendly) than she is.   _____

4.   Of the three individuals who volunteered, Ted is the one about whom
     I am (less) certain.   _____

5.   I don't believe I've ever seen a (beautiful) sunset than this one.   _____

6.   We make many printers, but the Model SX6 is the (fast).   _____

7.   No restaurant makes (good) hamburgers than Clown Alley.   _____

8.   Located next to the airport, Westchester is probably the (noisy) area in the city. _____

9.   Living in the suburbs provides (quiet) surroundings than in the city.   _____

10. Of all the applications we have received, this one seems the (sincere). _____

11. For this job we need the (skilled) employee in the department.   _____

12. I'm afraid Andrea has the (less) chance of being selected in the lottery. _____

13. No one works (slow) than Bob.   _____

14. DataSource is (likely) to be awarded the contract than CompuPro.   _____

15. This is probably the (unusual) request I've ever received.   _____

16. Juan has had (few) citations than any other driver.   _____

17. The office is certainly looking (good) today than yesterday.   _____

18. Everyone watching the video thought that Thomas looked (credible)
     than any other actor.   _____

19. It was the (bad) accident I've ever seen.   _____

20. Sharon's report had the (less) errors of all those submitted.   _____

If the underlined word or words in the following sentences are correctly expressed, write *C*. If they are incorrect, write a corrected form in the space provided.

Example: Because <u>less</u> people made contributions, we failed to reach our goal. fewer

1. He played his Internet music so <u>loud</u> that we couldn't work. _____

2. We have decided to increase our <u>point-of-purchase</u> advertising. _____

3. It is <u>a</u> honor to speak to your organization this afternoon. _____

4. Talking with her <u>won't</u> do <u>no</u> good. _____

5. The machine is running <u>quieter</u> since we installed a hood. _____

6. Todd and I felt <u>badly</u> about Kurt's accident. _____

7. The general manager should not become involved in this <u>conflict of interest</u> issue. _____

8. Ms. Edelstein was dressed <u>neatly</u> for the interview. _____

9. At present we are searching for a source of <u>inexpensive, accessible</u> raw materials. _____

10. Rex has been a member of <u>an</u> union for many years. _____

11. <u>These sort</u> of employees can make a company successful. _____

12. Most candidates completed the examinations <u>satisfactory</u>. _____

13. We are conducting the campaign from <u>house-to-house</u>. _____

14. We <u>couldn't hardly</u> imagine the time that went into the project. _____

15. She can't wait to take <u>a</u> one-week vacation. _____

16. The children were playing <u>quiet</u> when the guests arrived. _____

17. He <u>didn't</u> say <u>nothing</u> during the meeting. _____

18. You are a preferred <u>charge-account</u> customer at our store. _____

19. We expect a signed contract in the <u>not too distant</u> future. _____

20. Our customer mailing list is completely <u>up to date</u>. _____

In the following sentences, select the correct word(s).

1. Only the (a) two last, (b) last two speakers made relevant comments. _____

2. Craig is more stubborn than (a) anyone else, (b) anyone I know. _____

3. (a) Mrs. Smith reports that she has only one volunteer.
   (b) Mrs. Smith only reports that she has one volunteer. _____

4. Applications will be given to the (a) first five, (b) five first job candidates. _____

5. Los Angeles is larger than (a) any other city, (b) any city in California. _____

For each of the following sentences, underline any errors in the use of adjectives and adverbs. Then write the correct form. Mark C if the sentence is correct as written.

6. Unfortunately, we've had less applications this year than ever before. _____

7. We employees are real concerned about the new parking fee. _____

8. You can sure depend on my help whenever you need it. _____

9. He can be counted on to paint the room as neat as a professional would do the job. _____

10. The uniform you are required to wear certainly fits you good. _____

11. Because we have less work to do this week, we should finish soon. _____

12. The recently-enacted law has received great support. _____

13. Apparently we have picked the worse time of the year to list an office for rent. _____

14. Although it is a honorary position, the chairmanship is important. _____

15. We hadn't hardly reached shelter when it began to rain. _____

16. The Andersons made a round the world tour last year. _____

17. Because of their many kindnesses to us, I feel badly that we cannot reciprocate in some way. _____

18. If less people were involved, the new procedures could have been implemented earlier. _____

19. Festival promoters rented a 840-acre farm in Ulster County. _____

20. How much further must we drive tonight before stopping? _____

21. Less employment opportunities exist in that field; therefore, I am transferring to a different major. _____

22. My organization has selected the later of the two proposals you submitted. _____

23. Sam said he was sure he did good on his examination. _____

24. In order to farther her career, she is taking business classes. _____

Self-Help Exercises
Prepositions

LEVEL 1

Underline any errors in the following sentences. Then write the correct form. If the sentence is correct as written, write *C*.

1. You should of seen the looks on their faces! _____

2. No one except Mr. Levine and he had access to the company records. _____

3. I read the book and plan to attend the lecture too. _____

4. Just between you and I, this engine has never run more smoothly. _____

5. Some of the software programs we borrowed off of Jeffrey. _____

6. If you will address your inquiry too our Customer Relations Department, you will surely receive a response. _____

7. The director of human resources, along with the office manager and she, is planning to improve our hiring procedures. _____

8. We could of done something about the error if we had known earlier. _____

9. Because we are receiving to many spam messages, we are adding filters. _____

10. All salespeople except Ms. Berk and he were reassigned. _____

11. Did you obtain your copy of the team proposal off him? _____

12. Please get your passes from either Mrs. Bowman or he. _____

13. See whether you can get some change for the machine off of her. _____

14. Both the project coordinator and he should have verified the totals before submitting the bid. _____

15. The commission for the sale has to be divided between Ms. Carpenter and he. _____

16. Because to few spaces are available, additional parking must be found on nearby streets. _____

17. If you and he could of come yesterday, we might have been able to help you. _____

18. So that we may better evaluate your application, please supply references too. _____

19. You could of had complimentary tickets if you had called her. _____

20. The marketing manager assigned too many customers to Ann and I. _____

For each of the following sentences, underline any errors in the use of prepositions. Then write a correct form. Mark *C* if the sentence is correct as written.

1. We think that beside salary the major issue is working conditions. _____
2. Your support and participation in this new Web program are greatly appreciated. _____
3. The warranty period was over with two months ago. _____
4. Please come into see me when you are ready for employment. _____
5. Just inside of the office entrance is the receptionist. _____
6. The senior Mr. Wiggins left $3 million to be divided between three heirs. _____
7. Will you be able to deliver the goods like you said you would? _____
8. For most of us, very few opportunities like this ever arise. _____
9. Exactly what type software did you have in mind? _____
10. Some of the trucks were moved in to the garage at dusk. _____
11. When can we accept delivery of the electrical components ordered from Hellman, Inc.? _____
12. Because of your concern and involvement in our community action campaign, we have received thousands of dollars in contributions. _____
13. I know the time and date of our next committee meeting, but I do not know where it is at. _____
14. If you were willing to accept further responsibility, I would assign you the committee chairmanship. _____
15. Joanna could not help from laughing when she saw her e-mail. _____
16. Please hurry up so that we may submit our proposal quickly. _____
17. What style furniture is most functional for the waiting room? _____
18. After going into meet the supervisor, Carla was hired. _____
19. All parking lots opposite to the corporate headquarters will be cleaned. _____
20. Immediately after Kathy graduated high school, she started college. _____

In the following sentences, select the correct word.

1. Halle found that her voice was rising as she became more and more angry (a) at, (b) with the caller. _____

2. We know of no one who is more expert (a) in, (b) with cell phone technology than Dr. France. _____

3. Our specifications must comply (a) with, (b) to those in the request for proposal (RFP). _____

4. After corresponding (a) to, (b) with their home office, I was able to clear up the error in my account. _____

5. The houses in that subdivision are identical (a) to, (b) with each other. _____

6. If you (a) plan to attend, (b) plan on attending the summer session, you'd better register immediately. _____

7. A few of the provisions are retroactive (a) for, (b) to January 1. _____

8. Jeff talked (a) to, (b) with his boss about the company's future plans. _____

9. Standing (a) on, (b) in line is not my favorite activity. _____

10. She made every effort to reason (a) to, (b) with the unhappy customer. _____

11. Apparently the letters on the screen do not sufficiently contrast (a) with, (b) to the background. _____

12. The courses, faculty, and students in this school are certainly different (a) from, (b) than those at other schools. _____

13. Do you dare to disagree (a) to, (b) with him? _____

14. Being the leader of a business team is similar (a) with, (b) to coaching a sports team. _____

15. I am angry (a) at, (b) with the recommendation that we share offices. _____

16. The president insisted that he was completely independent (a) of, (b) from his campaign contributors. _____

17. He went on working oblivious (a) from, (b) to the surrounding chaos. _____

18. The figures on the balance sheet could not be reconciled (a) to, (b) with the actual account totals. _____

19. A number of individuals agreed (a) to, (b) with the plan. _____

20. Our office is convenient (a) to, (b) for many cafés and restaurants. _____

13 Self-Help Exercises
Conjunctions

LEVEL 1

Worksheet 1

Name four coordinating conjunctions:

1. _____   2. _____   3. _____   4. _____

When coordinating conjunctions connect independent clauses (groups of words that could stand alone as sentences), the conjunctions are preceded by commas. The two independent clauses form a compound sentence.

Compound Sentence: We hope to increase sales in the South, *but* we need additional sales personnel.

Use a comma only if the sentence is compound. When the words preceding or following the coordinating conjunction do not form an independent clause, no comma is used.

Simple Sentence: The bank will include the check with your monthly statement *or* will send the check to you immediately.

In the following sentences, selected coordinating conjunctions have been underlined. Mark *a* or *b* for each sentence.

  a = No punctuation needed   b = Insert a comma before the
                                            underlined conjunction

5. Marc Green is a specialist in information systems <u>and</u> he will be responsible
   for advising and assisting all our divisions.   _____

6. Marc Green is a specialist in information systems <u>and</u> will be responsible
   for advising and assisting all our divisions.   _____

7. This is an orientation session designed for all new employees <u>but</u> topics
   of interest for all employees will also be discussed.   _____

8. I have studied the plan you are developing <u>and</u> feel that it has real merit.   _____

9. We seek the reaction of the council <u>and</u> of others who have studied the plan.   _____

10. Our executive vice president will make the presentation in New York <u>or</u> he will
    unveil the plan in London.   _____

Worksheet 2

1. Name five conjunctive adverbs:

   1. _____ 3. _____ 5. _____

   2. _____ 4. _____

2. When a conjunctive adverb joins independent clauses, what punctuation mark precedes the conjunctive adverb? _____

3. Many words that serve as conjunctive adverbs can also function as parenthetical adverbs. When used parenthetically, adverbs are set off by what punctuation marks? _____

In the following sentences, words acting as conjunctive or parenthetical adverbs are underlined. Add necessary commas and semicolons to punctuate the sentences.

4. The company is planning nevertheless to proceed with its expansion.

5. Tour prices are contingent on double occupancy that is two people must share accommodations.

6. This organization on the other hand is quite small in the industry.

7. Our group will travel first to New York for the first product presentation then we will proceed to Paris for additional presentations.

8. Today's job market is very competitive however recent graduates can find jobs if they are well trained and persistent.

9. Most recruiters prefer chronological résumés consequently we advise our graduates to follow the traditional résumé format.

10. Human resources professionals spend little time reading a cover letter therefore it is wise to keep your letter short.

Worksheet 1

1. Name five subordinating conjunctions:

    1. _____   3. _____   5. _____

    2. _____   4. _____

Use *T* or *F* to indicate whether the following statements are true or false.

2. A phrase is a group of related words *without* a subject and a verb.   _____

3. A clause is a group of related words containing a subject and a verb.   _____

4. An independent clause has a subject and a verb and makes sense by itself.   _____

5. A dependent clause contains a subject and a verb but depends for its meaning
    on another clause.   _____

6. Conjunctions such as *because*, *if*, and *when* are used preceding
    independent clauses.   _____

Indicate whether the following groups of words are phrases (*P*), independent clauses (*I*), or dependent clauses (*D*). Capitalization and end punctuation has been omitted.

Example: he stood in a very long line   I _____

7. in the past year   _____

8. although she came to every meeting   _____

9. she came to every meeting   _____

10. during the period from spring to fall   _____

11. if sales continue to climb as they have for the past four months   _____

12. the director asked for additional personnel   _____

13. as soon as we can increase our production   _____

14. we can increase our production   _____

15. because your organization has financial strength   _____

16. in the future   _____

17. when he returns to the office   _____

18. fill out and mail the enclosed card   _____

19. we are reworking our original plans   _____

20. because your old résumé listed your work history and then went
    on to describe previous jobs in grim and boring detail disregarding their
    current relevance   _____

Worksheet 2

Add necessary commas to the following sentences. If a sentence requires no punctuation, write *C* next to it.

1. If you follow my suggestions you will help to improve the efficiency of our department.

2. You will help to improve the efficiency of our department if you follow my suggestions.

3. When completed the renovation should make the seventh floor much more attractive.

4. Let's discuss the problem when Ms. Gardner returns.

5. Drivers who park their cars in the restricted area are in danger of being ticketed.

6. Our latest company safety booklet which was submitted over six weeks ago is finally ready for distribution.

7. As you may know we have paid dividends regularly for over 70 years.

8. These payments provided there is no interruption in profits should continue for many years to come.

9. If necessary you may charge this purchase to your credit card.

10. Any employee who wishes to participate may contact our Human Resources Department.

11. James Gilroy who volunteered to head the program will be organizing our campaign.

12. I assure you that you will hear from Ms. Higgins as soon as she returns.

13. Before you send in the order may I see the catalog?

14. May I see the catalog before you send in the order?

15. We will submit the proposal within four working days if that schedule meets with your approval.

Worksheet 3

Use the information provided within parentheses to construct dependent clauses for the following sentences. Add subordinating conjunctions such as *who*, *which*, *although*, and *since*. The dependent clauses can appear at the beginning, in the middle, or at the end of the sentences.

Example: Dr. Cushman recently moved his practice to Miami Beach. (Dr. Cushman specializes in pediatrics.)

Dr. Cushman, who specializes in pediatrics, recently moved his practice to Miami Beach.

1. The original agreement was drawn between Mr. Hightower and Columbia Communications. (The agreement was never properly signed.)

   _____

   _____

2. Thank you for informing us that your credit card is missing. (This credit card has an expiration date of April 30.)

   _____

   _____

Combine the following clauses into single sentences.

3. (Your account is four months past due.) We will be forced to take legal action. We must hear from you within seven days.

   _____

   _____

4. Sally Horton won an award as this month's outstanding employee. (She works in the Quality Control Department.) Ms. Horton is an assistant to the manager in that department.

   _____

   _____

5. We are sending you four poster advertisements. They will appear in advertisements in magazines in April. (April marks the beginning of a national campaign featuring our sports clothes.)

   _____

   _____

LEVEL 3

The correlative conjunctions *both... and, either... or, neither... nor,* and *not only... but (also)* should be used in parallel constructions. That is, the words these conjunctions join should be similarly patterned. Compare the words that *follow* the conjunctions. For example, if a verb follows *either,* a verb should follow *or.* If the active voice is used with *neither,* then the active voice should be used with *nor.* Study the following examples.

Not Parallel: *Either* Vicki is typing the Collins' report *or* proofreading it. (The subject follows *either* and a verb follows *or.*)

Parallel: Vicki is *either* typing the Collins' report *or* proofreading it. (Both conjunctions are followed by verbs.)

Not Parallel: *Neither* have I pumped the gas *nor* was the oil checked. (An active-voice construction follows *neither* while a passive-voice construction follows *nor.*)

Parallel: I have *neither* pumped the gas *nor* checked the oil.

In the following, write the letters of the sentences that are constructed in parallel form.

1. a. We have neither the energy to pursue this litigation nor do we have the finances.
   b. We have neither the energy nor the finances to pursue this litigation. _____

2. a. You may either write a research report or a book report can be made.
   b. You may either write a research report or make a book report. _____

3. a. He is not only clever but also witty.
   b. Not only is he clever but he is also witty. _____

4. a. The Web site contains both information and it has an application form.
   b. The Web site contains both information and an application form. _____

Revise the following sentences so that the correlative conjunctions are used in parallel construction.

5. Either you can fax him your response or you can send him an e-mail message.

_____

_____

6. Our goals are both to educate motorists and also lives may be saved.

_____

_____

7. Neither does Tony have a job offer nor does he even have an interview lined up.

_____

_____

8. We knew either that we had to raise more money or begin selling stock.

_____

_____

9. Not only are businesses looking for employees who can work in teams but also can learn effectively in teams.

_____

_____

14 Self-Help Exercises
Commas

Add necessary commas to the following sentences. For each sentence indicate the number of commas that you added. If a sentence is correct, write *C*.

1. Your organization's use of cross-functional teams Mr. Wilson explains is why your company is able to develop so many innovative products. _____

2. By the way do all of your teams work well together and collaborate effectively? _____

3. To be most successful however all teams require training coaching and other support. _____

4. Our team leader is from Ames Iowa but is now working in Des Moines. _____

5. Developing effective collaborative teams on the other hand is not always possible. _____

6. The CEO's son Mark will be joining our team for the summer. _____

7. Send the shipment to MicroTech Systems 750 Grant Road Tucson Arizona 85703 as soon as possible. _____

8. It appears sir that an error has been made in your billing. _____

9. You have until Friday April 30 to make complete payment on your past-due account. _____

10. Mr. Franklin T. Molloy who is an advertising executive has been elected chairman of the council. _____

11. Anyone who is interested in applying for the job should see Ms. Sheridan. _____

12. The bidding closes at 10 p.m. EST. _____

13. You will in addition receive a free brochure outlining our wireless devices. _____

14. Our latest wireless technology provides support for high-traffic areas such as airports shopping centers and college campuses. _____

15. All things considered the company will be obligated to pay only those expenses directly related to the installation. _____

16. Only Mr. Hudson who is a specialist in information systems is qualified to write that report. _____

17. You can avoid patent trademark and copyright problems by working with an attorney. _____

18. We are convinced incidentally that our attorney's fees are most reasonable. _____

19. Mr. Van Alstyne developed the policy Ms. Thorson worked on the budget and Mr. Seibert handled compensation issues. _____

20. Sasha will travel to Italy Greece and Croatia next summer. _____

Add necessary commas to the following sentences. For each sentence indicate the number of commas that you added. If a sentence is correct, write *C*.

1. We must find a practical permanent solution to our Internet access problems. _____

2. For a period of six months it will be necessary to reduce all expenditures. _____

3. Melissa Meyer speaking on behalf of all classified employees gave a welcoming address. _____

4. We held a marketing meeting last week and we included representatives from all divisions. _____

5. I am looking forward to getting together with you when you are in Rochester. _____

6. We do appreciate as I have told you often your continuing efforts to increase our sales. _____

7. Consumer patterns for the past five years are being studied carefully by our marketing experts. _____

8. For some time we have been studying the growth in the number of working women and minorities. _____

9. After you have examined my calculations please send the report to Bill Thompson. _____

10. Please send the report to Bill Thompson after you have examined my calculations. _____

11. Would you please after examining my calculations send the report to Bill Thompson. _____

12. Our human resources director is looking for intelligent articulate young people who desire an opportunity to grow with a start-up company. _____

13. Call me as soon as you return or send me an e-mail message within the next week. _____

14. Beginning on the 15th of June Dell is slashing prices on laptop computers. _____

15. In 2013 we will unveil our most innovative hybrid vehicle. _____

16. As soon as I can check the inventory we will place an order. _____

17. On October 25 the president and I visited Sandra Goodell who is president of Sandra Goodell Public Relations. _____

18. You may submit a report describing when where and how we should proceed. _____

19. To begin the purchase process we will need your request by Thursday June 1 at the latest. _____

20. Any student who has not signed up for a team by this time must see the instructor. _____

Add necessary commas to the following sentences. For each sentence indicate the number of commas that you added. If a sentence is correct, write *C*.

1. Michael Ferrari PhD has written another book on consumer buying. _____

2. In 2010 our company expanded its marketing to include the United Kingdom. _____

3. By 2011 12 of our competitors were also selling in Great Britain. _____

4. In 2011 our staff numbered 87; in 2012 103. _____

5. It was in Taiwan not in mainland China where the lightest racing bike in the world was made. _____

6. Long before our president conducted his own research into marketing trends among youthful consumers. (Tricky!) _____

7. "We prefer not to include your name" said the auditor "when we publish the list of inactive accounts." _____

8. You may sign your name at the bottom of this sheet and return it to us as acknowledgment of this letter. _____

9. The provisions of your Policy No. 85000611 should be reviewed every five years. _____

10. Irving Feinstein MD will be the speaker at our next meeting. _____

11. Dr. Feinstein received both a BA and an MBA from Northwestern University. _____

12. Ever since we have been very careful to count the number of boxes in each shipment. _____

13. In his lecture Dr. Hawkins said "One species of catfish reproduces by hatching eggs in its mouth and growing them to about three inches before releasing them." _____

14. Did you say it was Mr. Samuels not Ms. Lambert who made the sale? _____

15. Ten computers were sold in January; nine in February. _____

16. Our figures show that 17365000 separate rental units were occupied in September. _____

17. "The function of a supervisor" remarked Sid Stern "is to analyze results not to try to control how the job is done." _____

18. By the way it was the president not the vice president who ordered the cutback. _____

19. "A diamond" said the therapist "is a chunk of coal that made good under pressure." _____

20. Whoever signs signs at her own risk. _____

Self-Help Exercises
Semicolons and Colons

15

LEVEL 1

Punctuate the following groups of words as single sentences. Add commas and semicolons. Do not add words or periods to create new sentences.

Example: Come in to see our new branch office; meet our friendly tellers and manager.

1. Our principal function is to help management make profits however we can offer advice on staffing problems as well.

2. Delegates came from as far as Dallas Texas Seattle Washington and Miami Florida.

3. Jerry looked up names Andrea addressed envelopes and Janelle stuffed the envelopes.

4. Thank you for your order it will be filled immediately.

5. Employees often complain about lack of parking space on the other hand little interest was shown in a proposed carpooling program.

6. Computers are remarkable however they are only as accurate as the people who program them.

7. This sale is not open to the general public we are opening the store to preferred customers only.

8. Some of the employees being promoted are Jill Roberts secretary Legal Department Lea Lim clerk Human Resources and Mark Cameron dispatcher Transportation Department.

9. We will be happy to cooperate with you and your lawyers in settling the estate however several matters must be reviewed.

10. In the morning I am free at 10 a.m. in the afternoon I have already scheduled an appointment.

11. The book was recently selected for a national award thus its sales are soaring.

12. Look over our online catalog make your selections and click to submit your order.

13. We hope that we will not have to sell the property but that may be our only option.

14. We are convinced therefore that you are the right person for the job.

15. We do not sell airline seats we sell customer service.

16. Our convention committee is considering the Hyatt Regency Hotel Columbus Ohio Plaza of the Americas Hotel Dallas Texas and the Brown Palace Hotel Denver Colorado.

17. As requested the committee will meet Thursday May 4 however it is unable to meet Friday May 5.

18. Market research involves the systematic gathering recording and analyzing of data.

Add colons, semicolons, or commas to the following sentences. Do not add words or periods. Write *C* after the sentence if it is correct.

1. Three phases of our business operation must be scrutinized purchasing, production, and shipping.

2. The candidates being considered for supervisor are Ned Bingham, Sean Davis, and Anna Donato.

3. George Steinbrenner, New York Yankees owner, said "I want this team to win. I'm obsessed with winning, with discipline, with achieving. That's what this country's all about."

4. Following are four dates reserved for counseling. Sign up soon.

   September 28   January 4
   September 30   January 6

5. At its next meeting, the board of directors must make a critical decision should the chief executive officer be retained or replaced?

6. This year's seminar has been organized to give delegates an opportunity to exchange ideas, plans, techniques, and goals.

7. The three Cs of credit are the following character, capacity, and capital.

8. Our Boston tour package included visits to these interesting historical sites the House of Seven Gables, Bunker Hill, the Boston Tea Party Ship and Museum, and Paul Revere's home.

9. I recommend that you take at least three courses to develop your language arts skills Essentials of College English 105, Business Communication 201, and Managerial Communication 305.

10. The speaker said that membership is voluntary but that contributions would be greatly appreciated.

11. Several of the tax specialists on the panel were concerned with the same thought government spending continues to rise while taxes are being reduced.

12. To determine an individual's FICO credit rating, companies use the following factors payment history, outstanding debt, credit history, inquiries and new accounts, and types of credit in use.

13. Scholarships will be awarded to Jill Hofer Jeremy Stone and Carolina Garay.

14. Our favorite Colorado resort is noted for fly fishing, mountain biking, tennis and hiking.

15. Our favorite Colorado resort is noted for the following fly fishing, mountain biking, and hiking.

Add colons, semicolons, or commas as needed. If a word following a colon should not be capitalized, use a proofreading mark (/) to indicate lowercase. Show words to be capitalized with (≡). Mark C if a sentence is correct as it stands.

1. There are three primary ways to make a credit check namely by e-mail, by U.S. mail, or by telephone.

2. Please order the following supplies Cartridges, paper, and labels.

3. Although we are expanding our services we continue to do business according to our original philosophy that is we want to provide you with flexible and professional investment services on a highly personal basis.

4. Employees who conduct Web research are taught this rule Evaluate the validity of all data found on the Web.

5. Dr. Ruglio's plane departed at 2 15 and should arrive at 6 45.

6. We invited Jeff, Kevin, Tony, and Tom but Tony was unable to come.

7. Three of our top executives are being transferred to the Milwaukee office namely Mr. Thomas, Mr. Estrada, and Mrs. Stranahan.

8. On our list of recommended reading is *Investment an Introduction to Analysis*.

9. The library, as you are already aware, needs space for additional books, particularly in the nonfiction field and even greater space will be required within the next five years.

10. Our airline is improving service in several vital areas for example baggage handling, food service, and weather forecasts.

11. Julie Schumacher was hired by a brokerage house and given the title of "registered representative" that is she is able to buy and sell securities.

12. Professor Wilson listed five types of advertising Product, institutional, national, local, and corrective.

13. We considered only one location for our fall convention namely San Francisco.

14. Many important questions are yet to be asked concerning our program for instance how can we meet our competitor's low prices in the Southwest?

15. If possible, call him as soon as you return to the office however I doubt that he is still at his desk.

16 Self-Help Exercises
Other Punctuation

Add any necessary punctuation, including end punctuation, to the following sentences. If a sentence is correct, write *C*.

1. Will you please e-mail this form to the I R S as soon as possible
2. You did say the meeting is at 10 a m didn't you
3. Mr Kephart is a C P A working for Berman, Inc
4. Do you know whether Donald L Cullens Jr applied for the job
5. Help The door is jammed
6. Will you please Ms. Juarez visit our Web site and register for your gift
7. What a day this has been
8. Although most candidates had A A degrees two applicants had B A degrees
9. Our C E O and C F O normally make all budget decisions
10. Cynthia asked whether invitations had been sent to Miss Tan Mr Roe and Ms Rich
11. All calls made before 9 a m E S T are billed at a reduced rate
12. Alan Bennett M D and Gina Caracas Ph D were our keynote speakers
13. How many FAQs (frequently asked questions) do you think we should post at our Web site
14. We are expanding marketing efforts in China France and the U K
15. Surprisingly, the C P U of this computer is made entirely of parts from the U S A
16. Please send the package to Laurie Adamski 5 Sierra Drive Rochester N Y 14616
17. Would you please check Policy No 44657001 to see whether it includes $50000 comprehensive coverage
18. Did you say the order was received at 5 p m P S T
19. Wow How much was the lottery prize
20. After Mike completed his M A he was hired to develop scripts for movie D V Ds

Write *T* (true) or *F* (false) after the following statements.

1. In typewritten or simple word processing–generated material, a dash is formed by typing two successive underscores. _____

2. Parentheses are often used to enclose explanations, references, and directions. _____

3. Dashes must be avoided in business writing since they have no legitimate uses. _____

4. Hyphens can be used to form compound words and compound numbers. _____

5. If a comma falls at the same point where words enclosed by parentheses appear, the comma should follow the final parenthesis. _____

Write the letter of the correctly punctuated sentence in the space provided.

6. a. Twenty seven couples will attend the marriage retreat.
   b. Twenty-seven couples will attend the marriage retreat.
   c. Twentyseven couples will attend the marriage retreat. _____

7. (De-emphasize)
   a. Directions for assembly, see page 15, are quite simple.
   b. Directions for assembly—see page 15—are quite simple.
   c. Directions for assembly (see page 15) are quite simple. _____

8. a. Eat, sleep, and read: that's what I plan to do on my vacation.
   b. Eat, sleep, and read—that's what I plan to do on my vacation.
   c. Eat, sleep, and read, that's what I plan to do on my vacation. _____

9. a. To file a complaint with the Better Business Bureau (BBB), call during normal business hours.
   b. To file a complaint with the Better Business Bureau, (BBB) call during normal business hours.
   c. To file a complaint with the Better Business Bureau (BBB) call during normal business hours. _____

10. (Normal emphasis)
    a. Sharon Hunt (who is an excellent manager) may be promoted.
    b. Sharon Hunt, who is an excellent manager, may be promoted.
    c. Sharon Hunt—who is an excellent manager—may be promoted. _____

11. a. "What is needed for learning is a humble mind." (Confucius)
    b. "What is needed for learning is a humble mind.": Confucius
    c. "What is needed for learning is a humble mind."—Confucius _____

12. a. You missed the due date (July 1;) however, your payment is welcome.
    b. You missed the due date; (July 1) however, your payment is welcome.
    c. You missed the due date (July 1); however, your payment is welcome. _____

13. (De-emphasize)
    a. Only one person knows my password—Denise Powell, and I have confidence in her.
    b. Only one person knows my password (Denise Powell), and I have confidence in her.
    c. Only one person knows my password; Denise Powell, and I have confidence in her. _____

14. (Emphasize)
    a. Our current mortgage rates: see page 10 of the enclosed booklet—are the lowest in years.
    b. Our current mortgage rates (see page 10 of the enclosed booklet) are the lowest in years.
    c. Our current mortgage rates—see page 10 of the enclosed booklet—are the lowest in years. _____

Write *T* (true) or *F* (false) for each of the following statements.

1. When the exact words of a speaker are repeated, double quotation marks are used to enclose the words. _____

2. To indicate a quotation within another quotation, single quotation marks (apostrophes on most keyboards) are used. _____

3. When a word is defined, its definition should be underscored. _____

4. The titles of books, magazines, newspapers, and other complete works published separately may be underscored or italicized. _____

5. The titles of chapters of books and magazine articles may be underscored or enclosed in quotation marks. _____

6. In the United States, periods and commas are always placed inside closing quotation marks. _____

7. Brackets are used when a writer inserts his or her own remarks inside a quotation. _____

8. The Latin word *sic* may be used to call attention to an error in quoted material. _____

9. Semicolons and colons are always placed outside closing quotation marks. _____

10. Use the apostrophe to make nouns plural. _____

Write the letter of the correctly punctuated statement.

11. a. "Jobs," said Mr. Steele, "will be scarce this summer."
b. "Jobs, said Mr. Steele, will be scarce this summer."
c. "Jobs", said Mr. Steele, "will be scarce this summer." _____

12. a. The manager said, "This file was clearly marked Confidential."
b. The manager said, "This file was clearly marked 'Confidential'."
c. The manager said, "This file was clearly marked 'Confidential.'" _____

13. a. *Chattel* is defined as a "piece of movable property."
b. "Chattel" is defined as a *piece of movable property*.
c. "Chattel" is defined as a "piece of movable property." _____

14. a. Do you know who it was who said, "Forewarned is forearmed."
b. Do you know who it was who said, "Forewarned is forearmed"?
c. Do you know who it was who said, "Forewarned is forearmed."? _____

15. a. "We warn all e-mail users to avoid messages that are 'flaming,'" said the CEO.
b. "We warn all e-mail users to avoid messages that are "flaming," said the CEO.
c. "We warn all e-mail users to avoid messages that are 'flaming'", said the CEO. _____

Complete Punctuation Review

Insert all necessary punctuation in the following sentences. Correct any incorrect punctuation. Do not break any sentences into two sentences.

1. Did you see the article titled Soaring Salaries of C E O s that appeared in *The New York Times*

2. This years budget costs are much higher than last years, therefore I will approve overtime only on a case by case basis.

3. The S.E.C. has three new members Dr. Carla Chang Professor Mark Rousso and Robert Price Esq

4. Needless to say all contract bids must be received before 5 pm E S T

5. We formerly depended on fixed-rate not variable rate mortgages.

6. The following representatives have been invited Christine Lenski DataCom Industries, Mark Grant LaserPro, Inc., and Ivan Weiner Image Builders.

7. Last year we moved corporate headquarters to Orlando Florida but maintained production facilities in Atlanta.

8. (Quotation) Did Dr. Tran say We will have no class Friday.

9. Graduation ceremonies for B.A. candidates are at 11 am, graduation ceremonies for M.B.A. candidates are at 2 pm.

10. As we previously discussed the reorganization will take effect on Monday August 8.

11. We feel however that the cars electrical system should be fully warranted for five years.

12. Will you please send copies of our annual report to Anna Golan and D B Rusterholz?

13. Although he had prepared carefully Mitchell feared that his presentation would bomb.

14. In the event of inclement weather we will close the base and notify the following radio stations KJOW KLOB and KOB-TV.

15. (Emphasize) Three excellent employees Gregorio Morales, Dawna Capps, and DaVonne Williams will be honored at a ceremony Friday June 5.

16. (Quotation) "Your attitude not your aptitude will determine your altitude, said Zig Ziglar.

17. By May 15 our goal is to sell 15 cars, by June 15 20 additional cars.

18. The full impact of the E P A ruling is being studied you will receive information as it becomes available.

19. If the fax arrives before 9 pm we can still meet our June 1 deadline.

20. Send the contract to Ms Courtney Worthy Administrative Assistant Globex Industries 7600 Normandale Boulevard Milwaukee WI 53202 as soon as possible.

21. (De-emphasize) Please return the amended budget proposal see page 2 for a summary of the report to the presidents office by Friday March 4.

22. Prospective entrepreneurs were told to read a *Success* magazine article titled A Venture Expert's Advice.

23. Larry Zuckerman our former manager now has a similar position with I B M.

24. If you really want to lose weight you need give up only three things, namely breakfast, lunch, and dinner.

25. As expected this years expenses have been heavy consequently we may have to freeze hiring for the next six months.

17 Self-Help Exercises
Capitalization

LEVEL 1

Write the letter of the group of words that is correctly capitalized.

1. (a) a case of german measles   (b) a case of German measles   _____
2. (a) in the field of marketing   (b) in the field of Marketing   _____
3. (a) the Hancock Building   (b) the Hancock building   _____
4. (a) for all Catholics, Protestants, and Muslims   (b) for all catholics, protestants, and muslims   _____
5. (a) an order for china and crystal   (b) an order for China and crystal   _____
6. (a) both Master's and Doctor's degrees   (b) both master's and doctor's degrees   _____
7. (a) the state of Oklahoma   (b) the State of Oklahoma   _____
8. (a) a class in conversational French   (b) a class in Conversational French   _____
9. (a) a memo from our Sacramento Office   (b) a memo from our Sacramento office   _____
10. (a) a British rock album   (b) a british rock album   _____
11. (a) our web site   (b) our Web site   _____
12. (a) traffic in the big apple   (b) traffic in the Big Apple   _____
13. (a) the King Edward room   (b) the King Edward Room   _____
14. (a) a holiday on Memorial Day   (b) a holiday on Memorial day   _____
15. (a) the waters of Delaware bay   (b) the waters of Delaware Bay   _____

Use proofreading marks to capitalize (≡) or to show lowercase (/) letters in the following sentences.

16. Bob's Chevron Station is located on Speedway Avenue in the next County.

17. Many employees of the Meredith Corporation plan to participate in the Company's profit-sharing plan.

18. Investigators from the securities and exchange commission insisted on seeing all E-Mail messages.

19. During the Winter i will enroll in management, english composition, and accounting.

20. The American Association Of Nurses will open its annual meeting in the Pacific ballroom of the Regency hotel in San Francisco.

21. Our persian cat and russian wolfhound cohabit quite peacefully.

22. Last Summer my family and i visited the grand canyon in arizona.

23. The two companies signed a Contract last april.

24. Interior designers recommended italian marble for the entry and spanish tiles for the patio.

25. A limousine will take guests from kansas city international airport directly to the alameda plaza hotel.

Write the letter of the group of words that is correctly capitalized.

1. (a) my uncle and my aunt   (b) my Uncle and my Aunt   _____

2. (a) Very sincerely yours,   (b) Very Sincerely Yours,   _____

3. (a) Send it to Vice President Lee   (b) Send it to vice president Lee   _____

4. (a) Volume II, Page 37   (b) Volume II, page 37   _____

5. (a) located in the western part of Indiana   (b) located in the Western part of Indiana   _____

6. (a) stored in building 44   (b) stored in Building 44   _____

7. (a) within our Human Resources Department   (b) within our human resources department   _____

8. (a) the Federal Communications Commission   (b) the federal communications commission   _____

9. (a) in appendix III   (b) in Appendix III   _____

10. (a) heading South on Highway 5   (b) heading south on Highway 5   _____

11. (a) the book *Ethics and Business*   (b) the book *Ethics And Business*   _____

12. (a) both federal and state laws   (b) both Federal and State laws   _____

13. (a) Q-tips and kleenexes   (b) Q-Tips and Kleenexes   _____

14. (a) orders from Sales Director Ali   (b) orders from sales director Ali   _____

15. (a) a trip to the east coast   (b) a trip to the East Coast   _____

Use proofreading marks to capitalize (≡) or to show lowercase letters (/) in the following sentences.

16. We received a directive from Ruth Jones, the Supervisor of our Administrative Services Division.

17. The President of our Company gave an address entitled "Leadership: What Effective Managers do and how They do it."

18. Gina Schmidt, customer service representative, attended a convention on the east coast.

19. To reach my home, proceed north on highway 10 until you reach exit 7.

20. Mayor Bruno visited the governor in an attempt to increase the city's share of State funding.

21. The best article is "Does your training measure up?" by Leslie Brokaw.

22. John put on his ray-ban sunglasses and took off in his jeep.

23. Sue's Mother and Father were scheduled to leave on flight 37 from gate 6 at phoenix sky harbor international airport.

24. Subject: task force meeting this friday

25. Taxicab, Bus, and Limousine service is available from the airport to the ritz-carlton hotel.

Write the letter of the group of words that is correctly capitalized.

1. (a) photographs sent from Venus to Earth   (b) photographs sent from Venus to earth   _____

2. (a) a room marked "private"   (b) a room marked "Private"   _____

3. (a) the Egyptian Room and the Sahara Room   (b) the Egyptian room and the Sahara room   _____

4. (a) the finest production on earth   (b) the finest production on Earth   _____

5. (a) from Senator-Elect Ross   (b) from Senator-elect Ross   _____

6. (a) speaks German and French   (b) speaks german and french   _____

7. (a) some asian cultures   (b) some Asian cultures   _____

8. (a) an envelope stamped "confidential   (b) an envelope stamped "Confidential"   _____

9. (a) our sales director, Joe Hines   (b) our Sales Director, Joe Hines   _____

10. (a) to ex-President Clinton   (b) to Ex-President Clinton   _____

Use proofreading marks to capitalize (≡) or to show lowercase (/) letters in the following sentences.

11. The returned check was stamped "Insufficient funds."

12. A paddleboat traveled south down the Mississippi river.

13. No one recognized ex-senator Thurston when he toured Napa valley.

14. We wonder, professor, if the gravity of Mars might be similar to that of earth.

15. The Organization's bylaws state: "On the third monday of every month, the Club's Treasurer will prepare the financial report."

16. The President of our Company has traveled to Pacific Rim Countries to expand foreign markets.

17. The secretary of state met with the president to discuss this country's National policy toward african nations.

18. British english is the Dialect taught in most countries where english is not a native language.

19. In malaysia we soon learned that muslims do not eat pork and that buddhists and hindus do not eat beef.

20. Although he was known as a "banker's banker," Mr. Lee specialized in Mortgage Financing.

NAME _____

Self-Help Exercises
Numbers

18

LEVEL 1

In the space provided write the letter of the correctly expressed group of words.

1. (a) for 24 employees   (b) for twenty-four employees   _____
2. (a) only 9 days left   (b) only nine days left   _____
3. (a) twenty-five dollars   (b) $25   _____
4. (a) on the thirtieth of May   (b) on the 30th of May   _____
5. (a) it cost 20 cents   (b) it cost twenty cents   _____
6. (a) (military style) 5 April 2012   (b) April 5, 2012   _____
7. (a) $2.05, 85¢, and $5.00   (b) $2.05, $.85, and $5   _____
8. (a) we started at 9 a.m.   (b) we started at nine a.m.   _____
9. (a) 2 Highland Avenue   (b) Two Highland Avenue   _____
10. (a) 226 Sixth Street   (b) 226 6th Street   _____

Underline any errors in the expression of numbers in the following sentences. Write the correct forms.

11. 194 businesses were sent the ethics survey on December 1st.   _____
12. 2 companies have moved their corporate offices to twenty-fifth avenue.   _____
13. Three of the least expensive items were priced at $5.00, $3.29, and 99 cents.   _____
14. If your payment of $100.00 is received before the 2 of the month, you will receive a discount.   _____
15. On February 1st the guidelines for all fifteen departments went into effect.   _____
16. Our office, formerly located at Two Ford Place, is now located at One Kent Avenue.   _____
17. Please call me at 815 611-9292, Ext. Three, before 4 p.m.   _____
18. On May 15th 2 performances will be given: one at two p.m. and another at eight p.m.   _____
19. 3 of our employees start at 8:00 a.m., and 5 start at 8:30 a.m.   _____
20. If reservations are made before the fifteenth of the month, the fare will be 204 dollars.   _____
21. Grossmont College offers a fifteen-hour training course that costs one hundred twenty-five dollars.   _____
22. Classes meet Monday through Thursday from 11:45 a.m. until one p.m.   _____
23. The Werners moved from 1,762 Milburn Avenue to 140 East 14 Street.   _____
24. Lisa had only $.25 left after she purchased supplies for forty-four dollars.   _____
25. On the third of January and again on the 18th, our copy machine needed service.   _____

Write the letter of the correctly expressed group of words.

1. (a) for 82 students in 3 classes   (b) for 82 students in three classes   _____

2. (a) an interest period of ninety days   (b) an interest period of 90 days   _____

3. (a) over the past thirty years   (b) over the past 30 years   _____

4. (a) two 35-day contracts   (b) 2 35-day contracts   _____

5. (a) he is 45 years old   (b) he is forty-five years old   _____

6. (a) line three   (b) line 3   _____

7. (a) nearly 2.6 billion units   (b) nearly 2,600,000,000 units   _____

8. (a) fifteen 50-page pamphlets   (b) 15 fifty-page pamphlets   _____

9. (a) Lois Lamb, 65, and
    John Lamb, 66   (b) Lois Lamb, sixty-five, and
    John Lamb, sixty-six   _____

10. (a) the child is 2 years
    4 months old   (b) the child is two years
    four months old   _____

Underline any errors in the expression of numbers in the following sentences. Write the corrected form.

11. We have received fifty reservations over the past 14 days.   _____

12. Tour guests will be transported in three thirty-five-passenger
    air-conditioned motor coaches throughout the fifteen-day excursion.   _____

13. 53 of the corporations had operating budgets that exceeded one million dollars.   _____

14. Only 10 telephones are available for the forty-eight employees in 5 offices.   _____

15. Chapter eight in Volume two provides at least three references to pumps.   _____

16. About 100 chairs are stored in Room Four, and another eight chairs
    are in Room 14.   _____

17. We ordered two thirty-inch desks and three chairs.   _____

18. Of the twenty requests we received, five were acted on immediately
    and three had to be tabled.   _____

19. The 2 loans must be repaid within 90 days.   _____

20. When she was only 24 years old, Mrs. Markham supervised
    more than 120 employees.   _____

21. Only two of the 125 mailed surveys were undeliverable.   _____

22. Frank Morris, sixty-four, plans to retire in one year.   _____

23. Linda Hannan and her fifteen-person company signed
    a three million dollar contract.   _____

24. She purchased new equipment to beam fifty-two World Cup games
    from nine locations to forty million avid soccer fans in Pacific Rim countries.   _____

25. The thirty-year mortgage carries an interest rate of eight percent.   _____

Assume that all of the following phrases appear in complete sentences. Write the letter of the phrase that is appropriately expressed.

1. (a) the tank holds just 9 gallons   (b) the tank holds just nine gallons   _____

2. (a) only a three percent gain   (b) only a 3 percent gain   _____

3. (a) 4/5 of the voters   (b) four fifths of the voters   _____

4. (a) a 50% markup   (b) a 50 percent markup   _____

5. (a) a one-half share   (b) a one half share   _____

6. (a) a decline of .5 percent   (b) a decline of 0.5 percent   _____

7. (a) he placed 3rd in the state   (b) he placed third in the state   _____

8. (a) in the nineteenth century   (b) in the 19th century   _____

9. (a) a 5-pound box of candy   (b) a five-pound box of candy   _____

10. (a) at least 95% of the stockholders   (b) at least 95 percent of the stockholders _____

Underline any errors in the expression of numbers. Write the corrected form.

11. A No. Ten envelope actually measures four and a half by nine and a half inches.   _____

12. The two candidates in the 33d Congressional District waged hard-hitting campaigns.   _____

13. Tests show that the driver responded in less than seven two hundredths of a second.   _____

14. Great strides in communication technology have been made in the 21st century.   _____

15. The desk top measured thirty and three-fourths inches by sixty and a half inches. _____

16. Payment must be received by the thirtieth to qualify for a three percent discount. _____

17. Our office was moved about fifty blocks from 7th Street to 58th Street.   _____

18. Temperatures in Phoenix were over one hundred degrees for 8 consecutive days.   _____

19. The notebook computer weighs just seven point nine four pounds and is fifteen and a half inches wide.   _____

20. Appropriation measures must be passed by a 2/3 majority.   _____

21. She ordered a nine by twelve rug to cover two-thirds of the floor.   _____

22. After completing Form Ten Forty, the accountant submitted his bill for 800 dollars. _____

23. By the year 2,014, the number of employees over the age of 55 will increase by 52%. _____

24. Nine different airlines carry over one hundred thousand passengers daily.   _____

25. The company car was filled with fifteen gallons of gasoline and one quart of oil. _____

Answers to Self-Help Exercises

Chapter 1 Self-Help Answers

1. c **2.** b **3.** c **4.** b **5.** c **6.** b **7.** b **8.** d **9.** b **10.** b

Chapter 2 Self-Help Answers

Worksheet 1

A. *Answers will vary.* **2.** Substitutes for a noun *he she it* **3.** Shows action, occurrence, or state of being *jumps works is* **4.** Describes nouns or pronouns *tall soft five* **5.** Modifies verbs, adjectives, or other adverbs *hurriedly very nicely* **6.** Joins nouns and pronouns to other words in a sentence *to for at* **7.** Connects words or groups of words *and but or* **8.** Shows strong feelings *Wow! Gosh! No!*

B. 1. pronoun **2.** verb **3.** adjective (article) **4.** adjective **5.** noun **6.** preposition **7.** noun **8.** conjunction **9.** pronoun **10.** verb **11.** adverb **12.** adjective **13.** interjection **14.** adjective (article) **15.** noun **16.** conjunction **17.** noun **18.** verb **19.** adjective **20.** adjective **21.** noun **22.** preposition **23.** adjective **24.** noun **25.** pronoun **26.** verb **27.** adverb **28.** conjunction **29.** adjective (article) **30.** adjective **31.** noun **32.** verb **33.** adverb

Worksheet 2

1. pronoun **2.** verb **3.** noun **4.** preposition **5.** noun **6.** conjunction **7.** adjective **8.** noun **9.** verb **10.** adverb **11.** verb **12.** noun **13.** interjection **14.** verb **15.** noun **16.** adverb **17.** verb **18.** pronoun **19.** verb **20.** verb **21.** adjective **22.** noun **23.** preposition **24.** noun **25.** adjective (article) **26.** adjective **27.** adjective **28.** noun **29.** verb **30.** conjunction **31.** adjective **32.** conjunction **33.** adjective **34.** conjunction **35.** adjective **36.** noun **37.** verb **38.** verb **39.** pronoun **40.** adverb **41.** preposition **42.** adjective (article) **43.** adjective **44.** adjective **45.** noun **46.** noun **47.** adverb **48.** verb **49.** preposition **50.** adjective (article) **51.** adjective **52.** noun **53.** preposition **54.** adjective (article) **55.** adjective **56.** adjective **57.** noun **58.** noun **59.** verb **60.** adverb **61.** verb **62.** adjective (article) **63.** noun **64.** pronoun **65.** verb **66.** preposition **67.** adjective **68.** noun

Chapter 3 Self-Help Answers

Worksheet 1

1. (S) applicant (V) received **2.** (S) speaker (V) made **3.** (S) telephones (V) rang **4.** (S) we (V) will hire **5.** (S) team (V) built **6.** (S) salespeople (V) received **7.** (S) manager (V) will send. **8.** (S) we (V) released **9.** (S) One (V) was given **10.** (S) computers (V) require **11.** (S) printout (V) was **12.** (S) One (V) sold **13.** (S) list (V) is **14.** (S) Everything (V) is covered **15.** (S) committee (V) was appointed **16.** (S) Mr. Thomas (V) is **17.** (S) copiers (v) are **18.** (S) Ms. Seymour (V) is **19.** (S) Mr. Torres (V) has been **20.** (S) offices (V) are

Worksheet 2

Sentence Variety: 1. b **2.** a **3.** c **4.** d **5.** a **6.** c **7.** b **8.** c **9.** a **10.** c **Sentence Patterns:** *Answers will vary.* **11.** voted **12.** fell **13.** arrived **14.** rang **15.** ended **16.** dropped **17.** policy **18.** virus **19.** package **20.** him **21.** the door **22.** documents **23.** good **24.** manager **25.** Mr. Jones **26.** Mary **27.** Mr. Smith **28.** John **29–33.** *Answers will vary.*

Worksheet 3

Sentence Types: 1. a **2.** c (period) **3.** d (question mark) **4.** b (period) **5.** e (exclamation mark) **6.** a **7.** c (period) **8.** b (period) **9.** a **Sentence Faults: 10.** c **11.** b **12.** d **13.** a **14.** a **15.** c **16.** d **17.** b **18.** a **19.** c **20.** b

Chapter 4 Self-Help Answers

Level 1

1. giraffes **2.** feet **3.** switches **4.** the Bushes **5.** boxes **6.** languages **7.** faxes **8.** sandwiches **9.** income taxes **10.** children **11.** successes **12.** values **13.** dresses **14.** branches **15.** recommendations **16.** women **17.** mismatches **18.** taxis **19.** loaves **20.** annexes **21.** beliefs **22.** the Rosses **23.** storms **24.** ranches **25.** The Joneses **26.** the Chavezes **27.** letters **28.** businesses **29.** computers **30.** wishes

Level 2

1. wharves **2.** chiefs of police **3.** 2010s **4.** the Wolfs **5.** embargoes **6.** LVNs **7.** size 10s **8.** amts. **9.** faculties **10.** by-products **11.** entries **12.** lookers-on **13.** companies **14.** knives **15.** courts-martial **16.** A's **17.** the Shermans **18.** memos **19.** valleys **20.** zeros **21.** lives **22.** yrs. **23.** the Murphys **24.** runners-up **25.** oz. **26.** journeys **27.** MBAs **28.** wolves **29.** the Kellys **30.** minorities

Level 3

1. data **2.** theses **3.** bacteria **4.** Chinese **5.** parentheses **6.** headquarters **7.** alumnae **8.** millennia **9.** genera **10.** news **11.** sheep **12.** alumni **13.** larvae **14.** bases **15.** memoranda or memorandums **16.** are **17.** is **18.** formulas **19.** analyses **20.** is

Chapter 5 Self-Help Answers

Level I

Worksheet 1

1. all employees' passwords **2.** this company's office **3.** the women's uniforms **4.** an employee's signature **5.** the supervisor's e-mail message **6.** all members' opinions **7.** the pilot's landing **8.** both partners' agreement **9.** Jeffrey's notebook **10.** the department's strengths **11.** the students' grades **12.** those people's customs **13.** a student's presentation **14.** the bank's credit

15. citizens' savings 16. Canada's mountains
17. the employer's requirements 18. all candidates'
résumés 19. the government's policies
20. both attorneys' fees

Worksheet 2

1. author's 2. drivers' 3. carpenter's 4. thief's
5. company's 6. employees' 7. CEO's 8. readers'
9. caller's 10. authors' 11. Gap's 12. customers
13. country's 14. employees' 15. organization's
16. president's 17. family's 18. attorney's 19. employees
20. farmer's 21. citizens' 22. companies 23. customer's
24. Children's 25. supervisor's

Level 2

1. public's 2. Ross's 3. company's 4. The suggestions of
my uncle's lawyer 5. editor in chief's 6. Brown's 7. RNs'
8. telephone number of the president's assistant 9. sales
10. brother-in-law's 11. England's 12. CBS's 13. the
Rodriguezes' 14. Wes's 15. Angeles 16. the Horowitzes
17. the Morrises' 18. architects' 19. James's 20. agents
21. Brault's 22. the Caldwells 23. Elvis's 24. Dallas
25. reporters'

Level 3

1. Clark and Clark's 2. aunt and uncle's 3. day's 4. Robin
and John's 5. Diana and Jason's 6. associate's 7. year's
8. Larry's 9. Jennifer's 10. Debbie's and Julie's
11. stationer's 12. bachelor's 13. month's 14. year's
15. day's 16. months' 17. master's 18. years' 19. year's
20. else's 21. classes' 22. bosses' 23. dollar's 24. tomorrow's 25. today's

Chapter 6 Self-Help Answers

Level 1

Worksheet 1

1–14. *Order of answers may vary.* 1–7. I, you, he, she,
it, we, they 8–14. me, you, him, her, it, us, them 15. I
16. she 17. he 18. they 19. she 20. we 21. she 22. he
23. she 24. he 25. I

Worksheet 2

1. me 2. him 3. them 4. me 5. her 6. him 7. her 8. them
9. us 10. me 11. it's 12. theirs 13. its 14. There's 15. hers
16. it's 17. yours 18. Whose 19. ours 20. You're

Level 2

1. them 2. I 3. her 4. We 5. me 6. me 7. her 8. he 9. him
10. I 11. himself 12. her 13. her 14. she 15. me 16. us
17. she 18. him 19. I 20. me 21. me 22. She and I
23. her 24. us 25. I

Level 3

Worksheet 1

1. she 2. he 3. they 4. she 5. him 6. she 7. she 8. he
9. me 10. they 11. he 12. him 13. her 14. I 15. she
16. she 17. I 18. him 19. I 20. she 21. he 22. him
23. she 24. she 25. he

Worksheet 2

1. he 2. me 3. its 4. she 5. us 6. there's 7. he 8. I 9. me
10. her 11. us 12. you're 13. her 14. him 15. yours 16. me
17. he 18. its 19. him or me 20. There's 21. him 22. me
23. I 24. their 25. she 26. I 27. me 28. us 29. she 30. there's

Chapter 7 Self-Help Answers

Level 1

1. her 2. his or her 3. his or her 4. their 5. their 6. he
or she 7. his or her lunch 8. him or her 9. her 10. their
pictures 11. her 12. his 13-15. *Order of answers may
vary.* Every employee must obtain his or her parking
permit in the supervisor's office. Every employee must
obtain a parking permit in the supervisor's office. All
employees must obtain their parking permits in the
supervisor's office.

Level 2

1. *her* instead of *their* 2. *its* instead of *it's* 3. *his or her*
instead of *their* 4. *his or her* instead of *his* 5. *his* instead
of *their* 6. *her* instead of *their* 7. *their* instead of *his*
8. *its* instead of *their* 9. *its* instead of *their* 10. *him or her*
instead of *them* 11. *her* instead of *their* 12. *his or
her* instead of *their* 13. *his or her* instead of *their*
14. *his or her seat* instead of *their seats.* 15. *its* instead
of *their* 16. *its* instead of *their* 17. *them* instead of *it*
18. *his* instead of *their* 19. *her* instead of *their*
20. *they* instead of *she or he*

Level 3

Worksheet 1

1. Whom 2. whom 3. who 4. whom 5. whom 6. whom
7. Who 8. Whom 9. Who 10. who 11. who 12. who
13. whom 14. who 15. Who

Worksheet 2

1. whoever 2. whoever 3. whomever 4. whomever
5. whoever 6. whoever 7. whoever 8. Whoever
9. whoever 10. Whoever 11. Who 12. who 13. who
14. whoever 15. whom

Worksheet 3

1. Whom 2. who 3. whom 4. whoever 5. whom
6. whom 7. Whoever 8. who 9. who 10. who 11. whom
12. whom 13. Who 14. Whom 15. whomever 16. whom
17. Whoever 18. whom 19. whom 20. whom 21. whose
22. who's 23. who's 24. whose 25. who's

Chapter 8 Self-Help Answers

Level 1

1. transitive 2. intransitive 3. linking 4. complements
5. helping 6. I 7. L—Jessica 8. T—addresses 9. I
10. L—consultant 11. T—pants 12. T—application
13. L—better 14. L—he 15. I 16. T—questions
7. T—gifts 18. I 19. L—justified 20. T—expectations

Level 2

Worksheet 1

1. Mark did not receive the text message until Monday
morning. 2. Dell shipped our order last week. 3. Sherri
Bradford must authorize withdrawals beginning next
week. 4. Mr. Stern asked Wyatt to be responsible for turning out the lights at the end of the day. 5. Management
forced employees who travel a great deal to surrender
their frequent-flier awards.

Worksheet 2

Answers may vary. 1. We must complete our departmental report before 5 p.m. 2. Mr. Smith wrote checks on an
account with insufficient funds. 3. Judges make decisions

in the courts that affect the daily lives of all Americans.
4. Management warned employees working with computers to change their passwords frequently.
5. Our CPA scrutinized our accounting records during the audit.

Worksheet 3

1. were **2.** was **3.** be **4.** would **5.** be **6.** rest **7.** were **8.** were **9.** be **10.** be

Level 3

Worksheet 1

1. your passing **2.** his investing **3.** Mr. Cortina's gambling **4.** C **5.** your criticizing **6.** your calling **7.** C **8.** my working

Worksheet 2

1. b **2.** b **3.** a **4.** b **5.** a
6. Completing the examination in only 20 minutes, Maria earned a perfect score.
7. To locate the members' names and addresses, we used the current directory.
8. Driving through the desert, we thought the highway seemed endless.
9. My knees shook and my voice wavered when I addressed the audience for the first time.

Chapter 9 Self-Help Answers

Level 1

1. is **2.** occurred **3.** is **4.** is **5.** is **6.** plans **7.** will sell **8.** supplied **9.** studies **10.** will analyze **11.** applied **12.** considered **13.** varies **14.** insists **15.** will appeal **16.** requires **17.** will demand **18.** tried

Level 2

Worksheet 1

1. rung **2.** froze **3.** hid **4.** chosen **5.** built **6.** drunk **7.** hung **8.** given **9.** gone **10.** bitten **11.** eaten **12.** sung **13.** swore **14.** sprang **15.** shaken **16.** worn **17.** written **18.** stolen **19.** taken **20.** gone

Worksheet 2

1. laid **2.** lie **3.** lying **4.** laid **5.** laying **6.** lie **7.** lay **8.** Lay **9.** lain **10.** lie **11.** lie **12.** lying **13.** lie **14.** lay **15.** lain **16.** lay **17.** lying **18.** lie **19.** laid **20.** laying

Level 3

1. has opened **2.** is planning **3.** had called **4.** has worked **5.** were seeing **6.** will be signing **7.** had broken **8.** have seen **9.** are considering **10.** were hearing **11.** rung **12.** drank **13.** choose **14.** driven **15.** saw **16.** gone **17.** saw **18.** eaten **19.** written **20.** rose **21.** sworn **22.** sank **23.** shrank **24.** begun **25.** forbidden

Chapter 10 Self-Help Answers

Level 1

Worksheet 1

1. provide (subject: sites) **2.** is (subject: supervisor) **3.** comes (subject: supply) **4.** think (subject: workers) **5.** is (subject: Everyone) **6.** was (subject: table) **7.** is (subject: list) **8.** needs (subject: equipment) **9.** has (subject: One) **10.** are (subject: copies) **11.** is (subject: furniture)

12. are (subject: Effects) **13.** have (subject: salespeople) **14.** are (subject: Profits) **15.** sounds (subject: one) **16.** was (subject: shipment) **17.** is (subject: Everyone) **18.** are (subject: subsidiaries) **19.** have (subject: Officials) **20.** was (subject: letter)

Worksheet 2

1. travels (subject: flow) **2.** are (subject: newspaper and magazines) **3.** is (subject: Coleman, Harris & Juarez, Inc.) **4.** are (subject: books) **5.** appear (subject: points) **6.** are (subject: stages) **7.** was (subject: No one) **8.** is (subject: member) **9.** are (subject: size and design) **10.** is (subject: unit) **11.** has (subject: American Airlines) **12.** provide (subject: seasons) **13.** Has (subject: van) **14.** is (subject: condition) **15.** is (subject: luggage) **16.** has (subject: salary) **17.** appears (subject: One) **18.** is (subject: American Medical Association) **19.** are (subject: ease and convenience) **20.** are (subject: Aggressiveness and delinquency)

Level 2

1. is (subject: Most) **2.** has (subject: The Committee on Youth Activities) **3.** deserves (subject: Each) **4.** is (subject: one [of your two competitors]) **5.** is (subject: work) **6.** is (subject: Either) **7.** were (subject: members) **8.** mention (subject: invoices) **9.** merits (subject: one) **10.** every one **11.** are (subject: you) **12.** has (subject: Each) **13.** belongs (subject: most) **14.** is (subject: group) **15.** is (subject: Some) **16.** has (subject: staff) **17.** Were (subject: any) **18.** has (subject: union) **19.** have (subject: employees) **20.** is (subject: Most)

Level 3

1. has **2.** is **3.** enjoy **4.** was **5.** was **6.** is **7.** favor **8.** are **9.** are **10.** am **11.** is **12.** is **13.** like **14.** are **15.** is **16.** need **17.** were **18.** are **19.** complain **20.** has

Chapter 11 Self-Help Answers

Level 1

1. more effective **2.** worst **3.** friendlier **4.** least **5.** more beautiful **6.** fastest **7.** better **8.** noisiest **9.** quieter **10.** most sincere **11.** most skilled **12.** least **13.** slower or more slowly **14.** more likely **15.** most unusual **16.** fewer **17.** better **18.** more credible **19.** worst **20.** fewest

Level 2

1. loudly **2.** C **3.** an **4.** won't do any *or* will do no **5.** more quietly **6.** bad **7.** conflict-of-interest **8.** C **9.** C **10.** a **11.** These sorts **12.** satisfactorily **13.** house to house **14.** could hardly **15.** C **16.** quietly **17.** didn't say anything *or* said nothing **18.** charge account **19.** not-too-distant **20.** up-to-date

Level 3

1. b **2.** a **3.** a **4.** a **5.** a **6.** fewer (for *less*) **7.** really (for *real*) **8.** surely (for *sure*) **9.** neatly (for *neat*) **10.** well (for *good*) **11.** C **12.** recently enacted **13.** worst (for *worse*) **14.** an (for *a*) **15.** had hardly **16.** round-the-world **17.** bad (for *badly*) **18.** fewer (for *less*) **19.** an (for *a*) **20.** farther (for *further*) **21.** Fewer (for *Less*) **22.** latter (for *later*) **23.** well (for *good*) **24.** further (for *farther*)

Chapter 12 Self-Help Answers

Level 1

1. should have (for *should of*) 2. him (for *he*) 3. C 4. me (for *I*) 5. from (for *off of*) 6. to (for *too*) 7. her (for *she*) 8. could have (for *could of*) 9. too (for *to*) 10. him (for *he*) 11. from (for *off*) 12. him (for *he*) 13. from (for *off of*) 14. C 15. him (for *he*) 16. too (for *to*) 17. could have (for *could of*) 18. C 19. could have (for *could of*) 20. me (for *I*)

Level 2

1. besides (for *beside*) 2. support for *or* support of 3. omit *with* 4. in to (for *into*) 5. omit *of* 6. among (for *between*) 7. as (for *like*) 8. C 9. type of software 10. into (for *in to*) 11. C 12. concern for 13. omit *at* 14. C 15. omit *from* 16. omit *up* 17. style *of* furniture 18. in to (for *into*) 19. omit *to* 20. graduated *from*

Level 3

1. b 2. a 3. a 4. b 5. b 6. a 7. b 8. b 9. b 10. b 11. a 12. a 13. b 14. b 15. a 16. a 17. b 18. b 19. a 20. a

Chapter 13 Self-Help Answers

Level 1

Worksheet 1

The order of Answers 1–4 may vary. 1. and 2. or 3. nor 4. but (students may also list *yet, for,* and *so*) 5. b 6. a 7. b 8. a 9. a 10. b

Worksheet 2

Answers may vary. 1. therefore, however, consequently, moreover, then (students may also list *accordingly, also, anyway, furthermore, hence, in fact, in other words, in the meantime, indeed, likewise, nevertheless, on the contrary, on the other hand, otherwise, that is,* and *thus*) 2. semicolon 3. commas 4. planning, nevertheless, 5. occupancy; that is, 6. organization, on the other hand, 7. presentation; then 8. competitive; however, 9. résumés; consequently, 10. letter; therefore,

Level 2

Worksheet 1

Answers may vary. 1. although, because, if, when, until (students may also list *after, as, as if, as though, before, even though, in order that, provided, since, so that, that, unless, where, whether,* and *while*) 2. T 3. T 4. T 5. T 6. F 7. P 8. D 9. I 10. P 11. D 12. I 13. D 14. I 15. D 16. P 17. D 18. I 19. I 20. D

Worksheet 2

1. suggestions, 2. C 3. completed, 4. C 5. C 6. booklet, which was submitted over six weeks ago, 7. know, 8. payments, provided there is no interruption in profits, 9. necessary, 10. C 11. Gilroy, who volunteered to head the program, 12. C 13. order, 14. C 15. days,

Worksheet 3

Answers will vary.

1. Although never signed, the original agreement was drawn between Mr. Hightower and Columbia Communications.
2. Thank you for informing us that your credit card, which has an expiration date of April 30, is missing.
3. Because your account is four months past due, we will be forced to take legal action unless we hear from you within seven days.
4. Sally Horton, who works as assistant to the manager in the Quality Control Department, won an award as this month's outstanding employee.
5. We are sending you four poster advertisements that will appear in magazines in April, which marks the beginning of a national campaign featuring our sports clothes.

Level 3

1. b 2. b 3. a 4. b
5. You can either fax your response or send an e-mail message.
6. Our goals are both to educate motorists and to save their lives.
7. Tony has neither a job interview nor even an interview lined up.
8. We knew that we had to either raise more money or begin selling stock.
9. Businesses are looking for employees who not only can work in teams but also can learn effectively in teams.

Chapter 14 Self-Help Answers

Level 1

1. (2) teams, Mr. Wilson, 2. (1) By the way, 3. (4) successful, however, training, coaching, 4. (2) Ames, Iowa, 5. (2) teams, on the other hand, 6. C 7. (4) MicroTech Systems, 750 Grant Road, Tucson, Arizona 85703, 8. (2) appears, sir, 9. (2) Friday, April 30, 10. (2) Molloy, who is an advertising executive, 11. C 12. (1) 10 p.m., 13. (2) will, in addition, 14. (2) airports, shopping centers, 15. (1) considered, 16. (2) Hudson, who is a specialist in information systems, 17. (2) patent, trademark, 18. (2) convinced, incidentally, 19. (2) policy, budget, 20. (2) Italy, Greece,

Level 2

1. (1) practical, 2. (1) months, 3. (2) Meyer, employees, 4. (1) week, 5. C 6. (2) appreciate, often, 7. C 8. C 9. (1) calculations, 10. C 11. (2) please, calculations, 12. (1) intelligent, 13. (1) return, 14. (1) June, 15. C 16. (1) inventory, 17. (1) Goodell, who 18. (2) when, where, 19. (3) process, Thursday, June 1, 20. C

Level 3

1. (2) Ferrari, PhD, 2. C 3. (1) 2011, 4. (1) 2012, 5. (2) Taiwan, China, 6. (1) before, 7. (2) name," said the auditor, 8. C 9. C 10. (2) Feinstein, MD, 11. C 12. (1) since, 13. (1) said, 14. (2) Samuels, not Ms. Lambert, 15. (1) nine, 16. (2) 17,365,000 17. (3) supervisor," remarked Sid Stern, results, 18. (3) way, president, vice president, 19. (2) diamond," said the therapist, 20. (1) signs, signs

Chapter 15 Self-Help Answers

Level 1

1. profits; however, 2. Dallas, Texas; Seattle, Washington; and Miami, 3. names, envelopes, 4. order; 5. space; on the other hand, 6. remarkable; however, 7. public; 8. Roberts, secretary, Legal Department; Lea Lim, clerk, Human Resources; and Mark Cameron, dispatcher, 9. estate; however, 10. 10 a.m.; 11. award; 12. catalog, selections, 13. property, 14. convinced, therefore, 15. seats; 16. Hyatt Regency Hotel, Columbus, Ohio;

Plaza of the Americas Hotel, Dallas, Texas; and the Brown Palace Hotel, Denver, Colorado **17.** requested, Thursday, May 4; however, Friday, **18.** gathering, recording,

Level 2

1. scrutinized: **2.** C **3.** said: **4.** C **5.** decision: **6.** C **7.** following: **8.** sites: **9.** skills: **10.** C **11.** thought: **12.** factors: **13.** Hofer, Stone, **14.** tennis, **15.** following:

Level 3

1. check; namely, **2.** supplies: cartridges **3.** services, philosophy; that is, **4.** rule: **5.** 2:15 6:45 **6.** Tom; **7.** office; namely, **8.** *Investment: An* **9.** field; **10.** areas; for example, **11.** representative"; that is, **12.** advertising: product **13.** convention, namely, **14.** program; for instance, **15.** office; however,

Chapter 16 Self-Help Answers

Level 1

1. IRS possible. [**Note:** If you don't feel comfortable using a period after a polite request, rephrase the sentence so that it is clearly a command: *Please e-mail this form to the IRS as soon as possible.*] **2.** 10 a.m., didn't you? **3.** Mr. CPA Inc. **4.** Donald L. Cullens Jr. job? **5.** Help! jammed! **6.** please, Ms. Juarez, gift. [**Note:** If you don't feel comfortable using a period after a polite request, rephrase the sentence so that it is clearly a command: *Please visit our Web site and register for your gift.*] **7.** been! **8.** AA degrees, BA degrees. **9.** CEO and CFO decisions. **10.** Tan, Mr. Roe, and Ms. Rich. **11.** 9 a.m., EST, rate. **12.** Bennett, MD, Caracas, PhD, speakers. **13.** site? **14.** China, France, and the UK **15.** CPU USA. **16.** Adamski, Drive, Rochester, NY 14616. **17.** No. $50,000 coverage. [**Note:** If you don't feel comfortable using a period after a polite request, rephrase the sentence so that it is clearly a command: *Please check Policy No. 44657001 to see whether it includes $50,000 comprehensive coverage.*] **18.** 5 p.m., PST? **19.** Wow! prize? **20.** MA, DVDs.

Level 2

1. F (use two hyphens) **2.** T **3.** F **4.** T **5.** T **6.** b **7.** c **8.** b **9.** a **10.** b **11.** c **12.** c **13.** b **14.** c

Level 3

1. T **2.** T **3.** F (enclose definition in quotation marks) **4.** T. **5.** F (enclose in quotation marks) **6.** T **7.** T **8.** T **9.** T **10.** F (use apostrophes to make nouns possessive) **11.** a **12.** c **13.** a **14.** b **15.** a

Complete Punctuation Review

1. "Soaring Salaries of CEOs" *The New York Times*? **2.** This year's last year's; therefore, case-by-case **3.** SEC members: Dr. Carla Chang, Professor Mark Rousso, and Robert Price, Esq. **4.** say, 5 p.m., EST. **5.** fixed-rate, not variable-rate, **6.** invited: Christine Lenski, DataCom Industries; Mark Grant, LaserPro, Inc.; and Ivan Weiner, **7.** Orlando, Florida, **8.** say, "We Friday"? **9.** BA 11 a.m.; MBA 2 p.m. **10.** discussed, Monday, August 8. **11.** feel, however, car's **12.** D. B. Rusterholz. **13.** carefully, "bomb." **14.** weather, stations: KJOW, KLOB, and KOB-TV. **15.** employees—Gregorio Williams— Friday, June 5. **16.** attitude, aptitude, altitude," **17.** cars;

by June 15, **18.** EPA studied; **19.** 9 p.m., **20.** Ms. Courtney Worthy, Administrative Assistant, Globex Industries, 7600 Normandale Boulevard, Milwaukee, WI 53202, **21.** (see page 2 for a summary of the report) to the president's Friday, **22.** *Success* "A Venture Expert's Advice." **23.** Zuckerman, our former manager, IBM. **24.** weight, things; namely, **25.** expected, this year's heavy; consequently,

Chapter 17 Self-Help Answers

Level 1

1. b **2.** a **3.** a **4.** a **5.** a **6.** b **7.** a **8.** a **9.** b **10.** a **11.** b **12.** b **13.** b **14.** a **15.** b **16.** station county **17.** company's **18.** Securities and Exchange Commission e-mail **19.** winter I English **20.** American Association of Nurses Ballroom Hotel **21.** Persian Russian **22.** summer I Grand Canyon Arizona **23.** contract April **24.** Italian Spanish **25.** Kansas City International Airport Alameda Plaza Hotel

Level 2

1. a **2.** a **3.** a **4.** b **5.** a **6.** b **7.** a **8.** a **9.** a **10.** b **11.** a **12.** a **13.** b **14.** a **15.** b **16.** supervisor **17.** president company Do How Do It **18.** East Coast **19.** Highway Exit **20.** state **21.** "Does Your Training Measure Up?" **22.** Ray-Ban Jeep **23.** mother and father Flight 37 Gate 6 Phoenix Sky Harbor International Airport **24.** Task Force Meeting This Friday **25.** bus limousine Ritz-Carlton Hotel

Level 3

1. a **2.** b **3.** a **4.** a **5.** b **6.** a **7.** b **8.** b **9.** a **10.** a **11.** Funds **12.** River **13.** Senator Valley **14.** Professor Earth **15.** organization's Monday **16.** president company countries **17.** national African **18.** English dialect English **19.** Malaysia Muslims Buddhists Hindus **20.** mortgage financing

Chapter 18 Self-Help Answers

Level 1

1. a **2.** b **3.** b **4.** b **5.** a **6.** a **7.** b **8.** a **9.** a **10.** a **11.** A total of 194 December 1 **12.** Two 25th Avenue **13.** $5 $.99 **14.** $100 2nd **15.** February 1 15 departments. **16.** 2 Ford Place **17.** (815) 611-9292, Ext. 3 *or* 815-611-9292, Ext. 3 **18.** May 15 two 2 p.m. 8 p.m. **19.** Three 8 a.m. five **20.** 15th $204 **21.** 15-hour $125 **22.** 1 p.m. **23.** 1762 14th **24.** 25 cents $44 **25.** 3rd

Level 2

1. b **2.** b **3.** b **4.** a **5.** b **6.** b **7.** a **8.** a **9.** a **10.** b **11.** 50 **12.** three 35-passenger 15-day **13.** Fifty-three $1 million **14.** ten 48 five **15.** Chapter 8 Volume 2 **16.** Room 4 8 chairs **17.** 30-inch **18.** 20 requests 5 3 **19.** two loans **20.** twenty-four years **21.** Only 2 **22.** 64 **23.** 15-person $3 million **24.** 52 40 million **25.** 30-year 8 percent

Level 3

1. a **2.** b **3.** b **4.** b **5.** a **6.** b **7.** b **8.** a **9.** a **10.** b **11.** No. 10 4 ½ by 9 ½ inches **12.** Thirty-third **13.** 7/200 **14.** twenty-first **15.** 30 ¾ inches by 60 ½ inches **16.** 30th 3 percent **17.** 50 blocks Seventh **18.** 100 degrees eight **19.** 7.94 pounds 15 ½ inches **20.** two-thirds **21.** 9 by 12 two thirds **22.** Form 1040 $800 **23.** 2014 fifty-five 52 percent **24.** 100,000 **25.** 15 gallons 1 quart